Promoting Recovery in Early Psy

Promoting Recovery in Early Psychosis
A Practice Manual

EDITED BY

Paul French
Associate Director
Greater Manchester West Mental Health NHS Foundation Trust, Manchester
Honorary Senior Lecturer, Department of Psychology,
School of Psychological Sciences, University of Manchester

Jo Smith
NMHDU Joint National Early Intervention Programme
Lead and Worcestershire EI Clinical Development Lead,
Worcestershire Mental Health Partnership NHS Trust
Worcestershire

David Shiers
NMHDU Joint National Early Intervention Programme Lead
Worcestershire

Mandy Reed
Consultant Nurse for Early Intervention in Psychosis
Bath

Mark Rayne
Programme Specialist in Service Development NHS West Midlands Regional
Development Centre
West Midlands

⊛WILEY-BLACKWELL

A John Wiley & Sons, Ltd., Publication

This edition first published 2010
© Blackwell Publishing Ltd

Blackwell Publishing was acquired by John Wiley & Sons in February 2007. Blackwell's publishing programme has been merged with Wiley's global Scientific, Technical, and Medical business to form Wiley-Blackwell.

Registered office
John Wiley & Sons Ltd, The Atrium, Southern Gate, Chichester, West Sussex, PO19 8SQ, United Kingdom

Editorial office
9600 Garsington Road, Oxford, OX4 2DQ, United Kingdom
2121 State Avenue, Ames, Iowa 50014-8300, USA

For details of our global editorial offices, for customer services and for information about how to apply for permission to reuse the copyright material in this book please see our website at www.wiley.com/wiley-blackwell.

Library of Congress Cataloging-in-Publication Data

Promoting recovery in early psychosis : a practice manual / edited by Paul French . . . [et al.].
        p. ; cm.
Includes bibliographical references and index.
ISBN 978-1-4051-4894-8 (pbk. : alk. paper)
1. Psychoses.   I. French, Paul, 1963–
    [DNLM: 1. Psychotic Disorders—therapy.   2. Psychotic Disorders—rehabilitation. WM 200 P957 2010]
    RC512.P67 2010
    616.89—dc22

                                                                                2009031823

A catalogue record for this book is available from the British Library.

Set in 9.5/12pt Palatino by MPS Limited, A Macmillan Company
Printed and bound in Malaysia by KHL Printing Co Sdn Bhd

1 2010

Contents

Theme 2 Raising community awareness

Editor biographies

Dr Paul French has worked in mental health services since 1986 and has always been interested in the provision of services for people with psychosis having worked in a variety of inpatient and community settings. He has a strong interest in At Risk Mental States (ARMS) and the integration of research-based interventions within clinical settings for these clients. He completed his PhD in psychological factors associated with ARMS at Manchester University in 2007. Currently, Paul is an Associate Director for Early Intervention in Greater Manchester West Mental Health NHS foundation Trust. He also an Honorary Senior Lecturer in the Department of Psychology, School of Psychological Sciences, The University of Manchester.

EI book dedication from Paul French
To Delia, Chloe, Nadia and Ben not only for their continued love and support but also their patience with my late nights finishing off projects that don't lend themselves to a 9–5 existence.

Dr Jo Smith is Joint National Early Intervention Programme Lead for NMHDU (National Mental Health Development Unit in England) supporting Early Intervention development and implementation across England.

Jo is a Chartered Clinical Psychologist and Early Intervention Lead for Worcestershire Early Intervention Service with Worcestershire Mental Health Partnership NHS Trust.

Jo was previously Chairperson of IRIS (Initiative to reduce the impact of psychosis) which published Clinical Guidelines and service frameworks for Early Intervention in Psychosis (2000) which formed the basis for the Department of Health Early Intervention Policy Information Guide. Jo was also a member of the UK Department of Health Taskforce for Early Intervention.

EI book dedication from Jo Smith
To Dave, Tim and Charlie for their love, support and patience and my Worcestershire EI team colleagues

and the young people and families with whom I have worked, to whom my part in this book is dedicated.

Dr David Shiers is GP advisor West Midlands, Joint lead with Dr Jo Smith of the National Early Intervention Programme, National Institute for Mental Health in England.

Mental illness was no more than a professional interest as a GP (25 years) in Leek until David's daughter Mary developed schizophrenia aged 16 in 1993. David co-founded with Jo and other close colleagues a West Midlands initiative called IRIS (Initiative to Reduce the Impact of Schizophrenia) to improve services for young people with psychosis and their families. Through IRIS, he and Jo led the development of the Early Psychosis Declaration in 2004. Endorsed by the World Health Organisation, the declaration has provided a guiding set of values and principles for the development of Early Intervention in the UK.

David has a particular interest in narrative as a better way of understanding complex care systems. He has published a variety of articles about improving services for those with severe mental illness from his perspective as a carer and GP.

EI book dedication from David Shiers
My special thanks to Mary and Ann both for inspiring me and for putting up with me being sat in front of the computer for too many long evenings on this project.

Mandy Reed works in Bath as a Consultant Nurse in Acute Adult Mental Health and as a Senior Lecturer at the University of the West of England (UWE). Prior to her current post, she co-led the set up and development of the then highly regarded Gloucestershire Recovery in Psychosis (GRIP) Early Intervention Service for 3 years. Her passion and challenge in her current role has been to work alongside traditional services promoting collaborative user- and carer-focused effective mental health services by sharing the evidence from Early Psychosis Services.

She is also Lead for the PSI (Thorn validated) Programme at UWE and a Non Medical Prescriber within the Bath and North East Somerset EI Team.

EI book dedication from Mandy Reed
To my amazing sons Oliver, Charles and Henry and in memory of my brother Paul who was born a generation too soon to benefit from the Early Psychosis Declaration.

Mark Rayne has worked in the mental health field for the past 25 years, previously working as a mental health nurse in Staffordshire and Walsall and for the past 5 years working for the National Institute for Mental Health and more recently CSIP as a programme lead supporting EI developments across the West Midlands.

Mark has been involved in EI for the past 8 years and prior to his Regional CSIP EI lead post was National EI Coordinator and Clinical Lead for EI in Walsall.

EI book dedication from Mark Rayne
In loving memory of my best friend Christian Pilbeam

Contributors

Lizzie Banks   Carer Consultant and Trainer, Gloucestershire.

Tom Barker   Chartered Clinical Psychologist, Worcestershire Mental Health Partnership NHS Trust, Worcestershire.

Mark Bernard   Clinical Psychologist and Honorary Research Fellow, Birmingham and Solihull Mental Foundation Health Trust, Birmingham.

Max Birchwood   Professor of Mental Health, University of Birmingham, Birmingham.

Paul Blackburn   Clinical Lead, Humber Mental Health and Teaching Trust, East Yorkshire.

Sarah J. Boldison   Development Consultant for South West Development Centre, Bristol.

Katerine Brunet   Clinical Psychologist, Birmingham and Solihull Mental Health Foundation Trust, Birmingham.

Frank R. Burbach   Consultant Clinical Psychologist, Somerset Partnership NHS and Social Care Trust, Somerset.

Richard Burden   Case Manager, Worcestershire EI Service, Worcestershire.

Graham Carr   Clinical Team Lead, Torbay Mental Wellbeing and Access, Devon Partnership NHS Trust, Torquay.

Emma Cotes   Chartered Clinical Psychologist, Birmingham and Solihull Mental Health Foundation Trust, Birmingham.

Tom Craig   Professor of Social Psychiatry, Institute of Psychiatry, King's College London, London.

Eric Davis   Visiting Professor of Mental Health, University of West England, Bristol.

Jos Dawe   Consultant Psychiatrist, Insight Early Intervention Service, Plymouth.

Guy Dodgson   Consultant Clinical Psychologist Northumberland, Tyne and Wear NHS Trust, Newcastle upon Tyne.

Gráinne Fadden   Consultant Clinical Psychologist, Director, Meriden Family Programme, Birmingham.

Alan Farmer   Consultant Psychiatrist, Worcestershire Mental Health Partnership NHS Trust, Worcestershire.

Paul French   Associate Director GMW NHS Foundation Trust and Honorary Senior Lecturer, University of Manchester, Manchester.

Tony Gillam   Clinical Manager, Worcestershire EI Service, Worcestershire.

David Glentworth   Lead Practitioner for Psychosocial Interventions, Greater Manchester West NHS Foundation Trust, Manchester.

Andrew Gumley   Chair of Psychological Therapy, University of Glasgow, Glasgow.

Chris Jackson   Consultant Clinical Psychologist and Honorary Senior Research Fellow, Birmingham and Solihull Mental Health Foundation Trust, Birmingham.

Satnam Singh Kunar   Specialist Registrar in Psychiatry, Coventry and Warwickshire NHS Partnership Trust, Warwick.

Clare Lamb   Consultant Child and Adolescent Psychiatrist, North Wales Adolescent Service, Conwy.

Helen Lester   Professor of Primary Care, University of Manchester, Manchester.

Ros Manning   Care of Gloucester EI.

Carly Mays   Community Engagement Officer, Tha National Trust Greenway, Devon.

Kate Macdonald   Managing Director, Jellycat Media Ltd, Hull.

Stephen McGowan Early Intervention Lead for Bradford and Airedale Early Intervention Service, Bradford.

Charles Montgomery Consultant Psychiatrist, Wonford House Hospital, Devon Partnership NHS Trust, Devon.

Elizabeth Newton Chartered Clinical Psychologist, Coventry and Warwickshire NHS Partnership Trust, Coventry.

Claire Park Department of Psychological Therapy, University of Glasgow, Glasgow.

Rowena Passy National Foundation for Educational Research, Berkshire.

Paul Patterson Birmingham Early Intervention Service and Birmingham University, Birmingham and Solihull Mental Health Foundation Trust, Birmingham.

Dan Pearson Consultant Therapist, Leicestershire Partnership Trust, Leicester.

Sharon Peters Carer Support Worker Cheltenham.

Paddy Power Consultant Psychiatrist, Institute of Psychiatry, King's College London, London.

Kathryn Pugh National Lead for MHA 2007 Implementation, Children and Young People's Workstream, The National Mental Health Development Unit, London.

Mark Rayne Programme Specialist in Service Development, NHS West Midlands, Birmingham.

Mandy Reed Consultant Nurse, Early Intervention in Psychosis Service-Bath and North East Somerset, Bath.

Imogen Reid Clinical Psychologist, Psychological Therapies Service (Swindon), Avon and Wiltshire Mental Health Partnership NHS Trust, Wiltshire.

Lindsay Rigby Research Cognitive Therapist, University of Manchester, Manchester.

Glenn Roberts Consultant in Rehabilitation Psychiatry, Exeter.

Diane Ryles Team Manager, Birmingham and Solihull Mental Health Foundation Trust, Birmingham.

David Shiers NMHDU Joint National Early Intervention Programme Lead, Worcestershire.

Alexa Sidwell Clinical Teacher and Senior Case Manager, Derbyshire Mental Health NHS Trust, Derby.

Swaran P. Singh Professor of Social and Community Psychiatry and Consultant Psychiatrist, University of Warwick, Coventry.

Gina Smith Consultant Nurse for Family Intervention/Clinical Lead for Carers, Avon and Wiltshire Mental Health Partnership NHS Trust, Wiltshire.

Jo Smith NMHDU Joint National Early Intervention Programme Lead and Worcestershire EI Clinical Development Lead, Worcestershire Mental Health Partnership NHS Trust, Worcestershire

John Somers Honorary Fellow, University of Exeter, Exeter.

Lynda Tait Research Fellow, University of Birmingham, Birmingham.

Lucie Taylor Mental Health Worker, Western Cheshire Primary Care Trust, Chester.

Ian Wilson Teaching Fellow, Manchester Dual Diagnosis Service, Manchester Mental Health and Social Care Trust and Teaching Fellow, University of Manchester, Manchester.

Iain Wright Clinical Lead for Early Intervention in Psychosis, Mersey Care NHS Trust, Liverpool.

Foreword

Some 20 years ago when addressing a local meeting of the 'National Schizophrenia Fellowship' (now RETHINK) in Birmingham, I spoke about the evidence for the clinical and ethical importance of getting help early when a psychosis is suspected. I felt I was saying something really important and my talk was well received. However, I vividly remember a young man putting his hand up at the end and asserting, with all the irony he could muster, '. . . that's very interesting but why would I want fast access to your *crap* services?'. Everyone applauded. He stole the show. Of course he was absolutely right. It prompted in me a lot of reflection about the quality of care and treatment young people receive in mental health services. There was at the time a lazy assumption that the unpleasant aspects of this severe mental illness was a rather inevitable consequence of the illness, the person and his family: the long treatment delay at the first episode, the high rate of compulsory detention, the high suicide rate and the low rate of employment. All that could be achieved was containment of the individual and his illness and, worse still, it was widely believed that communicating high expectations of recovery was giving young people and their families false hope–better to come to terms with the inevitable decline as quickly as possible.

And here we are 20 years later with dedicated early psychosis teams covering the whole country and offering a firm antidote to the dead hand of Kraepelinian fatalism. This has been a fascinating story about how services can be turned around through a combination of hard science and consumer and clinicians working together to make a difference. This has been a remarkable achievement that has been admired and copied worldwide. David Shiers and Jo Smith have worked tirelessly inside and alongside the Department of Health to make this happen and their chapter offers some very important messages about their experience and also important lessons about the application of the early intervention approach across the spectrum of youth mental health.

This book is special because it appears at the apex of a great deal of hard work, commitment and experience of working with this young group of people over the last 10 years: all the key players involved in the UK have shared their expertise with us to produce a 'state of the art' text for clinicians, consumers and service managers about how to promote recovery following the early appearance of psychosis. This book provides a comprehensive and thorough coverage of the nuts and bolts of early intervention from the science and practice of engaging young people in the recovery process through to the specific aspects of intervention and personal growth. It is a genuine 'how to do it' text that will be invaluable for services in the UK and internationally.

I am proud of the achievements of my colleagues writing in this book and hope that you will be as inspired as I have been by their energy, ingenuity and extraordinary skill.

Max Birchwood
Birmingham, January 2010

Chapter 1 **Introduction**

David Shiers and Jo Smith

There is one thing stronger than all the armies in the world; and that it is an idea whose time has come.

(Victor Hugo, 1862)

It feels timely to be bringing together a training resource about *Promoting Recovery in Early Psychosis* to support the rapid service development created by the current UK policy platform and proliferating research evidence. In this introduction, we want to paint a backdrop of how policy, research and practice have been harnessed to provide the context in which we hope practitioners will find this practice manual relevant and helpful.

Few could have anticipated 10 years ago prior to the outset of the National Service Framework for Mental Health (DH, 1999) the extraordinary shift in how we understand and treat psychosis, none more so than in the arena of Early Intervention (EI) bringing with it new hope for young people with emerging psychosis and their families. Significant advances in understanding the nature of psychosis have created a whole range of new treatment options included in the NICE Schizophrenia Guidance (NICE, CG82 updated 2009):

- emphasis on recovery
- modern pharmacological practice
- psychological interventions
- working with families

With the completion of the NSF, these treatment advances have been accompanied by major investment and redesign of community-based specialist mental health provision, so that now most young people with a first episode of psychosis in England can access a local EI service. With that in mind, this book has been written by mental health practitioners and service users and carers to make it accessible to a wide range of clinicians with the emphasis on skills development and sharing new and innovative EI team approaches.

However this book sets out to be more than just a collective guidance. The authors hope learning will be underpinned by a shared appreciation of the vision and values of the **Early Psychosis Declaration** (EPD) (see International Consensus Statement; Bertolote & McGorry, 2005) (Table 1.1).

What is important about the declaration is how it moves away from a disease and deficit model to one focused on improving health and building on attributes. This book is organised to reflect the five themes of the EPD, its component chapters contributing in their different ways to achieving its standards through collaborative and imaginative approaches embedded in the declaration's optimistic message of recovery. For instance, take the EPD theme 'Promoting recovery and the achievement of ordinary lives': what and who needs to be involved in helping a young person achieve this declaration standard? Certainly optimal health care and intervention is essential but is this sufficient? Ask yourself 'how might the young person be supported to secure a meaningful job: the importance of building self-esteem and motivation, of collaborative working with benefits agencies, youth agencies, job centres, and education providers?'

In this way, the book explores the declaration's five themes through contributions selected to encourage the co-production of health, acknowledging that health improvement requires integrated and collaborative care from many people and agencies beyond simply those of health services (Figure 1.1).

Table 1.1 What is the early psychosis declaration?

The EPD is a consensus about the standards of care that those developing early psychosis and their families should expect. First formed by some key people from across the UK with a special interest in early psychosis, the consensus (Bertolote & McGorry, 2005) gained the support of a number of organisations including World Health Organisation (WHO), the International Early Psychosis Association (IEPA), Initiative to Reduce the Impact of Schizophrenia (IRIS), Rethink and the National Institute Mental Health in England (NIMHE) with the ambition to:

- Establish a clear vision, some values and some actions required to achieve early intervention and recovery for all young people experiencing psychosis.
- Generate optimism and raise expectations from young people experiencing psychosis and their families that will influence the development of better services.
- Provide a framework for enabling those young people and their families to work alongside practitioners and services to:
  ○ Acknowledge the key shared concerns;
  ○ Develop a set of jointly agreed, valued and measurable goals;
  ○ Jointly commit to a set of strategic actions to achieve these goals.
- Attract and encourage practitioners from a wide range of health, social, educational and employment services to think about how they can better contribute to supporting these young people and their families.

For more information about the declaration – see www.iris-initiative.org.uk.

Figure 1.1 The 5 key themes of the Early Psychosis Declaration.

EI and reform of mental health practice in England

EI has participated over the last 10 years in a wider mental health reform enabled by a sociological and political process informed by evidence. However, the idea that it was desirable to treat conditions like schizophrenia earlier in their course is not new. Radical thinkers such as Harry Sullivan challenged (and may still challenge) traditionalists, convinced by Kraepelin's original description (1896) of 'dementia praecox'

as a single disease entity (schizophrenia) with a universally poor outcome.

I feel certain that any incipient cases might be arrested before the efficient contact with reality is completely suspended, and a long stay in institutions made necessary.

(H.S. Sullivan, 1927)

Some 60 years would elapse before treatment delay became firmly linked to outcome. In 1986, the Northwick Park study (Johnstone *et al.*, 1986) showed that individuals taking longer than 1 year to access services could expect 3 times more relapse in the subsequent 2 years than those who accessed services in under 1 year. These findings sparked intense research and clinical interest. One of that study's key authors helped to develop the North Birmingham EI service, the first UK EI service(s) (opening in 1989), mirroring service innovations in Australia, Scandinavia and the USA. Thus were laid the modern foundations for EI in the UK. And yet, research and innovative practice of themselves could not have generated the scale of reform that we have seen in England in the last 10 years. This modern era of EI development coincided with UK political sensitivity heightened by high-profile media concerns for public safety (e.g. the tragic killing of Jonathan Zito by Christopher Clunis; Benjamin Silcock entering a lion-cage). The existing UK policy of 'Care in the Community' became severely criticised for neglect of individuals by overburdened community mental health teams that relied excessively on crisis hospital admission and medication. Groups like IRIS (Initiative to Reduce the Impact of Schizophrenia) increased this pressure for change harnessing key researchers, early clinical innovators, users and family members, aligning with voluntary sector organisations such as Rethink and Making Space.

The stage was set for the traditional 'one size fits all' community mental health team approach to be challenged. Heralded in 1999 by the NSF Adult Mental Health, there followed a subsequent string of detailed policy guidance for EI (Table 1.2), including important Policy Implementation Guidance (DH, 2001) which put forward an EI service specification. New teams formed with discrete functions to deliver more intensive and focussed support at key points to break the cycle of crisis response and hospitalisation. These different 'functionalised' teams provided:

- *Early intervention:* intensive case management using age- and phase-specific interventions in the early phase of psychosis.

- *Assertive community treatment* where the patient resides – for example, for patients prone to a pattern of disengagement and relapse in crisis.
- *Home treatment/crisis response* at the point of crisis to avert the need for hospital admission.

These approaches have been continuously researched and developed which in itself distinguished this as a new era of mental health practice in England.

EI: Policy, practice and research

These radical reforms have been underpinned by a synergy between three essential elements, a continuing policy platform, a strengthening research evidence and evolving practice and service development.

Policy: We have already touched on the policy and political drivers – see Table 1.2 for a summary of key EI policy support. The NHS plan (DH, 2000) promised 50 new teams to cover England, configured to a national service blueprint (DH Policy Implementation Guide, 2001) to recruit 7,500 new cases each year and provide 3 years of evidence-based treatment. Full implementation in 2004 would achieve a 'steady state' (new cases balancing discharges) of 22,500 cases. However, this deadline had anticipated neither the complexities of both the service development itself nor some of the wider management and commissioning changes within the NHS and it became obvious that the planned implementation was stalling. The Department of Health restored the trajectory of anticipated caseload and service investment through its EI Recovery Plan (DH, 2006), and then maintained EI service(s) as a top mental health priority in the NHS Operating Framework (2007 to present). The important message here is that EI has enjoyed a sustained policy platform for the last 10 years and continues to hold the attention of policy makers.

Research: EI has enjoyed one of the most rapidly evolving growths in research curiosity of any field of mental health. The challenge is to translate new findings into tangible benefits. Indeed this book continually draws down from these discoveries. Put simply, 'Early intervention

Table 1.2 Policy development to support EI in the UK

National Service Framework Adult Mental Health (DH, 1999) Outlining a 10-year policy commitment. EI service development now becomes a firm policy intention.

NHS Plan (DH, 2000) Mental Health sits as a top priority within the wider plan for modernisation of the entire NHS. For EI the NHS Plan gave specific commitment to:

- Develop 50 EI teams, each serving populations of about 1 million by April 2004 so that, 'all young people who experience a first episode of psychosis, such as schizophrenia will receive the early and intensive support they need'.
- Reduce the DUP to a service average of 3 months (maximum individual 6 months) and continuous service support for the first 3 years.
- Create a comprehensive CAMHS service.

Priorities and Planning Framework 2003–2006 (DH, 2002) Set out the NHS Plan objectives against timelines, reaffirming EI service(s) as a priority with its own targets.

Policy Implementation Guide (DH, 2001–2002) The 'PIG' gave detailed service specifications: The EI model should provide care for 3 years for those aged 14–35 with emerging psychosis. EI service(s) were expected to develop with fidelity to the prescribed 'PIG' model, although flexibility was possible provided services could demonstrate anticipated outcomes were being met.

Core Interventions in the Treatment and Management of Schizophrenia (NICE, 2002) Values EI's role within the care pathway, supported by an evidence base of treatments.

NSF for Children, Young People and Maternity Services (DH, 2004)

Reinforces the commitment to ensure seamless provision of EI for those young people in transitional age, requiring that child and adolescent and adult mental health services effectively integrate through joint commissioning and collaborative working arrangements.

2004 Early Psychosis Declaration (World Health Organisation) Developed by IRIS and the International Early Psychosis Association, an international consensus about service targets to meet the needs of these young people and their families.

2004 NIMHE/RETHINK EI Development Programme A 3-year programme to support and guide the implementation of EI services and action the Early Psychosis Declaration (DS and JS are the national co-leads of this programme).

2006 EI Recovery Plan 2006/2007 required EI provision to 7,500 new patients in 2006/2007 in order to put EI development back on target **(DH, 2006) acknowledged the 2003–2006 trajectories** to provide EI to 22,500 patients by December 2006 was off-course.

2007/2008 NHS Operating Framework EI is a *continuing priority ... so that EI services are in place* **in all areas.**

2008 NHS Operating Framework EI is still present in 2008/2009 and expected to be in 2009/2010 framework.

---

in Psychosis' provides an evidence-based paradigm of care comprising of three concepts:

- Early detection of psychosis.
- Reduce the long duration of untreated psychosis.
- Importance of the first 3–5 years following onset (critical period) for later biological, psychological and social outcomes.

Worth highlighting has been the improved understanding of the cost impact of EI service(s). This has encouraged an 'invest to save' argument for commissioners of services which proves that, despite its higher running costs, EI service(s) can potentially save in the order of £5k in year one, rising to £14k by year three per case compared to treatment as usual (McCrone *et al.*, 2008). These savings reflect mainly reductions in admission and readmission rates achieved by EI service(s) impacting on more traditional pathways into mental health services by:

- Earlier detection, education and collaboration with primary care and community agencies;
- Stronger engagement and more age/phase appropriate intervention with individuals and families.

The impact of these cost savings has been projected to 2026 in an important strategy document 'Paying the Price' (McCrone *et al.*, 2008) which concludes:

Early intervention services for psychosis have also demonstrated their effectiveness in helping to reduce costs and demands on mental health services in the medium to long-term, and should be extended to provide care for people as soon as their illness emerges.

'Paying the Price' (McCrone *et al.*, 2008)

Practice and service development: England has enjoyed unprecedented growth in EI service(s). From 1998, as the NSF got underway there were two teams providing care for about 80 people. DH Local Delivery Plan Returns at March 2007 revealed 145 EI services serving 15,750 people, in the context of a positive trajectory towards full policy implementation. (Figure 1.2).

The growth of capacity, in terms of number of teams and number of cases 'on the books' is necessary but is not sufficient in itself. One way to look at this was to examine how EI teams complied with the Policy Implementation Guide. Early intervention self assessment data for 2007-2008 (DH and CSIP, November 2008) revealed only 5 % LIT's rated as 'red' (failing to meet the EI policy implementation guide (PIG), minimum fidelity criteria and to provide for at least 50% of caseload trajectory targets), 28% rated as 'amber' (meeting EI PIG and minimum fidelity criteria and providing for between 51 and 90% of their caseload trajectory targets) and 67% as 'green' (meeting EI PIG and minimum fidelity criteria and providing for between 91 and 100% of caseload trajectory targets. The National EI Programme conducted a service mapping exercise (October 2007) to assess service provision against the criteria used in the annual Durham assessment of local delivery plans – Figure 1.3.

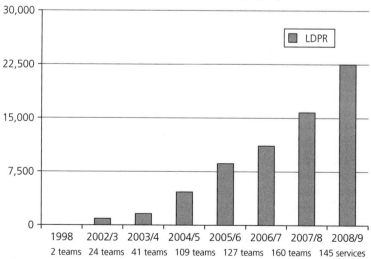

El provision across England
(15,750 cases at end of March 08)

Figure 1.2 EI provision across England.

Majority:

- provide for full age range (80%)*
*some rely on specialist CAMHS/adolescenet provision for 14–18 years

- capacity to provide 3 years intervention (78%)*
* some discharge cases earlier

- caseloads of 15 or less (81%)*
*some with higher caseloads have assistant care co-ordinators supporting case managers

Many:

- have early detection strategy (69%)
- monitor high risk or suspected FEP cases (58%) with further 23% with limited monitoring capacity

Fewer:

- systems in place for out of hours cover (48%)*
* majority rely on Crisis & HT

- offer flexible hours or evening opening*
* one team open for weekend access (South Essex)

Figure 1.3 National EI Programme mapping in October 2007 of service provision using the Durham annual assessment criteria for fidelity.

Table 1.3 Clinical effectiveness Outcome Data from Worcestershire EI service(s)

	National	**EI service(s) (3 years) 2003–2006 n = 78**
Duration of untreated psychosis (months)	12–18	5–6
% admitted in FEP	80	41
% FEP using MHA	50	27
Readmission	50	27.6
% engaged at 12 months	50	100 (79% well engaged)
Family involved (%)	49	91
satisfied (%)	56	71
Employed (%)	8–18	55
Suicide attempted (%)	48	21
completed (%)		0

Source: Smith, 2006.

Finally, the ultimate test of whether this policy imperative is really making a difference to peoples' lives is to assess how the service experience has changed. Can services demonstrate improvement in indicators of quality and outcome? That is precisely why the EPD has been so important in this whole service development with its focus on *co-production of health* rather than *reduction in illness*. EI service(s) have evolved with an ethos of audit and reflective practice centred on some key measures, many linked to the EPD. The routine collection of this type of data by EI service(s) was explored by the National EI Programme service mapping exercise (October 2007 unpublished) which revealed:

- Majority of EI service(s) measure DUP (79%), readmission (68%), employment (71%) and educational outcomes (68%).
- Fewer measure service engagement (59%), relapse (51%) and parasuicide (47%).

Table 1.3 illustrates the value of such reflective data from Worcestershire Early Intervention Service, a non-research–based EI service(s), replicable by many similar EI service(s) across England.

Table 1.4 Early intervention 2009 and the next 10 years: Some questions?

- *A youth mental health service model:* Given that 80% of long-term adult mental health disorders commence in those aged 15–25, will the EI model be extended to treat a wider range of young peoples' mental health disorders? If so will EI psychosis become embedded within a youth mental health service?
- *BME equity:* How will equality of access to EI service(s) and quality of outcome be assured for those from minority ethnic groups?
- *Early detection:* How will the emerging evidence for the benefits of early detection (*Chapter 11 Early detection and treatment opportunities for people with emerging psychosis. Paul French*) become embedded into practice and new service development?
- *Length of EI psychosis provision:* Will the current 3-year PIG model be extended to 5 years in the light of evidence for loss of the early benefits of EI (for instance in the elevated suicide rates seen when these young people are discharged to traditional community mental health services)?
- *EI psychosis as a trojan horse:* Can EI act as a culture-carrier, creating ripples into the still waters further down the care pathway (e.g. *PSI, family work, medicines*), reigniting interest in the therapeutic strengths of home, families and communities?
- *Offender pathways:* How might those clients presenting with offending behaviours avoid becoming entrapped within a criminal justice system and access EI service(s)?
- *EI for physical health pathways*: How can EI service(s) work with primary care to provide an EI paradigm for physical disorders in the face of growing concerns about premature deaths due to cardiovascular, respiratory and infective disorders? (Parks *et al.*, 2006)

EI practice and service development has benefited enormously from reflective practice; this illustration shows how the standards of the EPD can provide quality indicators able to drive local service improvement.

Final reflections

I have seen how much progress early intervention teams have made, how innovative they have been, and the impact they are having. I now believe that early intervention will be the most important and far reaching reform of the NSF era. Crisis resolution has had the most immediate effect but I think early intervention will have the greatest effect on people's lives.

Professor Louis Appleby, National Director for Mental Health October 10 2008 Policies and Practice for Europe (DH/WHO Europe Conference attended by 35 countries)

Now an established 'normal' part of the architecture of specialist services, EI psychosis has travelled from the margins to mainstream over the lifetime of the NSF, gathering momentum through a synergy of policy, research and practice. However what we have described is a journey and not a destination and we feel the next phase of consolidation is perhaps the most exciting. What might the next 10 years hold for EI service(s) (Table 1.4).

Table 1.4 shows some of the positive opportunities that the paradigm of EI may be able to influence. However there will also emerge risks and cautions, such as the ongoing financial recession or future NHS reorganisations. EI psychosis must avoid being a *victim* of these pressures, but provide a *solution*. Indeed, because of the central importance attached by EI to audit of care pathways, no other part of mental health provision is better equipped to be in touch with clients' journeys. Thus, EI, far from being a *problem* demanding resources, can offer an *answer* by demonstrating how to better use scarce resources.

So what has this EI voyage taught us? Much of the challenge is not about new money but about a different mindset which challenges 'Treatment as Usual' by seeing different ways of doing things. We hope this mindset, defined by the values and principles of the EPD, will be part of what the reader of this book takes away.

Useful information resources
IRIS website on www.iris-initiative.org.uk for

- Leaflet describing the aims of the declaration;
- Launch presentation declaration by Benedetto Saraceno;
- Toolkit for self-assessment of a service against the declaration's standards.

References

Bertolote, J. & McGorry, P. (2005). Early intervention and recovery for young people with early psychosis: Consensus statement. *British Journal of Psychiatry*, 187 (Suppl. 48), s116–s119.

Department of Health and CSIP (2008). *Self Assessment Report 2007–2008*. London: Department of Health.

DH (1999). *The National Service Framework for Mental Health*. London: Department of Health.

DH (2000). *The NHS Plan: A Plan for Investment, A Plan for Reform*. London: Department of Health.

DH (2001). *The Policy Implementation Guide on Mental Health*. London: Department of Health.

DH (2002). *Improvement, expansion and reform – the next 3 years: priorities and planning framework 2003–2006*. London: Department of Health.

DH (2001–2002). *The Policy Implementation Guide on Mental Health*. London: Department of Health.

DH (2004). *The National Service Framework for Children, Young People and Maternity Services*. London: Department of Health.

DH (2006). *Early Intervention Recovery Plan Duncan Selbie Letter to Chief Executives of Health & Social Care*. London: Department of Health.

Johnstone, E.C., Crow, T.J., Johnson, A.L. & Macmillan, J.F. (1986). The Northwick Park Study of first episodes of schizophrenia. *British Journal of Psychiatry*, 148, 115–120.

McCrone, P., Dhanasiri, S., Patel, A., Knapp, M. & Lawton-Smith, S. (2008). *Paying the Price. The Cost of Mental Health Care in England to 2026*. London: Kings Fund.

Kraepelin, E. [1896] (1987). Dementia praecox. In: J. Cutting & M. Shepherd (eds), *The Clinical Roots of the Schizophrenia Concept*, pp. 13–24. Cambridge: Cambridge University Press.

National Institute for Clinical Excellence (2009). *NICE Clinical Guideline 82: Core Interventions in the Treatment and Management of Schizophrenia in Primary and Secondary Care* (update of 2002 guidance). London: NICE.

Parks, J., Svendsen, D., Singer, P. & Forti, M.E. (2006). *Morbidity and Mortality in People with Serious Mental Illness*. National Association of State Mental Health Programme Directors, 13th technical report.

Sullivan, H.S. [1927] (1994). The onset of schizophrenia. *American Journal of Psychiatry*, 151 (Suppl. 6), 135–139.

Chapter 2 Duration of untreated psychosis and pathways to care

Katerine Brunet and Max Birchwood

Introduction

The early stage of psychosis is typically highly distressing not only for the individual but also for relatives and friends, yet it may take a considerable length of time for some people to reach treatment after experiencing their first symptoms of psychosis. This delay is commonly referred to as the duration of untreated psychosis, or DUP. Reviews of the literature indicate a mean DUP of approximately 2 years (Marshall *et al.*, 2005), while median values suggest that many people reach treatment within 6 months, with a small number experiencing delays of several years (Norman & Malla, 2001).

It is often within the DUP that young people experiencing voices, paranoia or unusual ideas may withdraw from important relationships or become excluded because of changes in their behaviour. College courses or early careers may be disrupted, with long-term consequences. Together with the psychotic experiences themselves, these life changes are likely to affect the way in which a young person comes to view themselves at a pivotal stage of their personal development. Perhaps not surprisingly, the risk of self-harm during this period is high, particularly when treatment delay is long (Harvey *et al.*, 2008). Surely, it is only proper that these young people are offered specialist help as quickly as possible.

In the UK, the Department of Health (DH) regards the reduction of DUP as a national priority, setting a median target of 3 months with no delay to extend beyond 6 months (DH, 2002). The Early Psychosis Declaration (Bertolote & McGorry, 2005) similarly requires treatment to be reached within 3 months of the onset of symptoms, and after no more than three attempts to find help.

A brief summary of the evidence

Does treatment delay influence the outcome of psychosis?

For several years, studies have attempted to determine whether or not those young people who experience longer treatment delays are likely to suffer a poorer prognosis. A recent meta-analysis of 26 first-episode psychosis (FEP) studies has now provided robust evidence that individuals who experience a longer DUP also experience poorer outcomes in terms of symptoms, quality of life and social functioning after 6–12months of treatment. Further evidence is needed for a conclusive understanding of the relationship after 12 months (Marshall *et al.*, 2005).

It has been argued that longer DUP does not *cause* poorer outcome but is simply a *characteristic* of those presentations that more commonly lead to a poorer prognosis (McGlashan, 1999). Nevertheless, the relationship is reported to be independent of a number of factors (Norman & Malla, 2001) including premorbid adjustment (how well someone was functioning before they became unwell), which has been proposed as the factor most likely to underpin the relationship (Marshall *et al.*, 2005). Studies reporting that some aspects of outcome are improved by reducing DUP through early detection strategies add further evidence for an independent relationship (Melle *et al.*, 2004). A greater understanding of DUP is therefore vital if we are to improve the prognosis and the quality of life of individuals experiencing FEP.

Who experiences long treatment delays?

The majority of help-seeking pathways involve some assistance from the young person's family or friends, who play a crucial role in recognising that there is a problem and supporting attempts to seek help. Assistance from relatives has been associated not only with shorter treatment delay (Morgan *et al.*, 2006a) but also with a lower likelihood of police involvement and compulsory admission (Cole *et al.*, 1995). Meanwhile, young people who are unemployed, living alone or homeless might take longer time to reach treatment, perhaps due to their social isolation (Barnes *et al.*, 2000; Morgan *et al.*, 2006a).

Families themselves might be influenced by previous experiences of services – we know that a family history of psychiatric hospitalisation contributes to longer DUP, perhaps due to a higher tolerance of unusual behaviour or an avoidance of psychiatric services following unpleasant past experiences (Verdoux *et al.*, 1998).

The influence of ethnicity has also been widely investigated. Although African–Caribbean and African individuals may not experience longer treatment delays than non African–Caribbean and African individuals, their pathways to care are thought to be more complex. For example, these groups are reportedly less likely to enter mental health services via their GP, more likely to enter services through the criminal justice system and more likely to be compulsorily admitted in comparison with White British individuals. In part, this may be due to these groups experiencing higher levels of unemployment and being more likely to live alone. It has also been argued that African–Caribbean individuals are perceived as more threatening by onlookers, and that high levels of stigmatisation in African–Caribbean communities lead friends and relatives to contact the police rather than mental health services during a crisis (Morgan *et al.*, 2005a, b).

Barriers to identification and treatment

Recognition of the early signs of psychosis or even a full psychotic episode can be hindered by the nature of its presentation as well as an individual's social context. An abrupt change in behaviour or florid affective symptoms might prompt a speedy reaction, and allow for easy identification of the problem as a psychosis (Morgan *et al.*, 2006a).

Presentations that are more ambiguous in nature might lead to lengthier delays in recognition and treatment. Poor premorbid functioning has been associated with longer delays, perhaps due to an absence of strong social networks (Larsen *et al.*, 1998) or because early signs of psychosis are confused with ongoing difficulties with adjustment. Similarly, where these early signs develop gradually rather than abruptly, they might be confused with an emerging depression or social phobia, and mask the appearance of an episode of psychosis. Presentation during adolescence might cause further ambiguity; unusual ideas, experiences and behaviour, social isolation and changes in functioning are all common features of adolescence (McGorry *et al.*, 1995). Indeed, the more these three factors are present (poor premorbid functioning, gradual development of early signs and adolescent onset), the longer may be the DUP (Brunet *et al.*, 2006).

Similarly, it might be that DUP is longer for young people whose difficulties are characterised by an absence of usual thoughts, feelings or behaviours rather than the presence of unusual behaviour (Malla *et al.*, 2002). In particular, it has been suggested that when a young person is finding it hard to experience pleasure, desire or motivation, their difficulties may be misinterpreted as depression or as a developmental characteristic of adolescence or young adulthood (Malla *et al.*, 2002) thus delaying the identification of an emerging psychosis.

Implementation into practice

A number of hurdles must be overcome before a young person receives treatment for FEP. The symptoms or distress needs to be recognised by the individual or by those around them and a search for help commenced. Those approached for help must recognise the problem as a mental health issue and refer to appropriate services. Mental health services must then recognise the presentation as a psychosis and begin appropriate treatment. DUP could then be viewed as a series of three phases rather than as a unitary concept, enabling us to identify and target barriers to care (Norman *et al.*, 2004; Brunet *et al.*, 2007; Power *et al.*, 2007). As depicted in Figure 2.1,

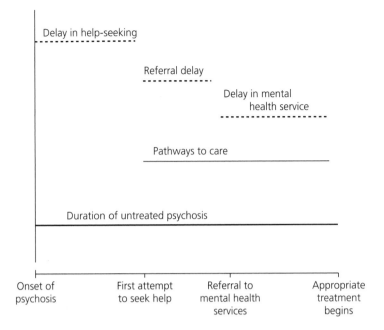

Figure 2.1 The components of treatment delay.

we might then view DUP as comprising: (1) a delay between the onset of first symptoms and the initiation of help-seeking (help-seeking delay); (2) a delay between the first attempt to seek help and referral to mental health services (referral delay) and (3) a delay between inception by mental health services and the commencement of appropriate treatment (delay in mental health services) (Brunet *et al.*, 2007).

Delays in each of these phases make significant contributions to overall DUP, though the relative impact of each phase and associated pathway barriers will vary between regions of the UK (Brunet, 2004; Morgan *et al.*, 2006a). Variations could result from differences in service structure and philosophy, the level of local knowledge and skills surrounding FEP, clarity of pathway and treatment protocols for FEP and cultural norms within local communities.

It seems to be essential then that a local audit of delays and care pathways is first carried out if interventions are to be targeted appropriately. Barriers that are identified within each of the delay phases can then be addressed through interventions in the community, primary care and secondary care services.

Early detection and community education

Results from the TIPS study in Norway and Denmark suggest that programmes of community education and early detection can be effective in reducing treatment delay. The original study compared three treatment sites (two in Norway and one in Denmark), each a self-contained healthcare sector providing the same package of drug and psychosocial treatments. One site featured an additional early detection programme aiming to reduce DUP. This programme adopted two tactics: (1) an educational and anti-stigma campaign aimed at professionals and the community in general and (2) the provision of a widely advertised early detection team offering advice and a response within 48 hours. Results suggest that DUP was dramatically reduced where these interventions were in place and that this improvement has been maintained in areas where the campaign continued (Melle *et al.*, 2004; McGlashan *et al.*, 2007). These strategies may have been effective partly as a result of attracting young people who would not otherwise have attended services, as well as reducing DUP for those who might have reached services at a later stage of illness.

Rather than a blanket educational campaign, the UK approach is currently characterised by the targeting of specific pathway players as identified by local pathway audits. For example, the Birmingham Early Intervention Service has made efforts to reduce treatment delay by forging strong links with local community leaders. These relationships are important in guiding services to accurately serve the particular needs of each community, particularly given the high level of ethnic diversity that characterises the city.

Having an Early Detection arm to Early Intervention Services is particularly important in this endeavour, as demonstrated by EDIT (Early Detection and Intervention Team) in Birmingham and Manchester, and OASIS (Outreach and Support in South London) (Broome *et al.*, 2005) in Lambeth. In Birmingham, for example, the EDIT provides community education through links with statutory and non-statutory services and members of the local community. Awareness training and education programmes are provided to help people to identify early warning signs of psychosis, and specific guidance given to promote help-seeking.

Relationships with schools, colleges, universities, hostels and youth services are particularly important to facilitating help-seeking. Individually tailored workshops inform professional staff and young people themselves about mental health issues, the signs to watch out for and how to access services. Educational toolkits are also being developed, including the use of multimedia such as the 'State of Mind' DVD that was co-developed by service users and a local school.

The Birmingham EDIT is also developing a youth-oriented website that young people and professionals can be directed to as an accessible source of information on mental health, the signs to look out for and who to turn to for help. The Internet is fast becoming an indispensable medium for communication with young people, with positive-mental-health sites aiming to reduce stigma and offer confidential advice and signposting.

Interventions in primary care

GPs play a particularly important role in pathways to care for early psychosis. Studies in

Birmingham and London have reported 72% and 63% (respectively) of individuals with FEP to have consulted their GP at some point during their pathway to care (Brunet, 2004; Power *et al.*, 2007). The benefits of early GP involvement include a clear association with reduced likelihood of police involvement, inpatient admission and compulsory admission (Cole *et al.*, 1995; Power *et al.*, 2007).

The potential for GPs to play a major role in the improvement of care pathways and reduction of delays has been targeted by the REDIRECT programme, described in more detail elsewhere in this book. This randomised control trial provides GP practices with an educational package focusing on early psychosis and is examining the impact on treatment delay and other variables. The training programme revolved around video-based vignettes of GP consultations for suspected psychosis, with practice-based exercises around key symptoms to look out for and questions to ask. Information booklets and tip sheets are provided, and refresher sessions arranged to reinforce the guidance (Lester *et al.*, 2005).

In a similar study, the LEO-CAT (Lambeth Early Onset Crisis Assessment Team) trial provided a group of GPs access to an early detection team in addition to an educational programme, and found that this package encouraged GPs to refer directly to mental health services, reducing the number of young people who experienced long delays before assessment and treatment (Power *et al.*, 2007).

Interventions in secondary care

Interventions targeting secondary care services are also crucial if treatment delay is to be reduced. Prior to the establishment of an Early Intervention Service in one locality we found that delays in secondary services contributed 35% of overall mean DUP (Brunet *et al.*, 2007). Qualitative information indicated a number of factors that may have contributed to the delays in mental health services. First, long waiting lists for an initial appointment were common. These delays were sometimes compounded when individuals failed to attend three initial appointments and were automatically discharged, necessitating a lengthy process of re-referral. After inception into mental health services, delays also occurred where ambiguous presentations led to misdiagnosis and a course of intervention before a psychosis was identified. In some cases, misdiagnosis was avoided through periods of drug-free assessment, again contributing to the postponement of 'criteria treatment'. Finally, once a thorough assessment had been completed and a psychosis identified, individuals sometimes declined treatment.

These observations are currently being explored both locally and nationally as part of the 'National Eden' evaluation study of Early Intervention Services (Lester *et al.*, 2006). This project will enable individual Early Intervention Services to audit local treatment delays and provide targeted intervention strategies. It may be that organisational changes could allow for more prompt initial appointments, and that more assertive approaches could avoid inappropriate discharge where clients are unable or unwilling to attend outpatient appointments. A greater focus on the improvement of initial service engagement in this group might also reduce treatment delay, amongst other benefits.

Most crucially, Early Intervention Services need to provide clarity in the definition of FEP and share this understanding with professionals from primary care, secondary care and voluntary services. This should be accompanied by a clear treatment protocol and clearly marked pathways into Early Intervention. In Birmingham for example, the EDIT offers regular training days for NHS and voluntary sector staff. Since opening its doors in 2002, contact with referring services has resulted in increasingly appropriate referrals, perhaps reflecting the impact of EDIT on local awareness and understanding of early psychosis in primary and secondary services.

The team now hopes to extend this programme to systematically train all Community Mental Health Teams, Consultant Psychiatrists, junior medical staff, Community Psychiatric Nurses and Clinical Psychologists in the early detection and recognition of emerging psychosis, with the aim of lowering the threshold for suspicion and referral to EDIT and Early Intervention teams. Training will utilise case studies and local DUP data to enable identification and problem solving of pathway barriers for each locality.

Most importantly, services need to be equipped to offer timely and appropriate treatment for the referrals that arise from these programmes. Of young people reaching services for a first episode of psychosis, we found 29% to have begun seeking help during the 'prodromal' or 'at risk phase' of their psychosis (Brunet *et al.*, 2006). Early detection teams such as EDIT therefore play an increasingly key role not only in the reduction of treatment delay, but also in the provision of expert care once young people arrive at the end of their pathway.

Case studies

Paula

Paula lived with her mother and father who had both experienced mental health problems while she was a child. Paula was often bullied because of this, and found it difficult to get on with other children at school. She managed to stay away from the bullies by skipping school and spending time on her own, and she began to fall behind with her school work. In the evenings, Paula did not have many friends to socialise with and she became anxious around children of her own age, though she did play with her younger sister's friends occasionally. As she entered puberty, Paula began spending more and more time alone, finding it difficult to relate to her family and experiencing increasing levels of anxiety.

Feeling comforted by spiritual beliefs, Paula immersed herself in a growing interest in religion, and spent more and more time researching different faiths and developing her own spiritual perspective. As Paula's fascination grew, she developed the idea that her purpose in life was to consider various religious perspectives and to uncover the truth amongst them. Her family noticed that she had become increasingly religious, but as Paula had always been quite withdrawn they did not consider this to be unusual, and were unaware of the extent of her beliefs.

When Paula was 18, a visiting aunt, Jackie, was keen for Paula to look for work in order to contribute financially to the running of the family home. On talking to Paula, her aunt realised that Paula was not lazy as she had believed, but was finding it difficult to leave the house because of her anxieties. Jackie wondered whether Paula was suffering from depression and asked her GP about this possibility next time she visited. Her GP suggested that Paula be encouraged to visit her own doctor, which Jackie mentioned to Paula's mother. Paula did not feel that there was anything wrong with her, and did not think that the doctor would understand her.

The issue was not raised again until Jackie visited again and noticed that Paula sometimes found it difficult to concentrate during their conversations. At these times, Paula was retreating into thoughts about the perspectives of various religions, and had begun to interpret these thoughts as being the voices of religious leaders. Worried that her aunt would think this weird, Paula told Jackie that she had a hearing problem for which Jackie arranged a GP's appointment. Paula's doctor could not find any physical problems with Paula's ears and referred her to a hearing specialist in response to Paula's vague description of the complaint. Several months later, the specialist reported no physical problems with Paula's ears.

Dissatisfied with this outcome, Jackie took Paula back to the GP who began to suspect from Paula's withdrawn presentation that she was experiencing symptoms of depression. When a prescription of antidepressants had no visible effect after several appointments, the GP referred Paula to psychiatric services. Paula first met with a psychiatrist 3 months later, but spoke very little while her aunt explained that she thought Paula was experiencing a depression. Paula was prescribed an alternative antidepressant and visited the psychiatrist twice more over a period of 4 months. During the second appointment, the psychiatrist noticed that Paula smiled to herself at times for no apparent reason and began to suspect that she was hearing voices. On further questioning, Paula admitted that this was the case and was referred to the local Early Intervention Service.

Matt

Matt was living alone when he first experienced problems with his mental health. As a child he had lived with his parents and sister, and had a wide circle of friends. He stayed in touch with the closest of these friends when he left school and began training as a mechanic. Matt had always enjoyed working with cars and got on well in his new job. A few months later, however, Matt was shocked when his parents separated and his mother began spending time with a man who behaved aggressively towards Matt and his sister. Matt felt that his mum started to act differently towards him, ignoring her boyfriends' aggressive behaviour and criticising Matt more than she had in the past. Matt did not feel welcome at home and moved into a bedsit that was some distance from his family and friends.

The suddenness of these changes left Matt with a sense of shock, and he struggled to cope with the mixed emotions that he felt towards his mother and her new boyfriend.

Having moved to another part of the city, Matt also found it more difficult to spend time with his friends, and to speak to them openly about his family's situation. His friends noticed that Matt was becoming more withdrawn and that he was behaving in a way that was unusual for him. They noticed him muttering to himself from time to time, and on one occasion saw him shouting as if he were in an argument with someone. When a friend visited him at his bedsit and saw a knife beside his bed, she became frightened and called the police. Hearing that Matt had been seen talking to himself, the police requested an assessment by a psychiatrist, who promptly referred Matt to the Early Intervention Service.

Implications and conclusions

The Department of Health (DH, 2002) and Early Psychosis Declaration (Bertolote & McGorry, 2005) both emphasise the reduction of treatment delay as an important target. Shorter delays are likely not only to improve the prognosis of a psychosis itself, but also reduce the impact of the illness on a young person's social, vocational and psychological development. These outcomes aside, more prompt treatment is likely to reduce the enormous distress commonly experienced by young people and their families during this difficult time.

Although Early Intervention Services are vital to the reduction of treatment delay, their existence alone is not sufficient to achieve this goal. Local audits are necessary to identify treatment and pathway barriers, and to inform targeted interventions in the community and in primary care and secondary care services. Early detection teams provide a linking of statutory and non-statutory services, Early Intervention and Community Mental Health Teams, and are key to the dissemination of clear protocols for identification and referral.

References

Barnes, T.R.E., Hutton, S.B., Chapman, M.J., Mutsatsa, S., Puri, B.K. & Joyce, E.M. (2000). West London first-episode study of schizophrenia: Clinical correlates of duration of untreated psychosis. *British Journal of Psychiatry*, 177, 207–211.

Bertolote, J. & McGorry, P. (2005). Early intervention and recovery for young people with early psychosis: Consensus statement. *British Journal of Psychiatry*, 187 (Suppl. 48), s116–s119.

Broome, M.R., Woolley, J.B., Johns, L.C. *et al.* (2005). Outreach and support in south London (OASIS): Implementation of a clinical service for prodromal psychosis and the at risk mental state. *European Psychiatry*, 20, 372–378.

Brunet, K.F. (2004). *Treatment delay in first-episode psychosis: Service configuration, pathways to care and the psychology of help-seeking.* Unpublished PhD Manuscript, University of Birmingham.

Brunet, K., Birchwood, M., Lester, H., Iqbal, Z., Thornhill, K. & Coles, S. (2006). Treatment delay and pathways to care in early psychosis: The trouble with ambiguous cases. *Schizophrenia Research*, 86, S40–S40.

Brunet, K.F., Birchwood, M., Lester, H. & Thornhill, K. (2007). Delays in mental health services and duration of untreated psychosis. *Psychiatric Bulletin*, 31, 408–410.

Cole, E., Leavey, G., King, M., Johnson Sabine, E. & Hoar, A. (1995). Pathways to care for patients with a first episode of psychosis – A comparison of ethnic groups. *British Journal of Psychiatry*, 167, 770–776.

Department of Health (2002). *The NHS Plan: Improvement, Expansion and Reform.* London: HMSO.

Harvey, S.B., Dean, K., Morgan, C. *et al.* (2008). Self-harm in first-episode psychosis. *The British Journal of Psychiatry*, 192, 178–184.

Larsen, T.K., Johannessen, J.O. & Opjordsmoen, S. (1998). First-episode schizophrenia with long duration of untreated psychosis. Pathways to care. *The British Journal of Psychiatry Supplement*, 172, 45–52.

Lester, H., Tait, L., Khera, A., Birchwood, M., Freemantle, N. & Patterson, P. (2005). The development and implementation of an educational intervention on first episode psychosis for primary care. *Medical Education*, 39, 1006–1014.

Lester, H.E., Birchwood, M. & Rogers, H. (2006). Eden: Evaluating the development and impact of early intervention services in the West Midlands. *Schizophrenia Research*, 86, S50–S50.

Malla, A.K., Takhar, J.J., Norman, R.M.G. *et al.* (2002). Negative symptoms in first episode non-affective psychosis. *Acta Psychiatrica Scandinavica*, 105, 431–439.

Marshall, M., Lewis, S., Lockwood, A., Drake, R., Jones, P. & Croudace, T. (2005). Association between duration of untreated psychosis and in cohorts of first-episode outcome patients – A systematic review. *Archives of General Psychiatry*, 62, 975–983.

McGlashan, T.H. (1999). Duration of untreated psychosis in first-episode schizophrenia: Marker or determinant of course? *Biological Psychiatry*, 46, 899–907.

McGlashan., T., Joa, I., Larsen, T.K. *et al.* (2007). Educational information campaigns are critical to reducing duration of untreated psychosis. *Schizophrenia Bulletin*, 33, 486–486.

McGorry, P., McFarlane, C., Patton, G. *et al.* (1995). The prevalence of prodromal features of schizophrenia in adolescence – A preliminary survey. *Acta Psychiatrica Scandinavica*, 92, 241–249.

Melle, I., Larsen, T.K., Haahr, U. *et al.* (2004). Reducing the duration of untreated first-episode psychosis: Effects on clinical presentation. *Archives of General Psychiatry*, 61 (2), 143–150.

Morgan, C., Mallett, R., Hutchinson, G. *et al.* (2005a). Pathways to care and ethnicity. I: Sample characteristics and compulsory admission – Report from the AESOP study. *British Journal of Psychiatry*, 186, 281–289.

Morgan, C., Mallett, R., Hutchinson, G. *et al.* (2005b). Pathways to care and ethnicity. 2: Source of referral and help-seeking – Report from the AESOP study. *British Journal of Psychiatry*, 186, 290–296.

Morgan, C., Abdul-Al, R., Lappin, J.M. *et al.* (2006a). Clinical and social determinants of duration of untreated psychosis in the AESOP first-episode psychosis study. *British Journal of Psychiatry*, 189, 446–452.

Morgan, C. Fearon, P., Hutchinson, G. *et al.* (2006b). Duration of untreated psychosis and ethnicity in the AE SOP first-onset psychosis study. *Psychological Medicine*, 36, 239–247.

Norman, R.M.G. & Malla, A.K. (2001). Duration of untreated psychosis: A critical examination of the concept and its importance. *Psychological Medicine*, 31, 381–400.

Norman, R.M.G., Malla, A.K., Verdi, M.B., Hassall, L.D. & Fazekas, C. (2004). Understanding delay in treatment for first-episode psychosis. *Psychological Medicine*, 34, 255–266.

Power, P., Iacoponi, E., Reynolds, N. *et al.* (2007). The Lambeth Early Onset Crisis Assessment Team Study: General practitioner education and access to an early detection team in first-episode psychosis. *British Journal of Psychiatry*, 191 (Suppl. 51), s133–s139.

Verdoux, H., Bergey, C., Assens, F. *et al.* (1998). Prediction of duration of psychosis before first admission. *European Psychiatry*, 13, 346–352.

Chapter 3 **Inpatient provision in early psychosis**

Tom Craig and Paddy Power

Introduction

Early psychosis (EP) services are now well established in Europe, North America and Australia. A guiding principle of these services is that treatment should begin as early as possible in the course of the illness. In keeping with the wider provision of mental health care, much of the emphasis is on community-based initiatives, for example the provision of specialised early assessment and community outreach teams providing care across the first 2–3 years following onset. Acute emergencies are managed as far as possible in the community either by the specialised service or by separate crisis and home-treatment teams that provide 24-hour care directly to the individual's home.

Yet, despite this effort, more than a half of people with a first episode continue to be admitted to hospital and 60–80% will be admitted at some point during the initial 3 years of the disorder (Power *et al.*, 1998; Sipos *et al.*, 2001; Sanbrook *et al.*, 2003; Craig *et al.*, 2004; Gould *et al.*, 2006). In one London UK Borough, for example, while there is an extensive network of community services including well-functioning crisis resolution teams (Johnson *et al.*, 2005), assertive outreach (Killaspy *et al.*, 2006) as well as a specialist Early Intervention Service (EIS), over 72% of people presenting with a first episode had been hospitalised and almost half detained compulsorily within the first 3 months after initial contact with mental health services. Crisis resolution teams had initially accepted a third of these people for home treatment but almost half were then hospitalised suggesting that crisis resolution teams have, at best, only a modest impact on admission in first-episode psychosis (FEP) (Gould *et al.*, 2006).

Why hospitalise?

The main reasons for admission to hospital for FEP have not changed substantially since the introduction of EP services, and boil down to providing a secure base in which to manage risk of harm to self and others while waiting for treatment to bring about symptomatic and behavioural change sufficient for the patient to be managed in the community. How far this improvement needs to go before discharge depends on the capacity of community services, the tolerance of risk and whether the inpatient care is incentivised to reduce length of stay. Priorities for admission include command auditory hallucinations that give compelling instructions to the patient to harm himself or others; depression with suicidal content; manic symptoms with antisocial disinhibited behaviour; intercurrent physical illness or nutritional problems and behavioural disturbances including severe self-neglect, disorganisation and dangerousness. Another common, though less immediately pressing, reason is a poor response to community treatment, typically because of protracted delays in starting medication or poor compliance; but here, the balance of a short-term gain has to be weighed against longer-term engagement in treatment.

There is a typical timeline to any admission starting with the rapid resolution of non-specific 'distress' and disruptive behaviours – for example anxiety, insomnia, agitation and excitement, followed closely by the implementation and maintenance of an appropriate drug treatment for distressing 'positive' symptoms. Although these symptoms respond rapidly to medication with a reduction in positive symptoms as early as the first week of treatment (Agid *et al.*, 2003), it is not unusual for it to take a week or two before a substantial overall improvement is achieved. During this time, effort may go into resolving factors such as poor nutrition, physical ill health or substance abuse that may impede recovery and require interventions in their own right. It is also good practice to begin planning for discharge and aftercare as soon as the patient arrives on the ward, with a gradual shift in emphasis towards community activities and involvement of the community care team.

Problems in the acute ward environment

The shift to community services over the past three decades has not been without consequence for what remains of hospital care. In Britain, as more and more patients are successfully managed at home, hospital wards have reduced in size and the case mix has narrowed with higher levels of acuity, compulsory detention and a corresponding increase in behavioural disturbance and risk (Barker, 2000; Quirk & Lelliott, 2001; SCMH, 2004). Hospitalisations are shorter now than they were in the 1980s, readmissions as a proportion of all admissions is rising as is average occupancy, which is well over 100% in many acute adult inpatient settings. Acute inpatient units are now managing a selected group of patients with very severe symptoms, a very poor level of functioning and at high risk to themselves or others. Rates of admission for minority ethnic groups, particularly people of African or Caribbean lineage in the UK, are over three times higher than the average, with a greater proportion of these originating from contact with emergency rooms and the criminal justice system and often resulting in involuntary detention and treatment (Leff, 2005).

In this climate, hospitalisation of a young person in their first episode of illness is almost certain to be a frightening experience and it is not surprising that symptoms akin to those in post-traumatic stress disorder (PTSD) have been reported (McGorry et al., 1991; Jackson, 2004). The circumstances of admission may include compulsion and in the initial phases may have involved interventions such as seclusion (i.e. removal from the open-ward setting

to a side room on their own) and physical restraint. Patients are confronted by the agitated, distressed and sometimes violent behaviours of other residents and meet older patients with chronic conditions that may well be taken as an alarming forewarning of a possible future. Thus, if hospitalisation is needed, it is important to minimise this trauma through attention to the environment, personal comfort, clear explanations of admission procedures and, where possible, minimisation of exposure to chronic illness.

Sadly, the quality of care in acute adult inpatient wards often falls well short of these ideals. In England, for example, hospital wards are frequently criticised by patients and staff (Greenwood et al., 1999; Rose, 2001). Patients complain of feeling unsafe and of experiencing harassment, threats and violence (Greenwood et al., 1999; MIND, 2004). They report that low staffing levels mean that nurses have too little time to talk and in one survey of 400 inpatients, a third said that staff had been frankly rude or patronising (Greenwood et al., 1999). The Sainsbury Centre for Mental Health one-day National survey of inpatient care in England 2003–2004 (SCMH, 2004) reported average vacancy rates for qualified nurses of 13%, sickness rates of 6.8% and the average use of temporary agency staff amounting to more than four full-time staff per ward. Only a quarter of the wards had adequate assistance (domestic and clerical) to ensure that the ward was clean, equipment in order and service user privacy and dignity were maintained. Other identified problems included the drain of better staff to new community services and problems with communication between the different elements of hospital and community services. In a recent survey of all acute inpatient mental health wards in England by the Healthcare Commission (HCC), significant variations between the quality of care received by patients were highlighted (HCC, 2008). This confirms that although improving inpatient care has been a key priority for all mental health trusts for some years, there is still a lot of work to be done. On a more positive note, Trusts that performed well in the survey demonstrate that it is possible to make a difference.

The HCC (2008) have identified the following priorities as the next steps:

- Putting a greater focus on the individual and care that is personalised;
- Ensuring the safety of service users, staff and visitors;
- Providing appropriate and safe interventions;
- Increasing the effectiveness of the acute care pathway.

A not surprising consequence of a system that prioritises the shortest possible length of stay is the gradual erosion of activities that rely on the development of therapeutic relationships (be they individual or group), which may never be given much chance to develop in the case of an acutely unwell, involuntary patient. However, high levels of inactivity and boredom have long been known to have a deleterious impact on the outcome of severe mental disorders (Wing & Brown, 1970). Poor quality of life and low satisfaction scores are correlated with inactivity (Kelly *et al.*, 2001). Patients offered activity engage earlier in ward groups, and activity scheduling on inpatient wards produced significant reductions in depression compared to supportive psychotherapy (Hopko *et al.*, 2003).

Improving the inpatient experience

In recent years, there has been a significant effort to address these problems. One suggestion has been to develop dedicated FEP inpatient facilities or to use existing non-hospital crisis centres as an alternative (Killaspy *et al.*, 2000). Unfortunately, dedicated FEP facilities are still very uncommon and most patients in the public sector will continue to be admitted to general acute ward facilities. With this in mind, there is still much that can be done to improve the experience. A number of helpful guidelines addressing standards of care (Royal College of Psychiatrists, 2006) and websites offering advice and examples of good practice have been produced (STARWARDS, 2008). Although concerned with all aspects of psychiatric hospital care, these guidelines are also relevant for inpatient care of individuals with FEP.

Implementation into practice

Although the average age of individuals with a first episode of psychosis is around 26 years, a significant minority will be under 18 years of age. How might inpatient settings be created to be more acceptable for younger people?

A: The physical environment is clearly an important factor in the overall experience of inpatient care and it has profound influences on both patients and staff (Holahan & Saegert, 1973; Tyson *et al.*, 2002). The ward environment should be youth-friendly and bright in design. Space, light and cleanliness are paramount as all too often acute wards in public mental health services are a ghastly combination of scruffiness and dilapidated ill-assorted furniture. Even quite simple changes to ward layout, cleanliness and homeliness can have quite profound impact on people (Holahan & Saegert, 1973). The benefits of open wards and minimal restraint for the well-being of both patients and staff have been known long enough to hardly warrant mention. Yet, locked wards remain with us and may even be an increasing trend that parallels the rise in the proportion of involuntary patients on the wards of a typical inner-city service. In such facilities, the need for space is even more pressing, both in terms of adequate ward-based recreational space and also access to a garden area that is both a safe and pleasant space for patients and visitors alike. Patients should ideally have their own rooms and en suite toilets. Their rooms should contain a safe to secure personal belongings and they should be able to lock their own doors (albeit with staff override capability and anti-barricade design). Men and women should have separate sleeping accommodation and, where possible, separate sitting room/quiet space. It is also important to take into account cultural sensitivities for young women. Many acutely unwell patients sleep poorly at night and it is helpful to have observable sitting-room space that can be accessed at night with access to soft drinks available at all times.

For young people under the age of 18, admission to a child and adolescent mental health services (CAMHS) specific inpatient setting is recommended though this is not without difficulties.

Older adolescents experiencing florid psychotic symptoms can be a very uneasy 'fit' in a traditional CAMHS ward. One option is to provide separate areas for adolescents with psychoses within the same complex, for example the EPPIC inpatient psychosis unit in Melbourne is separated from the Adolescent Inpatient Unit but is linked in the middle by a shared intensive care area.

B. Security: Security for patients, visitors and staff is paramount. Nonetheless, it should be discrete so as not to cause undue alarm. There should be clear lines of sight across the ward, the minimisation of blind spots and the removal or close monitoring of ligature points and of access to and from the building. Fire safety and evacuation need particular attention (the EPPIC unit was twice partly destroyed by fire). Security systems including personal alarms for staff are now routinely provided in most wards and staff need to be trained in their use including the importance of ensuring that furniture is not arranged so that access to the alarm is blocked. Entrance and exit points need to be carefully designed to minimise the risk of absconding or injury to those attempting to force their way out. Toughened glass double doors with an 'airlock' mechanism controlled by the reception provide security and prevent unwelcome visitors. Some wards have built-in intensive care areas so that disturbed patients can be nursed in-house away from the other residents and minimising the need for transfer to a different care team.

All wards need protocols for acceptable conduct for patients and staff to ensure a safe and therapeutic environment. Policies should be in place to cover searching and restraint, rapid tranquillisation, seclusion and what to do to limit the importation and use of illicit drugs. The latter may include regular drug screening, some restrictions on visiting, leave entitlements and liaison with the police. Failure to deal effectively with behaviours such as drug use, bullying or sexual exploitation on a unit can quickly escalate out of control, putting the safety of staff and residents at serious risk. To minimise these problem behaviours, information should be clearly displayed so that there is no misunderstanding about the consequences of antisocial behaviours on the unit. Likewise,

it should be incorporated routinely into patients' care plans so that patients view it as integral to their recovery and relapse prevention. Persistent antisocial activity such as drug use or stealing, despite cautions, should prompt immediate discharge if the patient has mental capacity and does not meet criteria for detention under the mental health act or cessation of leave until the care plan can be adhered to. In response to very high rates of illicit drug use and growing prevalence of the so-called 'dual diagnosis', a number of services now employ specialist dual diagnosis workers and provide drug education and intervention programmes during inpatient stay. Developing drug abuse strategies was said to be one of the most successful interventions by participants in the London-based Acute Care Collaborative (2006).

A more contentious issue for staff is the introduction of cigarette-smoking bans on inpatient units. Staff worry that such bans will provoke confrontations and violence though there is no evidence for this from studies of bans (Lawn & Pols, 2005). It is not uncommon for young patients to be introduced to cigarette smoking during their first hospitalisation and it has significant long-term health consequences as well as increasing the doses required of antipsychotic medications. If smoking is not banned completely, it should be confined to designated smoking areas, for example outdoors in secure gardens/courtyards attached to the daytime areas of the units. Counselling and nicotine patches should be provided to help with cessation.

C. Zoning observation policies: Patient risk assessment and monitoring systems are an essential component of acute ward management. One system that has been successfully introduced is called the 'zoning' system (Gamble, 2006), which assigns a red, amber or green code/zone to each inpatient and determines the level of risk, observation, 1:1 time with staff and leave entitlement. All newly admitted patients are maintained in the 'red zone' for the first 72 hours while being assessed and only downgraded to amber or green zone by agreement of the treating multidisciplinary team. Any staff member can increase the zone if they have immediate concerns about the level of risk. Furthermore, patients at immediate risk of self-harm, sexual exploitation or physical violence may be placed on 1:1 nursing observations immediately by the nurse in charge of a shift or one of the medical staff with review on a shift-by-shift basis.

Implication into practice

All inpatient settings have explicit or implicit rules about how residents and staff will interact. It is important to consider what can be done to minimise the problems of 'institutionalisation' and dependency.

D. Integration with community services: Unlike the 'total institution' studied by Goffman in the 1960s, modern acute services are far more permeable to the community (Quirk *et al.*, 2006). One of the possible strengths of a specialist FEP service ought, therefore, to be a close integration of the inpatient and community teams. For all patients coming on to the ward, there should be a documented individual in the community team who will be involved throughout the admission and provide continuing contact on discharge. For most people, this will be the community staff who was involved before admission though some admissions will be for individuals with no prior contact and others will be transfers from the wider mental health service. For these patients, it should be a priority to sort out discharge arrangements and involve the community team from as early a point as possible. Patients admitted in an emergency may be appropriately concerned about arrangements for looking after children, the security of their home or the welfare of pets. Good working links with community teams can go a long way towards allaying these worries. Information and good communication are key.

E. Improving the first encounter: How individuals and their families are greeted on the ward can have profound effects on longer-term service satisfaction and engagement. It may be possible to plan for an admission and for individuals or families to see the ward before admission though our own local attempts to arrange this have often been overtaken by events despite best intentions. At the very least, on arrival, patients

should be introduced to a member of staff who will oversee the admission and as soon as possible should receive introductory information about the ward and the inpatient programme. This ideally is provided both in writing and by explanation and covers the aims of the ward, the current therapy programme, a description of rights and responsibilities, visiting arrangements and policy on personal belongings including the use (or not) of mobile phones. In the UK, all involuntarily detained patients must be informed of their legal rights on the day of their admission or as soon as they have the capacity to understand. Other information, for example on the availability of advocacy, legal services, benefits and housing advice, interpreting services and complaints procedures, should be provided at an early stage as soon as the individual is sufficiently well to understand and take in the information.

F. Assessment: A comprehensive assessment of the patient's needs will typically take place over several days with refinements to initial formulations as the individual's mental state improves. Often, the initial information is very limited and complicated by language barriers, problems accessing collateral information or indeed difficulties on the part of the client and families in recounting events prior to admission. Carers' observations are however an essential source of information and one helpful way that they can communicate this is in a written synopsis of the patient's life history (requesting the same of the patient is often inadvisable until they have made a good recovery). In the immediate phase, as with any acute admission, the assessment needs to cover physical health, mental state and risk to self and others. The physical examination is easily regarded as a mundane necessity and likely to turn up little of relevance in a young person with a first episode of psychosis. Yet, there are many physical conditions that include psychotic symptoms and that can be mistaken at first presentation. For example, 1% of first admissions to the Lambeth Early Onset (LEO) ward had psychoses found to be secondary to undiagnosed conditions such as systemic lupus erythematosis (SLE), multiple sclerosis (MS), AIDS and epilepsy and significant numbers have conditions such as diabetes, asthma and pregnancy, which need to be taken into consideration in prescribing psychotropic medication or that might make physical restraint dangerous.

Care plans should always be developed collaboratively, and it is considered good practice for the patient to have his/her own copy. Initial care plans are likely to focus on immediate risk issues, including, for example, the risk of absconding and a plan for alerting informal carers or other people who might be at risk. However, it is important to move quickly beyond this initial phase to a comprehensive needs assessment around which to develop consensual treatment plans.

Implementation into practice

Boredom is the great curse of hospital admission and inactivity has long been known to be bad for recovery. Consider what are the therapeutic and activity ingredients needed in a modern early intervention setting.

G. Interventions: These include medication, psychological interventions, occupational and educational activities that for a young population will include access to a gym, computers, library and educational facilities. Inpatient psychosocial group programmes impact significantly on clinical outcome during the acute phase (Drury et al., 1996). However, it is difficult, if not detrimental, to engage acutely psychotic patients in challenging individual or group therapy interventions, and such programmes should contain a mix of activity-based sessions with low key talking therapies. The importance of physical activity both as a pleasurable way to occupy time and also for well-established benefits on mental and physical health hardly needs emphasising. This provision need not involve much by way of expensive equipment. Football for those well enough to leave the ward, basketball in a garden area or even table tennis tournaments do the job nicely (Iancu et al., 2004). Each patient should have individual contact with a member of staff at least once in each shift in addition to whatever participation is required for group-based activities and specialist psychological or social therapy. In practice, this means that the team nurses need to

allocate some protected time for this as a matter of routine and this in turn has requirements in terms of staffing levels and supervision (Acute Care Collaborative, 2006). Regular supervision sessions should be provided for any staff providing formal psychological interventions. For additional interventions, it is far more cost-effective or better received by patients, to bring in specialist staff on a sessional basis (e.g. benefits advisors, pharmacists, music therapists etc.) than to expect regular nursing staff to undertake these unfamiliar roles.

The National Institute for Clinical Excellence (NICE) guidelines for the management of schizophrenia (National Institute for Clinical Excellence, 2002) recommend that the choice of medication should be made jointly with the patient on the basis of an informed discussion of the relative benefits and side effects of medication and which may also involve the patient's advocate or informal carer as appropriate. There should be clear ward protocols for medical and nursing staff about medication regimens including emergency oral and intramuscular (IM) medication and these should be audited regularly to identify problem prescribing, for example by on-call staff. Electro conductive therapy (ECT) use is rarely required, but still has a role in the most extremely disturbed and life-threatening situations with severe catatonia, depressive or manic psychosis. In the LEO service, 0.5% of first-episode patients had treatment with ECT.

Frequent sessions with medical staff are crucial in the initial days of explaining, deciding and monitoring medication treatment. Families want quick access to the Consultant Psychiatrist, and it provides a good opportunity to discuss issues such as diagnosis, aetiology, risks, treatment, recovery and long-term prognosis. Meeting early with families allows staff to undertake carer needs assessments as well as risk assessments of any children involved. It is advisable to notify social services of any childcare arrangements while lone parents are in hospital and invite them to family meetings if safety/supervision issues are a concern. Carer group psychoeducation sessions are a helpful addition to individual family counselling and support. Formal family therapy may also be helpful in a small proportion of particularly stressed families. Finally, identifying other 'at risk' members of the family may help with referrals to appropriate services.

The most common initial psychological intervention on the LEO ward is psychoeducation, with individually tailored information about psychosis, its causes and treatment. Patients and carers usually have concluded that the episode is either stress- or drug-induced, and it is best if staff can elaborate this 'stress vulnerability model' with brief explanations of underlying genetic predispositions, neurodevelopmental factors and the impact of triggers such as drug use on dopamine systems. This allows for an explanation of how drugs aggravate the psychosis and medication reduces the symptoms. The most important aspect of this is the instillation of hope in recovery and to normalise the experience of aspects of the illness. This needs to be balanced with a pragmatic account of what to expect during the recovery phase, for example depression, cognitive difficulties, amotivation, social anxiety and stigma. Mention should also be routinely made of aggression and suicide, with advice on prevention and sources of help. Checks and advice should be given if relevant on driving restrictions, gun licences and certain occupational hazards. Finally, all patients and carers should be informed from the start that medication should be taken for a minimum of 18 months to minimise the risk of relapse and that in some cases it will need to be for longer.

The evidence for the benefits of very early implementation of cognitive behavioural therapy (CBT) for psychosis during an acute admission is weaker (Tarrier *et al.*, 2004), though psychological approaches to manage distress, the trauma of early treatment and strategies for staying well on recovery are essential. Whatever the specific therapeutic interventions for an individual case, it is obviously important that these are regularly reviewed and that their continuation beyond hospital is thought about and implemented in advance of discharge. The activity programme, both at an individual and ward-group level, should include appropriate evening and weekend activity and as soon as the patient's condition allows, should include access to local community facilities, including those facilitated or supported by the community mental health team that will provide care on discharge from hospital.

H. Staffing numbers and skills: All this, of course, requires staff in sufficient numbers with adequate skills and good morale. For a service dealing with patients many of whom will be experiencing their first admission to hospital, getting this right might be pivotal to future collaboration and outcome. First must come a strategy to develop and retain a core team, minimising reliance on bank and agency staff. This core team needs to be equipped with a number of basic skills and competencies that are regularly updated and maintained. All staff should receive regular professional and clinical supervision and there should be an ongoing programme of professional development. This will include an adequate budget for training including arrangements for cross-cover to allow staff to attend training courses. The staff need to be consulted in the development of the service and particularly on aspects of policies and procedures that relate to their practice. These guidelines and policies should be easily accessible and regularly monitored. Levels of sickness or other absence need to be monitored and positive actions taken to reduce absence levels. This is often a matter of addressing staff shortages and low morale. The availability of a reflective practice or staff support group can be helpful. Access to work-related counselling is also important.

All staff who undertake assessments or are involved in care planning should be trained in managing risk both of self-harm and of dangerousness to others. Qualified staff should all have training and support to provide basic psychological interventions such as problem solving, group facilitation and activity scheduling. Some services use standardised outcome measures of symptoms or social functioning that require additional training in their use.

I. The use of restraint and seclusion: Clearly, all forms of restraint and seclusion should be avoided except in the most extreme circumstances when patients are at an immediate risk of injuring themselves or others (NICE guideline, 2005). If manual restraint by staff is required, it should be very brief and undertaken by a 'response team' with sufficient number of staff trained in 'control and restraint' techniques to avoid injuries and minimise distress (Wright, 2003). The patient should be reassured, brought quickly to a quiet area of the ward away from other patients to avoid embarrassment, distress and intrusion from other patients. Staff with training in defusing highly volatile confrontations should then engage the patient to ascertain what the issues are and how they can be resolved. Usually, PRN oral and sometimes IM medication is required in these circumstances. The use of locked seclusion rooms – up to 30% admissions in some countries (Tunde & Little, 2004) – should be avoided, as it is a very punitive and intensely distressing experience for patients (it has never been used in the LEO service). After incidents and injuries, there should be routine systems in place for prompt debriefing of staff, patient and carers (Bonner *et al.*, 2002). Incidents are a regular occurrence on acute wards managing young people with psychosis, and it is useful to have clinical audit systems in place to monitor them so that hot spots or critical times can be identified and preventative mechanisms put in place.

An illustrative example: The Lambeth Early Onset Ward

The LEO inpatient unit opened in March 2001 as an open acute inpatient unit for patients aged 18–35 years. It is an L-shaped 18-bed (10 male and 8 female) ward with segregated gender areas at opposite ends joining as a communal day-activity area in the middle. Priority is given to first-episode patients and those who relapse during the subsequent 2 years while being followed up by the LEO Community Team. It is staffed by a multidisciplinary team of 27 full-time equivalent (FTE) clinicians (team leader, 22 nurses and nurses assistants, two part-time consultant psychiatrists, two junior trainee psychiatrists, half-time clinical psychologist, occupational therapist, sessional group therapists, sessional benefits advisor, part-time pharmacist, medical secretary and administrator). The consultant psychiatrists work across the other LEO teams to provide continuity of care. It is funded on a standard adult mental health (UK) funding profile with five nurses on daytime shifts and four at night.

The LEO Unit aims to provide a youth-friendly atmosphere that is safe, collaborative and therapeutic. The focus is on psychosocial interventions, low-dose medication and collaborative engagement with clients and carers in treatment decisions. A weekday group programme provides a mix of activity and cognitive-oriented groups to address recovery and relapse prevention issues. Every effort is made to manage acutely disturbed patients on close observations on the unit, and it also has access to a nearby Psychiatric Intensive Care Unit (PICU) – approximately 5% of patients spend part of their admission in PICU.

In the first 3 years of operation, the LEO Unit had 647 admissions (484 clients), of which only 38% were first-episode/LEO patients (Hutchinson et al., 2004). The remainder were patients who could not be accommodated on other wards because of bed pressures and who typically stayed in LEO until beds became available on their sector ward. There is an attempt to prioritise younger patients in the earlier years of their illness, although this has not always been possible, and represents a significant extra demand on the unit/service's resources. At various times, proposals have been made to lease six of the 18 LEO unit beds to one of the Trusts' other Borough's EISs. However, acute bed pressures and the reconfiguration of other wards in Lambeth has to date prevented these solutions from being realised.

In the first 3 years of operation, two-thirds of admissions were male with an average age of 25.7 (Hutchinson et al., 2004). Men were significantly younger than women at first admission but there were no differences in length of stay or use of involuntary orders. The proportion of individuals in the LEO service being admitted at some point in the first year of contact with services fell from 75% in standard care services prior to the introduction of the LEO service to 60% by 2004. Thirty percent were readmitted following a relapse at some point in the subsequent 2 years. Relative to other acute wards on the same hospital site over the same time period, the LEO unit has had much lower rates of involuntary admissions. The LEO community team followed up 94% patients on discharge from hospital (nearly 5% were discharged to other parts of the country or overseas).

Implications and conclusions

It seems inevitable that hospital treatment will continue to be needed in the management of EP for the foreseeable future. Paradoxically, as community alternatives become more effective, so the acuity and 'pressure cooker' nature of the inpatient environment rises. Now, as never before, attention needs to be given to the design of these environments including their location, physical characteristics, facilities, number and skills of staff, integration with community services and in particular how well they address the needs of young people with FEP.

References

Acute Care Collaborative (2006). www.londondevelopmentcentre.org.uk

Agid, O., Kapur, S., Arenovich, T. & Zipursky, R. (2003). Delayed-onset hypothesis of antipsychotic action: A hypothesis tested and rejected. *Archives of General Psychiatry*, 60, 1228–1235.

Barker, S. (2000). *Environmentally Unfriendly: Patients' Views of Conditions on Psychiatric Wards*. London: Mind.

Bonner, G., Lowe, T.,Rawcliffe, D & Wellman, N. (2002). Trauma for all: A pilot study of the subjective experience of physical restraint for mental health inpatients and staff in the UK. *Journal of Psychiatric and Mental Health Nursing*, 9, 465–473.

Craig, T.K.J., Garety, P.A., Power, P. *et al.* (2004). Lambeth Early Onset (LEO) service. *BMJ*, 329, 1067–1068.

Drury, V., Birchwood, M., Cochrane, R. & Macmillan, F. (1996). Cognitive therapy and recovery from acute psychosis: A controlled trial. I. Impact on psychotic symptoms. *The British Journal of Psychiatry*, 169, 593–601.

Gamble, C. (2006). The zoning revolution. *Mental Health Practice*, 10, 14–17.

Gould, M., Theodore, K., Pilling, S., Bebbington, P., Hinton, M. & Johnson, S. (2006). Initial treatment phase in early psychosis: Can intensive home treatment prevent admission? *Psychiatric Bulletin*, 30, 243–246.

Green C., Hutchinson W., McGuire P. Power P. (2004). An evaluation of a first-episode psychosis inpatient unit: A clinical audit of the first three years of the Lambeth Early Onset (LEO) Unit in south London. *Schizophrenia Research*, 70 (1) (Suppl.), 131–132.

Greenwood, N., Key, A., Burns, T., Bristow, M. & Sedgwick, P. (1999). Satisfaction with in-patient psychiatric services. Relationship to patient and treatment factors. *The British Journal of Psychiatry*, 174, 159–163.

HCC (2008). *The pathway to recovery: A review of NHS acute inpatient mental health services.* Commission for Healthcare Audit and Inspection. Available to download from: http://www.healthcarecommission.org.uk/serviceproviderinformation/reviewsandstudies/servicereviews/improvement reviewmethodology/adultacuteinpatientmental-health.cfm (accessed 19.8.08).

Holahan, C. & Saegert, S. (1973). Behavioural and attitudinal effects of large-scale variation in the physical environment of psychiatric wards. *Journal of Abnormal Psychology*, 82, 454–462.

Hopko, D.R., Lejuez, C.W., Lepage, J.P., Hopko, S.D. & McNeil, D.W. (2003). A brief behavioural activation treatment for depression; a randomized pilot trial within an inpatient psychiatric hospital. *Behaviour Modification*, 27, 458–469.

Iancu, I., Strous, R.D., Nevo, N. & Chelben, J. (2004). A Table Tennis Tournament in the Psychiatric Hospital: Description and suggestion for salutogenic implications. *International Journal of Psychosocial Rehabilitation*, 9, 11–13.

Jackson, C., Knott, C., Skeate, A. & Birchwood, M. (2004). The trauma of first episode psychosis: The role of cognitive mediation. *Australian and New Zealand Journal of Psychiatry*, 38, 327–333.

Johnson, S., Nolan, F., Hoult, J. *et al.* (2005). Outcomes of crises before and after introduction of a crisis team. *The British Journal of Psychiatry*, 187, 68–75.

Kelly, S., McKenna, H., Parahoo, K. & Dusoir, A. (2001). The relationship between involvement in activities and quality of life for people with severe and enduring mental illness. *Journal of Psychiatric and Mental Health Nursing*, 8, 139–146.

Killaspy, H., Dalton, J., Mcnicholas, S. & Johnson, S. (2000). Drayton Park, an alternative to hospital admission for women in acute mental health crisis. *Psychiatric Bulletin*, 24, 101–104.

Killaspy, H., Bebbington, P., Blizard, R. *et al.* (2006). The REACT study: Randomised evaluation of assertive community treatment in north London. *BMJ*, 332, 815–820.

Lawn, S. & Pols, R. (2005). Smoking bans in psychiatric inpatient settings? A review of the research. *The Australian and New Zealand Journal of Psychiatry*, 39, 866–885.

Leff, J. (2005). Pathways to care and ethnicity. 1: Sample characteristics and compulsory admission. *British Journal of Psychiatry*, 186, 281–289.

McGorry, P., Chanen, A., McCarthy, E., Van Riel, R., McKenzie, D. & Singh, B. (1991). Post-traumatic stress disorder following recent onset psychosis: An unrecognised post psychotic syndrome. *Journal of Nervous and Mental Disease*, 179, 253–258.

MIND (2004). *Ward Watch – MIND's campaign to improve hospital conditions for mental health patients. www.mind.org.uk.*

National Institute for Clinical Excellence (2002). *Clinical Guideline 1: Schizophrenia: Core Interventions in the Treatment and Management of Schizophrenia in Primary and Secondary Care.* London: NICE.

NICE (2005). *Violence: The Short-Term Management of Disturbed/Violent Behaviour in In-Patient Psychiatric Settings and Emergency Departments Clinical Guideline CG25.* National Institute for Clinical Excellence. http://guidance.nice.org.uk

Power, P., Elkins, K., Adlard, S. *et al.* (1998) Analysis of the initial treatment phase in first-episode psychosis. *British Journal of Psychiatry*, 172 (Suppl.), 171–176.

Quirk, A. & Lelliott, P. (2001). What do we know about life on acute psychiatric wards in the UK? A review of the research evidence. *Social Science & Medicine*, 53, 1565–1574.

Quirk, A., Lelliott, P. & Seale, C., (2006). The permeable institution: An ethnographic study of three acute psychiatric wards in London. *Social Science & Medicine*, 63, 2105–2117.

Rose, D. (2001). *Users Voices: The Perspectives of Mental Health Service Users on Community and Hospital Care.* London: Sainsbury Centre for Mental Health.

Royal College of Psychiatrists (2006). *Accreditation for Acute Inpatient Mental Health Services (AIMS): Standards for Acute Inpatient Wards.* London: Royal College of Psychiatrists.

STARWARDS (2008) http://starwards.org.uk/

Sainsbury Centre for Mental Health (2004). *Acute Care 2004: A National Survey of Adult Psychiatric Wards in England.* London: Sainsbury Centre for Mental Health.

Sanbrook, M., Harris, A., Parada, R. *et al.* (2003). The effectiveness of an early intervention team in the treatment of first episode psychosis. *Australian e-Journal for the advancement of Mental Health*, 2, 2–9.

Sipos, A., Harrison, G., Gunnell, D., Amin, S. & Singh S.P. (2001). Patterns and predictors of hospitalisation in first-episode psychosis. Prospective cohort study. *British Journal of Psychiatry*, 178, 518–523.

Tarrier, N., Lewis, S., Haddock, G. *et al.* (2004). Cognitive-behavioural therapy in first-episode and early schizophrenia: 18-month follow-up of a randomised controlled trial. *British Journal of Psychiatry*, 184, 231–239.

Tunde, A.M. & Little, J. (2004). Use of seclusion in a psychiatric acute inpatient unit. *Australasian Psychiatry*, 12, 347–351.

Tyson, G., Lambert, G. & Beattie, L. (2002). The impact of ward design on the behaviour, occupational satisfaction and well-being of psychiatric nurses. *International Journal of Mental Health Nursing*, 11, 94–102.

Wing, J.K. & Brown, G.W. (1970). Institutionalism and schizophrenia: A comparative study of three mental health hospitals 1960–1968. London: Cambridge University Press.

Wright, S. (2003). Control and restraint techniques in the management of violence in inpatient psychiatry: A critical review. *Medicine Science and the Law*, 43, 31–38.

Orygen Youth Health: http://www.orygen.org.auv

Chapter 4 **Developing youth-focused services**

Kathryn Pugh and Clare Lamb

Introduction

The Early Psychosis Declaration (EPD) describes the importance of 'comprehensive programmes for the detection and treatment of early psychosis' . . . with the 'important function of promoting recovery, independence, equity and self-sufficiency and of facilitating the uptake of social, educational and employment opportunities for those young people' (Bertolote & McGorry, 2005).

Detection and recognition are the first steps and rely on a better understanding and a reduction in the stigma currently associated with mental illness in general, and psychosis in particular. Indeed, the importance of raising community awareness and reducing the stigma which surrounds a diagnosis of psychosis was recognised by the EPD in requiring that all 15-year olds are equipped by mainstream education to understand and deal with psychosis, and that psychosis-specific training is available to teachers and other relevant community agencies. However, to be effective, this ambitious aim must be linked with provision of youth-focused, high-quality effective services for children and young people with first-episode psychosis. This need was recognised as a priority by the Department of Health and addressed specifically in the NHS Plan (Department of Health, 2000). This states that Child and Adolescent Mental Health Services (CAMHS) and Adult Mental Health Services (AMHS) should work together with commissioners to ensure that all young people in England, aged 14–35 years, with a first episode of psychosis receive early intervention by a designated Early Psychosis Service. Developing an Early Intervention Service (EIS) for first-episode psychosis, which genuinely meets the needs of young people presents service providers and commissioners with a range of opportunities and challenges.

This chapter considers the following questions:

- What do young people say they want from a mental health service?
- What other elements help to develop an inclusive and accessible EIS?
- What models of EIS have been adopted to meet these needs?
- What are the challenges faced in developing EISs, and how have these challenges been met?
- What are the top tips to help Early Intervention in psychosis services (EIS) survive and grow?
- What are some of the questions service providers and commissioners might consider to help develop reflective practice?

Background

The position and relationship of the EIS with respect to local Children's Services, Youth Services and Adult Mental Health Services is key, and will impact on the model of service provided. An EIS may choose to sit with 'high threshold' adult teams and become a service for young people with frank presentation of psychosis only, or alternatively with generic Youth Services or CAMHS, who will accept a broader range of presenting difficulties but may not be as experienced in identifying the early symptoms of psychosis.

EISs in England are not uniform. They can range from one or two dedicated staff 'bolted on' to existing services who can only offer a limited range of support, to comprehensive multidisciplinary teams, which are integrated well within adolescent and adult mental health teams and offer effective and accessible services which have the needs of the user at their core.

EISs offer young people the perspective that suffering from a severe mental illness does not mean the end of hope, nor should it mean the end of their dreams of a life with a career, a home and a family. Early Intervention in Psychosis (EIS) teams which build and measure themselves against criteria which are shaped and designed around and by young service users are much more likely to engage with young people and deliver a service which meets their needs. There has been considerable research into the type of services young people want. As EI services become the norm rather than the exception, teams must make sure that they are aware of what makes a service appealing and accessible to young people.

Developing youth-focused services

Young people between the ages of 14 and 25 may experience a prolonged period of uncertainty and turmoil in their lives. It is a crucial stage of social, personal and emotional development, a time for completing education, contemplating significant life choices regarding careers and moving away from home to become truly independent. The brain as well as the body of a young person is still developing and the early adult years are critical for the formation of self-image, social skills and impulse control (Young Minds, 2006). Young people experience pressure to achieve at school and/or to conform to different street cultures. Alcohol and drugs are readily available. They live in a stressful busy world with the domination of media, a decline in social cohesion, a reduction of opportunities to buy their own home or move into a job, which assures them of lifelong employment. Mental ill health in adolescents is rising (Collishaw et al., 2004) and the transition period from adolescence to adulthood coincides with the age of onset of a number of severe mental disorders including psychosis.

Do we have the mental health services to meet the needs of young people? There has been a wide range of policy initiatives from the government and considerable investment in England

in both adult and children and adolescent services. This very welcome investment has allowed many new community services to develop; however, services were under funded at the start and there is still a lack of capacity to support young people showing early signs of mental distress (Social Exclusions Unit, 2004; Street et al., 2004; HASCAS, 2006).

In the context of general service development, it would be reasonable to expect EISs for young people to be a priority. Psychosis 'ticks all the boxes' as an illness, which requires immediate attention and has the potential to become a lifelong condition. It is a serious mental illness which may require monitoring for many years and can significantly affect a young person's life chances, leading to dropping out of school or college, family breakdown, hospitalisation and in some cases, treatment under the Mental Health Act.

Evidence is emerging that early treatment not only leads to better individual outcomes for young people, but can lead to financial savings in the medium- and long-term treatment (Knapp et al., 2008). However, unfortunately, EI services still struggle to become a funding priority for commissioners. The funding problem may be because EI services were the last in the queue to be developed after Adult Crisis and Assertive Outreach Teams. It may reflect the split in how services are planned and funded. Despite a change in Government Policy (Department for Education and Skills & Department of Health, 2004), stating that CAMHS in England must provide a service up to 18 years by December 2006, in some parts of the country, 16- and 17-year olds are still left without services, as commissioners and service providers fail to agree about who should treat them. The different professional cultures of CAMHS and adult mental health have contributed to differences in theory and practice, including differences in eligibility thresholds for referral and in the level and style of intervention (Reder et al., 2000).

It is recognised that particular groups of young people at high risk of developing mental health problems in adult life may not be accessing mental health services, including those looked after by the local authority, young people from Black and Minority Ethnic communities, the homeless or those seeking refugee or asylum status (Richards & Vostanis, 2004).

EISs for psychosis must take these issues into account and must span the divide between CAMHS and AMHS. An effective EI service is one, which exists in a framework of positive relationships between the adult service, CAMHS service and commissioners as well as social services, education and local non-statutory and community services.

> *You need something in-between rather than just jumping from child to adult services . . . you need one specific person who will stick with you and not lots of different people who will just pass you on the whole time.*
>
> – Young person (Pushed into the Shadows, p. 36)

The Royal College of Psychiatrists NICAPS report (O'Herlihy *et al.*, 2001) identified a national problem with a general shortage of child and adolescent inpatient beds, the lack of emergency facilities available, inadequate inpatient provision for young people with severe and high-risk needs and the use of adult psychiatric beds for children and young people. The Young Minds' study 'Whose Crisis?' (Street, 2000) identified particular problems with inpatient provision for young people aged 16–19. There are a number of concerns about the adequacy and effectiveness of treatment and care for young people offered by adult psychiatric wards. A study for 11 Million, the Children's Commissioner report for England, highlighted the issues for young people treated inappropriately on adult psychiatric wards (11 Million, 2007). This has been addressed by changes to the 1983 Mental Health Act for England and Wales. The government has committed to introducing a duty on Hospital Managers in April 2010 to ensure that a young person under the age of 18 years, whether a voluntary or detained inpatient, is admitted to an environment suitable for their age, subject to their need (DH, 2007).

What do young people say about what makes a good service?

There is considerable research into what young people want from a mental health service (Howarth & Street, 2000; Smith & Leon, 2001; Street *et al.*, 2005; Garcia *et al.*, 2007). Young people want to be involved as a matter or course in planning services from the earliest point, and to be involved in designing evaluation and outcome measures. Service users want to know that when they have an input, their views will be listened to, respected and acted upon. Young people who are involved directly are more likely to be more satisfied. There is evidence that involving users in service development reduces anxiety and improves trust and relationships with professionals (Farrel, 2004).

Services need to be easily accessible, and how services are accessed must make sense to young people – can they, for example, self-refer and if not, why not?

Services must be there in a crisis. Young people in crisis are much more likely to act on impulse. However, a young person's criteria for what constitutes a crisis can be very different from a professional's perspective, and this needs to be explored. The environment where a service is provided is crucial. If EI teams use a clinic base for assessments and therapeutic work, that base needs to reflect the age of the young people. Young people are very sensitive to the potential stigma of attending a mental health clinic. Referral to a day hospital attended by much older service users is unlikely to meet developmental needs and does not send out a message of recovery. Some services have overcome the problem of the stigma of being in a statutory service by being located in a voluntary sector organisation such as in 'The Zone' in Plymouth. Voluntary sector 'shop front' services can be much more appealing (Macleod & Parker, 1986; DFES, 2005). Services must be multiagency, multidisciplinary and be prepared to cope with more than just the mental health issues – they must take a psychosocial approach. Providing an honest evaluation of young people's difficulties and encouraging them to aspire and achieve realistic goals are more likely to engage young service users and their families than offering a bleak picture of a lifetime of chronic ill health with no prospects. Young people rarely have one problem – for example, if their family cannot cope with their illness, they may become homeless, or if they have a substance misuse problem, they may fall between services. Young people want a service which does not pass them around like a parcel – they have very little interest in who is providing the service, be it a youth worker, social worker, psychiatric nurse or psychiatrist, they just want help.

If a young person under the age of 18 needs inpatient treatment, it must be in an environment, which reflects their developmental needs, particularly if circumstances mean they are admitted to an adult ward. Young people who have been placed on adult wards report lack of education, lack of treatment, poor discharge planning and limited access to treatment other than medication (11 Million, 2007). The needs of an individual will change during their stay as an inpatient – for example, a young person experiencing a psychotic crisis may not be well enough to access education initially, but as he/she recovers, the provision of education is vital.

Young people who have been detained on adult wards reported extreme stress and anxiety caused by the environment, as well as their illness.

I need treatment to get over my treatment.
– Young person (Pushed into the Shadows, p. 74)

If a young person has negative experiences on an adult ward including (at the extreme) verbal, physical or sexual abuse, they will be much less likely to engage with services in the future. This can lead to repeated presentations in crisis, with a cycle of admissions under the Mental Health Act and disengagement. In some areas, teams are able to access crisis houses where young service users and their families can be offered intensive support in an environment which is smaller and separate from a busy general ward where patients' ages can range up to 60 years.

Peer groups and friendship are extremely important to this age group. Services must enable young people with psychosis to maintain contact with their peers and social networks as well as their family. The EPD (Bertolote & McGorry, 2005) highlights the importance of early engagement and involvement of families and close friends in the care and treatment of the young person where appropriate.

There must be an awareness of the cultural needs of young people. Mental ill health carries differential levels of stigma in different communities. In many communities, prayer and faith play an important and beneficial role in young people's lives (Street *et al.*, 2005). Research has highlighted a high level of fear and suspicion of mental health services by many in the Black community (The Sainsbury Centre for Mental Health, 2002). Service design must reflect the needs of the community it serves.

Examples of different service models

Despite the challenges referred to above, in recent years there has been considerable development of innovative mental health services, including First-episode Psychosis Services that promote greater working between Child and Adult Mental Health Services (Maitra & Jolley, 2000) and which have responded to the needs identified by young people. Across England, Early Psychosis Services have been set up to span the traditional age range across CAMHS and Adult services and in some areas have acted as a catalyst to the further development of generic mental health services that bridge the transition age.

Research on service structure that bridges the 'transition' age recommends any or a combination of the following types of service:

- Designated service;
- Designated team within a service;
- Designated staff trained in adolescent work seconded to adult teams (Richards & Vostanis, 2004).

Designated service: Comprehensive multidisciplinary teams

In some areas, fully funded multidisciplinary teams exist whose main focus is the treatment of first-episode psychosis and who see all children and adults from 14 to 35 years. In order to meet the needs of the younger age group, these teams have designated sessional input from clinicians with training and expertise in Child and Adolescent Mental Health. In other areas, there are fully funded multidisciplinary teams designed to meet the generic mental health needs of older adolescents only. The majority of the latter link with or are part of the EIS for psychosis.

In both models, the teams tend to have good working relationships with the local Home Treatment and Crisis Resolution Teams as well as Social Services, Education, the local Youth Offending Team and Substance Misuse Service. Other common aspects include a mix of expertise from both CAMHS and Adult Mental Health, providing individual and family psychosocial and psychological interventions alongside medication. The teams promote a youth-centred and flexible approach with an emphasis on effective engagement of young people through outreach and joint working with other agencies. Many of these community services lack age-appropriate day provision and psychiatric inpatient services for the younger age group (Lamb, 2004).

Designated team within a service: The 'virtual team'

Another example of a model linking both CAMHS and adult teams is that of a 'virtual team' where designated members from the respective multidisciplinary teams work together to provide a range of skills and expertise to help meet the developmental and mental health needs of adolescents presenting with psychosis to either the CAMH or AMH service.

Designated team within a service: Teams based in youth services

There are examples of EISs that are embedded in the local Youth Service. The accessible, non-stigmatising 'shop front' setting and low threshold for self-referral can serve to facilitate early engagement with an NHS early psychosis service, providing interventions within the Youth Centre premises.

Designated staff seconded to adult teams: Liaison/link posts

In other areas, commissioners have funded 'clinical liaison' or 'link' posts to facilitate joint working by CAMHS and adult mental health teams, with adolescents experiencing psychosis. These generally comprise one or two clinicians, often community psychiatric nurses with expertise in working with adolescents. These individuals carry out assessments and some face-to-face work in addition to working jointly across both the adult mental health and CAMHS teams. The input provided will be less than in the case of a designated team.

Most of the models cited above have improved the mental health service offered by forging strong working links or formal partnership agreements with other agencies involved with young people. Successful partnerships have been formed with non-statutory and voluntary organisations as well as those from the statutory sector. However, there continues to be significant inequity in the level and effectiveness of service provided across the country.

How have EI teams developed across England to take account of children and young people under 18?

EI teams are not necessarily compliant with the Mental Health Policy Implementation Guide (PIG) when it comes to the age range they support. The degree to which they are 'Policy Implementation Guide' compliant varies, often dictated by the level of support and interest from local commissioners.

In a telephone survey carried out of EI teams in 2006, out of the 72 interviewed, 60% of the teams covered the 14–25-year-old range, 17% covered 16–25 year age range, 6% were restricted to 18–25 year age range and 21% covered other age ranges (Pugh & Law, 2006).

Some services reported difficulties in setting up services across the full age span (14–35) as suggested in the PIG. In one area, the EIP team was told it could not work directly with under-18-year olds because 'this was unethical'. In some areas, CAMHS was run by the PCT, but AMHS was run by a Mental Health Trust.

Staff experienced difficulties agreeing to the input and funding for CAMHS practitioners to take on a role in EI services. Some services had agreed locally on a different age band as a result of a needs assessment, which identified 16–25 years as the 'core' age group.

Several services reported difficulties in funding at inception, with commissioners for AMHS and CAMHS arguing about which budget should contribute to the creation of the team. CAMHS commissioners stated that the new investment in CAMHS should stay within what was regarded as 'core business', and that as the treatment of psychotic older teenagers had been the remit of adult services in the past, it should be resourced from adult services. In addition, adult services had traditionally been given more money over the years and the savings which EI purported to offer would be in beds on adult wards even if they accommodated 16- or 17-year olds. Hence it was proposed that adult services should 'pump prime' the EI team. AMHS commissioners viewed the CAMHS's growth monies as legitimate funding for an EI service as the funds allocated to AMHS had been spent on adult crisis and assertive outreach teams.

Respondents to the telephone survey reported that in areas where the creation of EI services had led to conflict rather than constructive debate, teams felt fragile and unsupported. Several teams were experiencing financial pressures, with posts frozen or cut, which made staff feel insecure and more likely to seek work elsewhere. Even well-established and high-profile teams felt vulnerable as the funding of the discrete teams could be cut altogether if Mental Health Trusts were under pressure to make savings.

Summary

In order to improve engagement of young people with early onset psychosis, it is of paramount importance to take note of national research data on the views of young people and their families with respect to what they want from a mental health service. This chapter has outlined the information available to date. In addition, services will need to ensure that they have consulted with young people and referrers in their local area. With respect to models of service, it is helpful to refer to information on what has worked elsewhere. We have described different models of EIS and the particular challenges and solutions of teams across the country. An important aspect of improving access to EIS is service development and working to ensure that a successful service survives in the current economic climate of the NHS. In conclusion, we will outline some 'Top Tips' to help an EIS survive and grow. We will then pose some questions for service providers and commissioners to help develop reflective practice with respect to improving engagement and access to services by young people with early onset psychosis.

Top tips for EI teams to survive and grow

EI services exist in a competitive arena, in an environment where even excellent services are vulnerable. A basic step to improving access is for the successful team to survive and grow. We think the following suggestions may help.

Improve communication: Good relationships with CAMHS or AMHS came about when team members actively worked to communicate with each other across the services. Successful teams particularly avoided seeming 'picky' or 'precious' about which referrals to accept. This can prove easier for the generic Youth Mental Health Service or CAMHS, as a broader range of referrals are accepted and, in the case of a young person who turns out not to have psychosis, their mental health needs can still be met by within the team without referring on. EI services which are stand-alone may find this process more difficult, and need to work continuously to remind referrers about what they can or cannot accept whilst making sure that referrals they do not accept have their mental health needs met by other more appropriate services. Communication within the community is vital. It can be achieved by work with schools and Further Education colleges on a regular basis, for example within the PHSE curriculum, to raise awareness of psychosis amongst young people and their teachers and also by outreach into faith communities, offering talks to community groups to tackle stigma.

Follow the money: Where funding is a problem, identify or create a champion from a key influencer, be it a commissioner, executive or non-executive director or local councillor. Seek out key decision makers and invite them to visit the team and to meet young people and their families in their user group forum. Ensure that the champion has information about the effectiveness and value of the service. Services should also keep a range of proposals ready to be tweaked and refined if new pots of money or 'use it or lose it' money becomes available. This often occurs just before the end of the financial year. Such plans need to include a variety of ideas and a menu of costs – for example, publications and leaflets the team or young people might find useful, gym sessions, activity days for young people or money for a carers group.

Information is power: EI services need to make sure that they audit their clinical outcomes and include quality-of-life scores, and publish the results. It is much more difficult to cut or curtail a service which is well thought of and popular with parents or carers.

Make every meeting count: Sitting on service planning committees makes it much more difficult for that committee to disinvest from the service, and can ensure that EI is 'first in the queue' for any investment or new plans.

Keep asking, keep listening: EI services have been and will continue to be commissioned and provided on the basis of guidance provided by the Mental Health PIG and informed by the experiences of other EI services. Services that have incorporated the views of young service users from their community from the outset have found this invaluable to assist them to develop a service that meets the needs of their client group. However, as this client group moves through the service and onto adult services or into full recovery, other young people join the service and their needs may change. Services engaged in continual reflective practice and which have a culture of continued feedback are more likely to continue to provide a service which their young people will use than services which remain fixed at a point in time.

References

11 Million, Office of the Children's Commissioner (2007). *Pushed into the Shadows, Young Peoples' Experience of Adult Mental Health Facilities*. London: 11 Million.

Bertolote, J. & McGorry, P. (2005). Early intervention and recovery for young people with early psychosis: Consensus statement. *British Journal of Psychiatry*, 187 (Suppl. 48), s116–s119.

Collishaw, S., Maughan, B., GoodmanR., *et al.* (2004). Time trends in adolescent mental health. *Journal of Child Psychology and Psychiatry*, 45 (8), 1350–1362.

Department for Education and Skills & Department of Health (2004). *National Service Framework for children, young people and maternity services*. London: Department of Health.

Department for Education and Skills (2005). *Youth Matters*. London: Stationery Office.

Department of Health (2000). *The NHS Plan*. London: Department of Health.

Department of Health (2001). *Mental Health Policy Implementation Guide*. London: Department of Health.

Department of Health (2007). *Mental Health Act 2007, Amendments to the Mental Health Act 1983*. London: Stationery Office.

Farrell, C. (2004). *Patient and Public Involvement in Health: The Evidence for Policy Implementation*. London: Department of Health.

Garcia, I., Vasiliou, C. & Penketh, K. (2007). *Listen Up! Person-Centered Approaches to Help Young People Experiencing Mental Health and Emotional Problems*. London: Mental Health Foundation.

HASCAS (2006). *CAMHS to adult transition*. www.hascas.org.uk.

Howarth, C. & Street, C. (2000). *Sidelined: Young Adults Access to Services*. London: New Policy Institute.

Knapp, M., McCrone, P. & Razzouk, D. (2008). Economics of early intervention services: A scoping review. *Report to the Department of Health, Personal Social Services Research Unit, London School of Economics and Centre for the Economics of Mental Health*. London: Institute of Psychiatry, King's College.

Lamb, C. (2004). National telephone survey of community mental health teams for older adolescents. *Presentation at DH/NIMHE Conference on Services for Early Intervention in Psychosis*. Spring 2004.

Macleod, R. & Parker, Z. (1986). Considerations in community mental health programmes for youth. *Canadian Journal of Psychiatry*, 31 (6), 568–574.

Maitra, B. & Jolley, A. (2000). Liaison between child and adult psychiatric services. In: *Family Matters: Interface Between Child and Adult Mental Health*, pp. 285–302. London: Routledge.

O'Herlihy, A., Worral, A., Bannerjee, S. *et al.* (2001). *National In-patient Child and Adolescent Psychiatry Study.* London: Royal College of Psychiatry Research Unit.

Pugh, K. & Law, S. (2006). Involving service users in EIP. *Presentation YoungMinds.*

Reder, P., McClure, M. & Jolley, A. (2000). Interface between child and adult mental health. In: P. Reder, M. McClure & A. Jolley (eds), *Family Matters: Interface between Child & Adult Mental Health.* London: Routledge.

Richards, M. & Vostanis, P. (2004). Interprofessional perspectives on transitional mental health services for young people aged 16 to 19 years. *Journal of Interprofessional Care*, 18 (2), 115–128.

Smith, K. & Leon, L. (2001). *Turned Upside Down: Developing Community-Based Crisis Services for 16–25 Year Olds Experiencing a Mental Health Crisis.* London: Mental Health Foundation.

Street, C. (2000). *Whose Crisis? Meeting the Needs of Children with Serious Mental Health Problems.* London: YoungMinds.

Street, C., Stapelkamp, C., Taylor, E. *et al.* (2005). *Minority Voices: Research into the Access and Acceptability of Services for the Mental Health of Young People from Black and Minority Ethnic Groups.* London: YoungMinds.

Social Exclusions Unit (2005). *Transitions: Young Adults with Complex Needs.* London: Social Exclusion Unit.

The Sainsbury Centre for Mental Health (2002). *Breaking the Circles of Fear: A Review of the Relationship Between Mental Health Services and African and Caribbean Communities.* London: The Sainsbury Centre for Mental Health.

YoungMinds (2006). *A Work in Progress: The Adolescent and Young Adult Brain: A Briefing Paper.* London: YoungMinds.

Chapter 5 **Strategies for engagement**

Lynda Tait, Diane Ryles and Alexa Sidwell

Introduction

Engagement of individuals with first-episode psychosis (FEP) into Early Intervention Services (EIS) and treatment is fundamental to achieving the aims of service delivery to reduce the impact of FEP on the individual and their families, and to facilitate recovery. Despite the significance of engagement, the evidence base underpinning effective engagement strategies is at an early stage, particularly engagement strategies that are useful and appropriate for young people. This chapter draws on lessons others and we have learned from the experience of working within EIS. In addition to discussing the key issues involved in facilitating engagement, our aim is to suggest active engagement strategies that have been found to be useful, with reflection on the reasons why other strategies were not as successful. However, we do not wish to be prescriptive; relationships are complex, and what works in one situation may not work in another. Our message is the importance of being creative and flexible with engagement strategies in forming collaborative partnerships with individuals with FEP. We aim to encourage working in partnership with individuals to identify their strengths, the personal goals they want to achieve and the kind of life they want versus what we think is in their best interests.

A brief summary of the evidence

What is engagement?

Engagement is a key concept regularly used in mental health services. However, despite its widely recognised importance, it is often difficult to say what it is. We have used a definition that emphasises the relational aspects of engagement with services, which is based on the recovery model applicable to community mental health services (Repper *et al.*, 1994; Tait *et al.*, 2002; Priebe *et al.*, 2005). Engagement involves developing a collaborative and trusting relationship with individuals, which is key to delivering effective services and support (Tait *et al.*, 2002). Client engagement is used to describe what happens in mental health services when clients develop a positive attitude towards the values of the service and the caseworkers they have most contact with. Engaged clients actively work in partnership with caseworkers to improve their own well-being and demonstrate a willingness to develop a genuine two-way relationship. A client who willingly arranges appointments, actively participates in managing and cooperating with treatment plans and seeks help when needed should be considered more engaged than someone who either passively accepts treatment or refuses it (Tait *et al.*, 2002). Furthermore, engagement is a continuous process; for example, an individual may engage, disengage and at some time in the future re-engage, and mental health professionals need to continue engagement efforts during the entire period of contact with individuals to maintain a collaborative and trusting relationship. Engagement is at the heart of everything we do. However, building effective relationships can be a challenge. The task for mental health professionals is to overcome barriers to engagement by thinking of creative ways to make services more acceptable and relevant to individuals with FEP, particularly young people whose needs are different from older adults (Malla & Norman, 2001; Haddock *et al.*, 2006).

Principles of engagement

As shown in Table 5.1, a range of attitudes and behaviours of mental health professionals are associated with encouraging engagement

Table 5.1 Principles of engagement

- Services delivered from non-stigmatising and easily accessible location.
- Services relevant and appropriate to individual needs.
- Low-key, informal and non-coercive engagement style.
- Emphasis on working in partnership with the person.
- Empathic listening to reach an understanding of personal goals and priorities.
- Demonstrating a genuine interest in the views and experiences of individuals.
- Increasing the involvement of individuals in clinical decision making.
- Focus specifically on the broader needs and aspirations of individuals.
- Psychoeducation individually tailored to the person's understanding.
- Being realistic about the pace of progress to expect and what can be offered.
- Taking a long-term perspective towards developing a good relationship.
- Client-centred flexibility (e.g. fitting in with the client's needs).

(Repper *et al.*, 1994; Tait *et al.*, 2003; Priebe *et al.*, 2005). Being a good listener and the ability to engage empathically and collaboratively are key skills for reaching an understanding of the other person's goals and priorities in fostering engagement (Sainsbury, 1998). Failure to listen to the views and experiences of individuals and encourage their full involvement in clinical decisions played a prominent role in disengagement from Assertive Outreach (AO) (Priebe *et al.*, 2005). Encouraging full involvement in decisions about care and listening to individuals in a sensitive and genuinely interested manner can help to achieve the goals of engagement and effective service delivery.

Challenges to engagement

The formation of a trusting relationship between mental health professionals and individuals with FEP is a crucial task for both parties (Tait *et al.*, 2002), the strength of which can determine the well-being of individuals with mental health problems (Priebe & Gruyters, 1993). Undoubtedly, the attitudes and characteristics of each can exert a significant influence on engagement (Perkins & Repper, 1996). Even so, the responsibility for developing and maintaining an effective relationship remains clearly with mental health professionals. Where services are inappropriate to individual needs or insensitively delivered, non-engagement with services as a reaction to those experiences can

be seen as a rational and active choice (Tait *et al.*, 2002).

Both the design of services and interpersonal behaviour of mental health professionals can be influential in the process of engagement. Individuals who tend to have an 'avoidance' coping/recovery style may be more likely to engage with a service that is 'on tap, but not on top': in other words, one that engages in a low-key, informal way, that keeps the individual in control of the relationship and focuses attention to the broader needs and aspirations of the person, in a normalising context (Tait *et al.*, 2004). Demanding and cajoling compliance with treatment, insensitive use of psychoeducation and stigmatising the individual (e.g. by admission to wards with more chronic patients) would stoke avoidance and disengagement in this group (Tait *et al.*, 2004).

Implementation into practice: Promoting engagement

The majority of the proposed engagement strategies were developed through experience working within stand-alone models of EIS, based in central Birmingham and South Staffordshire, both of which have adopted a modified AO approach and offer support to young people aged 14–25 (in central Birmingham up to age 30) years who are experiencing early onset psychosis. In line with the Early Psychosis Declaration (EPD) (Bertolote & McGorry, 2005), both teams offer 'youth-friendly' EIS, delivered in a low-stigma setting, to young people with FEP. Our services function with the philosophy that each young person has unique needs, strengths and ambitions. We aim to provide support and treatment within an atmosphere of hope and optimism, and an appreciation that time is needed to build collaborative and trusting relationships with young people and their carers.

Clinical case studies: Building positive personal relationships

Developing a positive personal relationship based on trust between young people and service providers has been identified as a key factor influencing the engagement process (O'Brien, 2001; Kirsh & Tate, 2006). Young people have the right to an honest and open discussion about their right to confidentiality, and when, and in what circumstances confidentiality may be broken. Young people need to be reassured that they are free to share other information that will be kept confidential. We have found that clearly setting out the limits of confidentiality and the sharing of confidences between a young person and a mental health worker has resulted in building trust and helping to reduce stress levels of the young person. The rights of parents and their right to information (for under age 16) needs to be negotiated carefully so that young people continue to feel they are entering into a trusting relationship.

> **Case study**
>
> *Jack (15 years old) met his EIS CPN who explained the issues around confidentiality. Jack discussed openly things that were concerning him, particularly about his relationships with his family and his future aspirations. These issues did not place him or others at risk, but the CPN was concerned that he would lose trust in her if she disclosed these with his family during the family sessions. The CPN explored the value of disclosure with Jack, that is to 'manage' his parents' concerns and anxieties. Role play/reversal was used to enhance his level of empathy, to think of his parents' feelings, concerns and actions. The CPN then negotiated with him what would be discussed with his parents before the family sessions.*

Usefulness of service

A good place to begin developing a trusting relationship is to help young people with practical and financial aspects of daily life (O'Brien, 2001; Weaver *et al.*, 2003), including housing and welfare benefits. Practical help to meet a person's immediate needs helps to increase confidence that the service can be useful and can lead to better understanding and the building of a long-term, trusting relationship. Practical support can be offered in ways that build a trusting relationship, for example, accompanying a young person to a leisure activity, such as the cinema, or to a job placement, helping to hang up curtains, helping with shopping or getting their nails painted. We have found that the adoption of these practical strategies have helped to build rapport and service credibility with young people, particularly when we have been able to tap into their personal interests.

> **Case study**
>
> *Charlotte had been admitted to the adolescent unit and two EIS team members went to meet her in hospital. They introduced themselves and took along a copy of Heat magazine and some chocolate, as they had found out about her interests.*

However, services should aim to develop practical living skills in young people, building independence and responsibility within a supportive framework whilst avoiding fostering dependence. Engagement in interventions needs to relate to the likelihood that these interventions will help the young person achieve their longer-term goals. Sometimes their goals may seem unrealistic and staff may have to find obscure connections between the activities and the goals. This involves caseworkers being sensitive to what would be meaningful to a young person, something that they will be comfortable with, enjoy and feel that they will benefit from. Services also need to be aware that as well as providing support and reducing the impact of psychosis, helping the young person to enjoy life and have fun is invaluable. Adult-trained health care staff may find it a challenge to negotiate through these issues. However, qualified Youth Workers are able to provide supervision on alternative approaches and dealing with 'unrealistic aspirations' sensitively so that staff can develop more youth-friendly skills that successfully engage young people into therapeutic programmes.

Case study

When Alex first sought help, he said, 'I was made to feel weird . . . they [i.e. EIS] treated you like a normal person'. He said the best thing about being in the service was rekindling his interest in making music and he learned to have fun again. He also learned self-help strategies to manage his positive symptoms, which he appreciated but saw as a means to recovery but not his main goal.

Realism

We have found it useful to be open and flexible about what can be realistically achieved and what we can offer. It can be a difficult task for workers in balancing the need for hope whilst also being honest about the risk of relapse. Establishing the young person's role in maintaining their own recovery can help promote their feelings of control and the development of realistic goals. Confidence can be increased if young people are encouraged to take responsibility for exploring solutions. It is important that services do not feel they should or are able to meet every need of service users and create dependency or unrealistic expectations. It is also useful to reflect on what can be done to support a person in achieving success and, if unsuccessful, what would help in learning from that experience. It is important to remember not to erode self-belief by deciding that an individual's aspirations are 'ill-founded' or to focus on the problems with their ambitions (Repper & Perkins, 2003).

Being supportive and non-judgemental

Individuals with mental health problems have successfully engaged with mental health professionals where they have felt understood (O'Brien, 2001). We have found it important to acknowledge that adolescents can be frustrating and challenging to work with. However, young people are more likely to ask for support when questions are framed in a sensitive manner and reflect a nonjudgemental approach. For example, if asked in a direct way about substance use or medication, a young person will be likely to react in a defensive manner. We have tried to listen to a young person's point of view and encourage a re-evaluation on the place substance use has in their lives, such as the significance of fitting in with the crowd to their identity, and then suggest alternative ways of dealing with the consequences of their motivation to feel accepted by others. We have found that highlighting the costs and benefits of a course of action has helped a young person to re-evaluate their choices.

Case study

John was a regular cannabis user, like his friends. He also dabbled with other recreational drugs. His team spoke to him about his drug use and told him about the links between drug use and relapse at every visit. He told a support worker that he believed that was all the team cared about. He said he had told his care co-ordinator he had reduced his intake, as he felt 'that's what they want to hear'.

We have found that the use of role reversal, within a non-judgemental approach, is a valuable technique to developing a young person's understanding of an alternative perspective; in essence, they establish their own solutions to problems.

Case study

Monica was unhappy about the time she had to be home in the evenings, causing arguments between her and her parents. EI staff asked Monica to role play her mother and advise staff, playing Monica, about the same issues. Monica developed a better understanding of her parents' concerns and was able to negotiate a compromise.

Pacing

Our teams take a standard holistic approach to the care offered and, particularly in the early stages, take a gentle approach. Focusing on getting assessments done is seen as important but is unlikely to be successful for some people who need a gentle approach. In making services attractive to young people and adults, we have found that finding out about a person's interests in the early stages is useful rather than focusing on symptoms or medication. In our experience, individuals tend to offer information about their life history that is more accurate when they feel they can trust workers. The information in the assessments is then more valid.

We have tried to make services non-threatening and comfortable for clients by being tolerant if a person is going at a pace that is slower than we would generally expect. It is important for the team not to replicate a parental role with the young person whilst being aware of the need for assessing negative symptoms. The challenge is to accept that recovery may not be a linear process and that some people will experience setbacks as part of the recovery process. Maintaining a positive view of future possibilities for clients may help to minimise any frustration experienced as a result of slower-than-expected progress.

Individual approach to maintaining contact

An individual approach is needed in maintaining contact with a young person. Contact once a week may be enough for one person, whereas with others, contact may be needed two or three times a week due to a young person needing a higher level of support or to manage crises. During initial meetings, regular contact may help cement the relationship; young people are often trying to make sense of the experience of psychosis at this time. The nature of contact might be a combination of home visits and engaging in social groups. As young people learn to self-manage, visits can be reduced to weekly and, in some cases, monthly. Contact should be discussed carefully so that young people do not feel either rejected or swamped

by the team. Daily visits during times of stress, if negotiated, can be seen as supportive and demonstrate an acknowledgement of the pressure the person is feeling.

> **Case study**
>
> *Kay is an independent young mum who sees her care co-ordinator fortnightly. However, during school holidays, the pressure of looking after her daughter coupled with friction with neighbours led to her feeling stressed and anxious. Daily supportive visits for 2 weeks whilst childcare was organised allowed Kay to 'offload' to team members and reduced her isolation, whilst planning strategies to reduce her stress.*

We have found that males tend to prefer 'whole team' visits (where several staff members attend), whereas females prefer fewer people and time-limited visits. The length of visits varies, with some young people tolerating only a short, 10-minute visit. A person in their late 20s may have very different attitudes to an adolescent. A flexible approach is needed also when planning visits. Some young people are comfortable with low-key, drop-in visits but others prefer planned sessions.

> **Case study**
>
> *Dave said he was 'not a planner' but agreed staff could call in when they were passing. Sometimes visits would be half an hour, at other times, his mobile phone would ring and he would say, 'got to go'.*

> **Case study**
>
> *Alison was upset when a team member dropped in unannounced to pass on a message. She had a friend with her who did not know she had a CPN and she was left worried as to how she could explain this visitor. It took several weeks and many apologies to resume an alliance with Alison. She has since specified only three members of the team who can visit and for planned appointments.*

This case study highlights the importance of caseworkers including the individual in decisions about the timing of visits and being responsive to a young person's priorities. Phoning beforehand or texting might also have signalled the caseworker's positive intent and understanding of the young person's needs.

Mental health professionals should expect some non-attendance and if young people fail to keep appointments, persistence in re-establishing contact is part of forming a trusting relationship. The effort made in being persistent may be interpreted as demonstrating commitment to the person, a factor important to facilitating engagement (Priebe *et al.*, 2005).

Case study

Saaed was initially slow to engage with his care co-ordinator or acknowledge he had any problems. He reluctantly agreed to fortnightly visits. Over several months, he gradually began to talk to his worker who focused on his career aspirations and avoided talk of 'illness'. After a year, they were able to discuss this reluctance. Ahmed said he thought his care co-ordinator must be 'really thick skinned' not to see how unwelcome her visits were initially and they laughed about this. By this time, they had developed a good understanding and his care co-ordinator explained that she felt it was worth the persistence.

Non-traditional methods of contact

Non-traditional methods of contact, using a variety of approaches, seem to work best with young people. For example, texting and email communication is now generally considered to be the approach that suits young people. Our EIS team members have used sending a text or email beforehand as a reminder of an appointment successfully. Texting care co-ordinators is helpful if privacy at home is difficult or just to say, 'I'm okay'. Texting may feel easier than verbalising difficult emotions and should be regarded as the normal way of communicating for young people, more so than formal letters.

Case study

Gemma had received phone calls and letters from the EIS team inviting her to see them for an assessment (at her home address). When she did not keep any of the appointments offered, the team sent information to her about the service and suggested that she text or call them when she felt ready. Her mother, GP and a Connexions worker were informed and advised to notify them if they became anxious or more concerned about Gemma. Two weeks later, Gemma texted the EIS Youth Worker asking for help and contact was established by meeting Gemma in the Connexions office.

This case study highlights the need for a more relaxed approach being led by the young person and not to be too 'assertive' or rush into making speedy contact. Levels of risk were managed by ensuring that those already engaged with Gemma were informed of how to initiate a rapid response from EIS, if required.

Occasionally young people have not wanted to engage but concerns from family members have initiated and maintained contact with the team. In these scenarios, staff members do not push for rapid contact but call to see family and offer support, information and reassurance.

Case study

Tom's mother contacted the team concerned that he was acting 'strangely' and isolating himself from everyone. EI staff visited but when Tom saw them, he ran off down the road. This continued for several weeks but staff persisted, offering Tom's mother advice and support, and left information for Tom. Eventually, Tom saw the EI staff after feeling reassured that they would not pressure him and was able to ask questions through his mother.

Including family and friends

With the permission of clients, engaging family members and friends is important to building a trusting relationship with a young person (Bertolote & McGorry, 2005). Key family members are engaged as early as possible in our services, and staff members present their involvement as normal and helpful. Staff members explain the benefits of carer and informal networks to help understand and increase the chances of helpful support. Young people seldom refuse, as long as confidentiality is clearly outlined and some contact is with the young person. For example, without engaging the family of young South Asian females, the team is unlikely to engage the young person. Family members may need reassurance that the service will be culturally sensitive.

Case study

Afya said she had lost confidence and had stopped going out. She was invited to the women's group and social group but her family asked if they could visit the centre first as they had worries that male service users might be present. A visit reassured them and Afya and her family are working well with the service.

Medication engagement

Compared to an adult, a young person with FEP is more likely to disengage from taking medication or to take it erratically (Remington, 2005). The reasons for not taking medication can outweigh the reasons for taking it. Apart from the perception that taking any medication is stigmatising, antipsychotic medication can have negative side effects, which a young person will be concerned about, such as increasing weight and altering sexual function: acceptance and attractiveness is extremely important to young people.

Research evidence supports low doses to minimise the risk of extra pyramidal side effects (Bertolote & McGorry, 2005; Remington, 2005) and we have found it also useful to offer information and advice, including dietary advice, for making informed choices and about side effects. It is also useful to link the reduction in psychotic symptoms to medication through monitoring progress through charting the reduction of symptoms after initiating medication. In our experience, the use of prophylactic medication is particularly hard to sell to a young person. Many believe they will not relapse and will prefer to take medication to improve

symptoms only when and if they occur. It is useful to explain to young people that we understand the reluctance to take tablets and the helpfulness of being honest about it in order to assess, for example, if it is the tablets that are not working or that they are not taking them.

Services need to view non-adherence with medication as the norm and work with the young person about when to restart medication. A useful approach is to discuss with the young person the issues relating to stopping medication and draw up management plans for if symptoms emerge.

Case study

Pete wanted to stop taking his medication, as he believed it 'did not work'. He discussed this with his CPN who explored the potential issues with him using a problem-solving approach, for example, what could be done if symptoms re-emerged. Early warning signs were identified with Pete and his mother and he agreed to a management plan where he or his mum contacted the team to discuss recommencing medication or increasing support. Pete's wish to stop taking medication was taken seriously and even when the potential for relapse was identified, a range of interventions was offered, not just medication.

Service accessibility

Services need to be accessible (Bertolote & McGorry, 2005) and getting the setting right, particularly for young people, is especially important. Engaging young people into mental health services has traditionally been problematic. Although not a choice for many services, being located in an easily accessible, non-stigmatising location can help to facilitate engagement. Fitting in with a young person's needs (client-centred flexibility), such as meeting people where they prefer, and preferably within their own environment, rather than in a formal setting, is a useful approach, especially where services have been set up in less user-friendly locations such as hospital sites. Services need to create links with agencies (Bertolote & McGorry, 2005) whose sole responsibility is to engage young people, for example, Connexions and Youth Service, who have a range of approaches to engaging young people in different settings, but whose main approach is to engage in the young person's arena rather than encouraging the young person to engage in theirs.

Case study

Staff and service users meet to play in a pool hall one afternoon a week. Darren spoke little to his care co-ordinator on home visits but agreed to attend and goes regularly. He is able to talk more freely with staff members in this group and has asked other group members about their coping strategies.

Case study

Carl's mum rang the GP, as she was worried he was becoming unwell like her brother who has mental health problems and lives in a hostel. Carl, aged 17, was invited to the local CMHT where his uncle attends to see a psychiatrist. He did not attend, as he did not want to ask for time from work and felt frightened going to a mental health unit at the psychiatric hospital. Nine months later, after an acute crisis and having lost his job, the EIS team supported by Home Treatment engaged him.

Staff/professional issues

In some cases, despite extensive efforts to engage someone on their terms, they do not want to engage or disengage from services. In these scenarios, the assessment and management of risk becomes a priority for the professionals involved. Where there is concern and action needs to be taken to ensure their or others' safety, the initiation of more assertive treatment can be traumatising and extremely challenging for staff. This issue requires consideration when things do not go to plan and good supervision and team working is crucial to ensuring that staff are supported.

Case study

Dan engaged well when discussing his beliefs and feelings at length and on his own terms. However, he made little progress with cognitive interventions and became increasingly despondent about the world and his future. The CPN and Youth Worker discussed their growing concerns in supervision where medication was recommended. The staff felt unable to push for this, as they were concerned that he would disengage. Eventually, the levels of risk (suicide) became so significant that they arranged for a psychiatrist to see him at home. Dan refused to take medication and was eventually sectioned and admitted to hospital. The CPN co-ordinated this inpatient admission, whilst the Youth Worker stood back. Dan's relationship with the CPN became strained and he refused contact with her but on his discharge agreed to see the Youth Worker whose focus was to continue offering him time to discuss his agenda. The Youth Worker spent time exploring the team's early anxieties and risk protocols with Dan and how this would affect their future relationship.

This case study clarifies the need to manage risk and ensure safety but also highlights the dilemma faced by many staff when concerns about an individual's safety outweigh their focus on engagement. Approaches can be adopted to resolve some of the longer-term issues around future engagement. It is crucial that young people are 'debriefed' following compulsory treatment, ideally involving those staff that had been working on their engagement. Reasons for decisions and actions need to be fully explained and a focus on preventative approaches can be useful, that is early warning signs.

Implications and conclusions

Engagement involves professionals and clients who influence each other in the course of developing a collaborative and trusting relationship in pursuit of a common goal or goals to achieve the clinical and social recovery of young people with FEP. However, it is the responsibility of mental health professionals delivering EIS to make their services attractive, easily accessible and relevant to young people with FEP: low engagement reflects a problem with the services offered as well as something about the client. Only when a collaborative and trusting relationship between mental health professionals and individuals with FEP has been developed can effective interventions be provided. The challenge to mental health professionals, however, is to be more creative and flexible with engagement strategies and tailor them to individual needs. In particular, the principles of age-appropriate care, and ways in which such approaches can be implemented in EIS, needs to be part of any training provided for mental health professionals. Health professionals should also make links with services whose primary focus is to engage young people to collaborate in delivering interventions and sharing skills so that young people can access the support that is necessary for their personal development and recovery.

Suggested further reading

Sainsbury Centre for Mental Health (1998). *Keys to Engagement: Review of Care for People with Severe Mental Illness Who Are Hard to Engage with Services.* London: The Sainsbury Centre for Mental Health. This is a review of both literature and policy, including the presentation of a small qualitative study on ways of working appropriate to engaging a group of people known as 'hard to engage', which is both useful and relevant to current policy.

Kaufman, S. (2001). Detached youth work. In: F. Factor, V. Chauhan & J. Pitts (eds), *The Russell House Companion to Working with Young People* is a useful general reference book for Youth Workers in the UK. Chapter 13 written by Sacha Kaufman is of particular interest for its reflection on non-judgemental approach to engaging young people.

Useful websites

www.nya.org.uk The government-funded National Youth Agency is committed to promoting young people's personal and social development. Useful publications and resources can be downloaded from the website.

www.youngminds.org.uk Young Minds is a national charity whose aim is to improve the mental health of young people. The website provides useful information, publications and resources to download.

References

Bertolote, J. & McGorry, P. (2005). Early intervention and recovery for young people with early psychosis: Consensus statement. *British Journal of Psychiatry*, 187 (Suppl. 48), s116–s119.

Haddock, G., Lewis, S., Bentall, R., Dunn, G., Drake, R. & Tarrier, N. (2006). Influence of age on outcome of psychological treatments in first-episode psychosis. *British Journal of Psychiatry*, 188, 250–254.

Kaufman, S. (2001). Detached youth work. In: F. Factor, V. Chauhan & J. Pitts (eds), *The rhp Companion to Working with Young People*, p. 246. Lyme Regis, Dorset: Russell House.

Kirsh, B. & Tate, E. (2006). Developing a comprehensive understanding of the working alliance in community mental health. *Qualitative Health Research*, 16 (8), 1054–1074.

Malla, A.M. & Norman, R.M.G. (2001). Treating psychosis: Is there more to early intervention than intervening early? *Canadian Journal of Psychiatry*, 46, 645–648.

O'Brien, L. (2001). The relationship between community psychiatric nurses and clients with severe and persistent mental illness: The client's experience. *Australian and New Zealand Journal of Mental Health Nursing*, 10, 176–186.

Perkins, R.E. & Repper, J.M. (1996). *Working Alongside People with Long Term Mental Health Problems.* London: Chapman & Hall.

Priebe, S. & Gruyters, T. (1993). The role of the helping alliance in psychiatric community care. A prospective study. *Journal of Nervous and Mental Disease*, 181, 552–557.

Priebe, S., Watts, J., Chase, M. & Matanov, A. (2005). Processes of disengagement and engagement in assertive outreach patients: Qualitative study. *British Journal of Psychiatry*, 187, 438–443.

Remington, G. (2005). Rational pharmacotherapy in early psychosis. *British Journal of Psychiatry*, 187 (Suppl. 48), 77–84.

Repper, J. & Perkins, R. (2003). *Social Inclusion and Recovery: A Model for Mental Health Practice.* Philadelphia: Elsevier.

Repper, J., Cooke, A. & Ford, R. (1994). How can nurses build trusting relationships with people who have severe and long term mental health problems? Experiences of case managers and their clients. *Journal of Advanced Nursing*, 19, 1096–1104.

Sainsbury, C. (1998). *Keys to Engagement: Review of Care for People with Severe Mental Illness Who are Hard to Engage.* London: Sainsbury Centre for Mental Health.

Tait, L., Birchwood, M. & Trower, P. (2002). A new scale (SES) to measure engagement with community mental health services. *Journal of Mental Health*, 11 (2), 191–198.

Tait, L., Birchwood, M. & Trower, P. (2003). Predicting engagement with services for psychosis: Insight, symptoms and recovery style. *British Journal of Psychiatry*, 182, 123–128.

Tait, L., Birchwood, M. & Trower, P. (2004). Adapting to the challenge of psychosis: Personal resilience and the use of sealing-over (avoidant) coping strategies. *British Journal of Psychiatry*, 185, 410–415.

Weaver, T.I.M., Tyrer, P., Ritchie, J. & Renton, A. (2003). Assessing the value of assertive outreach: Qualitative study of process and outcome generation in the uk700 trial. *British Journal of Psychiatry*, 183 (5), 437–445.

Chapter 6 Early intervention service models

Guy Dodgson and Stephen McGowan

Introduction

This book is concerned with how to ensure that an individual with first-episode psychosis (FEP) gets the right kind of help in a timely fashion to ensure that they make a good recovery. This chapter discusses how to ensure skilled professionals provide effective specialist care, consistent with best-practice evidence, policy guidance and the Early Psychosis Declaration. This chapter is concerned with how these professionals are organised and co-ordinated in ways that maximise their ability to offer effective services. This is service delivery.

The evidence base for the effectiveness of Early Intervention in Psychosis (EIP) stems mainly from specialist teams operating in urban areas, for example Birmingham, Lambeth (London) and Melbourne (Australia). The Mental Health Policy Implementation Guidance or MH-PIG (2001) gave a detailed description of how the British Government expected EIP teams to operate. This guidance was based on best practice within these specialist teams. Service delivery, therefore, is about translating best-practice principles and the vision expressed in the Early Psychosis Declaration, into a clinical setting. EIP services have been developed by service leads, who have attempted to translate these principles into practical and effective services. This process necessarily involves some compromises, for example due to demography, geography, staff/skill shortages, local nuances and variations and, of course, financial pressures. The challenge for service leads has been how much to compromise and what principles of EIP are non-negotiable.

In this chapter we will outline what we consider the critical components and core features

to be; explore the evidence base and policy drivers for the model proposed in the MH-PIG; outline the main service delivery models that have emerged in the UK and critically examine the relative merits and deficiencies of each. We will use examples of different services to highlight the complex needs and practical dilemmas that have influenced service design and show how a focus on core principles can lead to an effective service.

Core principles

EIP has sought to address the full range of needs of young people with FEP, from its focus on primary prevention, health promotion and anti-stigma, through help seeking, access and assessment, to best-practice interventions and recovery.

A summary of the evidence

We have seen previously the persuasive evidence base for the clinical components of EIP and the 'critical period' hypothesis (Birchwood *et al.*, 1998). In this section we will consider the evidence base for the service delivery models that pioneered EIP's emergence as a coherent service model and shaped UK policy.

At the time of its inclusion in the NHS National Plan (DH, 2000), EIP promised a remarkable reversal in the outcomes for young people with early psychosis – if only the right kind of interventions could be provided early enough by an appropriately configured service. Alongside Assertive Outreach and Crisis Resolution and Home Treatment, EIP was one of three new community models required by the 10-year reform plan described in the National Service Framework (NSF) for Mental Health (DH, 1999). In 2001 the MH-PIG provided highly structured directions for the establishment of new teams for clients with FEP in England.

The MH-PIG provided detailed plans for the development of discrete and specialist EIP services: Every young person aged 14–35 with an FEP would receive early and intensive support from a specialist team which would continue to help them through the first 3 years following their illness. The MH-PIG highlighted deficiencies in existing services and described a model service specification, defining whom the service is for, what it is intended to achieve and what it does. Significantly, it went so far as to define team sizes, skills mixes and management and operational procedures, including a framework and time-scales for service planning and implementation.

In December 2002, The National Institute for Clinical Excellence (NICE) published their clinical guideline on schizophrenia (NICE, 2002), detailing core interventions in its treatment and management, with appraisal of the underpinning evidence. Although criticised for including a large quantity of 'good practice points' as well as research-based recommendations, the guideline found good evidence for the component treatments within EIP, that is the use of low dose atypical antipsychotic medication for first episodes, Cognitive Behavioural Therapy, family interventions, Assertive Community Treatment (ACT) and home/non-hospital treatment models for the acute phase.

At the time, the guideline found insufficient evidence for the EIP team model, but called for further research studies to evaluate this. The service model described in the MH-PIG was extensively based on the North Birmingham model and the advice of the IRIS group (www. iris-initiative.com). Whilst many of the constituents of the UK EIP model can trace their roots back to the EPPIC service (McGorry et al., 1996), the proposed 'assertive outreach' model of team configuration and deployment derives from ACT in the USA. The NICE also appraised evidence for ACT in their guideline and concluded that whilst some caution was necessary in the interpretation of research findings into the UK context, when compared with standard care, ACT is more likely to improve contact and satisfaction with services, minimise the use of hospital services, improve the quality of life and improve work and accommodation status for people with severe mental disorders.

From a research perspective, much more is now known about the long-term trajectories of psychosis and their biological and psychosocial triggers. Delay in first treatment is linked strongly with poor outcomes (Norman & Malla, 2001; Marshall et al., 2005) and Harrison et al. (2001) showed how the outcome at 2/3 years strongly predicts the outcome 20 years later. More recently, a systematic appraisal of the evidence for EIP was undertaken for the Cochrane Database (Marshall & Rathbone, 2006). It found strong evidence for the link between a long duration of untreated psychosis (DUP) and poor outcomes. There is also encouraging evidence for the impact of EIP teams, for example, in terms of reduced bed days and improved mental states.

Establishing early intervention teams in practice

Despite the evidence for the effectiveness of these services and explicit performance targets, resistance to the implementation of EIP remained long into the 10-year plan. By highlighting the overall ineffectiveness of existing services, both adult and Child and Adolescent Mental Health Services (CAMHS), as well as the potentially harmful effects of conventional treatment, the MH-PIG managed to alienate many clinicians. Also, providing such detailed – and some would argue rigid – guidance caused offence to commissioners and managers, who perceived it as insensitive to local needs and as leaving little room for creativity in service planning. Moreover, the apparent complexity and costliness of these services were understood to be major causes for the early reluctance to develop new EIP services.

With regard to complexity, EIP is viewed as a considerably more complicated service model and implementation challenge than either Assertive Outreach or Crisis Resolution. The model itself is intricate, essential planning information needs to be gathered and there are a multitude of interfaces with other services both within and outside of Mental Health. Engaging stakeholders meaningfully in the planning process is vital, a new highly skilled workforce needs to be created and significant barriers may need to be overcome.

With regard to cost, it had been calculated that the implementation of EIP would cost mental health services an additional £5,000 per patient per year (SCMH, 2003), with government figures suggesting annual incidence rates of 15 people per 100,000 per year (DH, 2001). While mental health services have struggled with chronic staff shortages and a history of underinvestment, this alone represented a daunting challenge.

Against this backdrop, establishing new EIP teams in practice was never going to be easy. The different service models that have emerged owe as much to the issues discussed here as they do variations in local needs. It is, however, accepted that the specialist model prescribed in policy guidance will not be appropriate in all localities. For example, in rural areas the geographical dispersal of clients across large areas will determine the nature and intensity of the EIP service that can be offered. Furthermore, pre-existing services and how they are configured, the level of investment required to develop an EIP service, as well as the incidence and prevalence of psychosis, will differ from locality to locality, and in some preclude the development of stand-alone specialist teams.

In its guide to implementing EIP, the Sainsbury Centre (SCMH, 2003) called for 'local answers to local challenges' and for imaginative service design. It was argued that whilst certain core service ingredients were fundamental, the organisation of the means of delivery could be left to local discretion.

In response to questions about whether it was mandatory to conform to the MH-PIG in every detail, the National Institute for Mental Health in England (NIMHE) published guidance for commissioners and providers of mental health services on the scope for flexibility. 'Counting Community Teams: Issues in Fidelity and Flexibility' (NIMHE, 2003) described criteria against which proposed variations from MH-PIG models could be assessed. This guidance was intended to support the adoption of locally pertinent service delivery models, whilst averting the risk that different models would stray too far from the evidence base or simply seek to save money. Subsequently, more specific EIP fidelity guidance was produced and disseminated by the NIMHE (Table 6.1). The latter, whilst consistent with the MH-PIG, sought to reflect consensus in the field as to what constituted the critical components of an EIP service approach and has since proved consistent with emerging performance management frameworks for EIP teams.

Models of service delivery in EIP

As a result of the MH-PIG and the successive guidance described here, a small number of service delivery models have emerged as alternatives to the specialist team initially proposed. In this section we will describe these models and critically examine the relative merits and deficiencies of each, particularly with regard to each one's ability to deliver the critical components of an EIP approach.

When service developers have attempted to translate the above core principles into a service they have tended to use one of three service models. These three models are described below. They are often regarded as separate, discrete models. However, in reality, they form a continuum where it is the degree of centralisation of service delivery that changes.

1 **Specialist Team Model**
   The service is provided through a stand-alone specialist team. All staff work predominantly for the team and have a shared task to provide EIP services. This is the model proposed by the MH-PIG, based on evidence from early EIP and Assertive Outreach services.

2 **Dispersed or CMHT Model**
   The service is provided by staff (full- or part-time) embedded within an existing service, usually a Community Mental Health Team (CMHT). Staff are expected to follow the core principles of care, but often have limited contact with people in similar roles. This is the least expensive model to implement.

3 **Hub-and-Spoke Model**
   This model is a cross between the above two models. The service is provided by staff who are to be embedded in 'spokes', often CMHTs, and in the central 'hub'. The hub usually provides access to leadership, specialist skills and

Table 6.1 Minimum fidelity standards for new EIP services by December 2006 (NIMHE, 2005)

Involvement	• There is evidence of the full and meaningful involvement of child, adolescent and adult MH services, service users and carers and a broad range of partner agencies in service planning. • The service model must have the support of all key local stakeholders.

Teamwork	• EIP is provided by a discrete specialist team/s, each team seeing 120–150 clients, optimally.
	• OR – a hub and spoke or dispersed model that meets minimum standards for a 'team' definition, i.e.:
	  – A coherent group of specialist practitioners, whose sole/main responsibility is EIP, with common aims and objectives, philosophy of care and agreed care standards (NB – Optimum team capacity still applies).
	  – Explicit leadership that provides specialist supervision, work allocation, fidelity monitoring, service and staff development and performance management.
	  – The ability to provide Assertive Outreach to those clients that require it.
	  – Clarified medical responsibility for patients.
	• Up to four teams would comprise a Service (450 clients).

Interventions	• As per Policy Implementation Guide. • OR – the full range of best-practice interventions, pertinent to the stage of service development reached (as a minimum, recovery interventions by December 2006) – where – an explicit plan for the development of a comprehensive service for 14–35 year olds, within the lifespan of the NSF (2009), has been agreed and published.
Capacity	• Sufficient capacity to achieve SHA targets. • OR – sufficient capacity to meet the actual level of local need, where good quality audit/research has quantified this. Capacity must be based on care coordinator caseloads of 10–15 and an intention to see clients for 3 years.

Audit and Information	As a minimum, local information is gathered that will enable the:
	
	  – Accurate definition of local incidence rates.
	  – Mapping of current services.
	  – Measurement of DUP.
	  – Evaluation of outcomes (NB – This is a requirement where novel service models have been adopted).

support to the spoke workers. This model is often found in rural areas.

Many of the clinical interventions required to deliver an effective service to EIP service users and their families are easier to deliver in a specialist team. The strongest evidence base is also for this model. In some parts of England, this model needs to be compromised because of the geography of the area or other service-based factors (see Northumberland example). If a specialist team is not possible, then any compromise should have a mechanism for ensuring fidelity to the EIP model and the new ways of working described in this book. Dispersed models do not have this mechanism, which can make them appear cheaper as there is no need

to fund a manager or specialist staff such as psychiatrists. However, they are likely to be less effective and the roles of manager and psychiatrist will still be required, but will be provided by non-specialist workers. Therefore, the saving is notional not real.

Case studies

Tees and North East Yorkshire Case Study – Specialist Team

The Tees and North East Yorkshire EIP Service covers a population of 1.2 million. The area covered is boundaried in the north by Easington and Hartlepool but runs down to a rural patch of East Cleveland, which covers large areas of the North Yorkshire Moors. The service expects to have an incidence of just over 200 cases per annum. Originally the service was based together as one team with people being allocated geographical areas to work in. However, even in a specialist service, covering a relatively densely populated geographical area, there might still be populations that are best served by modified models and the service has recently added some geographical spokes for its most isolated communities.

In my view it is vital that the team is based together. In order to deliver a consistent, high quality, person centred and risk tolerant service it is essential that a team approach is taken and that this work is coordinated and directed from within.

(Sue Wadforth Hull and East Yorkshire EI Team Manager)

The strength of a large discrete service is the ability to employ people with specialist skills that are accessible to all clinicians within the service. The service employs a number of Band 7 sub-team managers with specialist skills and interests, which are accessible to the whole service. The service manager also works across the whole service, as do two CAMHS workers, enabling the service to see people under the age of 16. There is also a good blend of different disciplines and specialist skills within the team. The sheer size of the service enables it to be robust and to be able to manage issues such as sickness absence and annual leave independently. One difficulty for the service is that, as it covers different local authority and PCT areas, there are some organisational variations across localities. However, these are minimised by having one service with a shared ethos that enables greater consistency across the patch. There are further opportunities for development and the full realisation of the advantages that size and critical mass bring. For example, the size of population covered would enable a sizeable sample for the collection of research and audit data to demonstrate local need and service effectiveness. Also, further specialist skills could be brought into the service, particularly psychiatry and clinical psychology, to try and further enhance the clinical service offered. A further opportunity remains to develop early detection strategies, which would reduce the duration of untreated psychosis.

Craven Case Study – Dispersed / CMHT Model

Elsewhere, some areas have opted to provide EIP from pre-existing mental health teams. The rationale for this has usually derived from considerations relating to rurality, low incidence or both. The flexibilities process (NIMHE, 2003) has proved sympathetic to arguments for smaller and more rural services to opt out of the specialist stand-alone service models proposed in the MH-PIG and there has been a great deal of interest in whether such models can prove effective. An example of a rural community where a CMHT-based EIP model has been adopted can be found in the Craven Community Mental Health Service in North Yorkshire. This service serves a large part of the Yorkshire Dales but expects to see only eight new referrals per year. Early intervention is provided predominantly, by two community mental health nurses (one full-time and one part-time), one of whom also undertakes some EIP service development responsibilities. Both members of staff also carry out other generic duties, as well as contributing to the CMHT's Crisis Resolution and duty assessment functions. A partnership agreement with the local CAMHS service aims to enable an age-appropriate service for the under17s, and all adult clients come under the care of a single, team-based psychiatrist. The team operates out of the local general hospital and has the flexibility to deliver their service outside of core office hours when required.

Given the challenge of providing community-based specialist mental health services to a dispersed rural population, the Craven team recognise a number of strengths for their model. Being small and fully integrated with their community mental health colleagues, communication is optimised and there is ready access to the full range of staff and skills within the CMHT, which includes staff with expertise in employment, housing and dual diagnosis. This connectedness also enables sharing of EIP expertise and offsets some of the fragility of a very small team, since there is always a wider pool of staff to call upon in the event of high demand, sickness or absence. The Craven team feel that they are less likely than a larger or more distant service to be impersonal; they can pay attention to detail, can be more cognisant of specific local idiosyncrasies and are well connected to important related agencies in their own area – not the least primary care services. They are flexible and well placed to forge strong community links, and this model minimises the risk of service elements being provided a long way from clients' homes.

On the down side, it is acknowledged that smaller teams face a number of inherent difficulties, particularly with regard to key fidelity criteria. In common with Craven, such teams tend to have less complete and diverse skill mixes, fewer support workers and are less likely to have dedicated medical staffing. This means that they struggle to support the full breadth of interventions required for EIP, and the positive risk-taking ACT approach cannot be provided. The capacity for assessment and 'watch and wait' interventions in primary care can be disproportionally difficult to sustain in smaller teams, and the requirement to share key clinicians/roles can lead to non-specialist approaches. Without a dedicated EIP leadership function the Craven team have struggled to acquire specialist supervision and training, and their capacity for local needs assessment and service planning has been minimal. Given the complexity of EIP and the change management that is involved at so many levels, this is often the most vital element that is missing from small, low incidence and low resource developments.

The inherent fragility of the EIP function in this model demands a reliance on the wider mental health team, which in itself contains certain risks. EIP teams were expected to offer an alternative culture to that found in generic mental health teams, and the requirement for youth-focused, optimistic and engaging services was seen as central to the need to provide something distinctly different for the EIP client group. Whilst the values that the EIP approach is founded upon are not unique to them alone, it stands to reason that under this model the adult CMHT culture will dominate.

Although it is accepted that the problems posed by dispersed rural populations require careful consideration, some commentators have suspected perverse incentives for the adoption of CMHT-embedded EIP services, arguing that these models represent the least challenge to the dominant culture and also represent the least expensive option. Staff in Craven have themselves expressed concern that their existence and configuration may owe more to a requirement to achieve targets than a genuine desire by senior management to provide different and better services:

I can't help thinking that this job is more about ticking boxes than making a real difference. If you really wanted to provide a better service for young first episodes you'd do more than this.
(David Bright, Care Coordinator, Craven CMHT)

Nevertheless, satisfaction with these local teams is reported to be high and the commitment of the individuals involved is unquestionable. Some of the limitations of the dispersed/CMHT model described here are not insurmountable and, in fairness, some of the problems faced are problems of commissioning rather than problems of delivery. Nevertheless, it remains to be seen whether these models can progress to offer the comprehensive features required and produce outcomes comparable to the impressive results that are beginning to be seen in MH-PIG-compliant teams elsewhere.

Case studies

Northumberland Case Study – Hub and Spoke

The Northumberland EIP Service covers an area of 2,000 square miles with an expected incidence of 30 cases per annum, from the 310,000 population. The southeast corner of Northumberland is more densely populated and also has the highest levels of deprivation. In the first year of operation, only two full-time care coordinators would be required to manage the expected 30 cases. It was agreed that the best way to provide a service initially was to have part-time care coordinators embedded within CMHTs (spokes) and a clinical psychologist to provide specialist skills, leadership and to maintain fidelity to the MH-PIG (hub). The CMHT manager held clinical accountability for service users, and the sector psychiatrist provided medical cover. The clinical psychologist co-worked with and supervised the care coordinators to ensure that an EIP approach was used. This hub-and-spoke model was effective in reducing bed days, encouraging engagement and increasing employment rates. However, care coordinators were pulled into CMHT tasks, team working was restricted and there was limited ability to specialise.

When the team had been operational for 3 years and was managing 90 cases, it became feasible to develop the hub into a specialist team to enhance fidelity and the overall quality of service provided. However, the size of Northumberland made it more effective to retain some embedded workers in the more rural areas to reduce travel time. The service remains a hub-and-spoke model, but now has an enlarged centralised hub.

The hub and spoke model has pro's and cons. Undoubtedly having staff based in the areas they cover has benefits, as does proximity to other MH colleagues. On the downside it is hard to support and supervise spoke staff at a distance and in my view quality suffers sometimes because of this.

(Carol Anne Farquhar, Team Manager, Bradford and Airedale EI)

In this respect, the design limitations for new EI services can be compared to machine design. For example, vehicles that need to be strong and rugged are usually heavy and slow, whilst those that need to be fast are light-weight but

less durable. For service designers, each circumstance brings its own specific challenges and these exist on a continuum. Figure 6.1 provides a simple illustration of this continuum and also helps us to see how the optimum model of service might vary over time and may change as a service develops or as external factors change.

Implications and conclusions

In this chapter we have outlined critical components of the EI approach, explored the evidence base and policy drivers for the model proposed in the MH-PIG and outlined the main service delivery models that have emerged in the UK. We have used examples of different services to critically examine the relative merits of each. Table 6.2 summarises the benefits and deficits of the main service models that have emerged for EIP:

As can be seen, each model has strengths and weaknesses, and many question marks hang over the new and untested alternatives to the MH-PIG model. Whilst each local situation

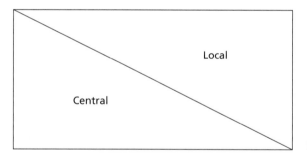

Figure 6.1

Table 6.2 Benefits and deficits of EIP service models

	Specialist	Dispersed	H & S
Evidence base to support	✓	X	X
Promotes team approach/ACT	✓	X	X
Promotes clear EIP value base/philosophy	✓	X	?
Consistency of practice	✓	X	✓
Promotes recruitment and retention	✓	?	?
Promotes development of specialist skills	✓	X	?
Promotes strong local presence	X	✓	✓
Value for money	✓	?	?
May benefit other community teams	?	✓	✓
Easy to ring-fence EIP resource	✓	X	?

demands its own set of solutions, there are often common themes, and certain core features are non-negotiable. Ultimately, the challenge is to establish the model that is most pertinent to the particular needs of a locality and to ensure that this model will deliver the core service features and clinical interventions that evidence shows are required for successful EI.

Cost will always be a major consideration and EI is costly – but no more so than any of the other new community mental health services that we are required to provide. The imperative is to ensure that EIP is good value for money and that the promised outcomes are achieved. This means making sure that money is spent wisely and financial benefits are realised, that teams are efficiently managed and clinically led towards a faithful interpretation of the chosen model and that a locality's unique strengths and needs are recognised and incorporated. With reference to the Early Psychosis Declaration, the ambition of EI is that young people and families affected by psychosis should be able to expect prompt assistance, services that really help (and that do not stigmatise), rapid and sustained recovery and, ultimately, ordinary lives – wherever they live. Appropriate models of service delivery are critical to the realisation of this ambition.

Suggested further reading

The Sainsbury Centre for Mental Health (2003). *A Window of Opportunity: A Practical Guide for Developing Early Intervention in Psychiatric Services*. London: The Sainsbury Centre for Mental Health.

Department of Health (2001). *Mental Health Policy Implementation Guide*. London: Department of Health.

References

Birchwood, M., Jackson, C. & Todd, P. (1998). The critical period hypothesis. *International Clinical Psychopharmacy*, 12, 27–38.

Department of Health (1999). *The National Service Framework for Mental Health*. London: Department of Health.

Department of Health (2000). *The NHS Plan: A Plan for Investment, a Plan for Reform*. London: Department of Health.

Department of Health (2001). *Mental Health Policy Implementation Guide*. London: Department of Health.

Harrison, G., Hopper, K., Craig, T. *et al.* (2001). Recovery from psychotic illness: A 15 and 25-year international follow-up study. *British Journal of Psychiatry*, 178, 506–517.

Initiative to Reduce the Impact of Schizophrenia (IRIS). Retrieved 2002, from www.iris-initiative.org.uk

Marshall, M., Lewis, S., Lockwood, A. *et al.* (2005). Association between duration of untreated psychosis and outcome in cohorts of first episode patients: A systematic review. *Archives of General Psychiatry*, 62, 975–983.

Marshall, M. & Rathbone, J. (2006). Early intervention for psychosis. *Cochrane Database of Systematic Reviews*, 4, CD004718.

McGorry, P.D., Edwards, J., Michalopoulos, C. *et al.* (1996). EPPIC: An evolving system of early detection and optimal management. *Schizophrenia Bulletin*, 22 (2), 306–326.

National Institute for Mental Health in England (2003). *Counting Community Teams: Issues in Fidelity and Flexibility*. NIMHE.

National Institute for Clinical Excellence (2002). *Clinical Guideline 1: Schizophrenia: Core Interventions in the Treatment and Management of Schizophrenia in Primary and Secondary Care*. London: NICE.

Norman, R.M.G. & Malla, A.K. (2001). Duration of untreated psychosis: A critical examination of the concept and its importance. *Psychological Medicine*, 31, 381–400.

The Sainsbury Centre for Mental Health (2003). *A Window of Opportunity: A Practical Guide for Developing Early Intervention in Psychiatric Services*. London: The Sainsbury Centre for Mental Health.

Chapter 7 Cognitive behavioural interventions in early intervention services

Elizabeth Newton and Emma Cotes

Introduction

This chapter will explore the use of cognitive behavioural therapy (CBT) for people with first-episode psychosis, treated within early intervention (EI) services. It will focus on the use of CBT for positive psychotic symptoms, as well as other difficulties which may be secondary to an episode of psychosis, such as social anxiety, low mood and low self-esteem. These are all common difficulties presented by clients seeking psychological support within EI.

The chapter begins by providing a brief resumé of the evidence base for cognitive behavioural interventions in psychosis, in general, and in EI, in particular. CBT is just one of a number of evidence-based, cost-effective interventions which, in line with the Early Psychosis Declaration (Bertolote & McGorry, 2005), should be made easily accessible within the early phase of psychosis, in order to aid recovery. CBT is well placed as an intervention in early psychosis because it has many values in common with those set out by this declaration. For example, CBT aims to develop acollaborative working relationship with the young person, which respects and draws upon their strengths and qualities. Furthermore, CBT aims to support the young person to set and achieve their own recovery, social and educational and vocational goals. Here, we draw upon our own experience as clinical psychologists working within EI to describe how such interventions have been put into practice, using case studies and narrative from service users to illuminate the text. We will also explore some of the obstacles and challenges faced when implementing psychological approaches in EI which have been developed for adults who have long-term difficulties.

A summary of the evidence

CBT for people with schizophrenia is advocated by UK guidelines for the treatment of schizophrenia (National Institute for Clinical Excellence, 2002), which recommend that it should be available to all people with a diagnosis with schizophrenia and that it should be routinely offered to people with persistent psychotic symptoms. Provision of CBT as an adjunct to medication is important because studies show that a significant group of individuals will continue to experience psychotic symptoms even when taking medication as prescribed (Johnstone et al., 1991). In addition, each psychotic episode may be associated with an increase in residual positive symptoms (Wiersma et al., 1998). The main aims of CBT for psychosis are to reduce the distress and impact on functioning associated with the symptoms of psychosis, to reduce emotional disturbance (such as anxiety and depression) associated with the psychotic episode and to help the individual arrive at their own personalised understanding of their difficulties (Garety et al., 2000). There is also evidence that CBT can reduce relapse rates (NICE, 2002).

Individual CBT interventions for treating psychotic symptoms (e.g. delusions and hallucinations) have been reported in the research literature for several decades. Although early work comprised case studies involving a small number of individuals, and thus lacked experimental controls (Beck, 1952; Hole et al., 1979), research has since moved on to evaluate the effects of CBT interventions for psychosis in a more systematic way. A series of randomised controlled trials have shown that CBT for people with psychosis can have a positive effect on residual positive symptoms and depression when compared with treatment as usual (TAU) or waiting list control groups (Garety *et al.*, 1994; Granholm *et al.*, 2002). CBT has been associated with a significant reduction in the severity of delusions when compared to supportive counselling or TAU (Durham *et al.*, 2003) and a significant reduction in complying with command hallucinations (Trower *et al.*, 2004). There is also evidence for the superiority of CBT over alternative interventions such as supportive counselling (Tarrier *et al.*, 1998), befriending (Sensky *et al.*, 2000) and psychodynamic supportive therapy (Durham *et al.*, 2003). Although it is beyond the scope of this chapter to discuss the findings on individual studies in depth, the interested reader is directed to Gaudiano's (2005) paper which provides a detailed overview of research conducted in this area.

Most recently, research has begun to focus specifically on evaluating CBT in early psychosis. Research in this area is in its infancy, and NICE (2002) states that the literature so far is too limited to come to any firm conclusion about its efficacy. In 1996, Drury *et al.* compared TAU with a cognitive therapy intervention in first-episode psychosis, and found that the CBT group experienced faster recovery times and had significantly fewer residual positive symptoms, at 9 months. The difference between the groups was no longer significant at a 5-year follow-up, but the CBT group still reported significantly greater perceived control over their illness, and participants who had suffered one (or no) relapse reported a reduced level of delusional beliefs (Drury *et al.*, 2000). The largest study to date focusing on first-episode clients has been the Socrates study (Lewis *et al.*, 2002; Tarrier *et al.*, 2004), which compared CBT with supportive counselling and TAU. Both the CBT and supportive counselling groups improved significantly on symptom measures (measured by the PANSS) in comparison to the TAU group at an 18-month follow-up (Tarrier *et al.*, 2004). Although there were no significant differences between the three groups in relation to relapse

or rehospitalisation rates, there was a trend towards significance for the CBT intervention to have a better effect on hallucinations in comparison with the supportive counselling group.

Research has also attempted to identify client factors associated with positive outcomes amongst those experiencing a first episode of psychosis. Jolley *et al.* (2003) suggest that it may be most useful to offer CBT to clients with persisting symptoms or affective disturbance following their episode of psychosis, rather than offering this type of intervention routinely to all individuals. Haddock *et al.* (2006) conclude that clients under 21 years of age may benefit more from supportive counselling, whereas those over 21 may benefit more from CBT. The younger age group were also rated as being significantly more difficult to engage in therapy by the therapists.

In addition to individual cognitive behavioural interventions for psychotic symptoms, there is a small but growing evidence base for the efficacy of cognitive behavioural group therapy for auditory hallucinations (Gledhill *et al.*, 1998; Wykes *et al.*, 1999; Chadwick *et al.*, 2000). These are one of the most common symptoms in psychosis with between 60 and 74% of people with a diagnosis of schizophrenia reporting that they hear voices (Wing *et al.*, 1974; Slade & Bentall, 1988). Between 20 and 50% of these continue to be distressed by hearing voices despite taking regular antipsychotic medication (Curson *et al.*, 1988). Individual CBT has been reported to have little impact on auditory hallucinations (Pilling *et al.*, 2002). Group cognitive behavioural approaches have been specifically designed to target auditory hallucinations. These provide additional group benefits, such as capitalising on social support, normalising and destigmatising symptoms and increasing coping repertoires. The need for early clinical intervention focusing on voices has been highlighted in order to reduce distress, increase coping and to abort or delay the development of secondary difficulties (Dhosse *et al.*, 2002; Escher *et al.*, 2002). It is also believed that hallucinations and beliefs about hallucinations may be more easily influenced by psychological therapy shortly after their onset (Bentall, 1994). We are aware of only one published study evaluating the effectiveness of voices groups with young people with recent onset of psychosis

(Newton *et al.*, 2005). This demonstrated that the experience of auditory hallucinations significantly improved over the treatment phase as predicted, with a significant increase in the amount of control that participants had over the voices, and a significant reduction in the voices' power. The young people were also engaging in more activities, following the group intervention.

A high proportion of individuals who experience psychosis may also experience co-morbid mood or anxiety difficulties. These difficulties require assessment and treatment in their own right, both because of the distress they cause and because they can act as stressors, which increase the chances of future relapse (Birchwood *et al.*, 1998). For example, Birchwood *et al.* (2000) found that 36% of clients in their study developed moderate depressive symptoms in the 12 months following an acute episode. Other studies have reported prevalence of depression in similar samples to be between 38 and 45% (Johnstone *et al.*, 1991; Addington *et al.*, 1998). Recent NICE guidance on the treatment of anxiety strongly suggests that CBT interventions should be offered to this group, because this type of therapy has the longest-lasting effect of any of the treatments available (NICE, 2004a). The NICE guidelines on depression conclude that psychological treatments using CBT principles can be as effective as drug treatments and therefore should be offered to those suffering with the symptoms of depression (NICE, 2004b).

Implementation into practice: Case studies

The next section of the chapter presents three different case studies, each illustrating the use of cognitive behavioural interventions in EI. Where possible, clients' views on the interventions that they have experienced are included. Following the case studies, issues relating to the practicalities and challenges of this work are discussed.

It is important to note that the CBT interventions described were only one aspect of the package of care that the clients were receiving from their EI team. Each client received regular case management support and medical reviews. During their time in EI, they would also have been offered family intervention, early signs (relapse prevention) work and support with vocational and social activities.

Steve: CBT for delusions

Steve was referred to the EI service following his first hospital admission. His case manager requested that he be referred to the team psychologist. He was a mature university student who had previously been working as a motor mechanic. Prior to his hospital admission, he had been struggling at university, having been required to change course. He had been admitted following a suicide attempt. He strongly believed that he had been systematically bullied and discriminated against by his university tutors, and also believed that his girlfriend and family members had knowledge about a conspiracy against him to ruin his life. He described suffering from low mood and anxiety, but did not feel that he was experiencing psychosis.

Steve believed that his treatment by the university tutors merited a compensation payout because he had been victimised and felt the change of course had been forced on him and would ruin his future career chances. He believed that his case had already been settled as an out-of-court settlement, and that the money had been paid to his girlfriend or relatives. Steve's girlfriend and parents agreed that he had been bullied at university but the beliefs about the financial settlement were delusional. These beliefs made it difficult for Steve to get on with his life, as he felt the payout would be transferred to him in due course and there was therefore no need to return to his course or look for a job. His partner was distressed because she was providing practical, emotional and financial support and Steve had been hostile and irritable towards her because he believed she was withholding information and money from him.

Steve met with the therapist happily because she was willing to discuss the situation with him. He was seen at his home weekly, and then fortnightly, over an 8-month period. At the start of the intervention, Steve described spending virtually all his time ruminating on his situation. He reported that he had 90% conviction in the belief that an out-of-court settlement had taken place and that he was 100% convinced that his family knew more about his situation than he did. When Steve was asked in a gentle and exploratory way how about he would feel and what he would do should there not be a payout (hypothetical contradiction), he said that he would be very depressed and would kill himself. In the formulation of his difficulties, this reaction was in line with the idea that he was suffering from underlying low self-esteem and without the esteem gained from the grandiose idea that he would soon be a wealthy man, Steve would feel worthless and depressed. Hypothetical contradiction had illustrated that a full modification (total change) of his delusional beliefs would lead to increased risk of suicide and therefore a partial modification (part change) of his delusional ideas was the goal of the intervention. The therapist aimed to modify his beliefs to acceptable alternatives which would reduce family tension and to enable Steve to begin to do some activities but would not make Steve feel depressed or suicidal. Activities were designed to give Steve a sense of achievement to improve his low self-esteem.

The intervention followed the structure laid out by Nelson (2005). Strategies used included mapping out a timeline of events which took place at university that Steve felt supported his beliefs. Although this evidence was not formally challenged at this stage, whilst the task was being completed, the therapist 'floated' a range of alternative explanations for some of the events. As the intervention progressed, Steve began to evaluate the evidence he was holding in support of his beliefs and to consider alternative views. Over time, Steve was able to begin to recognise that there was a possibility that an out-of-court settlement had not been reached, and the level of conviction in this belief fell from 90% to 50%. During the intervention, it was very important to monitor Steve's levels of hopelessness and suicidality because he had reported that he would kill himself should he not receive the money. This was done using formal assessment measures (the Calgary Depression Scale (Addington et al., 1990) and Beck Hopelessness Scale (Beck, 1988)). If these had increased, a new direction would have been taken. Family members were actively engaged by the therapist in encouraging Steve to find useful roles within the family that he could fulfil, in order to increase his self-esteem. For example, his brother asked him to help build a wall, which gave him a sense of achievement and lifted his mood. As Steve began to spend less time ruminating about his situation, he began to be able to engage in tasks outside the house, such as walking his dog and meeting friends again, and the level of tension between him and his girlfriend also reduced considerably. His level of conviction in the belief that his family knew more than he did fell from 100% to 30% over the course of therapy. After approximately 6 months, with no evidence of the out-of-court settlement money appearing,

he felt able to ask for some advice on how to make a complaint about a member of university staff, who he felt had treated him unfairly, and he also began to take on casual labouring work which improved his financial situation.

Gregory: CBT for co-morbid anxiety

Gregory was referred to psychology 6 months after being taken on by the EI service after making a good recovery from his psychotic symptoms. He was very concerned about severe anxiety, which was preventing him from doing social and vocational activities. At the time of the assessment, he was spending every day at home, but reported that his goals were to get a job and to socialise more.

Gregory described himself as a quiet and shy child who had always had a tendency to be anxious. He was given a diagnosis of dyslexia when he was young and had many experiences of failure related to this. He found things difficult at school, was placed into the bottom sets, where he received special help. He changed schools on a number of occasions, and failed his GCSEs. He later went on to attend college, where he resat these, and also took two A-levels, and did well. However, in comparison to his peers, he felt that he always found academic work more difficult. He believed that this was something to do with 'being a failure' rather than taking into account his specific learning disability. He reported that he had always felt anxious and had had low self-confidence.

Gregory continued to struggle academically when he went to university, and this seemed to be compounded by difficulties on the course with both lecturers and course content. He began to feel unwell. Encouraged by his family, he returned home, where he was diagnosed with a psychotic episode and treated by the EI service. At this point, there were a number of other life stressors; two of his grandparents died and his parents separated. It seemed that the experience of psychosis itself and the fact that this interrupted his life goals (e.g. he had not been able to work since this time) had a further negative impact on his self-confidence, heightened his anxiety and reinforced his beliefs about being a failure.

Since becoming unwell, Gregory had adopted a low-stress lifestyle. He spent a lot of time at home, sleeping, or working on his computer and avoiding situations that might provoke anxiety or that he did not feel confident about. He described suffering from physical symptoms of anxiety and panic, but he experienced these rarely, owing to his avoidance. This avoidance maintained his anxiety symptoms and concerns about not having the ability to achieve anything (e.g. getting a job). He was not able to learn that anxiety decreases the longer you stay in an anxiety-provoking situation or the more frequently you attempt it. Nor was he able to challenge negative automatic thoughts about situations which were causing him to feel anxious (e.g. 'I will say something stupid', 'I cannot do voluntary work') by collecting evidence to the contrary. In addition, when he was in anxiety-provoking situations, he described a number of safety behaviours which maintained his anxiety. For example, in a situation where he was fearful that he would make a fool of himself and imagined dropping his food or drink on the floor, he sat down and placed his drink on the table to prevent this from happening. This stopped him from learning that this was very unlikely to happen or what the outcome of this would be should it really occur (hopefully he would only feel silly or embarrassed for a few seconds and other people would react sympathetically and would not laugh at him and think he was stupid, which was his fear). He continued to worry about making a fool of himself by dropping food and drink at the next social event that he attended, which made him feel anxious.

Gregory described the underlying core beliefs and related negative automatic thoughts which contributed to the anxiety. For example, he held the core beliefs 'I am a failure' and 'I am incompetent'. He had a tendency to set himself very high goals which were extremely frightening to think about and therefore never attempted to achieve his goals. This maintained his anxiety, related beliefs and hopelessness.

Gregory received 20 sessions of CBT over a 6-month period. This included behavioural work, in which he and his psychologist worked through a graded hierarchy, exposing Gregory to a variety of anxiety-provoking situations and encouraging him to practice these until his anxiety diminished. In addition, cognitive work was undertaken to help Gregory to identify and re-evaluate negative automatic thoughts and underlying beliefs. In particular, this focused on his belief that he was a failure, which appeared to be related to his high levels of anxiety in new situations.

At the end of the sessions, Gregory had completed approximately three-quarters of the tasks on his hierarchy. This included activities such as going shopping, socialising in other people's houses, attending an activity group, talking to new people, clothes shopping, talking to people on the telephone and doing part-time work. He reported that the behavioural work helped him to understand his difficulties; in particular, he learnt that avoiding the activities and things that he was concerned about made his anxiety worse, rather than better. The behavioural work also provided evidence for Gregory that he did not fail when he tried new activities. This was useful in undermining his core belief that he was a failure. Cognitive work investigated evidence for and against the belief that he was a failure using both current and historical evidence. Gregory and his psychologist collated evidence to build up an alternative, more positive belief, of Gregory as successful. Gregory was able to make good use of tools such as anxiety diaries and coping cards to help with this work. His conviction in the belief that he was a failure fell from 100% to 65% over the time of the intervention. His anxiety as measured by the Beck Anxiety Inventory fell from a score of 29 (severe anxiety) to a score of 15 (mild to moderate anxiety). This was despite the fact that the latter rating was taken during a week in which Gregory had begun a new part-time job, which we might anticipate would raise his anxiety levels.

Gregory: 'I was diagnosed with psychosis and after my first episode I had feelings of worthlessness and being anxious. I had problems doing everyday things . . . for example, . . . holding drinks at social occasions, and having the catastrophic thought that I would always drop my drink. We did flow diagrams to demonstrate to myself how having the thought that everything is going to go wrong will come back and effect my performance, making me more anxious. Instead I should enforce the idea that I can do the tasks asked of me and have a positive image. Also we looked at what would be the worst that could happen if I did drop the drink and that the reaction would not be as bad as I imagine. We looked at past evidence of my achievements as my frame of mind made me look more at my failures rather than my achievements. This was to help me with my attitude that I always fail at things. I no longer even think of dropping my drink now and don't feel as worthless. I still suffer from illness from time to time but I think I cope better than I did before'.

Table 7.1 What participants said

What participants said:
Mark: 'I was talking to people who have similar experiences to myself, so it was quite helpful to understand and see the similarities between cases – which was quite remarkable how similar it was . . .'
Patience: 'Yeah [*talking to others in the group*] that helped a lot, cos you got to know people who was/who had the same problems as you and you can just/like . . .'
Jocasta: 'I have made a friend like/who's like/who's been through the same thing as me and she's just cool with it'. '[*I learned*] that there are more people . . . of my age group have this problem. I'm not the only person that's got this problem, so I don't have to feel like I'm crazy or anything like that'.
Angelo: 'A lot of the time I felt like what they were saying I knew about it already, cos we were talking about hobbies and interests and how many voices we hear, and what were the voices saying – um but I also learnt more things than what I came in with [. . .] how to cope with the voices, hobbies and interests and talking about it'.
Harinder: 'I could see what helped me and what didn't' . . . 'What made the voices, what made me stop hearing voices, and what didn't stop me from hearing voices.[. . .] So now I can see why playing football, watching TV, going out, helps, but if I just sit alone and keep listening to my voices its not going to help'.

(Excerpts taken from: More than just a place to talk: Young people's experiences of group psychological therapy as an early intervention for auditory hallucinations, Newton *et al.*, 2007.)

A first-episode voices group

Evidence for the effectiveness of voices groups is positive and growing. A large number of people with early psychosis will experience and be distressed by auditory hallucinations despite taking medication. It therefore makes sense for EI services to run a voices group programme. An additional advantage is that this approach represents a time- and cost-effective way of providing psychological therapy, because as up to 10 clients can be seen at once, by two therapists, in a closed group programme of only seven sessions (following the protocol of Wykes *et al.*, 1999).

Our experience of running voices groups in EI has suggested that they are well received by our clients, who value meeting other people with voices, and receive support from this. The groups also have a positive impact on symptoms, particularly in reducing levels of distress associated with voices, in increasing perceived control over the voices and in reducing their perceived power (see Table 7.2). We have followed the treatment protocol designed by Wykes *et al.* (1999) for groups of adults with auditory hallucinations. This protocol has also been successful in treating young people with distressing voices (Newton *et al.*, 2005). Sessions

are based on a cognitive behavioural approach using techniques such as Socratic questioning and guided discovery (the use of questioning to uncover and explore the meaning attributed to situations and to consider possible alternative views and ideas which may be less distressing) and coping strategy enhancement (finding and building upon successful coping strategies). Seven weekly, 1-hour sessions are run, each dealing with a particular theme:

Week 1 – The sharing of information about voices
Week 2 – Models of psychosis
Week 3 – Models of hallucinations
Week 4 – Effective coping strategies
Week 5 – Stigma and labelling
Week 6 – Improving self-esteem
Week 7 – Overall model of coping with voices

When working with EI clients, we have noted that it is useful to make the groups more active and less didactic (e.g. plenty of activities, exercises and small group discussions). It is an advantage if groups can be run outside working hours so as not to interfere with work and education, which are important both for symptom relief and personal development

Table 7.2 Examples of clinical assessment measures used prior to and immediately following a group for two clients

Scale used		Score before Group	Score following Group
PSYRATS auditory hallucinations scale (total score)	Client 1	29	27
	Client 2	23	19
Beliefs About Voices Scale (Revised): Malevolence	Client 1	3	5
	Client 2	10	6
Benevolence	Client 1	0	0
	Client 2	0	0
Omnipotence	Client 1	6	8
	Client 2	5	2
Engagement	Client 1	0	0
	Client 2	2	0
Resistance	Client 1	22	24
	Client 2	12	11
Number of coping strategies attempted	Client 1	14	19
Number of successful coping strategies	Client 2	14	18
	Client 1	8	13
	Client 2	11	13
Number of activities participating in on a regular basis	Client 1	16	43
	Client 2	31	35
Depression (Calgary Depression Scale)	Client 1	2	2
	Client 2	5	2
Anxiety (Beck Anxiety Inventory)	Client 1	3	1
	Client 2	7	0

for many of the young people attending. With the support of care coordinators, taxis and hospital transport, we have also found it helpful to provide transport in order to encourage participation.

Working with people with first-episode psychosis: Some challenges and some solutions

As mentioned in the introduction, most cognitive behavioural interventions for psychosis were designed for adults with a long history of difficulties. There is a dearth of literature on specific psychological treatments for young people with first-episode psychosis or on how or whether it is necessary to adapt adult interventions when working with this client group. However, CBT is used regularly with young people with psychosis in current clinical practice and we must therefore

suppose that clinicians believe it to have efficacy, despite the fact that the use of such therapies with this client group does not yet have a strong evidence base. Until the evidence base grows, 'treatment of younger cases is guided by the results of studies of adults', (Carr, 1999, p. 733). This may not always be appropriate. For example, young people with psychosis frequently do not have a diagnosis early on in their illness but still suffer from distressing positive symptoms – the literature frequently concentrates on people who have a diagnosis of 'schizophrenia' and long-term treatment-resistant positive symptoms. It may be that treatments for young people require different intervention goals to adult interventions; for example, to facilitate reintegration into education or work and peer social networks. Treatments also need to take developmental and educational level into account. For example, CBT relies on cognitive ideas and on tools such as homework and diaries, and this may be beyond the capability of the young person in treatment. The American Association of Child and Adolescent Psychiatry Practice Parameters (2001) recognise that in order for adult treatments to be successful with young people, clinicians should be prepared to make clinical adjustments to 'tune' therapies to patients' developmental needs.

In our clinical practice, we have sometimes found it necessary to make adjustments to the usual CBT format in order to work successfully with EI clients. Below, we use clinical observations and examples to describe some of the challenges faced when implementing CBT with our clients. Some of the changes that we have made to interventions in order to circumvent these difficulties are documented.

Beliefs about illness: Considerations for formulation and intervention

As demonstrated by the work carried out with Steve, we have frequently found in our clinical work that following a first episode of psychosis the client does not accept the medical model of their difficulties. In Steve's case, the therapist worked around this by utilising Steve's own ways of describing his difficulties such as 'being under a lot of stress' and 'not being able to get myself off the sofa' rather than using terms such as anxiety, depression or psychosis. In EI, we use a symptom- or problem-based approach, as advocated by Bentall (1990, 2004). This moves away from the need to talk about psychosis or diagnostic terms which may disrupt engagement and therapeutic alliance.

We also frequently draw upon a stress–vulnerability model of psychosis in order to illustrate how difficulties or unusual experiences may have occurred (Zubin & Spring, 1977). This can be explained to clients by using a 'bucket' analogy. For example, drawing a bucket for the client and filling it in together, adding cumulative layers of vulnerability and stress (e.g. Layer 1 – a family history of psychosis, Layer 2 – smoking cannabis, Layer 3 – exam pressure, etc.), which may act as precipitating or maintenance factors in our formulation of their difficulties. The

point at which the bucket overflows is identified as the point at which they experienced psychosis (or their difficulties in their own words, e.g. 'breakdown', 'stress', 'voices'). The therapist and client can identify an intervention plan together by identifying those 'layers in the bucket' about which something can be done, and then planning how to do this.

Destigmatising and normalising difficulties

Metacognitions can also be distressing. These are second-order beliefs about the experience of psychosis, or difficulties associated with this (e.g. hearing distressing voices, feeling paranoid) and their associated meanings (see Morrison et al., 2004). For example, a person who experiences voices will have first-order beliefs about the voices, which might include where they come from and how powerful they are. These beliefs will have consequences in terms of emotions, behaviour and further thoughts. However, they may also have the metacognition (second-order belief) that 'hearing voices makes people commit murder' and this too may impact directly, and negatively, upon the client's emotional state, thoughts and behaviour. For example, they may feel terrified and ashamed, the belief may affect their behaviour (the person may lock themselves in their house to avoid harming others). It may even exacerbate symptoms themselves, for example, the belief that hearing voices will make them murder somebody may make them feel anxious and this anxiety may increase the frequency of the voices.

In work with young people with psychosis, it is important to take a normalising and destigmatising approach when explaining psychosis and associated symptoms, in order to challenge negative beliefs and thoughts about symptoms and diagnosis, and to reduce associated stigma and secondary symptoms and consequences. Some useful ideas of how this can be done can be found in Nelson (1997). In the case of Steve, described earlier, once a strong rapport had been created, the therapist began to introduce the idea that psychosis is a state that can occur when any individual is under stress and a person's senses are in a state of elevated vigilance. The therapist described to Steve how this meant that individuals could find themselves looking very closely at everything that went on around them and sometimes cause them to misinterpret things as being 'significant' in some way. Using a series of analogies to destigmatise what Steve had experienced was very powerful. Prior to Steve's psychotic episode, he had worked as a car mechanic and the therapist introduced an analogy of the therapist feeling anxious and hypervigilant for noises and changes in the engine tone of her car following a mechanical breakdown. Following the breakdown, the therapist described how it was easy for her to misinterpret noises (which had probably always occurred but were outside her awareness) as signs of a further imminent breakdown. Using this analogy, Steve was able to begin to reconsider some of the situations where he felt strangers' gestures had personal significance, and identified that significant gestures and references to his situation from strangers seemed more frequent when he was feeling particularly anxious or irritated about his situation.

It can be useful to share personal experience of having experienced odd ideas or of hearing and seeing things that were not really there, in order to normalise such experiences. Videos, books and examples from other clients and research literature can also be used in order to normalise symptoms and help the client feel that they are not alone. Meeting other service users in group therapy itself can be both normalising and destigmatising. Qualitative work asking people about their experiences of being in a hearing voices group suggests that relief may be gained from meeting others, and may challenge negative beliefs about the meaning of symptoms, or stereotypes about people who have mental health problems (Newton *et al.*, 2007).

Time, frequency and location of sessions

When working with people experiencing psychosis, it is also important to ensure that the length of sessions suits each individual. For example, at the start of the intervention, Steve's concentration and ability to hold a conversation was quite limited. He was experiencing considerable distraction from his psychotic symptoms

and so initial sessions were short and frequent (e.g. 20 minutes twice per week). As concentration and the ability to tolerate psychological therapy improve, sessions can become longer and less frequent. Although not usual in adult mental health, another strategy is to have a tea break midsession, or to talk about something other than the difficulties for a few minutes, in order to refresh concentration. Similarly, group therapy sessions can be broken into shorter chunks by having one or two breaks for a drink, snack or walk, during the session. Again, Hazel Nelson (2005) describes many useful strategies for engagement of clients in psychological work.

The location of sessions also needs to be given careful consideration. McGovern (1994) identified that in routine mental health services, approximately 50% of clients are 'lost to follow-up' within 12 months. Symptoms, cognitive difficulties, reluctance to be seen in mental health settings and general disorganisation all contribute to young people missing outpatient appointments. EI has taken an assertive outreach approach in engaging its clients and this extends to psychology input. We offer people a choice in location of sessions, which can include a community location, the team base or a home visit. In addition, if the client has difficulty organising their time or remembering appointments, reminders by letter, telephone call or text messages can be used prior to the appointment. In early stages of engagement, or in treating difficulties that require exposure and/or behavioural experiments to be carried out, it may be appropriate to be creative with the venue of appointments. We have seen clients in places including art galleries, buses and fast food restaurants.

For young people with negative symptoms, sleep reversal, or those who just get up late, afternoon appointments lead to far fewer missed appointments. For those of our clients who work, we ensure that they can be offered appointments after work or college so that they do not have to take time off for frequent appointments. (Imagine how disruptive it could be to have up to three appointments per week for 3 years, and how popular you would be with your employer should this happen.)

This is respectful of their success in sustaining employment or education whilst overcoming their difficulties. It also avoids putting the client in a position where they may need to explain their situation to their employer (who may hold negative beliefs or stereotypes about mental illness), and indeed, having to choose between disclosure of their mental health problem or psychological therapy. Group sessions in EI are frequently run 'out of hours' in order to enable equal access to service users and family members who would not be able to attend daytime appointments. The frequency of sessions may also be reduced to less than one a week to better suit the client's schedule.

In summary, time, location and frequency of sessions need to be given careful consideration and to be discussed with the client during the assessment sessions. The client should be encouraged to pick a venue, time and frequency which will maximise their ability to engage in the work and the therapist should be encouraged to work flexibly and be enabled to do so by support of the EI team.

Negative symptoms and cognitive problems

Both the negative symptoms and cognitive problems associated with schizophrenia can have an impact on a client's ability to engage in CBT. For example, negative symptoms such as avolition can make it difficult for a client to motivate themselves to attend sessions or engage in therapeutic work. Alogia (poverty of thought), often associated with unresponsiveness and reduction in spontaneous speech, may make talking therapy difficult. Cognitive difficulties, such as poor memory, can make it very difficult to remember or test out the content of talking therapy. Executive functioning deficits (the most frequent cognitive problem associated with a diagnosis of schizophrenia) (Heinrichs *et al.*, 1984) may create problems with selecting goals and being able to plan stepwise progression towards them and with doing tasks requiring working memory (e.g. following conversations, remembering appointments) or cognitive shift (i.e. changing from one task or mental set to another whilst still keeping the other or others in mind). All of these will clearly impact upon the client's ability

to attend, make use of and respond to talking therapy.

If either negative symptoms or cognitive problems appear to be an issue, these may need assessment and treatment in their own right prior to the commencement of CBT. Psychological treatments for cognitive deficits such as cognitive remediation therapy (CRT) are well documented in the literature (for review, see Wykes & Van der Gaag, 2001). CRT is an intensive psychological therapy which has been shown to improve cognitive difficulties such as memory and executive functioning (Wykes *et al.*, 1999). Improvement of cognitive functioning prior to receiving CBT should improve a client's ability to benefit from this, as it is heavily reliant on skills such as attention, concentration memory and planning. (For example, the ability to be able to listen to and attend to what the therapist says, being able to think about and plan a response to their questions and to remember and utilise new ideas and behaviours in order to improve symptoms.) CBT itself can be used to improve negative symptoms. A treatment pack has been designed by Reid, Barker and Smith (2007) for tackling negative symptoms and motivational difficulties and is described in Chapter 15, Working with Motivational Difficulties, in this book.

Consideration can also be given to cognitive problems and negative symptoms within CBT sessions. For example, when a client has cognitive difficulties, CBT can be simplified, or tools can be used to work around these problems. For example, Steve had a poor verbal memory, and therefore information in sessions was drawn out in diagram form on big pieces of paper during each session. In the case of another client with memory problems, summary notes were written at the end of each session and were kept by the client to remind her of what had been discussed and the implications of this. Other strategies could include recording sessions or using diaries. In group therapy sessions, we routinely produce a summary sheet of what happened in the previous session and go through this at the beginning of the next session to help people to remember. For planning and motivational difficulties, SMART goals are frequently used (Shared, small and specific, Measurable,

Achievable, Realistic and Timed) to encourage a client to set a goal easily within their reach, and to have achieved it before the next session.

One common difficulty appears to be the ability of young people with psychosis to motivate themselves or to remember to do any homework for the following session. This can be both upsetting for the client, who has to say that they have not done it (possibly reinforcing underlying beliefs about inadequacy and failure), and frustrating for a therapist who, if used to working in adult mental health, may view this as a core part of CBT intervention. We have tackled this problem in a number of different ways by: (a) not setting homework; (b) changing our own expectations; (c) changing the nature of the homework by doing something that can be easily completed together in the next session or something that the client will have probably done and will be able to discuss even if they did not do it because it was homework; (d) doing things such as experiments together in the session rather than for homework; (e) using SMART goals as previously described or (f)sharing the homework with a supporter and asking them to help complete the homework (e.g. a case manager or family member).

Making therapy fun

We have found that there is rather too much discussion and didactic teaching in CBT for psychosis (both group and individual) for some of the young clients that we see. In group sessions, we have 'swapped' some of the didactic or group discussion tasks for exercises which involve 'doing' as well as 'talking', such as role-play and move-around quizzes. Therefore, each session offers a range of different learning opportunities (e.g. video, small group discussion, exercises). We use community outings to carry out group behavioural experiments together, which we video and then discuss during the following week's session. This provides the opportunity to complete SMART goals and test out new coping strategies with the support of other group members. Whilst continuing to use a clear cognitive behavioural framework, we have discovered that a little creativity can maintain the client's attention and enthusiasm in therapy and can make it more fun for both the clients and their therapists.

Implications and conclusions

In this chapter, we have reviewed the literature for CBT for psychosis. Most of this literature has been conducted on groups of clients who have a diagnosis of schizophrenia and have had symptoms for many years. Work to date suggests that CBT for psychotic symptoms is beneficial and that this work needs to be long term (e.g. 6 months and at least 10 sessions) to be effective (NICE, 2002). Less work has been done in the area of CBT for EI patients; in fact, NICE guidance suggests that there is insufficient evidence to draw any firm conclusions about whether short-term CBT is effective in early acute stages of illness. Similarly, there is very little (if anything) published on the treatment of co-morbid symptoms in psychosis or early intervention and whether CBT can be utilised in the same way as it can be in treating adults without psychotic difficulties. In EI, clinicians must be guided by a few preliminary studies, results described in conference presentations and also clinical information from colleagues using CBT in EI. One can only assume that clients find this work beneficial and clinicians feel that it is effective. Every day, across the UK, clinicians are using CBT to treat clients within EI who have a wide range of difficulties, for example, distressing voices, odd and worrying ideas and co-morbid problems such as anxiety and depression. We hope that the three examples given in the second part of this chapter give a flavour of the kind of work carried out on a day-to-day basis in EI. The final part of the chapter describes some of the adaptations made and differences we have encountered when implementing CBT in EI. We hope that some of the solutions we have found may be helpful for others who are engaged in implementing CBT with EI clients.

Suggested further reading

Hazel Nelson (2005). *CBT with Delusions and Hallucinations: A Practice Manual*. Cheltenham: Nelson Thorn Ltd.

Psychological Interventions In Early Psychosis. John Gleeson and Patrick McGorry (2004). Wiley, Chichester.

References

American Association of Child and Adolescent Psychiatry (2001). Practice parameter for the assessment and treatment of children and adolescents with schizophrenia. *Journal of the American Academy of Child and Adolescent Psychiatry*, 40, 4–23.

Addington, D., Addington, J. & Schissel, B. (1990). A depression rating scale for schizophrenics. *Schizophrenia Research*, 3, 247–251.

Addington, D., Addington, J. & Patten, S. (1998). Depression in people with first-episode schizophrenia. *British Journal of Psychiatry*, 172 (Suppl. 33), 90–92.

Beck, A.T. (1952). Successful outpatient psychotherapy of a chronic schizophrenia with a delusion based on borrowed guilt. *Psychiatry*, 15, 305–312.

Beck, A.T. (1988). *Beck Hopelessness Scale*. The Psychological Corporation, Harcourt Brace Jovanovich (San Antonio, Tex, New York).

Bentall, R. (1990). *Reconstructing Schizophrenia*. London: Routledge.

Bentall, R. (1994). Cognitive biases an abnormal beliefs: Towards a model of persecutory delusions. In: A.S. David & J.C. Cutting (eds), *The Neuropsychology of Schizophrenia*. London: Psychology Press.

Bentall, R. (2004). *Madness Explained Psychosis and Human Nature*. London: Penguin.

Bertolote, J. & McGorry, P. (2005). Early intervention and recovery for young people with early psychosis: Consensus statement. *British Journal of Psychiatry*, 187 (Suppl. 48), s116–s119.

Birchwood, M. & Iqbal, Z. (1998). Depression and suicidal thinking in psychosis: A cognitive approach. In: T. Wykes, N. Tarrier & S. Lewis (eds), *Outcome and Innovation in Psychological Treatment of Schizophrenia*. Chichester: John Wiley and Sons.

Birchwood, M., Iqbal, Z., Chadwick, P. & Trower, P. (2000). Cognitive approach to depression and suicidal thinking in psychosis – 1. Ontogeny of postpsychotic depression *The British Journal of Psychiatry*, 177, 516–528.

Carr, A. (1999). Child *and Adolescent Clinical Psychology. A Contextual Approach*. London: Routledge.

Curson, D.A., Patel, M., Liddle, P.E. & Barnes, T.E. (1988). Psychiatric morbidity of a long stay hospital population with chronic schizophrenia and implications for future community care. *British Medical Journal*, 297, 819–822.

Chadwick, P. Sambrooke, S., Rason, S. & Davies, E. (2000). Challenging the omnipotence of voices: Group cognitive behaviour therapy for voices. *Behaviour Research and Therapy*, 38, 993–1003.

Dhossche, D., Ferdinand, R., Van Der Ende, J. et al. (2002). Diagnostic outcome of self-reported hallucinations in a community sample of adolescents. *Psychological Medicine*, 32, 619–627.

Drury, V., Birchwood, M., Cochrane, R. & MacMillan, F. (1996). Cognitive therapy and recovery from acute psychosis: A controlled trial I. Impact on psychotic symptoms. *British Journal of Psychiatry*, 169, 593–601.

Drury, V., Birchwood, M. & Cochrane, R. (2000). Cognitive therapy and recovery from acute psychosis. A controlled trial 3: Five year follow-up. *British Journal of Psychiatry*, 177, 8–14.

Durham, R.C., Guthrie, M., Morton, R.C. et al. (2003). Tayside-Fife clinical trial of CBT for medication resistant psychotic symptoms – Results to 3 month follow-up. *British Journal of Psychiatry*, 177, 8–14.

Escher, S., Romme, M., Buiks, A. et al. (2002). Independent course of childhood hallucinations: A sequential 3-year follow-up. *British Journal of Psychiatry*, 181, 10–18.

Garety, P.A., Kuipers, L., Fowler, D., Chamberlain, F. & Dunn, G. (1994). Cognitive behaviour therapy for drug resistant psychosis. *British Journal of Medical Psychology*, 67, 259–271.

Garety, P.A., Fowler, D. & Kuipers, E. (2000). Cognitive-behavioural therapy for medication-resistant symptoms. *Schizophrenia Bulletin*, 26, 73–86.

Gaudiano, B. (2005). Cognitive behaviour therapies for psychotic disorders: Current empirical status and future directions. *Clinical Psychology: Science and Practice*, 12, 33–50.

Gledhill, A., Lobban, F. & Sellwood, W. (1998). Group CBT for people with schizophrenia: A preliminary evaluation. *Behavioural and Cognitive Psychotherapy*, 26, 63–75.

Granholm, E., McQuaid, J.R., McClure, F.S., Pedrelli, P. & Jeste, D.V. (2002). A randomised controlled pilot study of cognitive behavioural social skills training for older patients with schizophrenia. (Letter to the editor), *Schizophrenia Research*, 53, 167–169.

Haddock, G., Lewis, S., Bentall, R., Dunn, G., Drake, R. & Tarrier, N. (2006). Influence of age on outcome of psychological treatments in first-episode psychosis. *British Journal of Psychiatry*, 188, 250–254.

Heinrichs, D.W., Hanlon, T.E. & Carpenter, W.T. (1984). The Quality of Life Scale: An instrument for rating the schizophrenic deficit syndrome. *Schizophrenia Bulletin*, 10 (3), 388–398.

Hole, R.W., Rush, A.J. & Beck, A.T. (1979). A cognitive investigation of schizophrenia delusions. *Psychiatry*, 42, 312–319.

Johnstone, E.C., Owens, D.G.C., Frith, C.D. & Leavy, J. (1991). Clinical findings: Abnormalities of mental state and their correlates. *The Northwick Park follow-up study. British Journal of Psychiatry*, 159 (Suppl. 13), 21–25.

Jolley, S., Garety, P., Craig, T., Dunn, G., White, J. & Aitken, M. (2003). Cognitive therapy in early psychosis: A pilot randomized controlled trial. *Behavioural and Cognitive Psychotherapy*, 31, 473–478.

Lewis, S., Tarrier, N., Haddock, G. *et al.* (2002). Randomised controlled trial of cognitive-behavioural therapy in early schizophrenia: Acute phase outcomes. *British Journal of Psychiatry*, 181 (Suppl. 43), 91–94.

McGovern, D., Hemmings, P. & Cope, R. (1994). Long-term follow-up of young Afro-Caribbean's and white Britons with a first admission diagnosis of schizophrenia. *Social Psychiatry and Psychiatric Epidemiology*, 29, 8–19.

Morrison, A.P., Renton, J.C., Dunn, H., Williams, S. & Bentall, R.P. (2004). *Cognitive Therapy for Psychosis: A Formulation Based Approach*. New York: Brunner Routledge.

Nelson, H. (1997). *Cognitive Behavioural Therapy with Schizophrenia: A Practice Manual*. Cheltenham: Nelson Thornes Ltd.

Newton, E., Wykes, T., Landau, S., Smith, S., Monks, P. & Shergill, S. (2005). An exploratory study of young people's voices groups. *Journal of Nervous and Mental Disease*, 193 (1), 58–61.

Newton, E., Larkin, M., Melhuish, R., Wykes, T. (2007). More than just a place to talk: Young people's experiences of group psychological therapy as an early intervention for auditory hallucinations. *Psychology and Psychotherapy: Theory, Research and Practice*, 80 (1) 127–149.

National Institute for Clinical Excellence (2002). *Schizophrenia: Core interventions in the treatment and management of schizophrenia in primary and secondary care*. www.nice.org.uk. London: NICE.

National Institute for Clinical Excellence (2004a). Depression: Management of depression in primary and secondary care. Clinical Guideline 23. www.nice.org.uk. London: NICE.

National Institute for Clinical Excellence (2004b). Management of anxiety (panic disorder with or without agoraphobia and generalised anxiety disorder) in adults in primary, secondary and community care.

Clinical Guideline 22. www.nice.org.uk.London: NICE.

Pilling, S., Bebbington, P., Kuipers, E. *et al.* (2002). Psychological treatment of schizophrenia 1: Meta-analysis of family intervention and cognitive behaviour therapy. *Psychological Medicine*, 32, 763–782.

Reid, I., Barker, T. & Smith, J. (2007). Working with motivational difficulties. In: P. French, M. Read, J. Smith, M. Rayne & D. Shiers (eds) *Promoting Recovery In Early Psychosis*. Oxford: Blackwell.

Sensky, T., Turkington, D., Kingdon, D. *et al.* (2000). Randomised controlled trial of intensive CBT for patients with chronic schizophrenia, *British Medical Journal*, 317, 303–307.

Slade, P. & Bentall, R. (1988). *Sensory Deception: A Scientific Analysis of Hallucinations*. London: Croom Helm.

Tarrier, N., Yusopoff, L., Kinney, C. *et al.* (1998). Randomised controlled trial of intensive CBT for patients with chronic schizophrenia, *British Medical Journal*, 317, 303–307.

Tarrier, N., Lewis, S., Haddock, G. *et al.* (2004). CBT in first episode schizophrenia. 18-month follow-up of a randomised controlled trial. *British Journal of Psychiatry*, 184, 231–239.

Trower, P., Birchwood, M., Meaden, A., Byrne, S., Nelson, A. & Ross, K. (2004). Cognitive therapy for command hallucinations: Randomised controlled trial. *British Journal of Psychiatry*, 184, 312–320.

Wiersma, D., Niehuis, F.J., Slooff, C.J. & Giel, R. (1998). Natural course of schizophrenic disorders: A 15 year follow-up of a Dutch incidence cohort. *Schizophrenia Bulletin*, 24, 75–85.

Wing, J., Cooper, J. & Sartorius, N. (1974). *The Measurement and Classification of Psychiatric Syndromes*. Cambridge, UK: Cambridge University Press.

Wykes, T. & Van der Gaag, M. (2001). Is it time to develop a new cognitive therapy for psychosis – Cognitive Remediation Therapy (CRT). *Clinical Psychology Review*, 21 (8), 1227–1256.

Wykes, T., Parr, A. & Landau, S. (1999). Group treatment of auditory hallucinations: Exploratory study of effectiveness. *British Journal of Psychiatry*, 175, 180–185.

Zubin, J. & Spring, B. (1977). Vulnerability: A new view of schizophrenia. *Journal of Abnormal Psychology*, 86, 103–126.

Chapter 8 Cultural diversity in early psychosis

Swaran P. Singh and Satnam Singh Kunar

Introduction

In the UK, the ethnic minority population grew from 3 million in 1991 to 4.6 million in 2001; a rise of 53%. According to the population census of 2001 (Office for National Statistics), 7.9% of the UK population are from an 'ethnic minority' group with 1.8% of Indian origin, 1.3% Pakistani, 1% Black Caribbean, 0.8% Black African and a significant 1.2% of mixed ethnic heritage.

In common with population studies in the rest of Europe, ethnic minority groups are concentrated in the large urban centres, with nearly 46% in the UK living in Greater London, making up 29% of its population. Over 75% of all Black African and 61% of Black Caribbean individuals in the UK live in London and those of Indian origin are concentrated in London, Leicester and the West Midlands. Historically, the reasons for this geographical distribution have been predominantly economic. The large cities always attract a large pool of cheap, uneducated labour, which most immigrants to the UK, especially in the 1950s and 1960s, were.

Since the late 1980s, several studies have confirmed higher rates of psychotic disorders, more adverse pathways into care and greater use of the Mental Health Act (1983) amongst ethnic minorities as compared to the 'native' White population (Sharpley *et al.*, 2001; Singh & Grange, 2006; Singh *et al.*, 2007). This has caused great concern among minority groups, service providers and policy makers, with mental health services coming under intense scrutiny for any racist discrimination against minority groups which might explain these differences. In response to these concerns, the Department of Health has produced a document entitled Delivering Race Equality (DRE) which makes it incumbent upon mental health services to reduce these ethnic differences (The Department of Health, 2005). Specifically, DRE requires that 'disproportionate' admissions and detention of ethnic minority patients be reduced. However, recent evidence suggests that racism within mental health services cannot be considered the sole and sufficient explanation for ethnic differences in the rates and outcomes of psychotic disorders (Singh & Burns, 2006; McKenzie & Bhui, 2007; Singh, 2007a,b), with the Department of Health also acknowledging the fact that the reasons for ethnic differences are complex and do not always lie within the control of mental health services.

If mental health services are to be equitable and culturally appropriate to meet the needs of the contemporary multicultural and diverse Britain, service planners and commissioners must take into account the specific needs and wishes of ethnic minority groups. While the many causes for ethnic differences lie in larger societal problems such as deprivation and social adversity, there is much that services can and should do to meet the needs of this vulnerable patient group. In this chapter, we summarise the recent evidence confirming ethnic differences in early psychosis, explore the possible reasons for these differences and suggest ways in which services can ensure fairness, equity and appropriateness of care for all ethnic groups.

Incidence rates

Studies have now confirmed that some ethnic minority groups in the UK, particularly African-Caribbean and -Black African groups, are at increased risk of psychotic disorders

(Cantor-Graae, 2007). One of the earliest studies comparing the incidence of psychotic illness in ethnic groups in London, found that incidence rates in African-Caribbean and Asian populations compared to the white British population were 3.6 times higher (King *et al.*, 1994). Other British studies have found similar results (Moodley & Perkins, 1991; Wessely *et al.*, 1991; Van Os *et al.*, 1996).

The largest and most comprehensive epidemiological study conducted so far is the Aetiology and Ethnicity in Schizophrenia and Other Psychoses (AESOP) study. It was held in three UK centres (Nottingham, Bristol and south-east London) and focused on ethnicity, social risk factors and psychosis, particularly in the UK African–Caribbean population. Well-established and culturally neutral diagnostic instruments were used by researchers to identify all cases of first-episode psychosis. Clinical data was then presented to clinicians with all references to ethnicity removed, thereby ensuring that diagnostic judgements were made blind to the ethnicity of the patient. The AESOP study found that incident rate ratios for schizophrenia were high in all ethnic minority groups, being 9.1 in African–Caribbean groups, 5.8 in Black African groups and modestly increased rates in other minority groups. Rates were increased for both males and females. The study also confirmed that a similar incidence excess was apparent for manic psychosis as well but not for depressive psychosis. The study confirms that while all ethnic minority groups are at an increased risk of developing psychosis, there are perhaps additional risk factors to which some minority groups are selectively more exposed, hence explaining the differences between ethnic minority groups.

The AESOP study also found that separation from, and death of, a parent before the age of 16 were associated with a two- to threefold increased risk of psychosis. Separation from a parent was more common amongst Black Caribbean than white British patients and hence, it may have a greater impact in this population and thus contribute to the higher rates of psychosis in the Black Caribbean population (Morgan *et al.*, 2007).

Similar results have been found in studies in other European countries with large immigrant communities. A study in the Netherlands compared first admission rates for psychosis in the four largest immigrant groups in the country (from Surinam, The Dutch Antilles, Turkey and Morocco) with those of the native white Dutch population. Rates for immigrants from Surinam and The Dutch Antilles were two to five times higher than those for Turkish immigrants and for the native born population (Selten & Sijben, 1994). Other Dutch studies have yielded similar results (Selten *et al.*, 1997). These findings cannot be explained by hypotheses such as selective migration from Surinam to the Netherlands of those at risk of developing schizophrenia (Selten *et al.*, 2002) or due to prenatal exposure to influenza in Surinamese and Dutch Antillean immigrants to the Netherlands (Selten *et al.*, 1998).

Most studies looking at incidence rates have focused primarily on inpatients. A study in Malmo, Sweden, collected data on all patients with a possible psychotic disorder who made a first-in-a-lifetime contact with both inpatient and outpatient psychiatric services in the city. Results showed that first-generation immigrants had an increased risk of developing psychotic and schizophrenic illnesses compared with native Swedes. Risks for these disorders were not significantly increased in second-generation immigrants. The highest risks of developing a psychotic disorder were found in first-generation immigrants with 'black' (vs. 'neither black nor white' or 'white') skin colour and birthplace in a developing (vs. developed) nation (Cantor-Graae *et al.*, 2005).

British studies have also confirmed that various forms of early childhood and adult adversity as well as characteristics such as ethnic density may be particularly important in contributing to increased risk of psychosis in minority groups (Morgan & Fearon, 2007). Other risk factors for psychosis such as social exclusion, urban upbringing and discrimination are also more likely to occur in ethnic minority groups. Recently, attention has focused on the interaction between ethnic density and the incidence of psychosis. A 7-year prospective study in

The Hague, Netherlands found that incidence of psychosis was elevated most significantly among immigrants living in neighbourhoods where their own ethnic group comprised a small proportion of the population (Veling *et al.*, 2008). Higher ethnic density may mitigate against social adversity, provide greater social support or increase access to normalising explanations for anomalous experiences in individuals at high risk of developing psychosis, thereby preventing a transition into a psychotic disorder.

The higher incidence rates of early psychosis in ethnic minority groups is therefore an epidemiological fact, the causes for which are likely to be located in the adverse social experiences of ethnic minorities. Reducing these rates requires concerted action by a multitude of agencies that can tackle the sources of these adversities.

Pathways to care

An often reported finding is the adverse pathways into care experienced by ethnic minority groups in the UK. This has led to calls for a reduction in admission rates for ethnic minorities, especially admissions under the Mental Health Act (1983). Such ethnic differences are apparent even in first-episode cases where individuals have no previous experience of mental health care. There is also evidence that longitudinally, engagement between ethnic minority patients and mental health services deteriorates over time (Singh *et al.*, 2007).

Pathways to care are defined as 'the sequence of contacts with individuals and organisations prompted by the distressed persons' efforts, and those of his or her significant others, to seek help as well as the help that is supplied in response of these efforts' (Rogler & Cortes, 1993). Pathways to mental health are important and the different pathways taken in different societies reflect the cultural appropriateness of services, attitudes towards them and previous experience of them (Goldberg, 1999). Early intervention teams in psychiatry are based on the premise that the duration of untreated psychosis ought to be minimal as there is a 'critical period' in the early years of the development of psychosis that can improve the long-term prognosis of the illness if it is adequately treated during this period (Birchwood *et al.*, 1998). Early intervention services also aim to engage individuals both in voluntarily and in 'low stigma' settings to ensure that individuals have positive and non-coercive experiences of mental health care early in their contact with services.

Goldberg and Huxley's model (Goldberg & Huxley, 1980) of individuals passing through filters during their progress to secondary services does not always apply, as some people from ethnic minority groups will proceed through alternate routes to the National Health Service. They may have more faith in local community organisations, for example, places of worship, that may be more familiar to them and who they feel may be able to understand their experiences. This is especially so for those people who have no carers in their host country. Bhugra *et al.* (1997) found that only 1 in 36 African–Caribbean help-seeking individuals with schizophrenia had presented through their general practitioner (GP). Studies in London have also found lower rates of referral from GPs and higher numbers of referrals from the criminal justice system (Morgan *et al.*, 2005a,b). African–Caribbean families were more likely to access help for an ill relative through the police rather than medical services. A possible explanation for this may be that stigma of mental illness in African–Caribbean societies may mean that help is not sought until a crisis develops when behavioural disturbances attributable to illness are misconstrued as requiring legal rather than medical services (Singh & Burns, 2006). However, Indians and Pakistanis have lower rates of compulsory admission even though stigma is equally problematic in South Asia. The importance of the extended family unit in South Asians (even those of the second and third generations) may be a possible explanation for this and indeed, they are more likely to be brought to medical services by family members (Koffman *et al.*, 1997). There is evidence that pathways to specialist care vary with ethnic groups (Bhui *et al.*, 2003). Compared with white and south Asians who visited their GP, black patients were less likely to be referred to secondary services (Thomas *et al.*, 1993; Cole *et al.*, 1995). Compared with white individuals, black (Commander *et al.*, 1997) and south Asian individuals (Bhugra *et al.*, 1999; Burnett *et al.*,

1999) are more likely to be admitted to hospital following a domiciliary visit. The police were more likely to be involved in admissions or readmissions of black people (Thomas *et al.*, 1993; Commander *et al.*, 1999).

Engagement with services and help-seeking are dynamic, social and interpersonal processes, influenced by economic and educational status and cultural variations in how symptoms of mental illnesses are understood and the meaning attributed to these. Other factors include social isolation, not being registered with a GP and language barriers that contribute to poor engagement with services and more adverse pathways into care. A complex interplay between clinical presentation, social circumstances, risk management, local service availability and legal requirements for providing care interact in a complex manner to determine whether an individual is detained voluntarily or not. This complexity has not been adequately studied so far in the polarised debate which has pitched services against service users by attributing ethnic differences in detention rates on racism within services. In recognition of these gaps in our knowledge, the National Institute of Health Research has recently awarded a large programme grant to the Birmingham and Solihull Mental Health NHS Trust to explore this very issue by studying societal factors that determine and influence help-seeking in patients with early psychosis.

Reasons for ethnic differences in early psychosis

Secondary mental health services have been criticised by patients and their carers, advocate services and some within the service, for a number of reasons. They have been accused of being 'eurocentric'; western psychiatrists are likely to misinterpret behaviour from those of other cultures as being evidence of mental illness and use diagnostic labels to place all individuals in categories which may not be applicable to non-Europeans. A common assumption has been that black individuals experience longer delays in receiving appropriate treatment during the critical first episode but this theory has been challenged (Morgan *et al.*, 2006). The single

most serious accusation has been of institutional racism within psychiatry in the UK and that this is the reason why ethnic minorities, especially African–Caribbeans, have higher rates of psychotic illnesses and detention rates. Such simplistic notions are unhelpful especially if these serve only to alienate those who most need help. It is also deeply damaging to a profession built on trust (Singh & Burns, 2006). More research is needed to help identify factors that influence detention rates such as engagement, access, appropriateness of services and the application of the Mental Health Act, which should not be seen merely as a punitive measure but as a way of helping those most in need of services. It also provides safeguards for patients and allows them to challenge their detention. There is a risk that patient care may be compromised if staff are labelled as racist, as it will affect the relationship between an individual patient, their family, the local community and mental health services. Families may be seen as 'colluding' with staff when they contact psychiatric services, or families may turn away altogether from a system that is perceived as alien, racist and likely to inflict harm.

Provision of culturally appropriate services

Services must be able to provide a service that is sensitive, culturally appropriate and able to fulfil the needs of all sections of a diverse, multicultural society. This involves concerted action and a whole systems approach by all agencies including community groups, the voluntary and independent sectors, primary care and secondary mental health services.

Bhui and Bhugra (2002) have suggested a model of engagement with African–Caribbean patients. This would involve having an improved skills mix of the primary care team that would help to facilitate better levels of engagement with ethnic minority groups. Services ought to have an adequate provision of interpreters and staff ought to be more culturally sensitive to the local community. A recent article has found that ethnic minority groups in the USA are less likely to receive a range of psychosocial treatments, and this was especially so for minority groups with a severe personality disorder (Bender *et al.*, 2007).

This does bring to light the complex issue of service availability and delivery of specialised treatments such as psychotherapy. Bhui and Morgan give examples of issues that therapists should be aware of when treating those from a different ethnic background (Bhui & Morgan, 2007).

It is important for primary care, Child and Adolescent Mental Health Services and Early Intervention in psychosis teams to be involved in educational campaigns and offer outreach services at schools, colleges, youth or community clubs and universities. Many first contacts with mental health services will occur in these settings, and it is vital that students, youth workers and teachers are aware of how they can access services and the fact that those already under the care of services are able to access support at all times, both for themselves and their families. Knowledge of mental illness and help-seeking options can help to reduce stigma. Young people and their carers will want to know the possible implications of their illness to help with their recovery, future life and career aspirations.

Case studies

A 15–year-old boy from Togo, who arrived in England a few months ago with his mother, has been increasingly absent from school. He had, whilst at school, become isolative and quiet over the previous few weeks and teachers initially thought this was because of social isolation as he was new and his English was poor. Teachers had been very concerned and contacted his mother, who stated that he was not well but that he did not need to see a doctor. After a further few days, a senior staff member visited the home. The boy's mother would not let him into the house but he could hear the boy shouting from upstairs. Clearly concerned about the child's safety and fearing that he was possibly at risk, the staff member called the police who arrived promptly.

Implementations into practice

Is it possible the child was suffering with a mental illness?

What other methods could the staff at school have used to engage with the family?

It later transpired that the boy was mentally unwell and had been so for over a year.

His mother had not sought the help of services because she was not sure who to contact and was very socially isolated herself. She was also frightened as the boy's father had behaved in a similar way several years earlier and had walked out on the family.

What impact could the 'pathway to care' taken in this case have on future engagement with the family, and how could this be improved?

Other community engagement projects could include community and religious centres. The latter has been used, for example, to highlight the problems of poor diet, diabetes and hypertension in Sikh temples; mental health issues could also be discussed. It would certainly require the participation of senior members of staff, preferably from within those communities. This would also be a useful strategy to combat stigma. It is vital that people are made aware that services are available for mental health problems; this may not have been the case in their country of origin, and so may hold a degree of trepidation. The Department of Health has recently introduced Community Development Workers for black and minority ethnic communities, into the mental health workforce. Their role is essentially to enable individuals from minority groups to be better informed and more empowered on issues facing them so that mental health services can be commissioned more appropriately. At all levels, service users should be involved at a strategic level to put forward ideas about what they feel will benefit them and their communities.

General practice is the access point or 'front door' of the health service but there have been suggestions that it sometimes fails individuals from ethnic groups experiencing mental health issues. For example, British Asians are more likely to be given a physical diagnosis following a GP consultation (Wilson & McCarthey, 1994) and surprisingly, Asian GPs are reported to be poor detectors of psychiatric morbidity among Asian patients (Odell *et al.*, 1997). A possible reason for this may be that GPs' recognition of psychological problems can be masked by physical and social circumstances of the patient. This highlights the importance of training for GPs and related professionals, such as primary care nurses (Tait *et al.*, 2005) and health visitors, and the importance of close ties between primary care and community mental health teams to reduce the need for admission to hospital if possible. Prompt recognition and treatment can reduce the duration of untreated psychosis and improve outcomes in the longer term for the individual and their families (Brunet *et al.*, 2007).

The reasons for ethnic differences in the incidence and pathways in early psychosis are complex and multifaceted. Health services can and should attempt to mitigate the adverse effects of these differences, even if many such differences are due to more complicated societal factors, outside the remit of mental health services. Education and liaison with GPs, housing associations, social services, religious and other community groups and voluntary agencies must form the backbone of a shared care approach that is able to provide for the most vulnerable individuals in society.

References

Bender, D.S., Skodol, A.E., Dyck, I.R. *et al.* (2007). Ethnicity and mental health treatment utilization by patients with personality disorders. *Journal of Consulting and Clinical Psychology*, 75(6), 992–999.

Bhugra, D., Leff, J., Mallett, R. *et al.* (1997). Inception rates and one-year outcome of schizophrenia in west London. *Psychological Medicine*, 27, 791–798.

Bhugra, D., Corridan, B., Rudge, S. *et al.* (1999). Early manifestations, personality traits and pathways into care for Asian and white first-onset cases of schizophrenia. *Social Psychiatry and Psychiatric Epidemiology*, 34, 595–599.

Bhui, K. & Bhugra, D. (2002). Mental illness in Black and Asian ethnic minorities: pathways to care and outcomes. *Advances in Psychiatric Treatment*, 8, 26–33.

Bhui, K. & Morgan, M. (2007). Effective psychotherapy in a racially and culturally diverse society. *Advances in Psychiatric Treatment*, 13, 187–193.

Bhui, K., Stansfield, S., Hull, S., Priebe, S. & Mole, F. (2003). Ethnic variations in pathways to and use of specialist mental health services in the UK: Systematic review. *British Journal of Psychiatry*, 182, 105–116.

Birchwood, M., Todd, P. & Jackson, C. (1998). Early intervention in psychosis. The critical period hypothesis. *British Journal of Psychiatry*, 172 (Suppl. 33), 53–59.

Brunet, K., Birchwood, M., Lester, H. & Thornhill, K. (2007). Delays in mental health services and duration of untreated psychosis. *Psychiatric Bulletin*, 31, 408–410.

Burnett, R., Mallett, R., Bhugra, D. *et al.* (1999). The first contact of patients with schizophrenia with psychiatric services: Social factors and pathways to care in a multi-ethnic population. *Psychological Medicine*, 29, 475–483.

Cantor-Graae, E. (2007). Ethnic minority groups, particularly African-Caribbean and Black African groups are at increased risk of psychosis in the UK. *Evidence Based Mental Health*, 10(3), 95.

Cantor-Graae, E., Zolkowska, K. & McNeil, T.F. (2005). Increased risk of psychotic disorders among immigrants in Malmo: A 3 year first contact study. *Psychological Medicine*, 35(8), 1155–1163.

Cole, E., Leavey, G., King, M. *et al.* (1995). Pathways to care for patents with a first episode of psychosis: A comparison of ethnic groups. *British Journal of Psychiatry*, 167, 770–776.

Commander, M.J., Odell, S., Sashidharan, S.P. *et al.* (1997). A comparison of the socio-demographic and clinical characteristics of private household and communal establishment residents in a multi-ethnic inner-city area. *Social psychiatry and Psychiatric Epidemiology*, 32, 421–427.

Commander, M.J., Cochrane, R., Sashidharan, S.P. *et al.* (1999). Mental health care for Asian, black and white patients with non-affective psychoses: Pathways to the psychiatric hospital, in-patient and after-care. *Social Psychiatry and Psychiatric Epidemiology*, 34, 84–491.

Delivering race equality in mental health care (DRE). (Jan 2005). The Department of Health, Richmond House, 79 Whitehall. London. SW1A 2NS.

DH (1983). *The Mental Health Act*. London HMSO: Department of Health.

Goldberg, D. (1999). Cultural aspects of mental disorder in primary care. In: D. Bhugra & V. Bahl (eds), *Ethnicity: An Agenda for Mental Health*, pp. 23–28. London: Gaskell.

Goldberg, D. & Huxley, P. (1980). *Mental illness in the community: The pathways to psychiatric care*. New York: Tavistock.

King, M., Coker, E., Leavey, G. & Hoare, A. (1994). Incidence of psychotic illness in London: Comparison of ethnic groups. *British Medical Journal*, 309(6962), 1115–1119.

Koffman, J., Fulop, N.J., Pashley, D. & Coleman, K. (1997). Ethnicity and use of acute psychiatric beds: One-day survey in north and south Thames regions. *British Journal of Psychiatry*, 171, 238–241.

McKenzie, K. & Bhui, K. (2007). Better mental healthcare for minority ethnic groups – moving away from the blame game and putting patients first. Commentary on… Institutional racism in psychiatry. *Psychiatric Bulletin*, 31, 368–369.

Moodley, P. & Perkins, R.E. (1991). Routes to psychiatric inpatient care in an inner London borough. *Social Psychiatry and Psychiatric Epidemiology*, 26(1), 47–51.

Morgan C. & Fearon P. (2007). Social experience and psychosis insights from studies of migrant and ethnic minority groups. *Epidemiologica e Psichiatria Sociale*, 16(2), 118–123.

Morgan, C., Mallett, R., Hutchinson, G., Bagalkote, H., Morgan, K., Fearon, P. *et al.* (2005a). Pathways to care and ethnicity. 1: Sample characteristics and compulsory admission. Report from the AESOP study. *British Journal of Psychiatry*, 186, 281–289.

Morgan, C., Mallett, R., Hutchinson, G., Bagalkote, H., Morgan, K., Fearon, P. *et al.* (2005b). Pathways to care and ethnicity. 2: Source of referral and help-seeking. Report from the AESOP study. *British Journal of Psychiatry*, 186, 290–296.

Morgan, C., Fearon, P., Hutchinson, G. *et al.* (2006). Duration of untreated psychosis and ethnicity in the AESOP first-onset psychosis study. *Psychological Medicine*, 36(2), 239–247.

Morgan, C., Kirkbride, J., Leff, J. *et al.* (2007). Parental separation, loss and psychosis in different ethnic groups: A case control study. *Psychological Medicine*, 37(4), 495–503.

Odell, S.M., Surtees, P.G., Wainwright, N.W., Commander, M. & Sashidharan, S.P. (1997). Determinants of general practitioner recognition of psychological problems in a multi-ethnic inner-city health district. *British Journal of Psychiatry*, 171, 537–541.

Office for National Statistics, Cardiff Road, Newport. NP10 8XG.

Rogler, L.H. & Cortes, D.E. (1993). Help-seeking pathways: A unifying concept in mental health care. *American Journal of Psychiatry*, 150, 554–561.

Selten, J.P. & Sijben, A.E. (1994). Alarming admission rates for schizophrenia in migrants from Surinam, the Netherlands Antilles and Morocco. *Nederlands Tijdschrift voor Geneeskunde*, 138(7), 345–350.

Selten, J.P., Slaets, J.P. & Kahn, R.S. (1997). Schizophrenia in Surinamese and Dutch Antillean immigrants to the Netherlands: Evidence of an increased incidence. *Psychological Medicine*, 27(4), 807–811.

Selten, J.P., Slaets, J. & Kahn, R.S. (1998). Prenatal exposure to influenza and schizophrenia in Surinamese and Dutch Antillean immigrants to the Netherlands. *Schizophrenia Research*, 30(1), 101–103.

Selten, J.P., Cantor-Graae, E., Slaets, J. & Kahn, R.S. (2002). Odegaard's selection hypothesis revisited: Schizophrenia in Surinamese immigrants to the Netherlands. *American Journal of Psychiatry*, 159(4), 669–671.

Sharpley, M.S., Hutchinson, G., Murray R.M. & McKenzie, K. (2001). Understanding the excess of psychosis among the African-Caribbean population in England: Review of current hypotheses. *British Journal of Psychiatry*, 178, s60–s68.

Singh, S.P. (2007a). Institutional racism in psychiatry: Lessons from inquiries. *Psychiatric Bulletin*, 363–365.

Singh, S.P. (2007b). Institutional racism in psychiatry: Author's response. *Psychiatric Bulletin*, 370.

Singh, S.P. & Burns, T. (2006). Analysis and comment. Race and mental health: There is more to race than racism. *British Medical Journal*, 333, 648–651.

Singh, S.P. & Grange, T. (2006). Measuring pathways to care in first episode psychosis: A systematic review. *Schizophrenia Research*, 81(1), 75–82.

Singh, S.P., Greenwood, N., White, S. & Churchill, R. (2007). Ethnicity and the Mental Health Act 1983. *British Journal of Psychiatry*, 191, 99–105.

Tait, L., Lester, H., Birchwood, M. *et al.* (2005). Design of the Birmingham early detection in untreated psychosis trial (REDIRECT): Cluster randomized controlled trial of general practitioner education in detection of first episode psychosis. *BioMed Central Health Services Research*, 5, 19.

Thomas, C.S., Stone, K., Osborn, M. *et al.* (1993). Psychiatric morbidity and compulsory admission among UK-born Europeans, Afro-Caribbeans and Asians in central Manchester. *British Journal of Psychiatry*, 163, 91–99.

Van Os, J., Castle, D.J., Takei, N., Der, G. & Murray, R.M. (1996). Psychotic illness in ethnic minorities: Clarification from the 1991 census. *Psychological Medicine*, 26, 203–208.

Veling, W., Susser, E., Van Os, J., Mackenbach, J.P., Selten, J.P. & Hoek, H.W. (2008). Ethnic density of neighbourhoods and incidence of psychotic disorders among immigrants. *American Journal of Psychiatry*, 165(1), 66–73.

Wessely, S., Castle, D., Der, G. & Murray, R. (1991). Schizophrenia and Afro-Caribbeans. A case control study. *British Journal of Psychiatry*, 159, 795–801.

Wilson, M. & McCarthey, B. (1994). General Practitioner consultation as a factor in the low rate of mental health service use by Asians. *Psychological Medicine*, 24(1), 113–119.

Chapter 9 Antipsychotic medications and their use in first-episode psychosis

Alan Farmer

Introduction

In this chapter, I will mainly discuss the use of antipsychotic medication. Since the 1950s, these drugs have been an important part of the treatment for people with psychosis. The Early Psychosis Declaration, now an international consensus statement (WHO & IEPA, 2005), recognises the role of medication as part of a holistic, recovery-based model that provides biological, social and psychological support. Medication can provide symptomatic relief for mental and physical arousal, agitation and overactivity. It encourages a reduction in core symptoms of psychosis such as delusions and hallucinations although this action may be delayed. It may be useful to consider longer-term use as antipsychotic medication can reduce the risk of further episodes of psychosis.

We know that the prescribing of medication works best if there is a trusting, honest and open relationship between the prescriber and the patient. This is especially relevant when helping people experiencing first episode of psychosis (FEP). Medication is often regarded, especially by a young person, as incompatible with everyday life and their journey to reintegration and recovery. It is frequently seen as disempowering and sometimes dangerous, especially if the person's first experience had been rapid tranquilisation and distressing side effects when admitted in crisis to a psychiatric admission ward.

Individuals with FEP respond differently to medication than those with more established mental health problems with both increased rates of response and increased rates of side effects. An exhaustive account of the current evidence would be a book in itself and attract a more select readership! Remington (2005) has produced an excellent detailed summary. I will include scientific data where I feel this will inform good practice and I will provide references for further reading.

I hope this chapter will be a useful introduction for early intervention doctors and non-medical prescribers (NMPs). It should also be a useful resource for people with FEP, their families and carers and non-prescribing members of the multidisciplinary team. The aim is to enable us to make collaborative decisions on the basis of both the best evidence and the individual's circumstances.

A brief summary of the evidence

Whether I am prescribing or receiving medication, I always ask the following questions (Table 9.1):

Table 9.1 Questions to ask about medication

Questions to ask about medication
Why is medication being prescribed? Are there any alternatives?
What medication is being prescribed? Are there any differences between drugs?
What dose is being prescribed? I need it to work but want to avoid side effects.
What if it doesn't help?
Are any tests needed before the drug is started? What about monitoring?
What if a few doses are missed?
When can I stop and what might happen? Will I have to take it again?

Let us take our questions individually, briefly examine the current evidence and consider how we can implement these ideas in our day-to-day practice.

Why is medication being prescribed? Are there any alternatives?

'Early, effective interventions improve outcomes' is part of the Early Intervention mantra. Wyatt *et al.*'s (1998) review compared the impact of taking or not taking antipsychotic medication at an early stage of psychosis, suggesting a long-term benefit of early drug treatment. The broader topic of reducing the duration of untreated psychosis (DUP) is covered in detail in Chapter 2 of this book. We know that untreated psychosis can have a profound effect on social and psychological development. Whether untreated psychosis is 'biologically toxic' to brain function and development is controversial and needs further evaluation. There is ongoing discussion about the possible neuroprotective role of medication.

Implementation into practice

Antipsychotic medication can provide symptomatic relief for mental and physical arousal, agitation and overactivity. Side effects (detailed below) can emerge at higher doses and when the dose is rapidly increased. The initial experience of medication is very influential on longer-term attitudes and compliance and needs to be managed carefully. A short course of a tranquilising benzodiazepine (e.g. lorazepam or diazepam) can be a very useful adjunct in the initial, more florid presentation and reduce the need for a rapid titration to excessive doses of antipsychotic medication. Support, reassurance, relaxation techniques, distraction and a safe environment are also important in these initial stages.

Antipsychotic medication also encourages a reduction in the *positive symptoms* of psychosis such as delusions, hallucinations, thought disorder and bizarre behaviour. This effect is slower than the symptomatic relief and the effect will build over the first 3–6 weeks. Lieberman *et al.* (1993) found that 83% of people with FEP achieved remission within 1 year with sustained treatment. This is a great improvement when they compared studies of all episodes (around 30% of people with established psychosis are unresponsive to medication) and consistent with other FEP studies. I suggest that we prepare people with FEP for wellness rather than continuing disability. This is a key feature of the Early Psychosis Declaration (WHO & IEPA, 2005), which says that we should 'generate optimism and expectations of positive outcomes and recovery'. Lieberman *et al.* (1993) found that mean and median times to remission were 35.7 weeks and 11 weeks respectively. This delay in response was longer than expected and may be due to lengthy DUP prior to contact with services (around 52 weeks in many studies), the severity of illness at first contact and their strict criteria for remission. Being female, less ill at presentation, experiencing less extrapyramidal side effects (described below) and having no structural changes on brain scan predicted better results.

Whilst there is rarely an alternative to medication, it must always be embedded in a holistic package of care that involves psychological and social interventions and support for social systems. These are discussed in separate chapters. The absence of symptoms (remission) does not automatically lead to a sense of well-being, belonging and a meaningful life (recovery). Remission is the first station on the active journey to recovery.

What medication is being prescribed? Are there any differences between drugs?

Antipsychotic medication can be divided into older *typical* and newer *atypical* drugs. Studies that have shown clinical superiority of these newer drugs have most often studied people with established mental health problems rather than FEP. Studies that have focused on the FEP population have failed to show difference in effectiveness (summarised in Remington, 2005). So why do we prefer these newer drugs?

Older typical antipsychotic drugs (e.g. haloperidol, stelazine and chlorpromazine) have a characteristic, typical, side-effect profile. They provoke catalepsy (a condition characterised by muscular rigidity, fixed posture and decreased sensitivity to pain) in animal studies and in clinical use can be excessively sedating. They frequently cause extrapyramidal side effects; these include stiffness, tremor and difficulty in initiating movement. This is sometimes called drug-induced Parkinsonism due to the similarity to the neurological disorder. They can also cause acute dystonia, a sudden onset of painful muscle spasms. People with FEP are more likely to experience these side effects compared to people with more established mental health problems. Aguilar (1994) found high rates of dystonia (60%) when people with FEP were treated with haloperidol. The frequency was significantly related to younger age, severity of illness and the presence of negative symptoms (described below) at the start of treatment. People have a low tolerance of these side effects and find them distressing. They can affect attitudes towards medication and future compliance.

The typical drugs are also associated with a higher rate of tardive dyskinesia. This is the development of involuntary movements of the lips, jaw, tongue and facial muscles. In more serious cases, it can affect the arms and legs and it can be irreversible. Remington (2005) summarises the available data reporting that tardive dyskinesia is reduced by a factor of 5 to less than 1% per year if we prescribe atypical drugs. Even low doses of typical drugs are now thought to be associated with an increased risk of tardive dyskinesia in FEP.

The atypical antipsychotic drugs are not without their side effects. Extrapyramidal side effects can emerge at higher doses of some drugs. Others are associated with sedation, weight gain, raised prolactin, anticholinergic and hypotensive effects. Guides to relative adverse effects are found in most publications. Table 9.2 is derived from the Maudsley Prescribing Guidelines (Taylor *et al.*, 2007). The typical drugs, haloperidol and chlorpromazine, are included for comparison.

This is only a rough guide to relative incidence/severity and other side effects can occur (e.g. agranulocytosis with clozapine and photosensitivity with chlorpromazine – sunscreen is vital in sunny conditions). Prescribers should use more detailed information and keep up to date with new information. Paliperidone has been introduced since the publication of the guidelines. Its side-effect profile is similar to risperidone but initial reports suggest better tolerability.

Table 9.2 Antipsychotic comparison

	Sedation	Weight gain	Extrapyramidal	Anticholinergic	Hypotension	Prolactin elevation
Amisulpride	–	+	+	–	–	+++
Aripiprazole	–	+/–	+/–	–	–	–
Clozapine	+++	+++	–	+++	+++	–
Olanzapine	++	+++	+/–	+	+	+
Quetiapine	++	++	–	+	++	–
Risperidone	+	++	+	+	++	+++
Ziprazadone	+	+/–	+/–	–	+	+/–
Zotepine	+++	++	+	+	++	+++
Chlorpromazine	+++	++	++	++	+++	+++
Haloperidol	+	+	+++	+	+	+++

Key: +++ High incidence/severity
++ Moderate
+ Low – Very low

Implementation into practice

There are wide differences in the side-effect profiles of the atypical drugs. With this information, we can discuss with the person with FEP the relative risks and merits of the individual drugs and make informed choices about alternatives should side effects emerge.

Younger people are more susceptible to adverse effects and weight gain can be a problem. This can be associated with metabolic changes (e.g. glucose tolerance and lipid metabolism), and the implications for physical monitoring are discussed below.

Raised levels of prolactin can cause sexual dysfunction leading to amenorrhoea, impotence and at very high levels can cause lactation in both men and women. A persistently raised prolactin can also affect bone density and may increase the risk of osteoporosis and fractures in later life.

Quetiapine should be introduced slowly owing to its effect on the heart and has been associated with hypotension and potentially dangerous arrhythmias. It should be used with caution in people who already have a prolonged QT interval (the part of the ECG that represents recovery of contracted heart muscle in preparation for the next beat) or together with other drugs known to prolong the QT interval.

Many of the drugs discussed here can cause sedation. This can be therapeutic in the initial phase of treatment but can cause problems if the effect persists. Aripiprazole is not sedating and is not currently associated with metabolic, cardiac or hormonal effects. It can cause initial agitation, nausea and insomnia though the effectiveness of short-term symptomatic treatments for these problems is making aripiprazole a popular first-line choice for people with FEP.

Psychosis, especially schizophrenia, can be associated with *negative symptoms*, which include emotional flatness, reduction in speech and activity, poor motivation and loss of self-care skills. These often have a more profound effect on functioning and recovery than persistent positive symptoms. There is no convincing evidence that the atypical drugs are more effective at reducing negative symptoms due to the psychosis (primary negative symptoms). The beneficial effect that is often seen is probably

due to an individual's better clinical response to a new drug and a reduction in typical side effects (secondary negative symptoms). Thomas and Lewis (1998) give a good summary of this issue (not specific to FEP) but do conclude that 'whether the negative symptoms which respond are primary or secondary is beside the point if the patient improves'. Antidepressants may be effective in some cases though psychological and social interventions may prove more useful. I will discuss clozapine and depot antipsychotic medication at a later stage.

Implementation into practice

The choice of medication for people with FEP should be a collaborative process. People will need to take medication for a considerable length of time and a proportion will need long-term treatment.

The risk of tardive dyskinesia should guide us away from the older, typical drugs. The choice of atypical medication should be informed by their relative risk for other side effects.

The Early Psychosis Declaration (WHO & IEPA, 2005) suggests that low doses of atypical medication are offered as drug treatment of first choice. However, they accept that on a global scale there may be services with low levels of resources where low doses of typical drugs may need to be used.

Negative symptoms are difficult to treat. The most effective method is prevention; use medication that gives the maximum clinical response whilst minimising unwanted drug effects. Psychological and social approaches may provide alternatives to an acceptance of a sick-role, withdrawal and hopelessness.

What dose is being prescribed? I need it to work but want to avoid side effects

International Clinical Practice Guidelines for Early Psychosis, produced by the International Early Psychosis Writing Group (2005), suggest a 'start low, go slow' strategy for introducing atypical antipsychotic medication, giving people the best chance to respond to the lowest dose possible. A recent supplement of The Journal of Clinical Psychiatry (Weiden *et al.*, 2007) collected opinions from a range of experts. They included recommendations for initial dose and titration schedules for individuals with FEP. Table 9.3 is a summary of their findings.

Half to two-thirds of people experiencing FEP will show a response within 3 weeks at the initial dose. If the response has been inadequate, then the dose should be gradually increased at widely spaced intervals. In comparison with the above recommendations, The International Early Psychosis Writing Group (2005) suggests increasing medication at 2–3 weekly intervals. The decision ultimately depends on clinical response and risk.

From my experience with aripiprazole, I would suggest waiting 2 weeks before considering an increase and might reduce to a lower initial dose (5 mg) if side effects are poorly tolerated and/or unresponsive to symptomatic treatment. Any decision to increase the dose of any drug should be discussed with the individual with FEP, outlining the relative risks and benefits. Rapid titration is associated with high rates of side effects rather than a faster response and should be avoided with any antipsychotic drug. Benzodiazepines are useful additions when initial sedation is required.

What if my medication doesn't help?

The International Early Psychosis Writing Group (2005) and Maudsley Prescribing Guidelines (Taylor *et al.*, 2007) suggest that a change of medication should be considered if sedation or extrapyramidal side effects emerge or there is an inadequate response after 6–8 weeks. There has been concern that this represents a long period

of time for a young person with FEP to be on an ineffective drug. Leucht *et al.* (2007) combined the results of seven studies (all involving amisulpride vs. another antipsychotic though not specific to FEP) and found that people experiencing no improvement during the first 2 weeks of treatment were unlikely to respond by the end of 4 weeks. They suggest that these people may benefit from an earlier change of medication but accept that further evaluation is necessary.

Implementation into practice

Clinical practice would suggest that we already rarely persist with medication if there has been no initial response (around 2 weeks). A trial of 6–8 weeks is appropriate if there has been a partial response and we wish to see if there is further improvement, often with and increase in dose.

Returning to established guidelines, the National Institute for Clinical Excellence (2002) says:

'In individuals with evidence of treatment-resistant schizophrenia, clozapine should be introduced at the earliest opportunity. Treatment resistance is suggested by a lack of satisfactory clinical improvement, despite the sequential use of the recommended doses for 6–8 weeks of at least two antipsychotics, at least one of which should be an atypical'.

Clozapine is an atypical antipsychotic medication that is licensed for use in treatment-resistant schizophrenia. Whilst individuals may respond to the third or fourth drug, the likelihood reduces with each drug tried; down to less than 10% by the third drug. Clozapine is the only drug with evidence of effectiveness in treatment-resistant

Table 9.3 Recommendations for initial dosing strategies

	Usual starting dose (mg/day)	Interval between dose increases	Usual dose increment (mg)	Target dose range (mg/day)
Aripiprazole	10	1 week	5–10	10–25
Olanzapine	10	1 week	5	10–22.5
Quetiapine	150	3 days	150	300–800
Risperidone	1.5	1 week	1.5	2–6
Ziprazadone	60	4 days	40–60	100–200

Note: Quetiapine is licensed up to a maximum dose of 750 mg/day for schizophrenia in the UK.

schizophrenia (around 40%) and it should be considered as soon as treatment resistance is confirmed (Thomas & Lewis, 1998). Clozapine has a poor side-effect profile (see Table 9.2) and is also associated with agranulocytosis in around 0.8% of people. In this condition, there is a decrease in the white cells in the blood and a reduction in the body's ability to fight infection. In advanced cases, this can be fatal but the early stages are fully reversible. It is for this reason that regular blood tests are needed. Agranulocytosis is more common in children, adolescents (unfortunately treatment resistance is common in very early onset psychosis) and the elderly compared to young adults or middle-aged people. The Maudsley Prescribing Guidelines (Taylor *et al.*, 2007) has detailed information on starting clozapine as well as strategies for dealing with side effects and additional strategies if there is still a poor response.

Implementation into practice

The emergence of treatment resistance requires prompt and intensive investigation and intervention. We need to check that there are no complicating factors that may delay improvement. These include poor compliance, social stress, physical illness and substance misuse.

Clozapine is a decision that needs to be taken jointly with the individual with FEP and its benefits in treatment resistance weighed against possible side effects.

Cognitive behavioural therapy should also be considered for persistent symptoms. The wider issues of delayed recovery are covered in Chapter 21 of this book.

Are any tests needed before the drug is started? What about monitoring?

Rates of obesity, diabetes, high cholesterol (and other blood fats) and hypertension are increasing in Western and Westernised societies. These problems tend to occur together and have been called the *Metabolic Syndrome*. It is associated with increased risk of various disorders, especially heart attacks and strokes.

FEP can be (indirectly) associated with increased risk of health problems because:

1. Schizophrenia, a severe form of psychosis, is associated with increased risk of diabetes. Abnormal blood glucose results have been described at an early stage of the illness and may even be associated with a prodromal phase.
2. People with longer-term mental health problems have poor health compared to the general population.
3. Many antipsychotic drugs can be associated with weight gain and metabolic changes.

When working with someone with FEP, there is a real opportunity to address potential health risks. We invariably promote healthy lifestyle with advice about personal safety, healthy diet, regular exercise, promoting safe sex and help with reducing use of tobacco, alcohol and street drugs. We advise annual physical reviews in primary care. Barnett *et al.* (2007) is the most recent paper to address the issue of metabolic and cardiovascular risk in psychosis. They have adapted earlier recommendations from the American Diabetes Association and suggest a baseline measure of possible risk factors and monitoring during treatment with any antipsychotic drug (Table 9.4).

More frequent assessments may be indicated by pre-existing medical problems, family history and the seriousness of drug-induced metabolic effects. The body mass index (BMI) is calculated from weight and height. The normal value is 18.5–25, with a value above 30 associated with obesity. Waist measurements are quick and easy to do, with upper healthy limits of 94 cm for men and 80 cm for females. Healthy values are slightly reduced for South Asian populations as they experience higher rates of cardiovascular problems.

Barnett *et al.* (2007) also include a very useful flow chart for the assessment and management of metabolic risk factors and the Maudsley Prescribing Guidelines (Taylor *et al.*, 2007) includes more details of monitoring and interventions (including current evidence for weight-reducing drugs).

Prolactin should also be measured at baseline, at 6 months and then yearly unless prolactin-sparing drugs are used (see Table 9.4). Blood

Table 9.4 Baseline measure of possible risk factors and monitoring during treatment with any antipsychotic drug

	Initial visit	4 weeks	8 weeks	12 weeks	6 monthly	Annually
Personal/family history	X					X
Height/weight (BMI) or waist circumference	X	X	X	X	X	
Blood pressure	X			X	X	
Fasting plasma glucose	X	(X)	(X)	X	X	
Fasting lipid profile*	X			X	X	

(X): Finger prick tests can be used to identify early cases.
*Random total cholesterol/HDL cholesterol ratio may be used.

levels should be promptly rechecked on reports of sexual dysfunction in men or women.

These recommendations are examples of good practice and health promotion. The only mandatory investigations are regular blood tests for people taking clozapine (see above).

Implementation into practice

Weight gain and sexual dysfunction can be very distressing to a young person. It is often associated with low self-esteem and social anxieties, which can interfere with the recovery journey and may even increase the risk of relapse. Poor compliance (see below) may also be a complicating factor.

The Early Intervention Team in Worcestershire has developed good practice in relation to physical investigations and weight management. People with FEP are given information and encouraged to make active choices in relation to medication, which has led to improved compliance, weight loss and increased self-esteem. Care coordinators monitor for emerging side effects and are able to offer practical solutions, dose adjustment or a graded transition to alternative medication through close working with the team doctors and nurse prescriber.

Rates of tardive dyskinesia are reduced when atypical antipsychotic medication is used. Abnormal mouth movements are usually the first sign and are reversible in the initial stage; early detection is paramount. If the person with FEP is on a typical antipsychotic, then a switch to an atypical drug is indicated. If the person is already on an atypical drug, then a dose reduction or a switch to a drug with very low risk of tardive dyskinesia (quetiapine or clozapine) is suggested.

What if a few doses are missed?

The willingness to take medication is related to perceived beneficial effects, lack of side effects and the simplicity of the regime. Adherence can be related to insight but is more affected by attitudes towards medication and the relationship with the prescriber; many prescriptions are missed owing to ambivalence rather than active resistance. Adherence Therapy (www.adherencetherapy.com) is a development of Kemp's Compliance Therapy (1998). Training in Medication Management (Gray *et al.*, 2004) has also proved useful for professionals having most face-to-face contact with the client. Whilst not specific for FEP, both approaches may be useful strategies. A fuller discussion is unfortunately outside the remit of this chapter.

Implementation into practice

Poor or partial compliance with medication is around 50% across a range of health problems such as asthma, depression, diabetes and high blood pressure. It has been reported as high as 80% in schizophrenia. It is important to acknowledge and address this in FEP as missed doses can reduce the clinical response, contributing to social and psychological problems and increase the risk of relapse. It may be mistaken for treatment resistance with unnecessary escalation of doses or changes in medication.

Antipsychotic medication is also available as long-acting injections that can be given 2–4 weekly. Typical antipsychotic depot injections were widely used in the past but largely replaced by the oral atypical drugs. Since 2002, the atypical drug risperidone has also been available as a long-acting injection (Risperidone Consta). Recent reviews have challenged the view that this is an unpopular way of giving or receiving medication (Walburn *et al.*, 2001) and it can be very useful in enhancing adherence in an unmotivated, forgetful or disorganised individual. Initial results with younger people and those with FEP are encouraging. The Maudsley Prescribing Guidelines (Taylor *et al.*, 2007) more fully describes the use of long-acting injections and covers test doses, switching protocols and long-term management.

Another, more controversial, strategy has been the suggestion of financial incentives for taking medication. There are obvious ethical issues though clinical results have been encouraging (Claassen *et al.*, 2007).

When can I stop taking the tablets and what might happen? Will I have to take them again?

There is much debate into how long a person who has experienced FEP will need to take medication, especially if symptoms are in remission and they have made a full recovery. Owing to the varied findings and opinions, and the anxiety this issue causes in clinical practice, I have included a lot of research data in this section. It is disappointing that we can only come to limited conclusions and generalisations. It is truly 'work in progress', and I expect further developments in the next few years that will more fully inform our practice and the discussions we have with people with FEP.

Studies have reported relapse rates around 40–60% during the first year off medication after a successfully treated episode of FEP (Remington, 1995). This has led to a general consensus for continuing treatment during this initial period of remission. However, Robinson's (2004) 5-year study found the risk continuing at a significant level when people chose to stop medication even after 1 year of wellness. He reported relapse rates of 51% within 2 years rising to 78% over the 5-year period. This represented a fivefold increase in risk compared

to those on maintenance treatment. Gitlin *et al.* (2001), in a group of people with recent onset schizophrenia who had stopped medication after 1 year, found worsening of symptoms or relapse in 78% of the individuals by the end of the next 12 months and 96% by 24 months. These studies have led many professionals to consider longer periods of prophylactic medication. It is of concern that subsequent episodes may not respond as effectively to medication. Negative symptoms and treatment resistance may emerge or increase. Subsequent episodes are traumatic with the risk of increasing stigma and the psychosocial impact on the person and their social system.

So is it reasonable or feasible to ask a person who has made a good recovery from FEP to take medication on a long-term or an indefinite basis? The presence of side effects (e.g. weight gain, sedation and sexual dysfunction), which can reduce the sense of wellness, must be balanced against the risk of possible relapse. The increase in partial or non-compliance cannot be ignored.

The International Early Psychosis Association Writing Group (2005) suggests a pragmatic, collaborative approach:

1 Medication should be regularly reviewed to determine the minimum effective dose.
2 If a person with FEP had achieved full remission of symptoms, then withdrawal of medication can be considered after 12 months of remission.
3 If the episode was severe and slow to respond, a period of 2 years is suggested.
4 If the recovery has been incomplete, then the person may benefit from an extended period of medication up to 5 years.
5 Long-term medication is advisable for people who experience frequent relapses.

People with FEP (and their families, if appropriate) should be given the opportunity to complete early warning signs work prior to reducing and stopping medication. These strategies are covered elsewhere in this book. A gradual withdrawal of medication is associated with fewer problems over the first 6 months.

Short-term, *targeted*, medication can play an important part in relapse prevention. This is the use of medication only when particular signs or symptoms re-emerge. Targeted treatment has a poor reputation in people with longer-term mental health problems with high rates of relapse and hospitalisation; the review by Gilbert *et al.* (1995) found relapse rates of 50% compared to 16% for those on maintenance medication. However, there is a more positive picture for individuals with FEP. Gaebel *et al.* (2002) found that 2-year relapse rates in people with FEP were similar in targeted (42%) and maintenance treatment (38%). Gitlin *et al.* (2001) found that clinical monitoring and a low threshold for restarting medication prevented admission to hospital in a majority of people who experienced a return of symptoms of psychosis. However, he accepts that some symptoms may be non-specific, related to short-term stress, and not be part of a relapse (he refers to a study where 48% of early signs resolved with placebo!). Data from the German Research Network on Schizophrenia suggests that a combination of non-specific signs and symptoms is the most predictive of early risk and successful treatment (Gaebel & Riesbeck, 2007). This matches current clinical practice where the priority is to match interventions with the individual's relapse signature rather than textbook descriptions of psychosis.

There may be some groups who have a lower risk of relapse when stopping medication. Crow *et al.* (1986) found lower first-year relapse rates when DUP was less than 1 year. This was also true for those taking maintenance medication. Those remaining well without medication had higher occupational functioning than those maintained on medication. This finding has been replicated by the MESIFOS trial in The Netherlands (Wiersma *et al.*, 2007), who found that people with FEP receiving targeted treatment were more likely to achieve both social and symptomatic remission compared to those on maintenance medication (54% vs. 48%). Further research is needed to find predictors of successful discontinuation as this has obvious social and psychological implications. As well as DUP, shorter time to remission and better functioning at first presentation (e.g. employed,

in a relationship) may prove predictors of successful discontinuation with or without targeted treatment. In a recent study, 50% of people with FEP were well enough to discontinue medication at 1 year. Over the next 18 months, 40% of those were able to successfully stay off medication (Wunderink *et al.*, 2007).

Implementation into practice

The gradual discontinuation of medication, combined with early signs work and targeted treatment is possible for many individuals who experience FEP. Some will relapse and a few will develop a clinical picture of schizophrenia, which makes maintenance treatment necessary. However, supporting people coming off medication remains a major role for Early Intervention Services (EISs) and many will be successful in the short and long term.

Implementation and conclusions

Medication forms an important part of the wider treatment package for a person experiencing FEP. Drug regimens should be carefully tailored to this early, more responsive phase of illness and a young person's greater sensitivity to side effects. Low doses of atypical drugs are recommended as initial strategies with gradual increases, if necessary, to maximise the clinical response whilst minimising side effects; symptomatic remission rarely leads to recovery in the presence of distressing drug-induced physical problems.

We must also be vigilant in the prompt detection of treatment resistance. Poor or partial compliance, substance misuse and other physical, psychological or psychiatric conditions may lead to a disappointing response to medication; these issues merit specific treatments rather than ever-increasing doses of antipsychotic drugs.

The eventual stopping of medication is a common ambition for people who have experienced FEP. Even after a period of remission, this is not without risks but may be associated with social and psychological advantages. We are unable to say with certainty who will do well and who may experience further problems. Studies are emerging that may enable us to help people with FEP make the best decisions; even when this research data becomes available, we will still work with people as individuals, making joint decisions with them that reflect their unique circumstances.

All phases of prescribing should be a collaborative process and medication should not necessarily be seen as disempowering or disadvantageous if used appropriately. The development of NMPs in some EIS will hopefully give added benefit by improving access to collaborative prescribing decisions and concordance (Latter, 2005; Jones *et al.*, 2007), especially in those teams with little or no dedicated medical input. We can help by encouraging a sense of optimism and promoting expectations of positive outcomes and a journey towards recovery.

Suggested further reading

Taylor, D., Paton, C. & Kerwin, R. (2007). *The Maudsley Prescribing Guidelines* (9th edition). Informa Healthcare.

International Early Psychosis Association Writing Group (2005). International clinical practice guidelines for early psychosis. *British Journal of Psychiatry*, 187 (Suppl. 48), s120–s124.

Remington, R. (2005). Rational pharmacotherapy in early psychosis. *British Journal of Psychiatry*, 187 (Suppl. 48), s77–s84.

Thomas, C. & Lewis, S. (1998). Which atypical antipsychotic? *British Journal of Psychiatry*, 172, 106–109.

References

Aguilar, E.J., Keshavan, M.S., Martinez-Quiles, M.D. et al. (1994). Predictors of acute dystonia in first-episode psychotic patients. *American Journal of Psychiatry*, 151, 1819–1821.

Barnett, J.H., Werners, U., Secher, S.M. et al. (2007). Substance use in a population-based clinic sample of people with first-episode psychosis. *The British Journal of Psychiatry*, 190 515–520.

Claassen, D., Fakhoury, W.K., Ford, R. & Priebe, S. (2007). Money for medication: financial incentives to improve medication adherence in assertive outreach. *Psychiatric Bulletin*, 31, 4–7.

Crow, T.J., MacMillan, J.F., Johnson, A.L. & Johnstone, E.C. (1986). The Northwick Park study of first episode schizophrenia II. A randomised controlled trial of prophylactic neuroleptic treatment. *British Journal of Psychiatry*, 148, 120–127.

Gaebel, W. & Riesbeck, M. (2007). Results of the German Research Network on Schizophrenia (GRNS): Prodrome-based treatment in first-episode schizophrenia. *European Psychiatry*, 22 (Suppl. 1), S76.

Gaebel, W., Janner, M., Frommann, N. et al. (2002). First vs multiple episode schizophrenia: Two-year outcome of intermittent and maintenance medication strategies. *Schizophrenia Research*, 53, 145–159.

Gilbert, P.L., Harris, M.J., McAdams, L.A. et al. (1995). Neuroleptic withdrawal in schizophrenic patients: A review of the literature. *Archives of General Psychiatry*, 52, 173–188.

Gitlin, M., Neuchterlein, K., Subotnik, K.L. et al. (2001). Clinical outcomes following neuroleptic discontinuation in patients with remitted recent-onset schizophrenia. *American Journal of Psychiatry*, 158, 1835–1842.

Gray, R., Wykes, T.M., Edmunds, M. et al. (2004). Effect of a medication management training package for nurses on clinical outcomes for patients with schizophrenia: A cluster randomised controlled trial. *British Journal of Psychiatry*, 185, 157–162.

Jones, S., Hemingway, S. & Williams, B. (2007). Mental Health Nurses as non-medical prescribers – Entering uncharted territory. *Mental Health Nursing*, 27 (1), 14–17.

Kemp, R., Kirov, G., Everitt, B. et al. (1998). Randomised controlled trial of compliance therapy. 18-month follow-up. *British Journal of Psychiatry*, 172, 413–419.

Latter, S. (2005). Promoting concordance in prescribing interactions: The evidence base and implications for new generations of prescribers. In: M. Courtney & M. Griffiths (eds), *Independent and Supplementary Prescribing – An Essential Guide*. Cambridge: Cambridge Press.

Lieberman, J., Jody, D., Geisler, S. et al. (1993). Time course and biological correlates of treatment response in first-episode schizophrenia. *Archives of General Psychiatry*, 50, 369–376.

Leucht, S., Busch, R., Kissling, W. & Kane, J.M. (2007). Early predictors of antipsychotic nonresponse among patients with schizophrenia. *Journal of Clinical Psychiatry*, 68, 352–360.

National Institute for Clinical Excellence (2002). Guidance on the use of newer (atypical) antipsychotic drugs for the treatment of schizophrenia. *Health Technology Appraisal No. 43*.

Robinson, D.G., Woerner, M.G., McMeniman, M., Mendelowitz, A. & Bilder, R.M. (2004). Symptomatic and functional recovery from a first episode of schizophrenia or schizoaffective disorder. *American Journal of Psychiatry*, 161, 473–479.

Walburn, J., Gray, R., Gournay, K. *et al.* (2001). Systematic review of patient and nurse attitudes to depot antipsychotic medication. *British Journal of Psychiatry*, 179, 300–307.

Weiden, P.J., Preskorn, S.H., Fahnestock, P.A. *et al.* (2007). Translating the psychopharmacology of antipsychotics to individualized treatment for severe mental illness: A roadmap. *The Journal of Clinical Psychiatry*, 68 (Suppl. 7), 34–36.

Wiersma, D., Wunderink, A., Nienhuis, F.J. & Sytema, S. (2007). The MESIFOS-trial: Treatment strategies in remitted first episode psychosis. *European Psychiatry*, 22 (Suppl. 1), S76–S77.

World Health Organisation and the International Early Psychosis Association (2005). Early intervention and recovery for young people with early psychosis: Consensus statement. *British Journal of Psychiatry*, 187 (Suppl. 48), s116–s119.

Wunderink, L., Nienhuis, F., Sytema, S. *et al.* (2007). Guided discontinuation versus maintenance treatment in remitted first-episode psychosis: Relapse rates and functional outcome. *Journal of Clinical Psychiatry*, 68, 654–661.

Wyatt, R.J., Damiani, M. & Henter, I.D. (1998). First-episode schizophrenia. Early intervention and medication discontinuation in the context of course and treatment. *British Journal of Psychiatry*, 172 (Suppl. 33), 77–83.

Chapter 10 Working with diagnostic uncertainty in first-episode psychosis

Alan Farmer

Introduction

Whilst no area of medicine can claim to be an exact science, it is always seeking a further degree of certainty. Like the tale of Rumplestiltskin, we often feel that we will have power and authority over a disorder as soon as we can name it. I am, of course, talking from a medical point of view; no other member of the multidisciplinary team shares the psychiatrists' preoccupation (or delusion) and they have taught us a great deal about needs-led interventions and the importance of the person rather than the illness.

Diagnostic uncertainty is central to working with people with first episode of psychosis (FEP). Many problems may present with symptoms of psychosis (e.g. hallucinations and delusions). Equally confusingly, psychosis may initially present with a variety of other symptoms (e.g. preoccupations, withdrawal, depression and agitation). Often, a clinical picture of FEP can be further blurred by pre-existing problems of personality and street drugs as well as the challenging psychology of normal or abnormal adolescence.

In this chapter, I hope to explore the limits of normal experience and describe the main mental and physical health problems that may present with psychosis. I will discuss the association of psychosis with street drugs and personality and broach the difficult topic of when we might make a diagnosis of schizophrenia. I will finish with a reminder of the long-term instability of psychiatric diagnoses.

Who wants a diagnosis? Useful signposts or stigmatising labels?

Mental health problems have complex causes and explanations which are very particular to each individual. Risk factors are not specific; stressful life events, childhood adversity, migration and urban living are associated with depression as well as psychosis. We still have no diagnostic tests despite great leaps forward in brain imaging and gene mapping. Whilst our predictions might be guided by the best evidence available, it is often difficult to draw clear conclusions from research studies which usually involve people with more established mental health problems rather than people with FEP.

Rethink, a mental health charity, acknowledges that a correct diagnosis can be important, helping both the individual and carers to find positive ways of coping and sources of help such as local and national support groups. They say that accepting your diagnosis can often be an important first step, leading to an understanding of the value of ongoing support and treatment and improving the chances of recovery. More details can be found at www.rethink.org.

Implementation into practice

The term 'psychosis' in FEP is purely descriptive. It makes no assumption about the cause of the symptoms and does not leap to conclusions about longer-term outcomes. Approaches based on symptoms rather than diagnosis are thought to be less stigmatising (Bentall, 1990). Some people will eventually fit into a diagnostic category and we can help them make longer-term decisions about treatment and follow-up. However diagnoses such as schizophrenia can be stigmatising and demoralising to both the individual and their family. It should not be made until a clear clinical picture has emerged.

A brief summary of the evidence

Aren't we all a bit strange? Symptoms of psychosis in the general population

Symptoms of psychosis are not uncommon in people who never have a diagnosis or ever seek help. Up to 25% of young adults admit a non-drug–related delusion or hallucination at some point of time in their life and 5.5% of the British population reported psychotic symptoms in the absence of a psychotic illness. Paranoid thoughts and hallucinations can be more common in people with anxiety, alcohol-related problems and drug use and who have experienced victimisation or recent stressful life events. There is a complex interaction between psychosis, ethnicity and culture; studies have found over twice the rate of hallucinations in people of Caribbean origin living in the UK (Johns et al., 2004).

The American diagnostic system, the Diagnostic and Statistical Manual of Mental Disorders (DSM) included a description of a prodrome of schizophrenia in its revised 3rd edition (American Psychiatric Association, 1987). The nine symptoms included magical thinking, unusual experiences, social isolation and declining performance (American Psychiatric Association, 1987). Surveys of American high school students found that approximately half of them would meet these criteria and 10–15% experienced changes over an extended period of time (McGorry et al., 1995). These high rates suggest that these experiences are more often features of adolescence rather than a reliable predictor of psychosis. Its validity was repeatedly challenged and in the 4th edition of DSM it appears only as a retrospective description rather than a predictive entity (American Psychiatric Association, 1994). However, recent work has proved more useful in identifying 'at risk mental states' and their association with FEP though these are not specific to schizophrenia; this is covered in a separate chapter.

The situation is even more confusing in children. McGee et al. (2000) estimated that around 8% of healthy children can recall episodes with strange auditory or visual experiences. Normal development often includes an overactive imagination that can be mistaken for hallucinations or delusions. The concept of 'hearing voices' can be confused with experiencing memories or thinking to oneself. Time must be taken to develop a shared understanding; stories can be used to explore how they experience symptoms such as paranoia and hallucinations.

Of particular clinical interest is Hlastala and McClellan's (2005) study of young people with 'atypical psychotic symptoms'. Their symptoms were characteristically elaborate, often involved gaining rewards and were related to their immediate situation. Their social problems involved conflicts rather than the withdrawal and disinterest that can be common in psychotic illness. None of the young people developed an FEP over 2 years. They had, however, experienced high rates of abuse and neglect and the authors suggest their symptoms may be due to emotional or behavioural disturbances and post-traumatic experiences. These are not uncommon presentations and teams need to consider how they respond to these people's crises and help-seeking behaviours. I have found Youth Counselling Services very useful and would rather not inappropriately involve them in psychiatric services. I would advise against a diagnosis of psychosis, though accept that antipsychotic medication may help reduce aggression and disturbed behaviour. Cognitive behavioural methods or dialectical behaviour therapy may be useful in severe situations. I discuss personality and post-traumatic disorders in more detail below.

Differential diagnosis: Things we should be certain about

Interventions and support for people with FEP is largely based on the **symptoms** they seek help for. However, there are some important **diagnoses** that must be considered as specific treatments or investigations may be necessary (Table 10.1). I will discuss drug use and personality development in the next section.

Organic (physical) causes of psychosis

Doctors have a duty to exclude treatable medical conditions that may be mimicking psychosis. Physical causes may contribute to 5–8% of psychoses (Hyde & Lewis, 2003). However, in

Table 10.1 Important differential diagnoses

Important diagnoses to consider in FEP

- Organic (physical) causes of psychosis
- Affective (mood) causes of psychosis
- Traumatic causes of psychosis
- Developmental disorders and psychosis

routine practice, detailed physical investigations are often only done when there is marked cognitive decline, a consistently disappointing response to antipsychotic treatment or symptoms that are not typical of FEP (e.g. visual or olfactory hallucinations, disorientation or clouding of consciousness).

Epilepsy is the most common disorder that may present with psychosis, especially if the temporal lobe is involved. Individuals may display odd behaviour before, during (ictal) or after (post-ictal) any seizure. These can include hallucinations, memory problems or mood changes. Less common are brief inter-ictal or alternating psychoses. These can occur when seizures are less frequent or fully controlled. In these cases, confusion is rare but auditory hallucinations and paranoia are often present. Sachdev (2007) reviews the current literature and suggests there may be a common mechanism for all the brief psychoses associated with epilepsy. If there are concerns, an EEG and a specialist opinion are indicated. They can also advise on treatment as some antipsychotic drugs can make seizures worse.

Other causes of psychosis may be nutritional (e.g. B12 deficiency), metabolic (e.g. porphyria; the 'madness of King George'), hormonal (e.g. Cushing's syndrome) or infective (e.g. HIV or syphilis). Prescribed drugs such as steroids and dopamine agonists can also cause psychosis. A family history of physical health problems can alert us to inherited disorders such as Huntington's disease. More details can be found in textbooks of psychiatry or online at sites like www.emedicine.com.

Implementation into practice

Basic physical examination and baseline blood tests are important due to the links between physical health, mental health problems and their treatments. We need to incorporate these into routine clinical practice as many of the physical causes of psychosis can be identified or excluded with a thorough history and examination supplemented by laboratory tests. Investigations can be arranged by primary care doctors if an early intervention service does not have the necessary expertise or resources or if it is thought that the imposition of blood tests and brain scans will damage the initial engagement with the psychiatric team. If tests are needed, they should be arranged promptly and all results fed back as soon as they are available to allay anxiety and prevent an unnecessary additional preoccupation with physical health.

Affective (mood) causes of psychosis

A person with a manic episode can present with symptoms of psychosis and these usually mirror the raised mood. These include grandiose delusions and hallucinations that praise or encourage expansive plans. These symptoms are called 'mood congruent' and are most often accompanied by overactivity and an elated mood. Initial treatment with antipsychotic drugs is indicated. The clinical picture will become clearer after longer-term evaluation when mood stabilising medication may be considered as an alternative. A family history of mood disorder or previous episodes of depression may be a useful pointer.

People with severe depressive illness can also present with symptoms of psychosis. The symptoms are also mood congruent but now have a depressive, often nihilistic character. The person will believe that they are useless, that nobody likes them and may experience hallucinations that support this. They may develop delusions about their health and physical symptoms that cannot be explained by examination or investigations. These can present as bizarre delusions and I have met people who believe that they are already dead (Cotard's syndrome).

A low mood is common in all phases of psychosis (prodrome, acute, resolution and recovery phases); psychological and social interventions are important. However, a person with a depressive illness needs additional drug treatment.

The Calgary Depression Scale has been specifically designed to assess depression in people with psychosis (Addington *et al.*, 1993 or www.ucalgary.ca/cdss). In comparison with other assessment scales, there is less overlap with positive and negative symptoms of psychosis and side effects of medication that may lead to overdiagnosis of depression. Psychological factors are more reliable than behavioural or biological symptoms in detecting depressive illness secondary to psychosis (Table 10.2).

In depressive illness, antipsychotics will provide limited relief of symptoms and poorly target the root depression giving the impression of treatment resistance. Antidepressants should be used in most situations. Mood stabilisers are indicated if there is a history or strong suspicion of a bipolar illness (Kaye, 2005) as antidepressants may precipitate a manic episode or a period of instability of mood known as *rapid cycling*. Electro-convulsive therapy (ECT) can be a life-saving intervention in very severe illnesses when there is persistent suicidal behaviour or a refusal to eat or drink.

Traumatic causes of psychosis

I have already mentioned the link between stressful life events, victimisation and psychotic symptoms in the general population and the effect of abuse and neglect on children.

Post-traumatic stress disorder (PTSD) is a condition that may initially present as FEP. PTSD is a reaction to experiencing a serious threat to self or others with a response characterised by fear, helplessness or horror. Typical symptoms include flashbacks, dreams, withdrawal, flattened emotions, detachment from people and surroundings and an avoidance of anything that would remind the person of the trauma. Hallucinations, delusions and dissociative states (dreamlike states or feelings of unreality) can occur and lead to a suspicion of FEP. Correct identification of the problem and sensitive exploration of the traumatic event is important as the general principles of treating PTSD involve explanation and destigmatisation.

The onset of PTSD can be delayed for up to 6 months after the event. About 50% of people recover within 1 year but some experience long-term problems and personality change. Lifetime rates of 8% have been described and it is twice as common in women. High rates are found in the survivors of abuse, sexual assault, military combat/captivity, political/ethnic internment and genocide.

Developmental disorders and psychosis

The term autism was first used in 1910 by the Swiss psychiatrist Eugen Bleuler to describe self-absorbed behaviour in psychosis. In 1934, Leo Kanner introduced the idea of early infantile autism to describe some children's lack of interest in those around them. This 'aloneness' and an intolerance of change are the typical symptoms which affect 1–2/1000 children. Various autism spectrum disorders (approximately 6/1000 children) have been described; the most common is Asperger's syndrome, described in the 1940s by Hans Asperger. It shares the social awkwardness of autism but is not associated with language problems (early speech delay) or low IQ (US DSMIV criteria only).

Berney (2000) gives an excellent account of the current ideas surrounding autism and discusses the complex relationship with psychosis. Whilst

Table 10.2 Symptoms of depression

Symptoms of depressive illness

Biological

- Poor sleep with early morning waking (mood worst on waking)
- Poor appetite with weight loss
- Reduced energy/slowness

Psychological

- Feelings of hopelessness and sadness
- Loss of sense of pleasure
- Feelings of guilt and worthlessness
- Suicidal ideas
- Poor concentration and memory
- Psychosis

Social

- Withdrawal
- Reduced motivation

there is no association between schizophrenia and autism (in childhood or in adulthood), we do observe a high rate of psychotic symptoms. This may be due to social confusion, a tendency to literal, 'black or white' thinking and severe adjustment reactions, often to minor challenges or changes.

The association between Asperger's syndrome and FEP can be confusing in clinical practice. The transition from childhood through adolescence to adulthood is difficult for people who already may experience social difficulties and interpersonal awkwardness.

How do we differentiate between FEP and a longer-standing developmental disorder? A developmental history is always indicated as part of a full assessment of people presenting with FEP. This should give a picture of best level of functioning and any significant events during infancy, childhood and adolescence. Additional information can be sought from school records and Child and Adolescent Mental Health Service (CAMHS) notes; however, Asperger's syndrome has only been formally described and received particular attention since the 1980s. Fitzgerald and Corvin (2001) have produced an excellent summary on the differential diagnosis of Asperger's syndrome and Baron-Cohen et al. (2005) have produced the Adult Asperger Assessment which can be used with people who have not received a diagnosis in childhood.

Implementation into practice

People with Asperger's syndrome who are experiencing symptoms of psychosis are not usually excluded from first episode services and may benefit from medication and input from psychologists and occupational therapists.

They can be very gifted and may absorb themselves mastering esoteric topics. This is not to the extreme exclusion of all other activities that can be seen in people with autism. However, people with Asperger's syndrome can have difficulty appreciating or learning social rules and cues and are often socially isolated. This can make recovery from mental illness more difficult; group and social activities may cause distress, efforts to engage and interpersonal interventions may not be understood or seen as relevant.

Approaches have to be modified to incorporate the strengths of these individuals and progress may be slower than expected.

Street drugs, personality and psychosis

Telling the difference between FEP and personality development can be difficult. Parents or schools may ask that a young person be assessed as they are no longer the pleasant, outgoing person they remember and there has been a decline in appearance, hygiene and previous interests. This of course is most often a transient effect of normal adolescence. Personality disorders involve severe and persistent disturbance in thought, action and emotional response across a wide range of situations. It is associated with considerable personal and social disruption. These disorders emerge insidiously in late childhood and adolescence and continue into adulthood. Family members will also be able to provide invaluable background information.

Young people who are developing any personality disorder can present with social and psychological problems. The following disorders are more likely to include transient psychotic symptoms suggesting the possibility of FEP:

- *Schizotypal personality disorder*: The person may have difficulties with relationships. There may be odd ideas, experiences and behaviours but no persistent psychotic symptoms.
- *Paranoid personality disorder*: These people are sensitive and suspicious. They may overestimate their importance and abilities, easily bear grudges and be quickly angered by minor rebuffs or setbacks. There are no persistent symptoms of psychosis.
- *Schizoid personality disorder*: People may present as if they had negative symptoms of psychosis; a sense of detachment with limited emotional responses but no history of positive psychotic symptoms.
- *Borderline personality disorder*: A feeling of internal instability that leads to unpredictable and often sudden changes in thoughts, behaviour and mood. Paranoid ideas and hallucinations can occur but are usually transient and

related to the pervading mood or immediate situation.

We should never jump to conclusions about someone's personality; too often a young person with FEP is labelled as 'antisocial', 'immature' or 'borderline', especially if they are involved in illegal activity and use street drugs. This can lead to a denial of appropriate services and a further period of untreated active psychosis.

Implementation into practice

We may become aware of personality traits during a full assessment of unclear symptoms. Issues may also emerge in engagement or response to psychological or pharmacological interventions. Most of the time, these difficulties will be due to personal adaptation to trauma and long-term difficulties or behaviour that we may find difficult to understand. These can include coping strategies such as withdrawal to avoid victimisation or reduce social anxiety, substance misuse as anxiety management and temporary 'escape' from problems and emotional detachment and the rejection of help in people who have a history of abandonment and rejection. I find psychosocial and multidimensional case formulations invaluable (Alanen, 1997; Meaden & Van Marle, 2008) and have never given anyone a primary diagnosis of a personality disorder.

The association between street drugs and psychosis is particularly confusing (Table 10.3). Substance use and misuse is common in people with FEP and both problems reach their peak during adolescence and early adulthood. States of intoxication are common but we must consider that an independent or drug precipitated psychotic illness may be emerging. However, many people experience FEP without prior drug use and most people who use or misuse street drugs never develop a psychotic illness.

Cannabis is the most widely used illegal drug and has been the subject of most interest. Researchers have studied whether there is a link between using cannabis and developing psychosis as well as the direct effect the drug may have on the brain. This data is comprehensively summarised in Fergusson et al.'s (2006) review in the *British Medical Journal* and suggests that frequent use of cannabis increases the risk of psychotic symptoms and that cannabis may be accountable for 10% of psychotic illnesses.

Is psychosis related to drug misuse a distinct diagnosis? Do people present with different symptoms, need different treatment and have a different outcome to those whose FEP is unrelated to drug use? What is the risk that the person will develop further mental health problems?

Drug-induced psychoses are associated with an increased risk of longer-term mental health problems. Canton et al. (2007) found 25% of people in their 2005 study (see above) returned within a year with a non-drug–related psychosis. This group had poorer premorbid functioning, less insight, greater family history of mental illness. Arendt et al. (2005) found over 40% of people made a transition to schizophrenia or a schizophrenia-like illness within 3 years, some after a full recovery and a period of wellness lasting over a year. Young men were most at risk of making this transition. The role of street drugs should

---

Table 10.3 Characteristics of people with drug-induced psychosis

- Older at onset
- Less severe symptoms (positive and negative)
- Presence of visual hallucinations
- More likely to be in relationship
- More frequent comorbidity with antisocial personality disorder
- More frequent homelessness
- Less family support
- Higher frequency of substance misuse in parents

(Canton et al., 2005)

be considered in a differential diagnosis and drug precipitated illnesses can often occur at an earlier age (Addington & Addington, 1998). It may be missed due to denial or minimisation of drug use or poorly described due to initial confusion associated with states of intoxication and drug-induced episodes. Young people may also fear being refused help if the problem is judged by professionals as being 'self induced'. Requesting a urine sample for a drug screen is good practice when assessing a person with FEP and should be routine in admissions to hospital or crisis involvement with home treatment services.

Implementation into practice

If psychotic symptoms are due to drug use, then antipsychotic treatment may be brief with the longer-term focus on harm reduction or abstinence from the offending substance. Certain groups are at greater risk of making a transition to longer-term mental health problems.

Psychotic symptoms that persist despite stopping street drugs must not be ignored. Treatment will be necessary in line with current recommendations for psychosis. Untreated psychosis is invariably associated with serious psychological and social consequences and may also contribute to a return to harmful drug use.

People with FEP who continue to use street drugs have poorer functioning and a greater chance of relapse. Joint working with community drug teams is useful for people who use opiates or stimulants though they often have little to offer those whose drug of choice is cannabis. Motivational approaches may be a useful strategy to control drug use as well as encouraging engagement and compliance with medication. More general work on psychological and social functioning is also important and the role of alcohol should also be considered.

Diagnostic stability: Did we get it right?

In the 1930s, Masserman and Carmichael (1938) followed up 100 people admitted to a psychiatric hospital in Chicago. Within 1 year, 40% of the original diagnoses needed changing. Cooper (1967) studied almost 300 people admitted to hospital 4 times over a 2-year period in the 1950s.

They found that only 54% were given a consistent diagnosis and that the main reason for re-diagnosis was a change of doctor rather than a change of symptoms! Kendell (1974) studied the notes of 2000 people who were first admitted to hospital in 1964. Only 58% of people retained the same diagnosis over the next 5 years though Kendell commented that many changes represented a progression of some people's illnesses over a longer time period, for example confusional states to dementia, anxiety states to depressive illness and paranoid states to schizophrenia.

Schwartz *et al.* (2000) reviewed diagnoses at 6 months and 2 years after admission to hospital with FEP. At 6 months, around 25% met criteria for DSM-IV schizophrenia (American Psychiatric Association, 1994). Around 90% of them retained this diagnosis at 2 years. There was also a large group of people in the study (around 45%) whose psychosis was associated with a mood disorder. However, 21% of diagnoses were unknown or non-specific at 6 months but at 2 years a fifth of those had a formal diagnosis of a schizophrenic illness suggesting, in line with Kendell (1974), a transition from an unclear to a clear diagnosis in a number of people with FEP.

Risk factors associated with this progression included:

- Poorer premorbid adjustment in adolescence;
- Absence of drug or alcohol disorder;
- Duration of untreated psychosis longer than 3 months;
- A provisional diagnosis of schizophrenia on first assessment;
- Having a longer time in hospital;
- Being prescribed medication on discharge;
- Having more negative symptoms at 6 month review.

The presence of five or more of these factors gave a 50% risk of being diagnosed with a schizophrenic illness within the first 2 years.

There is growing interest in acute and transient psychotic disorders (ATPD). These have also been known as schizophreniform disorders. ICD-10 describes them as occurring within 2 weeks of a stressful event, sometimes within 48 hours. Whilst associated with clear and typical symptoms of psychosis, they resolve within days or weeks with complete recovery within 2–3 months (World Health Organisation, 1992). They make up around 5–6% of FEP though have been found to be twice as common in women and 10 times as common in developing countries (Susser & Wanderling, 1994).

Chen *et al.* (1996) and Amin *et al.* (1999) found around 80% of people diagnosed with schizophrenia during FEP still had this diagnosis after 3 years. This represents a considerable number of people whose FEP will be wrongly diagnosed as schizophrenia, a lifelong mental illness. Chen *et al.* (1996) is one of a number of studies finding these mistakes more often in non-Caucasian populations. For a diagnosis of schizophrenia, the American diagnostic system DSM-IV (American Psychiatric Association, 1994) requires psychotic symptoms to be present for 6 months. ICD-10 (World Health Organisation, 1992) only requires a period of 1 month. The use of stricter criteria makes little difference to the longer-term accuracy (Amin *et al.*, 1999); FEP is as unpredictable at 6 months as it is at 1 month.

Implications and conclusions

Diagnostic uncertainty removes the pressure to diagnose specific mental health problems at an inappropriately early stage. It involves a multi-disciplinary approach to need and risk. We must not rush into a diagnosis that can be misleading and damaging to young people with FEP. We must accept that illnesses may change and treat what needs to be treated, paying particular attention to important differential diagnoses and comorbidities.

An important part of the Early Psychosis Declaration (WHO & IEPA, 2005) is to challenge stigma and discrimination. We must avoid adding to the problem with inaccurate predictions of lifelong problems. We must also generate optimism and expectations of positive outcomes and recovery. It is also important to remain realistic and honest, providing help and support if a picture of longer-standing mental health problems emerges.

References

Addington, J. & Addington, D. (1998). Effect of substance misuse in early psychosis. *British Journal of Psychiatry*, 172 (Suppl. 33), 134–136.

Addington, D., Addington, J. & Maticka-Tyndale, E. (1993). Assessing depression in schizophrenia: The Calgary Depression Scale. *British Journal of Psychiatry*, 163 (Suppl. 22), 39–44.

Alanen, Y.O. (1997). *Schizophrenia: Its Origins and Need-Adapted Treatment*. London: Karnac Books.

American Psychiatric Association (1987). *Diagnostic and Statistical Manual of Mental Disorders* (3rd edition), revised. Washington DC: APA.

American Psychiatric Association (1994). *Diagnostic and Statistical Manual of Mental Disorders* (4th edition) Washington DC: APA.

Amin, S., Singh, S., Brewin, J. *et al.* (1999). Diagnostic stability of first episode psychosis. Comparison of ICD-10 and DSM-III-R systems. *British Journal of Psychiatry*, 175, 537–543.

Arendt, M., Rosenberg, R., Foldager, L. *et al.* (2005). Cannabis-induced psychosis and subsequent schizophrenia-spectrum disorders: Follow-up study of 535 incident cases. *British Journal of Psychiatry*, 187, 510–515.

Bentall, R.P. (1990). *Reconstructing Schizophrenia*. London: Routledge.

Baron-Cohen, S., Wheelwright, S., Robinson, J. *et al.* (2005). The adult Asperger assessment (AAA): A diagnostic method. *Journal of Autism and Developmental* Disorders, 35, 807–819.

Berney, T. (2000). Autism – An evolving concept. *British Journal of Psychiatry*, 176, 20–25.

Canton, C.L.M., Drake, R.E., Hasin, D.S. *et al.* (2005). Differences between early-phase primary psychotic disorders with concurrent substance use and substance induced psychosis. *Archives of General Psychiatry*, 62, 137–145.

Canton, C.L.M., Hasin, D.S., Shrout, P.E. *et al.* (2007). Stability of early-phase primary psychotic disorders with concurrent substance use and substance-induced psychosis. *British Journal of Psychiatry*, 190, 105–111.

Chen, Y., Swann, A. & Burt, D. (1996). Stability of diagnosis in schizophrenia. *American Journal of Psychiatry*, 153, 682–686.

Cooper, J. (1967). Diagnostic changes in a longitudinal study of psychiatric patients. *British Journal of Psychiatry*, 113, 129–142.

Fitzgerald, M. & Corvin, A. (2001). Diagnosis and differential diagnosis of Asperger syndrome. *Advances in Psychiatric Treatment*, 7, 310–318.

Fergusson, D., Poulton, R., Smith, P. *et al.* (2006). Cannabis and psychosis. *British Medical Journal*, 332, 172–176.

Hlastala, S. & McClellan, J. (2005). Phenomenology and diagnostic stability of youths with atypical psychotic symptoms. *Journal of Child & Adolescent Psychopharmacology*, 15, 497–509.

Hyde, T. & Lewis, S. (2003). The secondary schizophrenias. In: S.R. Hirsch & D.R. Weinberger (eds), *Schizophrenia*. Oxford: Blackwell Publishing.

Johns, L.C., Cannon, M., Singleton, N. *et al.* (2004). Prevalence and correlates of self-reported psychotic symptoms in the British population. *British Journal of Psychiatry*, 185, 298–305.

Kaye, N.S. (2005). Is your depressed patient bipolar? *Journal of the American Board of Family Practice*, 18, 271–281.

Kendell, R. (1974). The stability of psychiatric diagnoses. *British Journal of Psychiatry*, 124, 352–356.

Masserman, J. & Carmichael, H. (1938). Diagnosis and prognosis in psychiatry. *Journal of Mental Science*, 84, 893–946.

McGee, R., Williams, S. & Poulton, R. (2000). Hallucinations in nonpsychotic children. *Journal of American Academic Child & Adolescent Psychiatry*, 39, 12–13.

McGorry, P., McFarlane, C., Patton, G.C. *et al.* (1995). The prevalence of prodromal features of schizophrenia in adolescence: A preliminary study. *Acta Psychiatrica Scandinavica*, 92, 241–249.

Meaden, A. & Van Marle, S. (2008). When the going gets tougher: The importance of long-term supportive psychotherapy in psychosis. *Advances in Psychiatric Treatment*, 14, 42–49.

Sachdev, P. (2007). Alternating and postictal psychoses: Review and a unifying hypothesis. *Schizophrenia Bulletin*, 33, 1029–1037.

Schwartz, J., Fennig, S., Tanenberg-Karant, M. *et al.* (2000). Congruence of diagnoses 2 years after a first-admission diagnosis of psychosis. *Archives of General Psychiatry*, 57, 593–600.

Susser, E.S. & Wanderling, J. (1994). Epidemiology of nonaffective acute remitting psychosis vs schizophrenia: Sex and sociocultural setting. *Archives of General Psychiatry*, 51, 294–301.

World Health Organisation (1992). *The ICD-10 Classification of Mental and Behavioural Disorders. Clinical Descriptions and Diagnostic Guidelines.* Geneva: WHO.

World Health Organisation and the International Early Psychosis Association (2005). Early Intervention and recovery for young people with early psychosis: Consensus statement. *British Journal of Psychiatry*, 187 (Suppl. 48), s116–s119.

Chapter 11 Early detection and treatment opportunities for people at high risk of developing psychosis

Paul French

Introduction

It is important to elaborate what we mean by early detection of psychosis. Conventionally, it has referred to the early detection of an actual episode of psychosis, typically the first episode of psychosis (FEP) at the earliest possible opportunity. Shortening the duration of untreated psychosis (DUP), in other words, the time taken from the onset of psychosis to receiving treatment, seemed a worthy service objective which has been supported by evidence that longer DUP predicts a poorer prognosis (for a thorough review of DUP, see Chapter 2). However, research shows that it is now possible to identify individuals who are not yet psychotic, but through the presence of detectable signs and symptoms, can be considered to have an elevated risk of developing psychosis. These individuals are considered to have an At Risk Mental State (ARMS) for psychosis. This chapter will review the benefits of early detection of those at high risk of developing psychosis and examine potential treatment strategies that delay or prevent the onset of psychosis.

Background

For many years, we did not consider the possibility of intervening early with people with psychosis, as the dominant view typified by schizophrenia was a hopeless deteriorating course of illness, typified by the term 'chronic', one which raises the hackles of many service users, carers and clinicians. Today, we talk more readily about recovery and embrace the idea of recovery-orientated services, an important principle at the heart of early intervention in psychosis. Recovery is frequently associated with someone experiencing a frank episode of psychosis and their recovery is typically quantified as an absence of symptoms. However, recovery is now the topic of much research and clinical interest and it is becoming accepted that it is much more complex than merely the absence of symptoms. However, to truly embrace the possibility of recovery, we need to consider the possibility that people can recover from any point in the continuum; that is, we frequently refer to psychosis as a continuum from normal experiences at one end, through to high levels of distress and symptoms which are frequent and unremitting at the other end. A recovery model suggests that at any point on that continuum people can stop moving along it, arrest the progression and then, with the right conditions, retrace their steps to a point where they are able to manage their lives once again. The idea of early detection of people with an ARMS for psychosis embraces the fact that people can be identified as expressing signs and symptoms which would confer this notion of an elevated risk beyond the general population. Then, if left unchecked, these symptoms can progress and the individual would have a significantly higher chance of developing a full expression of psychosis. If we are to consider that this is possible, then two key factors are required; the first being the ability to identify people who are considered to be experiencing an ARMS; and the second, to cultivate an intervention or set of interventions which can assist in arresting the progression towards psychosis or manage the complex array of problems frequently experienced by this population.

Research findings indicate that it is possible to reliably identify people at an ultra-high risk of developing psychosis over a relatively short time frame. The work in this area has been pioneered by Alison Yung and her group in Melbourne (Yung *et al.*, 1996, 1998, 2006). What this group found through talking to young people who had experienced an FEP is that their psychosis did not just appear overnight; it typically grew out of some other problem. Interestingly, this group also explained that they attempted to get help in the early stages but their difficulties did not necessarily trigger a service response. Therefore, this appeared to indicate that a help-seeking population could be identified who were in the early stages of a developing psychosis before the onset of their FEP. Yung and colleagues set about operationalising their findings, and in a seminal paper (Yung *et al.*, 1998), published very impressive findings that a high-risk cohort could be identified, finding that 40% of their high-risk cohort went on to develop a psychosis over a 12-month time frame. The operationalised method of identification was through a mixture of state-and-trait factors. They not only included low level but detectable signs of psychosis (being able to pick up sub-threshold symptoms of hallucinations and delusional thinking) but also included factors associated with a family history (people with a first-degree family history and who were also experiencing an increase in stress at that time). This criteria is now widely accepted and utilised in numerous research and clinical teams globally for example (Lam *et al.*, 2006).

For some time, this criteria was operationalised through measures which were originally designed to be utilised with people with an established psychosis such as the Positive and Negative Syndromes Scale (PANSS (Kay *et al.*, 1987)). However, recent years have seen the development of measures specific to this population, and the Comprehensive Assessment of At Risk Mental States (CAARMS (Yung *et al.*, 2006)) developed by Yung and colleagues utilises their experience in this field to combine the various complexities of entry into a single measure. The other principal measure is the Structured Interview for Psychotic Symptoms (SIPS (Miller *et al.*, 1999)), which

again has good reliability, although it measures similar items to the CAARMS.

It is vital to utilise specific measures to define this population, as clinicians, we formulate our clients and explain away their problems as understandable. This is obviously a very important aspect of diagnosis and treatment, however, it means that potentially we would be less likely to understand someone's problems in terms of an emergent psychosis. It is also important to understand that an ARMS for psychosis can frequently emerge out of a set of symptoms which could be classified in multiple ways such as Post-Traumatic Stress Disorder, Obsessive Compulsive Disorder, Borderline Personality Disorder, Panic Disorder or even some complicated combination of any of these presentations. This fits more readily with a continuum rather than a categorical model and aligns with current thinking such as that espoused by McGorry and colleagues who have proposed a clinical-staging model to understand the onset and development of psychosis (McGorry *et al.*, 2006). The idea of the clinical-staging model embraces the fact that even people with a severe deteriorating illness will at some point start to recognise the onset of that illness, clinical staging helps define what symptoms may be associated with onset and offers a range of interventions which are staged through the development of the illness.

In the case of an ARMS client, it would make most sense to continue to assess in detail utilising specific measures as discussed, and if an intervention was required, then utilise an intervention which targeted the problems that initiated the help-seeking process.

In this instance, the GP is not directly treating an emergent psychosis, although with the family history, his age and elevated stress levels, this does place John in a high-risk category. Indeed, attempts to treat with an antipsychotic might have increased John's anxiety about his own mental state, possibly making him hypervigilant for psychotic-like symptoms which may appear. However, the GP was able to help John manage his poor sleep and then follow him up to review how things were going to maintain a watching

Case studies

John, an 18-year-old man, presented to his general practitioner (GP) with a range of difficulties, complaining that his sleep was poor, that he felt stressed at college and was unable to concentrate on his studies. John has a first-degree relative with a history of psychosis; so his GP was aware of this and asked more specific questions about psychotic-like symptoms which John denied.

It would make sense for the GP to initiate a close watching brief for John, reflecting a heightened period of concern despite the absence of psychotic symptoms. John does, however, have some other symptoms such as poor sleep whose successful treatment would help him to feel better in the morning and possibly function better at college. It would also be worth trying to work out what it was that was currently affecting John and were there any other factors or areas of concern or worry.

brief. He was then in a position to offer alternative support if things did not improve.

Should John have described a clearer history of psychotic-like symptoms, then the GP could have initiated a more assertive approach such as referral straight to an early detection team who could advise more readily on treatment options.

Currently, guidance from the International Early Psychosis Association (IEPA) suggests that treating ARMS with psychological strategies should be a first line of treatment and Yung (Yung *et al.*, 2007) recommends that early treatment should focus on non-psychotic difficulties such as anxiety, depression or substance-use problems.

An emerging evidence base suggests the use of a specific psychological intervention utilising Cognitive Behaviour Therapy (CBT). This approach has been utilised in the UK through the Early Detection and Intervention Evaluation (EDIE), single blind study (Morrison *et al.*, 2004, 2006). This study identified individuals who were considered as being at a high risk of developing psychosis according to the criteria described earlier. The participants were then randomised to either monitoring or treatment

plus monitoring. The treatment was cognitive therapy (CT) and the monitoring (assessment using the PANSS and other psychological measures) was undertaken every month, initially for a period of 1 year, although we did an additional study to follow the group at 3 years post-treatment. People were not prescribed any medication as part of the research protocol, and if they were taking antipsychotic medication at assessment, then they were considered ineligible, as it would make it impossible to understand if it was the medication or the CT that was contributing to a reduction in transition if this occurred. Results from the trial demonstrated a significant reduction in the transition to psychosis for ARMS clients over a 12-month time frame using multiple methods of classifying the transition to psychosis (Morrison *et al.*, 2004). The CBT utilised in this trial has been described more fully elsewhere (French & Morrison, 2004), but interestingly, we found that some benefits were maintained from a 6-month intervention remaining at 3 years (Morrison *et al.*, 2006). This paper also suggests that if measures of someone's suitability to CT are also examined, then an exploratory analysis demonstrated that significant results were obtained on a range of indicators. This indicates that not only can we identify people who are at a high risk of developing psychosis but also we are able to identify a group who may also make the most of CT interventions. A key factor for this intervention is someone's metacognitive beliefs, that is, how they think about their thoughts, these beliefs not only confer vulnerability (Morrison *et al.*, 2007) but are an amenable target of therapy.

Currently, there is limited evidence for utilising antipsychotic medication for ARMS. A trial in Australia found some benefits of a medication-based intervention, in combination with a number of other interventions, including CBT and case management (McGorry *et al.*, 2002), although these benefits were not significant at 12 months. Another trial found a trend in terms of significance when they undertook a double-blind trial of Olanzapine (McGlashan *et al.*, 2003) as an agent to prevent transition in ARMS clients.

In the USA, they have utilised a similar identification strategy, based on the approach pioneered by Yung and colleagues, although they have developed the SIPS and SOPS (Miller & McGlashan, 2000) as specific measures to assist with the identification of at-risk cases rather than relying on more general measures. They have adopted a medical intervention, choosing an atypical antipsychotic medication (olanzapine) as their primary intervention. The study is a double-blind randomised controlled trial (McGlashan *et al.*, 2003) with participants randomly allocated to receive either a placebo or olanzapine and taken for 1 year, followed by a further year of assessment with no medication. Due to problems with follow–up, this trial found no evidence to suggest the utilisation of olanzapine in ARMS cases.

For some time, the position regarding medication seems to be that of clinical equipoise (McGorry *et al.*, 2002), meaning that there is insufficient research evidence either way to determine whether medication is justifiable with at-risk clients. Some believe that the emergence of subclinical symptoms, heralding an ARMS, warrants the use of neuroleptic medication, whilst others believe that the initiation of neuroleptic medication in at-risk cases may expose large numbers of false positives to the side-effects of these medications unnecessarily, given the current accuracy of measures of risk (Bentall & Morrison, 2002). Bentall and Morrison (2002) also argue that the use of antipsychotic medication with this population risks intervening with psychotic experiences that cause no distress and may be valued by the person (or even functional). They also suggest that the distressing side effects of antipsychotic medication, including the newer atypicals, which commonly produce weight gain and sexual dysfunction, should be considered. Such side effects can have significant impact on self-esteem, especially in the age group in which many of the at-risk cases fall, and antipsychotic medications can still cause neuroleptic malignant syndrome, which can be fatal. Significantly, if medication is prescribed and it transpires that side effects are experienced, then there is the potential for this to adversely affect engagement with services in the future. Bentall and Morrison (2002) also note that the effects of such medication on the developing brains of adolescents are currently unknown. Such considerations make such pharmacological interventions problematic.

I believe that antipsychotic medication in at-risk cases is not justifiable as a first line of intervention, as large numbers of young people defined as being high risk, will not make the transition to psychosis but would have been unnecessarily exposed to the side effects of the medication. Indeed, McGorry *et al.*'s (2002) data certainly suggests that CT is a more acceptable intervention than even very low dose antipsychotic medication, and they advise that, 'some patients could be treated with psychological therapy alone as a first-line strategy' (p. 926). Recent guidelines (IEPA (International clinical practice guidelines for early psychosis, 2005)) recommend that people who are felt to be at risk of developing psychosis, and who are seeking help for subsequent distress or disability, should be engaged and assessed and, where relevant, offered:

- Regular monitoring;
- Interventions aimed at specific difficulties such as anxiety, depression or substance misuse and help with interpersonal, vocational and family issues where relevant;
- Psycho education and assistance to develop coping strategies for sub-threshold psychotic symptoms;
- Family support and education;
- Clear information about risks in relation to future mental health issues, delivered in a careful and considered way.

These guidelines should be delivered in low stigmatising environments such as home, primary care settings or youth-based services.

It is important not to assume that a psychological intervention is exempt from side effects. If a treatment can bring about positive change, then it may also bring about negative change. An obvious risk of intervening with an at-risk population is the possibility of unnecessary stigmatisation. The terminology used is also likely to be an issue in relation to this; it would seem to be needlessly stigmatising, not to mention inaccuracy given the false positives, to regard a high-risk population as prodromal, pre-psychotic or pre-schizophrenic. Rather, describing the population as distressed, help-seeking and at risk of developing psychosis would seem to be more accurate and less likely to pathologise or stigmatise individuals.

Another approach to develop intervention in ARMS cases has been to identify what has been termed 'initial and late prodromal clients' (Bechdolf *et al.*, 2005). In this approach, the research team identifies two stages for ARMS; in the initial stage, they offer cognitive interventions designed to minimise transition to the late stage, and in the late stage, they offer low dose antipsychotic medication (amisulpiride) designed to minimise the transition to full psychosis.

Implementation into practice

It is feasible to reliably identify individuals at an elevated risk of developing psychosis. However, we need to be mindful of the interventions that are offered. We need to ensure that we base our interventions around the problems that are present and not just what we think may emerge; this is where a psychological strategy, which has a focus on the problems the clients bring to therapy, can have a significant impact. Working with ARMS clients can be challenging but extremely rewarding, this is a client group with high levels of need and frequently limited support and resources which may be in the process of breaking down. However, it is easier to maintain existing resources than to recreate them not only for the service but also for the individual.

References

Bechdolf, A., Ruhrmann, S., Wagner, M., Kuhn, K.U., Janssen, B., Bottlender, R. *et al.* (2005). Interventions in the initial prodromal states of psychosis in Germany: Concept and recruitment. *British Journal of Psychiatry*, 187 (Suppl. 48), s45–s48.

Bentall, R.P. & Morrison, A.P. (2002). More harm than good: The case against using antipsychotic drugs to prevent severe mental illness. Journal of Mental Health, 11, 351–365.

French, P. & Morrison, A.P. (2004). Early Detection and Cognitive Therapy for People at High Risk of Developing Psychosis: A Treatment Approach, Wiley, Chichester.

International clinical practice guidelines for early psychosis. (2005). British Journal of Psychiatry, 187 (Suppl. 48), s120–s124.

Kay, S.R., Fiszbein, A. & Opler, L.A. (1987). The positive and negative syndrome scale (PANSS) for schizophrenia. Schizophrenia Bulletin, 13(2), 261–276.

Lam, M.M., Hung, S.F. & Chen, E.Y. (2006). Transition to psychosis: 6-month follow-up of a Chinese high-risk group in Hong Kong.

to prevent severe mental illness. *Journal of Mental Health*, 11, 351–365.

French, P. & Morrison, A.P. (2004). *Early Detection and Cognitive Therapy for People at High Risk of Developing Psychosis: A Treatment Approach*, Wiley, Chichester.

International clinical practice guidelines for early psychosis. (2005). *British Journal of Psychiatry*, 187 (Suppl. 48), s120–s124.

Kay, S.R., Fiszbein, A. & Opler, L.A. (1987). The positive and negative syndrome scale (PANSS) for schizophrenia. *Schizophrenia Bulletin*, 13(2), 261–276.

Lam, M.M., Hung, S.F. & Chen, E.Y. (2006). Transition to psychosis: 6-month follow-up of a Chinese high-risk group in Hong Kong. *Australian and New Zealand Journal of Psychiatry*, 40(5), 414–420.

McGlashan, T.H., Zipursky, R.B., Perkins, D., Addington, J., Miller, T.J., Woods, S.W. *et al.* (2003). The PRIME North America randomized double-blind clinical trial of olanzapine versus placebo in patients at risk of being prodromally symptomatic for psychosis. I. Study rationale and design. *Schizophrenia Research*, 61(1), 7–18.

McGorry, P.D., Yung, A.R., Phillips, L.J., Yuen, H.P., Francey, S., Cosgrave, E.M. *et al.* (2002). Randomized controlled trial of interventions designed to reduce the risk of progression to first-episode psychosis in a clinical sample with sub threshold symptoms. *Archives of General Psychiatry*, 59(10), 921–928.

McGorry, P.D., Hickie, I.B., Yung, A.R., Pantelis, C. & Jackson, H.J. (2006). Clinical staging of psychiatric disorders: A heuristic framework for choosing earlier, safer and more effective interventions. *Australian and New Zealand Journal of Psychiatry*, 40(8), 616–622.

Miller, T.J. & McGlashan, T.H. (2000). Early identification and intervention in psychotic illness. *Connecticut Medicine*, 64(6), 339–341.

Miller, T.J., McGlashan, T.H., Woods, S.W., Stein, K., Driesen, N., Corcoran, C.M. *et al.* (1999). Symptom assessment in schizophrenic prodromal states. *Psychiatric Quarterly*, 70(4), 273–287.

Morrison, A.P., French, P., Walford, L., Lewis, S.W., Kilcommons, A., Green, J. *et al.* (2004). Cognitive therapy for the prevention of psychosis in people at ultra-high risk: Randomised controlled trail. *British Journal of Psychiatry*, 185, 291–297.

Morrison, A.P., French, P., Parker, S., Roberts, M., Stevens, H., Bentall, R.P. *et al.* (2006). Three-year follow-up of a randomized controlled trial of cognitive therapy for the prevention of psychosis in people at ultrahigh risk. *Schizophrenia Bulletin*, 33, 682–687.

Morrison, A.P., French, P. & Wells, A. (2007). Metacognitive beliefs across the continuum of psychosis: Comparisons between patients with psychotic disorders, patients at ultra-high risk and non-patients. *Behaviour Research and Therapy*, 45 (9), 2241–2246.

Yung, A.R., McGorry, P.D., McFarlane, C.A., Jackson, H.J., Patton, G.C. & Rakkar, A. (1996). Monitoring and care of young people at incipient risk of psychosis. *Schizophrenia Bulletin*, 22(2), 283–303.

Yung, A.R., Phillips, L.J., McGorry, P.D., McFarlane, C.A., Francey, S., Harrigan, S. *et al.* (1998). Prediction of psychosis: A step towards indicated prevention of schizophrenia. *British Journal of Psychiatry*, 172 (Suppl. 33), 14–20.

Yung, A.R. Phillips, L., Simmons, J., Ward, K., Thompson, P., French, P. *et al.* (2006). Comprehensive assessment of at risk mental states. *Unpublished manuscript*.

Yung, A.R., Buckby, J.A., Cosgrave, E.M., Killackey, E.J., Baker, K., Cotton, S.M. *et al.* (2007). Association between psychotic experiences and depression in a clinical sample over 6 months. *Schizophrenia Research*, 91(1–3), 246–253.

Chapter 12 **Primary care liaison for individuals with first-episode psychosis**

David Shiers and Helen Lester

Introduction

A major strategy associated with early intervention in psychosis (EIP) is the ability to influence pathways to care. These pathways have been shown to be complex and often unsatisfactory in terms of the number of contacts and the time it can take before an individual with first-episode psychosis (FEP) is referred appropriately. Indeed, a recent systematic review (Marshall *et al.*, 2005) of 26 eligible studies involving 4,490 participants found a mean duration of untreated psychosis (DUP) of 126 weeks. Pathway to care data frequently highlights the importance of primary care in this process. This chapter will discuss these issues in depth, provide some insights into how primary care views individuals with psychosis and the paradigm of EI and highlight one particular strategy used in Birmingham to provide education about FEP specifically for general practitioners (GPs).

Overview of the evidence

Most people in the UK who have a psychosis live in the community and are registered with a GP. At any one time, a GP with a list of 2,000 patients will provide care for 10–20 individuals with established psychoses. People with established psychosis consult primary care practitioners 3–4 times more frequently and are in contact with primary care services for a longer cumulative time than patients without mental health problems (Kai *et al.*, 2000). Indeed, 30–50% of people with serious mental health problems are seen only in the primary care setting (Jenkins *et al.*, 2002).

There is evidence to suggest that many GPs believe they contribute little to the care of people with serious mental health problems (Bindman *et al.*, 1997), that the quality of communication between primary and specialist care about people with serious mental health problems can be variable (Lang *et al.*, 1997) and that GPs feel that the incidence of FEP is too low to warrant more active involvement.

The majority see their role as limited to physical illness and prescribing (Burns *et al.*, 2000). There is also some evidence that people with serious mental health problems are perceived as 'difficult' and as creating work, with the attitudes of inner city GPs particularly negative (Brown *et al.*, 1999). This of course, to some extent, reflects the negative stereotypes held by many in wider society, or at the very least, a perception of 'otherness', evocatively described by Jonathan Miller (Openmind 1999, 49, February/March):

There is a vast and very complicated unwritten constitution of conduct which allows us to move with confidence through public spaces, and we can instantly and by a very subtle process recognise someone who is breaking that constitution. They are talking to themselves; they are not moving at the same rate; they are moving at different angles; they are not avoiding other people with the skills that pedestrians do in the street. The speed with which normal users of public places can recognise someone else as not being a normal user of it, is where madness appears.

GPs' relative lack of enthusiasm and involvement may also reflect a paucity of formal training in mental health in the UK. A recent survey found that only one-third of GPs received any mental health training in the previous 5 years, while 10% expressed concerns about their training or mental health skills (MACA, 1999).

However, most GPs see one or two new cases each year, are frequently consulted at some point during a developing FEP (Skeate *et al.*, 2002) and are the most common final referral agent in the patient pathway. GP involvement also associates with less use of the Mental Health Act (Burnett *et al.*, 1999). Primary care, therefore, has a potentially pivotal role in reducing DUP and influencing the course and outcome of FEP. Problems with referral across the primary/secondary care interface can also delay diagnosis. A recent survey of GPs in West Midlands (unpublished thesis) highlighted frustrations with the specialist mental health care response:

Usually we get stuck in a closed loop. Often such youngsters have also has some involvement with alcohol or drugs and which ever avenue of help we seek, sends the referral back 'try a more appropriate referral'. I knew nothing of the EI service.

I would like one point of referral, not have to know about each individual service and which one to refer to; there also frustrations about being passed from pillar to post.

EIS development, however, heralds a different way of working across the primary/secondary care interface to provide better services for people with acute psychosis (both first episode and relapse). Indeed, primary care and EIS share a number of philosophical and clinical concerns. Both have a low threshold for referral, work with diagnostic uncertainty and are used to seeing and trying to help distressed families. These shared issues provide fertile ground for primary care and EI services to work closely together with a common objective of ensuring that a young person and their family access appropriate quality services in a timely fashion. We believe it is vital for EIP services to work closely with primary care, acknowledging its pivotal role in care pathways as the Early Psychosis Declaration highlights (see Table 12.1).

Primary care and the paradigm of EIP

In this section, we will explore the mindset of primary care, reflecting on the findings of a recent study (Lester *et al.*, 2005a) that offers insights into GP attitudes and behaviours about

Table 12.1   Early Psychosis Declaration

Early Psychosis Declaration Comprehensive programme	Relating to primary care Measured outcome
Improve access and engagement	
Walk-in responsive services usually provided in primary care settings should be equipped to deal effectively with early psychosis.	The mean DUP from the onset of psychosis is less than 3 months. The use of involuntary treatments in the first engagement is less than 25%.
Service interfaces are designed to support quicker and more effective engagements of young people.	Effective treatment will be provided after no more than three attempts to seek help.
Practitioner training	
All primary care sites are equipped to deal effectively with early psychosis.	Recognition, care and treatment of young people with psychosis are a routine part of training curricula of all primary care and social care practitioners.
Continued professional development is supported for all specialist staff working with young people with psychosis.	Specific Early Intervention training programmes are resourced and evaluated.

Source: Betolote and McGorry, 2005.

FEP. We will then use stories drawn from a series of pathway audits in the West Midlands to illustrate the complex nature of EIP and the problems that can occur when different parts of the NHS fail to communicate well. We will finally draw on emerging data from a case study of all EIS in the West Midlands (EDEN) to highlight potential problems in pathways both into and out of EIS.

A focus group study, based in the West Midlands, drew together 45 individuals with serious mental health problems and 39 GPs to discuss their views on providing and being on the receiving end of primary care. Patients and GPs both agreed on the value of GPs providing continuity of care and of knowing the person prior to the illness as well as their wider family and social context:

> You've got a familiar face who knows your story and you don't have to start from the beginning again. She's seen me deteriorate and come back again. I feel very safe in her hands (Patient).

Patients particularly valued GPs' generalism (rather than specialism) and their ability to navigate care systems. Indeed, they saw primary care as the 'cornerstone' of their care:

> I mean, the GP has to have some understanding of mental health but I don't expect my GP to know all of the issues to do with my illness. I would though expect him or her to refer me to a specialist person. The important thing is that somebody is looking after you so it's not just you on your own (Patient).

However, many of the GPs felt that their lack of specific mental health expertise meant they had little to offer:

> I know that I cannot look after people with severe and enduring mental health problems. I don't have the skills or the knowledge. I could not to do it well (GP).

Barriers to care were explored by the groups. Probing the 'did not attend' issue revealed how negative stereotypical attitudes held by some GPs could act as a barrier to early detection:

> They are notoriously bad at keeping appointments or turning up you know, so if you say you want to see them on a regular basis they probably won't keep the appointment and they'll turn up when you're not there (GP).

In contrast, many patients suggested that if they failed to attend an appointment, it was almost always because they were unwell:

> If someone had come and visited us when I was bad, that would have nipped it in the bud (Patient).

Gaming tactics of negotiating and facilitating access by exaggerating symptoms were described by patients, to help them obtain an urgent appointment with their GP. These same tactics were also described by some GPs in order to persuade psychiatrists to accept patients for further assessment and care:

> It's traumatic, the efforts needed to get help. No one wins, I feel bad having to do this, to sometimes have to exaggerate the distress I'm in, but I have to, to get the help I need (Patient).
>
> The focus is on risk assessment. But why do you have to be in crisis before you get help? You need to kick up a stink (to access specialist care) (Patient).
>
> I think that what we need is secondary care to be responsive when we need it. We don't ask for help very often, but when we do ask for help. We mean now, not after the week end (GP).
>
> Sometimes they have to be standing on a bridge before we can get people help and we have to exaggerate symptoms to get the psychiatrist's attention at an earlier stage (GP).

Critical pathways

Pathway audits in the West Midlands have highlighted the complexity of patient and family journeys (Table 12.2) and demonstrate the involvement of many other community agencies (Table 12.3).

The following stories are derived from cases in the West Midlands Pathway to Care Audits.[1] Identifying details have been changed to ensure anonymity.

Table 12.2 Pathways to care in the West Midlands Audit*

- DUP was 7–15 months
- For 54%, help-seeking began within 2 weeks of the onset of psychotic symptoms
- 80% were hospitalised
- 52% required use of the Mental Health Act (1983)
- 45% of these involved the police or criminal justice system
- Only one person achieved effective engagement via a psychiatric outpatient clinic appointment (n = 45)

*An audit of Pathways to Care for 45 people with FEP in the West Midlands (Macmillan *et al.*, 1998/1999).

Table 12.3 Pathway players in the West Midlands Audit

General psychiatrist	45	Health visitor	3
Family member	37	Work colleagues	3
GP	36	Private landlord	2
Police	22	Church	2
CPN	18	Occupational health	2
A&E	13	Friends	2
Social worker	11	General physician	1
Psychologist	5	Learning difficulties psychiatrist	1
Teacher/tutor	4	Forensic psychiatrist	1
Neighbour	4	Substance misuse service	1
Police surgeon	4	Homeless service	1
Hostel staff	4	Solicitor	1
Probation office	3	Ambulance service	1
Prison staff	3	Public health	1
Resource centre	3		

Case study

Christopher, aged 17 years, lived with his mother and siblings, and is working as a labourer. He consulted his GP with the complaint of noises in his ears. The next day, his mother telephoned the GP worried about Christopher's level of stress that had been building up for 6 months. The GP arranged to review Christopher the following week when it became clear that he had been hearing voices, and an urgent psychiatric assessment was requested.

This presentation is typical of many within the audits. In line with other studies, the GP was the most common point of first contact. Thirty-seven per cent of individuals with FEP described their GP's support as 'extremely helpful'. However, 63% described the support as 'fairly to not at all helpful'. Over half presented within 2 weeks of experiencing psychotic symptoms, but had been experiencing prodromal symptoms for between 2 and 6 months. Approximately, a quarter of individuals sought help themselves, but more usually a family member, usually the mother, first raised concerns with the GP.

The take-home message here is that GPs need a high index of suspicion and a low threshold for urgently referring a young person with a severe mental health crisis for specialist mental health assessment. It is particularly important that GPs are encouraged to listen to and act on family/parental concerns. Diagnostic uncertainty is the norm and such GP referral behaviour should be reinforced positively by EIPs. It is also important that helpful treatment options are offered to those who do not turn out to have psychosis but nevertheless need support and advice.

Case study

Steve was an academically bright teenager who suddenly appeared to lose interest in school and became defiant. Life at home became punctuated by frequent arguments, having previously related well to his family. He had several failed attempts to leave home, usually returning within a few weeks. After about a year, aged 18, he consulted his GP and was referred to psychology. The records describe treatment for anxiety with over-valued ideas but after three attendances, he declined further input. After a year of 'oddness', friends suggested to Steve that he might have schizophrenia after watching a programme on TV. His mother worried over Steve's paranoid thinking and preoccupation with food and his body. He returned home to his mum who took him to the family GP and assertively requested help including a request for CPN input.

As with many emotional problems, the presenting features in Steve's case were obscure. Only 7% of people in the audits showed clear evidence of psychosis, 50% reported less-specific emotional and psychological changes, 37% reported purely physical/somatic symptoms and 25% reported changes in work and social functioning. Detection is also more difficult when, as is common, psychosis takes several months to emerge from a prodrome of non-specific psychological and social disturbances of varying intensity. Indeed, it may be confused with normal adolescence, which can cause further diagnostic problems for primary care clinicians.

Case study

The waiting list to see the primary care CPN was longer than that for a psychiatrist so Steve was seen at outpatients. Complaints of low mood and hearing voices were documented and an antidepressant was prescribed with a 2-week follow-up. But in the meantime, he became acutely disturbed with delusions of grandeur and was directed back to his GP by his mother. The GP noted the bizarre behaviour but took no action until the mother returned the same day insisting something be done immediately. He was seen by the Consultant Psychiatrist and admitted that day.

The issue here is not simply that the GPs were poor at detecting psychosis. Often, the systems of specialist care do not support easy access. Indeed, one audit (n = 45) revealed that only one successful engagement with EIP took place through a psychiatric outpatient clinic. Of more importance is that parental fears and intuition were frequently ignored, in part explaining why it took between three and five contacts to achieve a successful pathway to care. The learning point for EIS is the need to think about how they make themselves accessible to GPs for discussing cases (pre-referral liaison) and facilitating youth-sensitive engagements.

Case study

Mathew, 18 years old, became obsessional and irritable over about 2 years, coinciding with him leaving home to start college. His tutor noticed a gradual deterioration in his attendance and that he appeared unable to concentrate and organise himself. The tutor particularly noticed that he returned, after the Easter break, apparently dressed in the same clothes. The tutor was sufficiently concerned about his physical and mental well-being that she actively sought help for him by contacting social services. Social services would not intervene without a self- or a GP referral. Once social services were involved, psychiatric assessment was arranged.

As Mathew's story illustrates, pathways to care can involve other community and youth agencies such as schools, colleges probation, housing and welfare services (see Table 12.2). Knowledge of local pathways may help EIS to identify these various agencies and liaise with them in terms of joint working and training issues.

Case study

Diane, aged 16, became increasingly withdrawn over a period of a few months. She had used cannabis and amphetamines. She had seemed troubled and less interested in her schoolwork, but it was not until a holiday away with a friend that it became more obvious that Diane might be unwell. On her return to school, her teacher noticed she seemed distant and preoccupied. Prompted by the teacher and her ex-husband, Diane's mum took her to see her GP. Diane revealed some paranoid thinking that included a description of the TV and radio talking to her. The GP felt she may have a psychosis and requested an urgent psychiatric opinion.

Diane's story demonstrates that the onset of psychosis is not constrained by age criteria. However, primary care is a cradle-to-grave service, and the pathways barrier for many people between the ages of 14 and 17 is difficulties in accessing a Child and Adolescent Mental Health Service (CAMHS). Typically, long waiting lists are compounded by services that are not necessarily equipped to deal with people with psychosis. As one mother in the audit stated: *Our daughter went from a CAMHS service that didn't do psychosis to an adult service that didn't do young people.*

If a 16-year old presents with ambiguous symptoms currently, they still risk sitting outside services until 17, by which time they may have an unambiguous and severe mental health problem that then causes them to be acutely admitted to an adult service under the Mental Health Act.

Case study

The EDEN study of 14 EIS across the West Midlands found that while there were some problems from the EIS perspective in terms of entry criteria and pathways to care, an even more worrying issue was the lack of exit strategies from EIS at the end of the 2–3-year treatment period. Most services had neither time nor staff capacity to make clear links with primary care and individuals were frequently discharged from a 'gold standard' service to primary care without prior notification or a plan for follow-up. Whilst all EIS prided themselves on their youth-sensitive approach, their community setting and their active strategies for assertively engaging young people once a referral had been made, few recognised the important role that primary care has to play in the referral pathway or the need to work in close partnership with the sector to improve entry and exit strategies (personal communication).

Indicators within the 2006 GP contract Quality and Outcomes Framework (QOF) now encourage GPs to document a 'comprehensive care plan' in the primary care record that should include a list of the individual's early warning signs and require the practice to actively follow up any one who has not attended their annual health check. However, people are still likely to fall through the pavement cracks between primary care and EIS if the two services do not actively liaise and work in partnership to ensure clear channels of communication and define agreed roles and responsibilities.

Developing an educational strategy

In Birmingham (UK), we have developed an educational programme in primary care to help GPs recognise and act appropriately when they see a young person with an FEP. The educational intervention is 'complex' in that it comprises a number of interconnected components that are likely to interact with one another. The programme was developed as the intervention in the REDIRECT study, a cluster randomised controlled trial (RCT) involving individuals with FEP in over 100 practices in Birmingham (Tait *et al.*, 2005). The REDIRECT study's hypothesis is that GPs in the 50 intervention practices who have received the educational intervention will refer young people with FEP more frequently and at an earlier stage to the EIS than those in the 50 control practices who have not participated in the educational intervention.

In developing the REDIRECT RCT and educational intervention, the study team adhered closely to the Medical Research Council (MRC) complex intervention framework (Campbell *et al.*, 2000), which provides guidance on using a stepped approach to the development and evaluation of complex interventions. This phased approach separates the different questions being asked and helps researchers establish the probable active components of the intervention.

We wanted to ensure that the training package addressed knowledge, attitudes and behaviours and was theoretically sound. We therefore developed the intervention through a combination of searching the literature for good practice, focus groups with GPs and individuals with FEP to gain a better understanding of the specific barriers to early recognition of FEP in primary care and mailing a short training needs analysis questionnaire to assess knowledge gaps to 50 GPs across the West Midlands.

The outcome of the theoretical and modelling work suggested the educational intervention needed to impart knowledge about important symptoms and signs evident in FEP, teach core questioning skills and encourage more positive attitudes towards young people with FEP. The REDIRECT study team therefore worked with a Birmingham-based EIS to develop a 17-minute video/CD-ROM with professional actors that included four vignettes showing how young people may present with an FEP in a primary care setting. The scenarios showed young people from different family backgrounds, some in education and others in work, confused and often frightened by their symptoms. The video also contained short discussion segments

between an acknowledged international expert in FEP and a GP, on issues such as symptoms and signs to be alert for in FEP, suggestions for how to phrase questions and the importance of referring all people with suspected FEP for specialist mental health assessment.

Specifically, the video imparted knowledge about key 'alert' indicators for FEP, suggesting that psychosis rarely presents 'out of the blue'. Warning symptoms of possible psychological vulnerability demonstrated on the video included:

1 irritability
2 losing concentration
3 depression
4 anxiety
5 feeling uneasy
6 constant tiredness
7 suspiciousness
8 rudeness
9 withdrawal from friends

The video vignettes and discussion sections highlighted the fact that psychosis rarely presents with a neat symptom parcel, and that positive and negative symptoms are rarely volunteered spontaneously and may need to be actively sought. If GPs suspect a developing psychosis, they were encouraged to ask the person about changes in other areas of life such as:

1 Social functioning, for example problems in relationships with friends and family;
2 Cognition, for example poor concentration and memory;
3 Mood, for example feeling depressed, anxious or irritable;
4 Thought content, for example preoccupation with strange thoughts or ideas (ideas of reference, delusions of harm, persecution or grandeur, auditory hallucinations);
5 Drug misuse;
6 Suicidal ideas.

If they had concerns, the video stressed the importance of keeping an 'active watching brief', to ensure that a line of communication and offer of care is maintained wherever possible through follow-up appointments, home visits or a telephone call. The video also included a vignette of a mother seeking help for her daughter and best practice in terms of the GP listening to and acting on the mother's concerns and proactively engaging with the young person through a home visit.

As aides-memoires and reinforcing information increase the effectiveness of an educational intervention, we also provided a short booklet reinforcing the information given in the video, and an A4-laminated checklist of key symptoms and questions which GPs could refer to easily in a consultation.

A booster session, held 6 months after the initial educational session, aimed to reinforce knowledge and skills gained in the initial educational session and to further encourage more positive attitudes towards young people with FEP. To help facilitate attitude change, two users of an EIS were invited to give a short talk describing their personal experiences of FEP. One, a secondary school teacher, used a short video she had made describing her experiences and then gave an update on her recovery. Both users gave GPs an insight into how profoundly the illness had affected their and their families' lives, how the psychosis had emerged, the role of primary care and their subsequent recovery. The video and talk were followed by an opportunity for the GPs to ask questions and discuss any issues raised by the session. The fact that GPs were in essence being educated by a service user who had been a secondary school teacher who had recovered to the point of now working as a paid member of an EIS also helped to disconfirm negative stereotypes of young people with FEP.

An evaluation of the training (Lester *et al.*, 2005b) showed that the most valued aspect of the initial video training was information about the symptoms and signs of FEP. The booster session was also well received, with most GPs agreeing it was effective in reinforcing their awareness and knowledge of FEP. Many GPs also commented positively on the unique opportunity it provided to gain an insight about FEP and recovery from a patient's perspective.

Implications for the future and conclusions

Early intervention is everyone's business. The incidence of FEP may be low at an individual practice level but the consequences for the person and their family can be devastating and long lasting. We know GPs are key pathway players, typically prompted by help-seeking initiated by families. Furthermore, the GP role may become even more important as the markers for those at highest risk (the so-called at-risk-mental-state) become more refined, as witness research which increasingly shows that very early detection and intervention may reduce the progression to psychosis (McGorry *et al.*, 2002; Morrison & French, 2004). We now await evidence for whether these findings can be translated into practical interventions that are widely available.

For primary care, the implications of these studies are considerable. They could, for example, shift the focus towards GP recognition and flagging up of those with key 'alert' indicators and a different access route to a youth-orientated specialist assessment and psychological treatment service. What may be needed is a way of working in which EIS recognise the strengths of primary care: the knowledge of the individual before the onset of psychosis, the ongoing relationship with the family and the long-term continuity of care that goes beyond the 3 years of EIS involvement. Indeed, the relationship between families and primary care and 'being in it for the long term' is a fundamental modus operandi of primary care. Armed with this understanding, EIS might consider a marketing strategy for the 'middle ground' of primary care. To sell the 'at risk mental state' concept to GPs, EIS must talk 'family practice' and 'young people with an acute mental health crisis'.

In summary, primary care practitioners need easy access to specialist advice and assessment for individuals with suspected FEP who could in turn be engaged within its less stigmatising and more easily accessible environment. EIS also have a role to play in helping to address GP knowledge gaps and attitudes towards young people with FEP. When such levels of partnership working are achieved, care pathways may be shorter and less traumatic and the Early

Psychosis Declaration an interesting historical footnote!

Suggested further reading

Shiers, D. & Lester, H. (2004). Early intervention for first episode psychosis. *British Medical Journal*, 328, 1451–1452.

Lester, H. (2001). 10-minute consultation: First episode psychosis. *British Medical Journal*, 323, 1408.

Useful website addresses

http://www.iris-initiative.org.uk

This UK EI website has a section devoted to practitioner learning which contains primary care guidance, endorsed by the Royal Colleges of GPs, Royal College of Psychiatrists and the British Psychological Society. Fact sheets, DVDs and articles can be viewed.

http://www.psychosissucks.ca/epi/

This Canadian website (Fraser South Early Psychosis Intervention (EPI) Program) promotes early detection, educates about psychosis and provides direction for seeking help.

http://www.eppic.org.au/

This Australian website described the work of the EPPIC group and includes information on a wide range of resources such as training manuals, videos and DVDs.

References

Betolote, J. & McGorry, P. (2005). Early intervention and recovery for young people with early psychosis: Consensus statement. *British Journal of Psychiatry*, 187, s116–s119.

Bindman, J., Johnson, S., Wright, S. *et al.* (1997). Integration between primary and secondary services in the care of the severely mentally ill: Patients' and general practitioners' views. *British Journal of Psychiatry*, 171, 169–174.

Brown, J., Weich, S., Downes-Grainger, E. & Goldberg, D. (1999). Attitudes of inner city GPs to shared care for psychiatric patients in the community. *British Journal of General Practice*, 49, 643–644.

Burnett, R., Mallett, R., Bhugra, G., Hutchinson, G., Der, G. & Leff, J. (1999). The first contact of patients with schizophrenia with psychiatric services: Social factors and pathways to care in multi-ethnic population. *Psychological Medicine*, 29, 475–483.

Burns, T., Greenwood, N., Kendrick, T. & Garland, C. (2000). Attitudes of general practitioners and community mental health team staff towards the locus of care for people with chronic psychotic disorders. *Primary Care Psychiatry*, 6, 67–71.

Campbell, M., Fitzpatrick, R., Haines, A. *et al.* (2000). Framework for designing an evaluation of complex interventions to improve health. *British Medical Journal*, 321, 694–696.

Jenkins, R., McCulloch, A., Friedli, L. & Park, C. (2002). *Developing a National Mental Health Policy*. London: Maudsley Monograph.

Kai, J., Crosland, A. & Drinkwater, C. (2000). Prevalence of enduring and disabling mental illness in the inner city. *British Journal of General Practice*, 50, 922–924.

Lang, F., Johnstone, E.C. & Murray, G.D. (1997). Service provision for people with schizophrenia: Role of the general practitioner. *British Journal of Psychiatry*, 171, 165–168.

Lester, H.E., Tritter, J. & Sorohan, H. (2005a). Patients and health professionals' views on primary care for people with serious mental illness: Focus group study. *British Medical Journal*, 330, 1122–1127.

Lester, H.E., Tait, L., Khera, A. & Birchwood, M. (2005b). The development and evaluation of an educational intervention on first episode psychosis for primary care. *Medical Education*, 39, 1006–1014.

Marshall, M., Lewis, S., Lockwood, A., Drake, R., Jones, P. & Croudace, T. (2005). Association between duration if untreated psychosis and outcome in cohorts of first episode patients. *Archives of General Psychiatry*, 6, 975–983.

McGorry, P., Yung, A., Phillips, L., Yuen, H. *et al.* (2002). Randomized controlled trial of interventions designed to reduce the risk of progression to first-episode psychosis in a clinical sample with sub threshold symptoms. *Archives of General Psychiatry*, 59, 921–928.

Mental After Care Association (1999). *First National GP Survey of Mental Health in Primary Care*. London: MACA.

Morrison, A., French, P., Walford, L. *et al.* (2004). Cognitive therapy for the prevention of psychosis in people at ultra-high risk: Randomized controlled trial. *British Journal of Psychiatry*, 185, 291–297.

Skeate, A., Jackson, C., Birchwood, M. & Jones, C. (2002). Duration of untreated psychosis and pathways to care in first-episode psychosis. *British Journal of Psychiatry*, 181, s73–s77.

Tait, L., Lester, H., Birchwood, M., Freemantle, N. & Wilson, S. (2005). Design of the BiRmingham Early Detection In untREated psyChosis Trial (REDIRECT): Cluster randomised controlled trial of general practitioner education in detection of first episode psychosis [ISRCTN87898421]. *BMC health services research*, 5 (1), 19.

Notes

1. North Staffs Pathways to Care prospective audit, n = 45 (Macmillan *et al.*, 1998/1999, unpublished).

Worcester Pathways to Care retrospective audit, n = 30 and GP workshop, n = 26 (Smith, 2000, unpublished).

Walsall Pathways to Care audit using casenotes review and structured interviews with individuals and families, n = 18 (Rayne, 2002, unpublished).

Gloucester GP Postal questionnaire, n = 15 (Davis, 2002, unpublished).

Chapter 13 **Raising community awareness for early psychosis**

Kate Macdonald and Paul Blackburn

Introduction

Early intervention (EI) services aim through intensive support to enable young people to get on with their lives rather than becoming long-term users of mental health services. Longer duration of untreated psychosis (DUP) is associated with worse symptoms and functioning, and less chance of remission in people with first episode psychosis (Marshall *et al.*, 2005). Raising awareness and reducing the stigma associated with psychosis in the general population are core components of EI. However, EI teams are rarely commissioned with the capacity to deliver a comprehensive early detection strategy.

Reducing stigma is key to improving help seeking in young people and their families and in enabling people to live ordinary lives in the future. This is not a simple task reflected in a recent report from the National Office of Statistics on Attitudes to Mental Illness (2007) which found that, overall, positive attitudes towards people with mental illness has actually decreased since 1994 (DH, 2004). This is despite a comprehensive policy drive launched via the National Service Framework (NSF) in 1999 (National Office of Statistics, 2007). Standard One (NSF) includes a requirement for health and social services to combat discrimination and promote social inclusion. The Social Exclusion Unit indicated that despite a number of campaigns aimed at addressing stigma and discrimination, there had been no significant change in attitudes with many people fearing to disclose their condition and less than 4 in 10 employers saying they would recruit someone with a mental health problem. In a follow-up report to the NSF it was restated that there is a need to tackle social exclusion for people experiencing mental health problems, to improve employment prospects and to oppose stigma and discrimination (DH, 2004). 'From Here to Equality' was published in 2004, a five-year plan (2004–2009) which aims to tackle stigma and discrimination on mental health grounds (NIMHE, 2004a). This strategy recognises the need for a sustained programme of work across government and in partnership with the voluntary and private sectors. It is also important to acknowledge that providing information on the causes and consequences of mental illness on its own does not change people's attitudes or behaviour. The strategy was developed following the recommendations of a scoping review which was undertaken on behalf of NIMHE by Mentality, Mental Health Media and Rethink, which made the following recommendations (Crepaz *et al.*, 2004).

1 Users and carers are involved throughout in the design, delivery, monitoring and evaluation of anti-discrimination programmes.
2 National programmes that support local activity demonstrate the most potent combination for efficacy.
3 Programmes should address behaviour change with a range of approaches.
4 Clear consistent messages are delivered in targeted ways to specific audiences.
5 Long-term planning and funding underpins programme sustainability.
6 Programmes should be appropriately monitored and evaluated.

The priority audiences include young people, the public sector, private, voluntary and professional organisations and the media and public.

Shift is part of the Care Services Improvement Partnership (CSIP) and was established in 1994 to build on the work of the Mind Out for Mental Health Campaign which ran between 2001 and 2004. It is a 5-year initiative which aims to tackle stigma and discrimination surrounding mental health issues. Shift's work programme is focusing on areas where people experience the most discrimination; the media, public organisations and employment (DH, 2006).

It is important that EI teams link in with this national work and there are opportunities to do so. However, what can they do on a local basis to raise awareness around the existence of their team, to reduce the stigma associated with mental health services and to raise specific awareness of psychosis? This chapter explores these questions, reviews the evidence base and gives a specific focus on approaches to engage with the local media.

The evidence

There have been a number of studies specific to EI teams which explore the impact of a multi-faceted media and education campaign aiming to reduce the DUP.

The TIPS Project (Early Treatment and Intervention in Psychosis) was an early example of this (Larsen *et al.*, 2001). As part of a multi-site international EI study, it targeted health care providers, education and the public through an education campaign delivered via radio, newspaper, cinema and TV media advertisements. Materials were distributed to every household across the county of Rogaland, Norway. They found that public awareness around psychosis increased from 45% to 73% and schizophrenia from 68% to 80% (Johannessen *et al.*, 2001). Help seeking increased and DUP was reduced from 1½ years to 6 months. A more recent study from the project reported that whilst numbers of first episode cases appeared at about the same rate over the two sites, the DUP differed significantly in the early detection area with a median DUP of 5 weeks compared with 16 weeks in the area without early detection (Melle *et al.*, 2004).

Another study carried out as part of the Early Psychosis Intervention Programme (EPIP) in Singapore found that a combination of public education and networking with primary health care providers reduced DUP from a median of 12 to 4 months in the experimental group. There was also an increase in the number of self and family referrals and a fall in police referrals (Chong *et al.*, 2005).

In Australia, the Compass Strategy (Wright *et al.*, 2006) used a health promotion model to guide the development, implementation and evaluation of a community awareness campaign aimed specifically at young people with the aim of improving mental health literacy and earlier help seeking amongst this group. The programme used the Precede–Proceed Model (Green & Kreuter, 1999) which incorporates development, implementation and evaluation phases. During the precede phase, priority intervention targets are established. These targets guide the development of the intervention stage (proceed), the impact of which is tracked through evaluation on factors identified as important targets in the assessment process.

The evaluation focused on process and impact of the programme. The process evaluation enabled a dynamic process of adjustment in response to problems or deficits. The impact was primarily measured by a telephone survey with independent samples of young people in both the experimental and comparison regions. Results of the process evaluation found that the website was the most frequently used resource. The most effective referral sources for the website were newspapers, schools, posters and general practitioners. Schools requested the most printed materials. The impact evaluation showed higher recall of mental health campaigns in the experimental region. Three factors showed significant change:

1 Beliefs regarding the risk of suicide associated with depression and psychosis increased or stabilised in the experimental region whilst it declined in the comparison region.
2 'Thinking that nothing can help' decreased as a barrier to help seeking in the experimental region compared whereas in the comparison region this belief was either stable or increases.
3 Self-identified depression significantly increased in the experimental region.

The evaluation also showed that there was a significant increase in help seeking in the experimental area during the implementation phase. Perceived prevalence of mental health problems also increased.

These studies demonstrate that comprehensive educational and media awareness raising strategies can impact on knowledge of psychosis and in help-seeking behaviour. In the UK, there have been no comparable studies specifically around raising awareness of psychosis although there has been work focusing on particular target groups, for example, with general practitioners (Tait *et al.*, 2005). However, there is an increasing momentum in the UK in campaigns which target mental health issues across the board on a national basis. Shift was described in the previous section but in addition, other initiatives which sit with voluntary sector organisations are gathering pace and complimenting this work.

The 'See Me' Campaign was launched in Scotland in 2002 through its website www.seemescotland.org.uk. It is an alliance of five Scottish mental health organisations (Highland Users Group, National Schizophrenia Fellowship (Scotland), Penumbra, The Royal College of Psychiatrists (Scottish Division) and the Scottish Association for Mental Health). The campaign combines local action, ongoing work with the media and periodic high profile advertising and PR activity supported by mass circulation of campaign materials. *See Me* follows a similar process and evaluation model to the Compass Project.

In July 2007, The Big Lottery announced £16 million in funding matched by £2 million from Comic Relief for 'Moving People', a 4-year programme which aims to emulate the success of See Me and other similar campaigns such as 'Like Minds Like Mine' in New Zealand. Like See Me, this is a partnership of mental health charities led by Mental Health Media, Mind, Rethink and the Institute of Psychiatry. This is the largest award for mental health ever given to a voluntary sector led initiative.

Scotland in 2003 and now England in 2007 have adopted a training programme aimed at the general public called Mental Health First Aid (MHFA). The programme was developed in Australia and is based on the principles of First Aid for physical health. It equips trainees with the skills to recognise symptoms, how to help in a crisis and how to guide people to access mental health services should it be necessary. The 12-hour course is aimed at front-line public sector workers and agencies, community groups, voluntary organisations and a range of public services as well as the general population. It includes a session on psychosis and the English version has been adapted to reflect current policy around EI services. A review of evaluation studies undertaken in Australia revealed statistically significant benefits 5–6 months post-training: improved concordance with health professionals about treatments, improved helping behaviour and greater confidence in providing help to others and decreased social distance from people with mental disorders.

Implementation into practice

The establishment in the UK of EI teams is seen as one of the strongest examples of a social movement to gain health improvement. The service style of EI means teams are already working alongside other organisations outside mental health services to enable young people to live ordinary lives (as per the aims of the WHO Early Psychosis Declaration, Bertolote & McGorry, 2005). Many have developed their own promotional materials and offer training around psychosis to target groups in the community. However, as studies described earlier and national policy states, providing information on the causes and consequences of mental illness on its own does not change people's attitudes or behaviour. Very few EI teams have been commissioned with the capacity to deliver a comprehensive programme. Clearly it makes sense for EI teams to link their awareness raising strategies to national initiatives. The challenge is for service leads to keep a handle on all the developments and strategies which are being implemented. There is recognition that the NHS is poor at taking a systems-based approach to implementing change. A Trust may have a social inclusion lead or health promotion department but that does not mean they necessarily liaise with EI as a matter of routine. EI teams need to take a proactive opportunistic approach in

Table 13.1 Engaging with the media

The media is interested in circulation and audience, not in campaigning for the well-being of the section of the population who experience mental health difficulties. Indeed in a recent survey commissioned by Shift it was found that 27% of newspaper reporting about mental health involved homicides or acts of violence with mental health service users are quoted in only 6% of the reports. The idea that mental illness is equated with violence is constant.

The media can, however be engaged in reporting 'human stories' or events/developments that are 'out of the ordinary'. The following are events/activities associated with PSYPHER which have attracted or achieved media attention. They are events and activities that are typical of EI services and have the potential to offer a different story to the general public.

engaging with leads locally and regionally looking at common agendas across policy frameworks to achieve their objectives.

The remainder of this chapter will focus on approaches PSYPHER (Psychosis Service for Young People in Hull and East Riding) has used to create partnerships with other organisations with the aim of raising awareness and delivering a comprehensive service which enables young people to get on with their lives. It will also look at strategies we have used to engage with the local media (Table 13.1).

PSYPHER is a stand-alone service which was officially launched in October 2004 but a project working initially to a hub-and- spoke model had existed for a number of years prior to this.

PSYPHER attempts to create a psychosocial culture in relation to client work and this means that the engagement of and collaboration with families and significant others is core service activity. Considerable focus is put on the 'fabric' of the everyday lives of service users. This involves attending to issues of social inclusion, daily activity (encouraging the continuation or initiation of education, training or employment), housing, etc. and having a belief and expectation that the young person can and will get on with their life. In addition, PSYPHER aims to bring about a cultural shift in how mental health difficulties are thought of and how services are delivered within the mental health system and in the wider community.

PSYPHER has taken an opportunistic approach in how it has delivered its health awareness raising strategies. It is acknowledged that this is not the ideal way to go about things. However, the team has never had specific funding to do this work. Until early 2006, it did have a strategic

lead who had the capacity to oversee the development of the team (holder of the vision) influencing the establishment of its culture to be one that reflected the aspirations of the EI programme rather than becoming just *better* treatment as usual. The lead was also able to engage with stakeholders on a strategic level to build links with external partners and develop initiatives aimed at both providing a comprehensive service but also raising awareness in the community at the same time.

One early piece of work was the Connexions-funded 'Making a Difference' Project. This was a national pilot for Connexions which created strong links between agencies, including Connexions Humber, CAMHS (Inter-Agency Link Team) and Hull and East Yorkshire Mind. It demonstrated how mental health and educational services can work together to develop a model that enables early detection and referral, and the training of a broad range of front-line staff. Developing a strong relationship with Connexions was a key way to open the door to a range of agencies who work with young people including education and youth agencies which is essential to reduce DUP and enable young people to re-engage with their lives quicker. As a result of this project, two senior primary care mental health workers were funded by the Primary Care Trusts in Hull and Behaviour Improvement Programme (BIP) in four schools with the aim of rolling the model out across the city. This project resulted in newspaper articles and a radio interview.

Creative activity and sport as a 'Hook' for media coverage

Service users are at the centre of PSYPHER's promotional activities. Following our experience of an Arts Council funded Arts in Health project (Pass It On), we recognised the positive impact creative activity had in acting as a catalyst to build confidence and enable service users to develop or improve their skills. We supported a bid for the development of a new service called Creative Connexions which is now a core funded project housed within Connexions Humber and have worked on a number of projects with them over the past 4 years. Service users designed our promotional materials and have made a number of films which we have used to raise the profile of the service. The team was also able to initiate a partnership with Leeds Xscape to offer snowboarding lessons to service users. A team member happened to also be a snowboard instructor at Xscape and was able to use this link to set up the programme promising media coverage. Again, we found that sport was an excellent way to increase the confidence of service users. It also provided an excellent media 'hook' with an article being written in a local magazine which went to every house in the city.

Our launch event was our first opportunity to actively engage with the media. BBC Humberside spent a day with the team talking to staff and service users about their experiences of psychosis and PSYPHER. A film crew came to Xscape to film a snowboarding lesson and this was shown on the early evening Look North programme. The launch itself was targeted at a range of audiences. It took place in the nightclub 'Asylum' at the University of Hull. The morning was taken up with formal presentations to professionals in agencies working with young people across Hull and East Riding. In the afternoon, a number of organisations including Creative Connexions, Hull and East Yorkshire Mind and the Warren (a youth agency in Hull) provided creative workshops in drama, dj-ing and various creative activities. In the evening, we had our first benefit gig again at the university profiling popular local bands and aimed at university students. A week later we had another gig at the Adelphi, a music club in Hull at which service users performed alongside local bands and dj's. These gigs were highly successful and we continue to put these on with

service users taking an active role in the design of promotional literature and organisation of the events. In 2006 we again worked with Creative Connexions and the Trust Arts in Health Department, on a music and creative arts project which culminated in a gig. A cd was produced of featured bands from the night with artwork developed by service users and promotional information on the service. These were given out free on the night. We also worked with film students from the University of Lincoln as part of their final year project to make an advert for the event which was shown hourly on the BBC Big Screen in the City Centre. This enabled us to communicate information on the service to a wider audience of shoppers.

From its origins in the local park, 'PSYPHER Tigers' football club was formed. Made up of service users, the club plays in a corporate league locally, and has been supported by a £10,000 grant from the Football Association. Service users wanted the team to be identified with PSYPHER because they are keen to contribute to the reduction of stigma associated with psychosis and demonstrate that they are 'normal' young people who just happen to have experienced psychosis. This was reported (with a team photograph) in the Hull Daily Mail. Hull City Football Club is keen to work with the team to contribute to the awareness raising campaign.

What all of the above activities have in common is that they have involved little or no cost to the EI team. Prior to every event we issued a press release which has resulted in coverage on local listings websites, newspapers and Radio Humberside. Publicity materials included flyers with information on the back about the service focused at different audiences. For example, the last campaign was entitled 'Keep Your Mate in Mind'. Materials are funded by the money we take on the door. This is a demonstration of how using activity which has a therapeutic impact can also be used to generate media coverage.

In recognition of the value of this work and the talent we saw amongst our service users, a social enterprise was established in 2006 called Jellycat Media Limited in partnership with Creative Connexions. When PSYPHER no longer had funding for its strategic lead, it became more difficult to continue with these activities since the team was increasingly pressured due to issues with capacity and funding. Jellycat works closely with PSYPHER and has taken over the management of promotional activity. It also supports staff to continue developing creative projects within the team and provides creative workshops which PSYPHER had established. This can be the first stage in building confidence and skills to enable an individual to be ready to access mainstream programmes provided by other organisations. Jellycat also provides a multimedia business service (including graphic design, web design and film production) giving young people who have experienced mental health problems opportunities to gain work experience working alongside freelance professionals. Future plans are to formalise an accreditation framework and to develop an apprenticeship programme enabling participants to be employed in the future. Jellycat aims to reduce the stigma of mental illness and demonstrate that young people, by training and working in the creative arts, can and do get on with their lives. A number of service users have already gone on to access training in music technology and event management and offer active support to Jellycat work.

A further core activity of Jellycat is to raise awareness of mental health problems and the need to seek help earlier through the development of innovative training materials geared to the needs of different organisations and the wider community. The organisation is currently working with CSIP on the adaptation and design of its MHFA materials for England. Service users also have the opportunity to receive training in delivering mental health awareness training and be paid for the training they provide alongside professional staff.

Implications and conclusions

This chapter reviewed national policy strategies to raise awareness and looked at the evidence base for delivering strategies focussing on psychosis. It was established that in order to effect behavioural and attitudinal change, any intervention has to be comprehensive. Whilst there are issues around EI teams receiving funding

to develop stand-alone campaigns, there are a number of exciting national initiatives developing in the UK which EI can *piggy-back* on to. It is important that team leaders remain alert to opportunities to influence this work, supported by their local and regional leads to do so. It is still essential that EI teams establish partnerships with local agencies in pursuit of their clinical objectives and given the style of working, this offers natural opportunities to engage the local media in reporting stories which raise the profile of their service. The experience of PSYPHER demonstrates that it is possible to develop projects with service users which both have therapeutic impact and contribute towards the goal of influencing the reduction of stigma in the general community.

References

Bertolote, J. & McGorry, P. (2005). Early intervention and recovery for young people with early psychosis: Consensus statement. *British Journal of Psychiatry*, 187 (Suppl. 48), s116–s119.

Chong, S.A., Mythily, S. & Verma, S. (2005). Reducing the duration of untreated psychosis and changing help seeking behaviour in Singapore. *Social Psychiatry and Psychiatric Epidemiology*, 40 (8), 619–621.

Crepaz Keay, D., Farmer, P., Gale E., Gibbons, M., Pinfold, V. & Seymour. L. (2004). *Scoping Review of What Works in Anti Stigma and Discrimination.* National Institute for Mental Health in England.

Department of Health (2004). *The National Service Framework – Five Years On.* London: Department of Health.

Department of Health (2006). *Action on Stigma: Promoting Mental Health, Ending Discrimination at Work.* London: Department of Health, HMSO.

Green, L.W. & Kreuter, M.W. (2001). *Health Promotion Planning: An Educational and Ecological Approach* (3rd edition) (Mayfield Publishing was purchased by McGraw-Hill in 2001; for the catalog description of this book and to order a review copy, to obtain copyright permissions to reprint from it, to identify sales agents outside the U.S. or your camps representative, go to: McGraw-Hill.

Johannessen, J.O., McGlashan, T.H., Larsen, T.K. *et al.* (2001). Early strategies for untreated first episode psychosis. *Schizophrenia Research*, 51 (1), 39–46.

Larsen, T.K., McGlashan, T.H., Johannessen, J.O. *et al.* (2001). Shortened duration of untreated first episode of psychosis: Changes in patient characteristics at treatment. *The American Journal of Psychiatry*, 158 (11), 1917–1919.

Marshall, M., Lewis, S., Lockwood, A. *et al.* (2005). Association between duration of untreated psychosis and in cohorts of first-episode outcome patients: A systematic review. *Archives of General Psychiatry*, 62, 975–983.

Melle, I., Larsen, T.K., Haahr, U. *et al.* (2004). Reducing the duration of untreated first-episode psychosis: Effects on clinical presentation. *Archives of General Psychiatry*, 61, 143–150.

National Institute for Mental Health in England (2004). *From Here to Equality*. London: NIMHE.

National Office of Statistics (2007). *Attitudes to Mental Illness*. TNS 2007, Attitudes to mental illness 2007,

Shift/CSIP. http://www.dh.gov.uk/en/Publication sandstatistics/Publications/PublicationsStatistics/ DH_076516

Tait, L., Lester, H., Birchwood, M., Freemantle, N. & Wilson, S. (2005). Design of the BiRmingham Early Detection In untREated psyChosis Trial (REDIRECT): Cluster randomised controlled trial of general practitioner education in detection of first episode psychosis [ISRCTN87898421]. *BMC Health Services Research*, 5 (1), 19.

Wright, A., McGorry, P.D., Harris, M.G., Jorm, A.F. & Pennell, K. (2006). Development and evaluation of a youth mental health community awareness campaign – The Compass Strategy. *BMC Public Health*, 6, 215.

Chapter 14 **Raising awareness in schools**

Rowena Passy, Carly Mays, Graham Carr, Glenn Roberts, John Somers and Jos Dawe

Introduction

This chapter is an exploration of the challenges and opportunities faced by one project that aimed to raise awareness about psychosis in schools and colleges. *On the Edge* was an interactive Theatre in Education (TIE) programme produced by Exstream Theatre Company that undertook a national tour between October 2004 and March 2005, performing to over 5,300 participants in 125 different audiences. Seventy-one performances were in 51 different schools and colleges where the target audience age was between 14 and 22; 9 performances were in 5 different universities where audience members consisted of staff and students; 5 performances were open to the public. The remaining 40 performances were for teachers and mental health professionals where the programme was used as a part of continuing professional development (CPD) and/or as a conference presentation. It is the performances in schools and colleges that are the focus for this discussion; we describe the challenges and opportunities that this programme brought, using data from the evaluation research to illustrate the points that we are making and to show how the programme affected some of those who participated. For the sake of brevity, throughout the chapter we refer to schools and colleges as 'schools' and to student audience members as 'participants'.

The context: Health education in schools

The foundations of good health can be laid early in life (Licence, 2004) and the central role that schools can have in health education has long been recognised (Warwick *et al.*, 2005). In the UK, there has been an increasing government

interest in this area of health promotion and health education (DfEE, 1997; DH, 1999; ODPM, 2004), and different national initiatives include the formal introduction of Personal, Social and Health Education (PSHE) into the National Curriculum (DfEE/QCA, 1999a, b) and setting up the National Healthy Schools Standard (NHSS) in 1999. The latter scheme is at the centre of the Government's goal to 'achieve a healthy population of young people' (DfES/DH, 2005, p. 1); it has the aim of helping schools to become healthy environments for pupils and staff (Schagen *et al.*, 2005) and currently has four different strands: PSHE, healthy eating, physical activity and emotional health and well-being.

The latter aspect of the NHSS can be seen as meshing with part of a greater understanding among educationalists that mental health forms a core part of children's general health (Weare, 2000; Hornby & Atkinson, 2003). Although progress in this direction can only be described as slow – a recent Ofsted report (Ofsted, 2005) suggests that teachers are largely unaware of mental health issues – a context is beginning to emerge in which awareness about mental health is gaining importance within the school environment. It is supported in principle by another government document that emphasises the importance of children's social and emotional well-being and of developing skills to strengthen their personal resilience (DfES/DH, 2005).

But how should students be educated on these matters? Clearly there are a variety of ways in which this can be done, including teacher-led and/or peer-led classroom sessions, bringing experts into schools and the so-called PSHE days where routine lessons are abandoned and the teaching day devoted to one particular topic; there are also examples of interventions where students are brought into contact with people who have mental health issues to help reduce stigma (Pinfold *et al.*, 2003; Schulze *et al.*, 2003). TIE brings a dramatic angle to such teaching; it has been a part of British educational pedagogy since the 1960s (Sextou, 2003) and has been used in areas such as sex and relationship education (Evans *et al.*, 1998), crime prevention (Allen *et al.*, 1999) and drug education (Winston, 2001). Drama's strength lies in its ability to engage participants with the narrative of the people whose story is portrayed and to encourage reflection on moral and social issues within a particular context rather than in the abstract (Winston, 1999); drama fosters empathy, whether it be with those who have been mistreated or ostracised (Day, 2002) or who provoke censure in some way (Edmiston, 2000, p. 68) by giving an understanding of the way in which different attitudes and behaviours arise. And, although it is difficult to generalise, there is broad agreement within evaluation research on TIE that both teachers and young people find drama an enjoyable, engaging and interesting way to learn about specific subject matters (Sawney *et al.*, 2003).

On the Edge can be seen as part of this tradition of teaching through drama; it uses the narrative of one young man's experience to show how psychosis affects all those close to the person who has the condition, and it offers insight into the different feelings and emotions that may be encountered in these circumstances. The programme's distinctiveness lies in the three different components of the programme, a method developed by John Somers, whose research shows that stretching audience contact with the storyline maximises its impact (Somers, 1996).

On the Edge: An interactive TIE programme on first episode psychosis

On the Edge grew out of the relationship formed between John Somers (Senior Lecturer in Applied Drama at the University of Exeter) and Dr Glenn Roberts (Consultant in Psychiatry in the Devon Partnership NHS Trust) when they collaborated in 2001 over an interactive play

that examined the effects of the foot and mouth epidemic on farming families. When Dr Roberts became the Consultant Lead for developing the early intervention (EI) service in Exeter, the partnership saw the chance to 'combat stigma, discrimination and prejudice by raising community awareness and educating 15-year olds about psychosis, alongside their teachers' (www.rethink.org/newcastledeclaration/) by creating a similar programme about first episode psychosis. As the development of the programme progressed, the national tour was designed to coincide with the formation of the EI in Psychosis teams that were being established over England in 2004/2005; the idea was to encourage links between schools and EI services by inviting members of the local EI teams and other local charities (such as Mind or Rethink) to a performance. The programme therefore had three target audiences: young people between the ages of 14 and 22 to comply with the Early Psychosis Declaration; mental health professionals to support the new EI services; teachers to inform and educate on an area in which there appears to be little formal training. And the three stated aims of the programme were to:

- Raise awareness of mental illness, specifically to increase knowledge and understanding of psychosis;
- Contribute towards reducing the stigma and discrimination surrounding mental illness;
- Raise awareness of available help and to improve help-seeking behaviour.

The programme was designed to consist of three elements that lasted for a minimum of 4 hours over 3 weeks. For the first element, the theatre company supplied a shoebox full of memorabilia which the teacher then explored with his or her class. Key questions were 'Who are these people?' and 'What is happening to them?' The intention was that the class should spend about 40 minutes – roughly the length of a lesson – to begin to develop a narrative about Terry Gardner, the central character and the (fictional) owner of the box. Participants were able to discover key facts about his life and to recognise that something was wrong but, because the box's contents gave parts of the story rather than the whole, they were unable to complete the story. In this way, the shoebox was designed to generate a sense of curiosity about what is happening to the people involved in the emerging story, to introduce facts and contextual information to save time during the performance and to generate the beginnings of an emotional attachment to the characters, particularly Terry, so that the audience would engage and empathise with his story.

The second element consisted of a 2-hour session of four parts that was brought by Exstream Theatre Company to the school approximately 1 week after the work with the shoebox. First, Graham Carr (the mental health nurse who travelled with the company and who facilitated the performance) would introduce himself and any other mental health professionals who were present, saying that they were available at the end of the 2-hour session to anyone who might want to talk. Next he would ask the students about the conclusions they had drawn from the shoebox session, reminding them of the items and allowing them to speculate further on what might be about to happen. The company would then present the play, which was designed to pick up the different threads of the shoebox and weave them into a coherent narrative; participants' familiarity with the characters was deepened into engagement with the story as they watched Terry's descent into first episode psychosis and his friends and family showing a variety of reactions. The second part was the hot seating, where the actors remained in role and the audience questioned them about feelings, motivations and actions. Students then broke up into small discussion groups, when each actor came out of role and facilitated the discussion on issues that arose from the performance. Finally Graham gave a power point presentation that clarified Terry's condition, informed on how it could be understood and showed different avenues of available help that could be sought in such circumstances. The presentation ended with a slide on which was written:

Keep it simple
Stay in touch

And, while the slide was shown on the screen, Graham said the key message of the whole programme:

Reaching out early leads to better recovery

This concluding statement was designed to be clear, easy to remember and to act as a bridge to the third and final component of the programme; it was reinforced by a postcard placed on each seat for the participants that had key points about psychosis and information on where to seek help. The final part of the programme was a classroom follow-up session approximately a week later, lasting for 1 hour. Led by the teacher and/or local EI services, it was intended to enable students to reflect on and consolidate knowledge gained through the programme. Each school was given a copy of the education pack 'Back from the Edge' that had been devised and assembled by Dr Roberts and that was intended to be used as a resource to support the session.

Evaluation

Evaluation of any arts project is complex (Woolf, 1999), and the research team decided to use both quantitative and qualitative methods to ensure a robust assessment of the way in which the programme was received. The data collected consisted of:

- Baseline questionnaires and 1-week post-performance questionnaires for students at schools, colleges and one university (from 29 institutions; not all completed both parts of this research);
- Evaluation forms from those attending non-student performances ($N = 474$);
- Interviews (72 interviews with 133 students, teachers and mental health professionals);
- Research diaries completed by the cast;
- Six-month follow-up research in schools and colleges, consisting of a shortened form of the questionnaire already used ($N = 402$) and 42 interviews with students.

As with any evaluation, the research methods have limitations. Problems with the quantitative methods rest with the smaller number of completed 1-week questionnaires than baseline, suggesting that those schools, colleges and universities who did complete both phases of the evaluation were more receptive to the project; participation in each of the qualitative methods was voluntary, which may mean that those with an interest in the subject matter were more likely to contribute to the research. Nonetheless, as we show in the conclusion, the programme had some considerable success in achieving its three aims. Let us now turn to the challenges and opportunities that arose in taking the programme into schools.

The challenges: Preparation

John Somers and Glenn Roberts convened an Advisory Group early in the development of the programme, for it had to rest on secure foundations if it were to engage the different audiences and fulfil the three aims of educating, challenging stigma and improving help-seeking behaviour. The different members of the Group, which consisted of themselves and nine others who were mental health professionals, arts therapists, service users and carers, ensured that the programme was drawn from a diversity of experiences and views, and that its development was subject to a continuous process of critical appraisal and negotiation. The challenges that the members of the Group set themselves were that the programme should be clinically relevant, portray an authentic experience and be dramatically effective; consideration was also given to the way in which participants should be cared for in the event that the programme raised personal issues that needed immediate attention.

For the programme to be clinically relevant, it needed to give accurate information to its participants. The major challenge here was to present a model of psychosis that was accessible to those who knew little about mental health issues while embracing the diversity of views on the psychotic experience that were represented within the Advisory Group. Agreement over these long-running controversies was neither expected nor reached, but a consistent focus on the educational content of the programme

for young people helped to channel the diversity of opinion into a spirit of co-operation; the result was the adoption of a broad model of psychosis that conformed with the one held by the majority of EI services. Justification of this model was included in the education pack that was given to schools and published on the NIMHE Knowledge Community (Roberts, 2004). Recognition of different approaches to treatment meant that Graham's presentation included both talking therapies and medication, although no specific drug was named. Although the Advisory Group members recognised that drug use can precipitate a psychotic episode, street drugs were not mentioned as a possible cause of psychosis because it was felt that drawing attention to the use of street drugs could distract the audience's attention from the subject of the programme – psychosis – and the issues that this particular condition might raise. In addition, they felt that to say that 'street drugs cause psychosis' risked losing credibility with the audience when young people can see for themselves that this is not always the case. These issues were recognised on the postcard that was given to all participants by including the statement:

Street drugs do not cause psychosis, but do make it worse and make recovery more difficult.

Thus the difficult issues of understanding the psychotic experience, different types of therapy and street drugs were carefully developed in recognition that the programme's portrayal may be seen as controversial.

The task of providing the audience with the portrayal of an authentic experience of psychosis was undertaken with equal care. Authenticity was used here in Heathcote's sense of 'for real' (Johnson & O'Neill, 1984, p. 175); participants were invited to become part of a young man's story that really could have happened. In this instance, the collaboration was enlarged to include drama specialists along with mental health professionals; John Somers wrote the original scenario and script fragments, which students then developed under his leadership as part of their final-year undergraduate course.

Members of the Advisory Group attended rehearsals, made contributions to the script, offered advice to the actors and invited them into mental health settings where they could gain a deeper understanding of the issues that they were bringing to life. This process ran alongside the debates on how to understand the psychotic experience and it took time, imagination and careful thought to produce a version of psychosis that was accessible, informative and non-threatening.

The last challenge for the preparation of the play was how to translate the aims of the programme in such a way that the human interest was balanced with the information carried within the drama, for it, too, needed to be authentic to be effective. Considerations here included how to include moments of light and shade together with development of the characters; dramatic techniques such as projected images to represent thoughts were used, along with stylised and naturalised drama, monologue and duologue. And, in contrast to a more conventional play that ends in some kind of dénouement, this play ended in a crisis whereupon the audience was first invited to understand the situation more deeply through hot seating each character and secondly, to move the story on in a positive fashion during the course of the discussion groups. During the development of the programme, the play was shown to schools in two separate pilot tours in order to draw on students' comments and reactions to develop the script, the hot seating and the format of the discussion groups; other influences on the programme came from teachers, particularly the Curriculum Advisor for Devon, from Carly Mays, the Project Director for Exstream Theatre Company and, in the final stages, from the professional actors who were to undertake the national tour of the programme.

The final aspect of preparation was concerned with caring for the participants, for it was anticipated that some might need immediate support after experiencing the programme while others would need help in the long-term. The issue of immediate support was resolved by NIMHE, which funded Graham Carr to travel with the company, and his duties included giving time to participants who wanted to talk after the 2-hour session was over. He also invited representatives from local EI services and mental health charities to the performance, thereby personalising the services to participants and encouraging longer-term links between schools and support systems. The long-term source of information on avenues of help had to be culturally acceptable to the student age group while not drawing attention to the person who was taking the information away. This particular challenge was solved by a postcard that had a colourful design on the front; the reverse side listed key points that had been raised during the course of the 2-hour session together with a list of websites and phone numbers where help could be accessed. One of these was placed on each chair before the 2-hour session began, allowing students to slip it unobtrusively into their bag should they so wish. In addition pens, stickers and balloons were provided by different mental health charities, all items that could be picked up simply for fun rather than showing a purpose.

Related to the issue of caring for participants, but also concerned with ensuring that the programme should run smoothly, the Project Director compiled a list of instructions and expectations that was to be sent to each participating venue. This included the rationale for the programme, explicit instructions on how to present the shoebox, instructions on the type of room required and a request that at least one teacher be present during the company visit in view of the sensitive nature of the subject matter. Contact teachers were encouraged to ring the company if they had any questions or difficulties with complying with the requests.

And so, at the end of 2 years of development, the tour began in October 2004 with the play, the actors and the different aspects of the 2-hour session as thoroughly and as carefully prepared as possible. In the next two sections, we discuss the challenges and the opportunities involved with touring the programme. Here we use comments from the evaluation data to illustrate the general points that we are making and to show the kind of impact that the programme had on different people. All comments are anonymous to protect the identity of the different people concerned.

The challenges: Touring

One of the major challenges of any tour is recognising how many people it was possible to reach within a given time and with the available funding. The balance here is important, for reaching too few people means that the programme is initially less attractive to funders or, when resources have been given, that the funders are provided with poor value for money. On the other hand, over-optimism means that the health and resilience of the cast suffers, with the possible result that the impact of the programme on the target audience can be diminished. Clearly we wanted to reach as many people as possible – and over 5,300 people is a considerable achievement – but we think, with hindsight, that the 6-month tour was too long for one cast of actors. The combination of the number of performances, the 6-month duration of the tour, the geographical area covered, the draining nature of the subject matter and the demands of the interactivity placed some strain on the cast and, by the end, they were very tired.

The other important challenge was creating an environment in which students could gain maximum educational benefit from the programme. The biggest issue in this context was time. Teachers are busy and a competitive education environment (Tomlinson, 2001) that places a premium on testing (Gorard *et al.*, 2002) means that there is little room for manoeuvre within the formal curriculum. *On the Edge* was relatively easily justified if it was booked through the subjects of Psychology or Health and Social Care, for instance, but the situation was less clear when the programme was booked through Drama or through PSHE:

The problem is that the PSHE programme is set ... for the whole year. It's very difficult to kind of squeeze this in ... I think it's enormously worthwhile and I think we ought to be more creative about this all the time ... but other people within the school don't feel it is and ... we're always playing that kind of, you know, push-me pull-you sort of game (male drama teacher, interview).

The lack of available curriculum time also affected the quality of support for the different components of the programme. In one school, for example, the (drama) teacher presented the shoebox and then asked the pupils in her class to devise a short piece on what they thought the programme was about, but in other schools the shoebox was shown to the class shortly before the theatre company arrived or, in some cases, not shown at all. While the effect of this is difficult to quantify, the cast diaries recorded a correlation between the students' preparation and the way that the performance was received:

The audience ... were very enthusiastic, especially during the hot seating. I thought it worth noting that the pupils seemed quite knowledgeable about the contents of the shoebox which suggested to me they had been well prepped. This seems to make such a difference to how schools receive this project. There is a pattern forming here. It seems like the better prepared an audience is, the more receptive they are to the performance and workshop (performance 53).

During the performance there were varying levels of support from teachers, ranging from wholehearted assistance and encouragement from all school staff who attended to no teachers present for the 2-hour session, despite the request that someone should be there. Lack of teacher support was frustrating for the cast and, at times, made their job of encouraging discussion and reflection difficult:

It was very frustrating to work with such a seemingly engaged group and yet receive no support from the staff around us. The teacher in the session talked throughout and even handed my group a register to fill out [during the discussion groups] (performance 19).

Finally, our research shows that 21 schools (41%) held a follow-up session and that 11 (22%) did not; 19 schools (37%) provided no data on this question. The reasons given for this suggest that this final session depended in part on the teacher's commitment to the programme. This, in turn, seemed to rest on their personal interest in mental health issues, their confidence in tackling the subject and their ability to create the necessary space; a quotation from a PSHE co-ordinator illustrates the low priority that training on/awareness of mental health issues is given in some schools:

> This is the first time, as a teacher, I ever seen anything to do with mental health and I've been a teacher for about nine years now ... I learned a huge amount from it, absolute huge amount ... You're now open to the fact that yeah, maybe that person's got it (male PSHE co-ordinator, interview).

These points suggest that the way that the project is brought into the school is of critical importance. In this case, the programme could have been more explicitly linked to other areas within PSHE through being framed as a way of exploring mental health issues within the context of EI; this opens links to topics such as obesity, bullying and smoking and may have encouraged thinking about mental health issues as a part of everyday life rather than a discrete area of expertise. It could also be presented as an anti-discrimination programme in the manner of, say, anti-racism initiatives, giving it a more immediate relevance to the current ethos of and movement towards inclusion within schools (DfES, 2001, p. 7).

The question of commitment to the three-part programme could be helped by a pre-performance meeting or presentation to groups of teachers to demonstrate the importance of each component of the programme, which may foster a more complete understanding of the importance of all three parts. Another suggestion could be to bring in local EI services to deliver the third part of the programme, thereby releasing teachers from the section about which they may feel uncertain. However, the central issue of including mental health issues as a formal part of every student's education remains, as yet, unaddressed; until this happens, we need to find imaginative ways of convincing schools of the importance of programmes such as ours.

Opportunities

The opportunities that this programme presented centred around making direct contact with young people and their teachers in an attempt to educate on psychosis, to challenge stigma and to leave a positive message about recovery. Interactive theatre can be a vibrant experience and the cast's diaries show levels of student engagement with the programme that were challenging and exciting:

> Very heated hot seating – one girl in particular shouted down dad (her reply to his 'do you have a mortgage?' was 'Mate! I live in the YMCA!') and grasped [the character] Scott perfectly – 'you're not really a hard man – it's all front because you're scared!' Brilliant fun! A fantastic show – lively audience clearly responding throughout (gasps, laughs etc) and very responsive in hot seating and panel. Most fun I've had in ages! (performance 90).

There were also humbling yet uplifting moments when the programme encouraged young people to talk about their own experiences:

> A young man on the front row who asked lots of questions made a public declaration that he suffered from schizophrenia, and had been hospitalised last summer. Now on medication and doing well at college – a public testimony. Wow! ... A really interesting show thanks to ... the young man who bared his soul to everyone, audience and us alike ... made the whole week worthwhile (performance 82).

This young man's declaration is a powerful illustration of the way in which the programme created a safe environment for discussion about psychosis and how he underlined two important messages of the play; mental health issues can happen to anyone and recovery is possible. Incidents such as this, together with the authentic portrayal of how families and friends are affected by psychosis, stimulated some participants into thinking in a new way about these issues:

> You stereotype like people with mental illness as being completely crazy and throwing bricks and like smashing plates and stuff like that but ...

when you saw that play, it's really good because it showed that he was just like normal and like he lived a normal life and yeah, like he did like races and things like that. But he didn't go mad, it was more in the mind than how he was acting (Year 11 female, interview).

The final opportunity was to facilitate and encourage connections between EI services, mental health charities and schools, and mental health professionals attended 31 of the school performances (61%). This was particularly important in the six schools where referrals to EI services were made immediately after the performance; one other school reported a young person seeking help soon after the company visit.

Conclusion

The evaluation shows that there were significant gains against each of the three aims of the programme. The quantitative data demonstrate a raised awareness among students about psychosis, including a belief that psychosis is a treatable condition and that a full recovery can be made; 91% of responding students felt that the intervention had helped them understand about psychosis either somewhat (55%) or a lot (36%). In the interviews, there was agreement among students that the programme had given them important information about psychosis that was empowering and that could be useful at any time in their lives.

The results for the second aim of reducing stigma are less clear-cut, but overall they suggest that the programme has had a positive effect on participants' attitudes towards mental health problems. The quantitative data shows that 53% of responding students felt it had helped their attitude towards psychosis become more positive and 89% believed they would feel more confident in supporting someone who was experiencing psychosis, while the qualitative data show the ways in which they have been encouraged to think about the complexity and reality of mental health issues. Students reported that the programme challenged stigma in a variety of thought-provoking ways, and the empathy shown towards the characters during the interviews suggests that an increased number

of students are open to the idea of helping and supporting those with mental health issues.

The final aim of the programme was to improve help-seeking behaviour and here, again, the data suggest some considerable success. The quantitative data show the number of students who knew where to seek help in the case of suspected mental illness rising from 37% in the baseline to 60% in the 1-week questionnaires (an increase of nearly 23%), with 76% of respondents reporting that they would be willing to consult a doctor. The qualitative data support and augment these findings. Almost all interviewees were able to say when and how they would access help, although this was tempered slightly by recognition that seeking and then accessing help may not be a straightforward process. The very act of seeking help implies that it is thought to be worthwhile which, in line with the quantitative data, suggests that the programme gave participants hope about recovery.

But the final word concerning the effectiveness of *On the Edge* comes from an interview with a young woman from an inner-city school in London:

... at the end they did a power point presentation thing where they told us all about it. And that, that's what shocked me, so many people had that problem and they were like Yeah, it doesn't matter what age you are, what sex, whatever, you can still get that illness ... But if you get help, it can get better. So it was like you learned more about it. because before any of this, psychosis, I thought it was well ... it's like what you see on TV, crazy people, people that are in mental homes and have like lots of problems in their life. But like, watching it made you [realise] it was something simple like his gran died. I know that's not something simple but do you know what I mean, it weren't like he was in debt and he was homeless and he didn't have no clothes, it was just his nan died and he couldn't get over it. And it makes you think; ... something that small can make something so big, make you feel that bad and that ill and that isolated (Year 10 female).

Such a comment provides a real and moving vindication of the programme.

References

Allen, G., Allen, I. & Dalrymple, L. (1999). Ideology, practice and evaluation: Developing the effectiveness of theatre in education. *Research in Drama Education*, 4 (1), 21–36.

Day, L. (2002). 'Putting yourself in other people's shoes': The use of Forum theatre to explore refuges and homeless issues in schools. *Journal of Moral Education*, 31 (1), 21–34.

Department for Education and Employment (1997). *Excellence in Schools*. London: Stationery Office.

Department for Education and Employment/Qualification and Curriculum Authority (1999a). *The National Curriculum: Handbook for Secondary Teachers in England*. London: DfEE/QCA.

Department for Education and Employment/Qualification and Curriculum Authority (1999b). *The National Curriculum: Handbook for Primary Teachers in England*. London: DfEE/QCA.

Department for Education and Skills (2001). *Inclusive Schooling – Children with Special Educational Needs*. Annesley: Department for Education and Skills.

Department for Education and Skills/Department of Health (2004). *Promoting Emotional Health and Wellbeing Through the National Healthy School Standard*. Wetherby: Health Development Agency.

Department for Education and Skills/Department of Health (2005). *National Healthy School status: A guide for schools*. www.dh.gov.uk/publications.

Department of Health (1999). *National service framework for mental health: Modern standards and service models*. http://www.dh.gov.uk/assetRoot/04/07/72/09/04077209.pdf (accessed 24.7.06).

Edmiston, B. (2000). Drama as ethical education. *Research in Drama Education*, 5 (1), 63–84.

Evans, D., Rees, J., Okagbue, O. & Tripp, J. (1998). Negotiating sexual intimacy: A PAUSE develops an approach using a peer-led, theatre for development model in the classroom. *Health Education*, 98 (6), 220–229.

Gorard, S., Selwyn, N. & Rees, G. (2002). 'Privileging the Visible': A critique of the National Learning Targets. *British Educational Research Journal*, 28 (3), 309–325.

Hornby, G. & Atkinson, M. (2003). A framework for promoting mental health in school. *Pastoral Care in Education*, 21 (2), 3–9.

Johnson, L. & O'Neill, C. (1984). *Dorothy Heathcoat: Collected Writings on Education and Drama*. London: Hutchinson.

Licence, K. (2004). Promoting and protecting the health of children and young people. *Child: Care, Health and Development*, 30 (6), 623–635.

Office of the Deputy Prime Minister (2004). *Mental health and social exclusion: Social exclusion unit report summary*. www.socialexclusion.gov.uk/download doc.asp?id=185 (accessed 20.02.06).

Ofsted (2005). *Healthy minds: Promoting emotional health and well-being in schools*. www.ofsted.gov.uk/publications/index.cfm?fuseaction=pubs.displayfile&id=3954&type=pdf (accessed 20.02.06).

Pinfold, V., Toulmin, H., Thornicroft, G., Huxley, P., Farmer, P. & Graham, T. (2003). Reducing psychiatric stigma and discrimination: Evaluation of educational interventions in UK secondary schools. *British Journal of Psychiatry*, 182 (4), 342–346.

Roberts, G. (2004). *What is psychosis: Diversity, disagreement and steps towards an international model of understanding*. http://kc.nimhe.org.uk/upload/glenn's%20dissonance%20oct%2091.doc.

Sawney, F., Sykes, S., Keene, M., Swinden, L. & McCormick, G. (2003). *It Opened My Eyes: Using Theatre in Education to Deliver Sex and Relationship Education. A Good Practice Guide*. London: Health Development Agency.

Schagen, S., Blenkinsop, S., Schagen, I. *et al.* (2005). Evaluating the impact of the National Healthy School Standard: Using national datasets. *Health Education Research*, 20 (6), 688–696.

Schulze, B., Richter-Werling, M., Matschinger, H. & Angermeyer, M. (2003). Crazy? So what! Effects of a school project on students' attitudes towards people with schizophrenia. *Acta Psychiatrica Scandinavica*, 107 (2), 142–150.

Sextou, P. (2003). Theatre in education in Britain: Current practice and future potential. *New Theatre Quarterly*, 19 (2), 177–188.

Somers, J. (1996). The nature of learning in drama education. In: J. Somers (ed.), *Drama and Theatre in Education: Contemporary Research*. North York, Canada: Captus.

Tomlinson, S. (2001). *Education in a Post-Welfare Society*. Buckingham: Open University Press.

Warwick, I., Aggleton, P. Chase, E. *et al.* (2005). Evaluating healthy schools: Perceptions of impact among school-based respondents. *Health Education Research*, 20 (6), 697–708.

Weare, K. (2000). *Promoting Mental, Emotional and Social Health*. London: Routledge.

Winston, J. (1999). Theorising drama as moral education. *Journal of Moral Education*, 28 (4), 459–471.

Winston, J. (2001). Drug education through creating theatre in education. *Research in Drama Education*, 6 (1), 39–54.

Woolf, F. (1999). *Partnerships for Learning: A Guide to Evaluating Arts Education Projects*. London: Regional Arts Board and the Arts Council of England.

Chapter 15 **Working with motivational difficulties in first-episode psychosis**

Imogen Reid, Tom Barker and Jo Smith

Giving up was not a problem. It was a solution because it protected me from wanting anything. If I didn't want anything, then it couldn't be taken away. If I didn't try, then I wouldn't have to undergo another failure. If I didn't care, then nothing could hurt me again. My heart became hardened.

(Deegan, 1996)

Introduction

Negative symptoms are an intrinsic aspect of psychosis (Gerbaldo *et al.*, 1997), and represent one of the three independent categories of symptoms, along with positive psychotic symptoms and disorganisation. Common negative symptoms include flattened affect and diminished emotional range, poverty of speech, curbing of interest and curiosity, reduced sense of purpose and social drive. Carpenter and colleagues (Carpenter *et al.*, 1988) have argued that it is possible to distinguish between primary and enduring negative symptoms (referred to as the 'deficit syndrome') and secondary and transient negative symptoms related to coping with positive symptoms, depression, side effects of medication or environmental deprivation. However, others have argued that multiple factors, including biological, psychological and social factors, may have an impact on the development and maintenance of negative symptoms and for each individual it is important to assess the relative contribution of these different factors and to plan relevant interventions accordingly (Morrison *et al.*, 2004).

Identifying negative symptoms of psychosis is important because of their potential prognostic value, particularly their association with poorer long-term functional outcomes, poor antipsychotic medication treatment response and their relationship to cognitive dysfunction. It has also been suggested that negative symptoms may be associated with delays in help seeking and hence a longer DUP.

This chapter will briefly review the literature relating to negative symptoms in first episode psychosis (FEP) and consider the importance of identifying and intervening early with individuals with FEP who are experiencing negative symptoms. For practical purposes, the chapter will specifically focus on interventions to address motivational difficulties which, although one manifestation of negative symptoms, may be particularly associated with poor longer-term quality of life outcomes. The bulk of the chapter will describe practical steps in the assessment of and intervention with motivational difficulties, supported by an illustrative case example to highlight issues relating to implementation in practice.

Negative symptoms in FEP: Evidence summary

Incidence of enduring negative symptoms in FEP

Estimates of the prevalence of enduring negative symptoms among individuals with FEP have varied across studies. Some studies (Fenton & McGlashan, 1994; Mayerhoff *et al.*, 1994) suggest that enduring negative symptoms are relatively rare, affecting about 10% of individuals whilst other studies suggest it may be as high as 31% (Gerbaldo *et al.*, 1997). Several studies have highlighted the considerable instability in negative symptoms in the first 12 months of FEP (Edwards *et al.*, 1999; Malla *et al.*, 2002).

Whilst the number of individuals initially showing negative symptoms may be relatively high, only a small proportion of individuals will continue to show persisting negative symptoms. Once identified the group which shows enduring negative symptoms appears to be relatively stable (Fenton & McGlashan, 1994; Mayerhoff *et al.*, 1994) and is associated with a relatively poor prognosis (Edwards *et al.*, 1999). The enduring negative symptom group has significantly longer duration of psychotic symptoms during first hospitalisation, longer durations of prodrome and DUP, a history of poor premorbid functioning, poorer quality of life scores, high levels of flattened affect at first presentation and lower remission rates at 1 year compared with individuals with transitory negative symptoms (Edwards *et al.*, 1999; Larsen *et al.*, 2000; Malla *et al.*, 2002). This suggests that enduring negative symptoms may be established well before the onset of prodromal symptoms and entry into treatment and may contribute to a greater delay in detection and initiation of treatment.

Predictive value of negative symptoms in FEP

Studies with FEP groups suggest that negative symptoms have predictive value which is greater than that for either positive or disorganised symptoms, and severe negative symptoms at the time of first hospitalisation may be a portent of poorer quality of life outcomes. Husted and colleagues (Husted *et al.*, 1992) showed that at 18-month follow-up, this negative symptom group had poorer social functioning, higher levels of residual pathology and poorer global functioning. Similarly, Ho and others (Ho *et al.*, 1998) found that severe negative symptoms moderately predicted later occupational impairment, financial dependence on others, impaired relationships with friends, impaired ability to enjoy recreational activities and poorer global functioning at 2-year follow-up. Since negative symptoms are known to correlate with poorer prognosis and social outcomes, their pervasive influence cannot be underestimated or ignored (McGlashan & Fenton, 1992; Ho *et al.*, 1998).

Intervention studies

While positive psychotic symptoms may be successfully relieved by antipsychotic medication, no drug has yet been approved specifically indicated for the treatment of negative symptoms. Although newer antipsychotic medications have claimed to have a better effect than first-generation antipsychotics, they have not met early hopes for a highly effective treatment for the alleviation of negative symptoms (Keefe *et al.*, 1999) and as such, negative symptoms often remain resistant to treatment using pharmacological intervention alone (Arango *et al.*, 2004). Malla and colleagues (Malla *et al.*, 2004) found only half of the individuals with negative symptoms showed improvements when treated with average doses of antipsychotic medications. In studies where negative symptoms have been shown to improve in response to antipsychotic medication, it has been argued that this may only be secondary to changes in positive symptoms or changes in depression severity (Rector *et al.*, 2003) rather than a direct impact on negative symptoms.

Psychosocial intervention trials have also largely focussed on positive symptoms with less emphasis on targeting or measuring the impact on negative symptoms. Some studies have reported moderate improvements in negative symptoms in individuals who receive CBT treatments for positive symptoms (Tarrier *et al.*, 2000, 2001; Haddock *et al.*, 2003). Again, it is unclear whether the effects on negative symptoms are secondary to the impact of CBT on positive symptoms.

Sensky and colleagues (Sensky *et al.*, 2000) specifically targeted negative symptoms, comparing CBT with a befriending intervention. Both CBT and befriending resulted in significant reductions in negative symptoms post treatment, although at 9 months follow-up, individuals who had CBT continued to improve while those in the befriending group did not. Rector *et al.* (2003) also specifically targeted negative symptoms, with the addition of CBT to enriched standard treatment. The addition of CBT led to moderate improvements in negative symptoms, although these effects were not significantly greater than those achieved by the enriched standard treatment group. However, at 6 months follow-up, 61% of individuals in the CBT group were experiencing clinically significant improvements in negative symptoms compared with only 31% in the enriched standard treatment group. Interestingly, the effect size changes between end of treatment and follow-up were almost identical to those reported by Sensky *et al.* (2000) at their 9 months follow-up. These two studies suggest that a greater length of time may be required to rehearse new skills if we are to impact on negative symptoms and 12–18 months may be required before significant improvements are observed.

Few intervention trials have specifically looked at reducing negative symptoms in FEP patients. Thorup and colleagues (Thorup *et al.*, 2005) evaluated an integrated treatment package with FEP and reported significant reductions in negative symptoms compared with standard treatment. It was not possible to identify a single therapeutic ingredient specifically responsible for these reductions in negative symptoms. Dyck and others (Dyck *et al.*, 2000) found that multifamily groups were successful in reducing negative symptoms, possibly by reducing expectations from family members.

The positive impact on negative symptoms of two quite disparate interventions suggests that effective interventions need to be tailored to the specific needs of the individual. Treatment guidelines recommend that to optimise functional outcomes for individuals with psychosis, psychosocial interventions should be combined with pharmacological management (Lauriello *et al.*, 2003). The enduring negative symptom group requires an intensive package involving higher than average doses of antipsychotic medication or the early institution of Clozapine therapy, combined with a more intensive set of psychosocial and cognitive interventions compared to the typical FEP intervention package.

Implementation in practice

In this section, we will discuss some practical strategies for working with individuals who are experiencing motivational difficulties. We will describe the main issues that need to be covered during an assessment and recommend some useful assessment measures. There are a number of cognitive and behavioural interventions that can be very useful in working with people who have motivational difficulties and their families and these will be outlined. We will discuss ways of addressing some of the common obstacles in implementing these interventions and highlight the importance of good supervision in doing this very challenging work.

Assessment

As with any other area of intervention, in working with people with motivational difficulties, the importance of a thorough and holistic assessment cannot be underestimated. As discussed elsewhere, motivational difficulties can occur in the context of other negative symptoms of psychosis. There are a number of assessment tools available which may be useful in assessing the full range of negative symptoms. A list of useful assessment tools is included in Table 15.1.

To gain a clearer picture of the impact of these difficulties on everyday functioning, tools such as the Social Functioning Scale or SFS (Birchwood *et al.*, 1990) and the Lancashire Quality of Life Profile (Oliver, 1992) can be invaluable.

As discussed earlier, within the literature, it has been recognised that other factors, such as depression and medication effects, may contribute to the development and maintenance of motivational difficulties. Thus, as part of the assessment it can be helpful to assess for levels of depression, using a measure such as the Calgary Depression Scale or CDS (Addington *et al.*, 1993) and the side effects of medication, using a measure such as the Liverpool University Neuroleptic Side Effects Rating Scale or LUNSERS (Day *et al.*, 1995). The presence of depression may indicate the need for specific treatment of depressive symptoms, either with antidepressant medication or using psychological intervention. If significant side effects are present and appear to be contributing to the individual's motivational difficulties, then a review of medication type, dosage and timing would be recommended.

A number of authors have also suggested that some individuals may manifest difficulties such

Table 15.1 Assessment tools

Assessment measure	Key characteristics
High Royds Evaluation of Negativity (HEN) Mortimer *et al.* (1989)	• 24-item scale • Observer based • Covers all aspects of common negative symptoms • Based on 5- to 10-minute interview
Negative Symptom Rating Scale (NSRS) Iager *et al.*, 1985	• 10 item, 4 subscales • Observer based • Based on 15-minute semistructured interview
Scale for the Assessment of Negative Symptoms (SANS) Andreasen, 1989	• Observer-based scale • Takes 30 minutes to complete
Subjective Experience of Negative Symptoms Scale (SENS) Selten *et al.*, 1993	• Derived from SANS • Self-rating scale • Assesses subjective distress and disruption to everyday functioning associated with negative symptoms

as social withdrawal or motivational difficulties as a response to distressing overwhelming positive symptoms. Therefore, it is helpful to carefully assess the presence of positive symptoms and delineate the relationship between these two domains. It has also been noted that some individuals may be fearful of relapse or symptom recurrence and may be avoiding exposure to demanding situations as a result. This needs to be assessed through a careful clinical interview. The Attitude to Relapse Scale (Smith, 2001) may also be a useful adjunct.

It is also vital to assess for any physical factors which may be contributing to the individual's difficulties such as the presence of viral infection, anaemia or underactive thyroid gland. Careful assessment of the individual's sleeping pattern and any factors which may be having a detrimental effect on sleep are also useful.

Many individuals with negative symptoms and motivational difficulties may show patterns of self-critical and negative thinking. This may further undermine their motivation. Individuals may anticipate failure, underestimate their personal resources to cope with difficulties and overcome obstacles and believe that there is no

point in trying things because failure will inevitably ensue (Rector *et al.*, 2005). In some cases, these negative styles of thinking may have been reinforced by previous experiences of failure, criticism from others or low expectations for success. Within the assessment process, it is important to identify any patterns of negative thinking which may be contributing to or exacerbating the individual's motivational difficulties. It is also useful to delineate any factors which may have contributed to the development and maintenance of these patterns of negative thinking.

So far the focus of the assessment process has very much been on the individual. However, it is important to also explore the environmental and social context of the individual. For example, it may be important to identify whether the young person has maintained contact with friends and whether they have any particular anxieties about engaging in social interaction, such as anxieties about explaining their mental health difficulties. Involving the family in the assessment process is also vital. Many family members struggle to understand or know how to respond to a young person who is struggling with motivational difficulties. Families may attribute this to laziness or may have expectations of the young person which are too high. Their response may be to become critical or demanding in an attempt to motivate the person. Alternatively, they may feel that it is not reasonable to have any expectations of the young person since they have been unwell and may have fallen into the pattern of doing everything for the individual with FEP.

In formulating meaningful goals for intervention, it is also vital to gain a clear picture of the young person's interests and aspirations prior to experiencing psychosis and currently. It is useful to ascertain whether they are still doing things that they find enjoyable or motivating and also to ask about what they would like to be doing in the future.

We have included a checklist of areas to cover in assessment and some suggestions for questions that you may wish to consider in Table 15.2 (Reid *et al.*, 2007).

Table 15.2   Assessment checklist

Individual Factors

Level of motivational difficulties

- What motivational difficulties and other possible negative symptoms have been identified?
- In what ways are they impacting on the individual's everyday functioning?
- How much distress are they causing to the individual?

Depression

- Is the person depressed?
- Can anything be done to alleviate these factors, for example review of medication?

Side effects

- Is the person experiencing side effects of medication?
- Can anything be done to alleviate these?

Positive symptoms and coping

- How long has the individual had psychosis?
- What positive symptoms have they presented with in the past?
- Are these still present?
- What strategies are they currently using to cope with these positive symptoms?
- How long has the individual been experiencing negative symptoms?
- Has the individual made attempts in the past to increase their levels of activity?
- If so, what happened, for example did they experience a recurrence of positive symptoms, were they unable to sustain this increase?
- What implications might this have for working with the individual, for example might they anticipate failure, are they likely to experience an increase in positive symptoms?
- How could these issues be addressed, for example might they benefit from help to learn new coping strategies?

Cognitive factors

- What are the person's beliefs about themselves, others or social relationships?
- What are the person's beliefs about likely failure or taking risks?
- What cognitive strategies might the person be employing to manage positive symptoms?
- Does the person have low expectancies for pleasure or success?
- Has the person internalised perceived stigma?
- Do they perceive themselves as having limited personal resources to deal with challenges?

Physical health

- Has the individual had a recent period of physical ill health, for example cough, viral infection, temperature or been recently diagnosed with anaemia, thyroid dysfunction or other physical health complaint?

(Continued)

Table 15.2   *(Continued)*

- Is the person experiencing any other physical health symptoms currently, for example aches and pains, fever, rashes?
- How long has the person been having negative symptoms? Have these symptoms only appeared after a recent infection or illness?
- When did the individual last see his/her GP for a physical health check and when did they last have a blood test?

Sleep/diurnal pattern questions

- What are the individual's usual waking and sleeping times? Do they have a regular sleep routine? Has this changed in any way: how, when and why? What did their sleep routine used to be?
- What is the individual's sleeping pattern like? Are they experiencing any difficulties with sleeping or has sleep been disturbed for any reason?
- Do they stay up late watching films or socialising/clubbing into the early hours?
- Has their diurnal pattern changed around so they tend to sleep in the day and be up and active during the night?

Personal background

- What was the individual doing prior to becoming unwell, for example were they working, studying, etc.?
- What skills or resources did they have?
- What interests or aspirations did they have?
- What interests or aspirations do they have now?
- What would they like to be doing in 3 months time?
- Is there anything that they do find particularly motivating?
- What blocks have been identified that may be impeding progress?

Environmental and social factors

- Are there any factors in the environment that may be exacerbating the individual's difficulties, for example overstimulation, understimulation, lack of social contact?
- What can be done to address these difficulties?
- Are there any social factors which may be exacerbating the problems, for example financial constraints?
- What can be done to address these difficulties?

Family/significant others

- What difficulties do the family/significant others report?
- What understanding do they have of the individual's difficulties, for example do they perceive the individual as being lazy, do they believe the individual is incapable of doing anything because they are unwell?
- What expectations do the family/significant others have of the individual?
- Are these realistic or are they aiming too high or too low?
- How do family members/significant others respond to the individual's difficulties, for example with encouragement, conflict, leaving them to it?
- What could be done to help the family/significant others in supporting the individual?
- Do the family/significant others need more information about psychosis?
- Would the family benefit from family intervention/BFT?
- Are there issues around loss and adjustment that need to be addressed?

Intervention

A number of core cognitive and behavioural tools can be extremely useful in assisting young people to overcome their difficulties and to move forward in the process of recovery. The tools we have found most useful and the circumstances under which they may be helpful are detailed in Table 15.3.

Table 15.3   Interventions commonly used in working with individuals with motivational difficulties

Intervention	Circumstances under which may be useful	Useful tips for using this tool
Keeping an activity diary	• To gain a clearer picture of how much someone is doing each day. • To identify what activities an individual is still able to do and what times of the day they tend to be most active.	• Information from the diary can be combined with other tools, for example to inform realistic goal setting and to challenge patterns of negative thinking if the person is underestimating how much they are able to do. • Discuss any anxieties the individual has about completing the diary, for example embarrassment about being seen to do too little.
Rating each activity in the diary for levels of enjoyment (Pleasure) and achievement (Mastery). A scale of 0–10 for each is typically used.	• To find out whether or not the individual is still engaging in activities which give them a sense of enjoyment and/or achievement. • To identify which activities, if any, the individual still gains some enjoyment or sense of achievement from.	• It is helpful to introduce this rating after the individual has become familiar with keeping the basic diary format. • If using the number-based ratings proves too complex, look at other strategies such as highlighting activities in different colours or placing an asterisk next to activities they enjoyed.
Activity scheduling – planning a daily schedule, including activities which give a sense of enjoyment and/or achievement.	• To assist individuals who may find it difficult to plan ahead. • To increase the number of activities that the individual is doing which give a sense of enjoyment and/or achievement. • To boost self-esteem and improve low mood.	• If the individual is struggling to plan ahead, it may be helpful to involve someone else such as a family member. • If the person finds it hard to come up with ideas of things that they could do, it can be helpful to construct a list of activities that they can choose from.
Teaching the individual to set SMART goals.	• To assist individuals who find it difficult to set goals or whose goals are vague, non-specific or unattainable in the short term. • To engender a sense of hope and to boost self-esteem through goal completion.	• If individuals consistently set under or over ambitious goals, then it is useful to explore the reasons for this. For example, individuals may set under ambitious goals if they are fearful of the possibility of relapse or if they have very negative beliefs about the implications of having had an episode of psychosis.

(Continued)

Table 15.3 (Continued)

Intervention	Circumstances under which may be useful	Useful tips for using this tool
Teaching the individual a structured approach to problem solving.	• To help individuals to identify and solve everyday difficulties in a constructive way. • This is a useful tool to help individuals address a wide variety of difficulties identified during assessment, for example resolving factors which are disturbing sleep, dealing with social situations, etc.	• If the individual really struggles to problem solve independently, it can be helpful to engage a family member or friend. However, it is important that they understand that their role is to help the young person work through the problem-solving steps and not to solve the problem for them.
Helping the individual to identify and challenge negative or self-critical patterns of thinking.	• To help individuals challenge negative thinking patterns which may be undermining their ability to engage in activities. • To improve self-esteem and low mood.	• If the individual experiences the same thought repeatedly, it can be helpful to write down useful challenges for them to refer to again in the future. • When working on challenging patterns of negative thinking, it is useful to check out whether any of these thoughts are being reinforced by negative or critical comments from others. This may need to be addressed through helping the person to develop assertiveness skills or if it is a family member through work with the family.
Helping the individual to recognise and celebrate successes – 'Nurturing the coach or cheerleader'.	• To ensure that individuals recognise signs of progress and are able to use positive self-talk to reinforce these steps forward. • This can be particularly helpful where individuals are minimising signs of progress or are engaging in unfavourable comparisons with others or with their previous levels of functioning.	• It can be helpful to identify specific things that the individual can say to encourage themselves and focus on things that have gone well. • Building in rewards or treats after successful completion of a goal can also be beneficial. • Briefing family members or friends as to how they can help the young person to celebrate successes can be very useful.
Developing a relapse prevention plan.	• This is particularly useful where individuals are fearful that increasing their levels of activity may result in symptom recurrence or relapse.	• This process should include discussion of trigger factors for relapse, identification of a relapse signature, development of a plan for responding should these signs emerge and a means of monitoring for the emergence of early signs of relapse.

Table 15.3   *(Continued)*

Intervention	Circumstances under which may be useful	Useful tips for using this tool
Developing strategies for managing residual positive symptoms.	• This may be a useful tool in cases where an individual is using social withdrawal as a means of managing residual positive symptoms and has few other coping strategies.	• A useful first step may be keeping a diary to identify when the target symptom gets worse, what the individual did to cope and how effective this was. • It can be helpful to introduce new coping strategies one at a time, ensuring that the person has a chance to practice them in session before they try them on their own. • Many people find that carrying a small laminated card summarising their coping strategies is very helpful.
Developing stress management skills.	• To assist individuals who have few coping strategies for dealing with stress.	• It can be useful to discuss with individuals that lack of activity and under stimulation may be as stressful as being in a situation where there are too many demands.

A full description of these interventions is beyond the scope of this chapter but full details can be found in relevant texts on cognitive behavioural interventions, such as Greenberger and Padesky (1995), Morrison *et al.* (2004) and Morrison (2002). Although the interventions are described separately, in practice they would often be used in combination with each other. For example, if an individual is struggling to complete a goal that they have identified, it may be helpful to explore what obstacles are preventing them from completing the goal. This may highlight a number of other useful areas for intervention such as problem solving to resolve practical obstacles or using techniques to challenge patterns of negative thinking, if the young person is not even attempting to undertake the goal because they are so convinced that their attempts will be unsuccessful.

As noted in the table, family members or friends may be invaluable allies in using some of these interventions but specific family-based interventions may also be necessary. Many family members find motivational difficulties particularly hard to understand and struggle to know how best to respond. Provision of clear information to family members about both the positive and negative symptoms of psychosis can be extremely helpful. In some cases, family members may underestimate the impact of such experiences and may expect the individual with FEP to carry on as before. This may result in conflict and criticism when the individual is unable to fulfil these expectations. Families may benefit from information which balances the hope of recovery with the need to have realistic expectations and to allow the individual enough time to recover. Other families may have expectations that are too low. For example, they may be very protective of the individual, believing that they are unable to do anything because they are 'unwell'.

Alternatively, they may be so fearful of triggering a recurrence of symptoms or receiving a negative response that they may avoid asking the individual to do anything. In such cases, it may be necessary to encourage the family to gradually increase the demands they make on an individual. It can also be important to encourage families to respond positively to any attempts by the young person to try to do more and to adopt a constructive, problem-solving approach when problems arise. Many of these skills are addressed within family interventions (Falloon *et al.*, 2004; Smith *et al.*, 2007) which include sessions on information giving, problem solving, goal setting and communication skills.

Common obstacles

There is an inherent challenge of engagement in working with individuals for whom lack of motivation is a key presenting difficulty. Very often, this lack of motivation will extend to participating in psychological therapy, particularly if this has not been initiated at the individual's own request. Individuals who have motivational difficulties are a heterogeneous group in terms of underlying causes and the varied potential functions served by symptoms. The challenge therefore in providing intervention to such individuals is to be sufficiently flexible in delivering an intervention whilst at the same time preserving the therapeutic elements of the interventions used. Clinicians may also find that it is necessary to systematically work with layers of maintaining factors, drawing on relevant tools as required in a flexible way in order to help break persistent symptom circles.

The most obvious and frequent obstacle encountered in working with motivational difficulties is non-completion of tasks agreed within sessions, such as record and diary keeping. Non-completion of tasks may arise for a number of reasons. An individual may be reluctant to complete an activity diary sheet due to embarrassment about how little he/she is doing, fear of criticism or ridicule from the therapist, or the individual may have difficulty remembering to regularly complete the form. A careful assessment is required of the reasons that tasks are not completed in order to generate effective remedies to overcome such obstacles. For example, the individual may require reassurance to allay any anxieties, or they may benefit from assistance or prompting from a supportive other person.

It is important to explain clearly a rationale for undertaking a therapeutic task that will in itself help to build openness to experimenting with suggested tasks. In activity scheduling work, for example, it can be helpful to inform individuals about the research by Gard and colleagues (Gard *et al.*, 2003) highlighting the discrepancy between anticipatory pleasure (the desire for something) and consummatory pleasure (enjoyment of something). This research found that people with psychosis tend to hold low expectancies for pleasure although once engaged in an activity, their ability to derive pleasure is not impaired. Low anticipatory pleasure may feed into a vicious circle of reduced motivation, reduced engagement in pleasurable activities and reduced experienced pleasure, thereby leading to further reduced motivation. Once this cycle has been explained, it may be helpful to build on this by encouraging the individual to carry out some monitoring for themselves by rating expected and actual pleasure, in order to highlight the extent to which this vicious circle may feed into the maintenance of their own motivational difficulties.

There may be more practical obstacles to the process of treating motivational difficulties such as the individual forgetting to carry out a homework task or confusion about the nature of the task. It is important therefore to be extremely clear in describing identified problems and homework tasks. Setting behavioural goals provides an opportunity to model and reinforce the use of a structured problem-solving approach, such as the use of SMART (Specific, Measured, Appropriate, Realistic, Timescaled) criteria. Using SMART criteria is an effective tool to reduce the risk that goals set may be too vague, overly ambitious and unattainable, or under ambitious. Potential obstacles to carrying out a task should also be anticipated at the planning stage and a troubleshooting plan developed to deal with these.

The process of using a structured problem-solving approach may also usefully highlight goals for psychological therapy that need to be addressed in order to progress the problem-solving work. Such goals may include grief work to help the individual to adjust to the impact of their mental health problems and accept associated losses such as the loss of previously held aspirations, or it may involve imparting information to counter unhelpful myths that exist about psychosis that can give rise to a particularly pessimistic outlook, particularly for someone who is experiencing FEP. Alternatively, an individual may be reluctant to undertake increased activities due to being fearful of doing anything that may trigger a further relapse. For such an individual, it is likely to be helpful to develop a relapse prevention plan including identified early warning signs, triggers and strategies to manage stress (Smith, 2001).

Unhelpful patterns of thinking are likely to contribute to the development and maintenance of motivational difficulties, and as such are an important focus of intervention. However, therapy-interfering cognitions that give rise to avoidance of implementing goals set in therapy provide an opportunity to identify and work with negative automatic thoughts as they arise. It is likely that these cognitions will reflect unhelpful patterns of thinking that contribute more generally to motivational difficulties, such as:

- Fear of failure ('I will get it wrong'; 'Others will notice, and will think I am no good');
- Fear of not coping ('I won't have the energy to do it'; 'I will never be able to study as well as I used to');
- Fear of exacerbation of symptoms and relapse ('It will stress me out, and my voices will be horrible');
- Fear of other people's responses; humiliation, hostility, stigma ('They will know I am a psycho'; 'I stand out').

Standard cognitive therapy strategies can be used to challenge such cognitions and develop alternative thoughts that help to build motivation, for example 'I usually enjoy football once I get there and get going'.

In our experience, there are some therapy characteristics that are essential in working with negative symptoms due to the challenges inherent in this work which have been highlighted. These include the need for therapy to be grounded in a creative and supportive problem-solving approach, and also the need for the therapist to be able to hold hope on behalf of the individual, and to be able to tolerate periods within therapy where it feels like little or no progress is being made. Clinicians working extensively with negative symptoms need to have good supervision and support in order to sustain their enthusiasm and creativity. Clinicians also need to be careful that they do not veer from grounding their input within a person-centred approach, towards pursuing goals or values held primarily by themselves, the services they work in or significant others such as relatives and carers.

Questions for clinicians

- Are there any assessment measures that it would be beneficial to use in this case?
- Have I considered all of the areas listed in the assessment checklist when conducting my assessment?
- What factors have contributed to the development and maintenance of the individual's motivational difficulties?
- Are there any risks that intervention will lead to unwanted psychological or emotional consequences (such as increased depression, stigma or feelings of low self-esteem)?
- Why is it important or helpful for the client to carry out this goal?
- When I encounter difficulties or obstacles, how can I ensure that I tackle these in a constructive way?
- What sources of support and supervision can I draw upon in working with individuals with motivational difficulties?

Clinical Case study

The following case study illustrates the process of holistic assessment discussed in the Assessment section. Several of the strategies described in the Intervention section were employed in working with the young man, Harry, and his family. The case study also illustrates the need to combine various strategies and to offer the interventions in a flexible manner, tailored to the needs of the individual.

Harry was a 22-year old man who was seen in psychology services 5 months after experiencing a first episode of psychosis. At the time of referral, Harry was living at home with his parents and younger sister. He had previously worked as an electrician but had been off sick for several months.

At school, Harry had been an average student with a good circle of friends. He had always been fairly conscientious and quiet. Prior to his episode of psychosis, Harry had been depressed for some time. He was involved in a minor car accident and became convinced that he had killed somebody during the accident. This belief persisted despite repeated reassurance and was a source of significant feelings of guilt and distress. He also became convinced that people in his neighbourhood were talking about his involvement in the accident and were plotting to punish him. As a consequence, he was reluctant to leave the family home. When he presented to mental health services, Harry was highly anxious and extremely preoccupied with the accident. Harry was diagnosed as having had a first episode of psychosis and was treated with antipsychotic medication.

By the time of his assessment by the psychologist several months later, he reported feeling 70% recovered. He felt less anxious and now accepted that no one had been harmed in the accident and that no one had been trying to punish him. Assessment with the Calgary Depression Scale, suggested there was no evidence of clinical levels of depression although Harry did report occasional low mood. However, Harry was reporting ongoing difficulties around poor confidence and motivation. Harry was spending much of his time at home, in bed or on his computer. He rarely went out although he had remained in contact with one of his friends who would visit him at his home. He was keen to return to work but was worried about being able to cope. Harry was extremely concerned about experiencing a recurrence of his difficulties in the future.

Harry's parents were also involved in the assessment process. They were very supportive towards Harry but had been given little information about how to help him. They were very fearful about the possibility of relapse and as a consequence had been avoiding placing any demands upon him.

Harry was seen for 14 sessions using a cognitive behavioural approach. During the early sessions, Harry and his psychologist agreed a shared problems list, a list of goals and a cognitive behavioural formulation of his difficulties. Although Harry had generally made a good recovery, it appeared that his high levels of anxiety about possible symptom recurrence and his lack of confidence about his ability to cope with stress, were leading him to avoid any situations where he could be exposed to demands or stress. However, this avoidance only served to reinforce his belief that he would not be able to cope with stress and would end up becoming unwell again. Harry's parents were similarly concerned about stress leading to a relapse and consequently avoided placing any demands upon him.

Harry was very keen to try and establish a more regular sleep pattern and improve his levels of confidence and motivation. Harry started keeping an activity diary. This suggested that he was spending much of his day in bed asleep. Harry was going to bed at 1.00 am and then sleeping through until midday. He reported feeling drowsy all the time. Harry's medication was reviewed by his psychiatrist and alterations were made to the dosage and timing of his medication.

Harry was introduced to the idea of using activity scheduling, planning activities each day which gave him a sense of achievement and/or enjoyment. When Harry struggled to complete planned tasks, a problem-solving approach was adopted to develop creative solutions. Harry was able to identify a number of enjoyable things that he could do but struggled to identify activities which gave him a sense of achievement. As he had a lot of practical skills, it was agreed that he would approach his family and ask if they had any jobs that needed to be done around the house. His parents gave Harry a list of jobs and he was then able to incorporate completion of these tasks gradually *into his activity scheduling. Harry was also encouraged to work towards the goal of gradually getting up earlier in the morning. This was seen as an important step in helping Harry to work towards his goal of returning to work. Harry started using an alarm in the morning, setting it slightly earlier each day. He also started to arrange to do things in the morning as an incentive to get up, including scheduling his appointments with the psychologist at progressively earlier times.*

Throughout this work Harry continued to express anxieties about being able to complete tasks properly and cope with stress. He also reported being worried about the possibility of recurrence of his psychotic symptoms. Harry was introduced to the use of thought diaries as a means of identifying specific anxious thoughts. His psychologist helped him to look at ways in which he could challenge these thoughts, using verbal challenging techniques and through the use of behavioural experiments. This largely focussed around Harry's confidence in driving and his perception that he would not be able to cope with any stress. Harry was provided with information about psychosis and relapse risk. Harry and his psychologist worked through a structured relapse prevention package, identifying Harry's relapse signature and clear actions that he, his family and other supporters could take.

Harry's family were actively involved throughout the intervention. They were given information about psychosis and specific advice around ensuring that they were able to ask Harry to help out with tasks around the home. They were also involved in the relapse prevention work in order to increase their confidence in being able to identify and respond to any future recurrence of Harry's difficulties.

As the sessions progressed, Harry's levels of confidence and motivation improved significantly. His activity levels increased and his activity diaries suggested a good balance between activities that were enjoyable and gave him a sense of achievement. Harry was able to get up in the morning when he had activities planned but still tended to sleep in late if he had not planned to do anything in the morning. Harry felt that the next important stage in his recovery was for him to return to work. Harry liaised with his employers and negotiated a graded return to work. He was keen to take this final step but had some

anxiety about how he would cope with going back to work. Within the sessions, the psychologist helped Harry to normalise these concerns and also identify some practical strategies that Harry could use to manage these anxieties, such as arranging to work alongside more experienced colleagues until he had built up his confidence.

Implications and conclusions

Negative symptoms cause considerable disruption in functioning and can be a source of distress for both individuals with FEP and their families. The presence of negative symptoms is predictive of poorer long-term outcome and so early detection and intervention are important before these difficulties become more entrenched. Although historically negative symptoms have engendered a sense of therapeutic pessimism, more recent studies have suggested that improvements can be obtained in the context of the use of cognitive behavioural strategies. We have described the importance of conducting a comprehensive, holistic assessment of the factors which may be contributing to the development and maintenance of motivational difficulties. In addition, we have discussed the way in which a range of cognitive behavioural interventions may be used to assist individuals with motivational difficulties. These interventions need to be offered in a flexible and creative manner and we have offered some practical suggestions for tackling common obstacles. We have also emphasised the importance of involving family members at every stage of the assessment and intervention process. It is acknowledged that working with individuals with motivational difficulties can be extremely challenging and we have emphasised the importance of regular supervision and support to ensure that the clinician is able to sustain their hope, creativity and enthusiasm. We have also found the following quotation from Deegan (1996) an inspirational reminder of the human cost of motivational difficulties and of how hard it can be for individuals to begin to initiate the process of change:

There are a number of things I tell students about how to work with people who appear to be hard of heart, apathetic, and unmotivated. First I help the student understand the behavior in terms of its existential significance. I want the student to grasp the magnitude of what it is they are asking a person to risk when they ask them to start to care about something again. It is not a crazy thing to try to protect such a vulnerable heart. Secondly, I ask students to suspend their perception of people as chronic mental patients and to try to see the individual as a hero. I ask them, could you have survived what this individual has survived? Finally, I try to help students understand that although they do not have the power to change or motivate the person with a psychiatric disability who is hard of heart, they do have the power to change the environment, including the human interactive environment, in which that person is surviving. When working with a person with a psychiatric disability who is hard of heart, who has given up and who is motivated not to care anymore, we must understand that this is a person who feels they have no power. They experience all the power to be in the hands of others. They experience what psychologists call an external locus of control. . . .

Suggested further reading

Brennan, G., Kerr, S. & Goldspink, S. (2000). Lack of motivation, confidence and volition. In: C. Gamble & G. Brennan (eds), *Working with Serious Mental Illness: A Manual for Clinical Practice*. Balliere Tindall, London.

Morrison, A.P., Renton, J.C., Dunn, H., Williams, S. & Bentall, R.P. (2004). *Cognitive Therapy for Psychosis: A Formulation Based Approach*. Brunner-Routledge. See Chapter 11 on Negative Symptoms.

Reid, I., Smith, J. & Barker, T. (2007). *Working with individuals who have motivational difficulties: A guide for staff and carers working with individuals affected by negative symptoms*. Avon & Wiltshire Mental Health Partnership NHS Trust and Worcestershire Mental Health Partnership NHS Trust.

References

Addington, D., Addington, J. & Maticka-Tyndale, E. (1993). Assessing depression in schizophrenia: The Calgary Depression Scale. *British Journal of Psychiatry*, 163, 39–44.

Andreasen, N. (1989). Scale for the Assessment of Negative Symptoms (SANS). *British Journal of Psychiatry*, 155, 53–58.

Arango, C., Buchanan, R., Kirkpatrick, B. & Carpenter, W. (2004). The deficit syndrome in schizophrenia: Implications for the treatment of negative symptoms. *European Psychiatry*, 19, 21–26.

Birchwood, M., Smith, J., Cochrane, R., Wetton, S. & Copestake, S. (1990). The Social Functioning Scale: The development and validation of a new scale of social adjustment for use in family interventions programmes with Schizophrenic patients. *British Journal of Psychiatry*, 157, 853–859.

Carpenter, W.T., Heinrichs, D.W. & Wagman, A.M.I. (1988). Deficit and nondeficit forms of schizophrenia. *American Journal of Psychiatry*, 145, 578–583.

Day, J., Wood, G., Dewey, M. & Bentall, R. (1995). A self rating scale for measuring neuroleptic side-effects. *British Journal of Psychiatry*, 166, 650–653.

Deegan, P. (1996). Recovery as a journey of the heart. *Psychiatric Rehabilitation Journal*, 19 (3), 91–97.

Dyck, D., Short, R., Hendrys, M. *et al*. (2000). Management of negative symptoms among patients with schizophrenia attending multiple-family groups. *Psychiatric Services*, 51, 513–519.

Edwards, J., McGorry, P., Waddell, F. & Harrigan, S. (1999). Enduring negative symptoms in first episode psychosis: Comparison of six methods using follow-up data. *Schizophrenia Research*, 40, 147–148.

Falloon, I., Mueser, K., Gingerich, S. *et al*. (2004). *Family Work Manual*. Meriden: The West Midlands Family Programme.

Fenton, W. & McGlashan, T. (1994). Antecedents, symptom progression and long term outcome of the deficit syndrome in schizophrenia. *American Journal of Psychiatry*, 151, 351–356.

Gard, D.E., Germans Gard, M., Horan, W.P., Kring, A., John, O.P. & Green, M.F. (2003). Anticipatory and consummatory pleasure in schizophrenia: A scale development study. A paper presented at the *Annual Meeting of the Society for Research in Psychopathology*, October 2003, Toronto, ON.

Gerbaldo, H., Georgi, K. & Piechl, D. (1997). The deficit syndrome in first admission patients with psychotic and non-psychotic disorders. *European Psychiatry*, 12, 53–57.

Greenberger, D. & Padesky, C. (1995). *Mind Over Mood*. The Guilford Press, New York.

Haddock, G., Barrowclough, C., Tarrier, N. *et al*. (2003) Randomised controlled trial of cognitive-behaviour therapy and motivational intervention for schizophrenia and substance use: 18 month, carer and economic outcomes. *British Journal of Psychiatry*, 183, 418–426.

Ho, B., Nopoulos, P., Flaum, M., Arndt, S. & Andreason, N. (1998). Two-year outcome in first episode schizophrenia: Predictive value of symptoms for quality of life. *American Journal of Psychiatry*, 155, 1196–1201.

Iager, A., Kirch, D. & Wyatt, R. (1985). A Negative Symptom Rating Scale. *Psychiatry Research*, 16, 27–36.

Husted, J., Beiser, M. & Iacano, W. (1992). Negative symptoms and the early course of schizophrenia. *Psychiatry Research*, 43, 215–222.

Keefe, R., Harvey, P., Lenzenwenger, M. *et al.* (1999). Efficacy and extra-pyramidal side-effects of the new antipsychotics olanzepine, quetiapine, rispiridone and sertindole compared to conventional antipsychotics and placebo: A meta-analysis of randomised controlled trials. *Schizophrenia Research*, 35, 51–68.

Larsen, T., Moe, L., Vibe-Hansen, L. & Johannessen, J. (2000). Premorbid functioning versus duration of untreated psychosis in one year outcome in first episode psychosis. *Schizophrenia Research*, 45, 1–9.

Lauriello, J., Lenroot, R. & Bustillo, J. (2003). Maximising the synergy between pharmacotherapy and psychosocial therapies for schizophrenia. *Psychiatric Clinics of North America*, 26, 191–211.

McGlashan, T. & Fenton, W. (1992). The positive–negative distinction in schizophrenia: Review of natural history validators. *Archives of General Psychiatry*, 49, 63–72.

Malla, A., Norman, R., Manchanda, R. & Townsend, L. (2002). Symptoms, cognition, treatment adherence and functional outcome in first-episode psychosis. *Psychological Medicine*, 32, 1109–1119.

Malla, A., Norman, R., Takhar, J. *et al.* (2004). Can patients at risk for persistent negative symptoms be identified during their first episode of psychosis? *Journal of Nervous and Mental Disease*, 192 (7), 455–463.

Mayerhoff, D., Loebel, A., Jose, M. *et al.* (1994). The deficit state in first episode schizophrenia. *American Journal of Psychiatry*, 151, 1417–1422.

Morrison, A.P. (ed.) (2002). *A Casebook of Cognitive Therapy for Psychosis*. Brunner-Routledge, East Sussex.

Morrison, A.P., Renton, J.C., Dunn, H., Williams, S. & Bentall, R.P. (2004). *Cognitive Therapy for Psychosis: A Formulation Based Approach*. Brunner-Routledge, East Sussex.

Mortimer, A., Lund, C. & McKenna, P. *et al.* (1989). Rating negative symptoms using the High Royds Evaluation of Negativity (HEN) scale. *British Journal of Psychiatry*, 160, 89–92.

Oliver, J.P.J. (1992). The social care directive: Development of a quality of life profile for use in community services for the mentally ill. *Social Work & Social Sciences Review*, 3, 5–45.

Rector, N., Seeman, M. & Segal, Z. (2003). Cognitive therapy for schizophrenia: A preliminary randomized controlled trial. *Schizophrenia Research*, 63, 1–11.

Rector, N.A., Beck, A.T. & Stolar, N. (2005). The negative symptoms of schizophrenia: A cognitive perspective. *Canadian Journal of Psychiatry*, 50, 247–257.

Reid, I., Smith, J. & Barker, T. (2007). *Working with individuals who have motivational difficulties: A guide for staff and carers working with individuals affected by negative symptoms*. Avon & Wiltshire Mental Health Partnership NHS Trust and Worcestershire Mental Health Partnership NHS Trust.

Selten, J-P, Sijben, N. & van den Bosch, R. *et al.* (1993). The subjective experience of negative symptoms: A self rating scale. *Comprehensive Psychiatry*, 34, 192–197.

Sensky, T., Turkington, D., Kingdon, D., Scott, J., Siddle, R. & O'Carroll, M. (2000). TRE: A randomised controlled trail of cognitive-behavioural therapy for persistent symptoms in schizophrenia resistant to medication. *Archives of General Psychiatry*, 57, 165–172.

Smith, G., Gregory, K. & Higgs, A. (2007). *An Integrated Approach to Family Work for Psychosis*. Jessica Kingsley, London.

Smith, J. (2001). *Early Signs Self Management Training Manual for Individuals with Psychosis*. Worcestershire Community & Mental Health NHS Trust.

Tarrier, N., Kinney, C., McCarthy, E., Humphreys, L., Winkowski, A. & Morris, J. (2000). Two-year follow-up of cognitive-behaviour therapy and supportive counselling in the treatment of persistent positive symptoms in chronic schizophrenia. *Journal of Consulting & Clinical Psychology*, 68, 917–922.

Tarrier, N., Kinney, C., McCarthy, E., Winkowski, A., Yusupoff, L. & Gledhill, A. (2001). Are some types of psychotic symptoms more responsive to cognitive-behaviour therapy? *Behavioural and Cognitive Psychotherapy*, 29, 45–55.

Thorup, A., Petersen, L., Jeppesen, P. *et al.* (2005). Integrated treatment a.meliorates negative symptoms in first episode psychosis – results from the Danish OPUS trial. *Schizophrenia Research*, 79, 95–105.

Chapter 16 **Early intervention and vocational opportunities**

Eric Davis, Richard Burden and Ros Manning

Introduction

Employment and occupational issues are central to the concept of recovery for mental health service users (Boldison *et al.*, 2007). Service users accessing early intervention (EI) services within the UK underscore the importance of being able to secure employment, training and educational opportunities (Rinaldi *et al.*, 2004).

The Social Exclusion Unit (SEU: ODPM, 2004) shows that people with a psychiatric mental health disability have the lowest employment rate at 21% of any discernible disabled cohort. This compares to a general population average of 73%. Also, once obtained, a job is twice as likely to be lost when compared to the general population. The economic costs are estimated to be £77.4 billion comprised of poor quality of life and shorter life expectancy, and the loss of employment and state benefits.

The SEU (ODPM, 2004) suggests that psychiatric disability may lead to and reinforce social exclusion in a number of ways:

- Stigma and discrimination;
- Mental health practitioners exhibit low expectations;
- Lack of emphasis upon the promotion of social and vocational outcomes;
- Engagement barriers to the community and access to a range of educational, training and vocational institutions.

The National Service Framework (NSF: Department of Health, 1999) was published by the Department of Health, UK, and described a blueprint for the future development of mental health services. Subsequently, the Mental Health Policy Implementation Guide (MHPIG) was published in 2001 (Department of Health, 2001). The MHPIG provided a detailed description of how some of the newer modernised mental health services would be rolled out. Among these services was EI in psychosis services. The importance of employment education and training is cited within the MHPIG (2001, p. 50).

More recently, the value of developing valid skills and roles has been recognised as a central part of the Recovery Movement. A prolific commentator upon this movement is Anthony (1993) who wrote that:

> *Recovery is a deeply personal, unique process of changing one's attitudes, values, feelings, goals, skills and/or roles. It is a way of living a satisfying, hopeful and contributing life even with the limitations caused by illness. Recovery involves the development of new meaning and purpose in one's life as one grows beyond the catastrophic effects of the mental illness.*

Implicit within Anthony's view and further explored by Davis *et al.* (2007) is that attempting to help users with first-episode psychosis (FEP) into valued occupation is more positive because it draws upon the individual's strengths instead of remaining pre-occupied with individual deficits.

The evidence

We know from the work of Bond (2004) that the individual placement and support (IPS) vocational model has been particularly effective in helping a more chronic population find a vocational niche. Bond found that on an average, the percentage of service users or 'consumers' obtaining jobs in a competitive employment environment nearly tripled when people were exposed to the IPS employment model (employment rates can reach 38% typically in this population compared to 10–15% in control populations). Bond identified a number of important components that helped people with longer psychiatric histories back into work:

- The service model focuses on competitive employment. The use of day treatment and sheltered employment is discouraged as they appear to not confer an advantageous benefit to helping people back to work.
- Eligibility for work is based on consumer choice. Thus, individuals are encouraged to clearly state their preferences for the type of jobs and roles that they think would be suitable for them.
- Job-retention strategies are important. This augments any attempt to acquire a job, as further support is deemed important.
- Vocational interventions are embedded within mental health services. Such integration is thought to work in an optimal fashion and certainly better than when vocational mental health services are provided separately.
- Attention to service-user preferences. There is some evidence to suggest greater job tenure for service users who are able to obtain a job much more closely approximated to their work expectations.
- Time-unlimited and individualised support. The ongoing support from a range of professionals and other valued people (including employers) means that the overall chances of success in the workplace are elevated.
- Benefits counselling. The critical issue here is that the fear of losing benefits could be a disincentive to either obtaining or retaining work, and discussion within this area can be helpful.

Although Bond and others have provided useful evidence to recommend the use of supported employment programmes such as IPS, nevertheless there has been far less work on attempting to examine such research within EI services and for those younger people with FEP. However, Rinaldi and colleagues (2004) examined the use of IPS-based supported employment in a first-episode group. They used a repeated measure within subjects' study design of supported employment with 40 FEP service users. This study showed that the IPS model was effective in helping FEP users into valued occupation. Unemployment fell from 55% to 5% and competitive employment rose from 10% to 41% over 12 months. Also, those who were in education or training at the baseline either maintained their education or training across this intervention or completed it within the research timescale. Again, the importance of job maintenance and retention was cited as being as important as job acquisition.

A second study by Nuechterlein *et al.* (2005) was conducted using a randomised controlled trial (RCT). In their RCT, 51 service users were randomised to either an active intervention or a traditional vocational rehabilitation control group. Participants were followed for 18 months (6 months intervention and 12 months follow-up). In the first 6 months, 93% of the active experimental group returned to work or study compared to 50% in the control condition. In the follow-up period, 93% in the active experimental condition remained in school or work compared to 55% in the control condition. In addition, it was noted that in the study, the active condition resulted in a significantly lower rate of treatment drop-out. Therefore, the Rinaldi and Nuechterlein studies indicate that the potential of IPS in FEP is at least as good as it appears to be from other research with a more chronic population with mental illness.

Implementation into practice

The creation of effective services means identifying the types of barriers that can exist towards employment for people with FEP. Thus, Boldison *et al.* (2007) and Lloyd and Waghorn (2007) identify a number of barriers. These include individual, practitioner, labour market and mental health organisation factors:

- **Individual barriers to employment**
  A combination of cognitive, positive, negative and disorganised symptoms may erode individual confidence and undermine attempts to secure employment or education. However, this can be helped by making sure that occupation is contained in the care plan and also

by learning how others may have coped in similar situations. It may also be helped with individual cognitive behavioural therapy intervention to tackle symptoms and underlying unhelpful cognitions.

- **Practitioners' barriers to employment**
  It is possible that certain mental health professionals do not subscribe to the view that service users can work or train successfully. By employing vocational specialists who work to create structural employment links, such scepticism can be overcome. This may also be helped by employing staff with optimistic attitudes in relation to recovery and the potential capacity for individuals to return to education or employment.

- **Labour market barriers to employment**
  Certain jobs and industries will only allow for fixed patterns of work (e.g. shifts/hours). Career counselling, job sampling and proactive job-searching may help establish preferences and work threshold. Furthermore, the fluctuating course of early psychosis may present some challenges to maintaining employment once earned. Time-unlimited support from a vocational worker would be expected to help with such sessions being held away from the workplace to help discuss performance management. Links to employment supervision to discuss flexibility in the workplace could be advantageous.

- **Mental health organisational barriers to employment**
  Employing trusts and provider organisations need to ensure that vocational outcomes comprise a core part of service business. The staff would need to focus on occupational issues as part of their ongoing development plans. Links to other organisations that can help to assist with practical work and advice ought to be formed.

Examples of early intervention services providing vocational opportunities

Many EI services prioritise efforts to help service users into employment, education or training. We have highlighted some examples of how EI services have implemented this in practice.

South West London Early Intervention Service has employed a half-time vocational specialist worker who is integrated within the team to provide evidence-based supported employment to specifically address the vocational needs of EI clients within the service. The vocational specialist not only assists clients to gain employment or return to education but also addresses the issue of job or course retention. Within 6 months of intervention by the vocational specialist, the proportion of clients in employment had risen from 10% to 28%, and by 12 months, to 40%. The proportion in education was constant at 33% for the first 6 months, with many clients moving on to gain competitive employment. There was only one client in the service without any form of vocational activity (Rinaldi & Perkins, 2007).

Camden EI service, North London, has developed VIBE which is a vocational support service led by the Occupational Therapist within the team working with young people (18–35) who have experienced an FEP. VIBE was set up in March 2004. VIBE aims to support young people with FEP to develop the skills to be able to access mainstream employment and educational opportunities. Their specific aims are to:

- develop activity programmes while users are recovering from the FEP to ensure that disabilities don't become entrenched;
- support them to access local providers of employment and education;
- run groups focused on developing appropriate skills to participate in education and employment;
- link with local mainstream education and employment providers to develop an understanding of this group;
- develop links with black and minority ethnic (BME) communities to engage with young people from BME communities.

The VIBE service won a Guardian award in 2006 for their work in successfully securing employment for young people from BME communities.

The Psychosis Services for Young People in Hull and East Riding (PSYPHER, www.herhis.nhs.uk) also contains as one of its central aims, a commitment to obtaining employment for people. PSYPHER believes that 'life interventions' have equal importance to clini cal interventions. Service users are encouraged to develop skills they already have or to develop new ones. The team has found that sport and creative activity have been catalysts to build confidence and move onto more formal education, training or employment. They have created a bank of 'PSYPHER Associates' who gain work experience and offer inspiration to other service users. The rationale for this was the recognition that many young people already have skills which the team could use (such as tennis coaching, musical ability). Others have been supported to develop skills in an area of their interest, for example, football coaches and snowboard instructing. PSYPHER has also established good links with non-statutory and statutory bodies locally to help young people back into education and work. They attempt to piggyback on other projects and initiatives wherever possible. As a result of this, many young people have moved into education and employment. In 2006, Jellycat Media Limited was established by the former Early Intervention Lead and the manager of Creative Connexions (a team established by Connexions Humber). This is a social enterprise set up to fill the gaps EI teams often have difficulty filling within the structures of the NHS. A core aim of the Jellycat is to provide opportunities for accreditation and formal training and employment in creative media for individuals who have experienced psychosis. It also aims to provide activities not routinely provided within the health setting or other statutory services which meet the needs of this group. These include providing creative workshops which are the first stage in building confidence and skills to enable an individual to be ready to access mainstream programmes provided by other organisations. The business end of the initiative offers multi-media services, including web design, graphic design and film production, which give young people opportunities to gain work experience and accreditation working alongside freelance professionals. Jellycat also provides mental health awareness training, research services and consultancy. Service users will have opportunities

to be trained in all aspects of the business. As the business grows, there will be opportunities for formal employment.

Many other EI services, including the Gloucestershire Recovery in Psychosis (GRIP) team where the authors work, also aim to encourage people into work, education or training and have formed links to local agencies such as Connexions and local youth, volunteer (e.g. Millennium Volunteers) and training agencies (such as The Prince's Trust) to provide work opportunities and training which help to build confidence and provide an initial step into meaningful occupation.

Case studies

How this gets operationalised in practice is illustrated using a case example of work carried out with Leah who used the GRIP EI team between 2004 and 2005.

Leah was born and raised in Cheltenham. Her parents were late middle aged when she was born and she also had a brother who was significantly older than her. The age gap was sufficiently great to preclude a 'normal' sibling relationship. There were certain difficulties at home that made childhood difficult.

The onset of illness was very quick. It occurred in the summer of 2004 when Leah was just finishing her second year at Sheffield University. She was engaged in work experience following the cessation of her studies and she distinctly remembers a friend saying 'you need to take a break or you will go under'. Leah reflects that her normal 'modus operandi' was to work very hard and to put too much on her plate rather than too little in terms of the number of tasks in which she was engaged.

She returned to Cheltenham for 2 weeks and was doing temping jobs – which uncharacteristically she wished she was not doing. Just prior to returning to the university, her parents went on a holiday. She found the fact that she needed to return to the university on her own for the first time stressful, particularly, as she had been also looking after the house. She went back to the university but found the pressure of not handing in her research project on time combined with a very busy social life in which she was president of the Dance Society and the lead bassist in an orchestra to be too much. She returned home one Friday early into the start of the autumn term after she was picked up by her mother whom she had phoned at 1.00 A.M. the previous morning.

Leah was admitted into the local inpatient unit at the Charlton Lane Centre the following Sunday. Meanwhile, Leah's dad and then boyfriend contacted GRIP via its website, currently being redeveloped, to request more information on psychosis and to raise their own mental health awareness. Within 7 days, the GRIP team was able to visit Leah in hospital. Leah herself described the hospital as being 'mental'. She said it was full of mental patients and there were lots of negatives because lots of unwell people were kept together. Leah wanted to leave the centre quickly. She said that, once she was out of hospital, the work that GRIP did was 'vital'. In particular, she felt that the weekly sports group on a Friday had been a huge benefit to combat her social isolation and to feel better about herself because of physical activity.

Leah felt that the structure provided by GRIP was quite a useful framework. She felt that the work, largely undertaken with her care co-ordinator at the time, was useful because it covered a number of core areas using the Care Programme Approach (CPA) process/framework. It was quickly identified that Leah would feel like she was getting back on her feet in optimal fashion by getting back to the university to resume her studies as she had 1 year left to complete her BSc. Prior to this, it was recognised that a series of intermediate steps would be useful in order to prepare Leah for her return to the university.

The return to the university was preceded by paid work. Leah and her case manager had discussed Leah starting some voluntary work, but she wished to earn some money. As GRIP had been based near the Cheltenham town centre, this was advantageous because visits to see her case manager meant that Leah was nearer to the job centre and to other potential employers. Leah was able to do a number of different jobs which included being a paid worker at the local government communication headquarters. She worked for 1 week at the Cheltenham Racecourse which helped to rebuild social confidence, and the routine associated with work, was also cited as being particularly useful.

Leah also felt that the unequivocal underlying support system from GRIP was essential. The ongoing encouragement from the team, in particular, her care co-ordinator, was much appreciated and certainly helped with the initial job search which then created the launch pad for a return to the university.

Returning to Sheffield University was also helped by GRIP contacting the Sheffield Early Intervention Team, in particular, a link person who was to become Leah's key worker in South Yorkshire. Leah commented that 'I had a similar support system as the one I had in Gloucestershire. This made all the difference to my confidence as I knew the team in Sheffield held the same values and spoke the same language as the GRIP team.'

Just at the time Leah was returning to the university, she was also asked by the GRIP team to attend an interview panel which was interviewing for new GRIP staff members. She was also asked to take part in a similar interview process in Sheffield who were also looking for new staff. She felt that this was also very advantageous.

Leah initially lacked confidence going back to the university but then felt that there was an advantage in her being a year older and therefore, in a wider sense, more mature. There were certain disadvantages in that because she had had a gap year, 'a gap year with a difference!' according to Leah that she did not really make friends in the way that she had in her original cohort. However, she very much wanted to finish her degree and she was also buoyed up by a clear demonstration of respect from her parents who were impressed that she had had the courage and determination to get herself back to the university. Leah was able to take on-board advice from GRIP and the Sheffield Early Intervention Team and maintained a good work/life balance in which she 'worked hard and played hard'. She was able to get a 2:1. Leah was very pleased with this. This then gave her the confidence to apply for a Masters course which was heavily research based in terms of its major content and she began this post graduate course in September 2006. At the time of writing, she has just finished her first research dissertation and her feedback on the course so far has been very good. The course is scheduled to end in October 2007 after which Leah feels that she may well be entitled to a break. Her future career may centre either on teaching or social work or a post in the NHS.

Implications and conclusions

Thus far, the chapter has described how policy and research have dictated that employment, education and training should form part of the wider, progressive EI services. Research (Bond *et al.*, 2004; Rinaldi *et al.*, 2004; Nuechterlein *et al.*, 2005; Boldison *et al.*, 2007) attests to the fact that such services can be delivered for both chronic and early-in-the-course populations.

- All service users will need to be offered the opportunity of employment, education or training. Being able to help provide educational opportunities as well as work is important due to the age range associated with EI services (Killackey *et al.*, 2006).
- Vocational intervention needs to be tailored to each service user and to reflect personal aspirations (Morrow *et al.*, 2002).
- Job-retention strategies will need to be provided alongside job acquisition as ongoing psychological factors may benefit from therapeutic input (Xie *et al.*, 1997).
- Job retention would expect to be enhanced via input from an EI vocational specialist on a time-unlimited and individualised basis (Gowdy *et al.*, 2003).
- Benefits counselling may help users move into work or training, as opposed to becoming 'trapped' into receipt of benefits (Mowbray & Megivern, 1999; Davis & Rinaldi, 2004).
- Different organisations (statutory and non-statutory) are capable of delivering vocational opportunities. What is key is that such services are flexible, proactive, capable of co-ordinating their efforts across agencies and can tailor-make their interventions for the individual service user.

It is also important that the staff exhibit a hopeful and positive attitude when working with young people so that occupational recovery, in its widest sense, is regarded not just as possible but probable. The expectations of staff and other potential 'enablers' can be crucial in promoting life opportunities. Thus, the extant research suggests that the above factors are necessarily intrinsic to future EI educational and vocational service development, and in developing access to appropriate educational and vocational opportunities.

In conclusion, it is important that young people with psychosis are offered the opportunity to engage in employment, educational and training opportunities to fully re-engage with society. Only in this way can fuller recovery begin and wider personal potential be realised.

Hopefully, as vocational interventions begin to bear fruit for this group of people, the functional aspects of individual recovery will continue within EI, and policy makers, managers and clinicians can continue to work together to improve further delivery of EI services.

Useful websites

- www.shift.org.uk SHIFT provides useful information on employment
- www.socialexclusionunit.gov.uk Social Exclusion Unit: Mental Health Section provides useful information on recovery from a government perspective
- www.herhisdev.nhs.uk PSYPHER website
- www.Jellycatmedia.com Jellycat Media Ltd
- www.eppic.org.au EPPIC: Influential Australian website that recognises the importance of occupational recovery

References

Anthony, W. (1993). Recovery from mental illness: The guiding vision of the mental health service system in the 1990's. *Psychosocial Rehabilitation Journal*, 16, 11–24.

Boldison, S., Davies, R., Hawkes, H., Pace, C. & Sayers, R. (2007). Employment, mental health and PSI: Operation is everyone's job. In: R. Velleman, E. Davis, G. Smith & M. Drage (eds), *Changing Outcomes in Psychosis: Collaborative Cases from Practitioners, Users and Carers*, pp. 194–210. BPS Blackwell, Chapter 11.

Bond, G. (2004). Supported employment: Evidence for an evidence-based practice. *Psychiatric Rehabilitation Journal*, 27 (4), 345–359.

Davis, M. & Rinaldi, M. (2004). Using an evidence-based approach to enable people with mental health problems to gain and retain employment, education and voluntary work. *British Journal of Occupational Therapy*, 67 (7), 319–322.

Davis, E., Velleman, R., Smith, G. & Drage, M. (2007). Psychosocial developments: Towards a model of recovery. In: R. Velleman, E. Davis, G. Smith, & M. Drage (eds), *Changing Outcomes in Psychosis: Collaborative Cases from Practitioners, Users and Carers,* pp. 1–21. BPS Blackwell, Chapter 1.

Department of Health (1999). *The National Service Framework for Mental Health: Modem Standards and Service Models.* London: Department of Health.

Department of Health (2001). *Mental Health Policy Implementation Guide.* London: Department of Health.

Gowdy, L., Carlson, L. & Rapp, C.A. (2003). Practice differentiating high-performing from low-performing supported employment programmes. *Psychiatric Rehabilitation Journal,* 26, 232–239.

Killackey, E., Jackson, H., Gleeson, J., Hickie, I. & McGorry, P. (2006). Exciting career opportunity beckons! Early intervention and vocational rehabilitation in first episode psychosis: Employing cautious optimism. *Australian and New Zealand Journal of Psychiatry,* 40, 951–962.

Lloyd, C. & Waghorn, G. (2007). The importance of vocation in recovery for young people with psychiatric disabilities. *British Journal of Occupational Therapy,* 70 (2), 50–59.

Morrow, L., Verins, I. & Willis, E. (2002). *Mental Health and Work Issues and Perspectives.* Adelaide: Aussienet – Australian Network for Promotion, Prevention and Early Intervention for Mental Health.

Mowbray, C. & Megivern, D. (1999). Higher education and rehabilitation for people with psychiatric disabilities. *Journal of Rehabilitation,* 65, 31–38.

Nuechterlein, K., Subotnik, K., Ventura, J., Gitlin, M., Green, M., Wallace, C. *et al.* (2005). *Advances in improving and predicting work outcome in recent onset schizophrenia.* Abstract No 117697. In: Abstract Viewer Savannah GA: International Congress on Schizophrenia Research.

Office of the Deputy Prime Minister (ODPM) (2004). *Mental Health and Social Exclusion.* ODPM Publications, Wetherby.

Rinaldi, M. & Perkins R. (2007). Implementing evidence based supported employment. *Psychiatric Bulletin,* 31, 244–249.

Rinaldi, M., McNeil, K., Firm, M., Koletsi, M., Perkins, R. & Singh, S. (2004). What are the benefits of evidence-based supported employment for patients with first-episode psychosis? *Psychiatric Bulletin,* 28, 281–284.

Xie, H., Dain, B., Becker, D. & Drake, R. (1997). Job tenure among people with severe mental illness. *Rehabilitation Counselling Bulletin,* 40, 230–239.

Chapter 17 **Substance misuse in first-episode psychosis**

Ian Wilson

Introduction

In the last few years, there has been an increasing awareness of the needs of a large group of people who are experiencing problems with their mental health and who also use drink and/or drugs. Traditional service approaches to these clients, by both mental health services and drug and alcohol agencies, have led to poor levels of engagement, problems with accurate detection and assessment, pessimistic attitudes and values among staff and restrictive 'gate-keeping' practices that have resulted in some services being exclusive rather than inclusive.

The result has been that some of the most vulnerable and chaotic clients have received the poorest of services, while commissioners of services have argued about responsibilities and funding streams. However, the tide of political, organisational and clinical direction has turned dramatically. There are now some excellent examples of good practice in joint commissioning, joint working and specialist service developments. Recent statements from the UK's Department of Health have underlined that 'dual diagnosis' represents the most important challenge for modern mental health services. Researchers, clinicians and service providers are attempting to respond to this challenge.

This chapter will explore issues of dual diagnosis when working with people experiencing a first or recent onset of psychosis. There will be a review of the current literature around issues of effective approaches in dual diagnosis. The evidence base for efficacious interventions will be summarised and an attempt will be made to comment on the issue of translating this research into effective treatments. Ways of improving staff attitudes and values towards this client group and improving their knowledge and skills, leading to better services, will be explored with the help of a recent document: Closing the Gap, Essential Shared Capabilities for Working with Dual Diagnosis (Hughes, 2006).

Prevalence rates in dual diagnosis

Due to increasing concern in the USA about the coexistence of mental ill health and substance use among their clients, the Epidemiological Catchment Area Study (ECAS: Regier et al., 1990) investigated a population of over 20,000 users of mental health services. The results showed that there was evidence of co-morbid substance misuse in the psychiatric population in excess of 50%. Lifetime prevalence of co-morbidity was found to be 47% in those individuals with a diagnosis of schizophrenia, 84% in those with personality disorders and 32% in those with an affective disorder. Rates of substance use appear to be higher among people with Severe & enduring Mentall Illness (SMI) than in the general population (Gibbins & Kipping, 2006). Prevalence studies in the UK have reported the prevalence of co-morbidity to range from 20% to 70%. For instance, in one study, 32% of people with schizophrenia were using illicit substances (Menezes et al., 1996); and in another study, up to 16% were using alcohol to excess (Duke et al., 1994). Working with people with a dual diagnosis has therefore become a routine part of any part of mental health care (Banerjee et al., 2002). In a recent review of the prevalence rates of cannabis use among people with psychosis, Green et al. (2005) used data from 53 different studies of treatment samples and five epidemiological studies. The authors found that prevalence estimates for current cannabis use were 23% and 11.3% for current misuse,

12-month use was 29.2% and 12-month misuse was 18.8%. Lifetime use and misuse rates were 42.1% and 22.5%, respectively.

A recent study investigating the prevalence rates of dual diagnosis across Manchester Mental Health and Social Care Trust (Holland & Schulte, 2006), which serves a culturally diverse and socially deprived urban population, showed some wide variations in the reported rates of dual diagnosis among clients from different parts of the service. For instance, reported rates among clients on psychiatric intensive care units (PICUs) are approximately 90%. A total of 71% of patients under the care of the assertive outreach service have co-morbid drug and/or alcohol problems. One community mental health team (CMHT) reported prevalence rates of 75%, while other CMHTs in different sectors of the city stated that they have rates as low as 10%. The mean rate across CMHTs is 29%. Several possible explanations for this huge disparity in prevalence can be suggested. It could be that drug and alcohol use is far more common in certain parts of the city or in certain groups of clients, possibly reflecting differences in class, gender, culture or ethnicity. Or it could be that there is a huge difference in the way co-morbidity is defined. Another reason might be because some teams are much more effective at detection and assessment of dual diagnosis than others.

A recent study into the prevalence of substance use among people with a first-episode psychosis (FEP) was undertaken by Barnett *et al* (2007). They used a representative sample of young people entering into an early intervention service (EIS) to record and measure current and lifetime substance use and to compare this with general population prevalence estimates from the British Crime Survey. They found that substance use among people with an FEP was twice that of the general population and was more common in men than women. A total of 51% of their clients reported cannabis abuse and 43% reported alcohol abuse. More than half the young people said that they had used Class A drugs and 38% said that they were using several substances at once. There appeared to be an association with the age at which the young erson used cannabis, cocaine, ecstasy and amphetamine and the age at which they later developed a psychosis. As the authors report, this association has serious public health consequences.

Much of the research into prevalence has been undertaken with users of mental health services. However, that is only one part of a complicated picture. There is also a high level of mental ill health among users of drug and alcohol services, many of whom will have had no assessment or treatment by secondary mental health services, primarily focused as they are on 'severe and enduring' mental ill health (which often means in effect the treatment of psychotic illness). A large survey of drug and alcohol treatment agencies (COSMIC Study: Weaver *et al.*, 2003) reported that:

- 74.5% of users of drug services and 85.5% of users of alcohol services experience mental health problems;
- 67.6% of drug treatment users and 80.6% of alcohol treatment users had depression and/or anxiety;
- 26.9% of drug treatment users and 46.8% of alcohol treatment users suffered from severe depression;
- the figures are 19% and 32.3% for severe anxiety;
- 7.9% of drug treatment users and 19.4% of alcohol treatment users have a psychosis.

These figures have real and significant implications for both the workers and users of drug and alcohol services. Even if successful outcomes are achieved in helping to reduce the impact of drink or drugs on someone's life, the effects of the coexisting mental health problem will often still be felt. As well as causing the person ongoing distress and disruption, it may also be a major factor in returning to substances in order to alleviate problems or to enhance mood. Drug and alcohol workers often find this frustrating and service users find it self-defeating and it can lead to pessimistic prognoses on both sides. Workers may not feel confident in detecting and assessing mental health problems. When they are able to identify them, they may be at a loss to address them. They might not have the skills needed to offer mental health interventions or the knowledge of services to know how or where to refer clients. Lastly, their attitudes and values concerning mental ill health may not reflect the kind of non-judgemental or empathic understanding that is helpful in ensuring optimistic outcomes.

These issues can be addressed through providing improved training, supervision and support of staff. Services can respond to their clients needs by encouraging networking between mental health and drug/alcohol services, enhanced joint working protocols and interagency care planning. There may be a case for specialist dual diagnosis workers to offer advice and individualised interventions to the most complex clients.

Effective interventions for dually diagnosed clients

Early studies

Research into effective interventions for dually diagnosed (DD) clients began in the 1980s. They examined the application of 'traditional' substance abuse interventions, consisting mainly of 12-step groups and other forms of abstinence-based programmes. These studies produced disappointing results, which led to pessimistic conclusions about the efficacy of interventions for those clients with coexisting mental ill health (Ley et al., 1999). However, these early studies seem to have failed to take into account the complex nature of dual diagnosis issues. It became clear to subsequent researchers that itwas necessary to design interventions that addressed a range of interrelated problems and concerns. Researchers in the USA began to look at the delivery of more comprehensive programmes incorporating assertive outreach and long-term rehabilitation, to positive effect. These projects began to offer interventions to clients who did not always acknowledge that they had either a substance use or a mental health problem or that these two factors were related. By the 1990s, projects began to incorporate principles of health behaviour change using a motivational interviewing (MI) approach (Miller & Rollnick, 2002), assertive outreach, comprehensiveness and a long-term perspective. However, most of

these initial studies were uncontrolled and should be viewed as 'pilot studies' (Detrick & Stiepock, 1992).

Integrated studies

Studies using a more robust methodology began to appear in the mid-1990s and eight fairly recent studies with 'experimental or 'quasi-experimental' designs support the effectiveness of integrated dual diagnosis treatments for DD clients (Godley et al., 1994; Jerrell & Ridgely, 1995; Carmichael et al., 1998; Drake et al., 1998; Ho et al., 1999; Barrowclough et al., 2001; Brunette et al., 2001; Haddock et al., 2003).

The critical components of successful trials appeared to be staged interventions, assertive outreach, MI, counselling about drug use and its effect on mental health and social support. Trials started to offer interventions based on a long-term perspective and on comprehensive integrated treatments. Successful trials also displayed an element of cultural sensitivity. The results of a 10-year follow-up study appeared to show sustained recovery among a group of clients in health-related outcomes and outcomes chosen as important by the participants themselves (Drake et al., 2006).

However, there is reason to be cautious about the findings from this research. Most of it was carried out in the USA, with a very different health service and social infrastructure compared to the UK. Is this research generalisable to services in the modern NHS? One of the studies (Barrowclough et al., 2001; Haddock et al., 2003) was carried out in the UK. It provided evidence of promising outcomes and has led to the instigation of the multicenter isradipine diuretic atherosclerosis study (MIDAS), a large multisite randomised controlled trial into the efficacy of MI and cognitive behavioural therapy (CBT), with an intention where appropriate to collaboratively make links between mental ill health and coexisting substance use. The result of this trial (which at the time of writing is still at the intervention stage) is awaited with interest, because it will produce the largest body of data into the efficacy of this form of treatment. There may be room for cautious optimism in UK settings. Graham (2003) recognised that there are potentially far more opportunities for co-working between EIS and drug and alcohol agencies. There is the likelihood that in the UK all agencies will share a 'harm reduction' approach based on client need and clinical effectiveness, compared to the situation in the USA, where the criminal justice system and the use of coercive interventions appear to be more the norm.

Other gaps in our knowledge of important issues for DD clients remain. There is limited information within the research on the cost implications of integrated services. It is therefore difficult to say if there would be possible savings resulting from more effective services for DD clients. There is a lack of specificity in the treatments described in the research and it is therefore hard to say which of the comprehensive interventions are most efficacious and for whom. Also, the research has been mainly directed at outpatient and community treatments. Very little of the investigation has taken place in in-patient settings.

Dual diagnosis and early intervention

High rates of substance use have been reported in clients entering mental health services for the first time. Cantwell *et al.* (1999), in a study of 168 young people presenting with FEP, reported that the criteria for drug use, drug misuse and alcohol misuse were met by 37% of the sample. Those most at risk of substance use in this group were young males. The link between using substances and experiencing an onset of a psychotic illness has been widely debated in recent years. It is still the subject of considerable concern and this section will attempt to summarise the major arguments. However, firstly, it is worthwhile to review what we know about patterns of substance use in society generally.

What are the patterns of drug use in the UK?

Substance use is a major issue for society throughout the world (Costa e Silva, 2002). The figures for drug use in the UK are among the highest in Europe: 35.6% of 16- to 59-year-olds used one or more illicit drugs in their lifetime (over 11 million people), 12.3% used one or more illicit drugs in 2008 (over 4 million) and 13.4% used Class A in their lifetime (Dodd *et al.*, 2004). Cannabis is the most widely used illicit drug in Europe (European Monitoring Centre for Drug & Drug Addiction, 2001). In the UK, cannabis is also the most commonly used street drug, with approximately 3.5 million users, followed by cocaine, ecstasy and amphetamine. Approximately, half of all 15- to 29-year-olds are said to have tried cannabis at some time in their lives.

Why do young people take drugs?

Young people choose to use drugs for many different reasons. One of the most obvious ones, but a reason that can be overlooked by parents, families or workers, is that they are enjoyable. Despite what others may think, young people often report that they have a lot of fun when under the influence of drugs. They also take them simply because they are so freely available. In most parts of the UK, it is now possible to gain access to most illicit substances. The price of various drugs has also been falling steadily. This is true of alcohol as well, which makes drugs and alcohol ever more accessible to more and more people. People also take substances out of curiosity and because they are bored.

However, some young people choose to use drugs because they can change how they feel and help them deal with emotional difficulties. This is especially attractive to someone who might be already experiencing problems in their lives or with their mental health. The user may find that when they take drugs their problems temporarily diminish and that they can aid social interaction.

Finally, sadly, for some young people, the use of drugs may become an established habit, which means that stopping their drug use would lead to physical or psychological withdrawal.

Cannabis and mental health

Cannabis is the most widely used illicit drug among young people. It is not surprising that it should have attracted worldwide attention from investigators who are interested in any possible links between its usage and the onset and course of mental health problems. The debate is a complicated one, with no easy answers.

Put simply, several recent studies (Arseneault *et al.*, 2002; van Os *et al.*, 2002; Zammit *et al.*, 2002) have suggested a causal link between the use of cannabis, especially if started at an early age, and the subsequent development of psychosis. The study by Zammit *et al.* (2002) is a good example of this theory. The study is a follow-up of a large group of people stretching over many years. In 1969, during the induction process for young conscripts into the Swedish armed forces (military service was compulsory at the time), people were asked to complete a medical questionnaire. One of the questions on this questionnaire was whether the young person had smoked cannabis. This large group of people was followed up on several subsequent occasions. Those who had reported cannabis use in 1969 were reported as having significantly more likelihood of developing a psychotic illness than those who said that they had not been smoking cannabis. However, can this be said to 'prove' a causal link between early use of cannabis and later development of psychosis?

There might be several confounding explanations for the link between the two. How accurate was the self-reporting? Were the young people who later went on to develop psychosis more likely to report their cannabis use than others? Were people who did not subsequently develop psychosis less inclined to admit to cannabis use? Were the group which developed psychosis already a different group of young people than their peers? Were there other factors that made them a different group – use of other drugs, including tobacco and alcohol, history of abuse, problems during their education, certain social or class differences? Some, but not all, of these questions have been answered by the researchers but the jury is still out about a clear 'causal link' between the use of cannabis and the development of psychosis.

However, it appears to be an irrefutable fact that the use of cannabis among young people with a vulnerability to psychosis can be a dangerous behaviour. A systematic review of the evidence pertaining to cannabis use and the occurrence of psychotic or affective mental health outcomes published in the *Lancet* in July 2007 (Moore *et al.*, 2007) showed an increased risk of any psychotic outcome in individuals who had ever used cannabis. Some young people seem to be 'super-sensitive' to even quite small amounts of the drug. Certain high potency types of the drug may have a crucial effect on some individuals. The 'super-strength' varieties (often known by the general name of 'skunkweed' because of its pungent smell, but in fact encompassing many different types and strains) seem to be particularly associated with the development of psychotic symptoms, possibly due to the high levels of one of the psychoactive substances found in them, THC. Families often tell services that the young person they care for had first experienced problems with thoughts, feelings and behaviours at the same time that they first noticed that cannabis was being used. The use of illicit substances causes families and carers great concern. It leads to arguments, bewilderment and, sometimes, despair for family members who see major changes in the young person and reach the conclusion that drug use is directly leading to mental health problems. Sometimes families decide that if the young person would stop using drugs, all the problems would disappear. Unfortunately, this is not always the case.

Detecting drug and alcohol use

It is essential that mental health workers are able to detect and assess drug and alcohol use in all the clients that they work with. Due to the high prevalence rates of use among young people, it is especially important when working with people experiencing a first or recent onset of psychosis. There is really no great secret about how to detect and assess substance use. It is a matter of asking the right questions at the right time. This, however, can only be undertaken if there is a degree of engagement built on the principles of honesty, trust and the display of non-judgemental attitudes towards the person and their lifestyle choices. From this essential basis the following questions can be helpful:

- Which drug(s)? How much?
- Which route? How often?
- For how long?
- How is the use being funded?

- What are the effects (both good and not so good)?
- What do you want to do about it?

What can we do?

As we have seen earlier in this chapter, there is a growing evidence base surrounding effective interventions for DD clients. These are based on comprehensive, integrated approaches that deal with all aspects of our clients' complex lives.

To assist the development of services for people with a dual diagnosis, Hughes (2006) has written an excellent document called 'Closing the Gap'. The purpose of 'Closing the Gap' is to provide a document to assist in the implementation of the Department of Health Dual Diagnosis Practice Implementation Guide (Department of Health, 2002). It also highlights the training and service developments that will be required to implement this in practice. This represents the first time that capabilities for working with combined mental health and substance use problems have been clearly identified and defined.

The document offers a comprehensive 'Capability Framework'. It highlights the roles and responsibilities of the various agencies in providing care for people with dual diagnosis. It states that care for those with serious mental illness and substance use should be provided by the mental health services (mainstreaming). The framework is divided into three sections: values and attitudes; knowledge and skills; and practice development. Each capability has three levels: core, generalist and specialist. Its aim is to establish core competencies for all staff that work with clients with coexisting mental health and substance use problems. This document complements other indicators of service and clinical development: The Knowledge & Skills Framework (Department of Health, 2003); Mental Health Care Group Workforce Team: National Mental Health Workforce Strategy (Department of Health, 2004a); The Drug & Alcohol National Occupational Standards (DANOS: Department of Health, 2004b); and The Ten Essential Shared Capabilities (Department of Health, 2004c).

'Closing the Gap' provides us with some important reminders of how to work effectively with young people who have a first onset of psychosis and who are simultaneously continuing to use drink and drugs. It clearly states that it is part of our role to work with this group of clients and that we need to encourage and sustain a degree of therapeutic optimism when we are working with them. We should acknowledge the uniqueness of individuals, be non-judgemental in our attitudes and values and whenever possible we should ensure that we attempt to display empathy about their present situation and how they have arrived there.

We need to develop our engagement skills and may well need to be particularly creative and opportunistic when working with hard-to-engage young people around issues of drug and alcohol use. When providing education and health promotion, the information should be individualised, should correspond, not conflict, with the client's existing knowledge and should be in a form and language that the client finds acceptable. A good example of dual diagnosis information that has been tailored to younger people can be found in the *'Out of Your Head'* Guides (Holland & Linnell, 2007). These booklets tell the stories of four people and were written following extensive collaboration with service users.

Interventions should be based around collaborative care planning and agreement on prioritising needs. MI techniques, relapse prevention work and CBT appear to provide the basis for successful interventions. For instance, the randomized controlled trial carried out in the UK referred to earlier in this chapter (Barrowclough *et al.*, 2001; Haddock *et al.*, 2003) used MI, CBT and family therapy with a DD population to attempt to improve symptoms of mental ill health and reduce substance use. This study showed that an integrated therapeutic approach could be efficacious and it has led to the much larger MIDAS which is currently being undertaken on several sites in the UK. A fuller description of the therapy can be found in Barrowclough *et al.* (2007). Their findings will be published over the next few years and should begin to establish clear evidence-based criteria for successful intervention packages.

Workers should be realistic about expecting that young people will change the way they behave because we 'think they should' or because they 'ought to' do so. Many young people, whether suffering from an early onset of psychosis or not, have individualised health behaviour models that may very well be different from our own. Their own mental or physical health may not be a high priority for them, and though they may decide to change their behaviours eventually, they may have decided that this is not the right time to do so. A randomized controlled trial by Edwards *et al.* (2006) compared an intensive cannabis-focused intervention for young people with an FEP with a less detailed psycho-education package. The cannabis-focused intervention, known as Cannabis and Psychosis (CAP), provided one-to-one therapy sessions designed to use MI principles to enhance the change process. The 'control' group received a basic education package concerning cannabis use and its connection with mental health problems. There were no significant differences between the cannabis-focused intervention group and the psycho-education group on cannabis use at the end of treatment and 6 months later. These authors therefore recommend that simple interventions based around providing acceptable information about cannabis use may be worth considering before attempting more intensive therapeutic input.

Case studies

Andrew is 19 years old. He first smoked cannabis with friends when he was 15. All his friends were smoking and he didn't want to feel left out. However, unlike the majority of his mates, he never really liked the sensation of being 'stoned'. Where most of them seemed to get a bit giggly and pleasantly relaxed, it always seemed to make him anxious and on edge. After a 'spliff' he sometimes believed that he was being followed or that he was going to be arrested by the police. These unpleasant experiences didn't make him quit smoking cannabis. In fact, he started to smoke it more regularly. Having been an able student at school, he achieved good GCSE results and then went

to 6th Form College. He began to struggle and before long he dropped out of college and was spending more and more time sitting at home alone. He had by now lost contact with many of his old friends. His behaviour was causing concern to his mother. She was especially worried about his continued cannabis use, which he no longer even bothered to try to hide from her. When she questioned him about it, he told her that it was none of her business, that all his friends smoked and that she didn't understand about his drug use or about his life in general.

When he was 18, the situation became untenable for everyone. Andrew's self care had deteriorated markedly and his behaviour had grown increasingly erratic. He could be heard talking loudly in his room and his speech patterns became more difficult to understand. His GP agreed to see him at home because Andrew would not attend the surgery. His GP referred him immediately to his local EIS for an initial assessment and they became involved in his care. It took 3 months for the service to engage with Andrew fully. At first, he was suspicious of the service and told workers that he didn't need any support. However, through consistency and honesty, workers gradually got to know him better and he agreed to talk to them about his thoughts and feelings. He described a range of hallucinatory experiences and unusual beliefs associated with them. He accepted the offer of a trial of anti-psychotic medication and his mental state slowly improved.

However, to his mother's disbelief and increasing despair, he continued to smoke just as much cannabis as he had before the involvement of the EIS. He often rolled his first 'spliff' to smoke with his morning cup of coffee and he would continue to smoke throughout the day. This caused arguments with his mother, and when she was offered a Carer's Assessment, Andrew's continuing use of cannabis was her stated number one priority.

Andrew's mother agreed to accept the offer of a cognitive-behavioural family intervention, to which his younger sister was also invited. This comprehensive intervention used strategies to enhance communication, techniques to reduce stress within the home and realistic goal setting to enable both Andrew and his mother to gradually regain their optimum functioning. The family was encouraged to address the issue of Andrew's cannabis use in an open and honest manner but which avoided arguments or criticism.

At the same time, Andrew was given the opportunity by his key worker to discuss his cannabis use without being judged and avoiding confrontation and argumentation at all times. An 'elicit/provide/elicit' approach was taken when providing him with information about cannabis and its potential effects on his mental state. This enabled the worker to understand clearly what Andrew already knew about cannabis and also elicited his own existing views about the part it played in his life and what, if anything, he wished to change about it. Information was given, with permission, which was individualised and which he found accessible and acceptable. The worker was then able to discuss with Andrew what he thought of the new information and what he wanted to do with it. Over the next 6 months, Andrew gradually reduced his cannabis use. He now smokes most weekends when he visits his friends. He seldom smokes during the week and, because his mother hates the smell of it in her house, he has agreed that if he does smoke at home, he will do so outside in the back garden. His mental state has continued to improve and he is thinking about going back to college to complete his A Levels.

Conclusion

Many young people experiment with drink and drugs. This can potentially lead to all kinds of problems. People with a vulnerability to the development of psychotic symptoms are no different from other young people in this regard. There used to be a great deal of 'therapeutic pessimism' surrounding people with psychotic illnesses who also use substances. A growing evidence base refutes these attitudes. DD clients can be engaged in a range of interventions that address both their mental health and their substance use needs. Families and carers can be supported with the distress these issues can cause. EIS should be flexible and skilled in their ability to work with young people who continue to use drink and drugs, even when these lifestyle choices appear to be affecting their mental health detrimentally. Clients will be taking substances for all kinds of reasons – because they believe that they help to relieve symptoms; because they think that

they reduce some of the side effects of medication; because they sometimes offer a quick way to feel a little better or to relieve boredom; because they are in an area of their lives that they still have some element of control over; that they would prefer to be labelled a 'drug user' than someone with a 'mental health problem'; and because substances are cheap, freely available and can be very enjoyable. By being collaborative and non-judgemental towards our clients, we can have conversations with them, which display empathy, avoid confrontation and support self-efficacy. This will, at the very least, aid the engagement process. Additionally, it can lead to some of our clients making sustained changes that can play an important part on their road to recovery from psychosis.

Useful websites

www.csip.org.uk/mentalhealthandcannabis
Care Services Improvement Partnership, Cannabis Toolkit
www.youngminds.org.uk/cannabis Young Minds
www.eastmidlands.csip.org.uk/dd/index
Education material – Out Of Your Heads guides (Mark Holland & Mike Linnell)
www.drugs.gov.uk
www.talktofrank.com
www.knowcannabis.org.uk

Suggested further reading

Baker, A. & Velleman, R. (2006). *Clinical Handbook of Co-existing Mental Health and Drug and Alcohol Problems.* London: Routledge.

Graham, H.L., Copello, A., Birchwood, M.J. & Mueser, K.T. (2003). *Substance Misuse in Psychosis: Approaches to Treatment and Service Delivery.* Chichester: Wiley.

Miller, W. & Rollnick, S. (2002). *Motivational Interviewing: Preparing People to Change Addictive Behaviour.* New York: Guilford Press.

References

Arseneault, L., Cannon, M., Poulton, R., Murray, R., Caspi, A. & Moffitt, T.E. (2002). Cannabis use in adolescence and risk for adult psychosis: Longitudinal prospective study. *British Medical Journal*, 325, 1212–1213.

Banerjee, S., Clancy, C. & Crome, I. (2002). *Co-existing Problems of Mental Disorder and Substance Misuse (Dual Diagnosis): An Information Manual*. London: Royal College of Psychiatrists Research Unit.

Barnett, J., Werners, U., Secher, S. *et al.* (2007). Substance use in a population based clinic sample of people with first episode psychosis. *British Journal of Psychosis*, 190, 515–520.

Barrowclough, C., Haddock, G., Tarrier, N. *et al.* (2001). Randomised controlled trial of MI, CBT and FI for patients with co-morbid schizophrenia and SUD. *American Journal of Psychiatry*, 158, 1706–1713.

Barrowclough, C., Haddock, G., Lowens, I. *et al.* (2007). Psychosis and drug and alcohol problems. In: A. Baker & R. Velleman (eds), *A Clinical Handbook of Co-existing Mental Health and Drug and Alcohol Problems*. London: Routledge.

Brunette, M.F., Drake, R.E., Woods, M. & Hartnett, T. (2001). A comparison of long-term and short-term residential treatment programmes for DD patients. *Psychiatric Services*, 52, 526–528.

Cantwell, R., Brewin, J., Glazebrook, C. *et al.* (1999). Prevalence of substance use in first-episode psychosis. *British Journal of Psychiatry*, 174, 150–153.

Carmichael, D., Tackett-Gibson, M., Dell, O. *et al.* (1998). *Texas DD Project Evaluation Report, 1997–1998*. College Station, Texas: A&M University Public Policy Research Institute.

Costa e Silva (2002). Evidence based analysis of the worldwide abuse of licit and illicit drugs. *Human Psychopharmacology*, 17, 131–140.Department of Health (2002). *Mental Health Policy Implementation Guidelines for Dual Diagnosis*. London: Department of Health.

Department of Health (2003). *Knowledge and Skills Framework*. London: Department of Health.

Department of Health (2004a). *Mental Health Care Group Workforce Team: National Mental Health Workforce Strategy*. London: Department of Health.

Department of Health (2004b). *Management Standards Consultancy for Skills for Health – Drugs and Alcohol Occupational Standards*. London: Department of Health.

Department of Health (2004c). *The Ten Essential Shared Capabilities – A Framework for the Whole of the Mental Health Workforce*. London: Department of Health.

Detrick, A. & Stiepock, V. (1992). Treating persons with mental illness, substance abuse and legal problems: The Rhode Island experience. *New Directions for Mental Health Services*, 56, 65–77.

Dodd, T., Nicholas, S., Povey, D. & Walker, A. (2004). *Crime in England and Wales 2003/2004*. London: Home Office Statistical Bulletin.

Drake, R.E., McHugo, G.J., Clark, R.E. *et al.* (1998). Assertive community treatment for patients with co-occurring severe mental illness and substance use disorder. A clinical trial. *American Journal of Orthopsychiatry*, 68, 201–215.

Drake, R.E., McHugo, G.J., Xie, H., Fox, M., Packard, J. & Helmstetter, B. (2006). Ten year recovery outcomes for clients with co-occurring schizophrenia and SUD. *Schizophrenia Bulletin*, 32 (3), 464–473.

Duke, P.J., Pantelis, C. & Barnes, T.R. (1994). South Westminster Schizophrenia Survey: Alcohol use and its relationship to symptoms, tardive dyskinesia and illness onset. *British Journal of Psychiatry*, 164, 630–636.

Edwards, J., Elkins, K., Hinton, M. *et al.* (2006). Randomized controlled trial of a cannabis-focused intervention for young people with first-episode psychosis. *Acta Psychiatrica Scandinavica*, 114 (2), 109–117.

European Monitoring Centre for Drug & Drug Addiction (2001). *2001 Annual Report on the State of the Drugs Problem in the European Union*. Brussels: European Monitoring Centre for Drug & Drug Addiction.

Gibbins, J. & Kipping, C. (2006). Coexistent substance use and psychiatric disorders. In: C. Gamble & G. Brennan (eds), *Working With Serious Mental Illness*. Edinburgh: Elsevier.

Godley, S.H., Hoewing-Roberson, R. & Godley, M.D. (1994). *Final MISA Report*. Bloomington Illinois: Lighthouse Institute.

Graham, H. (2003). A cognitive conceptualisation of concurrent psychosis and problem drug and alcohol use. In: H. Graham, A. Capello, M. Birchwood & K. Mueser (eds), *Substance Misuse in Psychosis: Approaches to Treatment and Service Delivery*. Chichester: John Wiley.

Green, B., Young, R. & Kavanagh, D. (2005). Cannabis use and misuse prevalence among people with psychosis. *British Journal of Psychiatry*, 187, 306–313.

Haddock, G., Barrowclough, C., Tarrier, N. *et al.* (2003). Cognitive behavioural therapy and motivational intervention for schizophrenia and substance misuse – 18 month outcomes of a randomised controlled trial. *British Journal of Psychiatry*, 183, 418–426.

Ho, A.P., Tsuang, J.W., Liberman, R.P. *et al.* (1999). Achieving effective treatment of patients with chronic psychotic illness and co morbid substance dependence. *American Journal of Psychiatry*, 156, 1765–1770.

Holland, M. & Linell, M. (2007). The "Out of Your Head" Guides. Manchester, Lifeline Publications.

www.lifelinepublications.org.uk/publications@life-line.org.uk.

Hughes, L. (2006). *Closing the Gap, Essential Shared Capabilities for Working with Dual Diagnosis.* University of Lincoln: Centre for Clinical & Workforce Innovation.

Jerrell, J.M. & Ridgely, M.S. (1995). Comparative effectiveness of three approaches to serving people with severe mental illness and SUD. *Journal of Nervous & Mental Disease*, 183, 566–576.

Ley, A., Jeffery, D.P., McClaren, S. & Seigfried, N. (1999). *Treatment programmes for people with both severe mental illness and substance misuse.* (Cochrane Review), Cochrane Library Issue 2 Oxford: Update Software.

Menezes, P., Johnson, S., Thornicroft, G. *et al.* (1996). Drug and alcohol problems among people with severe mental illness in South London. *British Journal of Psychiatry*, 168, 612–619.

Miller, W. & Rollnick, S. (2002). *Motivational Interviewing: Preparing People to Change Addictive Behaviour.* New York: Guilford Press.

Moore, T.H., Zammit, S., Lingford-Hughes, A. *et al.* (2007). Cannabis use and risk of psychotic or affective mental health outcomes: A systematic review. *The Lancet*, 370, 319–328.

Regier, D., Farmer, N. & Rae, D. (1990). Co-morbidity of mental disorders with alcohol and other drugs of abuse: Results from the Epidemiological Catchment Area (ECA). *JAMA: The Journal of the American Medical Association*, 264 (19), 2511–2518.

Schulte, S. & Holland, M. (2008). *Dual Diagnosis in Manchester, UK: Practitioners' Estimates of Prevalence Rates in Mental Health and Substance Misuse Services. Mental Health and Substance Use: Dual Diagnosis* 1, 2, 118–124.

van Os, J., Bak, M., Hanssen, M., Bijl R., de Graaf, R. & Verdoux, H. (2002). Cannabis use & psychosis: A longitudinal population study. *American Journal of Epidemiology*, 156, 319–327.

Weaver, T., Madden, P., Charles, V., Stimson, G. & Renton, A. (2003). Co-morbidity of substance misuse and mental illness in community mental health and substance misuse. *British Journal of Psychiatry*, 183, 304–313.Zammit, S., Allebeck, P., Andreasson, S., Lundberg, I. & Lewis, G. (2002). Self reported cannabis use as a risk factor for schizophrenia in Swedish conscripts of 1969: Historical cohort study. *British Medical Journal*, 325, 1199–1203.

Chapter 18 **Relapse prevention in early psychosis**

Andrew Gumley and Claire Park

Introduction

Prevention of relapse is a particular challenge in early psychosis. The construct of *relapse* does not necessarily have validity for individuals with psychosis and may unnecessarily pathologise their psychotic experiences. Efforts towards prevention of a second episode may inadvertently increase individuals' fearful expectations and sensitise them to catastrophically misinterpreting normal changes in emotional well-being. Furthermore, maintenance antipsychotics, the mainstay of relapse prevention, are not generally accepted by individuals with psychosis and 70% are expected to discontinue medication (Keefe, 2005). There is, therefore, an urgent need to develop acceptable psychological therapies which promote recovery and prevent recurrence of further episodes of psychosis.

The evidence base: Relapse prevention and emotional recovery

Emotional recovery and relapse prevention are two sides of the same coin (Gumley, 2007). The 2 years after the first episode appear to be a critical period in determining long-term outcome (Birchwood *et al.*, 1998). Relapse occurs in 20–35% at 1 year, 50–65% at 2 years and 80% at 5 years (Robinson *et al.*, 1999). Treatment of subsequent episodes of psychosis is less satisfactory than the first, with individuals being less likely to recover from their psychosis (Wiersma *et al.*, 1998). Relapse provides a basis for development of feelings of demoralisation and entrapment and has been linked to problematic emotional adjustment following psychosis. Feeling unable to prevent relapse is linked to development of depression (Birchwood *et al.*, 1993) and anxiety (Gumley *et al.*, 2004). Such negative feelings about psychosis are grounded in the reality of individuals' experiences and are associated with persisting psychotic experiences, more involuntary admissions, greater awareness of negative consequences and stigma of psychosis, being out of work and loss of social status and friendships (Rooke & Birchwood, 1998). Individuals in the early phase of psychosis are more likely to develop depression and suicidal thinking (Birchwood *et al.*, 2000; Iqbal *et al.*, 2000).

CBT for relapse prevention

Cognitive behaviour therapy (CBT) is effective in reducing the severity of positive and negative symptoms associated with schizophrenia (Tarrier *et al.*, 1993; Drury *et al.*, 1996a,b; Kuipers *et al.*, 1997; Tarrier *et al.*, 1998; Pinto *et al.*, 1999; Sensky *et al.*, 2000; Turkington *et al.*, 2002). Five trials provided post-treatment follow-up (Kuipers *et al.*, 1998; Sensky *et al.*, 2000; Tarrier *et al.*, 1999, 2000, 2004; Drury *et al.*, 2000). Whilst it should also be stated that reduction of relapse was a secondary aim of these studies, there was little evidence that CBT reduced relapse. Examination of treatment manuals adopted by trial investigators reveals that relapse prevention strategies are included (Kingdon & Turkington, 2004; Fowler *et al.*, 1995). These strategies focus on helping individuals recognise and respond to early signs of relapse by seeking help but do not specify particular cognitions or behaviours associated with development of relapse, nor do these manuals specify psychological strategies to address cognition or behaviour during relapse. Furthermore, these trials targeted reduction in positive psychotic symptoms as the principal outcome. Gumley and colleagues (1999) and Gumley and Schwannauer (2006) proposed that affect regulatory processes rather than psychotic symptoms should be the appropriate therapeutic focus for relapse prevention. There is evidence that optimising engagement and help-seeking, individualising early signs monitoring, availability of a therapist during crisis and providing prompt early psychological intervention at the appearance of early signs aimed at reducing emotional distress reduce relapse and readmission (Gumley et al., 2003).

Early signs of relapse

Relapse is defined as a recurrence of the symptoms of illness following a period of remission or the exacerbation of illness symptoms in the context of a period of partial remission. The construct of relapse, therefore, poses a number of problems in the context of early psychosis. It may require an acceptance on the part of the individual that they have an illness. This may be difficult for a significant proportion of individuals experiencing early psychosis. Acceptance of relapse may require submission to the idea of a powerful and recurrent illness which already carries strong connotations of stigma and shame.

The research literature (Table 18.1) shows that, on most occasions, a relapse is preceded by early signs including feelings of anxiety, depression, fear of relapse, suspiciousness, ideas of reference and low-level voices. Therefore, prediction (and prevention) of relapse should be feasible and effective using early signs monitoring. There are a number of critical issues in this literature.

1 Table 18.1 shows that individuals with psychosis (and their families) tend to be better at predicting relapse than clinicians. Individuals accurately predict relapse on about two-thirds of occasions, whereas health

Table 18.1 Studies of early signs and relapse in schizophrenia

Study	Nature of assessment of early signs	Number of relapses observed in the study	% success of predicting when a relapse will occur	% success of predicting when a relapse will not occur
Subotnik and Neuchterlein (1988)	Clinician	17	59	NR
Birchwood et al. (1989)	Individual with psychosis	8	63	82
Hirsch and Jolley (1989)	Individual with psychosis	10	73	NR
Tarrier et al. (1991)	Clinician	16	50	81
Gaebel et al. (1993)	Clinician	162	8	90
			14	70
			10	93
Marder et al. (1994)	Clinician	42	37	NR
			48	
Malla and Norman (1994)	Individual with psychosis Clinician	24	50	90
Jorgensen (1998)	Individual with psychosis Clinician	27	78	45
			30	58

professionals tend to predict relapse about 50% of the time. Therefore, relapse prevention relies on close collaboration with individuals with psychosis.

2 Although relapse is preceded by early signs such as those described above, increases in early signs symptoms are not necessarily followed by a relapse. Therefore, the potential for falsely identifying a possible relapse is high.

3 Experiences and symptoms defined as early signs are actually normally occurring. Symptom monitoring may actually sensitise individuals and their families to misinterpret normal changes in emotion, physiology, behaviour and thinking. This may actually produce threatening and catastrophic expectations that lead to increased feelings of fear, helplessness, embarrassment, hopelessness and shame. This, in turn, may actually inadvertently increase the risk of relapse rather than reduce it.

4 Monitoring for changes in emotion and thinking may in itself be a difficult task. Often, individuals with psychosis will have past experiences of loss, trauma or rejection, which are very painful, and focusing on monitoring potentially painful thoughts and feelings may heighten the very experiences that monitoring hopes to prevent.

5 Since psychosis is associated with experiences of hospitalisation perhaps in very traumatic and painful circumstances, remembering early signs can trigger painful and difficult memories.

6 Monitoring can contradict existing and long-standing coping strategies that involve a desire to avoid thinking about and re-experiencing painful memories and emotions.

7 Relapse prevention on the basis of early signs monitoring relies on individuals initiating help-seeking in the context of feeling vulnerable and threatened. Many individuals find help-seeking a challenge and may have experienced their relationships with others (including clinicians) as unhelpful, aversive or rejecting. Therefore, clinicians can create expectations on individuals to seek help in the context of high levels of distress, which, for some individuals, can outstrip their internal and external resources. This is particularly relevant for those who are more likely to have a more difficult and complex recovery.

Implementation into practice
'The relapse dance'

It seems to be that as soon as I get stressed out or upset I can go right, right down and the first thing I think about is I don't want to be here anymore, the first thing I think about is killing myself, and never hurting anyone else it is just me, I won't hurt anyone else it is just me I want to hurt, I feel like a failure and my mind, everything just goes, it's amazing it could be anything from making a sandwich wrong and the you get these feeling like I am wicked and it's weird, it's a weird, weird feeling.......sometimes if I am getting sick, I dream, very vivid dreams about my husband. I had one the other night there as well just every dream is about him and I don't feel rested cos I have been dreaming so bad. So it's a vicious circle, I seem to go into circles, doing well and then doing not so well and then doing really bad.

As is clear from this description of relapse, help-seeking in this context is a complex process. Seeking help when in distress implies that a person has an expectation that other people are helpful, reliable, trustworthy and caring. Seeking help when in distress also implies that the person is able to negotiate their way into the health service and articulate and explain their experiences and the kind of help that would be beneficial. There are a number of reasons that we should not assume these competencies. There is now considerable evidence showing that people with psychosis have experienced adverse life events including loss, trauma and abuse that compromise the capacity to seek help. Given the traumatic and distressing nature of psychosis, help-seeking may feel risky for many. Individuals with psychosis may fear increased medication, rehospitalisation and involuntary procedures. Individuals might also experience feelings of shame, guilt and embarrassment in relation to disappointing or letting their key worker down. This may result in an understandable and defensive delay in help-seeking. Given that the window of opportunity for intervention for early signs is narrow (2–4 weeks), delayed help-seeking may unintentionally result in key workers adopting a more crisis-driven and coercive responses to early signs, thus confirming individuals' negative expectations of help-seeking and increasing feelings of lack of control and entrapment in illness. This we refer to as the relapse dance. This is a dynamic, unfolding and interpersonal process. Therefore, perhaps it is not surprising that conventional CBT has struggled to demonstrate relapse prevention (Campbell, 2004). Psychological therapies focusing on reducing emotional distress, improving affect regulation and providing a secure base for help-seeking during crises are crucial components of staying well after psychosis (Gumley & Schwannauer, 2006).

The person in recovery

In order to support recovery, it is crucial to pay close attention not just to what individuals with psychosis say but how individuals construct and understand their experience of psychosis. We illustrate three narratives of recovery, which are referred to as Thwarted Recovery, Defended Independence and Freedom and Autonomy. These are not necessarily meant to be categorical but reflect important themes in how individuals might respond to their experience of psychosis and how this is reflected in the content and structure of their narratives in relation to speaking about recovery (Kerr & Gumley, 2008 in preparation).

'Thwarted recovery'

Thwarted recovery refers to a sense of psychosis as a powerful, overwhelming and uncontrollable experience. The individual might experience considerable trauma in relation to their experiences in the form of repeated and unwanted memories of psychosis.

Well, possibly the most significant thing, what I said earlier is that I have to think of the worst, the worst that can happen to me, is like I told you last week, is really quite severe, quite bad, I show chronic pain, mental anguish, and having to deal with that day in day out is quite wearing because

you expect that the situation would change after a while but my illness is regular enough for that not to change so I'm in a constant state of preparedness as it were.

This individual provides a vivid account of their response to psychosis. They feel preoccupied with the threat of recurrence, maintaining a constant state of vigilance in order to prevent relapse. However, the awful paradox is that in maintaining a state of preparedness, they remain in a state of high anxiety. Underneath this fearful state, this individual reflects on their experiences of loss in relation to their psychosis and their feelings of unresolved grief. Perhaps this is reflected in their temporary disorientation and absorption in the experience of talking and as they lose their place.

I got a tremendous, tremendous disappointment from being at University, thinking about it afterwards, just because, erm – \<sighs\>, after, the reason why I had to leave University was because of the illness, the illness, I lost my sanity, I lost my society, I lost my social life {speaking very fast} erm {3 secs}. Sorry, what was the question there?

The powerful and overwhelming nature of psychosis and significance of the loss is evocatively described below. In particular, the individual notes how voices they experience have access to very painful and unresolved memories that reinforce those feelings of fear, embarrassment and humiliation.

It is a total psychological experience. There is no strategies you can make. You just have to sit there and experience – abuse. And, the most important thing, and I said this to M, is my illness has my entire back catalogue. It has my entire diary, so it can pick things that have happened years ago, show a symbol of it, show a picture of it, and it's a horrible experience because you begin to relive those experiences. You don't have to relive them because they are generally bad experiences, of my schizophrenia, a lot of embarrassment, a lot of humiliation, and the reasons why they are so bad is that virtual every time I have an attack, the illness goes through them and makes you relive them to a certain extent.

The task of relapse prevention in this case is to begin to provide a context for the person to process, reorganise and reconstruct their traumatic experiences of psychosis and compassionately understand and respond to their feelings of shame, self-blame and humiliation that underpin their desire to seek safety through maintaining a state of preparedness and vigilance.

'Defended independence'

In contrast, defended independence reflects a different kind of response to psychosis that seems to have the goal of minimising preoccupation with psychosis and may reflect a more 'sealing over' or 'avoidant type' coping response.

How do you feel about being on medication at all? I don't like it.

What is it you don't like?
I don't know. It's just, \<short sigh\>. I just feel as if I will need to depend on it for the rest of my life – (um) – and I don't want to feel dependent on nothing.

What does that mean for you, when you think about being dependent on medication?
I don't know. I just feel that I need to rely on something to keep me well (right) and I don't want to rely on nothing. I would rather like not get a depot and stay out of hospital.

In the above narrative, this individual talks about their concerns about taking medication. Perhaps this reflects a desire for independence, and their fear that taking medication means that they are submissive and dependent.

Every time I would approach the staff, they would say, 'I'm too busy'.
How did you feel when they said that?
Rejected

Rejected? (Um hum) That is quite a strong feeling. What did you do when you felt like that?
F—them. If they didn't want to help me then that's their problem. So, I refused to take the tablets.

And so, in doing that, in refusing to take the tablets, was that like an act against the staff?
Aye. If they didn't want to help me, then what was the point in me being there?

So, it seems that would make you feel quite angry. Is that right?

It was, aye ... {3 secs} I didn't want to feel like that and they were making me feel like that. I felt worse going in that I do outside. That's why I don't want to go back into hospital. I am going to try my best to try and not go back into hospital, but I know that I will fail eventually.

This independent and sometimes angry stance belies a sensitivity to being rejected by others and perhaps a difficulty in forming trusting relationships. As we see, this independent stance may reflect an underlying vulnerability and insecurity.

Aye. My dad died in [Month 1] and – I became unwell in [Month 2].

How would you describe your relationship with your dad?
Oh, I loved him to bits. The two of us were best pals. We would go to the pub every single day. I wouldn't drink, I would just drink coke or Irn Bru, but my dad would drink, because he was a drinker but at the time I wasn't into it so I just drank Coke or Irn Bru. I had a motor at the time so I would pick him up, take him home and that was it. On the Saturday, we would go to the football and then go to the pub but ... {then speaking later of his father}...
 If we had done something wrong, he would shout at us and batter us but I loved him, he was brand new. We didn't talk for about a year, two years because he threw me out the house when I was {age}.

This defended independent stance may well be reflected in the literature. Individuals who use a sealing-over strategy tend to have lower levels of therapeutic alliance, are less likely to seek help in a crisis and are less likely to adhere to treatment. In addition, individuals who seal over also tend to have more negative views of themselves, tend to feel more insecure, rate their experiences of growing up as less caring and more abusive, feel less close to others and are more worried more about rejection. How do we possibly approach relapse prevention in the case of defended independence? Crucially, we want to develop a shared construction of the person's experience of psychosis. In addition, we also want to particularly focus on development of a trusting working alliance and understand how the person's coping prevents them from processing difficult and painful memories such as loss, or indeed how their response style reinforces and is reinforced by the reactions of others including staff. In addition, we may want to work with the person to develop more productive and fruitful coping responses, help them develop a capacity to reflect on and understand their emotional reactions to stressful events and develop coping that supports their autonomy but does not alienate others.

'Freedom and autonomy'

Finally, and in contrast to *defended independence and thwarted recovery*, we can understand a different kind of response to the experience of psychosis. This freely autonomous stance is evident where painful and difficult aspects of the experience of psychosis are neither minimised and avoided as in *defended independence* nor overwhelming, disorientating and preoccupying as in *thwarted recovery*. This narrative reflects an integration of painful aspects of experience, an acceptance of the experiences without submission and a valuing of relationships in the process of recovery.

> *I'm not ashamed by it in any way, shape or form and to be quite truthful – and this probably sounds really strange but – as much as there has been an awful lot of heartache surrounding my illness and my family, my mum, my dad erm my sister, my friends and stuff, and to an extent myself you know but – if I was to go back and change, if I had the power to go back and change that – I would say no because then I wouldn't be – who I am today with the insight that I have got and the experiences I have got so why – I wouldn't, I wouldn't change it. Elements of it, I would. Hurting other*

people but no \<takes a deep breath\>, the actual illness. You know......{and later reflecting on their recovery}

> *Recovery to me is about living... ....{7secs} about living your life and claiming back what you have lost basically. It is not lost, it's just in a wee cupboard somewhere, you know, you just need to find the key and get it back. Everybody's recovery is different, everybody's road to recovery is different. Mine has been a long process as well. It had not just been got ill, 'wahey I'm better'. It has been a long \<sighs\> process and a lot of trial and error to get to where I am just now. But it can be done.*

Role of the therapist

In particular, in relapse prevention work, we are concerned with the development of helpful coping responses in response to distressing emotions and difficult interpersonal situations. We are also crucially concerned with how a therapist and/or a service system is able to provide the individual with psychosis with a secure base which can provide a source of comfort, reassurance and safeness during times of distress and heightened risk of recurrence. In this way, the task of help-seeking becomes more achievable for those who have the greatest difficulty in being aware of and communicating their fears and concerns to others. Greenberg and Pascual-Leone (1997) and Greenberg *et al.* (1993) have also suggested that a pivotal task of cognitive interpersonal therapy is, in the context of a safe therapy relationship, to increase awareness of emotion by focusing attention on emotional experiences, and the development of a narrative enabling symbolic self-reflection on the fundamental experiential meanings embedded in personal experience. Siegel (1999) proposes five basic elements of discourse which foster a secure base:

Collaboration: Collaboration is developed through the careful negotiation of individuals' problems and goals within therapy, and the therapist's encouragement for the individual to develop an active, enquiring and explorative approach to understanding and resolving emotional distress.

Reflective dialogue: There is a focus on the person's internal experience, where the therapist attempts to make sense of client communications in their own mind and then communicate their understanding in such a way that helps the individual create new meanings and perspectives on their emotions, perceptions, thoughts, intentions, memories, ideas, beliefs and attitudes.

Repair: When attuned communication is disrupted, there is a focus on collaborative repair, allowing the individual to reflect upon misunderstandings and disconnections in their interpersonal experiences.

Coherent narratives: The connection of past, present and future is central to the development of a person's autobiographical self-awareness. The development of coherent narratives within therapy aims to help foster the flexible capacity to integrate both internal and external experiences over time.

Emotional communication: The therapist maintains close awareness not only of the contents of narrative, but also individuals' emotional communications. In focusing on negative or painful emotions within sessions, the therapist communicates and encourages self-reflection, understanding, acceptance and soothing.

The service system

Designing services to best meet the needs of emotional recovery and relapse prevention is an important but complex task. Goodwin *et al.,* (2003) proposed that a key function of multidisciplinary teams is to facilitate a 'secure base' through providing continuity and consistency of care during acute and recovery phases, by providing sensitive and appropriate responses to affective distress and by providing emotional containment during times of crisis. It is important to strike a balance between providing a reassuring supportive environment with encouragement to explore. Desynchronous approaches to recovery, relapse detection and prevention have the potential to produce ruptures in therapeutic alliance. For example, the basic approach of relapse prevention is the development of an accepting compassionate model of psychotic experiences. Catastrophic or anxious responses by staff to the re-emergence of low-level psychotic experiences are therefore considered desynchronous within this approach. An integral component of relapse prevention is the provision of team-based multidisciplinary training aimed at encouraging staff to reflect on their own beliefs, attributions and assumptions about recovery and relapse. Training should focus on helping staff identify and reflect on their own beliefs about psychosis, how they make attributions about individuals particularly during periods of high stress, how these attributions influence their own emotional and behavioural responses to relapse and how these attributions interact with individuals' beliefs, expectations and responses during periods of crisis.

Case study

In our experience of working together, many of the themes and ideas which we have expressed already were encountered. We do not want to describe a session-by-session account of 'who said what and when', or what particular techniques were helpful or not helpful. We would like to describe the tasks of recovery that we shared or collaborated on over a period of nearly 3 years. These tasks, which are outlined below, are not necessarily mutually exclusive, nor were they necessarily undertaken in the exact order they are presented. For example, the tasks of establishing and building trust, or establishing and developing hope were often returned to during times of distress and change.

Establishing and building trust

Establishing and building trust was a key part of learning to work together. In the beginning, everyone in the world seemed completely untrustworthy and the idea of developing any kind of trust was unthinkable. It actually seemed dangerous to put any trust in another person. In the beginning, it was our therapeutic relationship that was the basis for exploring and understanding trust. Later, we could use this as a basis to understand and develop trust in other people.

Establishing and developing hope

This was important to begin to develop some sense that things could improve. At the time, Claire was experiencing persisting and distressing voices that were persecuting and commanding. Learning how to understand and respond to these voices was important in beginning to build a sense of optimism and hope for recovery.

Learning to talk about feelings

This was a difficult process. There were a number of important fears with respect to the consequences of talking about thoughts and feelings. How would the team respond? How does one cope with opening feelings when this feels an alien way of talking? How do you talk about such experiences that form part of one's sense of failure and vulnerability? These were important questions throughout the process of recovery.

Building secure relationships

Secure relationships that foster growth and exploration but enable care and support are crucial in the process of recovery. Such relationships can also feel alien and frightening and increase one's sense of vulnerability, weakness and dependence. This may create conflicting and disorientating feelings. A key recovery task can be the building of secure-enough relationships through the therapeutic relationship or relationships with others such as nursing staff, family and partners. Where there is an instinct to shut off and not talk about such feelings, an important part of the therapeutic alliance is to support a reflection and understanding of these complex emotional responses.

Exploring sensitivity and insecurity

This provides a base for understanding emotional sensitivity in response to existing relationships or, indeed, in response to other people more generally. In particular, understanding and responding to feelings of anger, shame, fear and paranoia can be challenging and disorientating. This might mean finding ways to explore and understand these responses in day-to-day life and trying out new ways of coping.

Developing an emotional understanding

Finally, understanding where feelings come from can be an important part of recovery although this is not always obvious. For this reason, focusing on emotional resonance during therapy sessions can open up and allow the re-experiencing of painful memories that have laid down the basis of how we react in the here and now.

Claire's reflections on recovery

Although I found it difficult to relate to others during my psychosis, I also found others, including staff found it difficult to relate to me. I found I couldn't trust anyone and when things got really bad I took an overdose. This wasn't my first overdose, but it was a crucial turning point. I found myself in a psychiatric hospital again under Section and being considered for a 6-month section. I felt a mixture of feelings. On the one hand, I was relieved to be alive. One member of staff on the ward even commented how cheerful I was. On the other hand, I felt frightened, angry, confused controlled and the prospect of remaining under section only confirmed my expectations that I could not trust or be open with others. In the end and to my relief, the Section papers never went through. Since then being given the space and time to talk through my feelings, make choices for myself, build relationships with my family and my partner, and establish greater independence have been important parts of a recovery process that is still ongoing.

What the therapist learned about himself

As a clinical psychologist with a strong interest in cognitive therapy and a researcher interested in producing empirical data, I learned how to understand more deeply the interplay between theory, evidence and psychotherapeutic practice. I learned how to look beyond the theory, and to not just attend to what Claire said, but also how she spoke about her experiences. My practice changed as I became more aware of not just my limitations, but also some of the limitations of cognitive therapy as developed for people with psychotic experiences. I began to focus much more on the developmental and interpersonal basis of how we learn to regulate emotions and the implications for how others, including clinicians, respond in ways that are both helpful and unhelpful. I learned to focus more on emotion. In addition, to focus on experience as an opportunity to share in a process of reconstructing meaning, rather than simply offering and evaluating alternative meanings. The therapeutic process was one where a dynamic process of meaning-making was central.

Implications and conclusions

In this chapter, we have shown that there are a significant number of barriers to relapse prevention in early psychosis. We have also shown that relapse prevention and emotional recovery are two sides of the same coin. For those individuals at high risk of relapse, we need to develop an understanding of the complexity and sometimes contradictory nature of individuals' response styles. In doing so, the aim is to develop a compassionate understanding of the context and consequences of the person's coping. In entering such a process, a key vehicle of change is the therapeutic relationship which provides a context to establish security and trust to enable the development and reinforcement of reflective capacity and productive coping. This process is not without its challenges. Constructing a secure base can, for some, create feelings of vulnerability and threat that produce apparently contradictory or unexpected emotional or coping responses that in themselves can elicit confused or unhelpful reactions from services. This can produce and unintended confirmation of negative expectations of others. Therefore, these apparently contradictory responses need to be understood and explored in the person's life context. The development of a secure base for recovery provides a bridge for help-seeking, distress tolerance and distress reduction in the future. This has profound implications, not just for individual therapists, but also for how services reflect on their own helpful (and unhelpful) responses to individuals and their families.

Useful websites

http://www.scottishrecovery.net/ This is a useful website which provides information on recovery and provides reports on a large-scale project conducted in Scotland collecting individuals' narratives of recovery.

References

Birchwood, M. *et al.* (1989). Predicting relapse in schizophrenia: The development and implementation of an early signs monitoring system using patients and families as observers. *Psychological Medicine*, 19, 649–656.

Birchwood, M., Mason, R., MacMillan, F. & Healy, J. (1993). Depression, demoralisation and control over illness: A comparison of depressed and non-depressed patients with a chronic psychosis. *Psychological Medicine*, 23, 387–395.

Birchwood, M., Todd, P. & Jackson, C. (1998). Early intervention in psychosis. The critical period hypothesis. *British Journal of Psychiatry*, 172 (33), 53–59.

Birchwood, M., Iqbal, Z., Chadwick, P. & Trower, P. (2000). Cognitive approach to depression and suicidal thinking in psychosis. 1. Ontogeny of post-psychotic depression. *British Journal of Psychiatry*, 177, 516–521.

Drury, V., Birchwood, M., Cochrane, R. & Macmillan, F. (1996a). Cognitive therapy and recovery from acute psychosis: A controlled trial I. Impact on psychotic symptoms. *British Journal of Psychiatry*, 169, 593–601.

Drury, V., Birchwood, M., Cochrane, R. & Macmillan, F. (1996b). Cognitive therapy and recovery from acute psychosis: A controlled trial II. Impact on recovery time. *British Journal of Psychiatry*, 169, 602–607.

Drury, V., Birchwood, M. & Cochrane, R. (2000). Cognitive therapy and recovery from acute psychosis: A controlled trial. 3. Five-year follow-up. *British Journal of Psychiatry*, 177, 8–14.

Fowler, D., Garety, P. & Kuipers, E. (1995). Cognitive behaviour therapy for psychosis: Theory and practice. Chichester (UK): Wiley.

Gaebel, W. *et al.* (1993). Early neuroleptic intervention in schizophrenia: Are prodromal symptoms valid predictors of relapse? *British Journal of Psychiatry*, 163, 8–12.

Goodwin, I., Holmes, G., Cochrane, R. & Mason, O. (2003). The ability of adult mental health services to meet clients' attachment needs: The development and implementation of the service attachment questionnaire. *Psychology & Psychotherapy: Theory, Research & Practice*, 76, 145–161.

Greenberg, L.S. & Pascual-Leone, J. (1997). Emotion in the creation of personal meaning. In: M. Power & C.R. Brewin (eds), *The Transformation of Meaning in Psychological Therapies*. Chichester: John Wiley & Sons Ltd.

Greenberg, L.S., Rice, L.N. & Elliott, R. (1996). *Facilitating Emotional Change*. New York: Guilford Press.

Gumley, A., White, C.A. & Power, K. (1999). An interacting cognitive subsystems model of relapse and the course of psychosis. *Clinical Psychology and Psychotherapy*, 6, 261–279.

Gumley, A., O'Grady, M., McNay, L., Reilly, J., Power, K. & Norrie, J. (2003). Early intervention for relapse in schizophrenia: Results of a 12-month randomized controlled trial of cognitive behavioural therapy. *Psychological Medicine*, 33, 419–431.

Gumley, A., O'Grady, M., Power, K. & Schwannauer, M. (2004). Negative beliefs about self and illness: A comparison of individuals with or without co morbid social anxiety disorder. *Australian and New Zealand Journal of Psychiatry*, 38, 960–964.

Gumley, A.I. (2007). Staying well after psychosis: A cognitive interpersonal approach to emotional recovery and relapse prevention. *Tidsskrift for Norsk Psykologorening*, 5, 667–676.

Gumley, A.I. & Schwannauer, M. (2006). *Staying Well After Psychosis: A Cognitive Interpersonal Approach to Recovery and Relapse Prevention*. Chichester: John Wiley & Sons.

Hirsch, S.R. & Jolley, A.G. (1989). The dysphoric syndrome in schizophrenia and its implications for relapse. *British Journal of Psychiatry*, 156, 46–50.

Iqbal, Z., Birchwood, M., Chadwick, P. & Trower, P. (2000). Cognitive approach to depression and suicidal thinking in psychosis. 2. Testing the validity of a social ranking model. *British Journal of Psychiatry*, 177, 522–528.

Jones C, Cormac I, Silveira da Mota Neto JI, Campbell, C. Cognitive behaviour therapy for schizophrenia. *Cochrane Database of Systematic Reviews 2004*, Issue 3. Art. No.: DC000524. DOI: 10.1002/14651858.CD000524.pub2

Keefe, R.S.E. (2005). Comparison of atypicals in first-episode psychosis: A randomized, 52-week comparison of olanzapine, quetiapine, and risperidone. *European College of Neuropsychopharmacology 18th Congress*, 22–26 October 2005, Amsterdam.

Kerr, W. & Gumley, A. (Under Review). Individual with psychosis and staff perspectives on recovery in psychosis: talking the same language?

Kingdon, D. & Turkington, D. (2004). *Cognitive Therapy of Schizophrenia*. New York: Guildford Press.

Kuipers, E., Garety, P., Fowler, D. *et al.* (1997). London–East Anglia randomised controlled trial of cognitive-behavioural therapy for psychosis. I: Effects of the treatment phase. *British Journal of Psychiatry*, 171, 319–327.

Kuipers, E., Fowler, D., Garety, P. *et al.* (1998). London-East Anglia randomised controlled trial of cognitive-behavioural therapy for psychosis: III: Follow-up and economic evaluation at 18 months. *British Journal of Psychiatry,* 173, 61–68.

Malla, A.K. & Norman, R. (1994). Prodromal symptoms in schizophrenia. *British Journal of Psychiatry*, 164, 487–493.

Marder, S.R. *et al.* (1994). Fluphenazine vs placebo supplementation for prodromal signs of relapse in schizophrenia. *Archives of General Psychiatry*, 51, 280–287.

Pinto, A., La Pia, S., Manella, R., Giorgio, D. & DiSimone, L. (1999). Cognitive behavioural therapy and clozapine for clients with treatment refractory schizophrenia. *Psychiatric Services*, 50, 901–904.

Robinson, D., Woerner, M.G., Alvir, J. *et al.* (1999). Predictors of relapse following response from a first episode of schizophrenia or schizoaffective disorder. *Archives of General Psychiatry*, 56, 241–246.

Rooke, O. & Birchwood, M. (1998). Loss, humiliation and entrapment as appraisals of schizophrenic illness: A prospective study of depressed and non-depressed patients. *British Journal of Clinical Psychology*, 37, 259–268.

Sensky, T., Turkington, D., Kingdon, D. *et al.* (2000). A randomised controlled trial of cognitive behavioural therapy in schizophrenia resistant to medication. *Archives of General Psychiatry*, 57, 165–172.

Siegel, D.J. (1999). *The Developing Mind: Toward a Neurobiology of Interpersonal Experience*. New York: Guilford Press.

Subotnik, K.L. & Nuechterlein, K.H. (1988). Prodromal signs and symptoms of schizophrenic relapse. *Journal of Abnormal Psychology*, 97 (4), 405–412.

Tarrier, N., Barrowclough, C. & Bamrah, J.S. (1991). Prodromal signs of relapse in schizophrenia. *Social Psychiatry and Psychiatric Epidemiology*, 26 (4), 157–161.

Tarrier, N., Sharpe, L., Beckett, R., Harwood, S., Baker, A. & Yusopoff, L. (1993). A trial of two cognitive behavioural methods of treating drug-resistant residual psychotic symptoms in schizophrenic patients. *Social Psychiatry and Psychiatric Epidemiology*, 28 (1), 5–10.

Tarrier, N., Yusupoff, L., Kinney, C. *et al.* (1998). Randomised controlled trial of intensive cognitive behaviour therapy for patients with chronic schizophrenia. *British Medical Journal*, 317, 303–307.

Tarrier, N., Wittkowsky, A., Kinney, C., McCarthy, E., Morris, J. & Humphreys, L. (1999). Durability of the effects of cognitive-behavioural therapy in the treatment of chronic schizophrenia: 12-month follow-up. *British Journal of Psychiatry*, 174, 500–504.

Tarrier, N., Kinney, C., McCarthy, E., Humphreys, L. & Wittkowsky, A. (2000). Two-year follow-up of cognitive-behavioural therapy and supportive counselling in the treatment of persistent symptoms in chronic schizophrenia. *Journal of Consulting and Clinical Psychology*, 68, 917–922.

Tarrier, N., Lewis, S., Haddock, G. *et al.* (2004). Cognitive-behavioural therapy in first-episode and early schizophrenia. *British Journal of Psychiatry*, 184, 231–239.

Turkington, D., Kingdon, D., Turner T. & Insight into Schizophrenia Research Group. (2002). Effectiveness of a brief cognitive-behavioural therapy intervention in the treatment of schizophrenia. *British Journal of Psychiatry*, 18, 523–527.

Wiersma, D., Nienhuis, F.J., Slooff, C.J. & Giel, R. (1998). Natural course of schizophrenic disorders: A 15 year follow up of a Dutch incidence cohort. *Schizophrenia Bulletin*, 24, 75–85.

Chapter 19 **Trauma and first-episode psychosis**

Mark Bernard, Chris Jackson and Paul Patterson

Introduction

In our experience, gained through more than 15 years running a national network, listening to people who hear voices, many of them living with a diagnosis of schizophrenia; it is clear that there is a definite link between traumatic events and psychosis. On a daily basis, we see and hear terrible stories of sexual, emotional and physical abuse, and the impact of poverty, racism, neglect, and stigma on people's lives. ...The reduction of peoples distressing life experiences into a diagnosis of schizophrenia means that they are condemned to lives dulled by drugs and blighted by stigma and are offered no opportunity to make sense of their experiences. Their routes to recovery are hindered.

(Jacqui Dillon, Chair Hearing Voices Network)

As clinicians working in a busy Early Intervention Service for young people recovering from psychosis, this quote resonates with us for a number of reasons. First, with the growing body of empirical research supporting an association between trauma and psychosis (Morrison *et al.*, 2003), the need to identify, assess and intervene clinically with the consequences of trauma resulting from childhood experiences or from the impact of psychosis has become more pressing in recent years. Second, the quote indicates that a single diagnosis (usually one of schizophrenia) may mean that people's overt psychotic symptoms are treated medically but their underlying traumatic experiences are left untreated. Thus, the quote suggests that acknowledging people's distressing life experiences (including both early traumatic events and the trauma of psychosis), providing interventions

aimed at helping people making sense of their traumatic experiences and reducing the distress associated with these experiences may be crucial in facilitating and promoting recovery.

However, consistent with practitioners in other Early Intervention Services (Young *et al.*, 2001), it is our experience that people recovering from a first episode of psychosis are still not routinely assessed for childhood trauma or for trauma resulting from a first episode. Consequently, people may not receive appropriate psychosocial interventions for underlying trauma, as abuse is rarely spontaneously disclosed (Read & Fraser, 1998) or existing treatment may be fragmented and based on a partial understanding of their problem (Hermann, 1997). This lack of assessment (and corresponding lack of appropriate treatment) may be due to a range of factors including perceived lack of clinical skills, training around trauma and fear about inquiring about trauma and retraumatising individuals (see Cavanagh *et al.*, 2004). It is also likely that high caseloads and increasing administrative demands mean that clinicians, particularly care coordinators, simply do not have enough time to spend with clients to enquire about trauma.

In this chapter, we will consider issues around assessment and the different causal pathways between trauma and psychosis referred to above. First, we will consider the role that early adverse childhood events can play in the development of psychosis in adulthood. We will then consider whether psychotic symptoms and their associated treatment can cause symptoms of post-traumatic stress disorder (PTSD). A final model will then be considered that suggests that early adverse advents may result in biological and psychological vulnerabilities to later emotional and psychological distress including psychosis. We will then discuss recent developments in cognitive behaviour therapy (CBT) that attempt to treat trauma associated with psychosis.

Overview: Trauma and psychosis

The extensive overlap between symptoms of psychosis and PTSD can make assessment of both presentations difficult (McGorry et al., 1991; Morrison et al., 2003; Mueser & Rosenberg, 2003). Positive symptoms such as voices and delusions can be phenomenologically similar to the intrusions people experience in PTSD. DSM-IV (APA, 1994) states that in PTSD, the re-experiencing of trauma can include hallucinations and dissociative flashbacks. Similarly, following psychosis, people can experience negative symptoms, such as loss of affect, reduced speech, loss of motivation and energy and diminished interest in hobbies and personal relationships. These symptoms can mimic the emotional numbing and avoidance that are one of the defining features of PTSD outlined in DSM-IV (APA, 1994). The following case study illustrates the difficulty in assessing patients where trauma and possible psychosis may be present.

Case study to demonstrate assessment difficulties

Barbara was an 18-year-old female who was violently raped when she was 17 years old. She became addicted to heroin and her boyfriend continually told her she was cheap and dirty for being raped and that no one else (apart from him) would ever want her. After this relationship ended, she came off drugs with the help of her family and eventually began a new relationship. Two weeks later, her family reported that she had a breakdown. She stayed in her room crying, had aggressive mood swings, did not eat or wash, and reported she was hearing voices telling her she was 'cheap and dirty'. When she went outside the house, she felt that people were looking at her in a negative way like she was 'cheap' and consequently stopped going out. Following a psychiatric assessment, she received a diagnosis of psychosis and was commenced on antipsychotic medication. She was subsequently referred to an Early Intervention

---

Service, who carried out an extended assessment, which revealed no evidence of delusional thinking or bizarre behaviour. In addition, this assessment indicated that her voices were more consistent with intrusive re-experiences of her rape, and her social withdrawal was more consistent with emotional numbing and avoidance instead of negative symptoms of psychosis. It was then recommended that the medication was stopped, and Barbara was offered psychological therapy to understand her symptoms and deal with the rape.

This case study illustrates the importance of a thorough assessment, as the interventions people receive will be guided by their initial assessment. Furthermore, the feedback that people receive regarding their diagnosis may also play a role in their subsequent presentations. For example, Dunmore et al. (1999) found that interpreting initial post-traumatic symptoms as a sign of impending madness distinguished patients with a diagnosis of PTSD from those without a diagnosis of PTSD and recovered patients from those with persistent PTSD. This highlights the role that incorrect appraisals may play in presentations. Consequently, a wide-ranging and comprehensive assessment is essential when assessing patients presenting with possible symptoms of psychosis where there is a strong trauma history. Table 19.1 summarises key issues to consider when conducting such an assessment and some useful measures to consider in such cases are described in Table 19.2[1].

Can early traumatic life experiences cause psychosis in adulthood?

There is now substantial evidence suggesting a direct link between childhood trauma and psychosis (Read, 1997; Read et al., 2005). This link seems particularly strong for childhood sexual trauma and positive symptoms of psychosis, with the greatest association in order of strength being for voices commenting, ideas of reference, thought insertion, paranoid ideation, reading others' minds and visual hallucinations (Ross et al., 1994). More recent evidence suggests that the most consistent evidence is for the association

Table 19.1 Factors to consider when assessing trauma with psychosis

---

Factors to consider when assessing trauma with psychosis

- Has there been a thorough assessment of clients presenting problems?
- Are there current problems with serious substance misuse?
- Has an adequate trauma history (e.g. childhood abuse) been taken?
- Have symptoms of PTSD (i.e. intrusions and avoidance) been assessed?
- Has emotional distress (anxiety/depression) been assessed?
- Have psychotic symptoms been assessed and treated?
- Is the client in a recovery phase?
- Does the client have an 'integrating' or 'sealing' recovery style?
- Is the client currently suicidal?
- Has the client been hospitalised or been suicidal in the last 2 months?
- Is the client living in a reasonable stable environment with adequate social support?

Table 19.2 Assessment measures

Childhood Trauma: The Childhood Trauma Questionnaire (CTQ) (Bernstein *et al.*, 1997) is a 28-item self-report questionnaire with good validity and reliability. It assesses five different types of abuse and neglect including emotional, physical and sexual abuse, and emotional and physical neglect.

Trauma: Trauma History Questionnaire (THQ) (Mueser *et al.*, 1998) is a semi-structured interview used to assess exposure to different types of trauma such as sexual assault or unwanted sexual contact, physical attack, witnessing a trauma of another, sudden unexpected loss of a loved one and military combat.

Post-traumatic Stress Disorder (PTSD): PTSD can be assessed with either the Clinician-Administered PTSD Scale (CAPS) (Blake *et al.*, 1990) and/or the Impact of Events Scale-Revised (IES-R) (Weiss & Marmar, 1997). Both measures assess avoidance, intrusive re-experiences and arousal associated with trauma, which are the three defining criteria for PTSD in DSM-IV (APA, 1994). The CAPS is an interview-based measure with good validity and reliability. The IES is a self-report measure that also had good test–retest reliability and construct validity (Weiss & Marmar, 1997; Creamer *et al.*, 2003). People scoring above 33 on the IES can be regarded as meeting a diagnosis of PTSD (Creamer *et al.*, 2003).

Psychosis: The PANSS (Kay *et al.*, 1987) is a valid and reliable measure of positive (e.g. delusions, hallucinations, hostility) and negative symptoms (e.g. blunted affect, emotional withdrawal, social withdrawal) of psychosis and general psychopathology. General psychopathology and positive symptoms of psychosis can also be assessed more quickly with the Brief Psychiatric Rating Scale (BPRS) (Gorham, 1962).

Emotional Distress: Emotional distress is a key characteristic of both psychosis and trauma/PTSD. Thus, it is useful to assess anxiety using the Beck Anxiety Scale (BAI), which is a reliable and valid 21-item measure of anxiety (Beck & Steer, 1990). Depression can be assessed using the Beck Depression Inventory (BDI-II) (Beck *et al.*, 1996) or the Calgary Depression Scale (Addington *et al.*, 1993), which has been designed to assess depression in individuals with psychosis.

Experiences of Hospitalisation: The Psychiatric Experiences Questionnaire (PEQ) (Frueh *et al.*, 2005) can be used to assess distressing experiences within psychiatric settings (e.g. seclusion, restraint taking medication against will, inadequate privacy, physical/sexual assault). The Hospital Experiences Questionnaire (HES) (Shaw *et al.*, 1997) can be used to assess similar and additional (e.g. separation from family, loss of vocational role) distressing experiences.

---

between childhood abuse and voices and command hallucinations in adulthood (Read *et al.*, 2005) and that this relationship still exists without abuse/trauma in adulthood (Read *et al.*, 2003).

Read *et al.* (2005) summarise evidence showing that approximately 50% of people exhibiting auditory hallucinations report a history of either childhood physical or sexual abuse, but that this figure rises to approximately 70% if individuals have experienced both physical *and* sexual childhood abuse. In addition, the association between physical or sexual childhood trauma and auditory hallucinations continues even without subsequent trauma in adulthood (Read *et al.*, 2003). This finding suggests that childhood trauma is only reliably related to other positive symptoms (e.g. visual and olfactory hallucinations, delusions and thought disorder) in the presence of further trauma in adulthood.

It has also been recently demonstrated in two large (N > 4,000) semi-prospective studies (Janssen *et al.*, 2004; Spauwen *et al.*, 2006) that childhood trauma (i.e. emotional, physical, psychological or sexual abuse) before the age of 16 increased the likelihood of positive symptoms of psychosis in adulthood in a dose-response manner. Thus, individuals who experienced more frequent levels of abuse were more likely to develop corresponding pathology levels of psychosis and require health care interventions. Finally, in a cross-sectional interview-based population study, it has been found that participants who met the criteria for psychosis (n = 60) were 15 times more likely to have reported sexual abuse, 4 times more likely to have been bullied, 10 times more likely to have been taken into local authority care, 34 times more likely to have run away from home and 5 times more likely to have been the victim of serious injury, illness or assault (Bebbington *et al.*, 2004). Overall, sexual abuse was the best predictor of psychosis (3.9 times more likely), followed by running away from home (2.9 times more likely) and violence in the home (2 times more likely).

Can psychosis and its treatment cause symptoms of PTSD?

When I was ill, I went to the police station because I thought people were following me and picking on me. I thought people were out to kill me. Everywhere I looked I saw graffiti and I thought it was about me. I was always crying and felt uptight.

(Female, 23 years old)

When I was admitted to hospital, I felt that all my rights were taken away from me because I felt that the mental health service did not have the right to restrain and inject me ... dealing with the nurses was also hell. I would be injected just for ignoring them and badly manhandled. I was given no respect and ended up struggling with myself just to get myself to try to co-operate with them.

(Male, 21)

The two quotes above, taken from a study that asked people to write about the most distressing aspects of having psychosis (Bernard *et al.*, 2006), suggest that specific psychotic experiences (e.g. ideas of reference, paranoia, voices) or the treatment for psychosis (e.g. involuntary admission to hospital, restraint and seclusion) can be traumatising for individuals. One possible cause of this trauma may be the high level of distress associated with experiences (e.g. enforced seclusion, experiences of the self being controlled, visual hallucinations and thought insertion) involving a perceived loss of control (Shaw *et al.*, 1997). A number of studies have examined the contribution that symptoms of psychosis and their associated treatment can make to the development of post-psychotic PTSD. Morrison *et al.* (2003) reviewed seven studies, which looked at whether psychotic symptoms can result in symptoms of PTSD, and found that incidence of PTSD following psychosis ranged from 11% to 67%. They conclude that, despite some methodological flaws (e.g. reliance on self-reports, symptom overlap and small samples), the high rate of PTSD in response to psychosis has been replicated in many studies with different methodologies, and it is likely that some people (approximately 33%) may develop PTSD in response to psychotic experiences.

As indicated by the second quote above, admission to an inpatient setting can result in exposure to a range of distressing or potentially traumatising events, with up to 54% of patients being exposed to other violent or frightening patients, 59% experiencing seclusion and 34% experiencing restraint (Frueh et al., 2005). However, the contribution of such treatment experiences to the development of PTSD following psychosis is less clear. Some studies (McGorry et al., 1991; Meyer et al., 1999; Frame & Morrison, 2001) have not found a significant or strong relationship between the number or type (e.g. voluntary/enforced) of hospital admissions and severity or rates of PTSD, whereas others (Priebe et al., 1998; Morrison et al., 1999) found that hospital experiences can contribute directly to PTSD for some people. Shaw et al. (2002) found that people with post-psychotic PTSD did not actually have more unpleasant hospital experiences (e.g. involuntary admissions or number of admissions), but rated their experiences as more distressing, had more intrusive memories of them and also experienced higher levels of suicidal ideation. They also rated their psychotic symptoms as more distressing and had significantly more intrusive memories about their symptoms. This suggests that an important mediating variable for the association between people's traumatic experiences and levels of distress are the subjective appraisals that people make of their experiences. This was demonstrated by Jackson et al. (2004) who found that traumatic events (involuntary admission, detention) were not directly related to traumatic symptoms (i.e. level of intrusions and avoidance). Instead, participants who perceived their admission experiences as 'stressful' were more likely to meet a diagnosis of PTSD and to report higher levels of intrusions. Overall, perceived stressfulness of admission was highly correlated with intrusive memories of the first episode of psychosis. Consequently, this suggests that individual appraisals of traumatic events, rather than traumatic events per se, may play a pivotal role in the subsequent development of PTSD, which is consistent with current cognitive models of PTSD (see Ehlers & Clark, 2000).

Summary

There continues to be debate regarding the methods and sampling procedures used to investigate the relationship between trauma and psychosis. However, what seems certain is that exposure to childhood trauma including childhood sexual/physical abuse increases the risk of developing psychosis as an adult. Similarly, some individuals who develop psychosis will go on to develop symptoms of PTSD as a result of developing psychosis. However, exposure to childhood trauma does not necessitate the development of psychosis and not all people recovering from psychosis go on to develop PTSD. Thus, there are likely to be mediating variables in these relationships. We have already seen that the extent that people experience their psychotic experiences or experiences of hospital and treatment as stressful may be an important mediating variable. An additional framework will now be briefly considered.

Can early adverse events cause vulnerability to subsequent trauma and psychosis?

Recent theories have suggested that chronic or persistent developmental trauma may act as a risk factor for adult emotional disorder in general. Read and colleagues have suggested that such trauma exposure lead to changes in the hypothalamic–pituitary–adrenal axis (HPA) (Heim et al., 2000). Thus, childhood trauma such as sexual abuse (for some) may result in permanent dysregulation of the HPA-axis, which may result in many of the biological abnormalities (e.g. dopamine) that are sometimes documented in adult psychosis (Read et al., 2001). However, it is also possible that early adverse trauma or life experiences may also cause a psychological vulnerability to the development of psychosis in adulthood (Bentall et al., 2001; Garety et al., 2001) by increasing unhelpful responses to unusual adolescent perceptual experiences or 'at-risk mental states' (Yung et al., 1996). This may occur through the development of beliefs that, in turn, influence the processing of information about the self and the social environment. Specifically, following childhood trauma such as abuse and neglect, people may develop beliefs based on notions of defectiveness, vulnerability or being different or the 'odd one out', which predispose people to low self-esteem, depression, anxiety, PTSD, substance misuse in adulthood and psychosis. In relation to specific psychotic symptoms, it has been proposed that adverse childhood experiences may lead to the development of negative beliefs associated with social humiliation and subordination, which can lead people to be vulnerable to paranoia and commenting or attacking voices (Birchwood *et al.*, 2000).

This theory is supported by evidence that childhood trauma can lead people to be vulnerable to adult mental health problems in general such as anxiety and depression and psychosis. Bak *et al.* (2005) assessed self-reported childhood trauma in 4,045 people with no history of psychosis at baseline. Three years later they examined those who had subsequently developed psychosis in the intervening time period. They found that those who had been distressed by their recent psychotic experiences were significantly more likely to have reported a trauma history at baseline (43%) than those who were not distressed by their psychotic experiences (6%). Thus, individuals who reported childhood trauma were 10 times more likely to report distress in the face of anomalous experiences than those without self-reported trauma. In addition, for those with a prior childhood/ adolescent trauma history, distressing psychosis was associated with less subjective control over psychotic experiences and greater psychological distress. This finding is consistent with the notion that catastrophic appraisals of initial psychotic experiences (or at-risk mental states) are associated with greater distress (Morrison *et al.*, 2003), which may be an important variable in people's subsequent presentations. Bak *et al.* (2005) conclude that the cognitive and social vulnerabilities associated with early trauma provide a plausible explanation for their finding that individuals exposed to early trauma, when faced with early psychosis-like anomalous experiences (or at-risk mental states), display a reduced perception of control and a greater sense of distress.

Thus, an important consideration is a historical assessment of people's earlier life experiences and the examination of possible links with current symptoms or subjective reactions and appraisals of symptoms and treatment (Jackson & Birchwood, 2006). Consistent with this, Gumley and Schwannauer (2006) cite the example of how someone with a history of bullying may experience an involuntary admission as confirmation of their personal vulnerability and untrustworthiness of others. Alternatively, such an admission may generate fear, but the loss of control and humiliation associated with this may cause much more distress than the hospitalisation itself. This point is illustrated in the example of the young man (quoted previously) who was admitted against his will, and appeared to be most distressed by the loss of rights, restrictions and lack of perceived respect from nursing staff.

Jennings (1994) has also poignantly described how her daughter's childhood experiences of sexual abuse were replicated by common practices within the mental health system such as lack of acknowledgement of abuse, restraint, seclusion and being controlled and threatened on inpatient wards. It has been proposed that disempowerment and disconnection from others are the core psychological experiences of trauma (Hermann, 1997) and it is all too easy to see how these conditions may be replicated in the treatment of adults recovering from psychosis. Hermann (1997) also emphasises that recovery from trauma does not occur in isolation, but can only take place within the context of relationships with others. However, people's psychotic experiences often elicit concerns about personal safety and interpersonal trust (Gumley & Schwannauer, 2006), which can cause profound social isolation and directly impede recovery.

Individuals with a lifetime history of sexual assault are also more likely to report significantly higher levels of concern for personal safety and feelings of helplessness, fear and distress when admitted to an inpatient setting (Frueh *et al.*, 2005). Furthermore, traumatic experiences associated with intense fear, helplessness or horror have greater (non-significant) associations with adult psychosis than traumatic experiences not associated with fear and helplessness (Spauwen et al., 2006). Consequently, traumatic events that elicit strong emotional responses may be more implicated in the development of adult psychosis. This is consistent with theories positing a central role for emotions in the development of psychosis (Birchwood, 2003; Freeman & Garety, 2003) and evidence considered above on the pivotal role of subjective appraisals of experiences (Shaw et al., 1997; Jackson et al., 2004) in determining people's level of distress following psychosis and treatment.

Implementation into practice: Case study

The following case study illustrates some of the above points. Jason was a 20-year-old referred to an at-risk psychosis service due to low-level auditory and visual hallucinations, aggression, thoughts of harming others and low mood/suicidal ideation. The referral also reported that it had recently emerged that a male relative had physically and sexually abused him when he was a child on a regular basis. In the years following the abuse, he drank heavily and became aggressive. He began to feel that people were giving him dirty looks and putting him down. This developed into paranoia that people were laughing at him and frequently resulted in physical conflict that required police involvement. In the months leading up to his contact with services, he began to see a shadowy figure in his bedroom doorway every night while trying to sleep and heard someone trying to break into his house. He lost a series of jobs, as he did not like being told what to do by others and ended up in physical conflict with his superiors. However, he was keen to address these issues and therapy helped him to appraise his low-level hallucinations in the context of his abusive experiences, his current lack of sleep, alcohol use and high physiological arousal levels rather than signs of impending psychosis (Morrison et al., 2004). Over time, his anxiety and arousal levels lowered and his low-level hallucinations disappeared. Jason's therapy also included anger management. He began to channel his aggression in a more functional way through playing sport, which had the added bonus of improving his social functioning.

Summary

When assessing people with a first episode of psychosis, we need to consider the potential impact that early traumatic events may have had on people's subsequent biological and psychological development and the potential relationship between these early events and subsequent psychotic symptoms. In addition, people's appraisal of psychosis as a traumatic event and its associated treatment (Jackson et al., 2004) and people's efforts to assimilate and accommodate it (Gumley & Swanneur, 2006) are also important.

Recent interventions aimed at addressing symptoms of PTSD amongst people recovering from psychosis will now be considered.

Interventions aimed at treating PTSD

Interventions aimed at treating PTSD following psychosis or severe mental illnesses are in the preliminary stages. Jackson et al. (2009) conducted a randomised control trial with 67 participants recovering from a first episode of psychosis. Participants in the intervention condition received cognitive therapy aimed at reducing the emotional dysfunction (e.g. post-psychotic depression and low self-esteem) and PTSD experiences (intrusions and avoidance on the Impact of Events Scale) by challenging people's appraisals of their first episode of psychosis (e.g. loss, humiliation and entrapment). Results indicated that nearly 90% in the intervention group had significantly lower PTSD symptoms at 12-month follow-up compared to 55% in the control (treatment as usual) condition. In addition, only two participants in the intervention group experienced an increase or no change in PTSD symptoms, whereas 45% in the control group experienced an increase or no change in PTSD symptoms.

Jackson and colleagues (Jackson et al., 2004; Jackson & Birchwood, 2006) have also emphasised the role that recovery style plays when intervening clinically with people following psychosis. McGlashan (1987) suggested that people who 'seal over' adopt cognitive and behavioural strategies, which enable them to avoid reflecting on their psychotic experiences. In contrast, people who 'integrate' their experiences are curious about their psychotic experiences and are more likely to seek treatment and support. Evidence suggests that 'sealers' have poorer engagement with services (Tait *et al.*, 2003), report more negative early childhood experiences (e.g. rated parents as less caring and more abusive), have insecure adult attachment and a more insecure identity (Tait *et al.*, 2004). Furthermore, people who 'seal over' are more likely to report higher PTSD avoidance symptoms than 'integrators' (Jackson *et al.*, 2009), but may be less likely to engage with psychological therapy or other treatments, which may prevent them from emotionally processing their psychotic experiences or their prior experiences of trauma.

In an effort to examine alternative means of promoting emotional processing of psychotic events, Jackson and colleagues (Bernard *et al.*, 2006; Barton & Jackson, 2008) have recently conducted two small pilot studies on the potential of writing about psychosis and its related treatment on symptoms of PTSD. These studies are based on evidence that written emotional expression designed by Pennebaker (1997) can have wide-ranging physical and psychological health benefits (Smyth, 1998; Sloan & Marx, 2004), and national clinical guidelines recommend that all people recovering from a psychotic episode are provided with an opportunity to write a narrative of their illness (NICE, 2009). These studies found that both patients who wrote about their psychosis (Bernard *et al.*, 2006) and carers who wrote about their relative's psychosis (Barton & Jackson, 2008) reported lower avoidance symptoms of PTSD at 4-week follow-up compared to controls. Written emotional expression was never intended as a stand-alone treatment for PTSD and is not an adequate treatment for PTSD following psychosis. Nonetheless, it may be a useful technique for facilitating emotional processing following a psychotic episode that could be incorporated into broader cognitive programmes, particularly for participants who experience difficulties with open disclosure.

Mueser and Rosenberg (Mueser *et al.*, 2004; Rosenberg *et al.*, 2004) have recently pioneered an alternative cognitive approach to the treatment

of PTSD in severe mental illness. The therapy aims to increase awareness that trauma-related symptoms are understandable and learned responses to cope with traumatic events and aims to develop cognitive restructuring skills to reduce emotional distress by changing maladaptive beliefs and thoughts associated with the trauma. Mueser and colleagues highlight that at times clients may be experiencing distressing symptoms of psychosis and make the important point that therapy should be guided by the distress clients are experiencing. Thus, if there is greater distress associated with psychotic symptoms instead of those associated with trauma, then cognitive restructuring should be directed accordingly at these symptoms. This emphasis on distress is a useful therapeutic guide for clinicians who are uncertain whether the immediate focus of therapy should be directed at symptoms of PTSD or psychosis.

Existing evidence with three case studies (Hamblen *et al.*, 2004) has found clinically significant reductions in PTSD symptoms (two clients no longer met the criteria for PTSD symptoms at follow-up) and general psychiatric symptoms. Results from a pilot study (Rosenberg *et al.*, 2004) also found good retention of participants (86%) and no adverse effects from participation. In addition, 100% baseline rates of PTSD dropped to 64% at post-treatment, and 50% at follow-up, and there were significant reductions in emotional distress such as anxiety, depression, guilt and hostility. A recent randomised controlled trial by mueser and colleagues has cofirmed the effectiveness of this cognitive intervention in reducing PTSD symptoms in individuals with severe mental illness (Mueser *et al.* 2008).

Thus, at present, the cognitive approaches pioneered by Jackson *et al.* (2004a,b) and Mueser *et al.* (2004) are the most comprehensive and promising given their grounding in empirically validated approaches (i.e. cognitive therapy) for PTSD. Table 19.3 summarises some of the important issues raised by Mueser *et al.* (2004, see p. 122 for more details) and Jackson and Birchwood (2006) for care coordinators and clinicians to consider when offering cognitive therapy for PTSD following psychosis. Hermann

Table 19.3 Important issues to consider when offering cognitive therapy for PTSD following FEP

Important issues to consider when offering cognitive therapy for PTSD following FEP

- Is the client's care coordinator aware they are being offered CBT?
- Has the client received adequate information of what CBT will involve?
- Once therapy commences, is the therapist keeping the care coordinator aware of progress and particular problems?
- Have the client and care coordinator received psychoeducation on PTSD?
- Have the client and care coordinator been taught the difference between an intrusion and a positive symptom of psychosis?
- Is it sometimes necessary to shift focus away from symptoms of PTSD to positive symptoms of psychosis?
- Is the client aware why they developed symptoms of PTSD in context of their life experiences?
- Have client appraisals of symptoms been assessed?
- Are cognitive techniques being used to modify beliefs?
- Is a staying-well plan being implemented before termination of therapy?

Case study

The following case study illustrates how these recommendations may be utilised. Josie was a 25-year-old French woman who moved to the UK following the breakdown of her marriage. In the UK, she began to worry that her ex-husband had contacted her new employers. Josie's concentration at work deteriorated and she became increasingly concerned that her ex-husband had contacted the media and that people in general knew about her past. A concerned co-worker contacted mental health services and Josie was sectioned. This seemed to confirm her suspicions that she could not trust people and she became increasingly delusional and believed she was been poisoned and began hearing voices of her ex-husband. She attempted to abscond from the ward and attempted to take her life. Josie's psychotic symptoms were treated medically, but 2 months following her discharge assessment with the IES revealed that she was experiencing severe levels of PTSD associated with her recent hospital admission. Josie was trying to block out all thoughts of the admission, which was preventing her from processing these experiences, and resulting in severe intrusive re-experiences. Importantly, Josie was no longer experiencing suicidal ideation and had established a trusting relationship with her care coordinator. Nonetheless, she initially found it too difficult to openly discuss her experiences, but agreed to write them down. Following this, she engaged in psychological therapy, which focused on psychoeducation about PTSD and understanding

her psychotic symptoms in the context of her life experiences. It also addressed beliefs about personal vulnerability and related these to earlier life events, which provided her with a framework to understand her recent experiences. This then led onto emotional processing of her inpatient experiences through open discussion in therapy, further discussion of these experiences with her care coordinator while completing a relapse prevention exercise and a visit back to the ward to visit a friend she had made. Following 5 months of therapy, her PTSD symptoms (scores on the IES) had reduced dramatically, and her social functioning had improved.

(1997) has also highlighted the importance of a collaborative therapeutic alliance based on trust and safety when working with traumatised samples and the challenges inherent in this. This can be particularly important when working with people recovering from psychosis due to the potential for their experiences to disrupt their ability to trust others and to feel safe.

Conclusions

In the last 15 years, the relationship between early traumatic life events and psychosis in adulthood has received increasing recognition and empirical investigation. Similarly, the potential for psychotic experiences and their treatment to cause symptoms of PTSD is now acknowledged. Recent models based on an integration of biological, psychological and social factors are beginning to look at the interplay of these issues in more detail. In this chapter, we have attempted to illustrate the importance of careful assessment, therapeutic factors to consider when dealing with clinical cases involving trauma and psychosis and to outline recent cognitive behavioural interventions for trauma associated with psychosis. Continued development of trauma-focused interventions will hopefully ensure that people who experience trauma associated with psychosis are provided with the opportunity to make sense of these experiences and to help them deal with the trauma associated with psychosis (irrespective of its cause). Finally, it has also been demonstrated that training around enquiring about abuse and trauma histories has been shown to have a significant impact on the clinician's confidence and self-perceived abilities to both enquire about and respond to abuse disclosures (Cavanagh *et al.*, 2004). Together, the development of these two important strands should ensure that contrary to the experiences highlighted in the quote at the start of this chapter, trauma associated with psychotic experiences is acknowledged and recovery from trauma and psychosis is not neglected.

Suggested further reading

Larkin, W. & Morrison, A.P. (eds) (2006). *Trauma and Psychosis: New Directions for Theory and Practice*. London: Brunner-Routledge.

Kennerly, H. (2000). *Overcoming Childhood Trauma: A Self-Help Guide Using Cognitive Behavioural Techniques*. New York: New York University Press.

Read, J., van Os, J., Morrison, A.P., & Ross, C.A. (2005). Childhood trauma, psychosis and schizophrenia: A literature review with theoretical and clinical implications. *Acta Psychiatrica Scandinavica, 112*, 330-350.

Useful websites

http://www.psych.auckland.ac.nz/staff/Read/Read.htm

This website has useful information on the relationship between trauma and psychosis.

http://www.trauma-pages.com

This website has a wide range of information on trauma and PTSD for clinicians and researchers.

References

Addington, D., Addington, J. & Maticka-Tyndale, E. (1993). Assessing depression in schizophrenia: The Calgary Depression Scale. *British Journal of Psychiatry, 163*, 39–44.

American Psychiatric Association (APA) (1994). *Diagnostic and Statistical Manual of Mental Disorders* (DSM-IV) (4th edition). Washington DC: American Psychiatric Association.

Bak, M., Krabbendam, L., Janssen, I. *et al.* (2005). Early trauma may increase the risk for psychotic experiences by impacting on emotional response and perception of control. *Acta Psychiatrica Scandinvica, 112*, 360–366.

Barton, K., & Jackson, C. (2008). Reducing Symptoms of trauma in carers. A pilot study examining the impact of care giving experiences. *Australia and New Zealand Journal of Psychiatry, 42*, 693–701

Bebbington, P., Bhugra, D., Brugha, T. *et al.* (2004). Psychosis, victimisation and childhood disadvantage: Evidence from the second British Nationality Survey of Psychiatric Morbidity. *British Journal of Psychiatry, 185*, 220–226.

Beck, A.T. & Steer, R.A. (1990). *Manual for the Beck Anxiety Inventory*. San Antonio, TX: Psychological Corporation.

Beck, A.T., Steer, R.A. & Brown, G.K. (1996). *Manual for the Beck Depression Inventory* (2nd edition). San Antonio, TX: The Psychological Corporation.

Bentall, R., Corcoran, R., Howard, R., Blackwood, N. & Kinderman, P. (2001). Persecutory delusions: A review and theoretical integration. *Clinical Psychology Review, 21*, 1143–1192.

Bernard, M., Jackson, C. & Jones, C. (2006). Written emotional expression following first episode psychosis: Effects on symptoms of PTSD. *British Journal of Clinical Psychology, 13*, 405–415.

Bernstein, D.P., Ahluvalia, T., Pogge, D. & Handelsman, L. (1997). Validity of the childhood trauma questionnaire in an adolescent psychiatric population. *Journal of the American Academy of Child and Adolescent Psychiatry, 36*, 340–348.

Birchwood, M.J. (2003). Pathways to emotional dysfunction in first-episode psychosis. *British Journal of Psychiatry, 182*, 373–375.

Birchwood, M.J., Meaden, A., Trower, P., Gilbert, P., Meaden, A. & Plaistow, J. (2000). The power and omnipotence of voices: Subordination and entrapment by voices and significant others. *Psychological Medicine, 30*, 337–344.

Blake, D., Weathers, F.W., Nagy, L. *et al.* (1990). *Clinician-Administered PTSD Scale (CAPS)*. Boston: National Centre for Posttraumatic Stress Disorder, Behavioural Science Division.

Cavanagh, M.-R., Read, J. & New, B. (2004). Sexual abuse inquiry and response: A New Zealand training programme. *New Zealand Journal of Psychology*, 33, 137–144.

Creamer, M., Bell, R. & Failla, S. (2003). Psychometric properties of the Impact of Events Scale-Revised. *Behaviour Research and Therapy*, 41, 1489–1496.

Dillon, J. (2008). Asylum ONLINE (electronic version). Retrieved, 21 January 2008, from http://www.asylumonline.net

Dunmore, E., Clark, D.M. & Ehlers, A. (1999). Cognitive factors involved in the onset and maintenance of posttraumatic stress disorder (PTSD) after physical or sexual assault. *Behaviour Research & Therapy*, 37, 809–829.

Ehlers, A. & Clark, D.M. (2000). A cognitive model of posttraumatic stress disorder. *Behaviour Research Therapy*, 38, 319–345.

Frame, L. & Morrison, A.P. (2001). Causes of PTSD in psychosis. *Archives of General Psychiatry*, 58, 305–306.

Freeman, D. & Garety, P.A. (2003). Connecting neurosis and psychosis: The direct influence of emotion on delusions and hallucinations. *Behaviour Research and Therapy*, 41, 923–947.

Frueh, B.C., Knapp, R.G., Cusack, K.J. *et al.* (2005). Patients' reports of traumatic or harmful experiences within the psychiatric setting. *Psychiatric Services*, 56, 1123–1133.

Garety, P.A., Kuipers, E., Fowler, D., Freeman, D. & Bebbington, P.E. (2001). A cognitive model of the positive symptoms of psychosis. *Psychological Medicine*, 31, 189–195.

Gorham, D.E. (1962). The Brief Psychiatric Rating Scale. *Psychological Reports*, 10, 799–812.

Gumley, A. & Schwannauer, M. (2006). *Staying Well After Psychosis: A Cognitive Interpersonal Approach to Recovery and Relapse Prevention*. Chichester: John Wiley & Sons.

Hamblen, J.L., Jankowski, M.K., Rosenberg, S.D. & Mueser, K.T. (2004). Cognitive-behavioral treatment for PTSD in people with severe mental illness: Three case studies. *American Journal of Psychiatric Rehabilitation*, 7, 147–170.

Heim, C., Newport, D., Graham, Y. *et al.* (2000). Pituitary–adrenal and autonomic response to stress in women after sexual and physical abuse in childhood. *Journal of American Medical Association*, 284, 592–597.

Hermann, J.L. (1997). *Trauma and Recovery: From Domestic Abuse to Political Terror*. London: Pandora.

Jackson, C. & Birchwood, M. (2006). Trauma and first episode psychosis. In: W. Larkin & A.P. Morrison (eds), *Trauma and Psychosis: New Directions for Theory and Practice*. London: Brunner-Routledge.

Jackson, C., Knott, C., Skeate, A. & Birchwood, M. (2004). The trauma of first episode psychosis: The role of cognitive mediation. *Australian and New Zealand Journal of Psychiatry*, 38, 327–333.

Jackson, C., Trower, P., et al., (2009). Improving psychological adjustment following a first episode of psychosis: A randomised controlled trial of cognitive therapy to reduce post psychotic trauma symptoms. *Behaviour Research and Therapy*, 47, 454–462.

Janssen, I., Krabbendam, L., Bak, M. *et al.* (2004). Childhood abuse as a risk factor for psychotic experiences. *Acta Psychiatrica Scandinavica*, 109, 38–45.

Jennings, A. (1994). On being invisible in the mental health system. *Journal of Behavioural Health Services and Research*, 21, 374–387.

Kay, S.R., Fiszbein, A. & Opler, L.A. (1987). The positive and negative syndrome scale (PANSS) for schizophrenia. *Schizophrenia Bulletin*, 13, 507–518.

McGlashan, T.H. (1987). Recovery from mental illness and long-term outcome. *Journal of Nervous and Mental Disease*, 175, 681–685.

McGorry, P.D., Chanen, A., McCarthy, E., van Riel, R., McKenzie, D. & Singh, B.S. (1991). Posttraumatic stress disorder following recent-onset psychosis: An unrecognised post psychotic syndrome. *The Journal of Nervous and Mental Disease*, 179, 253–258.

Meyer, H., Taiminen, T., Vuori, T., Aeijaelae, A. & Helenius, H. (1999). Posttraumatic stress disorder symptoms related to psychosis and acute involuntary hospitalisation in schizophrenic and delusional patients. *The Journal of Nervous and Mental Disease*, 187, 343–352.

Morrison, A.P., Bowe, S., Larkin, W. & Nothard, S. (1999). The psychological impact of psychiatric admission: Some preliminary findings. *Journal of Nervous and Mental Disease*, 187, 250–253.

Morrison, A.P., Frame, L. & Larkin, W. (2003). Relationships between trauma and psychosis: A review and integration. *British Journal of Clinical Psychology*, 42, 331–352.

Morrison, A.P., French, P. Walford, L. *et al.* (2004). Cognitive therapy for the prevention of psychosis in people at ultra high risk: A randomized controlled trial. *British Journal of Psychiatry*, 185, 291–297.

Mueser, K.T. & Rosenberg, S.D. (2003). Treating the trauma of first episode psychosis: A PTSD perspective. *Journal of Mental Health*, 12, 103–108.

Mueser, K.T., Goodman, L.B., Trumbetta, S.L. *et al.* (1998). Trauma and posttraumatic stress disorder in severe mental illness. *Journal of Consulting and Clinical Psychological*, 66, 493–499.

Mueser, K.T., Rosenberg, S.D., Jankowski, M.K., Hamblen, J.L. & Descamps, M. (2004). A cognitive-behavioural treatment program for posttraumatic stress disorder in persons with severe mental illness. *American Journal of Psychiatric Rehabilitation, 7*, 107–146.

Mueser, K.T., Rosenberg, S.D., Xie, H., *et al.*, (2008). A randomised controlled trial of cognitive-behavioural treatment for posttraumatic stress disorder in severe mental illness. *Journal of consulting and clinical psychology, 76*, 259–271.

National Institute for Clinical Excellence (NICE) (2009). *Schizophrenia: Core Interventions in the Treatment and Management of Schizophrenia in Primary and Secondary Care. National Clinical Practice Guideline Number 82.* London. Nice.http://www.nice.org.uk/nicemedia/pdf/CG82FullGuideline.pdf.

Pennebaker, J.W. (1997). Writing about emotional experiences as a therapeutic process. *Psychological Science, 8*, 162–166.

Priebe, S., Broker, M. & Gunkel, S. (1998). Involuntary admission and posttraumatic stress disorder symptoms in schizophrenia patients. *Comprehensive Psychiatry, 39*, 220–224.

Read, J. (1997). Child abuse and psychosis: A literature review and implications for professional practice. *Professional Psychology: Research and Practice, 28*, 448–456.

Read, J. & Fraser, A. (1998). Abuse histories of psychiatric inpatients: To ask or not to ask? *Psychiatric Services, 49*, 355–359.

Read, J., Perry, B.D., Moskowitz, A. & Connolly, J. (2001). The contribution of early traumatic events to schizophrenia in some patients: A traumagenic neurodevelopmental model. *Psychiatry, 64*, 319–345.

Read, J., Agar, K., Argyle, N. & Anderhold, V. (2003). Sexual and physical abuse during childhood and adulthood as predictors of hallucinations, delusions, and thought disorder. *Psychology and Psychotherapy: Theory, Research, and Practice, 76*, 1–22.

Read, J., van Os, J., Morrison, A.P. & Ross, C.A. (2005). Childhood trauma, psychosis and schizophrenia: A literature review with theoretical and clinical implications. *Acta Psychiatrica Scandinavica, 112*, 330–350.

Rosenberg, S.D., Mueser, K.T., Jankowski, M.K., Salyers, M.P. & Acker, K. (2004). Cognitive-behavioral treatment of PTSD in severe mental illness: Results of a pilot study. *American Journal of Psychiatric Rehabilitation, 7*, 171–186.

Ross, C.A., Anderson, G. & Clark, P. (1994). Childhood abuse and positive symptoms of schizophrenia. *Hospital and Community Psychiatry, 45*, 489–491.

Shaw, K., McFarlane, A. & Brookless, C. (1997). The phenomenology of traumatic reactions to psychotic illness. *Journal of Nervous and Mental Disease, 185*, 434–441.

Shaw, K., McFarlane, A., Brookless, C. & Air, T. (2002). The aetiology of post psychotic posttraumatic stress disorder following a psychotic episode. *Journal of Traumatic Stress, 15*, 39–47.

Sloan, D.M. & Marx, B.P. (2004). A closer examination of the written disclosure paradigm. *Journal of Clinical and Consulting Psychology, 72*, 165–175.

Smyth, J.M. (1998). Written emotional expression: Effect sizes, outcome types, and moderating variables. *Journal of Consulting and Clinical Psychology, 66*, 174–184.

Spauwen, J., Krabbendam, L., Lieb, R., Wittchen, H-U. & van Os, J. (2006). Impact of psychological trauma on the development of psychotic symptoms: Relationship with psychosis proneness. *British Journal of Psychiatry, 188*, 527–533.

Tait, L., Birchwood, M.J. & Trower, P. (2003). Predicting engagement with services for psychosis: Insight, symptoms, and recovery style. *British Journal of Psychiatry, 182*, 123–128.

Tait, L., Birchwood, M.J. & Trower, P. (2004). Adapting to the challenge of psychosis: Personal resilience and use of sealing over (avoidant) coping strategies. *British Journal of Psychiatry, 185*, 410–415.

Weiss, D.S. & Marmar, C.R. (1997). The impact of event scale-revised. In: J.P. Wilson & T.M. Keane (eds), *Assessing Psychological Trauma and PTSD*, pp. 399–411. New York: Guildford Press.

Young, M., Read, J., Barker-Collo, S. & Harrison, R. (2001). Evaluating and overcoming barriers to taking abuse histories. *Professional Psychology: Research and Practice, 32*, 407–414.

Yung, A.R., McGorry, P.D., McFarlane, C.A., Jackson, H.J., Patton, G.C. & Rakkar, A. (1996). Monitoring and care of young people at incipient risk of psychosis. *Schizophrenia Bulletin, 22*, 283–303.

Note

1. These measures should only be used by clinicians with appropriate training or access to supervision.

Chapter 20 Suicide prevention in early psychosis

Paddy Power

Introduction

Suicide is one of the most tragic outcomes of psychotic disorders, highlighting the despair and distress that many patients experience. The early years of illness are when most suicides occur (Westermeyer *et al.*, 1991). On average, 5.5% of people with psychosis commit suicide within the first 5 years of follow-up (Heilä & Lönnqvist, 2003). Suicide is the commonest cause of unnatural death during the first 10 years of follow-up (Craig *et al.*, 2006). Life-time suicide rates are: 4–10% for schizophrenia and 6–15% of people with affective psychosis (Brown, 1997; Inskip *et al.*, 1998; Siris, 2001; Palmer *et al.*, 2005). Psychotic disorders account for 20–37% of suicides in people with mental illness (Burgess *et al.*, 2000; Hiroeh *et al.*, 2001; Hunt *et al.*, 2006) and schizophrenia alone accounts for almost a third of all youth suicides (Hunt *et al.*, 2006).

The devastating impact of these suicides on friends, family, fellow patients, communities and staff is a graphic reminder of the anger, regret, hopelessness and despair that many people experience with these illnesses. Their deaths can become a focus for identification for fellow patients or relatives, potentially increasing their own risk when faced with similar circumstances. Bereavement for affected families and friends is especially protracted, often complicated by intense feelings of unresolved guilt and remorse. Even staff, despite their training and support, face considerable challenges coping with such incidents with questions about their culpability and involvement. Services themselves come under considerable pressure and very public incidents can threaten their viability, particularly new services.

The factors that contribute to suicide in psychosis are complex, making risk assessment and prediction especially difficult. No one factor can be relied upon and it is important to take account of the individual nature of each person's risks. Most patients will experience some degree of suicidal ideation during the course of their illness (Power *et al.*, 2003). Only a minority with act upon their suicide intentions and it is relatively rare for these attempts to be fatal. Acute psychotic symptoms may only contribute directly to about 10% of suicides (Nordentoft *et al.*, 2002), while most suicides may have far more to do with the social, psychological and emotional impact of people's illnesses. Hopelessness and depression during the recovery phases are key mediators of suicide. Indeed, they might even be considered normal reactions given the often profound challenges people face during their recovery.

For most people with psychosis, suicide is only a fleeting consideration. However, for up to a quarter, suicide becomes a serious and persistent preoccupation for days and weeks (Power *et al.*, 2003). They especially need close attention during these phases, with interventions to address the underlying causes. The fact that most survive is a testament to the help, support and treatment that they receive. Sadly, despite every effort, clinicians and carers can never fully protect every person. Acknowledging this may help to limit the guilt and shame experienced by those left behind after suicides.

There is encouraging evidence that early intervention reduces the risk of suicide in psychosis (McGorry *et al.*, 1998; Power & Robinson, in press; Bertelsen *et al.*, 2007; Harris *et al.*, 2008). Rates of suicide among early intervention (EI) services are relatively low compared with the traditional services (Power & Robinson, 2009). In addition, certain treatments and psychosocial interventions have been shown to reduce levels of suicidality in early psychosis (Nordentoft *et al.*, 2008; Power & Robinson, in press). Finally, risk management systems in services can provide additional protection by identifying and monitoring those at highest risk.

This chapter will attempt to describe the 'what', 'when', 'why', 'who' and 'how' in suicide and psychosis before covering some of the interventions that might reduce the risk of suicide in this very vulnerable population.

What is suicide?

Not all self-inflicted deaths in psychosis are suicides in the true sense. Legally, the death must be (a) unnatural, (b) self-inflicted and (c) with intent (O'Carrol *et al.*, 1996). Coroners require evidence that the person intended: (a) to take the action; (b) to harm himself/herself by that action; (c) to die as a result of that action and (d) at the time of the action was capable of understanding the likely consequences of the action. This is often difficult to prove. In reality, people are often quite ambivalent about killing themselves during attempts (Andriessen, 2006). The consequence is that coroners tend to under-report, while clinicians over-report deaths due to 'suicide'. This leads to confusion about the true rates of 'intentional deaths' in psychosis and the factors that might contribute. A way round this is for services to report self-inflicted unnatural deaths among their patients as either (a) true suicides; (b) suspected suicides; (c) unintentional self-inflicted deaths; (d) accidental deaths or (e) undetermined deaths.

There is similar confusion about what constitutes 'suicide attempts'. This makes interpretation and comparisons of surveys from different centres particularly suspect (Wagner *et al.*, 2002). One option is to categorise 'non-suicidal deliberate self-harm' incidents as separate to 'suicide attempts' (Muehlenkamp & Gutierrez, 2004). In clinical practice, however, people often present with both forms of self-harm and there is reasonable justification to view them along a continuum of self-harm. It would also

be very naive to rely on such a dichotomous distinction when determining access to particular services.

When are people most at risk of committing suicide in first-episode psychosis?

The risk of suicide in psychosis is 0.5–1% each year during the initial 5 years of follow-up. Most suicides occur in the post-psychotic recovery phase, usually within several months of discharge from hospital (Drake *et al.*, 1984; Craig *et al.*, 2006; Hunt *et al.*, 2006) – unfortunately a time when clinicians tend to be less concerned about the risks.

It is possible that people are at even greater risk of suicide during the prodrome and DUP (duration of untreated psychosis). Only one unpublished study, Sireling, L. (personal communication), has examined this so far and its findings suggest that an even greater proportion of suicides in people with psychosis occur before any contact with mental health services. This has important implications for early detection and access to mental health services.

In the initial prodromal phase, one study revealed alarming levels of suicidality at initial presentation, with over 90% experiencing suicidal ideation and 24% with a history of suicide attempt (Adlard, 1997). By the time psychosis emerges and people present to mental health services, 50% will have experienced recent thoughts of suicide (Nordentoft *et al.*, 2002) and 25% will have already attempted suicide (Nordentoft *et al.*, 2002; Addington *et al.*, 2004). Suicide attempts are one of the main reasons for presenting to mental health services (Harvey *et al.*, 2006), and it is more likely to occur among those with depressive psychosis, psychomotor retardation and longer DUP.

After initial presentation, people with first-episode psychosis continue to experience very high levels of suicidality for several weeks after which the intensity drops rapidly in the initial 3 months of follow-up before rising quickly again from the fourth month onwards and remaining relatively high for up to 18 months follow-up (Power *et al.*, 2003).

Why do some people with psychosis become suicidal?

There are many reasons why people become suicidal but two main factors appear to contribute in psychotic disorders: psychotic symptoms themselves and emotional reactions such as depression and hopelessness. The former contributes to the initial peak of suicide risk seen in the acute psychotic phase, while the latter contributes to the peak during the post-psychotic recovery phase. This distinction is important as it helps to determine risk and which interventions might be most effective. Whatever the rationale for committing suicide, many suicidal patients struggle at length with their suicidal urges and can be still quite ambivalent when they come to formulate plans and begin to act upon their thoughts. The lethality of the final act is heavily dependent on chance, the reversibility of the method chosen and whether help is sought or available in time.

In psychotic states, the process of suicidality is complex, disturbed and unpredictable. Emotional factors may still be relevant but psychotic symptoms themselves may be a more important independent driver, for example intense paranoia, command hallucinations and impaired judgement. A disregard for personal safety may result in unintentionally lethal actions, for example wandering in front of traffic, off platforms, lighting fires and threatening armed police. Catatonic states may result in profound neglect, dehydration, exposure and fatal blood clots. Relatively mild or even unintentional self-destructive urges may easily result in lethal consequences in such disturbed states. Yet, remarkably, most people still maintain an intact sense of self-preservation and help-seeking despite these urges.

Major episodes of mood disorder (manic/depression) have a much more predictable impact on people's suicidality in psychosis. Acute depressive or mixed affective episodes are particularly risky (Hawton et al., 2005b), especially as the depression begins to lift and people regain their ability to act upon their tortured preoccupations, self-loathing and guilt. High levels of anxiety and agitation increase this risk. In manic psychotic episodes, suicidality is rare though one should remain alert to the risk of unintentional self-harm.

Most suicides actually occur during the recovery phase after the psychosis has remitted. This is the period when patients emerge from their psychosis to face some of the most difficult emotional challenges of returning to a normal life. The trauma of the psychosis itself might induce PTSD-like symptoms afterwards, heightening the risk of subsequent suicide (Tarrier et al., 2007). Emotional reactions such as anger, self-loathing, shame, revenge, anxiety, fear, panic, emptiness, loneliness, resignation, depression, hopelessness, reckless abandon and a wish to escape an impossible situation can precipitate a suicidal state. Males take longer than females to recover (Power et al., 1998). Recovery may be a slow, frustrating and disheartening process for individuals. In addition, people may be expected to return to the very situation that precipitated their psychosis while at the same time support is being withdrawn in the belief that the risks have abated. It can be an intensely lonely time for people with long periods of social isolation and inactivity. Rejection, alienation, stigma and precipitation into the social milieu of the chronically mental ill will add to the sense of distress, loss, hopelessness and despair. This can be worse if they have had prior experience of these illnesses, for example through a relative. The realisation of the same illness in themselves can precipitate intense emotional reactions. This is particularly pronounced if they have also lost a parent through suicide.

Unfortunately, most patients are likely to relapse (Robinson et al., 1999) and most relapses occur between the end of the first and third years of follow-up. The realisation and psychological impact of these relapses may induce profound despair and hopelessness. This is particularly relevant to patients whose previous experience of psychosis has been especially traumatic or associated with suicidality.

Patients who have already attempted suicide once are particularly prone to further attempts (see underlying risks below). Previous attempts may also represent significant unresolved traumas that compound future suicidal experiences.

However, it is important to mention that not all suicide attempts have a negative influence. It may be a life-affirming experience for some people, a test of their fate and resolve to survive overwhelming adversity. It may prompt help-seeking and elicit empathic reactions in others. It can also be an opportunity for engaging in psychotherapeutic interventions and in the most difficult to engage a rationale for assertive engagement or use of mental health legislation.

Who is most at risk of suicide in psychosis?

Hawton *et al.*'s (2005a) very helpful literature review (19 studies) describes who is most at risk of suicide in schizophrenia. Being male, of White ethnicity, higher educational background and IQ, living alone or away from family, a family history of suicide and recent losses are associated with greater risk of suicide. However, being married, having children and employment do not confer any protection in schizophrenia. Suicide risk is greater in those with a younger age of illness onset (Westermeyer *et al.*, 1991), longer DUP (Verdoux *et al.*, 2001; Clarke *et al.*, 2006), command hallucinations, agitation, impulsivity, worthlessness, hopelessness, fear of disintegration, poor adherence to treatment, co-morbid depression, drug use, suicide ideation and a history of suicide attempts (Hawton *et al.*, 2005a). Hawton *et al.* (2005a) found that there is conflicting evidence about whether 'insight' into one's illness increases one's risk of suicide. Negative symptoms such as flat affect appear to protect against suicide.

How do people with psychosis attempt suicide?

People with psychosis tend to chose methods that are particularly violent such as hanging, jumping in front of a moving vehicle or from a high place and cutting one's wrists (Harkavy-Friedman *et al.*, 1999; Hunt *et al.*, 2006). During acute phases of psychosis, the methods tend to be more bizarre, unpredictable and 'opportunistic', for example self-immolation. Fire safety, cigarette lighters, hanging points, sharps, glass, electrical appliances all should be routinely part of any risk management policy in residential units accommodating acutely psychotic patients. 'One to one' observations by staff may be needed for several days in particularly unpredictable patients.

Assessing suicide risk in patients with first-episode psychosis

One of the initial difficulties with assessing risk in someone with first-episode psychosis is that there is often very little history upon which to rely. One needs to consider the effect of a wide range of more subtle risk factors and extrapolate them into the future in order to identify potential risk factors downstream, for example the risk they might lose their partner or custody of a child or how they might react to their illness once they start to recover and gain insight. This really requires an intimate understanding of what to expect with these illnesses and how different people react differently to changing circumstances as these conditions evolve over the first few years. It is not for the faint-hearted, and everyone presenting with first-episode psychosis should be thoroughly assessed as soon as possible by a senior experienced clinician such as a consultant psychiatrist.

How does one assess suicide risk initially?

Suicide risk assessment and formulation is central to the initial clinical assessment in psychosis. It should always be undertaken by experienced mental health clinicians, and ideally initial assessments should be conducted in pairs so each clinician can collaborate in building the initial risk formulation and plan. The clinical record should routinely incorporate a clear suicide risk assessment, formulation and management plan as part of the initial assessment documentation (the one consistent finding of suicide inquiries is criticism about the lack of documentation and communication between staff).

How does one enquire about suicide in the initial interviews? Timing is important and ideally one should give enough time first to develop rapport and an understanding of some of the issues before asking whether the person has ever thought of suicide. One way of introducing the topic is to ask how the person is being affected by what has been happening, whether it is getting them down, how desperate they feel and if they ever thought of ending it all. If they have been thinking of or actually attempted suicide, one should ascertain where the person is situated along the continuum of suicidality from *ideation, intent, plans and actions* (such as procuring the *means* and making an *attempt*) (Power & Robinson, 2009). Try to identify what has made them feel this way, what emotions they are experiencing, whether it is driven by psychotic features, what their rationale for suicide is, what plans they have made and what is stopping them from doing it.

Ensure that you have left yourself enough time to explore the risk further if patients reveal they are suicidal as you may have to revise your plans and put in place preventative measures, for example supervision by family, crisis team, hospital, etc. You should also leave enough time to 'debrief' patients after any discussion about suicide, as such inquiries may prompt patients to re-evaluate their future and potentially trigger feelings of hopelessness.

If someone has been suicidal in the past, you should make a detailed record of each episode, listing the dates of suicide attempt, methods chosen, reasons and outcomes. This should form the basic template for future risk assessments, so that a chronological record can be maintained throughout a person's contact with services. The details should be checked with family, carers and other agencies involved so that a comprehensive picture is developed.

Some people will be very guarded at the initial assessment, fearful that if they mention being suicidal then they will be immediately hospitalised. To avoid this, it is helpful to explain that fleeting thoughts of suicide are a common reaction to their circumstances and that these feelings will tend to subside once they get help and treatment. If you believe that they can be managed at home as long as certain safeguards are in place, it is essential to negotiate an agreement that they will inform carers or staff as soon as it becomes unbearable so that more help can be provided. Those who are mute, partly catatonic or extremely guarded should

be managed with great caution, particularly if they manifest high levels of anxiety, agitation, perplexity and unpredictability. Their confused and distressed behaviour may result in self-injurious actions, for example wandering in front of traffic or fire-setting.

The initial risk formulation and provisional risk management plan

Ideally, the initial formulation and provisional risk management plan should be developed collaboratively at the first meeting with all involved. At the end of the assessment, the clinician should summarise what his/her concerns are and together work out sensible ways of managing the risks over the subsequent few days. Contingencies should also be discussed and 24-hour emergency contact details provided. Potential means (e.g. ropes, stockpiles of tablets) should be made inaccessible and carers should always be involved in the risk management plan. Staff need to be aware of the greater mediums for instant communication available to young people, for example text messaging or Facebook (that might be used to express suicide intentions) and staff should incorporate these into their risk management plan.

Some people will refuse to allow carers to be informed. Surveys show that close family members and carers are usually unaware of their relatives' suicide preoccupations or attempts (Rascón et al., 2004). Therefore, our recommendation is that if the carer is to be given any responsibility for supervision, they must first always be informed of the risks and be part of the suicide prevention plan. The same principle applies to any agencies or staff involved in the immediate care of the patient. If the patient is hospitalised, then all staff on each shift should be made clearly aware of an individual patient's risk and the level of supervision/observation required, for example 1:1 nursing at arm's length. If one wishes to respect the person's confidence, then one should never at the same time place another person (carer or professional) unwittingly in a position of having to supervise that risk without that knowledge.

Additional factors to consider during the suicide risk assessment

As one builds a more comprehensive formulation of suicide risk during the initial interviews, it is helpful to explore a number of additional biological and psychosocial risk factors for suicide in psychosis. Biological risks include familial risks (not only of suicide attempts but of impulsivity and aggression) (Korn *et al.*, 1995; Spirito & Esposito, 2006); alcohol and substance abuse (Verdoux *et al.*, 1999); chronic illnesses, for example diabetes, autoimmune disorders, multiple sclerosis; SSRI antidepressants (particularly in adolescents) and antipsychotic side effects such as akathisia and dysphoria (Hansen & Kingdom, 2006). Psychosocial factors include a history of adversities such as childhood sexual and physical abuse (Fennig *et al.*, 2005); major losses, separations, bereavements, family rejection, unemployment, debts, homelessness, recent arrest and imprisonment (Kerkhof & Diekstra, 1995). Suicide is much more common among people from certain countries (e.g. Eastern Europe) and very uncommon among people from Muslim countries (WHO, 2007). Understanding how social networks may form around common experiences such as self-harm may help reduce the potential for copycat phenomenon. Poorly coordinated and unresponsive services may contribute to suicide (Desai *et al.*, 2005). Preventable issues such as unchecked dispensing practices, medication storage, inadequate systems for management of high-risk clients, record keeping, staff supervision, cover for therapists on leave and lack of audits all may contribute to risk in suicidal patients.

Suicide risk assessment schedules as an adjunct to assessment

There are numerous of assessment schedules now available to rate suicidality – for a review of these, see Goldston (2000). However, they provide limited benefit in clinical practice and are best left to the realm of research. Although very useful as an aid to a comprehensive clinical suicide risk assessment, they cannot be relied upon on their own and no schedules exist that are specifically designed to assess suicide risk in psychosis. Their particular value is in providing a standardised measure of suicidality that can be monitored and reviewed during follow-up.

> *Suicide risk monitoring:* Routine risk assessment and management systems should be an integral part of any mental health service. An alert should be triggered within the service for any patient assessed to be a suicide risk and the service should remain on high alert until a formal review has determined that the risk has subsided. This basic assessment and monitoring of risk should be regularly reviewed, given the transient nature of suicidality. It should happen particularly during: (a) the transition from prodrome to psychosis; (b) the early phase of recovery; (c) early relapse if it occurs and (d) during phases when there are rapid fluctuations in mental state. Comprehensive reassessments of suicide risk should be made after any behaviour suggestive of a suicide attempt. This should trigger a reappraisal of the care plan and a formal review with the patient, carer, treating team and any other agencies involved. The increased risk should also trigger more frequent contact with the service until the risk has subsided, mediated ideally via one of the risk management systems described below. The full risk assessment should be reviewed again whenever a transfer occurs from one team to another, for example discharge from hospital.

The management of suicide risk in psychosis

The suicide risk assessment and formulation should determine which specific interventions are likely to be most effective. There is no 'one size fits all' remedy and certain interventions may be wholly inappropriate for a given individual even if research evidence generally supports their use. One's formulation should determine the immediacy of the risk, what is driving that risk and what resources are available to minimise that risk. If a person is clearly intent on suicide or has command hallucinations telling them to kill himself/herself, then immediate hospitalisation is generally the safest option unless 24-hour supervised care can be safely provided at home (sometimes appropriate in children).

Acute containment of risk

Services should have clear guidelines for emergencies. The immediate priority is to ensure the person's safety, supervision, removal of potential methods of self-harm and if necessary safe access to hospital beds. Extra staff may need to be called upon for assistance, for example for one-to-one observations. Clinicians should apply the principle of the least restrictive intervention needed to achieve a safe and effective outcome (Schwartz, 2000). All staff on a shift should be aware of the risk, the supervision required and any restrictions imposed to prevent access to means of self-harm, for example cigarette lighters, cords, sharps and so on. Places of containment (e.g. hospital bedrooms) should be checked to ensure minimal risk of self-harm. The person's treating team should be involved as soon as possible so that they can decide on which interventions might be most appropriate and who should provide them.

Tackling the causes of suicidality

It is helpful to determine whether the patient's suicidality is driven by: (a) the acute symptoms of psychosis; (b) complicating mood disturbance; (c) pre-existing co-morbid conditions, for example personality disorder; (d) the individual's internal psychological reaction to the impact of their illness; (e) external factors such as reactions of significant others and losses; (f) PTSD features related to a previous suicide attempt or death of a significant other and finally, (g) suicide pacts between patients. This will help to tailor individual packages of interventions and identify the goals to be achieved.

Before tackling the underlying causes of suicidality, it is essential to ensure that standard treatment for psychosis is in place – simply engaging patients better in standard treatment will reduce the risk of suicide (Dahlsgaard et al., 1998). Any additional effect of specific suicide preventative therapies is unfortunately likely to be small (Bronisch, 1996; Van der Sande et al., 1997b; Power et al., 2003). Integrating these additional interventions is likely to have the most benefit.

Treatment considerations in psychosis

Atypical antipsychotics (e.g. risperidone, quetiapine, olanzapine and sertindole) may have a suicide preventative effect compared to conventional antipsychotics (Barak et al., 2004; Kerwin & Bolonna, 2004). Clozapine may actually have a specific effect on reducing suicidal ideation (Meltzer, 2005). Adding antidepressants during the acute psychotic phase of depressive psychosis is advisable (Wijkstra et al., 2006) but not in the acute psychotic phases of schizophrenia or schizoaffective disorders (Levinson et al., 1999) unless complicating depression fails to respond to antipsychotics alone (Mamo, 2007). However, adding antidepressants in post-psychotic depression does appear to provide limited benefit (Siris, 2001) without risking the return of psychotic symptoms (Whitehead et al., 2003). Lithium may have a role in reducing suicide risk in affective disorders (Cipriani et al., 2005) and electroconvulsive therapy (ECT) is the still the most effective treatment for severe affective psychosis (Mukherjee et al., 1994). ECT should also be considered in severe suicidal depression complicating schizophrenia spectrum disorders (Mamo, 2007).

Individual and group-based psychological interventions would be expected to reduce the risk of suicide but the evidence is unfortunately very limited (Van der Sande et al., 1997a; Brown et al., 2005). Indeed, one needs to be careful of the potential for some therapies to aggravate the risk (Power et al., 2003). There is only one CBT intervention that has been specifically designed for suicidal young people with psychosis (LifeSPAN therapy) and the effect was limited (Power et al., 2003). Debriefing after suicide attempts is advisable and may help reduce subsequent morbidity (Schwartz, 2000).

Psychosocial interventions that protect the person's developmental trajectory, sense of 'self' and instil a sense of recovery, hope, support and social integration are likely to minimise the potentially disruptive impact of an episode of psychosis. Social policies, housing, benefits, employment schemes, user groups and parenting support all help reduce social exclusion. Family psychoeducation and systemic family work may reduce tensions, 'expressed emotion' and the burden of care at home, thereby protecting the family against disintegration and reducing the risk of suicide (Lipschitz, 1995).

Service considerations in suicide prevention

EI services may protect against suicide (McGorry *et al.*, 1998; Harkavy-Friedman, 2006; Bertelsen *et al.*, 2007; Harris *et al.*, 2008) by reducing initial delays in treatment (Melle *et al.*, 2006) and providing more intensive help during the recovery phase (Nordentoft *et al.*, 2008). Suicide rates in EI services appear to be about 50% lower than rates reported elsewhere (Power & Robinson, 2009). More general service considerations such as improving communication, switching to electronic record keeping, enhanced care plans and engagement, for example the Care Program Approach in the UK, may likewise impact on suicide risk (Appleby *et al.*, 2006).

Staff training programs in suicide prevention have been shown to provide a significant reduction in suicide rates (Rihmer *et al.*, 1995). These include training packages for non-health and health professionals (Davidson & Range, 1999; Fenwick *et al.*, 2004; Green & Gask, 2005; Stone *et al.*, 2005). The benefits of basic 'first aid' training can extend to all staff (including reception staff), families (Rascón *et al.*, 2004) and patients themselves (Brown *et al.*, 2005).

> *Self-help books* for both suicidal patients and survivors of suicide include *Choosing to Live* (Ellis & Newman, 1996), *Stronger than Death: When Suicide Touches Your Life* (Chance, 1997) and *Questions and Answers about Suicide* (Lester, 1989). Helpful Internet sites include the American Association of Suicidology (http://www.cyberpsych.org/aas.htm), the Suicide Education and Information Centre (www.suicideinfo.ca), the Suicide Awareness Voices of Education (http://www.save.org) and Friends for Survival (http://www.friendsforsurvival.org/suggested_books.htm).

Case study

The Zoning System (Ryrie et al., 1997; Gamble, 2006) is one of a number of risk management systems available in mental health services. It is recommended because of its ease of administration and usefulness in clinical practice. It has been successfully introduced in Early Intervention services such as the Lambeth Early Onset (LEO) service in London (Power et al., 2007) and includes both inpatient and community risk management protocols. Patients are categorised at daily team handovers into three levels of risk (low = green, moderate = amber, high = red) (Ryrie et al., 1997; Gamble, 2006). This assessment is supplemented by a risk assessment questionnaire undertaken when the team makes initial contact with the patient. All new patients to one of the teams are placed in the red zone until the multidisciplinary team decides otherwise. A highly visible board/chart is kept in each team base with a list of the team's patients in each of the three zones. Any clinician may move a patient up into a higher risk zone at any time if they are concerned about the patient but a patient's zone may not be downgraded until the team has made a decision to do so at its regular multidisciplinary clinical review meeting. The zoning system is linked to a patient management protocol that determines the intensity of supervision and frequency of observations/contact; for example, an inpatient in the red zone must have a nurse accompany them while on leave (if in red zone and high-profile observations, then no leave is permitted and whereabouts must be confirmed every 15 minutes). The system also determines the frequency of risk assessment reviews and means that red-zone patients are frequently evaluated and discussed at each team meeting and shift handovers. It is also a useful audit and management tool for evaluating service demand, incidents, caseloads and staffing levels.

The future of suicide prevention in psychosis

Estimates suggest that a sizeable proportion of people who commit suicide suffer from either untreated or treated first-episode psychosis (Power & Robinson, 2009). More needs to be done to highlight this tragic and potentially preventable situation. As the focus moves towards prevention and early intervention, there is evidence that this can minimise the risk of suicide. However, there are still major challenges ahead to improve on the fairly rudimentary systems currently available to assess risk and there is a danger that markers of risk might themselves attract additional stigma and social consequences. More specific proven interventions are needed for those most at risk. However, the mainstay of suicide prevention in psychosis is to ensure that sound evidence-based treatment of psychosis is provided without delay and throughout the critical period. This is best embodied in the model of early intervention. Early Intervention provides hope not just for a better future for many people with these illnesses, but also extra protection against these tragic incidents.

References

Addington, J., Williams, J., Young, J. & Addington, D. (2004). Suicide behaviour in early psychosis. *Acta Psychiatrica Scandinavia*, 109, 116–120.

Adlard, S. (1997). *An analysis of health damaging behaviours in young people at high risk of psychosis.* FRANZCP Dissertation, Melbourne: The Royal College and New Zealand College of Psychiatrists.

Andriessen, K. (2006). On 'intention' in the definition of suicide. *Suicide and Life-Threatening Behaviour*, 36, 533–538.

Appleby, L., Shaw, J., Kapur, N. *et al.* (2006). *Avoidable Deaths: Five Year Report into the National Confidential Inquiry into Suicide and Homicide by People with Mental Illness.* London: Stationary Office.

Barak, Y., Mirecki, I., Knobler, H. Y., Natan, Z. & Aizenberg, D. (2004). Suicidality and second generation antipsychotics in schizophrenia patients: A case-controlled retrospective study during a 5-year period. *Psychopharmacology*, 175, 215–219.

Bertelsen, M., Jeppesen, P., Petersen, L. *et al.* (2007). Suicidal behaviour and mortality in 547 first-episode psychotic patients: The OPUS trial. *British Journal of Psychiatry*, 191 (Suppl.), s140–s146.

Bronisch, T. (1996). The relationship between suicidality and depression. *Archives of Suicide Research*, 2, 235–254.

Brown, S. (1997). Excess mortality of schizophrenia: A meta-analysis. *British Journal of Psychiatry*, 171, 502–508.

Brown, G.K., Ten, H.T., Henriques, G.R., Xie, S.X., Hollander, J.E. & Beck, A.T. (2005). Cognitive therapy for the prevention of suicide attempts: A randomized controlled trial. *Journal of the American Medical Association*, 294, 563–570.

Burgess, P., Pirkis, J., Morton, J. & Croke, E. (2000). Lessons from a comprehensive clinical audit of users of psychiatric services who committed suicide. *Psychiatric Services*, 51, 1555–1560.

Chance, S. (1997). *Stronger Than Death: When Suicide Touches Your Life.* New York: W. W. Norton & Co.

Clarke, M., Whitty, P., Browne, S. *et al.* (2006). Suicidality in first episode psychosis. *Schizophrenia Research*, 86, 221–225.

Cipriani, A., Pretty, H., Hawton, K. & Geddes, J. R. (2005). Lithium in the prevention of suicidal behaviour and all-cause mortality in patients with mood disorders: A systematic review of randomized trials. *The American Journal of Psychiatry*, 162, 1805–1819.

Craig, T. J., Ye, Q. & Bromet, E. J. (2006). Mortality among first-admission patients with psychosis. *Comprehensive Psychiatry*, 47, 246–251.

Dahlsgaard, K.K., Beck, A.T. & Brown, G.K. (1998). Inadequate response to therapy as a predictor of suicide. *Suicide and Life-Threatening Behaviour*, 28, 197–204.

Davidson, M. W. & Range, L. M. (1999). Are teachers of children and young adolescents responsive to suicide prevention training modules? Yes. *Death Studies*, 23, 61–71.

Desai, R.A., Dausey, D.J. & Rosenhack, R.A. (2005). Mental health service delivery and suicide risk: The role of individual patient and facility factors. *American Journal of Psychiatry*, 162, 311–318.

Drake, R.E., Gates, C., Cotton, P.G. & Whitaker, A. (1984). Suicide among schizophrenics: Who is at risk? *Journal of Nervous and Mental Disease*, 172, 613–617.

Ellis, T.E. & Newman, C.F. (1996). *Choosing to Live.* Oakland: New Harbinger Publications.

Fennig, S., Horesh, N., Aloni, D., Apter, A., Weizman, A. & Fennig, S. (2005). Life events and suicidality in adolescents with schizophrenia. *European Child and Adolescent Psychiatry*, 14, 454–460.

Fenwick, C. D., Vassilas, C. A., Carter, H. & Haque, M. S. (2004). Training health professionals in the recognition, assessment and management of suicide risk. *International Journal of Psychiatry in Clinical Practice*, 8, 117–121.

Gamble, C. (2006). The zoning revolution. *Mental Health Practice*, 10, 14–17.

Goldston, D. (2000). Assessment of suicidal behaviours and risk among children and adolescents. *Technical report submitted to NIMH under Contract No 263-MD-909995.*

Green, G. & Gask, L. (2005). The development, research and implementation of STORM (Skills-based Training on Risk Management). *Primary Care Mental Health*, 3, 207–213.

Hansen, L. & Kingdom, D. (2006). Akathisia as a risk factor for suicide. *British Journal of Psychiatry*, 188, 192.

Harkavy-Friedman, J.M. (2006). Can early detection of psychosis prevent suicidal behaviour? *American Journal of Psychiatry*, 163, 768–770.

Harkavy-Friedman, J.M., Restifo, K., Malaspina, D. *et al.* (1999). Suicidal behaviour in schizophrenia: Characteristics of individuals who had and had not attempted suicide. *American Journal of Psychiatry*, 156, 1276–1278.

Harris, G.H., Burgess, P.M., Chant, D.C., Pirkis, J.E. & McGorry, P.D. (2008). Impact of a specialized early psychosis treatment programme on suicide. Retrospective cohort study. *Early Intervention in Psychiatry*, 2, 11–21.

Harvey, S.B., Dean, K., Morgan, C. *et al.* (2006). How often does deliberate self-harm precipitate first presentation to services with psychosis? Findings from the AESOP study. *Schizophrenia Research*, 86, S56–S57.

Hawton, K., Sutton, L., Haw, C., Sinclair, J. & Deeks, J. (2005a). Schizophrenia and suicide: Systematic review of risk factors. *British Journal of Psychiatry*, 187, 9–20.

Hawton, K., Sutton, L., Haw, C., Sinclair, J. & Harris, L. (2005b). Suicide and attempted suicide in bipolar disorder: A systematic review of risk factors. *Journal of Clinical Psychiatry*, 66, 693–704.

Heilä, H. & Lönnqvist, J. (2003). The clinical epidemiology of suicide in schizophrenia. In: R.M. Murray, P.B. Jones, E. Susser, J. Van Os & M. Cannon (eds), *The Epidemiology of Schizophrenia*, pp. 288–316. Cambridge: Cambridge University Press.

Hiroeh, U., Appleby, L., Mortensen, P. & Dunn, G. (2001). Death by homicide, suicide, and other unnatural causes in people with mental illness: A population-based study. *Lancet*, 358, 2110–2112.

Hunt, I.M., Kapur, N., Windfuhr, K. *et al.* (2006). Suicide in schizophrenia: Findings from a national clinical survey. *Journal of Psychiatric Practice*, 12, 139–147.

Inskip, H., Harris, E.C. & Barraclough, B. (1998). Lifetime risk of suicide for affective disorder, alcoholism and schizophrenia. *British Journal of Psychiatry*, 172, 35–37.

Kerkhof, A.J. & Diekstra, R.F. (1995). How to evaluate and deal with acute suicide risk. In: R.F. Diekstra,

W. Gulbinat, I. Kienhorst & D. de Leo (eds), *Preventive Strategies on Suicide*, pp. 97–119. Leiden: E.J. Brill Press.

Kerwin, R. W. & Bolonna, A. A. (2004). Is clozapine antisuicidal? *Expert Review of Neurotherapeutics*, 4, 187–190.

Korn, M.L., Brown, S.L., Kotler, M., Gordon, M. & Van Praag, H.M. (1995). Biological aspects of suicide. In: R.F. Diekstra, W. Gulbinat, I. Kienhorst & D. de Leo (eds), *Preventive Strategies on Suicide*, pp. 311–337. Leiden: E.J. Brill Press.

Lester, D. (1989). *Questions and Answers about Suicide*. Philadelphia, PA: The Charles Press.

Levinson, D. F., Umapathy, C. & Musthaq, M. (1999). Treatment of schizoaffective disorder and schizophrenia with mood symptoms. *The American Journal of Psychiatry*, 156, 1138–1148.

Lipschitz, A. (1995). Suicide prevention in young adults (age 18–30). *Suicide Prevention: Toward the Year 2000*, 25, 155–170.

Mamo, D. (2007). Managing suicidality in schizophrenia. *The Canadian Journal of Psychiatry*, 52 (Suppl.), s59–s70.

McGorry, P. J., Henry, L. & Power, P. (1998). Suicide in early psychosis: Could early intervention work? In: R. Kosky & H. Eshkevari (eds), *Suicide Prevention: The Global Context*, pp. 103–110. New York: Plenum Press.

Melle, I., Johannesen, J.O., Friis, S. *et al.* (2006). Early detection of the first episode of schizophrenia and suicidal behaviour. *American Journal of Psychiatry*, 163, 800–804.

Meltzer, H. Y. (2005). Suicidality in schizophrenia: Pharmacologic treatment. *Clinical Neuropsychiatry: Journal of Treatment Evaluation*, 2, 76–83.

Muehlenkamp, J. J. & Gutierrez, P. M. (2004). An investigation of differences between self-injurious behaviour and suicide attempts in a sample of adolescents. *Suicide & Life-threatening Behaviour*, 34 (1), 12–23.

Mukherjee, S., Sackeim, H. & Schur, D. (1994). Electroconvulsive therapy of acute manic episodes: A review of 50 years experience. *American Journal of Psychiatry*, 151, 169–176.

Nordentoft, M., Jeppesen, P., Abel, M. *et al.* (2002). OPUS study: Suicidal behaviour, suicidal ideation and hopelessness among patients with first-episode psychosis. One-year follow-up of a randomised controlled trial. *British Journal of Psychiatry*, 181 (Suppl. 43), s98–s106.

Nordentoft, M., Larsen, T., Bertelsen, M. & Thorup, A. (2008). The challenge of suicidal behaviour in early psychosis. *Early Intervention in Psychiatry*, 2, 1–2.

O'Carrol, P., Berman, A., Maris, M., Moscicki, E., Tanney, B. & Silverman, M. (1996). Beyond the tower of Babel: A nomenclature for suicidology. *Suicide and Life-Threatening Behaviour*, 26, 237–252.

Palmer, B.A., Pankratz, V.S. & Bostwick, J.M. (2005). The lifetime risk of suicide in schizophrenia: A re-examination. *Archives of General Psychiatry*, 62, 247–253.

Power, P., Elkins, E., Adlard, S., Curry, C., McGorry, P. & Harrigan, S. (1998). An analysis of the initial treatment phase of first episode psychosis. *British Journal of Psychiatry*, 172 (Suppl. 33), 71–77.

Power, P., Bell, R., Mills, R. *et al.* (2003). Suicide prevention in first episode psychosis: The development of a randomised controlled trial of cognitive therapy for acutely suicidal patients with early psychosis. *Australian and New Zealand Journal of Psychiatry*, 37, 414–420.

Power, P., McGuire, P., Iacoponi, E. *et al.* (2007). Early intervention in the real world: Lambeth Early Onset (LEO) and Outreach and Support in South London (OASIS) service. *Early Intervention in Psychiatry*, 1, 97–103.

Power, P. & Robinson, J. (2009). Suicide prevention in first-episode psychosis. In: P. McGorry & H. Jackson (eds), *The Recognition and Management of Early Psychosis: A Preventative Approach*, pp. 257–282. Cambridge: Cambridge University Press.

Rascón, G.L., Gutiérrez, L.M.D.L., Valencia, C.M., Díaz, M.L.R., Leanos, G.C. & Rodríguez, V.S. (2004). Family perception of the suicide attempt and suicidal ideation of relatives with schizophrenia. *Salud Mental*, 27, 44–52.

Rihmer, Z., Rutz, W. & Pihlgren, H. (1995). Depression and suicide on Gotland: An intensive study of all suicides before and after a depression-training programme for general practitioners. *Journal of Affective Disorders*, 35, 147–152.

Robinson, D., Woerner, M. G., Alvir, J.M.J. *et al.* (1999). Predictors of relapse following response from a first episode of schizophrenia or schizoaffective disorder. *Archives of General Psychiatry*, 56, 241–247.

Ryrie, I., Hellard, L., Kearns, C., Robinson, D., Pathmanathan, I. & O'Sullivan, D. (1997). Zoning: A system for managing case work and targeting resources in community mental health teams. *Journal of Mental Health UK*, 6, 515–523.

Schwartz, R.C. (2000). Suicidality in schizophrenia: Implications for the counseling profession. *Journal of Counseling and Development*, 78, 496–499.

Siris, S. (2001). Suicide and schizophrenia. *Journal of Psychopharmacology*, 15, 127–135.

Spirito, A. & Esposito, S. C. (2006). Attempted and completed suicide in adolescence. *Annual Review of Clinical Psychology*, 2, 237–266.

Stone, D.M., Barber, C.W. & Potter, L. (2005). Public health training online: The National Centre for Suicide Prevention training. *American Journal of Preventive Medicine*, 29 (Suppl. 2), 247–251.

Tarrier, N., Khan, S., Cater, J. & Picken, A. (2007). *Social Psychiatry & Psychiatric Epidemiology*, 42, 29–35.

Van der Sande, R., van Roojijen, L., Buskens, E. *et al.* (1997a). Intensive in-patient and community intervention versus routine care after attempted suicide. A randomised controlled intervention study. *British Journal of Psychiatry*, 171, 35–41.

Van der Sande, R., Buskens, E., Allart, E., van der Graaf, Y. & van Engeland, H. (1997b). Psychosocial intervention following suicide attempt: A systematic review of treatment interventions. *Acta Psychiatrica Scandinavica*, 96, 43–50.

Verdoux, H., Liraud, F., Gonzales, B., Assens, F., Abalan, F. & van Os, J. (1999). Suicidality and substance misuse in first-admitted subjects with psychotic disorder. *Acta Psychiatrica Scandinavia*, 100, 389–395.

Verdoux, H., Liraud, F., Gonzales, B., Assens, F., Abalan, F. & van Os, J. (2001). Predictors and outcome characteristics associated with suicidal behaviour in early psychosis: A two-year follow-up of first-admitted subjects. *Acta Psychiatrica Scandinavica*, 103, 347–354.

Wagner, B. M., Wong, S.A. & Jobes, D.A. (2002). Mental health professionals' determinations of adolescent suicide attempts. *Suicide & Life-threatening Behaviour*, 32 (3), 284–300.

Westermeyer, J., Harrow, M. & Marengo, J. (1991). Risk for suicide in schizophrenia and other psychotic and non-psychotic disorders. *Journal of Nervous and Mental Disease*, 179, 259–266.

Whitehead, C., Moss, S., Cardno, A. & Lewis, G. (2003). Antidepressants for the treatment of depression in people with schizophrenia: A systematic review. *Psychological medicine*, 33, 589–599.

Wijkstra, J., Lijmer, J., Balk, F.J., Geddes J.R. & Nolen W.A. (2006). Pharmacological treatment for unipolar psychotic depression: Systematic review and meta-analysis. *British Journal of Psychiatry*, 188, 410–415.

World Health Organisation (WHO) (2007). http://www.who.int/mental_health/prevention/suicide/suicideprevent/en/index.html.

Chapter 21 **Managing treatment resistance in first-episode psychosis**

Charles Montgomery and Glenn Roberts

Introduction

Early intervention (EI) has quickly taken root in part because politicians and service planners easily accept that the pre-existing norm of 'late intervention' has no merit and is fraught with an accumulating list of additional problems that add to suffering and inhibit recovery. But the current convention of marking the end of the duration of untreated psychosis (DUP) with prescription of antipsychotic medication risks diverting a broad, person-centred and holistic EI approach into a narrow 'medical model' based on drug treatment. For the 60% who respond well to help from EI services, this may matter little, although only a minority will have no further episodes and the risk of recurrence can emerge even 10 years later (Power *et al.*, 2006). For the 10–20% who respond poorly and have persisting symptoms and disabilities, and for the additional 30% whose relapses confirm them as having a long-term condition, the limitations of a narrow medical formulation of treatment becomes increasingly significant. Currently, guidance on treatment resistance is confined almost entirely to issues related to medication (NICE, 2002).

Alongside continued interest in developing and implementing evidence-based treatment, there is also a growing interest in 'Recovery' (CSIP *et al.*, 2007), which has arisen from people who have lived with the experience of long-term and recurrent mental disorders, and its hope and creative potential is equally applicable to people with delayed recovery from first episodes. Kleinman's (1998) observation that 'Chronicity arises in part by telling dead or static stories' underlines that our words, meanings and guiding concepts can create or crush our sense of hope and opportunity. Hence, we prefer the concept of 'delayed recovery' over 'treatment resistance', for in reality, people do not 'resist' our treatments so much as experience their limitations, and we want to uphold hope for personal recovery even when symptoms or disabilities persist.

Engaging with the paradox: enhancing recovery for people with delayed recovery

Research on delayed recovery has so far focused almost exclusively on a failed response to medication. Conventionally, a 20% decrease in the total score on the Brief Psychiatric Rating Scale (BPRS) is usually regarded as a positive outcome but clearly a person with a high initial BPRS score could achieve a 20% reduction but remain significantly disabled. A more holistic and pragmatic approach would view delayed clinical recovery as continuing illness-related disability despite adequate trials of medication and a comprehensive psychosocial package of therapy and support. What we mean by 'comprehensive treatment' is a moving target as there is some evidence that more rigorous treatment approaches do result in better levels of functioning, but there are few services that can offer everything that may be of possible benefit and the hope that EI approaches will result in fewer people entering the delayed recovery group has yet to be demonstrated. In the most advanced EI services, about one in five people have delayed recovery at 3 months, which EPPIC refers to as 'prolonged recovery' (Edwards *et al.*, 2002).

Alongside this sobering statistic, it is worth remembering that there is also good evidence for recovery even many years after inception.

Harrison *et al.* (2001) found that global outcomes at 15 and 25 years were favourable for over half of all people followed up and an appreciable number of people recovered for the first time between 15 and 25 years after inception, which they suggested undermined the post-Kraepelinian paradigm of inevitable chronicity and deterioration. There is always a possibility of some degree of improvement and recovery.

Alongside continuing clinical developments, there are major developments in understanding the concept of recovery itself. The contemporary recovery movement credits Antony (1993) with the most widely accepted definition of recovery. Like many (Ralph & Corrigan, 2005), he makes a distinction between clinical and personal recovery and argues that the *person* with a mental illness can recover even when the *illness* is not cured, and that the process of personal recovery can proceed in the presence of continuing symptoms and disabilities. This way of thinking about recovery has arisen from people's lived experience (CSIP *et al.*, 2007) and engages with the seemingly paradoxical assertion that you can *be* well even if you *have* a long-term illness. It acknowledges that recovery from the consequences and stigma associated with severe mental illness are often harder than recovery from the illness itself. A recovery approach incorporates a sound understanding of evidence-based treatment but simultaneously seeks to understand and support people regaining or developing a satisfactory pattern of living and control over their life with a capacity for self-management, according to their own values. The EI practitioner working with people in delayed recovery is therefore presented with a significant challenge – how to cultivate the capabilities and qualities needed to take a broad, holistic, inclusive and person-centred approach alongside advanced clinical and psychosocial skills whilst remaining well grounded in the painful and difficult realities that such journeys represent for all concerned. Embarking on such journeys depends first on building an understanding of why someone has delayed recovery, which may offer clues of what is needed to help.

Understanding and intervening in delayed recovery

Understanding: the disorder, the person, the context and the service

The disorder

A long DUP is closely associated with delayed recovery and appears to have at least three components: delay in help-seeking, delay in referral and delay in provision of mental health services (Brunet *et al.*, 2007) (Box 21.1). Clarke *et al.* (2006) looked at 171 people presenting with first-episode psychosis (FEP) in South Dublin. The range of DUP was from 2 weeks to 240 months with a mean of 17.9 months. They found that a longer DUP was associated with a significantly poorer functional and symptomatic outcome at 4 years. A similar finding was reported by Perkins *et al.* (2005) who suggest that DUP may be a potentially modifiable prognostic factor. A long DUP is very often associated with an insidious onset of psychosis (Morgan *et al.*, 2006) and it has long been known that a gradual onset of predominantly negative symptoms (motivational difficulties and social deficits) signals poor treatment responsiveness. In the past, there was a notion that this group was the result of institutionalisation and that their disabilities were acquired; this is now known not to be the case as a number of studies have shown the presence of neuropsychological deficits in first-episode patients (Bilder *et al.*, 2001), which may represent a distinctive and biologically distinct subgroup (Kirkpatrick *et al.*, 2001). Associated findings include frontal lobe impairment, dysfunctional eye movements and executive performance deficits with marked and progressive brain abnormalities on successive CT or MRI scans (Salisbury *et al.*, 2007).

Box 21.1 Characteristics of the disorder

- Long DUP with insidious onset
- Cognitive impairment associated with negative symptoms
- An association with depression
- An association with substance misuse

The presence of more subtle cognitive impairments are often associated with negative symptoms and problems in everyday living skills and are increasingly being reported as an important mediator of treatment response (Green, 1996). This is leading to a growing interest in EI services developing skills in cognitive enhancement strategies.

The possibility that active psychosis and therefore DUP could in some way be neurotoxic is an attractive hypothesis and has some supporters but is unproven. The possibility that newer atypical antipsychotics have neurocognitive benefits over older traditional drugs is similarly tempting but unestablished (Bowie *et al.*, 2006; Harvey *et al.*, 2006; Keefe *et al.*, 2007).

The person

Whereas psychosis associated with affective symptoms tends to be predictive of a good response to treatment, depression coexisting with schizophrenia very often results in incomplete recovery (Birchwood *et al.*, 2000) (Box 21.2). Symptoms of depression can be confused with negative symptoms but are very important to differentiate as co-morbid depression is the single most important predictor of suicide in schi-zophrenia. There is an increasing awareness of the dysphoric effects of antipsychotic medication on some people; this tends to be an idiosyncratic reaction which does not affect everybody but it should routinely be asked about when medication has been started. Depression can also be a significant feature in early recovery when the hitherto protective effects of delusional beliefs are lost following the gaining of insight. The individual can have an experience of insight, in effect awakening to a painful reality, which can produce a reactive type of depression. In delayed recovery, there is a particular need to focus on the person struggling with their problem and not just on the problem.

The context

Co-morbid substance misuse is a huge problem in FEP and is over-represented in the impaired recovery group (Box 21.3). There is a strong rela-tionship with non-adherence to treatment (Margolese *et al.*, 2004) and other more complex

---

> **Box 21.2 Characteristics of the person**
>
> - An earlier age of onset
> - Poor premorbid personality
> - Gender: female patients show a better response to treatment
> - Presence of soft neurological signs

> **Box 21.3 Characteristics of the context**
>
> - An association with criminality
> - High expressed emotion within the family plus an atmosphere of criticism
> - Loss of accommodation
> - Loss of educational tenure/work

---

associations (Verdoux *et al.*, 2005). Causal links have been postulated between cannabis use and psychosis (Fergusson *et al.*, 2006; Skosnik *et al.*, 2006) and cannabis use is known to be high amongst patients with established psychosis (Green *et al.*, 2005). In the UK, cannabis abuse has been reported in 51% of patients and 55% had used Class A drugs although this was thought to be an underestimate of true drug use (Barnett *et al.*, 2007). A prospective 15-month follow-up study of over 100 patients in Australia (Wade *et al.*, 2006) found 53% with a diagnosis of substance misuse at follow-up. Substance misuse was independently associated with increased risk of hospital readmission, a longer time to remission of positive symptoms and an earlier and increased risk of relapse of positive symptoms.

The service

Every established and well-functioning EI team can expect to have between 10 and 20% of their caseload with significant disabilities (Box 21.4). This can be difficult to cope with and is in breach of the idealistic optimism that commonly characterises EI services. There may be a parallel between the EI team's sense of failure and that of the family's tendency to blame itself for 'failing' a persistently ill family member. In the face of ongoing suffering and disability, it is easy for EI teams to develop one of two patterns

---

Box 21.4 Characteristics of the service

- High Duration of Unprescribed Clozapine (DUC)
- Failure to take whole-life focus
- Low morale
- High staff turnover – inconsistent care
- Low recovery awareness

---

of responding: a sense of despondency and a wish to refer on quickly to a rehabilitation and recovery (R&R) team or a partial denial of the situation resulting in anguished attempts to offer more therapy/different therapy/better therapy with better qualified therapists. In both these scenarios, there can be an aversion to the early prescription of clozapine arising from the mistaken belief of either 'that's what R&R teams do' or that, whilst pursuing a psychotherapeutic agenda, the use of clozapine will give the wrong message signifying the end of the road. It is as though the prescription of clozapine is mistakenly viewed as a last-resort intervention which somehow confirms the team's failure. Current guidance supports the use of clozapine after no longer than 18 weeks of impaired response (NICE, 2002), but it is almost always a great deal longer and given the significant possibility of a favourable response, this 'Duration of Unprescribed Clozapine' (DUC) may effectively extend the DUP even after the individual has been engaged in (ineffective) early treatment.

Intervention: biopsychosocial support

Medication in delayed recovery

Failure to respond adequately to one atypical, taken at its recommended dose reliably for at least 6 weeks, will prompt a switch to a different atypical for a further trial. It is frustrating to both the patient and clinician that the response to antipsychotic medication appears so 'hit and miss' with wide variation in benefits between people taking the same dose of the same medication. Experience has taught us to be explicit at the outset about this variation and to enlist the individual's interest in pursuing the medication

that will best suit him or her stating that 'we might not get it right first time'.

If after a second trial (again at an adequate dose for at least 6 weeks), disabling symptoms remain, combining atypicals is an option (although there is a very limited evidence base for this). A recent multicentre audit of prescribing of antipsychotic medication for inpatients in 47 mental health services in the UK, involving 3,132 patients (Harrington *et al.*, 2002), found that 48% were receiving more than one antipsychotic drug. In the majority of cases, the reason for this polypharmacy was that a single agent was not effective, although it was not clear that the addition of a second drug had provided marked benefits. There is, however, some evidence that augmenting the atypical clozapine with another antipsychotic, in particular amisulpride, can be helpful (for a review of other augmentation strategies, see Kerwin & Bolonna, 2005).

Clozapine: Clozapine is the most effective antipsychotic medication available and for some patients can dramatically reduce their symptoms and improve their level of functioning (McEvoy *et al.*, 2006). It is the only antipsychotic that is clearly superior over the rest and is specifically indicated for 'treatment-resistant schizophrenia'. Kane's now classic study (1988) compared clozapine with chlorpromazine in 268 patients meeting strict criteria for treatment resistance. After 6 weeks, using a range of clinically relevant criteria, 30% of the patients receiving clozapine could be classified as responders compared to just 4% of the chlorpromazine group. Many well-conducted studies have since confirmed the benefits of clozapine particularly in this delayed recovery group (Wahlbeck *et al.*, 2001).

Most studies have shown that up to 60% of patients showing delayed recovery following treatment with other atypicals will respond to clozapine; half of these within 6 weeks with the remainder responding by 6 months. Current guidance (NICE, 2002) restricts its use to patients who have failed to respond to an adequate trial of two antipsychotics, one of which must be an atypical. Common side effects include excess saliva, sedation and weight gain, and the less common but more serious complication of loss of white blood cells (neutropenia) and cardiac complications are kept under careful review through registration with the Clozapine Patient Monitoring Service (CPMS), regular blood tests and other reviews at 'clozapine clinics' (for more details of clozapine prescribing and management of side effects, see Taylor *et al.*, 2005).

Switching to clozapine is always carried out under the guidance of a Consultant Psychiatrist, often as an inpatient exercise but increasingly on a carefully supervised outpatient basis.

Psychosocial interventions in delayed recovery

Along with more complex medication regimes, this group requires highly skilled psychosocial support to minimise the impact of ongoing psychotic symptoms. Cognitive behavioural therapy for psychosis, in different forms, has shown good results for reducing positive symptoms. COPE (Cognitively Orientated Psychotherapy for Early Psychosis) has been devised and extensively evaluated by Jackson *et al.* (1998) in Melbourne. A therapeutic approach designed specifically for the delayed recovery group has been developed, the Systematic Treatment of Persistent Psychosis programme (STOPP), in four phases:

1 Developing a collaborative working relationship.
2 Exploring and coping with psychosis.
3 Strengthening the capacity to relate to others.
4 Finishing and moving on.

The therapy is individualised and flexible and incorporates a variety of psychoeducational materials. A number of psychological techniques are employed, which are described elsewhere in this book, including the introduction of coping strategies, problem solving, reality testing, diary exercises, challenging erroneous beliefs and exploring the meaning of voices. The aim of the therapy is to strengthen the sense of self and to develop a way of thinking that separates self from illness (see Edwards *et al.*, 2004).

For completeness, we would also mention the relatively undeveloped but attractive possibility of Cognitive Remediation for people with pronounced cognitive deficits. A recent study by Ueland and Rund (2005) involving 25 adolescents showed modest benefits at 12 months compared to psychoeducation alone. It consists of four modules – cognitive differentiation, attention, memory and social perception – but few services have the training, skills or capacity to deliver a typically 30- to 40-session therapeutic programme.

A strategic team approach to improving treatment for delayed recovery

EI teams need a secure mechanism for identifying clients in delayed recovery at the earliest opportunity. There needs to be an expectation that good progress can be made by 3 months and a mechanism for reappraisal if this is not the case. We suggest that a strategic care planning meeting should be called for all clients showing delayed recovery at 3 months to review of the original assessment and formulation so as to identify factors which may be impeding recovery. This leads to an action plan which guides the ongoing work with the client (see Box 21.5).

We suggest that each EI team should have a reliable means of identifying the delayed recovery group and should devise a delayed recovery protocol that includes the early use of clozapine as there is evidence that the proportion of people who show a good response to clozapine (around 60%) increases if its use is brought forward in the course of the illness (Lieberman *et al.*, 1993).

Beyond improved treatment: steps towards personal recovery

The skilful deployment of evidence-based treatment is mostly directed at the disorder, and success or failure is measured in clinical parameters such as changes in symptoms, disabilities and use of services. Taking up an emphasis on personal recovery also greatly extends our thinking by focusing on the person who has the problem, how they are coping with it and how the rest of their life is developing in the context

---

Box 21.5 Suggested format for strategic care plan review meeting for clients in delayed recovery at 3 months

Review the original assessment and previous treatment

Review possible co-morbidity, especially depression, undetected borderline learning difficulties, substance misuse, personality disorder, Aspergers syndrome.

Review the possibility that the client is complicating their recovery with recreational drug use.

Has the client had EEG and CT scan of brain to exclude rare intracranial causes of psychosis?

Has the client had full blood screen to exclude undiagnosed medical condition (i.e. hypothyroidism/diabetes)?

Has the client participated in:

1. Psychoeducation
2. Cognitively orientated psychotherapy
3. Family work

Reformulate:

Can we come to an understanding of the delayed recovery in terms of:

the disorder

the person

the context

the service

How do these variables interact – what and where are the possibilities for change?

Respond with an action plan:

Are there ongoing stressors in the client's immediate environment that can be modified?

Is there an indication for enhanced/specific psychological or behavioural work?

Is the client isolated and unoccupied and if so would a supportive occupational programme be helpful?

Is the client concordant with medication? If not, concordance therapy.

If yes, has the client had second atypical for 6 weeks?

If yes, consider clozapine.

Is the client using recreational drugs? If yes, assertive counselling on drug misuse and further psychoeducation.

---

of their mental heath problem and use of treatments. It begins to engage with people's preferences, hopes and strengths and the pursuit of wellness, not merely the extinction of symptoms. It is important to emphasise though that services cannot make people recover, for personal recovery pivots around the individual taking an active stance and becoming an active agent in their own recovery process. As Coleman commented (1999), 'Recovery is not a gift from doctors but the responsibility of us all . . .' Narratives from people who have used services describe how developing the capacity to become active in their own recovery hinges on people feeling able to exercise choice and regaining a sense of personal responsibility and control over their lives, whether or not they continue to have symptoms and disabilities. Services can help or hinder this process, and the development of recovery-oriented practice, practitioners and services (Shepherd *et al.*, 2008) may depend on a constructive shift in power relationships (Roberts & Hollins,

2007) so that services of the future are experienced as 'on tap, not on top' (Perkins, 2007). Paradoxically, an overemphasis on treatment can impede recovery as people (patiently) wait to get better rather than learning how to actively participate in making things better for themselves. These new developments are at an early stage but there are some impressive accounts of how things can work out if people are supported to re-establish a secure sense of personal identity apart from that derived from illness (Anonymous, 2007; Morgan, 2007). Developing recovery-oriented services will be a challenge for both staff and those who use services and will be accompanied by a range of new practices and opportunities such as supporting self-management, self-directed care, peer support and recovery coaching, and we suggest that this is entirely compatible with the core values, philosophy, hopes and objectives of EI services.

Case study

To illustrate some of the issues these themes raise, here is Mary's story:

Mary was a quirkily attractive19 year old, pale and thin, who liked to wear brightly coloured flowery dresses and who would not have been out of place smiling up at you from the fashion pages of a Sunday magazine. With hindsight, her parents think she developed psychosis when in her sixteenth year. Her school failure and increasing reclusiveness was put down to use of cannabis. Her family became alarmed as she lost contact with all her friends and they could hear her pacing about all night although it was difficult to talk with her as she felt that her family was constantly hassling her, which in their concern they were. One day she finally admitted to hearing a whispering voice for years, which more recently had become louder, more persistent and occasionally threatening to her. She was scared and wanted protection and help.

A GP referral to the EI team resulted in the Consultant Psychiatrist visiting Mary at home and a trial of low-dose antipsychotic medication. There was some initial improvement but on stopping it she became a lot worse believing that her stepmother was a witch who was trying to poison her, which led to compulsory admission.

She resumed medication at a higher dose and was soon able to talk about a voice which she believed to be her stepmother's whom she felt was controlling her mind. She also said she thought her stepmother had got people on TV and the radio to taunt her in a coded way and it was doing her head in. After 4 weeks, she was discharged back home better but still symptomatic; the EI team visited weekly.

The family tensions increased but attempts to work together as a family broke down amidst hostile accusations by Mary. Increasing medication to relieve her voices resulted in distressing medication side effects including painful breasts and a switch to a different antipsychotic.

Since she had become unwell, Mary had postponed her application to college and it was now approaching the time for reapplication. Mary was adamant she wanted to apply but was clearly very stressed by this prospect. When two members of the team visited the house later that morning, they found Mary's bedroom door locked and she had gone. She was found later that evening by the police, hitchhiking at a motorway service station, scared and

dishevelled – saying she had to attend an interview in London and was worried that her stepmother had hired a hit man to kill her. Assessment led to a further compulsory admission. By now, a year had passed since her first referral to the EI team and she was clearly not doing well.

A strategic care planning review meeting was called involving the ward staff and the EI team, following which an intensive programme of support was instigated which included weekly CBT, family support and a switch to clozapine. Mary was initially very reluctant to consider clozapine due to the regular blood tests but education, support and persistent encouragement from the nursing staff won through, as did the example of a fellow patient who was making good progress. She had the usual initial side effects of sedation and excessive salivation but engaged with learning how to overcome these problems and a sense of partnership working gradually emerged.

As she improved, she was able to communicate more freely about the considerable build-up of family tensions, which now appeared realistic. Four months later, she was supported by the EI team in leaving both hospital and the family home for supported accommodation and 6 months later she was continuing to recover slowly, looking after herself well with an offer of part-time voluntary work at a friend's picture-framing workshop. She now values taking her clozapine on the basis that it 'keeps the voices from getting at me', and has regular contact with her care coordinator and a clinical psychologist for CBT. She also attends a hearing voices group and can relate too much of what her peers experience. She visits the family home for dinner on Sundays and hopes to get to college next year.

Learning points

This is more an example of typical rather than best practice.

1 Low-grade negative symptoms, especially with insidious onset, can be difficult to differentiate from normal adolescent moodiness.
2 Mary had a long DUP, over 2 years, and her early symptoms were both masked and compounded by her cannabis use.

3 A therapeutic dose of medication is not nec-essarily an acceptable dose to the individual, and troublesome side effects predict discon-tinuation.

4 Switching antipsychotic medication can lead to a worsening of symptoms and to relapse.

5 A strategic care planning meeting led to con-structive change and a trial of clozapine that should have been triggered much earlier in her delayed recovery.

6 Instigation of clozapine needs careful moni-toring by skilled and trained staff that are familiar with negotiating and working aro-und the many problems associated with start-ing up and have a robust sense of therapeutic optimism.

7 Delusional beliefs associated with psychosis can offer insights into real-life conflicts and concerns often metaphorically or thematically.

8 Recovery is a process which takes time and depends on supporting people to get a life that they value, not merely what we offer – the aim is to re-enter society as a citizen.

9 Formal therapies and peer-supportive and self-help approaches can be complimentary and gain in value if efforts are made to facili-tate them working together.

Implications and conclusions

The diagnosis of psychosis, and particularly schizophrenia, is experienced as a highly stig-matising 'life sentence' partially because of the associated implications of chronicity and hope-lessness. The whole EI agenda is underpinned by hope that with early and effective interven-tion, the life trajectory of people who develop psychotic disorders can change for the better. As research into the effectiveness of EI service delivery develops worldwide, the outcomes to two crucial questions are eagerly awaited: first, will the proportion of FEP individuals with delayed recovery decline? Second, once delayed recovery is established, can extra ben-efit be gained from more intense psychosocial therapies?

At present, optimal treatment still results in up to 20% of people with delayed recovery. It is essential that EI teams identify this group at

the earliest opportunity and develop compre-hensive care plans within the first 3–6 months. There is also a need to look ahead and ensure a positive handover to rehabilitation services for people who have persisting needs over the longer term.

We have argued against regarding people or their problems as 'treatment resistant' when, in reality, they are experiencing the continuing lim-its of our effectiveness. We are also concerned that the associated narrow focus on symptoms inflates them so that they become everything. An emphasis on improving the effectiveness of clinical treatment can be powerfully augmented by an emphasis on personal recovery, which is gaining prominence as a values-led, humanis-tic and person-centred approach applicable to all people with long-term conditions. A broader focus on the person with the problem widens the possibility of useful intervention to anything and everything that is experienced as support-ing hope and promoting wellness. This takes in a broad view of the person and their context, their preferences and hopes for the future.

We also value an emphasis on people being *in* recovery as an ongoing process with advances and setbacks. This is about learning how to live and how to live well in the context of con-tinuing problems (Deegan, 1988). We suggest that this is both fully compatible with EI philosophy and practice and a source of hope and inspiration for the people we work with and ourselves too. We have much to learn from those who have lived with and beyond the limitation imposed by persisting symptoms and disability. The future of working for recovery with those who have delayed or complex pathways will be in close collaboration with them as a shared journey, learning together.

Suggested further reading

Care Services Improvement Partnership (CSIP), Royal College of Psychiatrists (RCPsych) and Social Care Institute for Excellence (SCIE) (2007). *Joint Position Paper: A Common Purpose: Recovery in Future Mental Health Services.* London: Social Care Institute for Excellence (ISBN :978-1-904812-24-1).

Edwards, J., Wade, D., Herrmann-Doig, T. & Gee, D. (2004). Psychological treatment of persistent positive symptoms in young people with first-episode psychosis. In: J. Gleeson & P. McGorry (eds), *Psychological Interventions in Early Psychosis*. Chichester: John Willey & Sons Ltd (ISBN: 0-470-84436-1).

Power, P., Smith, J., Shiers, D. & Roberts, G. (2006). Early intervention in first episode psychosis and its relevance to rehabilitation psychiatry. In: G. Roberts, S. Davenport, F. Holloway & T. Tattan (eds), *Enabling Recovery: The principles and Practice of Rehabilitation Psychiatry*. London: Gaskell Press.

Suggested websites

- www.recoverydevon.co.uk – the home base of Recovery Devon, with many resources linked to recovery-oriented and self-management approaches.
- www.rethink.org/recovery/ – go to 'Rethink's self-management programme', then go to 'Further Information' – the experiences and views of self-management of people with a diagnosis of schizophrenia (publication).
- www.rcpsych.ac.uk – go to 'publications', then 'leaflets', then 'schizophrenia'.

References

Anonymous (2007). Psychosis: A personal perspective. *Context*, 93, 27–29.

Antony, W.A. (1993). Recovery from mental illness; the guiding vision of the mental health service system in the 1990's. *Psychosocial Rehabilitation Journal*, 16 (4), 11–23.

Barnett, J.H., Werners, U., Secher, S.M. *et al.* (2007). Substance use in a population-based clinic sample of people with first-episode psychosis. *British Journal of Psychiatry*, 190, 515–520.

Bilder, R.M., Goldman, R.S., Robinson, D. *et al.* (2001). Neuropsychology of first-episode patients. *American Journal of Psychiatry*, 155, 337–343.

Birchwood, M., Iqbal, Z., Chadwick, P. *et al.* (2000). Cognitive approach to depression and suicidal thinking in psychosis. *British Journal of Psychiatry*, 177, 516–521.

Bowie, C.R., Reichenberg, A. Patterson, T.L. *et al.* (2006). Determinants of real-world functional performance in schizophrenia subjects: Correlations with cognition, functional capacity, and symptoms. *American Journal of Psychiatry*, 163 (3), 418–425.

Brunet, K., Birchwod, M., Lester, H. & Thornhill, K. (2007). Delays in mental health services and duration of untreated psychosis. *Psychiatric Bulletin*, 31 (11), 408–410.

Clarke, M., Whitty, P., Browne, S. *et al.* (2006). Untreated illness and outcome of psychosis. *British Journal of Psychiatry*, 189 (3), 235–240.

Coleman, R. (1999). *Recovery: An Alien Concept*. Gloucester: Hansell Publishing.

Care Services Improvement Partnership (CSIP), Royal College of Psychiatrists (RCPsych) and Social Care Institute for Excellence (SCIE) (2007). *Joint Position Paper: A Common Purpose: Recovery in Future Mental Health Services*. London: Social Care Institute for Excellence.

Deegan, P.E. (1988). Recovery; the lived experience of rehabilitation. *Psychosocial Rehabilitation Journal*, 11 (4), 11–19.

Edwards, J., Maude, D., Herrmann-Doig, H. *et al.* (2002). A service response to prolonged recovery in early psychosis. *Psychiatric Services*, 53, 1067–1069.

Edwards, J., Wade, D., Herrmann-Doig, H. & Gee, D. (2004). Psychological treatment of persistent symptoms in young people with first episode psychosis. In: J. Gleeson & P. McGorry (eds), *Psychological Interventions in Early Psychosis, A Treatment Handbook*. Chichester: John Wiley and Sons, Ltd.

Fergusson, D.M., Poulton, R., Smith, P.F. *et al.* (2006). Cannabis and psychosis. *British Medical Journal*, 332, 172–175.

Green B., Young, R. & Kavanagh, D. (2005). Cannabis use and misuse prevalence among people with psychosis. *British Journal of Psychiatry*, 187, 306–313.

Green, M.F. (1996). What are the functional consequences of neurocognitive deficits in schizophrenia? *American Journal of Psychiatry*, 153 (3), 321–330.

Harrington, M., Lelliot, P., Paton, C. *et al.* (2002). The results of a multi-centre audit of the prescribing of antipsychotic drugs for inpatients in the United Kingdom. *Psychiatric Bulletin*, 26 (11), 414–418.

Harrison, G., Hopper, K., Craig, T. *et al.* (2001). Recovery from psychotic illness: A 15 and 25 year international follow up study. *British Journal of Psychiatry*, 178, 506–517.

Harvey, P.D., Patterson, T.L., Potter, L.S. *et al.* (2006). Improvement in social competence with short-term atypical antipsychotic treatment: A randomized, double-blind comparison of quetiapine versus risperidone for social competence, social cognition and neuropsychological functioning. *American Journal of Psychiatry*, 163 (11), 1918–1925.

Jackson, H., McGorry, P., Edwards, J. *et al.* (1998). Cognitively orientated psychotherapy for psychosis (COPE). *British Journal of Psychiatry*, 172 (Suppl. 33), 93–100.

Kane, J.M., Honigfeld, G., Singer, J. *et al.* (1988). Clozapine for the treatment-resistant schizophrenic: A double blind comparison with chlorpromazine. *Archives of General Psychiatry*, 45, 789–796.

Keefe, R.S.E., Bilder, R.M., Davis, S.M. *et al.* (2007). Neurocognitive effects of antipsychotic medications in patients with chronic schizophrenia in the CATIE trial. *Archives of General Psychiatry*, 64, 633–647.

Kerwin, R. & Bolonna, A. (2005). Management of clozapine-resistant schizophrenia. *Advances in Psychiatric Treatment*, 11, 101–106.

Kirkpatrick, B., Buchanan, R.W., Ross, D.E. & Carpenter, W.T. Jr. (2001). Separate disease within the syndrome of schizophrenia. *Archives of General Psychiatry*, 58, 165–167.

Kleinman, A. (1998). *The Illness Narratives: Suffering, Healing and the Human Condition*. New York: Basic Books.

Lieberman, J.A., Jody, D., Geisler, S. *et al.* (1993). Time course and biological predictors of treatment response in first-episode psychosis. *Archives of General Psychiatry*, 50, 369–376.

Margolese, H.C., Malchy, L., Negrete, J.C. *et al.* (2004). Drug and alcohol use amongst patients with schizophrenia and other related psychosis: Levels and consequences. *Schizophrenia Research*, 67, 157–166.

McEvoy, J., Lieberman, J.A., Stroup, S.T. *et al.* (2006). Effectiveness of clozapine versus olanzapine, quetiapine, and risperidone in patients with chronic schizophrenia who did not respond to prior atypical antipsychotic treatment. *American Journal of Psychiatry*, 163, 600–610.

Morgan, C., Abdul-Al, R., Lappin, J. *et al.* (2006). Clinical and social determinants of duration of untreated psychosis in the AESOP first episode psychosis study. *British Journal of Psychiatry*, 189 (5), 446–452.

Morgan, G. (2007). My road to recovery. A talk to the Royal College of Psychiatrists Annual Conference, June2007.http://www.rcpsych.ac.uk/mentalhealth-information/viewpoint/recovery.aspx.

National Institute of Clinical Excellence (NICE) (2002). *Clinical Guideline 1 Schizophrenia: Core interventions in the treatment and management of schizophrenia in primary and secondary care*. At www.nice.org.uk or available free from NHS Response Line 0870 1555 455 quoting reference number NO176.

Perkins, D., Gu, H., Boteva, K. & Lieberman, J. (2005). Relationship between duration of untreated psychosis and outcome in first-episode schizophrenia: A critical review and meta-analysis. *American Journal of Psychiatry*, 162 (10), 1785–1804.

Perkins, R. (2007). *Making It! An introduction to ideas about recovery for people with mental health problems*. London: South West London & St. George's Mental Health NHS Trust (www.swlstg-tr.nhs.uk).

Power, P., Smith, J., Shiers, D. & Roberts, G. (2006). Early intervention in first episode psychosis and its relevance to rehabilitation psychiatry. In: G. Roberts, S. Davenport, F. Holloway & T. Tattan (eds), *Enabling Recovery: The Principles and Practice of Rehabilitation Psychiatry*. London: Gaskell Press.

Ralph, R. & Corrigan, P. (2005). *Recovery in Mental Illness: Broadening Our Understanding of Wellness*. Washington: American Psychological Association.

Roberts, G. & Hollins, S. (2007). Recovery: Our common purpose? *Advances in Psychiatric Treatment*, 13, 397–399.

Salisbury, D., Kuroki, N., Kasai, M.D. *et al.* (2007). Progressive and interrelated functional and structural evidence of post-onset brain reduction in schizophrenia. *Archives of General Psychiatry*, 64, 521–529.

Shepherd, G., Boardman, J. & Slade, M. (2008). Making recovery a reality. Sainsbury Centre for Mental Health. Policy paper (www.scmh.org.uk).

Skosnik, P.D., Krishnan, G.P., Aydt, E.E. *et al.* (2006). Psychophysiological evidence of altered neural synchronization in cannabis use: Relationship to schizotypal. *American Journal of Psychiatry*, 163, 1798–1805.

Taylor, D., Paton, C. & Kerwin, R. (2005). *The Maudsley 2005–2006 Prescribing Guidelines*. London: Informa Healthcare.

Ueland, T. & Rund. B.R. (2005). Cognitive remediation for adolescents with early onset psychosis: A one year follow-up study. *Acta Psychiatrica Scandinavica*, 111 (3), 93–201.

Verdoux, H., Tournier, M. & Courgnard, A. (2005). Impact of substance use on the onset and course of early psychosis. *Schizophrenia Research*, 79, 69–75.

Wade, D., Harrigan, J. Edwards, P.M. *et al.* (2006). Substance misuse in first-episode psychosis: 15 month prospective follow-up study. *British Journal of Psychiatry*, 189, 229–234.

Wahlbeck, K., Cheine, M. & Essali, M.A. (2001). Clozapine versus typical neuroleptic medication for schizophrenia (Cochrane Review). In: *The Cochrane Library*, 4. Update Software, Oxford.

Chapter 22 Nurturing hope in early psychosis: A conceptual model to guide intervention

Dan Pearson

Introduction

As the title suggests, this chapter is concerned with the significant role that hope plays in the experiences, well-being and recovery of those challenged with the diagnosis of first-episode psychosis. In particular, it addresses the pragmatic question: 'How might hopelessness be ameliorated or hope inspired'?

Anyone reading this who has experienced early psychosis at first-hand or has worked with service users and families who are struggling will know that the first onset of psychosis is, for most, an immensely traumatic, frightening, confusing and emotional time. By its very definition, psychosis involves aspects of experience that are removed from the individual's, or families', previous relationships with the world. Perceptual processes and belief systems are compromised; self-esteem and self-confidence can be affected; school, college or work careers can break down and family relationships can be put under immense stress. It is not uncommon at the beginning that those involved might find themselves overwhelmed with feelings of powerlessness and hopelessness. Although for many those difficulties and the associated feelings of despair will be fairly short-lived, others – those who experience a delayed recovery, who recover quickly but subsequently relapse, who are more conscious of lost dreams or failed expectations or who experience greater prejudice and discrimination – might find themselves struggling with escalating levels of hopelessness or, potentially, oscillating between hope and despair.

This chapter presents a model of understanding hope that offers a structure for generating strategies to challenge hopelessness and to inspire and nurture hope. The potential utility of the model is analysed in comparison with other, pre-existing and validated models of hope and hopelessness. Its practical application is then illustrated through an exploration of 'hope-focused therapy' with two individuals with first-episode psychosis.

Research into the significance of hope and hopelessness in early psychosis

The concept of hope is frequently highlighted in relation to experiences of psychosis, and has been described as an integral and essential requirement for recovery (May, 2004). Until now, however, actual research into the significance of hope and hopelessness in this field has been limited, and, in the specific arena of early psychosis, has been almost non-existent.

There is, in contrast, an extensive and expanding body of research relating to the role of hope in the fields of academia, sports performance, social relationships, physical health, palliative care and bereavement (Snyder, 2000, Snyder et al., 2002) as well as a separate body of work that has examined the impact of hopelessness (or despair) in relation to depression and suicidality.

Hope has been shown to have positive correlations with self-belief, self-worth, self-esteem and self-confidence, as well as athletic ability and performance, and subjective perceptions of scholastic competence and physical appearance (Snyder et al., 2002).

Hopelessness, on the other hand, has been linked with lack of motivation and engagement in treatment processes, and poorer outcomes in those suffering from chronic or terminal illness

(Abramson *et al.*, 1989). In conjunction with helplessness, hopelessness (or despair) has also been identified as a proximal mediator between depression, suicidal ideation and suicidal attempts (Minkoff *et al.*, 1973; Abramson *et al.*, 1989) – a finding that has special significance in relation to this book given the extremely high incidence of co-morbid and secondary depression amongst those individuals with first-episode psychosis, as well as the acknowledged high risk of successful suicide (Aquilar *et al.*, 1997; Jackson & Iqbal, 2000).

Hopelessness has been associated with restricted help-seeking behaviour, poor concordance with medication regimes and reduced collaboration in counselling or psychotherapy processes. In early psychosis, these factors might be linked to greater delays in accessing treatment (Duration of Untreated Psychosis), reduced efficacy of the care package once initiated and a generally more worrying prognosis.

There are a number of insights from the more general hope and hopelessness research that seem to have particular relevance and potential generalisation for those struggling or working with early psychosis:

- The presence of hope inspires motivation, collaboration and persistence, greater belief or faith in treatment regimes, more positive interpretations of feedback or responses from others and, generally, improved outcomes.
- Hopefulness and hopelessness are both important. The absence of one is not the same as the presence of the other, and whilst some people respond well to a reduction in hopelessness, others appear to need to actively feel hopeful.
- Hope is learnt and appears to be reciprocally connected to achievement – the more successful the person is, or has been in the past, the more hopeful they are likely to be in any current or future endeavours and, consequently, the more effective they are likely to be in what they do.
- Success and achievement also impact on the person's sense of self-worth or self-esteem, with greater self-esteem being linked to more confidence and hopefulness and, consequently, greater likelihood of success.

- Hope and hopelessness are contagious. Hope can be caught both from positive, optimistic attitudes of the therapist as well as from the person's natural social network, whilst hopelessness can be engendered and exacerbated by negativity, powerlessness or hopelessness in others (Repper, 2005).

Implementation into practice – developing an integrative model of hope and a broad approach to the inspiration and nurturing of hope

I said in the introduction that this chapter would focus primarily on the clinical applications of a model of hope developed by myself. That model is, however, very new and has yet to be validated through rigorous study of its implementation. To place it in context, therefore, I will first describe the most established models of hope and hopelessness and then highlight where this new model expands or differs in its shape and utility.

The most highly validated model of hope, in relation to the psychological therapies, has been developed by Rick Snyder and colleagues in Kansas (Snyder, 2000, Snyder *et al.*, 2002). In their model, hope is a future-orientated, change-focused construct. In other words, hope relates to the possibility that things in the future might be better than they are now; or, at least, better than our fears of how they might otherwise be. They have proposed three key elements in the development and maintenance of hope:

- A commitment to a clearly identified goal;
- The capacity to generate or identify strategies to achieve that goal (Pathway Thoughts);
- A belief in one's own ability to pursue those strategies to the point of success (Agency Thoughts).

In essence, they say, people learn from experience. Experiences of success or failure in setting clear goals and in developing and pursuing strategies for change inform the person's beliefs in themselves and the level of hopefulness that they might connect with when faced with life's next challenge. Attitudes of hopefulness inform action and a feedback loop means that the outcomes of those actions then influence future hopefulness.

Although the development of understandings in relation to hope has progressed almost completely independently from those relating to hopelessness, with very little cross-referencing in the literature, there is considerable similarity between Snyder's thoughts and those of the leading researchers in the field of hopelessness (Abramson *et al.*, 1989).

Issues of self-belief and learning from success are also placed at the heart of their thinking. Similar to Snyder, the process is seen as circular and potentially self-maintaining – lack of self-belief resulting in defensive practice, restricted goal selection and less committed action, with cognitive biases to attention, interpretation and remembering of events sustaining a story of self as disempowered and ineffective. They differ, however, first, in not distinguishing between what Snyder terms 'Agency' and 'Pathway' thoughts, and, more importantly, by focusing on the relationship between hopelessness and disempowerment. Since empowerment and powerlessness are relational considerations – in other words, products of interactional experience – the person's sense of hopelessness can be seen to

be influenced by the actions of others rather than as simply residing within the individual.

My own research into hope, although comparatively limited at this stage, has taken a different path to that of Snyder's or Abramson's groups:

(i) In focusing specifically on the experiences of those struggling with the first onset of a psychotic illness;
(ii) In exploring the stories of service users side-by-side with those of their families;
(iii) In asking directly about their recommendations as to what I, myself, or others might do in the future to encourage hope in the people with whom we worked.

The model presented here evolved from the challenge of trying to make sense of the many different strategies identified by participants as having helped specifically with hopefulness during difficult times. As a consequence, the model (see Figure 22.1) offers a comprehensive framework that both helps to explain how and why certain attitudes or approaches might make a difference to hope and provides guidance on

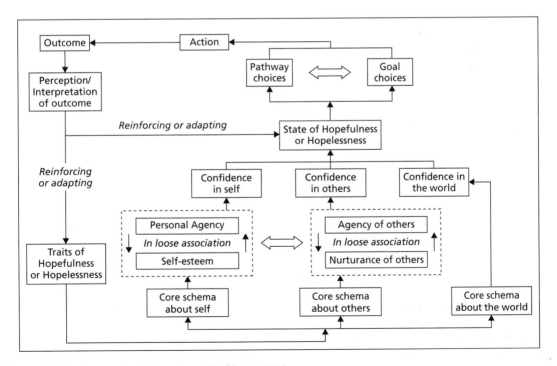

Figure 22.1 Pearson's relational model of hope 2006.

developing new targeted strategies for the amelioration of hopelessness and the inspiration or nurturance of hope.

In essence, this model takes both Snyder's and Abramson's ideas and locates them within a wider relational frame, with more complex differentiation with regard to factors that contribute to agency thoughts and pathway thoughts and a different perspective on the relationship between agency/pathway thoughts and goals. In addition, more attention is given to the metacognitive analysis of experience, and to the relationships between 'traits' and 'states' of hopefulness.

The model suggests that the sense of hopefulness that any person experiences in a given situation reflects an interaction between their confident attitudes to themselves, others and the world. Both 'confidence in self' and 'confidence in others' include ideas about agency – personal or other – and esteem or worth – self-esteem and 'received esteem' (which is defined in terms of the warmth, nurturance and respect received from others).

Personal agency is presented as connected not just to a history of achievement or success (as Snyder and Abramson have prioritised), but also to knowledge, including knowledge about available or appropriate strategies, which indicates a slightly different relationship between agency and pathway thoughts to that proposed by Snyder.

This model also proposes more complexity in relation to goals, including questions about what is appropriate or achievable, as well as distinctions between the pursuit of general or specific goals, a focus on hope or hopelessness, a concern with the short- or long-term future and the targeting of hopeful goals for themselves or others.

The information processing, or metacognitive analysis, of experience is seen as having the capacity to reinforce or modify both situational 'states' of hope or hopelessness and more long-term 'traits' or tendencies to these respective positions.

Implications for clinical practice: The inspiration of hope in therapy

The limited research that addresses therapeutic approaches to hope mostly seems to treat hope and hopelessness as two constructs occupying opposite ends of a single continuum of experience. Discussions relating to the inspiration of hope are often inextricably interwoven with those concerning the amelioration of hopelessness. One clear exception to this is the 'Hope Therapy' developed by Snyder and his colleagues, which advocates an active, transparent and direct focus specifically on the encouragement of hope (Snyder, 2000; Snyder & Taylor, 2000). They have argued that where problems, or lives, have become saturated with despair, a continuing focus on hopelessness risks crystallising the negativity of experience. In contrast, they have noted that a focus on hope has the potential to encourage more positive, motivated and creative thinking about the future. 'Hope Therapy' is targeted towards the three components of hope prioritised within Snyder's model:

- Goals
- Pathway Thoughts
- Agency Thoughts

Snyder and his colleagues have suggested that identifying and addressing of blocked goals, the development by the person of 'navigational tools' with which to progress in their lives and the encouragement of improved self-esteem, agency and, in time, emancipation from a dependency on the therapist should be central components that underpin all psychotherapies. Snyder and Taylor (2000) have further pointed out that both agency and pathway thoughts can be improved simply by the action of the individual initiating therapy.

The idea of an active, focused approach to hope in therapy has also been supported by John Cutcliffe (1996, 2004), a leading authority on bereavement counselling and suicidology. He has challenged, however, the overt and direct nature of Snyder's recommendations, arguing instead for a more implicit or intrinsic approach. Hope, he has suggested, should be interwoven in the very fabric of the therapy process, rather than addressed as a defined or separate intervention. All therapy, he has said, should be infused with attitudes and processes that nurture or inspire hope, including, amongst other things, showing 'unwavering commitment', 'experiencing a caring, human–human connection', 'facilitating the release of painful emotion', 'providing unconditional and continual support', 'freeing the client to talk', 'employing therapeutic touch', 'purposefully using silence' and 'avoiding colluding with ..... denial and/or hopelessness' (2004, p. 127).

Cutcliffe's ideas have resonated strongly with concerns raised in recent years regarding the effects of professional pessimism or hopelessness, which is often consequent to the negativity with which certain mental health difficulties are viewed (May, 2004). It has been suggested that this 'Therapeutic Pessimism' is causal in the occurrence of significantly more poor outcomes in both the short and long term, especially in those diagnosed with psychotic illness or crisis (Repper, 2000, 2005). Repper (2005) has described this in terms of hope and hopelessness being 'infectious and catching' (p. 17). She has noted that all clinicians need to be self-aware in relation to the attitudes of hope or hopelessness that they take into a therapy encounter, and that they should take time, through supervision and training, to address any more negative expectations that they might have.

Whilst Snyder's model focuses primarily on just the three target areas noted above, and Cutcliffe's and Repper's approaches prioritise the therapeutic relationship, the new model being presented here offers a multitude of loci at which to intervene. It also transcends the explicit and implicit split in the Snyder and Cutcliffe disagreement, by offering ideas about both attitudinal interventions and more direct problem solving and cognitive exploration.

One way of categorising or distinguishing between interventions is to think in terms of:

(i) Attitudes or processes that are enacted within the therapeutic relationship;
(ii) Conversations with the individual in relation to their experiences, attitudes and strategies;
(iii) Work in the context of their relationships – with family, friends, peers, work colleagues or community.

Hopefulness in the therapeutic relationship

In the model presented, this would come under the general heading of 'Confidence in Others'. It might include:

- *Validation of the person.* Warmth, empathy and caring, smiling, sharing, being flexible, listening attentively, not judging, being consistent and remembering the person's story.
- *Optimism about the person's unwellness, circumstances and future.* This 'optimism' would need to be knowledgeable (evidence-based), person-focused and individually meaningful, rooted in an appreciation, of the person's unique history, experiences, circumstances, hopes and ambitions, and reflecting a language, imagery and metaphors that have relevance to them.

Hopefulness in conversations with the individual in relation to their experiences, attitudes and strategies

Conversations with the individual in relation to their experiences, attitudes and strategies might take many different forms, or pay attention to a variety of different considerations, including:

- *Exploring confidence in self or the world.* This might involve attending to issues of empowerment, achievement, knowledge and self-esteem or, perhaps, supporting the person to view the world in less hostile or more predictable ways and to focus particularly on aspects of their circumstances that are within their scope to influence.
- *Subjective experiences of hopefulness or hopelessness and their impact on pathway and goal choices.* For many people, their state of hopefulness or hopelessness would not be something that was at the forefront of their awareness. Directly asking about hope brings this consideration to their attention and can have the effect of crystallising whatever hopeful attitudes are dominant in the person's experience at the time. It might also make possible the modification or accentuation of what is felt. Furthermore, since hopeful feelings fluctuate with context, there will be

'windows of hope' in which the person is more able to connect with a positivism about the future, and to generate motivation to act.

- *Appropriate goal setting or problem solving.* Goal choices can become compromised by the person's ability to identify any meaningful or appropriate future goals, as well as by feelings of powerlessness and hopelessness that undermine belief or motivation. Goal choices need to be clear and relevant. They might relate to the well-being of self or someone else, to a diminution of hopelessness or an increase in hope. They might be focused on the short or long term. In all instances, however, since success or failure will contribute to the person's continuing sense of hope or hopelessness, it is important that goals are realistically achievable and that selected strategies can be followed.
- *Analysis of the outcomes of implemented problem-solving strategies.* Feelings of hopefulness can be learnt and those of hopelessness unlearnt. Success can feed a better state of hopefulness in the here-and-now as well as to help build a very different attitude, or trait, of hopefulness in the longer term. For that to happen, experiences of achievement need to be first noticed and then assimilated. Dominant narratives, or personal stories, of failure or uselessness need to be exposed to scrutiny in the light of the new evidence of the person's capacity for success. Whether in relation to therapeutic experiments, crisis management and problem solving, or more general lifestyle choices, detailed analysis of the outcomes has the potential to maximise the hopefulness that might be harvested from any situation as well as to minimise any potential negativity arising from subjective perceptions of failure or inadequacy.

Hopefulness in work with the person in the context of their relationships

From the model, it is obvious that an individual's sense of personal agency and their attitudes of self-worth or self-esteem might be indirectly, though intrinsically, influenced by their experiences of others. The person's sense of hopefulness can also be affected more directly by their 'confidence in others', in relation to other people's preparedness to protect them, to intervene to resolve problems, to provide empathy, warmth and respect and, perhaps, even to hold hope for the person at times that when are unable to hold onto it themselves. Each of these concerns might relate to the importance that the person places in their relationships with their therapist, psychiatrist or key worker, in addition to their natural support networks, including family, friends, work colleagues and, perhaps, even God.

- *'Agency of Others'* refers to interventions or situations in which another individual acts to address or resolve a problem on behalf of the person. Such agency might be concerned primarily with the processes of decision making or of practical intervention and might include emotional and practical support.
- *'Nurturance by Others'* includes experiences of empathy, caring and warmth, of respect and acceptance or belonging. For those individuals who are most influenced by their beliefs about how they are viewed by others, these experiences impact strongly on their sense of self-esteem or self-worth, and, more indirectly, on their trust in themselves. More generally, the manner in which another person offers practical support – in particular, whether it is offered with warmth, caring and respect – might significantly affect the way that support is experienced, the trust that is invested in it and its likely efficacy.

Hope might be inspired or nurtured by supporting the person's family and friends, or even other involved professionals, to be more effective in the support that they offer, or more clear and explicit in the warmth, respect and caring that they feel. 'Intervention' might include maximising the benefits arising from those relationships that are already hope-inspiring or, alternatively, addressing some of those less helpful, less nurturing relationships that might previously have been experienced as compromising hopefulness.

Below, two case studies are described where intervention focused on addressing hope in the therapeutic relationship. Names and some other identifying features have been changed to protect anonymity.

Adam is 19. The youngest of three children, he is the only one still living at home with his parents. He was first diagnosed with a psychotic illness 15 months prior to his referral, by which point he had experienced three admissions to hospital, dropped out of school and disconnected from all of his previous friends. He felt that the prescribed medications had done little to contain his crises or manage his distress. He had spent significant time talking with his key worker about social engagement and occupation, but had responded to all plans or recommendations with the ubiquitous 'Yes, but ...'. When I first met him, he described himself as unmotivated to engage in therapy or to try to change his life. Conversations around staying well or relapse prevention had failed to identify any clear patterns to the contexts or triggers of his crises, and he felt unable to identify any early signs by which he might pre-empt another crisis. He had settled into a state of 'learned helplessness', convinced of his inability to affect his own well-being and feeling hopeless about the prospect of change. Asked about hopes or ambitions for the future, he struggled to see beyond his sense of inadequacy and was unable to describe any meaningful or clear goals of any kind. His parents were devastated by his situation. In response to his hopelessness and apathy, they fluctuated between taking over and doing things for him, encouraging him towards goals, which he regarded as unrealistic, offering him hope for the future, which he interpreted as well meant, but irrelevant blanket reassurance, and retreating into their own feelings of bereavement. The families' shared sense of loss and hopelessness was fuelling a vicious cycle of apathy, withdrawal, failure and rejection.

Charlotte is 28, University educated and employed in a challenging, professional job. She is an only child of parents who divorced when she was 5 years old. She lives alone, is very close to her mother and does not speak about her father. I first met her shortly after her discharge from hospital following a cannabis-triggered psychotic episode. Her initial crisis was very brief and she appeared to improve rapidly, returning to work with a minimal delay. That optimistic start, however, was followed by a slow decline characterised by deep suspiciousness of others, including her mother, work colleagues and the key worker, and an increasingly depressed, unmotivated, helpless and fatalistic attitude to her circumstances and future. Her compliance with medication and attendance at scheduled appointments had become a little haphazard and the key worker was concerned about her potential for disengagement. In addition, she had recently reported some vague expressions of suicidal ideation linked to feelings of hopelessness, which had raised concerns about her risk to self.

The inspiration of hope was not at the centre of the request for my involvement with either Adam or Charlotte, and neither was it the primary focus of our early conversations together. It did, however, become increasingly significant over the course of our work together. It is also fair to say that the inclusion of hope in the discussions with both was initially at my instigation, and was not explicitly acknowledged as a topic of discussion, in either instance, until after it had been implicitly present for some time. It should be noted that this was an organic process rather than a strategic decision. Hope conversations with Adam involved his parents on several occasions, but with Charlotte were on her own.

Addressing hope in the therapeutic relationship

Although for very different reasons, both Adam and Charlotte were quite uncertain about investing in a therapeutic relationship with me and early conversations were focused on disentangling their cynicism, mistrust and fear of myself, personally, and my intentions, professionally.

In terms of the model of hope, described, Charlotte's suspiciousness of others, at least at first, made it difficult for her to accept any positive regard from me, or to believe that I might be able to help her find a pathway out of the rut that she found herself in. She was convinced that I would judge her and so was reluctant to disclose details of her thoughts and feelings. Adam, on the other hand, was more prepared to talk openly, but was sensitive to being patronised, and was quite dismissive of anything that he experienced as positive or encouraging.

Hope-inspiring approaches involved, amongst other things, valuing Adam and Charlotte through a gentle expression of empathy; showing interest through listening and remembering; using languages and images that fitted with them; providing a context of boundaried consistency and reliability; focusing on their strengths and being cautiously positive about the potential efficacy of the therapy; making sense of their recent experiences in relation to their histories, experiences and their own narratives of their lives; asking lots of open questions to elucidate their understandings and, in particular, when offering observations, always avoiding any imposition of my interpretations. Engagement with Charlotte, in addition, required a direct exploration of her attitudes to trust with regard to the therapy process, and to me as a person, which included actively encouraging her not to share information with me before she was ready, as well as jointly drafting the initial assessment letter to her GP and Consultant Psychiatrist.

Addressing hope in Adam's and Charlotte's experiences, attitudes and strategies for dealing with difficulties

Both Adam and Charlotte experienced themselves as failing in their lives – academically, vocationally, financially and socially. Their attentions were skewed towards noticing, interpreting and remembering failures and their capacities to report positive experiences were compromised. Adam described himself as unable to define goals for his future, because he was unable to separate any desires or ambitions from his feelings of intimidation about the journey involved or convictions about his inability to sustain the energy to succeed. When he had identified goals in the recent past, they had tended to be inappropriate and overly ambitious and had resulted in further experiences of failure. Charlotte had experienced

herself as successful in the past, but had absorbed an extremely pessimistic understanding of her illness and felt overwhelmed by images of future loss, limitation and loneliness.

The inspiration of hope with Adam involved noticing small instances of enjoyment, pleasure or success in his life, and helping him to remember half-forgotten experiences of achievement in the past. We set small challenges, with bite-sized goals to help him to experience success in action, and then carefully analysed these experiences to encourage an assimilation of hope-inspiring interpretations.

The inspiration of hope with Charlotte involved a careful, respectful teasing apart of the story of illness that she had constructed, including the roots of her knowledge and her level of commitment to the understandings held. This non-impositional stance allowed her space to question her understandings, to set a more appropriate timescale for her recuperation and to develop a 'staying-well' plan that included an appreciation of resiliencies as well as vulnerabilities, together with potential triggers and early signs. In particular, her paranoia was reframed in terms of 'exaggerated mistrust', which was examined in relation to a historical lack of trust in others.

Addressing hope in relationships with family and friends

My conversations with Charlotte to date have included little focus on hope in her relationships with others, except for myself, although we do have an agreement to think about her attitudes to friendships at some point in the future.

With Adam, however, considerable attention was given to his relationship with his parents. We have spent time addressing everyone's fears as well as their feelings of desperation and despair. Adam and I together have provided his parents with more detailed information about his mental health problems, including more 'realistic-but-hopeful' understandings than had previously been held. Finally, I have worked with Adam's parents on their being more discriminatory and consistent in their support and praise of him, and on their setting more appropriate expectations of him.

Conclusions and implications

Hope is a complex construct. It is future-oriented and change-focused. It involves a personal investment in both the identification and pursuit of a desired goal. It is fundamentally relational and incorporates aspects of confidence in self and others, relating to experiences of agency and of esteem. Both hope and hopelessness have the potential to be self-perpetuating and they are contagious in that they can be, both, passed on directly and purposefully and caught from others by accident.

Research suggests that hope and hopelessness are strongly interrelated, but that the absence of one is not the same as the presence of the other, and interventions that seek to rebalance the scales of hope–hopelessness might involve either, or both, moderating or reducing hopelessness or inspiring and nurturing hopefulness.

There are a great many possible strategies that might affect the balance of hope and hopelessness and the model presented provides some guidance for those wishing to generate their own interventions to target these attitudes or feelings. It is important, though, to acknowledge that none of the strategies reported in the descriptions of the therapy conversations with Adam and Charlotte were special or unique to the inspiration of hope. In the case studies, however, these approaches were bound together with a 'glue of hopefulness' and we all felt that this consideration of hope added something extra to the process.

My final point is this: Whether or not, in reading this, you feel able to trust the model that has been presented, it is important to recognise that hopefulness and hopelessness are incredibly powerful factors in the experiences of all those who are faced with the first onset of psychosis. I believe that it is essential that they are, at some level, always taken into account in the therapy or treatment offered to those who are struggling.

Suggested further reading

Cutcliffe, J.R. (2004). *The Inspiration of Hope in Bereavement Counselling.* London: Jessica Kingsley Publishers.

Snyder, C.R. (ed.) (2000). *Handbook of Hope.* San Diego: Academic Press.

Flaskas, C., McCarthy, I. & Sheehan, J. (2007). *Hope and Despair in Narrative Family Therapy: Adversity, Forgiveness and Reconciliation.* London and New York: Routledge.

References

Abramson, L.Y., Metalsky, G.I. & Alloy, L.B. (1989). Hopelessness depression: A theory-based subtype of depression. *Psychological Review*, 96, 358–372.

Aquilar, E.J., Haas, G., Manzanera, F.G. *et al.* (1997). Hopelessness and first episode psychosis: A longitudinal study. *Acta Psychiatrica Scandinavica*, 96, 25–30.

Cutcliffe, J.R. (1996). Critically ill patients' perspectives of hope. *British Journal of Nursing*, 5 (11), 687–690.

Cutcliffe, J.R. (2004). *The Inspiration of Hope in Bereavement Counselling.* London: Jessica Kingsley Publishers.

Jackson, C. & Iqbal, Z. (2000). Psychological adjustment to early psychosis. In: M. Birchwood, D. Fowler & C. Jackson (eds), *Early Intervention in Psychosis: A Guide to Concepts, Evidence and Interventions.* New York: John Wiley and Sons.

May, R. (2004). Making sense of psychotic experience and moving towards recovery. In: J.F.M. Gleeson & P.D. McGorry (eds), *Psychological Interventions in Early Psychosis: A Treatment Handbook.* New York: John Wiley and Sons.

Minkoff, K., Bergmann, E., Beck, A.T. & Beck, R. (1973). Hopelessness, depression and attempted suicide. *American Journal of Psychiatry*, 130, 455–459.

Repper, J. (2000). Adjusting the focus of mental health nursing: Incorporating service users' experiences of recovery. *Journal of Mental Health*, 9 (6), 575–587.

Repper, J. (2005). Travelling hopefully. *Mental Health Today*, 16–18.

Snyder, C.R. (ed.) (2000). *Handbook of Hope.* San Diego: Academic Press.

Snyder, C.R. & Taylor, J.D. (2000). Hope as a common factor across psychotherapy approaches: A lesson from the Dodo's verdict. In: C.R. Snyder (ed.), *Handbook of Hope.* San Diego: Academic Press.

Snyder, C.R., Sympson, S.U., Michael, S.T. & Cheavens, A. (2002). Optimism and Hope constructs: Variants on a positive expectancy theme. In: E.C. Chang (ed.), *Optimism and pessimism: Implications for Theory, Research and Practice.* Washington DC: APA.

Chapter 23 Family interventions for first-episode psychosis

Frank R. Burbach, Gráinne Fadden and Jo Smith

Introduction

One of the fundamental objectives of the WHO Early Psychosis Declaration (EPD) Consensus Statement is to 'generate optimism and expectations of positive outcomes and recovery so that all young people with psychosis and their families achieve ordinary lives' (Bertolote & McGorry, 2005). The statement goes on to detail the 5-year outcomes that a comprehensive and effective programme would deliver to people with early psychosis and their families, and the interventions, both pharmacological and psychological, that would be required to attain these. In addition to advocating that services involve families, key supporters and communities as partners in care, the consensus statement recommends the routine availability of family interventions and practical psychosocial support. Families' needs in terms of 'better access to information and education, social, economic, practical and emotional support' can be met in a variety of ways. These include self-help and support groups (see Chapter 26), provision of information about early psychosis, assessments and packages of care for key family members (see Chapter 24) and through single and multiple family intervention (FI) and therapy.

Although there is a substantial evidence base for family interventions, concerns have been raised about the ability of staff to implement family work following training. However, one might anticipate that issues in implementing family work in Early Intervention (EI) services would be less than in generic services, given that the UK Department of Health (DH) has stipulated small caseload size and a family-oriented approach in these services: 'Care must be taken to engage and support **all** those

important to the service user' (DH, 2001). In this context, EI services need to consider how best to facilitate access to a range of family-based services and, specifically, when to offer formal rather than routine family interventions.

This chapter examines the evidence base underpinning family interventions in first-episode psychosis (FEP), explores issues relating to the implementation of FI in the context of family-oriented EI services and provides examples of family interventions in two NHS EI service contexts.

Summary of the evidence

There is a clear rationale for working with families in early psychosis. Between 60% and 70% of young people live with or are in close contact with their parents, grandparents and family of origin (Addington & Burnett, 2004). Many have young brothers or sisters who are affected by their sibling's difficulties (Fisher et al., 2004). Others are already in relationships and are parents of young children. Frequently, it is family members who initiate and sustain engagement with services, and EI services may engage with family members first, if individuals will not engage (De Haan et al., 2002, 2004; Sin et al., 2005; Boydell et al., 2006; Singh & Grange, 2006).

The available literature on the impact of emerging psychosis on families highlights how traumatic this can be (Martens & Addington, 2001). High levels of distress are common, and are present whether or not the young person is living at home. High expressed emotion (EE) is reported as present in over 50% of families, but the evidence for its predictive value is equivocal, with the weight of evidence suggesting that high EE during the first 2 years is probably not predictive of relapse (Huguelet *et al.*, 1995; Patterson *et al.*, 2000; Bachmann *et al.*, 2002; Heikkila *et al.*, 2002). 'Illness' factors such as symptom type and severity, age of onset, diagnosis or length of illness are not associated with EE or distress (Heikkila *et al.*, 2002), which appears to be linked more with functional difficulties such as disorganisation, impaired interpersonal functioning, difficult behaviour and social withdrawal (Tennakoon *et al.*, 2000). The family's perceptions of behaviour and their psychological appraisal of the impact of the mental health difficulties on them have also been identified as significant predictors of distress and poor psychological well-being for relatives (Addington *et al.*, 2003, 2005a; Raune *et al.*, 2004). For some families, the trauma and shock is so great that, initially, they are in denial (Slade *et al.*, 2003), and issues of grief and loss are common (Gleeson *et al.*, 1999). Families struggle to understand how health systems work, and identify finding a way through the 'service maze' as one of their primary needs (White, 2002).

Family interventions for people with FEP have been developed against a background of substantial evidence of the efficacy of FI for people with multiple episodes of psychosis. A number of randomised controlled trials indicated that the inclusion of family work with standard care, including medication, significantly reduces relapse rates, improves social functioning, reduces 'family burden' and reduces overall treatment costs (see Pharoah *et al.*, 2002; Pilling *et al.*, 2002; Pitschel-Waltz *et al.*, 2001). To date, the evidence base for family work in early psychosis is rather limited and although detail on the content of what should be offered requires further study (Penn *et al.*, 2005; Askey *et al.*, 2007), family approaches appear to be beneficial (Haddock & Lewis, 2005). Brief family psychoeducational approaches that typically consist of stress management, problem solving, the provision of information and relapse prevention strategies result in positive outcomes or changes from high to low EE (Goldstein *et al.*, 1978; Zhang *et al.*, 1994; Rund *et al.*, 1995; White, 2002). There is also evidence that systemic family therapy and a crisis management approach can result in lower readmission rates (Lehtinen, 1993; Seikkula *et al.*, 2006). Results from the Calgary Early Psychosis Program have consistently shown positive effects for family members in terms of improvements in psychological well-being and reductions in levels of distress and negative aspects of caring (Addington *et al.*, 2002, 2005b). The other theme that emerges from the literature is that families may benefit from different types of help being offered at different phases of psychosis (Gleeson *et al.*, 1999; Shannon *et al.*, 1997). This phased approach is summarised in Table 23.1. See also other chapters in this section for a fuller discussion of other interventions (Chapters 24–26).

While there are issues with the quality of family studies in early psychosis (Askey *et al.*, 2007), there is sufficient evidence that working with the family is critical for effective EI services. In addition, leading practitioner-researchers from IRIS (2000) in the UK (see Table 23.2) and EPPIC in Australia (Shannon *et al.*, 1997) have produced comprehensive guidelines for practice.

Implementation into practice

Family needs and service delivery

As the development of EI-specific services is relatively new, there have been few studies to date looking at the delivery of family work in practice. Slade *et al.* (2003) compared a specialist EI service with generic Community Mental Health Teams and found that while all staff acknowledged the importance of family work in psychosis, the EI staff, who had smaller caseloads and who had access to supervision, engaged in significantly more family work. The EI staff 'described their work as largely supportive and psycho-educational, with formal family therapy sessions being quite rarely undertaken'. The idea that FEP families do not necessarily require the detailed family intervention developed for families coping with recurrent or long-standing problems presents a challenge in terms of service design and delivery. The majority of families will benefit from some psychoeducation and support, while a small number may still require specialist family work. Staff in EI teams tend to come from generic services and are therefore not necessarily experienced in family work. The challenge is how EI services

Table 23.1   The needs of first-episode families: the stage model (from Shannon *et al.*, 1997)

Focus 1	Focus 2	Focus 3
The impact of the psychosis on the life of the 'family system' as a whole.	The impact of the psychosis on individual family members.	Interaction between the family and the course of psychosis.
Stage 1: Before detection: Perceptions and explanations		
The need to access appropriate treatment as soon as possible.	The need to feel safe, and to feel that the young person is safe.	The need for accurate information about the early warning signs of psychosis.
The need for consensus regarding the explanation for the change in behaviour.	The need to access appropriate treatment.	The need for information about appropriate sources of help.
		The need to minimise conflict regarding the young person's behaviour.
Stage 2: After detection: Grief and stress		
The need for effective treatment for symptoms of psychosis.	The need for effective treatment for symptoms of psychosis.	Education about the role of the family in treatment, especially for home-based acute phase management.
The need for information which minimises potential for conflict regarding treatment.	The need for practical and emotional support to minimise the impact of trauma.	
	The need to understand what has happened to their relative.	
	The need for repeated, clear messages about psychosis and its treatment.	
Stage 3: Towards recovery: Coping, competence and adaptive functioning		
The need for early identification and more aggressive treatment for treatment-resistant psychosis.	The need for early identification and more aggressive treatment for treatment-resistant psychosis.	The need for ongoing information regarding treatment during recovery phase (e.g. prophylactic role of medication).
The need for identification and intervention for more complex family issues (e.g. severe marital conflict, abuse).	The need for early identification and treatment of 'at-risk' family members (e.g. depression, acute stress).	The need for information regarding appropriate level of care as recovery progresses.
		The need for information regarding early warning signs of relapse.
		The need to encourage positive, low EE behaviours.
		The need to improve communication and problem-solving skills.

Table 23.1   *(Continued)*

Stage 4: First relapse and prolonged recovery: A view into the future

Need for effective acute-phase treatment for relapse. Need to reach consensus regarding longer-term prognosis.	Need for effective acute-phase treatment for relapse.	Need for psychoeducation and communication training for ongoing 'high EE'.
Need for assistance (e.g. family therapy) for complex, ongoing systemic problems such as enmeshment.	Need for access to ongoing community supports (e.g. Schizophrenia Fellowship). Need for treatment for depression and chronic stress problems.	

Table 23.2   IRIS guidelines

General aims of family work:
- To provide an effective treatment for the client.
- To address the needs of all family members who are affected by their relative's psychosis.

The main aims of the involvement of family in the early phase:
- To provide a complete picture of the build-up to psychosis.
- To engage them in a collaborative therapeutic process.
- To deal with the crisis of psychotic illness in the family.
- To identify and respond to the needs of individual families.

Guiding principles of family work:
- A collaborative working relationship is established between the client, family members and the professionals who are working with them.
- The difficulties faced are seen in an objective way and the combined efforts of all three – client, family and professionals – are seen as the best way of addressing issues.
- The value base underlying the approach is non-judgemental towards family members. Their past or current attempts to deal with the psychosis are valued and are seen as their best efforts to cope with a complex and unfamiliar situation within the limits of their current resources.
- The focus of the work is here-and-now and towards the future. There is an emphasis on positive achievements, and difficulties are addressed in a constructive way, arriving at a range of potential solutions that can be tried out.
- There is an emphasis on the honest and open sharing of information with all family members including the client.

Key tasks in family work:
- To engage the family in a therapeutic working relationship with professionals.
- To provide family members with the time to talk about what has been happening, to normalise their reactions and provide them with empathic support.
- To interview family members individually in order to get a picture of how each understands their situation, is affected by what is happening and can contribute to getting family life back on to an even keel again.
- To assess how family members relate to each other and how they as a unit address the issues with which they are faced.
- To provide the family with knowledge and to help them to deal with the situations they face as a result of psychosis.
- To help them to make contact with other people in similar situations to reduce feelings of isolation and stigma.

can meet DH guidance and provide a comprehensive service to young people and those who are important in their social networks. How can services best meet families' basic needs as part of routine care within EIS, as well as flexibly responding to the more complex needs of particular families?

A helpful heuristic may be to consider families' needs in terms of a hierarchy (Mottaghipour & Bickerton, 2005; Pearson *et al.*, 2007), although families' needs will not necessarily present in single categories and will not necessarily develop in a step-wise manner. When first involved with services, families tend to require information (about mental health issues, treatment options, how services work etc.) and the opportunity to talk about their traumatic experiences. This commonly includes a need to discuss their experiences related to the development of psychosis, their difficulties in accessing appropriate help and feelings of fear, anger, loss and grief. Many will also welcome further help with solving problems (e.g. about roles, chores or achieving goals) and improving communication (e.g. when misattributions result in patterns consisting of criticism and withdrawal), and some will seek more in-depth exploration of issues. In our experience, some families engage more with psychoeducational interventions, while others are more interested in reflecting on family relationships and interactions in the context of family history and cultural issues. A detailed discussion regarding family needs by Pearson *et al.* (2007) is summarised in Figure 23.1.

Mottaghipour & Bickerton's (2005) 'pyramid of family care' model similarly proposes a minimum level of care to meet families' basic needs for information regarding illness and orientation to the mental health service, and in a hierarchical fashion builds more specialist interventions to meet more complex family needs. This has implications for the training of staff and the provision of services. All staff will need to possess an ability to form supportive therapeutic relationships with families, be able to provide relevant information in a manner which takes into account the families' current knowledge and beliefs, and have some ability to enable families to reduce stress levels by improving communications, and developing coping strategies and problem-solving skills. In some circumstances, families may require more complex psychotherapeutic intervention, for example where pre-existing relationship problems are impacting on the person with FEP or in situations of pre-existing trauma or abuse. The traumatising effect of the onset of psychosis and the guilt,

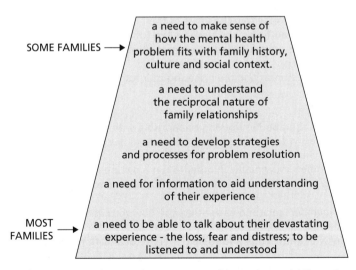

SOME FAMILIES →

a need to make sense of how the mental health problem fits with family history, culture and social context.

a need to understand the reciprocal nature of family relationships

a need to develop strategies and processes for problem resolution

a need for information to aid understanding of their experience

MOST FAMILIES →

a need to be able to talk about their devastating experience - the loss, fear and distress; to be listened to and understood

Figure 23.1 Family needs – The relationship between 'Breadth' and 'Depth' (from Pearson *et al.*, 2007).

denial, anger or hopelessness that frequently accompany this may also require the more skilled input of an experienced therapist. Although the ideal scenario may be for all EIS staff to be sufficiently well trained to respond flexibly to the full range of family needs, in reality, these more complex needs are often best met either by having some staff on the team who have received more specialist training and therefore have a more developed level of therapeutic skill, or through co-work with a more experienced family therapist, or referral to specialist psychotherapeutic services.

Service examples

In essence, what we are recommending is the incremental establishment of a range of local services for family members/significant others affected by FEP. Whilst we recognise that specialised services develop in the context of pre-existing local services and in response to local needs, it may be helpful to consider the implementation of family work in two NHS EI service settings.

Worcestershire EI Service

The Worcestershire EI Service, established in 2002– 2003, provides an example of a family-centred service with a range of services appropriate to families' needs at different points in time during their contact with the service (Figure 23.2). Families are routinely engaged in the services from the point of initial assessment and the team adopts a collaborative approach to clinical care decisions, involving the client and their family members. The majority of families (89%) meet regularly with members of their relatives' care team and in a recent service review, two-thirds had been actively involved in the production of their relative's care plans. Besides involvement in the clinical care process, 'routine family support' also includes crisis counselling and informal psychoeducation.

All members of the Worcestershire EI team are trained in Behavioural Family Therapy (BFT) and all families are made aware of and offered formal family intervention at some point in their contact with the EIS. BFT usually involves a number of assessment meetings with individual family members and the family unit followed, where agreed, by a series of (weekly) family sessions focusing on family psychoeducation and enhancing communication and problem-solving skills. However, only 20–25% of the caseload will be in receipt of formal FI at any one time related to both family need and team capacity limitations. As the sessions take place in the evenings, each case manager typically is able to offer formal family intervention to a maximum of two families.

Some families' needs are met through the other aspects of the service (e.g. routine family support and group psychoeducational sessions) but when families are clearly not coping, structured family sessions will be recommended. Typically, all families will receive routine family support from their case manager from the outset unless the individual does not consent to family contact, which is rare. Family members will also be encouraged to attend a relative's psychoeducation group during their first 12 months with the service (see Chapter 26 for more information on group-based interventions). Family intervention may be offered at any point during their 3 years with EI. Owing to families' ongoing relationship with the service as part of routine care, they are usually happy to take the advice of the team regarding the form of FI which might be of most help. Although, on occasions, families do prematurely discontinue family work when the clinicians involved feel that it would still be helpful. The take-up of formal FI is, thus, affected by a range of issues including the particular needs of families, the individual case manager's clinical judgement as well as the way in which case managers introduce the idea of BFT and its potential benefits.

We would suggest that it is the range of family-based services provided by the Worcestershire EI Service that enables an effective response to families' varying needs. In addition, it should be noted that, ideally, any family group interventions should be specific to EI families as relatives tend not to attend groups where families have more long-standing difficulties.

Worcestershire Early Intervention Service - Developing a Family Centred EI Service

Service background

- Service opened Jan 2003 (South), November 2004 (North)
- 560,000 catchment population
- Mixed urban/rural geography
- Anticipated incidence rate of 15–20 new cases per 100,000 per year countywide (based on local audit figures)
- Based in Worcester city
- Outreach to market towns of Malvern, Droitwich, Pershore, Evesham, Redditch, Bromsgrove, Kidderminster and surrounding rural areas (70–100k per town)

Family work as part of routine case management

- Families engaged in the service from the initial assessment
- Informal psycho-education for family members
- Collaborative approach to clinical care decisions involving the client and their family members
- Crisis counselling and help for family members
- Service satisfaction data has measured family satisfaction with the EI service:
  - 100% of families were aware of the content of their relative's care plan and 66.7% had been actively involved in its production
  - 88.9% of families meet regularly with members of their relative's care team
  - 71.4% of those who had received family intervention work felt it was helpful
  - 66.7% of families were "very happy" with the service their relative was receiving from the EI team. The remaining 33.3% were "quite happy" with the service
- Quote from a family involved with the service: *'the support, care, help, advice, guidance and counselling has been excellent for my son, my wife and myself in understanding and accepting this health condition'*

Formal family interventions

- All members of the EI team are trained in Behavioural Family Therapy (West Midlands Meriden Family Intervention Programme)
- All EI families are offered family intervention
- Formal family intervention is offered to address family needs not met by routine family support
- Focus on family psycho-education and enhancing communication and problem solving skills within the family unit

Group family psychoeducation sessions

- An opportunity for family members (including siblings) to meet with other families involved with the EI service
- Eight weekly 2-hour sessions focus on learning more about psychosis amongst others with similar experiences
- Opportunity to share experiences and discuss the impact of having a relative who has experienced psychosis
- Recent pre–post-group evaluation measured:
  - Knowledge about psychosis
  - Distress about their relative's difficulties
  - Perceived control over their relative's illness
  - Perceived support and ability to cope with their relative's illness
  - Optimism about their relative's future

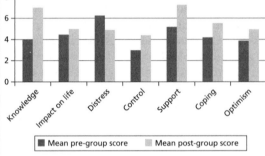

Pre–post-group evaluation

■ Mean pre-group score   ■ Mean post-group score

Support for siblings

- Specific information booklet developed for siblings, which was written with the help of 2 siblings involved in the service
- Brothers and sisters routinely involved in family intervention work
- Siblings are invited to attend the family psychoeducation group
- The service has helped link siblings together for peer support through facilitating the exchange of email addresses
- Quote from a service user's brother about the value of attending an EI family psychoeducation group:

  'There are a lot of people in the same boat as us, and in a way that's reassuring. Good information which has helped me understand about my brother's illness'

Carers' open evenings

- Quarterly meetings open to all family members of those involved with the EI service
- Informal atmosphere and an opportunity to meet other families with similar experiences in a relaxed environment
- Regular talks and presentations, along with time for attendees to meet each other and interact.
- Recent topics have included the roles of the different professionals within the EI team and services provided by the local Carers Unit.

Carer involvement in service development

- Service users and family members involved in rewriting, illustrating and launching the service's promotional prospectus.
- EI trust fund initiative is due to be led and coordinated by family members of EI service users.
- EI families regularly contribute to local family intervention training courses

Figure 23.2 Worcestershire EI service.

Somerset EI and Family Intervention (FI) services

In Somerset, a smaller 'hub and spoke' EIS was established in 2006–2007, in the context of an existing county-wide FI service. The FI service had been created through the delivery of a 1-year multidisciplinary course in each of the four service areas, with management agreement that all staff trained in FI would be able to devote half a day a week to the delivery of FI (Burbach & Stanbridge, 1998, 2006). Half of the EIS staff were also part of the FI service and faced the challenge of deciding whether to work with particular families as part of routine care or to refer them to the FI service where they had the further option of being one of the co-therapists working with the family. In the early stages of the new EI service, the EI/FI worker in one of the service areas referred approximately half of the caseload to the specialist FI service at an early stage, whereas an EI/FI worker in another area made fewer referrals to the FI service but tended to find herself dealing with increasingly complex family issues after having engaged with her families as part of routine family support. As the EI service developed, especially following the increase in the potential families that could be referred to a relatively finite capacity FI service, guidelines concerning routine and formal family work were recently agreed (Figure 23.3). Although in many cases, routine family work was sufficient to meet families' needs, and best provided by the EI worker, for families that expressed more complex needs it seemed more appropriate for an FI team member to join the EI worker to deliver formal FI, or to refer the family on for formal FI. The possible permutations were discussed on a case-by-case basis in the regular EI team and FI team supervision meetings, and other options available to all families and carers in Somerset such as generic rather than psychosis-specific services were also considered, including a formal carer's assessment and carer's support, a carers' education programme and carers' support groups.

On the rare occasions that the individuals do not wish their families to be involved in their care, it is explained that relatives are entitled to their own independent support and they are referred for a Carer's Assessment. On other occasions, the needs of the service user and other family members appear to be best met separately. In these situations, the family members may be seen in the FI service while the EI case coordinator focuses on the young person with psychosis. There are many permutations, for example, recently, the EI worker and an FI team colleague worked with a young woman with psychosis and her partner, while her parents were seen by two other therapists in the FI service. In our experience, however, the majority of young people with FEP can be engaged in FI with significant others. This is usually parents, but can also include siblings, partners, friends and professionals such as housing support staff. The key to successful engagement in the Somerset 'cognitive-systemic' FI approach appears to be the flexible, collaborative approach. The approach is to respond to families' expressed needs as well as trying to incorporate family needs as assessed by clinicians, agree therapeutic goals collaboratively, ascertain whether sessions have been useful and agree whether to have further family meetings on a session-by-session basis (Stanbridge *et al.*, 2003). It is interesting to note that in more clearly delineated approaches based on assessed needs such as BFT, where family members' needs are assessed and a series of family sessions are agreed, there is also a similar focus on flexibility and briefer interventions when working with people with FEP (Fadden & Smith, 2008).

The content of FI with FEP

The recommendations for meeting families' needs made by Gleeson *et al.* (1999) included a crisis-oriented approach with an initial focus on eliciting feelings from the often bewildered or traumatised family members, with techniques such as problem solving or communication training being introduced later. These have since been endorsed by other leading writers in the field (Addington & Burnett, 2004). We recommend an individualised approach

---

ROUTINE FAMILY WORK

(All families can expect an EI worker to offer the following:)

- Exploration of distress and provision of emotional support
- Exploration of contexts relatedto client's symptoms/problems
- Initial Carers Assessment (and signposting on to carers services)
- Involving the family in care planning and reviews
- Provision of information about psychosis and other mental health issues, coping strategies and services
- Encouraging realistic expectations and helping the family to maintain a sense of hope
- Assessment of need for formal FI

FORMAL FAMILY INTERVENTIONS

(Family needs-led sessions convened by FI trained co-therapists)

- Reducing stress/burden and encouraging realistic expectations
- Enhancing family members' skills for coping with psychotic symptoms
- Enhancing the ability to anticipate and solve problems
- Helping the family to communicate more clearly
- Identifying early warning of relapse and agreeing a plan of action
- Liaison and advocacy with mental health and other services
- Enabling change in the family interaction system
- Helping the family to be reflective, explore options, reach a shared understanding, deal with strong feelings (e.g. anger, guilt) and encourage a sense of personal agency

It is recognised that in less complex presentations the first six of the above can also be met within Routine Family Work

---

INDICATORS FOR FAMILY SUPPORT SERVICE (FORMAL FI)

- COMPLEX NEEDS
  - High level of family stress/distress/chaos
  - High risk of relapse
  - Concurrent (physical/mental health) problems in other family members
  - Relationship difficulties maintaining problems
  - Hopelessness or other strong feelings (e.g. guilt, denial)/poor coping strategies
- Pre-existing client/family risk factors (e.g. history of abuse or violence; developmental issues)
- Family unable to access other resources/services effectively
- EI worker's relationship with the client might be jeopardised by routine family work

---

PROCEDURE FOR REFERRAL FOR FORMAL FI

- Discuss Family Support Service with family members (give leaflet)
- Discuss reasons why formal FI is appropriate/agree basic goals

---

Figure 23.3 Somerset's guidelines for routine and formal family work.

tailored to the specific needs of each family, with a range of family services being available to meet the family's needs at different points in time.

Training implications

It is interesting to note that in a recent national survey of psychosocial interventions (PSI) skills within EI teams (Brabban & Kelly, 2006), the

South West and West Midlands regions reported the highest numbers of EI staff with formal PSI and family work qualifications. Both of the services described in this chapter have systematically attempted to develop the workforce in this manner and are now able to draw on this somewhat larger pool of trained staff. However, training alone does not guarantee implementation of FI – this requires a strategic, whole-systems perspective as discussed below.

With regard to the content of training programmes, we would make the following recommendations. In order to provide flexible multifaceted family work, staff should be trained in psychoeducational family interventions such as those developed by Barrowclough and Tarrier (1992), Falloon et al. (2004) and Kuipers et al. (2002) and to have specific knowledge of issues relating to early psychosis. In particular, they will need to feel confident in discussing issues regarding diagnostic uncertainty and be competent in dealing with the feelings evoked by the onset of psychosis. Skills in crisis-oriented counselling and collaborative, competency-based therapy (Bertolino & O'Hanlon, 2002) will also be helpful in encouraging an increased sense of agency and hope for the future amongst family members. Staff also need skills in working with children. In Somerset, it has also proved useful to train staff to explore interactional patterns and to provide them with a working knowledge of the way in which families develop over time. This facilitates the exploration of family stress in a normalising, non-blaming manner.

It is undoubtedly helpful to be more extensively trained, and the recent UK report on training and skills in EI services recommends the development of EI-specific family intervention training such as that currently offered through the Meriden Programme in the West Midlands (Brabban & Kelly, 2006). However, the skills listed above should not be regarded as a prerequisite for working with families with FEP. Much of what is described as 'routine family work' can be provided following relatively brief packages of training such as Somerset's 3-day course in Family Oriented Practice (Stanbridge & Burbach, 2004, 2007), which is generic in nature. Courses focused on psychosis, such as

Behavioural Family Therapy, can introduce key specialist family intervention skills to staff in only 5 days. Successful implementation of these new skills on completion of the training, however, will depend upon the ready availability of high-quality ongoing supervision (Fadden et al., 2004; Fadden, 2006) and the maintenance of a service context which facilitates family work. In Somerset, we have found that supervision is crucial in the maintenance of the service and also in ensuring its quality (Burbach & Stanbridge, 2008). This takes place in local monthly team supervision sessions, quarterly county-wide 'study days' and is built into our routine practice as each pair of therapists also reflect on their clinical work before, during and after each family session. Whilst one of the functions of this range of approaches to clinical supervision is to ensure safe and ethical practice, the prime function is to facilitate reflective practice (Schön, 1983) and thereby enhance the effectiveness of therapy. Building in a range of supervision processes is important to support staff carrying out this at times complex and demanding work.

Case study

This case study describing family work that took place over a 3-year period will illustrate the various forms of family work including psychoeducational intervention, informal carer support via a case manager and more formal family intervention (both behavioural family intervention and systemic family work).

Connor, aged 17, was referred to the Early Intervention Service after a 2-year period of alcohol and cannabis use. This had been associated with a decline in school performance, truanting, stealing from his parents and trouble with the police. Experimentation with amphetamine and cocaine triggered psychotic experiences. Relationships with his family deteriorated and there was some physical aggression between Connor and his father.

During an extended 6-month assessment period, the EI team provided family psychoeducation regarding substance abuse and psychosis, referred him to other agencies who helped him

to come off drugs and to secure employment in a local dog sanctuary and helped him to repair relationships with his family. The team concluded that Connor's problems were drug induced and he was transferred to 'monitoring' only.

However, 4 months later, Connor's parents contacted the EIS to report that his psychotic symptoms had returned, apparently linked to stress at work. His psychotic symptoms were treated with low-dose antipsychotic medication. His mood subsequently dropped and he became uncommunicative, spending long periods sleeping in his bedroom, neglecting his personal hygiene and failing to carry out even basic home care tasks (e.g. washing up, making his bed and keeping his room tidy). This was a source of major friction for his parents who saw him as lazy and 'wasting his life away' in bed.

The case manager held a number of joint sessions with Connor and his parents but behavioural family intervention had little impact. Connor's parents declined an invitation to join a local early intervention relatives group 'in case they met people who knew them'. They also felt they had sufficient information from an information booklet, Internet and discussions with the case manager. However, Connor had slipped back into substance misuse, accompanied by psychotic symptoms and incidents of aggression particularly directed at his father, which led to increased parental frustration and threats to make Connor homeless.

The case manager then sought the help of a psychology team colleague to work with Connor and his family to address their current difficulties and the family tensions these were creating. Connor failed to attend the first two family sessions and his parents vented their frustration at the lack of progress and the detrimental impact on 'family life'. They experienced constant tension on returning home from work (wondering what state the house or Connor might be in), reported problems with Connor borrowing and stealing money, aggression towards his dad and felt Connor was 'using' them. They noted increased marital tension and arguments between themselves and were split between natural parental concern and understandable anger at Connor's behaviour, particularly the drug and alcohol use, which they felt was within Connor's control.

They were encouraged, in Connor's absence, to use the sessions to consider the relationship between themselves and Connor and to what extent their own actions might be contributing to Connor's difficulties; e.g. doing too much for Connor, lending money to Connor, which may be funding his drug purchases, not setting clear limits and threatening consequences that they did not actually follow through. Although accepting that this might be a useful focus for sessions if Connor failed to attend, informal feedback via the case manager following the session suggested that they had felt judged and blamed for Connor's behaviour. This was broached directly at the next session and it was noted that all of their actions were understandable as caring parents and their intentions were clearly to support Connor. In spite of their frustrations and the damaging effect of Connor's behaviour on their relationship with him, there was clear evidence of their concern and caring. It was noted that their efforts at trying to manage and alter their situation appeared to have had little impact and that it may be valuable to use a dispassionate facilitator to develop a new perspective on their situation. There was discussion about how they would like things to be different and how this might be achieved.

At this point, Connor unexpectedly arrived at home and joined the session. He was briefed on the discussion to date and was asked in what ways he felt that his parents' lives had altered since his difficulties began. He observed that they rarely saw any friends now, rarely went out socially either independently or together, rowed constantly and were sleeping in separate bedrooms. He felt he could do nothing right, was treated like a child and felt bullied and intimidated by his dad. He observed 'from the moment I come up the drive and even before I come in Dad is already working himself up to have a go at me'. These observations were explored. His parents noted that the loss of contact with friends was through embarrassment at the situation with Connor, feeling that they could not compete with positive stories about their friends' offspring. They now felt too tired to do anything in the evenings and the rows reflected the general tension in the home and disagreement between them over the best way to handle their difficulties with Connor. They acknowledged Connor's comments about anticipatory tension but felt this was understandable in view of the difficult behaviour they had previously had to deal with when he arrived home drunk/heavily drugged. They were surprised that Connor had registered these adverse changes to their lives as they had perceived him to be self-concerned and detached from family life.

Connor for the first time apologised for the difficulties that he had caused them and noted how difficult his life had been compared to his sister Amy whom he perceived as 'the favoured child' and 'lucky'. He said he had always felt that his dad did not like him and had dominated him with criticism. His parents acknowledged he had been bullied at school and he said this had left him feeling low in confidence and a failure in his parents' eyes. Several sessions were spent identifying goals for change, individually and collectively, and also how they might support one another in making small changes. On the basis of a previous shared interest in tennis, his parents were encouraged to take this up again for tension relief and to build social contacts. Mum took up an evening fitness class and dad renewed a former interest in animal husbandry and bought some poultry to help with stress management and to build a leisure interest. His parents were encouraged to have a weekend away and subsequently booked their first holiday together as a couple for a number of years. Connor joined an assertiveness course at the local college to help build his confidence and began exploring the possibility of moving to an independent flat with the help of his case manager.

Further work dealt with Connor's observations that he felt treated like 'an incapable child'. He was encouraged to look for opportunities to demonstrate his maturity and ways he could command his parents' respect. His parents were encouraged to try positive rather than negative monitoring, noting those occasions when Connor was acting responsibly. Feedback revealed that there were many occasions where Connor was active, for example washing up, tidying, vacuuming, which had been missed or taken for granted. The more these were acknowledged, the more frequently they occurred. Connor was encouraged to tackle tasks independently on his car, for example changing the oil and fitting a stereo. Connor's father was surprised at how able Connor actually was. He realised through family discussion how his own high standards and abilities undermined confidence in both his wife and Connor. He realised that he set unrealistic expectations for his family which they all struggled to live up to and he began to hold back on advice giving, letting others do things in their way and learning to wait to be asked rather than offering unsolicited advice, which was perceived as implicit criticism, or doing things for his family which undermined confidence in their own abilities. He was able to observe a growing confidence in Connor, improvements in family tension and noted a relief of his own sense of responsibility for everything.

Over a series of fortnightly sessions for a 6-month period, family tensions gradually eased. Connor's parents began to go out more and to recontact friends. They played tennis together and independently several times during the week, and also enjoyed several short breaks and a week's holiday away. Connor's behaviour gradually improved. He stopped using drugs and alcohol and his paranoia eased. He started a part-time mechanic's course at a local college. Connor was eventually supported by his case manager, parents and sister to move to a flat nearby, which his family helped him to paint and furnish. He was able to invite his parents round for coffee and meals and sought their support with budgeting and domestic management tasks. The changes in family dynamics were summarised in a comment from Connor concerning his dad, noting: 'He treats me like an adult now. I feel now I have my own flat and am coping that he treats me with respect and as an equal. My dad even asked me to help him last week with a job he could not do on his own. I was made up!' The need for family sessions was subsequently reviewed and stopped after 9 months of formal family intervention. Further progress was reviewed in the course of routine contact by the case manager with Connor and his family.

Implications and conclusions

Working with the family and others who are important in the young person's social network ensures that their difficulties are understood in a social context. It facilitates the establishment of effective collaborative working relationships between the individual, family and health care

Table 23.3 Recommendations to maximise implementation of FI post-training

1. Ensure support for the training programme at the highest organisational level.
2. Ensure appropriate service context and sufficient resources are available to enable practice post-training (protected time, smaller caseloads, access to assessment materials).
3. Ensure post-training expert clinical supervision is available.
4. Use a team-training approach or ensure that there is a local 'critical mass' of trained practitioners.
5. Involve families/carers in the training programme and in the design and governance of the service.
6. Appoint local service leads/champions who are responsible for the development and maintenance of the service.

services. Offering help at this early stage supports the family's understanding, the way in which they relate to each other, and their adjustment to the major changes they face in their lives. It also helps to minimise the risk of problems developing for individuals and for the family as a whole. All of the well-established EI services such as those in Melbourne, Australia (Shannon *et al.*, 1997; Gleeson *et al.*, 1999; Crisp & Gleeson, 2008), Calgary, Canada (Addington & Burnett, 2004) and Birmingham, UK (Fadden *et al.*, 2004) as well as the two services described in this chapter identify family work as a core component of what should be delivered in order to maximise family functioning and to minimise risks of long-term difficulties. However, evidence from developing EI services in the UK suggests that while staff offer a minimum level of support and advice to families, they often feel ill-equipped to offer more structured types of help, and quote issues such as lack of materials and resources, and lack of confidence in dealing with children (Slade *et al.*, 2003). However, as a result of the substantial literature investigating difficulties involved in implementing family interventions following training (Fadden, 1997; Bailey *et al.*, 2003; Brooker *et al.*, 2003), there is now a growing consensus regarding the key requirements to maximise service delivery (see reviews by Brabban & Kelly, 2006; Brooker & Brabban, 2004) (Table 23.3).

This chapter has discussed some of the key ingredients – clear policy guidance, clinical guidelines, training programmes and guidance regarding implementation post-training – which are available to support the delivery of family interventions within EI services and we hope that the service examples and case study will encourage all EI services to develop the range of support available to families.

References

Addington, J. & Burnett, P (2004). Working with families in the early stages of psychosis. In: P. McGorry & J. Gleeson (eds), *Psychological Interventions in Early Psychosis: A Practical Treatment Handbook*. Chichester: John Wiley & Sons Ltd.

Addington, J., Coldham, E.L., Jones, B., Ko, T. & Addington, D. (2002). Family work in an early psychosis programme: A longitudinal study. *Acta Psychiatrica Scandinavica*, 106 (Suppl. 413), 101.

Addington, J., Coldham, E.L., Jones, B., Ko, T., Addington, D. (2003). The first episode of psychosis: The experience of relatives. *Acta Psychiatrica Scandinavica*, 108, 285–289.

Addington, J., McCleery, A. & Addington, D. (2005a). Three-year outcome of family work in an early psychosis program. *Schizophrenia Research*, 79, 107–116.

Addington, J., Collins, A., McCleery, A. & Addington, D. (2005b). The role of family work in early psychosis. *Schizophrenia Research*, 79, 77–83.

Askey, R., Gamble, C. & Gray, R. (2007). Family work in first-onset psychosis: A literature review. *Journal of Psychiatric and Mental Health Nursing*, 14, 356–365.

Bachmann, S., Bottmer, C., Jacob, S. *et al.* (2002). Expressed emotion in relatives of first-episode and chronic patients with schizophrenia and major depressive disorder – a comparison. *Psychiatry Research*, 112, 239–250.

Bailey, R., Burbach, F.R. & Lea, S. (2003). The ability of staff trained in family interventions to implement the approach in routine clinical practice. *Journal of Mental Health*, 12, 131–141.

Barrowclough, C. & Tarrier, N. (1992). *Families of Schizophrenic Patients: Cognitive Behavioural Intervention.* London: Chapman & Hall.

Bertolino, B. & O'Hanlon, W.R. (2002). *Collaborative, Competency-based Counselling and Therapy.* Boston: Allyn and Bacon.

Bertolote, J. & McGorry, P. (2005) Early intervention and recovery for young people with early psychosis: Consensus statement. *British Journal of Psychiatry*, 187 (Suppl. 48), s116–s119.

Boydell, K.M., Gladstone, B.M. & Volpe, T. (2006). Understanding help-seeking delay in the prodrome to first episode psychosis: A secondary analysis of the perspectives of young people. *Psychiatric Rehabilitation Journal*, 30 (1), 54–60.

Brabban, A. & Kelly, M. (2006) *Training in Psychosocial Interventions within Early Intervention Teams: A National Survey.* NIMHE/CSIP National PSI Implementation Group.

Brooker, C. & Brabban, A. (2004) *Measured Success: A scooping Review of Evaluated Psychosocial Interventions Training for Work with People with Serious Mental Health Problems.* NINHE/Trent WDC.

Brooker, C., Saul, C., Robinson, J., King, J. & Dudley, M. (2003). Is training in psychosocial interventions worthwhile? Report of a psychosocial intervention trainee follow up study. *International Journal of Nursing Studies*, 40, 731–747.

Burbach, F.R. & Stanbridge, R.I. (1998). A family intervention in psychosis service integrating the systemic and family management approaches. *Journal of Family Therapy*, 20, 311–325.

Burbach, F.R. & Stanbridge, R.I. (2006). Somerset's family interventions in psychosis service: An update. *Journal of Family Therapy*, 28, 39–57.

Burbach, F.R. & Stanbridge, R.I. (2008). Setting up a family interventions service. In: F. Lobban & C. Barrowclough (eds), *A Casebook of Family Interventions for Psychosis.* Chichester: Wiley and Sons.

Crisp, K. & Gleeson, J. (2008). Working with families to prevent relapse in first-episode psychosis. In:

F. Lobban & C. Barrowclough (eds), *A Casebook of Family Interventions for Psychosis.* Chichester: Wiley and Sons.

De Haan, L., Peters, B., Dingemans, P., Wouters, L. & Linszen, D. (2002). Attitudes of patients toward the first psychotic episode and the start of treatment. *Schizophrenia Bulletin*, 28 (3), 431–442.

De Haan, L., Welborn, K., Krikke, M. & Linszen, D.H. (2004). Opinions of mothers on the first psychotic episode and the start of treatment of their child. *European Psychiatry*, 19, 226–229.

Department of Health (DH) (2001). *The Mental Health Policy Implementation Guide.* London: HMSO.

Fadden, G. (1997). Implementation of family interventions in routine clinical practice following staff training programs: A major cause for concern. *Journal of Mental Health*, 6 (6), 599–612.

Fadden, G. (2006) Training and disseminating family interventions for schizophrenia: Developing family intervention skills with multi-disciplinary groups. *Journal of Family Therapy*, 28, 23–38.

Fadden, G. & Smith, J. (2008). Family work in early psychosis. In: F. Lobban & C. Barrowclough (eds), *A Casebook of Family Interventions for Psychosis.* Chichester: Wiley and Sons.

Fadden, G., Birchwood, M., Jackson, C. & Barton, K. (2004). Psychological therapies: Implementation in early intervention services. In: P. McGorry & J. Gleeson (eds), *Psychological Interventions in Early Psychosis: A Practical Treatment Handbook.* Chichester: John Wiley & Sons Ltd.

Falloon, I.R.H., Mueser, K., Gingerich, S. *et al.* (2004). *Family Work Manual.* Birmingham: Meriden Family Programme.

Fisher, H., Bordass, E. & Steele, H. (2004). Siblings' experience of having a brother or sister with first-episode psychosis. *Schizophrenia Research*, 70 (Suppl. 1), 88.

Gleeson, J., Jackson, H.J., Stavely, H. & Burnett, P. (1999). Family intervention in early psychosis. In: P.D. McGorry & H.J. Jackson (eds), *The Recognition and Management of Early Psychosis: A Preventive Approach.* Cambridge: Cambridge University Press.

Goldstein, M.J., Rodnick, E.H., Evans, J.R., May, P.R.A. & Steinberg M.R. (1978). Drug and family therapy in the aftercare of acute schizophrenics. *Archives of General Psychiatry*, 35, 1169–1177.

Haddock, G. & Lewis, S. (2005). Psychological interventions in early psychosis. *Schizophrenia Bulletin*, 31, 697–704.

Heikkila, J., Kartsson, H., Taminien, T. et al. (2002). Expressed emotion is not associated with disorder severity in first episode mental disorder. *Psychiatry Research*, 111, 155–165.

Huguelet, P., Favre, S., Binyet, S., Gonzalez, C. & Zambala, I. (1995). The use of the Expressed Emotion Index as a predictor of outcome in first admitted psychiatric patients in a French speaking area of Switzerland. *Acta Psychiatrica Scandinavica*, 92, 447–452.

IRIS (2000). *Early Intervention in Psychosis: Clinical Guidelines and Service Frameworks*. Birmingham: West Midlands IRIS (Initiative to Reduce the Impact of Schizophrenia), West Midlands Partnership for Mental Health.

Kuipers, L., Leff, J. & Lam, D. (2002) *Family Work for Schizophrenia: A Practical Guide* (2nd edition). London: Gaskell.

Lehtinen, K. (1993). Need-adapted treatment of schizophrenia: a five-year follow-up study from the Turku project. *Acta Psychiatrica Scandinavica*, 87, 96–101.

Martens, L. & Addington, J. (2001). Psychological well-being of family members with schizophrenia. *Social Psychiatry and Psychiatric Epidemiology*, 36, 128–133.

Mottaghipour, Y. & Bickerton, A. (2005). The pyramid of family care: A framework for family involvement with adult mental health services. *Australian e-Journal for the Advancement of Mental Health*, 4 (3) www.auseinet.com/journal/vol4iss3/mottaghipour.pdf.

Patterson, P., Birchwood, M. & Cochrane, R. (2000). Preventing the entrenchment of high expressed emotion in first episode psychosis: early developmental attachments pathways. *Australian and New Zealand Journal of Psychiatry*, 34, S191–S197.

Pearson, D., Burbach, F. & Stanbridge, R. (2007). Meeting the needs of families living with psychosis: Implications for services. *Context*, 9–12.

Penn, D.L., Waldheter, E.J., Perkins, D.O., Mueser, K.T. & Lieberman, J.A. (2005). Psychosocial treatment for first-episode psychosis: A research update. *American Journal of Psychiatry*, 162, 2220–2232.

Pharoah, F.M., Mari, J.J. & Streiner, D. (2002). *Family intervention for schizophrenia (Cochrane Review)*. In: The Cochrane Library, Issue 3. Oxford: Update Software.

Pilling, S., Bebbington, P., Kuipers, E. *et al.* (2002). Psychological treatments in schizophrenia: 1. Meta-analysis of family intervention and cognitive-behaviour therapy. *Psychological Medicine*, 32, 763–782.

Pitschel-Walz, G., Leucht, S., Bauml, J., Kissling, W. & Engel, R.R. (2001). The effect of family interventions on relapse and rehospitilization in schizophrenia: A meta-analysis. *Schizophrenia Bulletin*, 27, 73–92.

Raune, D., Kuipers, E. & Bebbington, P.E. (2004). Expressed emotion at first-episode psychosis: Investigating a carer appraisal model. *British Journal of Psychiatry*, 184, 321–326.

Rund, B.R., Aeie, M., Borchgrevink, T.S. & Fjell, A. (1995). Expressed emotion, communication deviance and schizophrenia. *Psychopathology*, 28, 220–228.

Schön, D. (1983). *The Reflective Practitioner: How Professionals Think in Action*. London: Temple Smith.

Seikkula, J., Aaltonen, J., Alakare, B., Haarakangas, K., Keranen, J. and Lehtinen, K. (2006). Five-year experience of first-episode nonaffective psychosis in open-dialogue approach: Treatment principles, follow- up outcomes, and two case studies. *Psychotherapy Research*, 16, 214–228.

Shannon, M., Burnett, P. & Gleeson, J. (1997). *Working with Families in Early Psychosis*. Victoria: EPPIC Statewide Services.

Sin, J., Moone, N. & Wellman, N. (2005). Developing services for the carers of young adults with early-onset psychosis – listening to their experiences and needs. *Journal of Psychiatric and Mental Health Nursing*, 12, 589–597.

Singh, S.P. & Grange, T. (2006). Measuring pathways to care in first-episode psychosis: A systematic review. *Schizophrenia Research*, 81, 75–82.

Slade, M., Holloway, F. & Kuipers, E. (2003). Skills development and family interventions in an early psychosis service. *Journal of Mental Health*, 12 (4), 405–415.

Stanbridge, R.I. & Burbach, F.R. (2004). Enhancing working partnerships with carers and families in mainstream practice: A strategy and associated staff training programme. *The Mental Health Review*, 9 (4), 32–37.

Stanbridge, R.I. & Burbach, F.R. (2007). Developing family inclusive mainstream mental health practice. *Journal of Family Therapy*, 29, 21–43.

Stanbridge, R.I., Burbach, F.R., Lucas, A.S. & Carter, K. (2003). A study of families' satisfaction with a family interventions in psychosis service in Somerset. *Journal of Family Therapy*, 25, 181–204.

Tennakoon, L., Fannon, D., Doku, V., O'Ceallaigh, S., Soni, W. & Santamaria, M. (2000). Experience of care-giving: relatives of people experiencing a first episode of psychosis. *British Journal of Psychiatry*, 177, 529–533.

White, A. (2002). *Working with families: Evaluation of an integrated positive approach to recent onset psychosis*. Presentation at the BABCP 30th Anniversary Annual Conference. University of Warwick, UK.

Zhang, M., Wang, M., Li, J. & Phillips, M.R. (1994). Randomised-control trial of family intervention for 78 first-episode male schizophrenic patients. *British Journal of Psychiatry*, 165 (Suppl.), 96–102.

Chapter 24 **Sharing care with families**

Mandy Reed, Sharon Peters and Lizzie Banks

Introduction

The Early Psychosis Declaration (EPD) (Bertolote & McGorry, 2005) gives great emphasis to the notion of family engagement and support and sees this as encompassing not only better access to information and education, but also social, economic, practical and emotional support. This chapter will focus on identifying ways of engaging and supporting carers individually alongside the other interventions provided by Early Intervention in Psychosis Services (EIS) and provides a rich narrative in the form of the experiences of two of the authors who are mothers of individuals who have had a first episode of psychosis (FEP). It will also highlight the symbiotic relationship of the recovery journey the carer needs to make alongside their loved one who has experienced an FEP. The case study will highlight the obstacles carers can face when trying to get professional help for a loved one contrasted by the experience of feeling listened to and supported once in contact with an EIS.

Although professionals provide a range of assessments, deliver treatments and offer support to families, their contact with both the individual themselves (unless hospitalised) and their families will only be for a tiny percentage of the time that families are living with the individual. This means that, in the majority of cases and for the majority of time, families are providing the majority of care (Addington & Burnett, 2004; Reed & Stevens, 2007). Good practice for professionals is therefore to engage, involve and support the families in a range of ways as the primary care givers. The very nature of 'sharing the care' with carers limits the potential for quantitative studies but relies heavily on the rich narrative of carer and user experiences, which can inform phenomenological research as this chapter will demonstrate. Throughout the chapter, direct quotes will be used to emphasise the carer's perspective and thus bring to life the evidence base and literature, giving meaning to the reality of sharing the care.

Without the carer's input the professionals are working in the dark. They have no idea what the individual or the carer was like before the illness, or of the family dynamics. They have a baseline from which to measure improvement, but only by listening can they set a target. Whether this is achievable is not the point, aiming for it is the important thing. This is what gives hope.

Summary of the evidence

A key component of the EPD (Bertolote & McGorry, 2005) is the focus on engaging and supporting families in order to help them feel respected and valued as partners in care. The target in the EPD is for 90% of families to feel this way. Given that between 60 and 70% of individuals experiencing an FEP are still living at home with their families (Addington *et al.*, 2003) and therefore the crucial components of the whole care package that the individual receives, a close working relationship with them can only be common sense. Unfortunately, this has not been the case historically within mental health services where families have often felt excluded by professionals who have colluded with the individual in not sharing information under the ill-interpreted guise of confidentiality (RCP, 2004) or stigmatised and looked down upon as somehow having caused the difficulties in their loved one (Östman & Kjellin, 2002).

Studies dating back to the 1980s have demonstrated a clear link between the level of support a family receives (through dedicated behavioural family interventions [FIs]) and the likelihood of relapse for the individual who has already experienced a psychotic episode (Falloon *et al.*, 1982; Leff *et al.*, 1982). Equally, a meta-analysis of FI studies highlighted the effectiveness of a combination of interventions for the individual and their family, most notably effective medication and FI (Pitschel-Walz *et al.*, 2001). The effectiveness of FI is not only firmly entrenched in government mental health policy (DH, 1999, 2001), but also remains a core component of psychosocial training courses and the subject of a number of training manuals (Smith *et al.*, 2007). For a fuller discussion of behavioural FIs within FEP, see Chapter 23. Family and carer education and support groups form the other main component of high-quality care (McFarlane *et al.*, 1995; Addington & Burnett, 2004). These are also discussed in more detail in Chapter 26.

Approximately, 60–70% of individuals experiencing an FEP are still living at home with their families (Addington *et al.*, 2003). Even when not living at home, it is more likely to be parents who notice the first signs that something is not right with their son or daughter (Boydell *et al.*, 2006). Delays and regression in emotional and psychological maturation are commonly experienced, which can contribute to parents supporting their offspring at home for longer than would have been the case had the individual not developed an FEP (Addington & Burnett, 2004). This in turn often leads to high levels of stress and worry and sense of burden as carers and families attempt to understand and come to terms with what is happening to their loved one (Kuipers & Raune, 2002; Rose *et al.*, 2006). The family's perceptions of their loved one's behaviour and their psychological appraisal of the impact of the mental health difficulties on them have been identified as significant predictors of distress and poor psychological well-being for relatives (Raune *et al.*, 2004; Addington *et al.*, 2005).

The sense of burden commonly experienced in caregivers has been identified as primarily related to worrying about the future of their loved one (Rose *et al.*, 2006). Dealing with sadness and grief, handling disruptive behaviour and knowing how to talk to the individual were highlighted as the top three concerns of families in the same study (Rose *et al.*, 2006).

Early Intervention in Psychosis literature highlights that when carers feel supported both informally and formally by mental health services and involved in their loved ones' care, they experience a reduction in the collateral psychosocial damage (Addington & Burnett, 2004) and feel better equipped to continue caring for their loved one (Reed & Stevens, 2007; Fadden & Smith, 2008).

Implementation into practice

Involving carers of an individual with an FEP needs to be addressed in a number of ways and underpins all aspects of high-quality Early Intervention in Psychosis work. As such, involving families and carers needs to be incorporated from how the team receives initial information through involvement in day-to-day care planning right through to promoting recovery for the carers as well as the individual with an FEP.

Gathering information from families as part of the initial assessment

When an individual with a possible FEP comes to the attention of mental health services, a thorough assessment from a range of sources is undertaken within EIS. Evidence shows that it is often family members who recognise that the individual is having some kind of mental health problem before they realise or acknowledge they do themselves (Boydell *et al.*, 2006). By having an 'open' referral system and embracing the concept of collaborative working, services are able to gain valuable information from relatives, carers, friends and other professionals involved. Within EIS, the importance of gathering information over a period of time to build up an accurate picture is fundamental to the approach, with the ability to hear the concerns of carers and others, which is an explicit part of the process. The Relative Assessment Interview adapted for FEP by Gleeson *et al.* (1999) offers a useful semi-structured interview for clinicians gathering information as part of their assessment process and is therefore useful in its own right and should be incorporated wherever possible into this phase of care. The structure of the interview allows the individual carer the opportunity to tell their story at the same time as gaining an understanding of how much knowledge the person already has about psychosis.

It is also important that wherever possible, carers have a Carers Assessment as part of the initial assessment process for each individual with FEP. This is best undertaken directly by a member of the EIS team but can also be undertaken by a local non-statutory agency such as Rethink or a Carer Support Worker. If another agency is involved in the Carers Assessment, it is important to have a good working relationship with them so that important information that could enhance the assessment process is not lost. Giving a carer the space to tell their story whilst acknowledging the often painful journey they have been through before getting into contact with services can be both cathartic and restorative psychologically. It also provides an important opportunity to begin to promote hope and optimism for the recovery of the individual with FEP and their loved ones (Addington & Burnett, 2004).

No one, not even another carer, can know what it's really like behind your closed doors with someone so extremely unwell. I felt so responsible for not having been able to stop my son from getting ill – I think the guilt will always be there however irrational that is.

Confidentiality

Good communication between all involved is at the heart of collaborative mental health care and underpins the spirit of the EPD (Bertolote & McGorry, 2005). It is important for EIS to find ways to establish and maintain safe and consistent ways of communicating with not only the individual with FEP, but also their carers, families and wider social networks. Often, carers

have been or have felt excluded from sharing important information with professionals either on the grounds of confidentiality or by not being believed (RCP, 2004).

All the time my son was in hospital I felt excluded. I was unable to build any sort of rapport with the staff at any of the three hospitals he moved between. It's a question of 'we know best so don't try to interfere or give us your opinions'. Just occasionally a member of staff would recognise me, say hello or smile and that would give me a real lift! You just feel sort of impotent in this situation and too exhausted to get angry....that comes later!

When information can be shared openly between all concerned, it is possible to enhance care and proactively manage potential risky situations (DH, 2007). It can also support and sustain the carer through difficult periods in the individual's recovery.

When I was forced to leave the house for periods each day because I needed a break from my son's behaviour, it was really helpful to make a mobile call to his care worker to ask advice or just let off steam. If she was ever unavailable, I knew she'd get back to me as soon as possible. It was equally reassuring to know I could walk into the office at any time, and because they had a 'whole team approach', there was usually someone to whom I could off load! In fact just knowing they were available probably meant I bothered them less than if I'd not been made to feel so welcome!

The concept of engagement with carers

Engaging with families and carers is as essential as engaging with the young person themselves and is important whether or not the individual with FEP wishes to themselves. The EPD and national policy guidance (Bertolote & McGorry, 2005; DH, 2001) identify the need for EI teams to be flexible and opportunistic in their range of interventions. This can very often mean working with and supporting the family who are likely to be actively seeking support, in contrast to the individual with an emerging FEP. By listening to family and carer concerns and gathering information from them, it is possible to work with the individual at a distance until such time as they are either ready to engage themselves with services or to have enough information to hand to help inform an assessment under the Mental Health Act (DH, 1983) should one become necessary. Giving carers information about the nature of an FEP as well as their right to request an assessment under the Act, if needed, can help to reduce some of the delays in the individual receiving effective treatment for their FEP and is one of the key targets of the EPD (Bertolote & McGorry, 2005).

I don't see how my son would have got on his road to recovery had his care worker not involved me. All through his illness he was very reluctant to 'engage' with services, so often meetings would be between his care worker and myself with a token appearance from him. My son really hated the thought of my discussing him with others but it was important to be seen to be working with just one member of the team, and slowly he came to realise that our sole and joint aim was to get him to a point where his future looked brighter.

The concept of engagement with carers also embraces skills in individual workers to be empathic and non-judgemental whilst giving accurate and honest information and feedback to them. In day-to-day practice, this can mean providing enough information to help carers differentiate between different types of behaviour including that driven by substance misuse or the psychosis as opposed to that driven by the kind of acting out adolescent/developmental behaviour most people will experience at some time or another during their journey as parents. This kind of psychoeducation can also be delivered through a group intervention (see Chapter 26 for fuller discussion of this kind of intervention).

As the parent carer of a young person with any illness it's easy to get into mothering/smothering mode and to make too many allowances for poor behaviour. It took his care worker to point out that my son's level of physical and verbal abuse was unacceptable, illness or no illness. Working

together on setting boundaries reinforced what was expected of my son.
Sometimes I needed his care worker to question my concerns and make me rethink whether some of his behaviour wasn't so much indicative of his illness but more of his age. Isn't it quite normal for a 17 year old to lock himself away, be uncommunicative and unwashed and swear more than is acceptable? So it was more a question of a deviation from this 'norm' that would indicate an EWS.

Workers also need to remember to reflect and take the time to engage according to the family's and client's needs rather than following a professional or service-led agenda. Although most practitioners would describe themselves as non-judgemental, there is often a tension between courses of action that workers believe may minimise the risk of relapse and allowing/supporting the individual and their families to take potential risks that is felt could jeopardise the recovery of all concerned. Being able to take risks is an important part of life, as is making and learning from mistakes. Somehow this has become less acceptable once an individual has experienced a psychotic episode with any mistake being taken for an EWS. This view is often also transferred to carers without respecting the value of their knowledge of their loved one and own life experiences.

I think, as a parent, I had a gut feeling of what would be most helpful in our situation, and this was to relocate away from the bad memories to somewhere more peaceful. It was a huge gamble and involved a lot of careful planning but it paid off. Now my son, who barely left the house for the year after he came out of hospital, is out and about in the village making a life for himself and feeling a useful and respected member of the community. Yet I still recall the look on his care worker's face when I mentioned my plan. Yes I knew a house move is one of the most stressful events yet I also knew it was right for us. However, I only had the courage to follow it through because the team was in the wings to pick up the pieces if it went wrong. Whatever they thought inwardly they did not judge my decision but just stood back. This gave me a feeling of at last taking charge of the situation and helping to get my son's life back on track.

Involvement in care planning, early warning signs and contingency planning

As carers are likely to be integral to the life of the individual with FEP, it is important to not only gather information from them during the assessment and engagement phase, but also to involve them as active members of a person's social network, care plan and EWS work whenever practicable. Information sharing between carers and professionals can provide a useful source of practical information such as the best time of day to call around or particular likes and dislikes. Evaluations from a number of EIS have shown that carers are routinely involved in the care plans of their loved ones (Fadden & Smith, 2008). This can also help to promote awareness of behaviours that keep Expressed Emotion (EE) down even if the family is not engaged in formal FI (Shannon *et al.*, 1997).

Professional and carer involvement means that both information and practical help can be shared, whether it be updating any changes in condition or providing lifts to appointments.

Looking back I realise how beneficial it was to have two perspectives on my son's recovery, and for two very different reasons. Firstly, as his 24/7 carer, there were long periods when there seemed little change in his condition from day to day, week to week which was disheartening, even depressing at times. However, his care worker, visiting periodically, was able to see a very slow but sustained improvement. And her letting me know this just gave me enough hope to keep going!

Conversely, being around my son all the time meant that I could detect very subtle changes in my son's appearance, behaviour, and attitude. I could then alert his care worker to what may be an EWS so she could arrange an interim visit – for example T's beanie hat was one indicator of his mood. He'd worn it day and night at the height of his illness, but once recovering he'd left it off. However, if he appeared in the doorway with it pulled down to his eyes, and particularly if

accompanied by increased swearing, I knew to be extra vigilant for other signs of possible relapse and to be ready to contact the 'team'. Nowadays, months down the road in his recovery, I'm relieved to say that a 'beanie' day just indicates that it's cold outside!!!

Recovery for carers

Dealing with sadness and grief is a fundamental concern expressed by carers (Gleeson *et al.*, 1999; Rose *et al.*, 2006). Alongside these feelings is the need to understand how to best deal with difficult behaviour and develop sensitivity about the 'right' way to talk to their loved one (Rose *et al.*, 2006) and the attributions attached to the development of mental health problems (Addington & Burnett, 2004). Carers can be said to work through a range of emotions when coming to terms with a serious illness in a loved one, which are similar to the experience of bereavement.

The emotions that a carer experiences are often not just to do with the present situation. When your child is acutely unwell you get on and deal with the day to day problems and think you're coping quite well under the circumstances. However, once he was recovering I know there was space for all sorts of 'past' to come bubbling up. So then you're trying to hold things together whilst haunted by all sorts of other issues. It's absolutely exhausting and not at all productive unless you're allowed to talk about these anxieties.

Worden (1991) identifies four 'tasks of mourning' in bereavement, describing the process as a series of pieces of work the bereaved needs to engage with in order to progress through their loss and ultimately be able to move on with their life. These are transferable as 'tasks of caring' for a young person with FEP in the following ways: to accept the reality of the mental health problem affecting the individual, to work through the pain of what may be lost as a result of the FEP and to adjust to an environment in which the individual may have different goals and expectations and to move on with their own lives (Table 24.1). An FEP can not only

Table 24.1 Tasks of caring for carers

1. In the majority of cases and for the majority of time, families provide the majority of care for an individual with an FEP, which needs to be acknowledged explicitly in all interactions.
2. When families feel involved with the care of their loved one and supported by professionals, they feel better equipped to carry out this often-protracted role.
3. Recovery for carers is as important as recovery for the individual with an FEP.

affect the development and educational progress of the person concerned, but also delay or limit the career of their carers owing to the extended responsibilities often experienced (Addington & Burnett, 2004).

You get so bogged down in the illness and so used to your child functioning at a certain level that it's hard to recall how he was before, or what you should be expecting as he recovers. Because he got ill at the age of 15 it was really difficult to know what he would have been like by the age of 20 had he not done so. So in a way you've got no gauge as to what you're aiming for, let alone what to realistically expect. We're at a point now where I feel I've got my son back plus more – I feel by hanging on in there and having the safety net of the EIS we've now got a far stronger relationship than if he'd never had psychosis and I'm able to invest in other parts of my life again.

Clinical case study

One of the authors of this chapter tells the story of her long journey to get the help her son needed from mental health services following his development of an FEP after the traumatic loss of his father. As is unfortunately too often the case, he only got help and treatment after coming into contact with the criminal justice system and through detention under the Mental Health Act (DH, 1983). In contrast to her struggle to get help for her son, she describes the difference it made feeling 'listened to' once she found she was able to self-refer to her local EIS. This included helping Adam to get appropriate care and providing psychoeducation and support for the whole family including his two brothers.

As a mother of a son with mental illness, the issue, which was closest to my heart, was

that I needed to know the professionals knew how my son was before he became ill. I felt he had lost his identity, and that this would give them a baseline to work from – I needed people to know my son, not just his mental health illness.

The trigger point for our journey was the tragic, sudden death of my lovely husband. At that time, Adam was just 18 years of age and was very close to his dad. As a family, we all suffered, but Adam seemed unable to move forward, taking solace in the bottle, smoking cannabis in a big way, isolating himself from his family and friends and becoming very hostile, mainly towards me. He left home and started living rough, walking the streets and looking like a down and out. I spent a lot of time tracking him down, only for him to move on again. I reported him missing to the police; this kind of behaviour went on for a long time.

To cut a long story short, my GP told me there was nothing he or I could do for Adam unless he harmed himself or someone else, which he did; he pushed a bottle in his brother's face during an argument. That, as it happened, was the only way we got help. His brother and I pressed charges, this way we were told someone would have to do something. He was given bail, but decided to run again. After four long months, he was picked up in Bournemouth, transferred to prison, and held on remand. I wrote to the Prison Governor expressing my concerns about Adam's state of mind. He read my letter and referred Adam to the 'In Reach Mental Health Team' within the prison. Thank goodness, for the first time someone was listening to me! Adam went to Crown Court where the Judge also listened to what I had to say, and ordered an assessment to be done. He was referred to our local psychiatric hospital under a Section of the Mental Health Act.

I often wondered whether the families of people suffering with mental illness were given a second thought, about how much suffering they went through before the services got involved. On more than one occasion, I had to bare my soul and that of my son, in an office full of strangers on the hospital ward. However, by this stage I had heard of the local EIS and that I was able to make contact with them directly for help and support.

In the short meeting I had with a member of the team I was able to tell her so much to her. She listened, understood and explained to me that Adam needed to be referred to them, which I was able to do. I also realised how traumatic the experience of supporting Adam, with the combined effects of losing a life long partner had been, but it needed someone to tell me, for I had not recognised the stress I was under. I had not given myself any credit for how I had coped so far, although I had lost my job and relationships with family and friends had suffered.

One of the very important roles that team played was explaining the illness to Adam's brothers. Because of Adam's behaviour, his brothers were very disparaging of him, until they took the time to explain the situation to them. Now the relationship they have is much better, not the relationship you would want for your children and not what I imagined they would have when they were growing up, but still, a relationship. Even though Adam was encouraged to attend sports and social groups that were organised by the team, at times I became frustrated at the pace of improvement. It was so slow; I think I must have driven Adam's care coordinator mad (pardon the expression). I was always phoning wanting to know why

and when? It is very hard for families to come to terms with a different person; it feels like a black cloak has shrouded my son and I know he is under there, but he cannot find his way out. Adam's care coordinator was very patient, even if I was not, and it was helpful to know that I could talk to any other member of the team if he wasn't available or we were between family work sessions. At this time, I also found a lot of comfort in talking to other carers of young men with psychosis. The team ran a Carer's Group, which I found extremely helpful, and I have made long lasting friendships with other carers who understand, accept and need no explanation. Working with the team also helped me to recognise that my role and experience as a carer was valid, not just to Adam but also to other people. As a result I now work as a Carer Support Worker for the local care network in Gloucestershire and have helped others to get the kind of support which helped me.

Implications and conclusions

A range of assessments, engagement strategies and support strategies are essential to collaborative working and care sharing with families and carers of an individual with FEP. The personal experiences described by two of the authors of this chapter who are mothers of individuals with FEP is supported by the growing evidence base about best practice for families and carers in EIS (Addington and Burnett, 2004; Fadden and Smith, 2008). It also demonstrates how their personal recovery journeys are influenced by

Table 24.2 Top five things which help carers to share with the professionals

1. Having an open referral system to EIS that allows families and carers to gain information and support either when the individual with FEP does or does not wish to have contact themselves with services.
2. Gathering information from families and carers as a routine part of the assessment process by EIS to gain an understanding of how things were before the difficulties began and of the family dynamics.
3. Involving families and carers routinely in care and contingency planning. When information can be shared openly between all concerned, it is possible to enhance care and take positive risks (either intervening early or offering additional support to minimise the impact of a potential recurrence).
4. Being able to access support and advice informally outside of planned meetings (e.g. FI or CPA reviews).
5. Supporting the development of links with other carers (e.g. through taking part in and facilitating carers meetings, helping to compile a carers pack or in research projects).

Table 24.3 Important principles of sharing care

1. To accept the reality of the mental health problem affecting the individual.
2. To work through the pain of what may be lost as a result of the FEP.
3. To adjust to an environment in which the individual may have different goals and expectations and to move on with their own lives.
   (With thanks to Worden, 1991)

not only their appraisal of the development of an FEP in their loved ones (Addington *et al.*, 2003), but also by the range of both formal and informal support offered by the EIS involved. When setting up EIS, it is therefore important to pay attention to building this level of support into the work of all team members and, wherever possible, also having a carers champion or lead within each team. Engaging with carers and families not only promotes recovery for the individual with an FEP, but also recovery for themselves (Tables 24.2 and 24.3).

Though it's a dreadful illness, if it has to be suffered then it's imperative to somehow find the positives and not to end up as 'victims' of psychosis. Being encouraged to get involved in related areas, be it facilitating carers meetings, helping to compile a carers pack or in research, gives you another focus and helps you feel 'useful' in an otherwise bleak period in your life. Three of us were really surprised when asked if we'd like to compile a Carer's Information Pack. Our meetings in the team's office always involved a lot of hysterical laughter, which we can now see was a huge release of all the stress that we'd borne individually as single parents for a collective total of about 12 years!! It was just what we needed and helped forge lasting friendships.

References

Addington, J., Coldham, E., Jones, B., Ko, T. & Addington, D. (2003). The first episode of psychosis: The experience of relatives. *Acta Psychiatrica Scandinavica*, 108, 285–289.

Addington, J. & Burnett, P. (2004). Working with families in the early stages of psychosis. In: J.F.M. Gleeson & P.D. McGorry (eds), *Psychological Interventions in Early Psychosis – A Treatment Handbook*. Chichester: John Wiley & Sons Ltd.

Addington, J., McCleery, A. & Addington, D. (2005). Three-year outcome of family work in an early psychosis program. *Schizophrenia Research*, 79, 107–116.

Bertolote, J. & McGorry, P. (2005). Early intervention and recovery for young people with early psychosis: Consensus statement. *British Journal of Psychiatry*, 187 (Suppl. 48), s116–s119.

Boydell, K.M., Gladstone, B.M. & Volpe, T. (2006). Understanding help-seeking delay in the prodrome to first episode psychosis: A secondary analysis of the perspectives of young people. *Psychiatric Rehabilitation Journal*, 30 (1), 54–56.

Department of Health (DH) (1983). *Mental Health Act*. London: HMSO.

Department of Health (DH) (1999). *The National Service Framework for Mental Health*. London: HMSO.

Department of Health (DH) (2001). *Policy Implementation Guide for Mental Health*. London: HMSO.

Department of Health (DH) (2007). *Best Practice in Managing Risk: Principles and Guidance for Best Practice in the Assessment and Management of Risk to Self and Others in Mental Health Services*. London: HMSO.

Fadden, G. & Smith, J. (2008). Family work in early psychosis. In: F. Lobban & C. Barrowclough (eds), *A Casebook of Family Interventions for Psychosis*. Chichester: Wiley and Sons.

Falloon I.R.H., Boyd, J.L. & Mcgill, C.W. (1982). Family management in the prevention of exacerbations of schizophrenia. *New England Journal of Medicine*, 306, 1437–1440.

Gleeson, J., Jackson, H.J., Stavely, H. & Burnett, P. (1999). Family intervention in early psychosis. In: P.D McGorry & H.J. Jackson (eds), *The Recognition and Management of Early Psychosis: A Preventive Approach*. Cambridge: Cambridge University Press.

Kuipers, E. and Raune, D. (2002). The early development of expressed emotion and burden in the families of first onset psychosis. In: M. Birchwood, D. Fowler, & C. Jackson (eds), *Early Intervention in Psychosis: A Guide to Concepts, Evidence and Interventions*. Chichester: John Wiley and Sons Ltd.

Leff, J., Kuipers, E. & Berkowitz, R. (1982). A controlled trial of social intervention in the families of schizophrenic families. *British Journal of Psychiatry*, 141, 121–134.

McFarlane, W.R., Lukens, E., Link, B. *et al.* (1995). Multiple-family groups and psycho education in the treatment of schizophrenia. *Archives of General Psychiatry*, 52, 679–687.

Östman, M. & Kjellin, L. (2002) Stigma by association, psychological factors in relatives of people with mental illness. *British Journal of Psychiatry*, 181, 494–498.

Pitschel-Walz, G., Leucht, S., Bauml, J., Kissling, W. & Engel, R. (2001). The effect of family interventions on relapse and rehospitalisation in schizophrenia: A meta-analysis. *Schizophrenia Bulletin*, 27 (1), 73–92.

Raune, D., Kuipers, E. & Bebbington, P.E. (2004). Expressed emotion at first-episode psychosis: Investigating a carer appraisal model. *British Journal of Psychiatry*, 184, 321–326.

Reed, M. & Stevens, C. (2007). Shared caring for a first episode of psychosis: An opportunity to promote hope and recovery. In: R. Velleman, E. Davis, G. Smith & M. Drage (eds), *Changing Outcomes in Psychosis – Collaborative Cases from Practitioners, Users and Carers*. Oxford: BPS Blackwell.

Rose, L.E., Mallinson, K., Gerson, L.D. (2006). Mastery, burden, and areas of concern among family caregivers of mentally ill persons. *Archives of Psychiatric Nursing*, 20 (1), 41–51.

Royal College of Psychiatrists (RCP) (2004). *Carers and confidentiality in mental health – Issues involving information sharing*. Booklet produced as part of Partners in Care Campaign available from www.partnersin-care.co.uk accessed 28.2.07.

Shannon, M., Burnett, P. & Gleeson, J. (1997). *Working with Families in Early Psychosis*. Victoria: EPPIC Statewide Services.

Smith, G., Gregory, K. & Higgs, A. (2007). *An Integrated Approach to Family Work for Psychosis – A Manual for Family Workers*. London: Jessica Kingsley.

Worden, J.W. (1991). *Grief Counselling and Grief Therapy – A Handbook for the Mental Health Practitioner* (2nd edition). London: Routledge.

Chapter 25 The needs of siblings in first-episode psychosis

Jo Smith, Gráinne Fadden and Lucie Taylor

Introduction

Psychosis in the family can be like a big cloud. It can be overwhelming. You think your family will never be the same...

(Sibling: Fisher *et al.*, 2004b)

Within the field of psychosis, research into the impact of psychosis on the family has predominantly focused on parents and spouses and largely ignored the impact on siblings. This is surprising given the importance of sibling relationships in the life cycle, the potential vulnerability of well siblings to developing psychosis themselves and the likelihood that the majority of individuals with first-episode psychosis (FEP) will be living with siblings in the family home. There have been few published studies looking at the needs of siblings coping with FEP or service models for how these might be addressed. Anecdotal clinical evidence suggests that siblings identify specific information and support needs which are rarely addressed, other than in the context of family intervention when siblings are still often not included.

This chapter will identify and summarise the existing literature and in the case study will provide insights from a sibling perspective of the impact of FEP and the needs arising from this. Based on clinical experience, we will identify implications for interventions with siblings and offer practical advice to inform more sensitive support for siblings coping with FEP.

Evidence summary

Nature of sibling relationships

Sibling relationships tend to be of longer duration than those with our parents, partners, peers and children and persist with varying degrees of intimacy and investment throughout the life cycle (Dunn, 2000). During childhood and adolescence, sibling relationships provide companionship, and both emotional and practical support (Goetting, 1986). The onset of psychosis in adolescence or early adulthood may be critical in terms of the potential disruption to and mutual loss of an important reciprocal relationship.

Numbers of siblings coping with FEP

Audit data from Worcestershire Early Intervention Service (EIS) (Smith *et al.*, 2008) reveals that the majority of individuals with FEP are living with siblings. In a caseload of 66 first-episode individuals, 89% of individuals had siblings (113 in total). Although the majority of siblings (68%) were aged 19 years or older, 4.4% were under 10 years, 9.7% were between 10 and 14 years and 17.7 % were 15–18 years old.

Impact of psychosis on siblings

I don't know how to talk to X. anymore. We used to get on really well. I worry about him when I'm at university, not knowing how he is and how mum and dad are coping with him. When I came home at Christmas, he just ignored me. At times I'm frightened of him, and I can't forget the time he cut his wrists. What's more, I feel guilty about how I seem to be getting on with my life and he seems stuck.

(Sibling: Worcestershire EIS)

The majority of studies have been retrospective or explored the impact on siblings coping with longer-term psychosis. They reveal a pervasive impact on sibling lives (Marsh *et al.*, 1993) where siblings report similar levels of subjective burden as parents and offspring (Solomon & Draine, 1995). UNAFAM (Union Nationale des Amis et Familles de Malades Psychiques) highlighted three periods of greatest vulnerability for siblings including onset of the illness when stress levels are considerable (Davtian, 2003). Siblings reported a lack of information, fears about developing problems themselves and anxieties about future burden. They identified principal sources of information about psychosis as family (63%) and the media (49%).

The limited research on first-episode siblings has mainly focused on grief experiences (Miller *et al.*, 1990; Fisher *et al.*, 2004a). However, one study (Fisher *et al.*, 2004b) revealed similar findings to accounts of siblings coping with longterm mental health difficulties. Siblings reported a pervasive adverse impact on family relationships and emotional well-being, neglect of personal needs, difficulties in sustaining friendships, impaired academic performance and increased burden and responsibilities. They felt ignored by psychiatric services accompanied by a wish to be more involved in the care of their affected sibling, and to receive more support and guidance from professionals.

A recent sibling guide to psychosis produced by the Canadian Mental Health Association, based on experiences of siblings from three EI services in Canada (Mulder & Lines, 2006), described a lack of information and understanding of psychosis, uncertainty and helplessness, emotional burden, family tensions and disruption to family life, a sense of responsibility for their affected sibling and difficulties coping with psychotic symptoms, aggression, suicide and self-harm.

A large sibling survey carried out by Rethink (Canning, 2006) rated access to advice and support as inadequate. Siblings were seeking accessible information, including sibling-oriented information packs (84%), dedicated sibling website space (76%) and publications on how best to support as siblings (77%). They also wanted to be actively involved through newsletters (65%), Web-based chat rooms and discussion forums (63%) and to have the opportunity for direct contact with other siblings through a local support group or Web-based sibling network (53%).

Implementation into practice

It would have been nice to be consulted about how my brother was before and what we think would help him now. We'd like to be involved in his care planning or something like that…

(Fisher et al, 2004b)

Several information leaflets targeting siblings coping with psychosis have been published, which provide information and coping advice. There are also a number of sibling websites (see resource list). Family intervention has often been regarded as the vehicle for whole family support but, in practice, practitioners tend to be better at talking to parents and spouses and not necessarily the whole family. In a chapter on family intervention with siblings (Smith *et al.*, 2008), we have described providing support to siblings coping with FEP in the context of family intervention. We identify issues for consideration when working with siblings and training and service implications, informed by the published literature and clinical experience.

Specific issues for siblings

There are a number of issues when thinking about working with siblings (Smith *et al.*, 2008). See Table 25.1.

Service development and training implications

A number of staff training and service development issues arise when working with siblings:

- **Working with siblings who may be children**
  This can be novel for staff that may only have been trained in adult work and are currently working in adolescent or adult (rather than child) services. Although the majority of siblings will be adults, one can expect approximately a fifth of siblings who are under 16 years with a small but significant number who may still be in primary years. This presents a challenge when working with families who have siblings across a very wide

Table 25.1 Things to consider when working with siblings

Recognising the valuable role of siblings and the resources they have to offer: Siblings who share the same room, attend the same school, share the same friends or interests are often the first to observe changes in behaviour and functioning and awareness that something is wrong. They can also be important social allies and provide considerable social support.

Getting the balance right in enlisting sibling support and encouraging independence: A balance needs to be struck between identifying and mobilising sibling support and helping siblings hold reasonable boundaries in relation to demands that might be placed upon them. It is important to help siblings maintain emotional well-being, sustain friendships and role performance and address personal needs and goals although these may not necessarily be raised as explicit needs by siblings themselves related to feelings of guilt or concerns about selfishness.

Taking a whole-family perspective: Trying to keep a balance in family discussions and ensuring that formal family intervention is not dominated by parental narrative and views. There is an implicit assumption that siblings do not have any difficulties of their own (either independent of or secondary to coping with psychosis in the family). Although service involvement may be related to the affected sibling, it is important to take a broader perspective and ensure that parents (and services) are not making demands on siblings to offer support at the expense of their own needs for care and that siblings also receive appropriate parental support (and where appropriate specialist service support) for their personal needs and difficulties.

Addressing peer support needs of siblings: Providing peer sibling email contacts, directing them to young people and sibling websites, providing contact details for linking with national sibling networks and groups (see resource list).

Flexibility in timing of sessions which include siblings: Fitting involvement around everyday family routines and commitments including mealtimes, school timetables, afterschool activities, clubs and homework demands.

Raising awareness about siblings' own potential genetic vulnerability as a higher risk group themselves with an emphasis on the importance of taking care of their personal health and well-being. This needs sensitive handling to avoid inadvertently raising anxiety levels by oversensitising naïve siblings to potential genetic risk. A family history of a psychosis increases the risk that other family members might have similar problems. Where a brother or sister (including a non-identical twin) has a psychosis, the risk for siblings will increase to 10%; if it is an identical twin that has a psychosis, the risk will increase to 50% (Maynard & Smith, 2003).

Being sensitive to confidentiality issues, which relies to some degree on how much the affected sibling wants their peer siblings to be involved. This can be difficult when an individual understandably wishes to preserve their independence, autonomy and privacy while their difficulties are having a direct impact on family life, relationships and the well-being of other family members. This can be aided by offering concurrent individual and family support options and identifying those needs which may best be addressed individually from those that would benefit from sibling involvement. The Royal College of Psychiatrists and The Princess Royal Trust of Carers 'Partners in Care' Campaign produced a useful leaflet addressing confidentiality issues with carers (Allison et al., 2004).

---

age range including appropriate pitch of information and available information materials (particularly for the younger age group), attention span and concentration limitations, different levels of understanding and potential contribution to any family discussion.

- **Collecting routine information about siblings**
  A simple means to prompt case managers to ask about siblings and potential needs for support is to include the routine completion of a simple family genogram at baseline assessment to reveal numbers, names and ages of all sibling members and whether or not they are living at home.

- **Assessing the needs of siblings**
  Services need to be more 'family-centred' when working in the early phases of psychosis, to recognise and acknowledge the broader impact on all family members. Family Intervention offers a format of individual

assessments prior to intervention, which lends itself well to formally assessing the impact on individual siblings and provides the opportunity to speak with siblings directly. Interestingly, informal conversations with parents reveal that many may avoid asking about the impact on siblings in fear of increasing their burden and having to stretch support beyond the affected sibling. Equally, siblings acknowledge that they hold back on revealing the true impact on themselves for fear of increasing burden and responsibilities on their parents.

- **Ensuring availability of specific resources for siblings**
  Services need to have a range of resource materials available for siblings appropriate for different age groups as well as details of sibling websites, books and other resources which siblings might wish to access.
- **Service capacity constraints**
  Even in a well-resourced service, there may be limits on team capacity to meet all sibling needs identified, particularly in relation to offering dedicated individual or group support to siblings, in addition to routine Family Intervention. Ideally, there should be capacity and flexibility to offer a range of support as required including individual sessions, access to a psychoeducational group and peer support opportunities as well as family intervention. However, there are also realistic limits on available resources in most services to meet the potential plethora and combinations of needs and support options that may arise. Realistically, the majority of support to siblings will be in the context of Family Intervention. However, the limits of providing one mode of support also need to be acknowledged. It can also be difficult to target individual sibling needs within a group-based intervention.

Sibling engagement

How can we effectively respond to concerns raised by siblings and engage them in family work to try and address these? Guidance to assist the engagement process, adapted from our recent chapter (Smith *et al.*, 2008), is listed in Table 25.2.

Service response to the needs of siblings
Comment in relation to her brother using cannabis and developing a psychosis:

It made me weigh a lot of choices and my own lifestyle. A consequence has been brought to my attention. No one says this could happen to you. But you never know.

(Sibling: Mulder & Lines, 2005)

When training staff in working with siblings, we have found it helpful to ask staff to imagine themselves as a sibling with a brother or sister who has recently developed psychosis, prompted by the following questions:

- **How do you think you might feel?**
- **What issues might this raise for you?**
- **How might your age influence your reactions?**

Several sibling publications (Maynard & Smith, 2003; Mulder & Lines, 2005) include guidance for siblings in relation to the help they should be seeking. This also offers a useful framework to guide services:

- **Helping siblings learn about psychosis** including prevalence to reduce feelings of isolation, common symptoms to help make sense of experiences, how long their sibling might take to recover, what they can expect to happen and personal genetic risk/vulnerability.
- **Encouraging siblings to talk about thoughts, feelings and reactions** including feelings of guilt, anger and loss and discussing difficulties in coping/adjusting with family and close friends.
- **Encouraging siblings to carry on with life:** Having fun, talking and doing ordinary things, keeping in contact with friends, staying involved with regular activities, sports and hobbies, keeping their identity, valuing personal successes, making plans for the future and challenging guilty feelings that might stop them doing this.

Table 25.2 Guidance to assist engagement

Normalising without minimising difficulties that may be identified as potentially natural tensions and concerns which might arise within any family and among siblings of different ages regardless of mental health problems in the family. Acknowledging that feelings and emotions they may be experiencing are normal and understandable. Emphasising that psychosis is *nobody's fault.*

Foster their partnership and support in the recovery process of their affected sibling while addressing their personal support needs by encouraging them to look after themselves and giving permission to carry on with their life, interests and friendships.

Showing genuine concern for what the family has had to deal with in trying to cope with serious mental health problems in the family without any specialist education or training and often handling difficult behaviours such as hallucinations, delusions and aggression, which may appear unpredictable and can generate fear and anxiety in family members.

Involving all siblings in family discussion and seeking to hear and understand their personal perspectives on the difficulties facing the family so ensuring that everyone has an opportunity to express their views and opinions so that no individual dominates discussion or feels left out, excluded and alienated.

Tailoring involvement to suit the age of the siblings is particularly important when working with very young siblings who may struggle to maintain attention and concentration. Setting tasks for younger siblings such as holding a watch to act as timekeeper and enlisting them to help to hand out information materials can be used as tactics to help them to feel included. Similarly, using visual materials (including asking them to draw pictures) to support verbal discussion is another helpful strategy to engage younger children. Encouraging parents to talk to younger-age siblings with the support of materials such as 'Making Time to Talk' (NSF Scotland, 2005) and bedtime stories designed to prompt discussion about mental heath problems with this age group (Lloyd, 2002; Ironside, 2003).

Getting siblings to identify positive outcomes they would like to see both individually and for the family as a whole, particularly seeking to convert critical comments into more constructive goals for change while providing hope and realistic optimism about the potential for change and recovery.

Being flexible (within reasonable limits!) in timing of and venue for family sessions, such as arranging family meetings at home, at the end of the day and fitting around family routines such as evening mealtimes, regular school and homework demands and personal social commitments to facilitate attendance of siblings.

Acknowledging and positively reinforcing sibling attendance and involvement, commending them for making time to attend family sessions and thanking them for their personal contributions to discussion that takes place.

- **Mobilising support:** Knowing what is available including information packs, websites, education programmes, activity breaks, support options including peer support opportunities.

- **Helping siblings set appropriate limits on and having realistic expectations of what they can do**: Offering only the amount of help and support that they feel comfortable with, acknowledging the reality of the situation and its special demands, letting go of what they cannot change.

- **Helping them to think about how to handle difficult situations or behaviours** including when their sibling talks to themselves, says weird stuff or does strange things, is withdrawn, sleeps excessively, behaves aggressively or threatens self-harm and what to say to friends.

- **Helping them to learn how to relate** when their sibling does not want to do the fun things they used to, when they do not know if they can fully trust them anymore, when their sibling is still using illicit drugs.

- **Helping them to identify what they can do to help:** Being there to talk to, being positive, encouraging and giving genuine compliments, finding things they can still do together, encouraging their sibling to do things they are good at, being oneself, showing care and offering support when parents are getting stressed out. A recent 'World Café' workshop (World Café Community, 2002) held with siblings (Smith & Taylor, 2007) identified 'tips' for professionals working with siblings:

- **Giving siblings space to talk about being a sibling separately from family:** Offer siblings a separate individual Carer's Assessment and the opportunity for 1:1 sessions with professionals so that siblings can be more open and feel less embarrassed and can share concerns which they do not feel able to share with parents; reassure siblings that if they do not engage in initial assessments or support that is offered that the offer of help is still open and that it is never too late to engage with or seek help from services; employ specialist workers trained to work with siblings.

- **Recognise the potential risks and costs as well as the benefits of talking about concerns and problems at home with peers:** Encourage discretion and careful thought about who is the right person to talk to as friendships can be very fickle and the costs may outweigh gains, particularly the potential for gossip, teasing or isolation.

- **When providing information:** Modify information so that it is age specific and age sensitive, keep jargon to a minimum, be honest and make sure you give siblings something to take away and read.

- **Not making assumptions about siblings:** Even those from within same family may react differently or may be in a different place at any one time, or may have different needs; these needs will change over time and at different ages. Do not make any assumptions about closeness of sibling relationships and recognise that some siblings may choose to detach.

- **Valuing the unique relationship that siblings have:** Where siblings will know many things that parents will never know; recognising the 'pull' of a sibling blood relationship and not overusing siblings; avoiding placing siblings in a spying role (and the feelings of guilt and betrayal that this may engender); being clear about how you will use information and what you ask from

siblings; clarifying the role of siblings and the boundaries on this; discussing assumed responsibilities with siblings to alleviate unnecessary worrying about responsibilities and giving siblings permission not to be a carer.

- **Supporting parents in addressing sibling needs:** In fulfilling their role and responsibilities as parents of siblings, encouraging them to make time for siblings so siblings feel included, supporting siblings in getting on with their own lives and helping to relieve siblings from an assumed sense of responsibility.

Service example

There are a lot of people in the same boat as us and in a way, that's reassuring…(the group provided) good information which has helped me understand my brother's illness.

(Sibling: Worcestershire EIS)

It may be helpful to consider the implementation of support to siblings within an NHS EIS setting. The Worcestershire EIS has already been described elsewhere (see Ch 23). Established in 2002, it provides a family-centred service including support to siblings (See Ch 23 fig 23.2). Demographic data about siblings is collected routinely through the assessment process which includes completion of a family genogram to collect details about sibling numbers, names, ages and whether living at home or not.

In consultation with EI siblings and based on earlier sibling materials produced by the Young People and Early Psychosis Intervention (YPPI) Centre in Australia (Horn & Howe, 2002), the Worcestershire EIS produced an information booklet for siblings giving information about psychosis and answering common concerns and questions (Maynard & Smith, 2003). Siblings are offered informal psychoeducation from the case manager supported by age-appropriate sibling information materials and access to website resources, including our own Worcestershire EIS siblings booklet.

Unless the affected sibling does not consent to sibling involvement (which is rare), siblings will also be invited to participate in formal

Behavioural Family Therapy (BFT) intervention at some point during involvement with EIS. BFT usually involves individual assessment meetings with all family members (including siblings) prior to joint family sessions where the focus is on family psychoeducation, early signs monitoring and enhancing family communication and problem-solving skills (Fadden & Smith, 2008).

Additionally, some sibling needs are met through the invitation to attend a relative's psychoeducational group. Ideally, group psychoeducational interventions should be specific to EI siblings as siblings may be reluctant to attend groups where parents or spouses may also be present. However, in practice, this is not always possible, related to staffing capacity constraints but this has not inhibited sibling involvement to date. Typically, we have engaged between two and four siblings in any psychoeducational group who have attended to gain information and the opportunity to meet other siblings and family members coping with similar situations and difficulties to themselves. Siblings present in psychoeducational groups have also been able to offer a sibling perspective to parents and spouses who may be present. In a couple of instances, parents and siblings from the same family have acknowledged that this was the first occasion that they had talked so openly as a family about their difficulties and gained an understanding from a whole-family perspective.

The service has also helped individual siblings link together where access to peer sibling support is requested through negotiating and facilitating the exchange of sibling email addresses between consenting sibling pairs.

We would suggest that it is the range of support to siblings provided by the Worcestershire EIS that enables an effective response to sibling needs.

Clinical case study

Lucie is a sibling of an older brother with psychosis. In this account, she provides an insight into the impact of early psychosis from a sibling perspective. The case study emotively describes initial confusion in understanding and dealing with emerging psychosis in the family. The shock and helplessness in not knowing how best to respond to bizarre or difficult behaviour, the adverse emotional toll (including feelings of isolation, anger, loss, resentment and guilt), disruption to family life and the struggle to cope with difficult situations and behaviours including side effects of medication, psychotic and anxiety symptoms:

I was sixteen when my brother suffered with his first episode of psychosis. . .

My brother came into the house telling us all he had just been trying to drive his car through two bollards and had terrorised a learner driver. We went to look at his car and found that this was not the case. Needless to say, we were all confused at what he was saying.

The first time my brother became ill his behaviour was so bizarre I don't think any of us knew what was going on. Me and my brother had always had a stupid sense of humour and it took us a few moments to realise he was talking rubbish for no apparent reason. I think the hardest thing to come to terms with was how quickly my brother became ill – it literally was overnight. There was no time to get used to the way he was, we had to start managing straight away. We all handled him differently and at times one of us would be more impatient with him than the others and this caused conflict amongst us all. I was often shocked at the things he came out with and when he said something strange, we would say 'well that's what you think because you are unwell at the moment but we don't think that'. Often, he would leave me speechless and I felt so helpless that I couldn't wave a magic wand and bring my brother back. I think before I fully accepted what my brother was suffering with we were already in the thick of it. I remember one of the worst evenings where I watched my brother literally crawl the wall, it was like a scene out of the exorcist and a side effect of his medication we had not been warned about.

The four walls of our house had never seemed so small and I quickly learned how uncomfortable it made people for me to talk about my brother's illness and soon learned it made others more at ease to say he had suffered a 'break down' rather than mention anything to do with his mental health.

I did not know anyone else that had the same or even a similar situation to me and I remember feeling very alone. Very few people understood what I was going through and I became less sociable. This was partly to do with the guilt of going out and leaving mom and dad to handle him, but also because I just did not have the energy and enthusiasm that I used to for socialising. As stupid as it sounds, I couldn't fully concentrate on enjoying myself when I was out. Unfortunately, my brother became ill around Christmas and so this completely ruined this season. This made me feel quite resentful and we were very isolated at a time that would usually be crammed with family and friends. We were cautious of my brother being around young cousins because of some of the odd things he used to say. My brother was so unpredictable, very angry one minute, very anxious and frightened the next.

He experienced very vivid delusions and thought he was our late grandfather, thought he needed a wheelchair and thought he could talk to God. On many occasions, when I or mom and dad planned to use public transport, my brother would become obsessed with the thought that there was a bomb on it. None of us could put the television on as my brother experienced voices and thought he was being sent messages through the TV. Needless to say, this made trying to live our lives as we had before my brother got ill an impossibility.

Unfortunately, amongst everything else my pet rabbit died and my brother in his confused state thought he had killed him so I was unable to properly grieve for a treasured animal. My brother spent two periods of time in hospital. He escaped from one and we had to receive an extremely distressing phone call to inform us so. I never went to see him in hospital. I just could not cope with seeing him there. Now, I feel riddled with guilt, as he often requested me to visit and it is something I have never forgiven myself for.

At the time, I felt very neglected by my parents as all their time, energy and thoughts went into my brother. This was not without the understanding that my brother's needs were much greater than my own, but, at times, important things for me were not acknowledged. My brother, at his worst, would only sleep in my bed with me. However, this was very fidgety disrupted sleep as he would be up very early fretting and needing reassurance. This was extremely physically and emotionally draining. Although my brother was very draining for the majority of his illness, we would laugh at some of the things he did and said because that was the only way of getting through. He would

insist on making cups of tea with cold water and the tea bag still in the mug. We would then have to look convincing that we were enjoying the cold drink. My brother has suffered two more episodes and all have presented us with different symptoms and challenges. I know that I owe a lot of my coping ability to the fact that I had an extremely understanding and supportive boyfriend. I know that things could have been a lot different for me with regard to finishing my degree, for example. I would have greatly appreciated the opportunity to have talked with other siblings in the same situation as I know my main struggle was feeling like I was alone. We did not really have positive support from any service. We felt very let down from the time when mom first went to see the GP and he told us to just carry on managing him at home to when we were not advised about potential side effects of his medication. I am sure an E.I service would have really made a difference had we been made aware of its existence. Luckily my story has a happy ending, my brother has been well now for two years and we are closer than ever. I do worry about my brother's illness returning but as a family we monitor him closely and he has an extremely good relationship with his Community Nurse.

Implications and conclusions

I want him to have an easy life. He does not have that and I wish that for him. It's not the way I expected it to be – but it's OK.

(Sibling: Mulder & Lines, 2005)

The UNAFAM study (Davtian, 2003) highlighted a 'no man's land' for siblings where they face a number of paradoxes:

- They have too little information yet they know too much.
- They are often involved but without a defined role or knowing what is expected of them.
- They experience difficulties but asking for help may risk making themselves more vulnerable.
- They often find themselves in the dilemma of choosing compassion or abandonment.

Working with siblings presents another challenge to stretched EI services in terms of broadening their scope to include support to siblings. Services (and parents) need to be sensitive to siblings' experiences and difficulties. We need to provide siblings with accurate information about what they may be dealing with at home and address their anxieties and support needs. While acknowledging the useful role that siblings may play in the recovery of their affected sibling, we also need to be mindful of setting appropriate boundaries on assumed responsibilities, ensuring that siblings' needs for distance are also supported and siblings are appropriately protected from undue burden of care.

Suggested further reading

Lamb, W. (1998). *I know this much is true.* London: HarperCollins Publishers. (This is a novel about twins where one has schizophrenia, and may be helpful for staff in understanding the impact on siblings. Not suitable for children).

Loudon, M. (2006). *Relative Stranger: A Sister's Story.* Canangate Books. ISBN: 1841956759.

Neugeboren, J. (1997). *Imagining Robert: My Brother, Madness and Survival.* New York: William Morrow and Company, Inc.

Safer, J. (2003). *The Normal One: Life with a Difficult or Damaged Sibling.* Delta Books. ISBN-10: 0385337566; ISBN-13: 978-0385337564.

Secunda, V. (1997). *When Madness Comes Home: Help and Hope for the Children, Siblings and Partners of the Mentally Ill.* Hyperion Books. ISBN-10: 0786861711; ISBN-13: 978-0786861712.

Simon, C. (1998). *Mad House: Growing Up in the Shadow of Mentally Ill Siblings.* Penguin. ISBN-10: 0140274340; ISBN-13: 978-0140274349.

Information booklets

Froggatt, D. (2001). *Leave My Stuff Alone – A Story for Young Teen Siblings.* Canada: WFSAD.

Horn, K. & Howe, D. (2002) and Maynard & Smith (2003). *For Brothers and Sisters, Information About Psychosis.* Young People and Early Psychosis Intervention (YPPI) Centre Australia.

Ironside, V. (2003). *The Wise Mouse.* London: YoungMinds (for age 5–11 years).

Lloyd, H. (2002). *Children Can Understand.* West Midlands: The Meriden Family Programme.

Maynard, C. & Smith, J. (2003). *Information About Psychosis for Brothers and Sisters.* UK: South Worcestershire Early intervention Service.

Mulder, S. & Lines, E. (2005). *A Sibling's Guide to Psychosis: Information, Ideas and Resources.* Canada: Canadian Mental Health Association.

NSF Scotland (2005). *It's About You Too!* (age 8–10 years) download from www.nsfscot.org.uk.

NSF Scotland (2005). *Need to Know* (age 11–14 years) download from www.nsfscot.org.uk.

NSF Scotland (2005) *Making Time to Talk* (for parents with a mental illness wanting to talk to children about mental illness) download from www.nsfscot.org.uk.

Sherman, M. (2006). *I'm Not Alone: A Teen's Guide to Living with a Parent Who Has Mental Illness* www.seedsofhopebooks.com.

Schizophrenia Society of Ontario (2006). *When Your Brother or Sister Has Schizophrenia* www.schizophrenia.on.ca.

Useful websites

www.sibs.org.uk

Generic website for siblings producing information sheets, regular newsletter, sibling support, training workshops for siblings.

www.rethink.org/siblings

New online national network for siblings to share experiences and get support set up by Rethink mental health charity.

www.champsworldwide.com

For children aged 5–12 years who have an adult family member with a mental illness.

References

Allison, S., Fadden, G., Hart, D., Launer, M. & Siddle, J. (2004). *Carers and Confidentiality in Mental Health. Issues Involved in Information Sharing.* London: Royal College of Psychiatrists, Partners in Care Campaign www.partnersincare.co.uk.

Canning, L. (2006). *Rethink Siblings Survey.* London: Rethink.

Davtian, H. (2003). UNAFAM study of the needs of siblings. *EUFAMI Newsletter*, 11, 14–16.

Dunn, J. (2000). State of the art: Siblings. *The Psychologist*, 13, 5, 244–248.

Fadden, G. & Smith, J. (2008). Family work in early psychosis. In: F. Lobban & C. Barrowclough (eds), *A Casebook of Family Interventions for Psychosis.* Chichester: Wiley and Sons.

Fisher, H., Tobitt, S., Saleem, S. & Steele, S. (2004a). Siblings' and mothers' grief reactions to the diagnosis of psychosis in a young family member. *Schizophrenia Research*, 70 (Suppl. 1), 88.

Fisher, H., Bordass, E. & Steele, H. (2004b). Siblings' experience of having a brother or sister with first-episode psychosis. *Schizophrenia Research*, 70 (Suppl. 1), 88.

Goetting, A. (1986). The developmental tasks of siblingship over the life cycle. *Journal of Marriage and the Family*, 48, 703–714.

Marsh, D., Dickens, R., Koeske, R. *et al.* (1993). Troubled journey: Siblings and children of people with mental illness. *Innovations and Research*, 2 (2), 13–23.

Miller, F., Dworkin, J., Ward, M. & Barone, D. (1990). A preliminary study of unresolved grief in families of seriously mentally ill patients. *Hospital and Community Psychiatry*, 42 (12), 1321–1325.

Mulder, S. & Lines, E. (2005). *A Sibling's Guide to Psychosis. Information, Ideas and Resources.* Toronto, Canada: Canadian Mental Health association.

Smith, J. & Taylor, L. (2007). Family work in early psychosis: Working with siblings. A 'World Café' workshop. *Meriden Family Conference: Working with Families: Developing Caring Partnerships*, Stratford-Upon-Avon, March 2007.

Smith, J., Fadden, G. & O'Shea, M. (2008). Interventions with siblings. In: F. Lobban & C. Barrowclough (eds), *A Casebook of Family Interventions for Psychosis*. Chichester: Wiley and Sons.

Solomon, P. & Draine, J. (1995). Subjective burden among family members of mentally ill adults: Reactions to stress, coping and adaptation. *American Journal of Orthopsychiatry*, 65 (3), 419–427.

World Café Community (2002). Café to go: A quick reference guide for putting conversations to work. Whole Systems Associates. wwwtheworld-cafe.com.

Chapter 26 **Group-based interventions**

David Glentworth and Mandy Reed

Introduction

Families of individuals with a first-episode psychosis (FEP) present with a range of problems and needs, which can be thought of as ranging from an expressed wish for some information and reassurance to chronic and severe interpersonal and practical problems that can threaten the well-being of both the client and the rest of the family. In FEP, service response needs to be prompt, flexible, meaningful and acceptable to a wide range of relatives and carers. The provision of a short psychoeducational/therapeutic group has a high level of face validity for carers, clients and services as it 'ticks the boxes' of providing information, support, contact with services, normalisation and peer interaction. It is easily protocolised and can be delivered by experienced clinical staff and carers.

This chapter will focus on the development of group-based interventions for families and carers within early psychosis, which support one of the primary aims of the early psychosis declaration (EPD) (Bertolote & McGorry, 2005) of promoting hope and optimism for all concerned. A rationale for the approach is highlighted focusing on the potential for peer support and normalisation. Within the UK, a number of early intervention services (EIS) have developed group-based interventions as part of their range of interventions (e.g. Worcestershire and Somerset). This chapter will describe two different models from different EIS, one in Salford and one in Gloucestershire, along with lessons learnt from developing this model of service provision. The Salford EIS has developed a rolling 5-week psychoeducation programme for individuals and their families, whilst the Gloucestershire EIS developed a 10-week programme which targeted carers specifically. In addition, a case study is given from the Salford programme

to highlight the benefits to all family members including the individual with an FEP. The Early Psychosis Prevention and Intervention Centre (EPPIC) model for family psychoeducation groups (EPPIC, 1997) was used as the basis for designing both courses with some adaptation for local needs.

A brief summary of the evidence

The evidence for the effectiveness of structured family interventions (FIs) in FEP has been discussed elsewhere in this book in some detail (see Chapter 23). Other types of interventions to support families and carers are discussed in Chapter 24 (individual support) and Chapter 25 (sibling support). These demonstrate that high-quality EIS offer a range of interventions to support families and carers including group-based interventions. The services we describe here have taken account of the literature on the experiences of families and their needs with particular emphasis on those factors which predict the development of distress and (in the long run) less helpful ways of coping.

Tennakoon et al., (2000) have found that even at first episode (defined as less than 12 weeks since the client's first exposure to neuroleptics), key relatives are already having to develop coping strategies in response to clients' problems and are experiencing distress. It might be important to note, however, that at this early stage the relatives recruited into the study had levels of psychiatric morbidity similar to the general population.

In addition, it is clear that among these coping responses are the development of relationships between families and clients that are categorised as 'High Expressed Emotion'. These relationships are not as predictive of poor outcome for clients as they are later in the course of disorders, but they develop quickly, perhaps in over half of cases (Heikkila *et al.*, 2002). Moreover, there is evidence that such coping styles are related to relatives' appraisal of the illness rather than its severity (Raune *et al.*, 2004) and that they may arise in loss and grief (emotional overinvolvement) and attempts to 'correct' behavioural changes and deficits (criticism and hostility) (see Chapter 23 and Patterson *et al.*, 2000 for further discussion).

In addition to the development of factors that predict poor outcomes for clients, relatives often express high levels of dissatisfaction with services. De Haan *et al.*, (2002) in a survey of 377 carers of people with FEP found that one-third were 'dissatisfied or very dissatisfied' with specific aspects of care, including advice, information and help with regaining structure and routine. Research in the UK, prior to the set-up of an EIS highlighted that only 10% of those carers interviewed for the study had received a carers assessment, with the majority feeling excluded from their loved one's care and expressing a wish to receive more information about psychosis (Davis, 2002 unpublished document). Addington *et al.*, (2005), however, demonstrated that early recruitment of relatives into an appropriate intervention resulted in an extremely high level of uptake of services (80% initially and 63% at 2 years) and high levels of expressed satisfaction. This research also confirmed that relatives' distress varied not according to the severity of clients' problems but with their appraisal of the impact and consequences of the illness (Addington *et al.*, 2003). Qualitative research on the response to and recovery of families from a family member's illness also highlights the importance of cognitive change and social support. Rose *et al.*, (2002), for example, interviewed 17 families 3 times over 2 years and identified important themes and stages in families' adaptation. Among them were the importance of managing grief, loss and stigma and reaching a 'stance of cautious optimism for the future'.

Other research emphasises the importance for relatives of the urge to find 'meaning' in the illness of their relative. Processes such as blaming oneself for the illness (Ferriter & Huband, 2003), the need to separate signs of illness from

developmental characteristics (Czuchta & McCay, 2001) and agonising over the ethics of trying to 'control' or 'manage' clients (Muhlbauer, 2002) have been identified.

Finally, it has been shown that social network support is important in the amelioration of family members' experience of burden and distress (Magliano *et al.*, 2002). Unfortunately, it may also be the case that relatives feel stigmatised by and 'inferior' to professional staff and that this may be a barrier to engagement with services (Östman & Kjellin, 2002).

It has been our intention, therefore, to develop models of engaging, intervening with and supporting families in early psychosis that will meet these challenges. The essential requirements of such a strategy address many of the issues highlighted in both in the literature and through local research, as highlighted in Table 26.1. Addressing these issues introduces participants to a model of collaboration with services, places their needs close to the centre of the Care Programme Approach (CPA) process (DH, 1990) and gives them sufficient information about services so that they might advocate more effectively for their own and their relative's needs. A key aspect which promotes this is that carers should be involved in the planning and running of groups wherever possible (Reed & Davis, 2007).

Finally, from an organisational standpoint, a suitable strategy will use resources efficiently, use existing staff skills and expertise and be sustainable over time. We have found within our services that brief psychoeducational groups, facilitated in such ways as to maximise essential therapeutic group processes such as universality are able to meet the requirements outlined above. We believe strongly that the group environment is especially suited to introduce relatives to alternative and hopeful models of illness, normalisation of their experience and reduction of stigma by access to an appropriate peer group and social network.

Implementation into practice

One of the central aims of the family programmes is to engage with the widest possible range of families, carers, friends and other supporters. On assessment for the service, all

Table 26.1   Essential requirements for group intervention strategy

---

- It is normalising rather than stigmatising.
- It recognises and validates families' experiences and efforts to cope.
- It is collaborative and recognises and makes use of families' strengths, skills and resources.
- It is flexible and easy to access.
- It has strong face validity for relatives.
- It meets expressed needs for information and fits with the evidence from studies (see above) that relatives' recovery journeys incorporate search for meaning and explanation.
- It is set up to address key beliefs and understandings of the illness.
- It promotes a hopeful model of recovery both for the client and the family.
- It recognises heterogeneity of client outcome.
- It is able to provide an appropriate peer group and social support for relatives.

---

clients are offered a rationale for the involvement of their family and/or friends or other key supporters in the service. The approach to offering a rationale to the person with FEP is to both strongly normalise the approach and to use the assessment to identify problems, values and concerns that can be used to individually tailor a rationale for the individual and the family.

Normalisation and rationale

It is recommended that a family programme such as this, incorporating as it does group psycho-education, is presented as the *default* mode of operation for the service; that is it is made clear to potential participants that this approach is offered as routine to everyone who accesses the service. Families often assume that services will blame them for the illness of their child and an approach offering help to them can be interpreted as implying that the roots of pathology lie within the family or in the parenting of the child. It is best not to assume that services will be seen automatically as benign and helpful and to make strenuous efforts to promote the service as a 'brand' with messages that incorporate the principles outlined above, for example that it recognises and values carers' experiences and contributions and offers essential, up to date information. Provision of information should be supported with a brochure or leaflet which reflects this strong 'brand' and where possible includes testimony in the form of comments from previous participants. See Chapter 24 for other aspects of collaborative care.

The rationale offered to carers and relatives can be even more effective when it addresses the idiosyncratic needs, concerns and experiences of relatives. The clinician or worker can use their assessment of the carer's key experiences, worries, concerns and feelings to adjust the rationale so that it seems particularly relevant and meaningful. For example, where a relative expresses confusion about the cause of the illness or perhaps even worries whether they might have contributed to it themselves, it can be useful to outline how these are concerns regularly expressed by relatives who come to the group and that the content is especially designed to help them answer these kind of questions for themselves.

Setting up the group

It is important that key stakeholders should be involved in the planning and running of this form of intervention. To this end, carers have been involved in the planning and running of the groups and each programme has been designed with a mixture of in-house and local experts. This enables the staff delivering the psychoeducational aspects of the course to feel a sense of ownership in the material. Each group or course has sufficient dedicated facilitators to provide continuity each week; in practice, this has meant that a minimum of three people (team members and carers) are involved in the facilitation of each module so that at least two are present at each week's session. In order to maximise uptake, we have also found it useful to pay special attention to the needs of the target population. Both Gloucestershire and Salford services have found that groups run in the early evening have been well attended. Workers should attempt to be responsive, however, to the needs of parents who have school-age children or people who live in localities where it may be considered inadvisable to venture out after dark, especially where they have to rely on public transport. In order to maximise ease of access to the intervention, it may be necessary at times to vary the times and locations at which the groups or courses are offered. In Salford, for example, after the third cohort of carers, it was evident that proportionately far fewer carers from the most socially deprived areas of the city had completed the groups. In response, the next group was run in the community room at the middle of the local authority housing development in the city centre. This enabled pedestrian access from the majority of the most deprived wards in Salford. Preferably, the venue should be accessible by public transport and in a non-hospital environment. It is not uncommon for parents and other friends and relatives to associate the 'mental hospital' with some unpleasant memories (possibly of the client's initial treatment experiences) or to hold preconceptions about it. Holding the meetings at a venue such as a community centre reinforces the message of recovery and cautious optimism that the programme is trying to convey.

At the start of each course or group, members are provided with a folder to keep handouts and other information in. Group members are given copies of all presentations along with a range of other leaflets and information found helpful by carers. Ground rules and boundaries around confidentiality, mutual respect and timekeeping are agreed during the first session, whilst each week starts and ends with a recap of the previous week and homework/pleasant event scheduling for the following one. The start of this and every subsequent week begins with the facilitators reviewing the previous week and checking if group members have any questions or whether the content or conduct of the groups have raised any uncomfortable issues for them. This is followed by a round where each person briefly talks about their week and raises issues they wish to talk about that week.

Although both programmes are relatively short, at 5 weeks in Salford and 10 weeks in Gloucestershire, it is essential that time is allowed for networking and informal support to take place amongst participants. This may be in dedicated sessions (Gloucestershire) or during breaks for refreshments.

The programmes

In Salford, the programme (Table 26.2) consists of five 1.5-hour sessions over consecutive weeks. Each session adheres to the general format of two separate 'presentations' from the facilitators or a guest presenter with a break between them and time set aside at the beginning and end of the meeting for discussion and 'socialisation'. The programme is adjusted according to the needs of the participants and we have developed sessions on Understanding Challenging Behaviour, Understanding the Benefits System and The Mental Health Act that we can deliver should participants express a strong desire. In Gloucestershire, the programme (Table 26.3) consisted of ten 2-hour sessions, also over consecutive weeks and included a broader range of topics in the standard format.

Leadership of the groups

One of the primary foci of the programmes is to encourage the development of the range of benign beliefs about illness and patient behaviour that might prevent or delay the formation of interpersonal difficulties and relatives' distress. To this end, we find that the group workers,

Table 26.2 The Salford group programme

Week 1	**Introduction to the programme**
	What is psychosis?
Week 2	**What causes psychosis?**
	Medical treatments
Week 3	**Psychosocial treatments**
	What services are available?
Week 4	**Substance use**
	Stress management – 1
Week 5	**Stress management – 2**

Table 26.3   The Gloucestershire group programme

Week 1	**The Importance of carers, carers assessments and care plans**
Week 2	**What is psychosis?**
	The work of the EIS team
Week 3	**Medication question and answer session**
	The impact of drugs and alcohol
Week 4	**CBT for psychosis**
Week 5	**Introduction to family interventions (FIs)**
	Recognising stress and setting boundaries
Week 6	**Problem solving – Falloon's (1985) six-step method for family work**
	Planning for future personal support
Week 7	**Dealing with professionals**
	Hospital admission
Week 8	**Money management and the benefits system**
Week 9	**Family communication**
	Psychosis and the legal system
Week 10	**(Social event with food and drinks provided)**
	Evaluation of the group + repeat of pre-course questionnaires
	Planning for ongoing support networks – led by the group themselves

whilst ensuring that the format is flexible enough to address individual families' concerns within a collaborative framework, must have enough confidence in the salience of the 'core messages' to assert the importance of the key modules by relating them to participants' and patients' needs. Facilitators must be able, therefore, to take a leadership and 'expert' role within the group, rather than be purely a 'moderator'.

Maximising therapeutic gains in the group

Targeting key attributions

The psychoeducation and other information offered in the group is especially geared towards introducing models of client symptoms, behavioural changes and 'illness' that have been shown to be associated with or underpin positive adaptation to psychosis and thus predict better outcomes for the client and relative. For

example, it has been shown that consistently 'high-EE' relatives are more likely to attribute 'problem' behaviour to aspects of the person rather than the illness and to believe that the client has some 'control' over these behaviours (Barrowclough et al., 1996). Similarly, relatives who ascribe greater severity and chronicity to the illness or who have high levels of self-blame are more likely to experience high levels of distress (Fortune et al., 2005).

'Blame' and control

The central aims of the initial sessions are to acknowledge the search for explanation and meaning when the well-being of a family member changes, to normalise models of illness that relatives commonly arrive at or are presented with and to present and discuss a multifactorial model of illness that encompasses a range of factors which contribute to the onset and maintenance of psychosis.

The activities that take place in the group to support these aims are:

- Presentation about the core symptoms and experiences in people experiencing psychosis;
- Watching a video of a person who has experienced psychosis describing his symptoms and his recovery journey;
- Guided discussion amongst the group members about the symptoms and causes of psychosis in which the facilitator elicits families' models of illness and highlights similarities and differences.

The main demand upon the facilitator in these discussions is to elicit and to recognise statements that reflect high levels of self-blame for the illness or attributions of blame or control towards the client. The facilitator can then invite a comparison with the empirical evidence that has been presented or, more usually, ask the group to discuss the beliefs and attributions. It is a characteristic of psychoeducational groups that information and knowledge from 'experts' is valued less highly than that of other participants (Buksti et al., 2006) and the therapist is often well advised to use the disparate knowledge and ideas of the varying participants to help introduce flexibility into dysfunctional beliefs rather than trying to insist that everyone subscribes to a favoured empirically based model.

Timeline

Unhelpful, pessimistic, catastrophic and stigmatising views of mental illness are commonplace in society. As a result of this, relatives of clients who have been offered a diagnosis or description of their illness such as 'schizophrenia' or 'psychosis' can experience difficulty in accepting and accommodating to it. It is common for parents to question a diagnosis or minimise problems, dismissing them as 'one offs' or 'just down to the drugs' if it seems that the client's problems do not fit with the demonised model of the 'schizophrenic' as mad and dangerous. Alternatively, on becoming aware of the nature of the client's problem, relatives may immediately assume the worst possible outcome. For example, one mother who attended the

Salford group was consumed by the concern that the future for her son lay inevitably as a 'down and out'. She could summon up no image of him in the future other than as 'an alcoholic, raggedy tramp in the gutter'.

It is therefore one of the essentials of the groups that participants have access to representations of illness that foster a degree of cautious optimism. To this end, it is helpful to have service users or a carer who can tell a personal story of recovery. It also helps if the group is reasonably heterogeneous in that participants themselves have different experiences of psychosis and recovery.

Socialisation to the care process

Services often seem to assume that both clients and their supporters have an inbuilt knowledge of the structure of mental health services and the processes by which they work. The reality is that many 'lay' people who come into contact with mental health services for the first time have never imagined that there is any difference between a psychiatrist and a psychologist, that there are nurses who do not work in hospitals or that social workers' main activity is to take children into care. The sessions on service provision are important not only as they act as an 'A to Z' of services, providing basic information on the statutory and legislative background to the CPA (DH, 1990) and the Mental Health Act (DH, 1983), but also as they present a collaborative model of working with clients that puts emphasis on the needs and rights of the family.

In addition, feedback on the programmes has consistently shown that families value the opportunity to meet and question professionals from a range of backgrounds; to learn the difference between a psychiatrist and a psychologist for example!

Assessments and evaluation

Pre- and post-assessments in both Salford and Gloucestershire include the General Health Questionnaire (GHQ) (Goldberg & Hillier, 1979) and the Experience of Caregiving Inventory (ECI) (Szmukler et al., 1996). In Gloucestershire, a locally derived assessment has also been used to determine what proportion of time each week a carer spends on caring as opposed to other activities such as work, recreation or household duties (Holland, unpublished tool). At the end of the courses, participants in both programmes also take part in a general evaluation of the taught and written course content, making recommendations for future groups and indicating what kind of ongoing support they would like and if they would be prepared to get involved in future groups or other types of training. All participants demonstrated an improved sense of well-being and increasing levels of hope and optimism for the future of not only their loved ones but also their own.

Peer support and involvement in service delivery

All attendees have found the group a positive experience with many of them continuing to meet up on an informal basis or keep in touch by email. Following the first group in Gloucestershire, three carers supported by one of the authors reviewed all the written information they had been given to develop a specific Carers Information Pack for the Team. Carers also became involved in recruitment for the Gloucestershire EIS and had input to formal and informal training programmes. As a result of this level of involvement, one member from the first group has since become a Carer Support Worker and there are several others looking for similar roles.

Issues for consideration/lessons learnt/obstacles encountered

The successful establishment, development and maintenance of a group FI, as with other aspects of a high-quality EIS, depend on a number of factors, including commitment at a service management level and the presence of a skilled, committed and motivated workforce (Bertolote & McGorry, 2005). These factors are common to a range of interventions and initiatives, however, and during the process of establishing the groups, we have had to answer a number of specific questions.

In order to ensure that the intervention is successful, it must be embedded within a service in which carers are recognised and valued and their needs addressed. To this end, service structures should formally incorporate carers in steering groups, recruitment and all team training and development. We would recommend that in setting up the intervention, carers should be part of a small working group planning the groups meeting approximately monthly for a period of 6 months prior to the start of the first intervention and subsequently as part of an ongoing project group.

In setting up the groups, it was necessary to consider whether clients as well as relatives should be invited. In Salford, the decision was made to open the invitation to the entire household to minimise the risk that clients would be suspicious about motives for talking to their relatives without them. In practice, very few of the groups in Salford have been attended by clients. Where they have, facilitators have found that this challenges them to present information in a form that is acceptable to service users themselves and to help them feel comfortable in an environment where carers' distress at the client's difficulties is evident.

In some groups, it is difficult to maintain a successful balance between affording relatives and carers the space in which to express their distress and difficulties and obtain peer support and the delivery of psychoeducation and the other central 'messages' of the group. Relatives find the informal support they give and receive of enormous benefit. This should be reflected in the formal structure of the group whilst taking care not to compromise the other, necessary aspects.

Finally, the experience in both Salford and Gloucester has been that it became much more difficult to sustain the intervention after the departure of key personnel for whom the intervention reflected a key clinical interest. We would strongly suggest that the importance of carer's needs should be formally reflected in the structure of teams and that one or more members of the team should be identified as family or carer 'specialists'. Although carers' needs should be the business of all the team, in practice we have found that structured interventions are difficult to maintain in the absence of an identified leader or advocate who has both the skills and power to maintain the profile and momentum of the groups.

Clinical case study (Alex, Maria and Chloe Morrison)

Alex was admitted to hospital after experiencing the first onset of psychosis whilst studying at University. Subsequently, he lived with and was supported during his recovery by his mum Maria and sister Chloe. Alex had 15 sessions of cognitive behaviour therapy (CBT) with a therapist from the Salford EIS, starting whilst he was an inpatient and continuing after his discharge home. He also attended the Family and Friends group with Maria and Chloe. All three were asked to reflect on their experiences of the group and the part it played in their 'recovery' and the development of their understanding of Alex's problems.

Alex

I remember that I seemed to be the only 'patient' there. Initially I felt a bit anxious and strange about this but the group was run in a way that made it comfortable to talk about my illness. I believe that we got the information that we needed about the illness and especially about all the help that Mum and Chloe could get. If there was one fault its that it probably would have been better if it had started as soon as I had got out of hospital, although thinking about this I probably wouldn't have gone at the time as I would not have been well enough!

Maria

The consultant at the hospital told me to find out as much information as I could about the illness. The group helped me make sense of all the information by discussing it with other people. You tend to think 'is it anything I've done?' when it happens and this was deliberately discussed. You learn that nobody truly knows what causes psychosis and that it's not because you gave them milk before they were 2. It was good to meet all the different professionals and to find out what other help was available. I think that it would have been more helpful to me if it had gone on a little longer but I know that for some people there it was difficult for them to commit even to the five weeks, especially those whose relative was still unwell.

Chloe

The information was OK, especially for my mum who wants to know everything about the illness, but it was perhaps a little too 'jargony'. It was helpful for me to be in a group at the time because I needed to know that there were other people out there and it wasn't just our family. You don't tell anyone else when the illness starts and because no one else talks about it you wouldn't know how common psychosis is. If there is anything I'd change it would be to include a 'cooling off' period at the end of the group. I went to subsequent Family and Friends groups to talk about my experiences and found that everyone was 'best mates' with each other. Giving extra time for people to meet and get to know each other would be good as you can then carry on supporting each other after the group has finished.

Implications and conclusions

A fundamental aspect of meeting the EPD is 'to ensure that families are not alienated or disempowered by encouraging better access to information, education, social, economic, practical and emotional support' (Bertolote & McGorry, 2005). This chapter has described and discussed a range of ways in which EIS can address engage and support families and carers through group interventions. Although the programmes described here vary in length, the content is broadly similar and both have had very positive outcomes for the individuals involved.

However, in order to deliver this level of psychoeducation and support, EIS need to not only recruit staff with the right attitudes and skills (DH, 2004; RCP, 2004) for working with families and carers, but also to have protected time for staff to deliver a comprehensive range of interventions. The experience of setting up the group interventions as described in this chapter has involved a considerable amount of commitment and dedication by the team members involved, which has proved hard to sustain once those key team members have moved on. Support and understanding of the importance of group-based interventions at a senior managerial level is essential to help protect the time needed to plan, implement and review a comprehensive range of services above and beyond basic care coordination of individuals with an FEP (Bertolote & McGorry, 2005). EIS that fail to get high-level organisational support and do not identify dedicated carer leads within the team skill mix will rely on the enthusiasm and goodwill of individuals attracted to this kind of work to develop group-based interventions on an ad hoc rather than consistent basis.

As seen in the two service examples discussed in this chapter, the key components of group-based psychoeducational support address the same range of topics (see Tables 26.1 and 26.2). Both services chose to run their groups in the early evening to facilitate maximum attendance and provided refreshments to promote informal networking and the development of peer support, which in many cases carries on post-completion of the formal group intervention. Most importantly, carers were involved in the design and delivery and evaluation of the groups, contributing to their own recovery processes as a result.

References

Addington, J., Coldham, E.L., Jones, B., Ko, T. & Addington, D. (2003). The first episode of psychosis: The experience of relatives. *Acta Psychiatrica Scandinavica*, 108, 285–289.

Addington, J., Collins, A., McCleery, A. & Addington, D. (2005). The role of family work in early psychosis. *Schizophrenia Research*, 79 (1), 77–83.

Barrowclough, C., Tarrier, N. & Johnson, M. (1996). Distress, expressed emotion and attributions in relatives of schizophrenia patients. *Schizophrenia Bulletin*, 22, 691–702.

Bertolote, J. & McGorry, P. (2005). Early intervention and recovery for young people with early psychosis: Consensus statement. *British Journal of Psychiatry*, 187 (Suppl. 48), s116–s119.

Buksti, A.S., Munkner, R., Gade, I. *et al.* (2006). Important components of a short-term family group programme. From The Danish National Multicenter Schizophrenia Project. *Nordic Journal of Psychiatry*, http://www.informaworld.com/smpp/title~content=t713691698~db=all~tab=issueslist~branches=60 - v6060, 3 May 2006, 213–219.

Czuchta, D. & McCay, E. (2001). Help-seeking for parents of individuals experiencing a first episode of schizophrenia. *Archives of Psychiatric Nursing*, XV (4), 159–170.

De Haan, L., Kramer, L., van Raay, B. *et al.* (2002). Priorities and satisfaction on the help needed and provided in a first episode of psychosis. A survey in five European Family Associations. *European Psychiatry*, 17, 425–433.

Department of Health (DH) (1983). *Mental Health Act*. London: HMSO.

Department of Health (DH) (1990). *The Care Programme Approach*. London: Department of Health, HMSO.

Department of Health (DH) (2004). *The Ten Essential Shared Capabilities – A Framework for the Whole of the Mental Health Workforce*. London: HMSO.

Shannon, M., Burnett, P., & Gleeson, J., (1997) *Working with Families in Early Psychosis*. Victoria: EPPIC Statewide Services.

Falloon, I. (1985). *Family Management of Schizophrenia*. Baltimore: Johns Hopkins University Press.

Ferriter, M. & Huband, N. (2003). Experiences of parents with a son or daughter suffering from schizophrenia. *Journal of Psychiatric and Mental Health Nursing*, 10, 552–560.

Fortune, D.G., Smith, J.V. & Garvey, K. (2005). Perceptions of psychosis, coping, appraisals, and psychological distress in the relatives of patients with schizophrenia: An exploration using self-regulation theory. *British Journal of Clinical Psychology*, 44, 319–331.

Goldberg, D.P. & Hillier, V.F. (1979). A scaled version of the General Health Questionnaire. *Psychological Medicine*, 9, 139–145.

Heikkila, J., Kartsson, H. & Taiminen, T. (2002). Expressed emotion is not associated with disorder severity in first episode mental disorder. *Psychiatry Research*, 111, 155–165.

Magliano, L., Marasco, C., Fiorillo, A., Malangone, C., Guarneri, M. & Maj, M. (2002). The impact of professional and social network support on the burden of families of patients with schizophrenia in Italy. *Acta Psychiatrica Scandinavica*, 106, 291–298.

Muhlbauer, S. (2002). Navigating the storm of mental illness: Phases in the family's journey. *Qualitative Health Research*, 12 (8), 1076–1092.

Östman, M. & Kjellin, L. (2002). Stigma by association, psychological factors in relatives of people with mental illness. *British Journal of Psychiatry*, 181, 494–498.

Patterson, P., Birchwood, M. & Cochrane, R. (2000). Preventing the entrenchment of high expressed emotion in first episode psychosis: Early developmental attachments pathways. *Australian and New Zealand Journal of Psychiatry*, 34, S191–S197.

Raune, D., Kuipers, E. & Bebbington, P. (2004). Expressed emotion at first episode psychosis: Investigating a carer appraisal model. *British Journal of Psychiatry*, 184, 321–326.

Rose, L., Mallinson, R. & Walton-Ross, B. (2002). A grounded theory of families responding to mental illness. *Western Journal of Nursing Research*, 24 (5), 516–536.

Reed, M. & Davis, E. (2007). Carers psycho education groups for a first episode of psychosis. *Meriden Programme Newsletter*, 3 (1), 6–8.

Royal College of Psychiatrists (2004). *Carers and confidentiality in mental health – Issues involving information sharing*. Booklet produced as part of Partners in Care Campaign available from www.partnersincare.co.uk accessed 28.2.07.

Shannon, M., Burnett, P., & Gleeson, J. (1997). *Working with families in Early Psychosis*. Victoria: EPPIC Statewide Services.

Szmukler, G.T., Burgess, P., Herman, H., Benson, A. & Colusa, S. (1996). Caring for relatives with serious mental illness: The development of the 'Experience of Caregiving Inventory'. *Social Psychiatry and Psychiatric Epidemiology*, 31 (3–4), 137–148.

Tennakoon, L., Fannon, D., Doku, V. *et al.* (2000). Experience of caregiving: Relatives of people experiencing a first episode of psychosis. *British Journal of Psychiatry*, 177, 529–533.

Chapter 27 **Roles of different professionals**

Iain Wright

Introduction

Arguably, despite a considerable effort to develop community-focused mental health care provision, Community Mental Health Teams have remained remote and insular from other community agencies. The development of new approaches to working towards recovery with individuals with first-episode psychosis (FEP) has demanded a shift in attitude, requiring a move out of the comfort zone to the outside world – the community.

Such recovery practice requires Early Intervention in Psychosis (EIP) practitioners to modify and develop new relationships with a wide range of individuals, professionals and agencies within the community if they are to reach, and meet the needs of individuals with FEP. Arguably, EIP teams require a more collaborative therapeutic relationship than other emerging specialist teams owing to the complex range of interventions and services that EIP requires. In turn, this requires recognition of the distinct roles that key disciplines will play in service provision.

The National Service Framework (NSF) Policy Implementation Guide describes the professionals and skills required to support an individual with FEP in their recovery. Rather than explore the role of each individual EIP professional or interfacing agency and its professionals, it may be more resourceful to examine the current drivers and influences for EIP services, and strategies which can be used to develop productive partnerships. This chapter will aim to discuss some of the challenges of engaging with a wide range of different professionals, exploring how their unique contributions can be valued and maximised.

The situations discussed relate to the author's experiences whilst coordinating the development of a new EIP service.

Summary of the evidence

People with long-term difficulties only show improvements in clinical state or social functioning when they have access to the relevant therapeutic input and practical assistance (Brooker et al., 1994; Ford et al., 1995). Teams must either deliver relevant interventions themselves or have access to them.

(Brooker & Repper, 2001, p. 76)

What does the NSF policy guidance has to say about EIP service aims?

The NSF Policy Implementation Guide (DH, 2001) provides the blueprint when making business case decisions about the range of skills and disciplines required. It is worth reminding ourselves of the key aims of EIP when considering the skills and blend of team members needed to provide an evidence-based approach.

- Reduce the stigma associated with psychosis and improve professional and lay awareness of the symptoms of psychosis and the need for early assessment.
- Reduce the length of time young people remain undiagnosed and untreated.
- Develop meaningful engagement, provide evidence-based interventions and promote recovery during the early phase of illness.
- Increase stability in the lives of service users, facilitate development and provide opportunities for personal fulfilment.
- Provide a user-centred service, that is a seamless service available for those from age 14 to 35 that effectively integrates child, adolescent and adult mental health services, youth and other services (DH, 2001).

These aims require an EIP service to deliver a wide range of functions both at the level of the individual with FEP and at the level of the community in which he/she lives. Sometimes overlooked, consideration of the community in which the team operates is a distinctive feature of a PIG-compliant provision. Williams *et al.* (1994) reinforce the importance of a good understanding about the community when describing how diversity amongst team members should reflect the demographic characteristics of the locality, and also that attitudes and personal abilities are also important. By achieving an appropriate diversity of background and culture, the team will be better able to meet a diverse range of needs, and thereby become enabled to deliver real choice for service users.

'Team working' — what helps and what hinders?

West's (2002) study involved 400 care teams and 200 team members and sought to explore the key aspects of teams. The methodology included quantitative and qualitative study of team working and outcomes using a variety of approaches. West showed that the quality of team working was directly related to the effectiveness of the team.

Positive qualities of team working . . .
- Having clear objectives
- High levels of participation
- Commitment to quality
- Support for innovation
- Reflective practice

. . . Lead to teams that work better together:
- More effectively
- More innovatively
- With lower staff turnover
- With team members who experience better mental health

Teams with high levels of effectiveness and innovation achieve this through communication, integration and regular meetings. Furthermore, teams with greater diversity of occupational groups are associated with higher levels of innovation. West concluded that health care teams which enjoyed strong team working could demonstrate higher quality and innovation of the service and greater well-being of team members.

Of equal importance, West viewed effective leadership as essential if teams were to function at their optimum level. Conversely, unclear leadership or where situations of conflict arose over leadership could result in less effective team working:

- Less participation
- Less commitment to quality
- Lower support for innovation
- Poorer team mental health
- Lower levels of effectiveness and innovation

The specialist team model is broadly based upon that of the Community Mental Health Team (CMHT) and case management (Onyett, 1998), with clear roles and responsibility regarding care coordination. In a well-funded and appropriately staffed EIP service, the ability to have rapid and flexible access to a range of disciplines and experience (both clinical and life) all sharing a common aim and philosophy relating to EIP is paramount. However, whilst such a range of professions and skills is vital, the relationships, attitudes and interpersonal skills are also relevant to the success of the team (Brooker and Repper, 2001). Successful teams are able to combine these characteristics within an egalitarian approach to team working, so that the relationships between team members mirror the relationship with the service user. Such an approach enables practitioners to:

- Convey an optimistic attitude towards recovery.
- Respect an individual with FEP and their family, and develop a collaborative approach to the therapeutic relationship.
- Work within a service user-led philosophy of care.
- Demonstrate a flexible and innovative approach to 'helping'.
- Integrate and explore local community groups and agencies to help ensure that identified needs are met using a wide range of services.

- Embrace an egalitarian approach to service organisation that reflects the relationship with individuals with FEP.
- Develop the EIP service in such a way that it reflects the needs and priorities of service users.

How do teams embrace recovery practice?

Team members should be encouraged to discuss their interests and beliefs to generate a strategic approach to gaining greater understanding of local communities and issues. Onyett (1998) has developed the useful concept of 'linking', to describe a collaborative approach to identifying resources which promote a positive outcome for the individual with FEP. Onyett sets out guidelines for actively linking with other agencies and resources to meet identified needs. Some of these guidelines can be used to assist the EIP team and practitioners to develop links with other agencies.

Keep the aims of linkage in sight – A client may be receiving help from a variety of agencies, both statutory and 'third sector'. This requires agencies to work in a way that aligns efforts to identify and achieve shared objectives whilst at the same time avoiding unnecessary duplication of effort. The potential synergy of such working relationships can provide enormous 'added value' to clients and increased job satisfaction to practitioners. For example, EIP services are working with Community Drama students at the Liverpool Institute for Performing Arts to develop mental health promotion activities for local schools, thereby meeting the needs of the EIP service and the college.

Establish contacts – The EIP service should invest time to properly explore and understand the geographical area they cover, identifying potential allies and opportunities. Informal networking and introductions are valuable ways to explore and discover new liaisons and partnerships. Potential partner agencies will require a clear understanding of their respective remit and responsibility if they are to develop meaningful collaborative relationships. Time invested in understanding the objectives and drivers of different agencies, that is 'where they are coming from', can avoid misunderstandings. For example, different agencies may respond differently to risk and boundaries of confidentiality, requiring each agency to have a mutual understanding and respect for each other when these situations arise. As partnerships strengthen, practitioners can successfully navigate these complex issues whilst still working within their respective organisational constraints.

Be personal – Make a concerted effort to navigate the bureaucratic rapids and identify pools of individuals who can bring about a solution, and get things done. It may seem obvious, but picking up the phone and speaking to others whom you have met and are on first-name terms will pay dividends.

Be consistent – It may be appropriate to use role play to develop a common language or script, to ensure that the whole EIP service will be reading from the same chart to convey a consistent message when describing the team's role, aim, philosophy and objectives. This will also encourage growing confidence when approaching other agencies and professionals.

Use the team – Onyett also reminds us that a great source of expertise and experience lies within your own team. New ways of working might formalise this concept, but to be effective this requires a supporting and trusting climate within the team. No matter how experienced an individual is, there is always more to learn. Be helpful and enthusiastic in sharing your own knowledge, and do not be afraid to seek the advice of others. This will work with other agencies too, and in doing so will enhance the pool of knowledge and experience available to each.

Implementation into practice

(The teams and professions described are not an exhaustive list, and the author apologises if particular disciplines are not included.)

The way in which our service has developed is fairly typical of other EIP services; the background of frequent organisational change within the NHS; competition for finite resources with other services; competition for the recruitment of suitably qualified and experienced staff; the achievement of targets and concurrently providing a safe, efficient and quality service.

Working collaboratively with a range of agencies and disciplines requires a sound appreciation and awareness of the roles, aims and priorities of your colleagues. This lets you understand, anticipate and overcome possible obstacles to developing collaborative approaches. The difficulties experienced and the model of team working utilised, combined with individual personalities and professional beliefs and approaches, will directly influence the solutions required. Keep in mind when developing partnerships that the destination is the same even if individual agencies and disciplines need to take different routes to reach it. And key to achieving that sense of *shared destination* is the cultivation of respect between agencies. Being respectful of what each person brings, an individual's knowledge and experience and their contribution to a *shared destination*, must be an underpinning principle of Early Intervention (EI) practice, whether that is working with a service user, another team member or another agency.

New Ways of Working

The introduction of New Ways of Working (NWW) has brought about a critical shift – it involves rethinking values, ways of working and roles to deliver person-centred care. EIP is an example of a relatively new mental health service provision and presents a good opportunity to re-evaluate and reconsider how services are organised and provided. Indeed, NWW, in many ways, reflects how EIP services have gone about developing new, enhanced and changed roles for mental health staff, for example Support, Time and Recovery Workers, Graduate Mental health Workers, Non-Medical Prescribing, physical health assessment and psychological therapies. Consultants see people according to need rather than as routine, work with a smaller number of complex cases and provide advice and consultancy to support team members.

One of the issues arising from the implementation of the NSF (DH, 1999) is that the development of specialist teams with a specific remit and skills mix may have been at the expense of an overall team approach. A minority of Trusts currently provide a so-called 'Functional Model' employing a Specialist Inpatient Consultant Psychiatrist, or consultant psychiatrist who works across the acute care pathway in crisis and inpatient services. For NWW to be successful, the leadership of each service will be paramount in developing a climate of cooperation to maintain continuity of care for the individual with FEP. Local discussion and agreement should clarify who takes responsibility through the care pathway across the interface between EIP, CRHT and inpatient services where the individual's needs are placed at the centre of the approach, so that care is needs-led and not service-led. Whatever is agreed should reflect the importance of continuity of care.

Change can evoke concern. There may be perceived 'risks', such as changing roles, surrendering roles and tasks, and devolved roles, for example non-medical prescribing, clinical leadership, responsible clinician and training requirements. This should be recognised and supported whilst concurrently refocusing upon valuing person-centred care – sharing tasks/work, demonstrating flexibility whilst having a clear understanding of, and value for the individual professional contribution. Each team member will react differently to changes in responsibility and authority, some 'jumping ship', and others 'bracing the mainsail'. Professionals should focus upon their strengths, and develop new skills and capabilities to enhance the range of interventions available within their team. Good leadership is crucial to ensuring that individuals are skilled and capable of the tasks required of them, and appropriate supervision and support is in place. A truly multidisciplinary team lets each member play to their strengths in an atmosphere in which skills and knowledge are shared across the team. Joint working between professionals, according to the needs of the individual, for instance flexible to time and place of being seen, will enhance the experience of the service and help provide positive engagement.

To support the implementation and development of NWW, the National Mental Health Workforce Programme (NIMHE: DH, 2007) has developed the Creating Capable Teams Approach (CCTA), an 'off-the-shelf' product that can be delivered by an experienced facilitator. It is a five-step approach with a *defined workforce focus*, which requires the support of an identified senior sponsor, the team leader and the Senior Management Team.

The aims of the CCTA are to:

- Support the integration of NWW and New Roles into the structures and practices of a multidisciplinary team, within existing resources.
- Support teams to review their services on the basis of the skills and capabilities required to meet service user and carer needs and enable them to utilise the opportunities and flexibilities that New Ways of Working and New Roles offer.
- Allow teams the opportunity to be proactive and directly involved in reviewing their workforce, and plan more creatively for the future that is 'a bottom up approach'.
- Produce a team profile and workforce plan, which will feed into the organisation's workforce planning process.

Traditionally, these are the disciplines associated with community mental health teams. The successful integration and closer collaborative style required by EIP services means that an approach is required which can meet the client's needs responsively, flexibly and appropriately. Initial assessments are conducted jointly, and this requires a willingness to share and support colleagues through the assessment process. To enhance engagement, the venue for therapeutic sessions has to be negotiable with the client, and requires team members to be flexible and willing to utilise alternative meeting places. Traditional methods of organising your working day may be challenged; for example, questioning the utility of the traditional clinic appointment, being

responsive and available for assessments and reviews.

Criminal justice liaison team

In our Trust, we are honoured to work alongside a beacon Criminal Justice Liaison Team (CJLT). This is a criminal justice–based mental health liaison service which addresses the needs of mentally disordered offenders at points of criminal justice system. The team is regularly involved in the assessment and management of risk, working with partner agencies, for example Police and Probation. The CJLT not only works within Adult Mental Health Directorate, but across the Trust acting as a central point of contact for any Trust service user anywhere in the criminal justice system. We have been able to learn valuable lessons from the CJLT. Indeed, there are similarities between CJLT and EIP:

- Developed from small beginnings;
- Required to forge relationships with agencies other than within the health system;
- Act as ambassadors for mental health and the Trust;
- High profile;
- High expectations.

The CJLT has provided the EIP service with a chart to map our journey. They too have had to navigate uncharted waters previously unexplored by mental health services, and overcome problems associated with different professional backgrounds, vocabularies and training. Combined with this were common misconceptions around mental health services and the individuals using the services. The journey of the CJLT began in similar circumstances to our own service. The local commissioners identified a need, and funded a lead professional, Marian Bullivant RMN, to develop the role. For Marian to make the required inroads to the police stations, magistrate courts and Bridewells in Liverpool was initially intimidating and frustrating, as at the time these places were largely a male domain, with little understanding, time or patience for the mental well-being of others. However, Marian rose to the challenge with great determination, a sense of humour, and the energy and drive to develop professional relationships within the criminal justice system. Things began to change. Referrals gradually became more frequent as awareness grew regarding the mental health and well-being of those who had been arrested and were going through the court process. Individuals with mental health problems could expect to be treated appropriately, whether that meant diverting them away from the criminal justice system to mental health services, or ensuring that they were supported through the criminal justice process.

As time has progressed, a sense of mutual respect and professional recognition has enabled the CJLT to attract further investment in additional services and roles which benefit clients:

- Provide advice to mental health teams about the criminal justice system and process, and act as a conduit of information and advice from the police.
- Develop the police post of Mental Health Police Liaison Officer; this especially has acknowledged the need and demonstrated the willingness of the criminal justice system to develop links with mental health services.
- Support mental health service users going through the criminal justice system, providing advice and support about what to expect, what to do, how to address the magistrate etc.
- Support the criminal justice system by chasing up court reports, and answering the queries of its Judges.
- Involvement in a rolling training programme for Police cadets.
- Coordination of Multi Agency Public Protection Arrangements (MAPPA) and HRAM meetings.

Marian and the CJLT show just what can be achieved in terms of *getting a foot in the door* of other services with whom mental health services may not have traditionally had a relationship. They show how important it is to take the necessary time and effort to develop a real understanding of the roles and responsibilities for

services and professions with which we must develop links. Each organisation will have basic tenets, some of which will be universal, and others that unique to itself:

Universal aspects:
1. Risk management
2. Health and safety
3. Confidentiality
4. Statutory responsibilities

Unique aspects:
- Age range
- Geographical coverage
- Roles
- Responsibility
- Response times
- Hierarchy
- Organisational structure
- Policies and procedures
- Function and form

By understanding and appreciating each other's roles, their differences and similarities can be explored and identified, and a complementary wider team approach developed:

- **Language:** Politically correct, formal, informal
- **Vocabulary:** Use of technical terms, jargon
- **Attitude:** Helpful, inquisitive, challenging, inclusive
- **Response:** Emergency, timely, unhurried
- **Attire:** Formal, uniform, casual
- **Philosophy:** Recovery, support, law and order, justice, education
- **Purpose:** Help, prevent, promote, nurture

Education

Schools and educational establishments have been notoriously difficult for EIP services to access (French & Morrison, 2004). Direct approaches to educational establishments can be hit and miss, with success largely depending upon the individuals involved being committed to collaboration and enabling access to the school. I have experienced successful joint working with school nurses as an effective way of working with schools.

Experience has shown that, as with the CJLT, understanding and aligning the aims and targets of specific agencies are the key to agencies working well together. Overcoming the stigma surrounding mental health often lies at the heart of what needs to be tackled if we are to create new and successful relationships with agencies outside mental health. By presenting your ideas in a way that addresses what is important for that particular organisation can form the basis for shared actions, which will create win–wins for both organisations.

The Academic Registrars Council chaired by Peter Saunders (Liverpool John Moores University) has led the development of a special approach in Higher Education relating to the mental well-being of students (Academic Registrars Council [ARC] Conference Liverpool, Unpublished proceedings). Significantly within the Student Support Service at John Moores University, a mental health practitioner post has been established to enhance, and accelerate, the access of students to appropriate mental health care. This link between John Moores University and the Adult Mental Health Services has generated a shared understanding of each organisation's systemic and functional peculiarities, and facilitated smoother and more successful navigation of mental health services.

The importance of student mental health and well-being is now recognised by Educational Services. Colleges and Universities acknowledge the value of enhancing support and developing links with mental health services, in terms of improved educational outcomes such as course completion, student satisfaction and academic results. EIP Teams are well placed to develop an effective interface with Higher Education, by which each organisation can gain. For individuals with FEP in higher education, this can mean having improved outcomes because of rapid access to EIP services.

By way of example, my own EIP service has recently formed a collaboration with the internationally recognised Liverpool Institute of Performing Arts (LIPA). The partnership is robust and looking to a number of positive outcomes with shared benefits:

- An additional student support resource for LIPA, not only to help individuals with FEP, but also to help signpost other individuals to appropriate services and organisations.
- LIPA and the EIP service working together to develop innovative approaches to mental health promotion through the creation of music and drama productions that benefit the student's knowledge and skills in relation to both their learning and development and their own mental health.
- Touring these productions out to schools and colleges, thus fulfilling the requirements of LIPA to offer community involvement, whilst at the same time enabling EIP services to access these settings to promote awareness about psychosis.

Conclusion

Remember the common goal – recovery and optimum quality of life
Achieving this goal, as a natural extension of the recovery principle, requires EIP services to collaborate with other agencies, education, police, probation, Youth Offending Teams, Job Centre Plus, Housing services, leisure services etc. Service users are experts about themselves; these agencies are experts about themselves. Acknowledge this, allow each to play to their respective strengths and develop the sense of a wider collaborative team built around the service user. Fundamentally, it is the nurturing and growth of healthy human relationships which will make this come about.

Communicate
Listen
Understand

Develop professional skills and techniques in approaches which enable you to be an ambassador for your EIP service, enhancing the reputation of the service
We all have an essential part to play in improving the chance of achieving an ordinary life for individuals with FEP. All those who encounter individuals within the specified age range, either within mental health services or without, potentially influence the outcome for

those individuals. Find new exciting and innovative ways to work together to improve the experience, and outcomes, for all concerned.

Services should aim to offer an approach to care that we ourselves would choose to receive. There are some simple tests of any service. Put yourself in the shoes of the service user and ask:

- Is this a service that I would choose for myself or a member of my family?
- Is it putting me at the centre of its service ethos?
- Is it helping me on my journey to recovery?
- Is it working collaboratively with other agencies who are helping me recover?

To realise fully a truly recovery-oriented, collaborative and user needs–led modus operandi, we must do unto ourselves as we would do to others. These tests can be translated into a value base reflected in the qualities, ideologies, philosophy and vocabulary of those providing the service and valued by those receiving that service. By doing so, a greater sense of honesty and genuineness will be demonstrated, with enhanced outcomes for both the service user and the service practitioners in terms of engagement, satisfaction and recovery.

Identify the attributes and attitudes that EIP services have in common with other agencies

- Acknowledge the priorities for other agencies and services.
- Relationships between EIP services and other agencies can come about in the most unexpected of circumstances.
- There is often a shared willingness to develop unique and innovative solutions to supporting students and young people.
- Agencies that support students and young people are ideally placed to offer resources, activities, advice and information to aid in the recovery of individuals with FEP.

Suggested further reading

Department of Health (DH) (2007). Mental health: New ways of working for everyone. Developing and sustaining a capable and flexible workforce.

Department of Health (DH) (2007). Creating capable teams approach (CCTA) best practice guidance to support the implementation of new ways of working (NWW) and new roles.

Useful websites

http://www.nimhe.csip.org.uk/our-work/workforce.html

www.skillsforhealth.org.uk/careerframework/graph.php

www.newwaysofworking.org.uk

References

Brooker, C. & Repper, J. (eds) (2001). *Serious Mental Health Problems in the Community: Policy, Practice & Research*. London: Baillière Tindall.

Brooker, C., Falloon, I., Butterworth, A., Goldberg, D., Graham-Hole, V. & Hillier, V. (1994). The outcome of training community psychiatric nurses to deliver psychosocial intervention. *British Journal of Psychiatry*, 165, 222–230.

Department of Health (DH) (1999). National service framework for mental health: modern standards and service models. London: Department of Health.

Department of Health (DH) (2001). *The Policy Implementation Guide on Mental Health*. London: Department of Health.

Department of Health (DH) (2007). *New Ways of Working for Everyone – A Best Practice Implementation Guide National Mental Health Workforce Programme*. London: Department of Health.

Ford, R., Beadsmoore, A., Ryan, P., Repper, J., Craig, T. & Muijen, M. (1995). Providing the safety net: Case management for people with serious mental illness. *Journal of Mental Health*, 1, 91–97.

French, P. & Morrison, A.P. (2004). *Early Detection and Cognitive Therapy for People at High Risk of Psychosis: A Treatment Approach*. Chichester: John Wiley & Sons.

Onyett, S. (1998). *Case Management in Mental Health*. Cheltenham: Stanley Thornes (Publishers) Ltd.

West, M. (2002) Health Care Team Effectiveness Project. *The Research Findings Register*. Summary number 847. Retrieved 19 February 2007, from http://www.ReFeR.nhs.uk/viewrecord.asp?id= 847.

Williams, M.L., Forster, P., McCarthy, G.D. & Hargreaves, W.A. (1994). Managing Case Management: What makes it work? *Psychosocial Rehabilitation Journal*, 18, 49–60.

Chapter 28 Shared capabilities in mental health practice

Gina Smith and Sarah J Boldison

Introduction

In the early days of the creation of the Early Psychosis Declaration (EPD) (Bertolote and McGorry, 2005), discussions amongst the working group in Newcastle (of which Gina was a member) kept returning to the purpose of the declaration and the desire that it achieve real change. It was agreed that an important feature of the EPD was that it should inform consumers, both service users and carers, of what to expect from an effective mental health service. Indeed, it was a declared strategic objective that the EPD should raise the expectations of consumers as a sensible and legitimate way to drive change. In this respect (and in many others), we feel the EPD is also extremely useful in helping service providers define what their service should achieve, thereby making it easier for practitioners to examine how they perform against some desired outcomes.

We want to draw parallels between the EPD and the 10 Essential Shared Capabilities (ESC) (DH, 2004b) as two influential frameworks for thinking about how we improve services for young people with emerging psychosis and their families. Just as the EPD provides a framework for good mental health services for those coping with first-episode psychosis, the ESC provides a framework for practitioners, defining the skills and knowledge required to enable them to be as effective as possible. In this chapter, we will describe how the ESC evolved and provide some examples of their broad utility, whilst recognising that we are still in the early stages of creating a truly modern and innovative mental health workforce, capable of whole systems thinking in action.

As yet, it appears that training courses focusing on first-episode psychosis are scarce and arguably such bespoke training may even be undesirable. We hope to demonstrate through this chapter that it is unnecessary for workers delivering early interventions for psychosis to attend training courses designed only around first-episode psychosis, and that they may be better served by a more generic programme. Nonetheless, as in our programme at the University of Bath, individualised learning objectives are important, to ensure that any course attends to each student's particular requirements, to equip and develop him or her to fulfil their role in practice.

Brief summary of the evidence

For several decades, there has been a growing shift from hospital to community-based services for people experiencing severe mental health difficulties, with an emphasis on home treatment wherever possible. This has required mental health practitioners to work more closely with families (Mohr *et al.*, 2000) as well as with a range of agencies including housing, social services, employment services, the voluntary sector and primary care. Nowhere is this more necessary than in services designed to support young people with psychosis and their friends, families and networks.

A wealth of research evidence informs our understanding of the common skills needed by mental health practitioners to enable them to provide effective care and treatment. Much of this was reviewed in *Pulling Together* (SCMH, 1997). However, because it predated the publication of the National Service Framework

for Mental Health (NSF) (DH, 1999), this publication suffers from a lack of context and is
without a description of a comprehensive, evidence-based service (including effective EI)
that the NSF has since made explicit. With this
in mind, the Capable Practitioner project was
commissioned (SCMH, 2001) to *identify a broad
unifying framework which encompasses the set of
skills, knowledge and attitudes required within the
workforce of mental health practitioners to effectively
implement the NSF* (p. 4). However, this analysis
of capabilities is itself limited to include only
those working within Adult Mental Health
Services, due to the project's finite resources.
Nonetheless, the resulting list of capabilities is
of relevance to practitioners working with Older
People as well as Child and Adolescent Mental
Health Services.

The Capable Practitioner framework (SCMH,
2001) pioneered the recognition that workers
in the field of mental health needed more than
a set of predetermined competencies, but that
they also required a framework of values and
attitudes, plus sufficient knowledge to enable
them to apply the competencies within increasingly complex service settings. Consequently,
the term *capability*, which embraces these
additional dimensions, has tended to displace
the term *competence* (Table 28.1).

The influence of the Capable Practitioner
project findings (SCMH, 2001) is very apparent within the subsequent, more workable ESC
framework (DH, 2004b), as seen in the 10 capabilities listed below:

1. Working in partnership
2. Respecting diversity
3. Practising ethically
4. Challenging inequality
5. Promoting recovery
6. Identifying people's needs and strengths
7. Providing service user–centred care
8. Making a difference
9. Promoting safety and positive risk taking
10. Personal development and learning

These have provided a potential framework
for the whole mental health workforce. We recognise that to intervene early in cases of psychosis,
this workforce comprises not just mental health
workers per se, but anyone who may come into
contact with young people experiencing, or
at risk of, or recovering from a first episode of
psychosis. The ESC (DH, 2004b) is designed to
apply equally to those from a professional background such as nursing and social work, as well
as to those without a professional psychiatric
accreditation. Thus, they can apply to relevant
workers in youth services, housing and education who have an interest in mental health.

Implementation into practice

Which term, practitioner or clinician? Throughout this chapter, the term *practitioner* is
favoured to that of *clinician*, to acknowledge
that mental health workers practice within a
broad range of settings and offer a wide range
of interventions. We feel the word clinician is
too rooted in health and may exclude essential
contributions from social care, the voluntary
and community sector, education, or indeed
the legal system. Furthermore, we use the word
practice to describe both the interventions and
the context in which these interventions take
place. This aligns with much of the literature on
whole systems working and the thinking that

Table 28.1 Capability

The term capability includes:
• A commitment to ongoing personal and professional development;
• A means to identify workers' skills and values;
• An emphasis on reflective practice;
• A means to implement effective evidence-based practice;
• An ethical component that embraces cultural values and social awareness within professional practice.

underpins current policy on mental health practice (Hudson, 2006), as well as linking with the social capital (McKenzie & Harpman, 2006) and lifelong learning (DH, 2001a) agendas.

What triggered the development of the ESC? Whilst there is undoubtedly a shift in the culture of mental health care delivery towards offering choices to people who use services and their families, many continue to report *not being heard, being marginal to assessment and care planning, and being rendered helpless rather than helped by service use* (DH, 2004b, p. 1). This, alongside tragedies such as those reported in the Bennett Inquiry (Norfolk, Suffolk and Cambridgeshire Strategic Health Authority, 2003), led the UK government to provide a list of the capabilities, the ESC, required by the whole mental health workforce to ensure the delivery of the NSF (DH, 1999) and the NHS Plan (DH, 2000). Indeed, it is intended that these ESCs should form the basis for all mental health worker training for professional and non-professionally affiliated staff, both pre- and post-qualification, as well as being included in induction programmes and any ongoing staff development.

What was the process for creating the ESC? The ESC evolved through a project coordinated by the Sainsbury Centre for Mental Health (SCMH) and the National Institute for Mental Health in England (NIMHE), led by a national steering group chaired by Roslyn Hope, Director of the NIMHE National Workforce Programme. The process involved consultation with carers, service users, practitioners, managers and academics, plus a number of focus groups in order to seek further opinions and feedback.

The Ten Essential Capabilities that emerged from a rigorous development process undertaken by the National Institute for Mental Health in England and the Sainsbury Centre for Mental Health can best be described as:
The basic principles that underpin positive practice.

So what? As with all new initiatives, there were some academic programme designers (ourselves included) who enthusiastically embraced the ESC, whereas others (possibly those with a longer history than us of delivering university programmes) saw it as just another passing phase. At any strategic workforce development meetings, we would opportunely emphasise our strong support for the framework. Gratifyingly, it appears our support would seem well placed as the ESC becomes increasingly acknowledged as the foundation for new training initiatives (www.newwaysofworking.org.uk).

How does this apply to EI practitioners? Lisa Hill provided an important way of thinking about the qualities of a generic EI practitioner in her interpretation of the ESCs for EI practice. These are discussed in some detail in the accompanying Chapter 29, Training Clinicians in Early Intervention.

See 5.3.1, 10 Essential Capabilities Framework as applied to EI Practitioners.

The quality of mental health training courses can be assessed using the National Continuous Quality Improvement Tool for Mental Health Education (Brooker & Curran, 2005). This is a particularly useful tool as it may be used to evaluate a range of programmes 'varying in length from one-day induction training to four-year undergraduate/postgraduate degrees' (p. 4). Whilst it is unlikely to be possible for practitioners to assess courses personally in such a rigorous way, everyone is entitled to enquire of those delivering training how its quality is assured.

How did our training programme make practical use of the ESC? Our Postgraduate Mental Health Practice programme at the University of Bath was designed with an equal emphasis on expanding knowledge to inform practice, and the development and implementation of practice skills. Students are therefore req-uired to identify a mentor in their workplace who works with us to monitor and evaluate the student's skills. Within our university role, we spend time with these mentors, ensuring they understand our programme and its values, which includes explaining how all our modules are underpinned by the ESC framework (DH, 2004b). We were surprised how rarely these experienced mental health practitioners had prior knowledge of this document, and yet it was always widely appreciated whenever we did discuss it. This suggests the Government dissemination strategy for such valuable resources as the ESC needs to be reconsidered, to ensure they reach busy practitioners not formally engaged in an education programme. That may change as the framework for ongoing professional and personal development is brought in by the NHS Agenda for Change pay structure (http://www.nhsemployers.org/pay-conditions/agenda-for-change.cfm). Accompanied by good use of appraisal processes, staff will be prompted to maintain an up to date awareness of new deve-lopments such as ESC. For those employing workers not bound by Agenda for Change (DH, -003), it may be useful to consider other strategies and incentives that encourage lifelong learning. This may be through formal qualifications or evidence gathered and displayed through practice portfolios, in keeping with the broad policy push across all organisations to build and implement National Occupational Standards (NOS) (www.ssda.org.uk).

Although there is much to be praised within the Capable Practitioner report (SCMH, 2001), we found its list of capabilities (67 in total) too long to be really helpful, either to us in the classroom or to workers in practice. Neither was it obviously applicable to practitioners such as youth workers, who would not necessarily recognise themselves as central to mental service provision. Thus, we were delighted by the timely publication of the ESC (DH, 2004b), coinciding as it did with the latter stages of our curriculum development.

Broader government guidance that informed our programme development and our links with mentors and managers in practice came from the National Mental Health Workforce Strategy (NIMHE, 2004), which is illustrated in Table 28.2.

This guidance recognises that *staff are the means of delivering effective services and need to be valued and supported in doing so* (p. 2). We assert that training embracing the ESC will enable staff to define their values, knowledge and skills in a way that will create such supportive work environments. This is particularly pertinent to EI for Psychosis services, where the compelling evidence for potential effectiveness can only be realised if practitioners are not overwhelmed and feel in control of their workload made up of people who may be very unwell. Other parts of secondary mental health services, particularly generic community teams, may also be struggling to cope with the impact of service redesign decreed, as they perceive it, by the NSF (DH, 1999) and NHS Plan (DH, 2000). In such cases, addressing the structure and skills of the workforce through collaborative partnerships can be a useful way to 'unstick' people's thinking and find ways to introduce new service objectives, in this instance EI, into an overloaded system.

Creating a workforce that can provide individuals with some real choices is vital if young people with psychosis are to engage willingly

Table 28.2 Aims of the National Mental Health Workforce Strategy

---

Aims of the National Mental Health Workforce Strategy (NIMHE, 2004):

1. Improve the design of the workforce to make it meaningful to local people in local services.
2. Increase the number of people in the workforce by retaining current staff and developing creative recruitment strategies to attract new people.
3. Make best use of specialist staff groups, facilitating new ways of working across professional boundaries.
4. Create new roles to complement existing roles.
5. Revise education and training programmes, increasing the focus on shared capabilities.
6. Develop change management and leadership skills in all organisations that provide mental health services.

---

with mental health services. Section 11 of the Health and Social Care Act (DH, 2001b) places a legal duty (which has become a legal requirement since January 2003) on the NHS to involve the public as well as individual service users in the planning and development of health services. The ESC, especially 'Working in Partnership', prepares practitioners to make this sometimes difficult requirement a reality, thus delivering on the government promise to provide service users and carers choice (CSIP, 2006). This is underpinned by the wider strategy *Improving the Life Chances of Disabled People* published by the Prime Minister's Strategy Unit in 2005.

Is the ESC sufficient by itself? The creation of a list of capabilities does not by itself identify the skills required to carry out the various interventions listed in the NSF (DH, 1999) and NHS Plan (DH, 2000). NOS (www.skillsfor-health.org.uk) provided us a valuable assessment of competence that allows the measure of a practitioner's fitness to carry out a particular task or skill. In practice, this approach is complemented by the framework suggested by Benner (1984) that illustrates how workers move from a novice position towards becoming an expert practitioner. We find that this model is well understood by students, mentors and managers, and encourages the use of supervision thus promoting effective, reflective and safe practice.

Nevertheless, it can be hard in practice to appreciate how all the various guidance, from a range of sources, fits together coherently to improve services to service users and their carers. Here again we were helped by the ESC document through its diagram that illustrates how the complementary frameworks fit together. With permission, we have reproduced this diagram in Figure 28.1.

Within the structure created by the ESC, an important underpinning aspiration of the course team was to work in the spirit of Appreciative Inquiry (Hammond, 1998). This theory *suggests that we look for what works in an organisation [resulting in] a series of statements that describe where an organisation wants to be, based on the high moments of where they have been* (p. 7). This supported us all to explore what was working and further build upon our own and our organisation's strengths.

Despite the ESC's many positives, it can be criticised for sometimes feeling overly prescriptive. For example, if the ESC *Making a Difference* is interpreted in isolation, then a worker may attempt to make a difference alone and end up behaving in a bossy manner. However, if *Making a Difference* is always routed through another

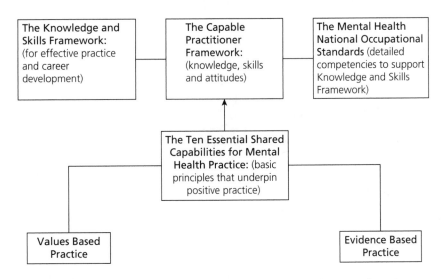

Figure 28.1 Relationship between the ESC, NOS, capable practitioner framework and KSF.

ESC *Working in Partnership*, then the outcome will always be based on a service user's and/or carer's preferences. This inspired us to find a more engaging way to encourage implementation of the ESC, rather than merely presenting the capabilities as a 'pick and mix' list.

Through discussion amongst the course development team, comprising service users, carers, academics and practitioners from a range of professional backgrounds, the notion of a tree germinated and flourished (Figure 28.2). This picture provided a catalyst for discussion and ideas that enabled us to easily demonstrate and discuss our belief that all other ESCs were rooted in 'Personal Development and Learning'.

And indeed, if 'Respecting Diversity', Practising Ethically' and 'Challenging Inequality' form the roots of the tree, 'Working in Partnership' is the trunk that supports all the rest.

Within a tree, there will be a number of creatures; each of these has a story to tell:

- In designing this course, inspired by one of our team member's experience as a beekeeper, we were influenced by the behaviour of bees. The bee collects nectar, in doing so pollinating other flowers. She takes her forage to the hive where nectar is passed around and the source of the sweetest nectar is revealed to others. The nectar is converted

Figure 28.2 Pictorial depiction of how the Essential Shared Capabilities fit into our learning and development landscape. "Tree with beehives" reproduced by permission of the University of Bath.

in her body to honey, which she ripens, and stores in cells made from wax exuded when young. This store is sealed and kept for future needs of the colony.

- Similarly, a mental health worker collects knowledge and skills, at the same time making links with other practitioners, service users and their support network. They share their knowledge and skills with others. They are constantly working to enhance their skills, incorporating reflective practice into their working lives in order to develop the highest-quality support they can offer, converting knowledge to practical wisdom for the good the greater society.
- The themes of networking, cooperation and cross-fertilisation permeate the whole of our Mental Health Practice programme.
- The earthworms denote important strategies that support any mental health workforce. Recruitment and retention policies when working well are often (like the worms) invisible, yet play a vital role in maintaining the fertile ground in which all learning and development begins, and is sustained.
- The birds illustrate a number of local and national policies that support individual practitioners. Some such as job descriptions and appraisals should be common to all, whereas the Knowledge and Skills Framework (DH, 2003) is health specific. Each of these may be either soaring high to view the wider landscape or nesting and taking care of a small number of eggs that need nurturing in order to thrive.
- The badger was placed in the picture by David Shiers – we leave it to him to share the secret!

Case studies/narrative

Rather than describe case work done with an individual or group of service users, we have chosen to discuss as *case studies* illustrations of how we collaboratively develop the knowledge and skills of our students on the Mental Health Practice programme at the University of Bath.

Our overarching programme aim has been to generate a real optimism in the students, a confidence that they could and would make a positive difference in others' lives. In the ESC (DH, 2004b), we found an ideal structure on which to build. We will now relate working examples for each of the ESC, taken from our own or our students' practice, or some classroom activity, or the more general administration of the programme, leaning towards examples we feel will be of most relevance and interest to those working with first-episode psychosis:

Personal development and learning

- Within our course philosophy, we include Mezirow's Charter of Andragogy, as this succinctly describes the model of adult learning that underpins our entire programme (www.bath.ac.uk/health/programmes/mhp).
- The use of portfolios is not new and is indeed used by a wide range of professional groups to record a person's individual development and skills acquisition. In our experience, portfolio learning has not always felt valued. We wanted to give renewed emphasis on this method of demonstrating knowledge and skills by using it as the main way to assess learning within our programme.
- We wanted to link appraisal in the workplace with an individual student's learning objectives. This proved difficult to achieve initially but now, 3 years on, such appraisal systems are commonplace and established in many mental health settings.
- Experienced mental health workers can register directly for our Postgraduate Diploma, providing they can demonstrate adequate learning from experience. Such accreditation of prior experience and learning (APEL) opportunities is not unique, but what has been unusual is the help we offer to prospective students. Through two 2-day workshops, candidates receive guidance on how to prepare and submit an Extended Practice Development Portfolio. This can then be used to show that they have acquired the necessary practice-based skills and the appropriate academic skills to join the Diploma without the requirement to complete the Postgraduate Certificate.

Challenging inequality

- Carers and service users have participated equally in classroom teaching, curriculum planning and course design, at the same rate of pay as workers from professional backgrounds.
- Recognising that university course fees were unaffordable to most voluntary organisations, we have successfully sought funding from our local Strategic Health Authority to enable students working in such organisations to attend the course at no direct cost to their employers.

Practising ethically

- We place a strong emphasis on values-based practice (Woodbridge & Fulford, 2004).
- We invited and successfully recruited Kim Woodbridge to be our external examiner, to shine a strong spotlight on ethics and values whilst significantly enhancing our learning in this area.

We repeatedly draw attention to the principles of good governance, using the Good Practice Guide in Governance in Public services (www.opm.co.uk/ICGGPS/download_upload/standard.pdf). This emphasised the value of workers' tracking the emerging evidence in their field of practice, encouraging them to disseminate this within their team, enabling the whole team to be as up to date as possible.

Respecting diversity

- Our core programme delivery team comprises a social worker, an occupational therapist and a nurse. We have also worked with a diverse range of others to design and deliver our programme.
- Students on our courses have come from a wide range of service settings. We have had students from traditional backgrounds of nursing and social work, studying alongside experienced counsellors, now working as mental health workers in primary care, members of the voluntary and community sector, as well as people who use services and those who care for them. This diversity provides an

enriching, if at times challenging, environment in which to learn and develop practice.
- There are different levels of academic and practice skills amongst our student cohorts. This has been greatly valued and encouraged a good deal of sharing and helping each other.

Working in partnership

- Information and resource sharing in the classroom, in the spirit of Appreciative Inquiry (Hammond, 1998), has been encouraged throughout the programme; this appreciative approach enables all students, even the quietest, to find their voice and bring items of interest to others.
- We have valued opportunities to work with career academics to deliver this programme, adding to the richness of learning. The core team have all held other positions, making them effectively lecturer practitioners. In spite of some of the challenges this posed, we would recommend this approach to partnership working to others setting up a similar programme.

Promoting recovery

- The promotion of recovery and hope, recognising and building on personal strengths and resiliencies of individuals remain central to our programme. We have been mindful of the language used, as this can differ across primary and secondary care and the voluntary and community sectors. Had we had students from education or youth services, this would have further informed our use of language and enriched all students' learning.
- One highlight the course team arranged was a performance of *On the Edge* staged at the University. This play was attended by those associated with the course, as well as many others from within the University, serving to further raise the profile of mental health and well-being within the University and in particular the importance of taking action early if psychosis is suspected.

Providing person-centred care

- Within our practice and our programme, we prefer the term 'person centred', to 'service user centred', as all service users are people and we are all potential users of mental health services.
- Students are introduced to the EPD (Bertolote and McGorry, 2005), encouraging them to embrace and share the optimism that this declaration fosters.

Identifying people's needs and strengths

- The University of Bath has a strategy to promote students' mental health. Any user of mental health services (including those for first-episode psychosis) as well as individuals with emerging symptoms would be well supported by services and resources identified within this strategy. Indeed, people with personal experience of mental health problems are welcomed as students by both academic and non-academic staff, thereby enhancing familiarity with mental health issues in order to support students appropriately by recognising their strengths and needs.
- Appreciative Inquiry (Hammond, 1998) fully supports a focus on strengths and learning from experiences.

Promoting safety and positive risk taking

- By teaching the skills of reflective practice in the first few days of the programme, a climate for learning from experience can be created, which then fosters a culture of positive risk taking. Students use portfolios to keep a clear record of decisions made in practice, which can be further discussed in supervision to promote the cycle of learning (Kolb, 1984).
- Sharing the emerging thinking about good and bad stress (Smith et al., 2006) promotes an understanding that we sometimes need to take risks for the sake of the potential learning. This is particularly pertinent for psychosis, where too much caution, sometimes referred to as emotional overinvol-vement (Brown et al., 1972), may hinder recovery.

Making a difference

Here we would like to share the words of our students:

> The course has been truly inspirational, both in my development as a practitioner and as a person.
> This course has changed my life. I feel more confident about my abilities – and who knows where it might take me.
> This course gets you to ask empowering questions: What can I learn from this?

Implications and conclusions

A particular appeal of the ESC for us is that they can apply equally to workers at any stage of their career (Benner, 1984). They are also as meaningful to a mental health worker in primary care as to a nurse, social worker, occupational therapist or psychiatrist in secondary care or a worker in a voluntary organisation with a role in promoting mental well-being. Thus, we are confident that the ESC will be meaningful to anyone providing early interventions for psychosis, and in whatever setting.

We are pleased to note that since adopting the ESC, the landscape surrounding our tree appears much more fertile. For example, we are seeing the 10 ESCs referred to in many of the new publications to support workforce development (www.newwaysofworking.org.uk) and in the recent documents promoting the Improving Access to Psychological Therapies programme (DH, 2007). They are also completely coherent with other service development tools such as *The Seven Effective Habits of Child and Adolescent Mental Health Services* (Kingsbury & York, 2006).

We find that the way the ESCs are applied has an impact on whether or not they are 'user-friendly'. We have therefore devised something of a hierarchy, in the form of a tree, to inform their delivery and to help make links with other initiatives. This ensures that 'Personal and Professional Development', including reflective practice, is the foundation of all we do and 'Making a Difference' is the overall aim of all our interventions.

References

Benner, P. (1984). *From Novice to Expert: Excellence and Power in Clinical Nursing Practice*. Menlo Park: Addison Wesley.

Bertolote, J. & McGorry, P. (2005). Early intervention and recovery for young people with early psychosis: Consensus statement. *British Journal of Psychiatry*, 187 (Suppl. 48), s116–s119.

Brooker, C. & Curran, J. (2005). *National Continuous Quality Improvement Tool for Mental Health Education*. Centre for Clinical and Academic Workforce Innovation: University of Lincoln.

Brown, G.W., Birley, J.L. & Wing. J.K. (1972). Influence of family life on the course of schizophrenic disorders: a replication. *British Journal of Psychiatry, 121*, 241–258.

Care Services Improvement Partnership (CSIP) (2006). *Our Choices in Mental Health – A Framework for Improving Choice for People Who Use Mental Health Services and Their Carers*. London: Department of Health Publications.

Department of Health (DH) (1999). *National Service Framework for Mental Health*. London: The Stationary Office.

Department of Health (2007). *Improving access to psychological therapies (IAPT) programme: Computerised cognitive behavioural therapy (cCBT) implementation guidance*. http://www.dh.gov.uk/en/Publication sandstatistics/PublicationsPolicyAndGuidance/ DH_073470.

DH (2000). *National Health Service Plan*. London: The Stationary Office.

DH (2001a). *Working Together Learning Together*. London: Department of Health Publications.

DH (2001b). *Health and Social Care Act*. London: Department of Health Publications.

DH (2003). *Delivering Race Equality Programme*. London: Department of Health Publications.

DH (2004a). *The Knowledge and Skills Framework*. London: Department of Health Publications.

DH (2004b). *The Ten Essential Shared Capabilities*. London: Department of Health Publications.

Hammond, S. (1998). *The Thin Book of Appreciative Inquiry* (2nd edition). Australia: The Thin Book Publishing Company.

Hudson, B. (2006). *Whole Systems Working. A Guide and Discussion Paper*. Integrated Care Network. http://www.dhcarenetworks.org.uk/_library/Resources/ ICN/ICN_Whole_Systems.pdf

Kingsbury, S. & York, A. (2006). *The 7 Helpful Habits of Effective CAMHS* (2nd edition). www.camhsnetwork.co.uk

Kolb, D.A. (1984). *Experiential Learning: Experience an the Source of Learning and Development*, New Jersey: Prentice-Hall.

McKenzie, K. & Harpman, T. (2006). Meanings and uses of social capital in the mental health field. In: K. McKenzie & T. Harpman (eds), *Social Capital and Mental Health*. London: Jessica Kingsley Publishers.

Mohr, W., Lafuze, J. & Mohr, B. (2000). Opening caregiver minds: National Alliance for the Mentally Ill's provider education program. *Archives of Psychiatric Nursing*, 14 (5), 235–243.

National Institute for Mental Health in England (NIMHE) (2004). *National Mental Health Workforce Strategy*. London: Department of Health Publications.

Norfolk, Suffolk and Cambridgeshire Strategic Health Authority (2003). *Independent Inquiry into the Death of David Bennett*.

Published by the Norfolk, Suffolk and Cambridgeshire Strategic Health Authority; Victoria House; Capital Park; Fulbourn; Cambridge; CB1 5XB Web: www .nscstha.nhs.uk.

Sainsbury Centre for Mental Health (SCMH) (1997). *Pulling Together*. London: Sainsbury Centre for Mental Health.

SCMH (2001). *The Capable Practitioner Framework*. London: Sainsbury Centre for Mental Health.

Velleman, R., Davis, E., Smith, G. & Drage, M. (2006). *Practice in Changing Outcomes In Psychosis*. Blackwell Publishing, Oxford.

Woodbridge, K. & Fulford, K.W.M. (2004). *Whose Values?* London: Sainsbury Centre for Mental Health.

Chapter 29 **Training clinicians working in early intervention**

Eric Davis, Mark Rayne, Ian Wilson, Lindsay Rigby

Introduction

The Early Psychosis Declaration (EPD, 2005) began life in Cheltenham, Gloucestershire in 2000. From this earliest stage the importance of a radically different approach to treatment and care was signalled by those service users, carers, academics and practitioners who attended.

- Was it right that a person with an emerging psychosis should be treated in the same way that someone with established condition?
- Was it helpful to ignore the traumas experienced by their families as they watched their loved ones experience the early phase?
- Did staff have the necessary attributes to respond?

As these initial ideas crystallised through first its iteration as a Newcastle declaration (NIMHE, 2002) and then ultimately as the EPD, one of the five key concerns expressed was the need to redress the inadequate training of specialist staff. And perhaps the most important challenge raised by those contributing to the EPD was whether the staff held the right attitudes which could hold up hope for these young people and their families through the very difficult early phase?

Early psychosis declaration

Guideline 4 extract relating to specialist practitioner training

- Continued Professional Development is supported for all specialist staff working with young people with psychosis
- Specific Early Intervention (EI) training programmes are resourced and evaluated

This chapter relates to the guideline of the EPD associated with the provision of practitioner learning. It is concerned with the evidence base underpinning practitioner training efforts. In addition, the process of the development and design of a training programme for EI practitioners in the form of a CD-ROM is described. Finally there is a reflection on this process and some implications for trainers are discussed in terms of pragmatic implementation.

The evidence

Brooker and Brabban (2004) evaluated a number of psychosocial intervention courses enabling staff to work with people with serious mental health problems. They examined a number of variables across a range of psychosocial intervention courses.

(i) PSI training had a generally positive effect on the attitudes and beliefs that trainees held about psychotic conditions (particularly beliefs about the cause of psychosis and improving therapeutic optimism). There were a number of difficulties examining attitude change in more detail due to the design of different studies that were reviewed. However where comparison was possible an improvement in attitude was evident.
(ii) From 13 studies reviewed only 2 failed to find a significant increase in knowledge but this was attributed to small sample sizes.
(iii) Skill acquisition: the level of expertise attained varied in a number of studies although some of the variation could be explained by different methods used to rate skill development. Gray et al. (2003) found that the strongest factors to influence skill

acquisition was the level of clinical skills in evidence pre-training, academic qualifications and attendance rates at the courses.

(iv) Behavioural change (implementation of PSI skill): practitioners developing PSI knowledge and skills commonly report barriers to implementation within the host organisation. This affects both individual psychological management and family management. Consistently reported barriers to implementation include: having a critical number of staff trained in the team
- caseload sizes too large
- insufficient backing from senior management to structurally adapt to absorption of newer training.

Furniss and Davis (2007) also report upon barriers to the implementation associated with PSI training and of how these can be overcome. Other factors that can potentially help practitioners to implement PSI skills are whole team training (Bailey *et al.*, 2003; Burbach & Stanbridge, 2006), access to appropriate supervision and organisational support.

(v) Benefits to service users and carers: six out of the seven reported studies were able to demonstrate improvement of service user symptoms. With regard to impact for carers too few studies and variation in what outcomes were measured made valid conclusions difficult to draw.

Conclusions: Brabban and Kelly (2006) comment upon training in EI. They state that too few staff in EI services for psychosis are properly trained and competent enough to deliver PSI for example Craig (2003). Fadden *et al.* (2004) suggested that practitioners working in new EI teams had often been drawn from existing community teams and traditional mental health settings and could lack the confidence and skills when working with young people with first episode psychosis.

Recommendation: From their survey Brabban and Kelly (2006) specifically recommend the development of an EI training programme (such as the CD-ROM detailed in this chapter).

It could be argued that many of the qualities demanded of EI Practitioners are subsumed within Table 29.1. Here the Ten Essential Capabilities (2004) are analysed and applied to EI training.

The capabilities described in Table 29.1 provide a link between the knowledge, skills, attitudes and clinical practice required of EI practitioners to effect positive outcomes for users and carers, and the ambition contained within the development of the EI training CD-ROM to facilitate such development, which is described below.

Development of the EI training CD-ROM

Rather than provide an illustrative clinical case history the authors of this chapter have chosen to provide a case history to demonstrate how a service need, in this case an educational programme deficiency, could be met through problem-solving and collaborative working.

The idea to create a bespoke EI training CD-ROM arose when representatives from three independent groups, all separately working to construct training resources for EI practitioners, came together at a SW hothouse in 2004. The first author (ED) in his previous capacity as EI Lead to NIMHE SW RDC convened two 'hothouses' in the SW Region with the aim of generating a working template to underpin a training programme. Service users, carers, managers, practitioners, commissioners, non-statutory staff and academics collectively identified a range of content areas for further development. Also, and in an early attempt to populate the CD with training materials, a range of academics and practitioners were approached from the International Early Psychosis Association (IEPA) conference held in Vancouver, Canada (2004) for help with practical training materials such as power point presentations and research literature. The response from the IEPA experts was overwhelmingly positive with many practitioners and academics giving freely of their time and expertise to help develop the training programme and provide practical materials.

The second author, MR had initiated training for EI practitioners in the West Midlands based on the findings of a training needs analysis.

Table 29.1   Essential capabilities and their relationship to EIP

Essential capability	Capability	Key components	Relationship to EI programme
Working in partnership	How capable are you at developing and maintain ing constructive working relationships with service users, carers, families, colleagues, members of the public and wider community networks?	This capability concerns the engagement of all those involved in receiving or providing mental health care, maintaining those relationships and bringing them to an appropriate end. This includes working positively with any tensions created by conflicts of inter-est or aspiration that may arise between the partners in care.	Includes multidisciplinary teamwork, cross boundary work and work with wider community networks. The focus with service users and their families and carers is on the development of partnership working who are viewed as partners in care rather than passive recipients of services. Service users and carers are central to this programme.
Respecting diversity	How capable are you of working in partnership with service users, carers, families and colleagues to provide care and interventions that not only make a positive difference but also does so in ways that respect and value diversity?	To respect and value diversity including age, race, culture, disability, gender, spirituality and sexuality.	This programme provides a learning environment, where existing beliefs about age, race, culture, disability, gender, spirituality and sexuality can be examined and challenged. All therapeutic interventions are set within a framework that acknowledges and respects diversity.
Practising ethically	How capable are you of recognising the rights and aspirations of service users and their families, acknowledging power differentials and minimising them whenever possible?	This includes providing treatment and care that is accountable to service users and carers within the boundaries prescribed by national (professional), legal and local codes of ethical practice.	This is reflected throughout the key aspects of the programme and is specifically addressed in medication management and substance abuse module and also includes communication and the ability to respond to the needs of people in an ethical, honest, non-judgemental manner.
Challenging inequality	How capable are you of addressing the causes and consequences of stigma, discrimination, social inequality and exclusion for service users, carers and mental health services.	This includes creating, developing or maintaining valued social roles for people in the communities they come from. It is particularly important to understand the nature and consequences of stigma and discrimination. Social inequality and exclusion have a potentially devastating effect on the recovery process and will make it difficult for service users to achieve their rightful place in society.	The programme explores this capability further and explains that to challenge inequality you will need to: Understand the effects of exclusion and discrimination. This is addressed throughout the programme.

(Continued)

Table 29.1 *(Continued)*

Essential capability	Capability	Key components	Relationship to EI programme
Promoting recovery	How capable are you of working in partnership to provide care and treatment that enables service users and carers to tackle mental health problems with hope and optimism to work towards a valued lifestyle within and beyond the limits of any mental health problem.	Recovery is about recovering what was lost: rights, roles, responsibilities, decision-making capacity, potential and mental well being. Recovery is what people experience themselves as they become empowered to achieve a meaningful life and a positive sense of belonging in the community.	Within this programme it is vital that candidates understand that recovery is a process that is unique to each person. Understand the essential role of hope in the recovery process. Accept that recovery is not about the elimination of symptoms or the notion of cure.
Identifying people's needs and strengths	How capable are you of working in partnership to gather information to agree health and social care needs in the context of the preferred lifestyle and aspirations of service users their families, carers and friends?	'The focus of this capability is on helping the service user and those involved with them to describe their experiences in such a way as to identify their strengths and formulate their needs.	This programme ensures that candidates carry out (or contri-bute to) a systematic, whole sys-tems assessment that has, as its focus, the strengths and needs of the service user and those family and friends who support them. Working in a way that acknow-ledges the personal, social, cultural and spiritual strengths and needs of the individual. Working in partnership with the individual's support network to collect information to assist an understanding of the person and their strengths and needs.
Providing service user centred care	How capable are you of negotiating achievable and meaningful goals; primarily from the perspective of service users and their families?	This also includes influencing and seeking the means to achieve these goals and clarifying the responsibilities of the people who will provide any help that is needed, including systematically evaluating outcomes and achievements.	Working alongside the service user to help them to describe their goals as precisely as possi-ble in a way that is meaningful to them. Helping the service user to iden-tify their goals and aspirations. Identifying the strengths and resources within the service user's wider network which have a role to play in supporting goal achievement.
Making a difference	How capable are you of facilitating access to and delivering the best quality, evidence-based, values-based health and social care interventions to meet the needs and aspirations of service users and their families and carers?	This capability is concerned with ensuring that people have access to interventions and services that have proven effectiveness in addressing specific needs. It is essential that people are able to use services that value them and those that support them and that will help to make a positive difference.	To begin to explore this capability further and in order to make a difference the programme enables you to: Understand the notions of evidence-based and values-based 'best practice' as enshrined in NICE guidance and Psychosocial Interventions Training, etc.

Table 29.1   *(Continued)*

Essential capability	Capability	Key components	Relationship to EI programme
Promoting safety and positive risk taking	How capable are you of helping the person to decide the level of risk they are prepared to take with their health and safety?	This includes working with the tension between promoting safety and positive risk taking, including assessing and dealing with possible risks for service users, carers, family members and the wider public. This capability focuses on the issues of risk to the individual and society and how this can best be addressed in a manner that values all those concerned.	To begin to explore this capability further and in order to practice in a way which promotes safety and positive risk taking the programme examines how you demonstrate the ability to develop harmonious working relationships with service users and carers particularly with people who may not wish to engage with mental health services.
Personal development and learning	How capable are you of keeping up-to-date with changes in practice and participating in life-long learning, personal and professional development for yourself and colleagues through supervision, appraisal and reflective practice.	This capability focuses on the need for the practitioner to take an active role in their own personal and professional development. In the same way that service users should be viewed as active partners in their care, not passive recipients, practitioners should be active participants in their own development.	This requires individual candidates on the programme to be proactive regarding their personal development and learning. Reflecting on their past learning. Assessing themselves and setting learning goals for the programme. Revisiting their learning goals, making further assessments, mapping progress and completing a development and learning plan for the future.

While there was positive initial feedback, various further unmet training needs were identified, both in terms of content and the capacity from expert practitioners and expert 'users-by-experience' to actually deliver the training. MR, in his capacity as EI Lead to NIMHE WM RDC, was able to raise these issues with EI lead colleagues from other regions.

The third working group looked to address EI training needs in the NW Region. Paul French, EI Lead to NIMHE NW RDC positively influenced planning in this Region to this end. In 2004 the third and fourth authors (IW and LR) were commissioned by Manchester Strategic Health Authority to design and produce a training programme for EI practitioners in the Region.

Through the SW hothouse in 2004 these three regions teamed up to combine efforts to produce the eventual training CD-ROM. Much of the content coordination and actual CD design was overseen by IW and LR. The final stage in the realisation of this CD-ROM as a nationally available resource was through the National EI Programme where the coordination of the sharing and development costs was achieved. The training resources were all given freely and with pride. The costs were simply those of creating the CD-ROM. This constitutes one of the most effective products of the National EI Programme, a demonstration of what could be achieved by cooperation and collaboration within a nationally coordinated and regionally delivered programme.

The CD-ROM training package was developed to fulfil two primary objectives:

1. Train EI staff in evidence-based interventions designed to help young people experiencing a first or recent episode of psychosis
2. Provide easily accessible training materials that EI team staff could use to promote

awareness of psychosis and of MH services to a wide range of potential 'stakeholders' of the service. These included families and carers, GP's, teachers, youth workers and voluntary agencies who work with young people.

IW and LR were seconded from their clinical roles for one day a week each for 6 months. Besides training materials and research literature made available from the SW and WM regions they undertook a further comprehensive literature search of relevant databases. This provided further information and materials judged suitable for including within this developing training programme.

Designing the training programme

Specific training objectives for the CD were identified:

1. Include all the main clinical components of EI and service delivery.
2. Make the training accessible to potential 'stakeholders' coming from a wide range of existing knowledge, experience and skills.
3. Make the package flexible to allow for variation in terms of available venues, time allocation and trainee numbers.
4. Produce a training package that could be delivered by trainers with varying levels of training experience.

The programme pack combines a variety of training materials and styles. Power point slide presentations are accompanied by well-developed background notes to enable trainers less familiar with the core material to familiarise themselves with some of the evidence base. Case studies include detailed guidelines for trainers alongside clear instructions for their use. The programme pack also includes a range of interactive small and large group exercises to meet the needs of 'active learners'. For each subject area a training rationale is provided with explicit aims and objectives. Trainers are encouraged to plan sessions effectively and a suggested time allocation is suggested for the delivery of each training component. For each training session trainers are provided with preparatory reference lists, reading lists as well as the materials and resources themselves.

Content of the training programme

The programme covers four key issue areas:

1. An introduction to psychosis, including models of illness and well being, signs and symptoms and a normalising rationale.
2. Engagement and assessment. This section offers some key advice to workers and carers about non-judgemental and supportive interactions with young people who may be in emotional distress.
3. An introduction to the range of possible interventions, including biopsychosocial interventions and an introduction to the concept of recovery from mental ill health.
4. 'Navigating the System', a section that provides an overview of primary and secondary mental health care provision and describes voluntary sector provision.

Each of the four areas are further subdivided into specific sections that may be presented sequentially or as stand alone sessions depending on the identified training needs.

Delivery of the finished product

The training package was initially provided in two forms: a 'hard copy' in booklet form; and an electronic version. The training programme was designed to be accessible and informative to trainers themselves so they could identify relevant session training materials with ease. The sessions were colour coded so that they dovetail with pre-existing knowledge levels, catering for 'basic' and 'advanced' knowledge. A range of learning styles were catered for by providing different session formats for example activist, theorist, reflector and pragmatist. Evaluation materials were included for each session.

Entitled 'Early Intervention in Psychosis: Training and Resource CD-ROM' endorsement was received from NIMHE, Rethink and IRIS and the resource was launched at the IEPA conference in Birmingham, UK (2006) in delegate packs. Subsequently NIMHE have also made the CD available through its national EI network with many services now in receipt of the CD-ROM, using the resource, and evaluating it positively. The initial print run was quickly exhausted, but work is planned for an updated and amended version. The material will also become accessible in e-form on the NIMHE website.

Using the training material

Authors IW and LR, in particular, have used the CD-ROM extensively since its completion. It now forms the basis for several teaching units on the University of Manchester's pre-registration nurse training units working with complex and enduring mental illness in the community, at Diploma in Professional Studies in Nursing (DPSN) and Bachelor in Nursing (BNurse) programmes.

Because of its versatility, the CD-ROM also forms the 'spine' of a programme developed to help a Family and Carers Group in Manchester living or in close contact with service users suffering from first or early onset psychosis. To date, this material has been rated as positive by families and carers seeking to enhance their understanding of, and response to, early psychosis. Using the 'basic' level of material has proven to be most appropriate. The early sessions describing normalising models of mental illness and explanations regarding the possible causes of psychosis are particularly popular, leading to interesting discussions between carers about their own experiences and personal illness models.

Future possibilities

The CD-ROM, from its initial launch in 2006, continues to be popular amongst EI teams across the UK. Its use has been positively reported anecdotally by staff, users and carers. However, a systematic qualitative and quantitative nationwide evaluation has yet to be carried out on its effectiveness. Such work could inform a content update, and the identification of new subject matter to be included in the production of future training materials. Given the goodwill generated within the UK (and international) EI network by the collaboration which created the current CD-ROM, both future evaluative and training endeavours can expect to benefit from the contributions of a wide range of personnel with appropriate EI expertise.

Implications for EI trainers

From a perusal of the wider evidence base, we offer a number of recommendations for trainers who wish to deliver EI training:

1. For knowledge and skills to be implemented it is vital that training is supported by provider organisations (e.g. NHS Trusts) at their most senior level (Furniss & Davis, 2007). Thus ensuring that senior management appreciates the value of training EI practitioners must be pursued. It may be a 'selling point' to be able to offer a high quality 'ready-to-go' EI CD-ROM training package?

2. Whole-team training should be considered. For example, in the related field of family work such an approach helps with practical implementation of learned skills (Bailey et al., 2003; Burbach & Stanbridge, 2006).

3. The inherent structural configuration of EI services must be considered when planning a training approach. In a specialist EI team with defined caseload ratios of 1:15 maximum, the nature of the work requires the delivery of PSI approaches to people with psychosis and their carers (Rolls et al., 2002). Supervision and peer support may be easier to access if a 'critical mass' of suitably PSI-trained personnel can be amassed (Brabban & Kelly, 2006).

Conclusion

The advent of newer services such as EI has created a real opportunity to improve the mental health of people suffering with psychosis, and to help those who routinely care for them. However judging the success of EI policy implementation by numbers of teams or counting of cases is not sufficient. The real success of EI will only be realised by the quality of the service experience and thus the training and development of the EI workforce must lie at the heart of this implementation.

We have tried in this chapter to outline the characteristics of an EI workforce that are fit for purpose in terms of attitudes, knowledge and skills. In achieving those characteristics we believe it is vital to seize opportunities to train and develop in the workplace and hope practical tools such as the CD-ROM described in this chapter will be helpful to EI trainers.

Acknowledgement
The authors wish to acknowledge the contribution made by Christian Pilbeam to this chapter.

Useful Website:
www.thorn-cheltenham.org.uk

Training Resource
IRIS/NIMHE/Rethink Early Intervention in Psychosis Training CD-Rom

References
Bailey, R., Burbach, F.R. & Lea, S.J. (2003). The ability of staff trained in family interventions to implement the approach in routine clinical practice. *Journal of Mental Health*, 12 (2), 131–141.

Bertolote, J. & McGorry, P. (2005). Early intervention and recovery for young people with early psychosis: Consensus statement. *British Journal of Psychiatry*, 187 (Suppl. 48), s116–s119.

Brabban, A. & Kelly, M. (2006). *Training in Psychosocial Interventions within Early Intervention Teams: A National Survey*. NIMHE/CSIP National PSI Implementation Group.

Brooker, C. & Brabban, A. (2004). Measured Success: A Scoping Review of Evaluated Psychosocial Interventions Training for Work with People with Serious Mental Health Problems NIMHE/Trent WDC.

Burbach, F. & Stanbridge, R. (2006). Somerset's family interventions in psychosis service: An update. *Journal of Family Therapy*, 28, 39–57.

Craig, T. (2003). A step too soon or a step too far? Early intervention in psychosis. *Journal of Mental Health*, 12 (4), 335–339.

Furniss, D. & Davis, E. (2007). Using effective management strategies to facilitate the delivery of PSI. In: R. Velleman, E. Davis, G. Smith & M. Drage (eds), *Changing Outcomes In Psychosis: Collaborative Cases from Practitioners, Users and Carers*, pp. 211–227. BPS Blackwell.

Fadden, G., Birchwood, M, Jackson, C. and Barton, K. (2004). Psychological therapies: Implementation in early intervention services. In: J. Gleeson & P. McGorry (eds), *Psychological Interventions in Early Psychosis: A Treatment Handbook*. Chichester: Wiley.

Gray, R., Wykes, T. & Gournay, K. (2003). The effect of medication management training on community mental health nurses clinical skills. *International Journal of Nursing Studies*, 40, 163–169.

Rolls, E., Davis, E. & Coupland, K. (2002). Improving serious mental illness through interprofessional education. *Journal of Psychiatric and mental Health Nursing*, 9, 317–324.

Chapter 30 Clinical supervision in early intervention teams

Tony Gillam

Introduction: Why clinical supervision might be helpful in early intervention teams

Early Intervention (EI) Teams work intensively with young people experiencing a first episode of psychosis and their families and carers. This work presents considerable challenges to team members. For example, intervening early in psychosis may mean it is far from clear (to patient, carer or clinician) what it is with which we are dealing. This 'diagnostic uncertainty' can be confusing for the professional trying to plan, on a day-to-day basis, how best to intervene.

The EI model requires that team members adopt an assertive outreach approach to individuals, yet hard-to-engage young people may feel there is a fine line between early inter*vention* and inter*ference* or harassment. The EI clinician has to strike a precarious balance between intervening early enough, assertively enough and not irritating clients to the point where they disengage.

There is often an expectation, if not a requirement, that EI teams will provide outcome audit data and be active participants in gathering research into first episode psychosis. Services may want to collect data on duration of untreated psychosis and pathways to care, for example, whilst also being required to draw up care plans, risk assessments and carers' assessments. How do we meet these expectations (often involving lengthy interviews and copious paperwork) without jeopardising engagement? How do we find the time for recording clinical activity (inputting data in 'near-real time', writing up notes, updating care plans), and still find time to *do* clinical work.

Amid this plethora of demands, clinicians may feel there is little spare time for discussing their work in a considered way, little time to reflect on practice. Yet, there is an additional expectation that practitioners will be 'reflective practitioners' committed to 'lifelong learning', to be constantly improving their practice, ensuring it is evidence-based, and ensuring they are not so burdened by their work that they themselves become burnt-out. Clinical supervision can be seen as an important means of maintaining a healthy, effective team.

Defining clinical supervision

Definitions of clinical supervision are not value-free and a review of a variety of definitions will illustrate how and why the concept has come to prominence. One simple definition provided by the Nursing and Midwifery Council (NMC) states: 'Clinical supervision is a practice-focused professional relationship, involving a practitioner reflecting on practice guided by a skilled supervisor' (NMC, 2002).

Supervision has been in use in the fields of clinical psychology, psychotherapy and counselling for many years. Social work has also long placed an emphasis on regular individual caseload review and supervision (Kadushin, 1992). Other professions such as nursing and occupational therapy began to give serious consideration to supervision from the 1990s onwards. That said, by no means is it universally available to members of these professions, one commentator remarking that "clinical supervision, for the most part, remains a curiosity rather than the norm" (Driscoll, 2000:10). As for the medical profession, the view seems to be that supervision has a vital role in medical education but that 'current supervisory practice in medicine has very little empirical or theoretical basis' (Kilminster & Jolly, 2000).

In 1993, the Report of the UK's Chief Nursing Officer defined supervision as 'a formal process of professional support and learning which enables individual practitioners to develop knowledge and competence, assume responsibility for their own practice and enhance customer protection and safety of care in complex clinical situations' (Department of Health, 1993). This emphasis on 'customer protection' is explained by the year of publication – 1993 was the year Beverly Allitt (a nurse working on a paediatric ward) was convicted of murdering four children, attempting to murder three and causing grievous bodily harm to six. The Department of Health placed renewed emphasis on the importance of supervision as a mechanism for public protection, something that had been implicit in the concept since the earliest days of social work supervision.

Many nursing authors offer a broader definition, arguing that supervision refers to a range of strategies including preceptorship, mentorship, supervision of qualified practice, peer review and the maintenance of identified professional standards. Thus, it is both a personal and a professional experience (Butterworth & Faugier, 1992). Brennan and Gamble (2006) see supervision as part of a clinical support structure which also includes, along with preceptorship and mentorship, appraisal, professional development and lifelong learning (Brennan & Gamble, 2006:400).

Common features of supervision

While models of supervision vary, they tend to encompass three main aspects:

- personal and professional support
- an educational function
- a quality assurance function

So, for example, Kadushin (1992) described three elements:

- supportive
- educational and
- managerial.

Supportive supervision focuses on worker morale and job satisfaction. It can be seen as helping to prevent 'burnout'. Educational supervision addresses deficits in the worker's knowledge, attitude and skills. It can be seen as promoting reflection and reflective practice. In managerial or administrative supervision the emphasis is on the correct, effective and appropriate implementation of the organisation's policies and procedures (Kadushin, 1992).

Some may argue that managerial supervision is a quite separate thing to clinical supervision. Brennan and Gamble, for example, seem to criticise the 'mixing up of managerial agendas with clinical agendas' suggesting this only adds to the confusion felt by professionals (Brennan & Gamble, 2006:401). Onyett, by contrast, stresses the primacy of the administrative function of supervision:

The word 'supervision' is often used too loosely in a context where clarity is critical. It is commonly used to describe a relationship that is more akin to peer consultation or mentoring. In social services, the term is used more precisely and in accordance with the dictionary definition, which stresses 'inspection' and 'control'....

(Onyett, 2003:175).

With all these variations in emphasis, it is reassuring to find surprising similarities between different models. For example, as can

Table 30.1 Models of supervision

Models of supervision

Common features	Kadushin's Model	Proctor's Model
Personal and professional support	Supportive	Restorative
An educational function	Educational	Formative
A quality assurance function	Managerial	Normative

Based on Proctor (1987) and Kadushin (1992).

be seen in Table 30.1, Proctor's (1987) model of supervision (comprising restorative, formative and normative elements) seems to mirror Kadushin's model (1987) closely.

Evidence for effectiveness

Despite the assertion that 'current supervisory practice in medicine has very little empirical or theoretical basis' (Kilminster & Jolly, 2000), there has been some research into the effectiveness of supervision. Much of this seems to relate to supervision of nurses rather than of other professions. This may reflect a range of views across disciplines. Some professions (e.g. clinical psychology and social work) place a high value on supervision (and may be less likely to feel the need to question it). Others (e.g. nursing and occupational therapy) may feel they need to justify the time spent away from direct contact with patients.

Butterworth et al. (1997) showed evidence of an increase in measurable emotional exhaustion and depersonalisation in a control group of nurses *not* receiving supervision. This study demonstrated that these effects were stabilised and, in some cases, ameliorated upon the introduction of supervision. Interestingly, those providing supervision showed difficulties similar to the unsupervised control group when acting as supervisors *without* receiving supervision in their own right. The researchers concluded that there was clear evidence that clinical supervision and mentorship had a beneficial effect on staff while, in those circumstances where it had not been introduced, or indeed had been withdrawn, there were measurable detrimental effects on the workforce (Butterworth et al., 1997).

Subsequent research into the effects of supervision (Teasdale et al., 2001) found no significant difference in burnout between supervised and unsupervised nurses but supervised nurses felt more supported and felt they coped better at work, this effect being more marked among more recently qualified nurses. This might suggest supervision is a luxury in a busy clinical team although, arguably, having staff who feel more capable and supported could be seen as worthwhile in itself.

Brennan and Gamble (2006) highlight another rationale for supervision which has particular relevance for EI teams. This is with regard to the provision of psychosocial interventions (which are seen as core work in EI). They remind us of the evidence that practitioners stop delivery of these interventions if adequate clinical support is not available. This leads Brennan and Gamble to argue that 'if the availability of psychosocial interventions is to increase it is essential that services attend to the provision of quality supervision and that psychosocial practitioners are encouraged to provide supervision as well as looking for it.' (2006:411). Thus, supervision is seen as part of a culture which promotes mutual support, reflective, evidence-based practice and, in particular, the delivery of challenging but essential psychosocial interventions.

Implementation in practice

When I became Clinical Team Manager of Worcestershire's EI Team, there was already a model of supervision arrangements in place. This had been developed as part of the service's operational policy and there was, for example, a clear expectation, explicit in my job description, that I would provide supervision to case managers. The model has required little change or adaptation but, as part of the preparation for this chapter, I thought it timely to evaluate supervision arrangements within the team. Other teams may want to adopt and, perhaps, adapt the model for their own use.

The current model is that shown in Figure 30.1, but requires some elucidation. It describes a vibrant ethos of supervision taking place within the team and extending beyond it. It includes individual and group supervision, and intervention-specific supervision as well as supervision of individual cases or caseloads. It includes mono-disciplinary and inter-disciplinary supervision and, in the case of students and trainees, mentorship.

There are various strands, reflecting differences between disciplines. Clinical psychology has a rigorous system for providing and receiving supervision. A consultant clinical psychologist (the service's Clinical Development Lead) provides supervision to the more senior clinical

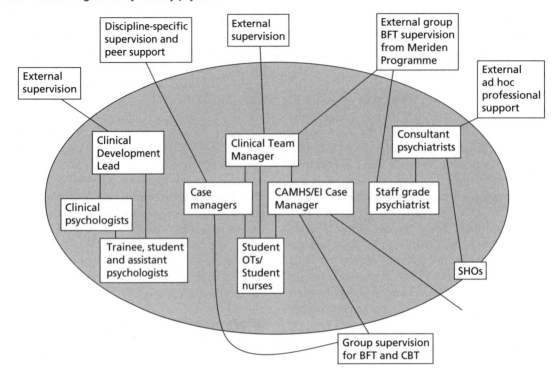

Figure 30.1 Supervision structure

psychologist in the team as well as personal and professional development supervision to the other psychologist in the team. The more senior of the team's two psychologists also provides week-on-week clinical supervision to the less senior one. The psychologists supervise any psychology assistants, psychology trainees or psychology students on placement with the team. The consultant clinical psychologist receives supervision externally, as do the consultant psychiatrists, (although on a more ad hoc basis). One of the consultant psychiatrists supervises the staff grade psychiatrist and both consultant psychiatrists supervise any Senior House Officers (SHOs) on placement with the team.

My own remit, as Clinical Team Manager – and a Community Psychiatric Nurse (CPN) by background – is to supervise case managers, be these CPN/Case Managers, Occupational Therapist (OT)/Case Managers or Social Workers. (In fact, the team does not, at the time of writing, have a

social worker.) The OT/Case Manager also receives peer group supervision with fellow OTs (and I would likewise expect any case managers of other disciplines to make arrangements for supervision specific to that discipline). This additional discipline-specific support or supervision seems unnecessary in the case of the CPN/Case Managers, because of my own nursing background. Where student nurses or OTs are on placement with the team these would be supervised/mentored by a case manager of the respective discipline.

Seconded to the team from the local Child and Adolescent Mental Health Service (CAMHS) is a CAMHS/EI Case Manager. This CPN receives clinical supervision from me and CAMHS-orientated supervision from a senior CAMHS nurse.

Supervision is available to all team members for specific psychosocial interventions. Thus, a locality-based group supervision of Behavioural Family Therapy (BFT) is available monthly, provided by BFT trainer/supervisors. (The EI team includes two BFT trainers, most of the team are BFT-trained and BFT practice, training and supervision are seen as central to the work of the team.) More recently, we have discussed the need for a similar arrangement for the group supervision of Cognitive Behavioural Therapy (CBT) and negotiations are underway for this to be provided (by a psychologist) to members of the EI team who practice CBT (this includes not only the clinical psychologists but also one of the CPN/Case Managers).

As BFT trainers, the staff grade psychiatrist and I both have access to external BFT supervision provided by the Meriden West Midlands Family Interventions Programme. As regards my own personal supervision, this is split between 'managerial supervision' (which is provided by my line manager) and clinical supervision for which I have an arrangement with a senior EI nurse – my 'opposite number' as it were – in neighbouring Herefordshire's EI Service. This latter arrangement is a mutual co-supervision not unlike the concept of 'co-counselling', which involves two individuals getting together and each taking turns to be counsellor (or in this case 'supervisor') and then client (or supervisee), having equal time in the two roles.

Too much of a good thing?

When enumerating the multifarious forms of supervision with which the team is involved, the question arises, is there such a thing as too much supervision? Certainly, a balance has to be struck between all the other work the team has to do. In some professional cultures there is a ratio of hours spent in clinical practice balanced against hours spent receiving supervision of that practice. For example, some clinical psychology trainees are expected to receive 1 hour of supervision for every 5 hours of clinical practice. For case managers, the frequency of supervision sessions is usually every 2-4 weeks. With a current establishment of six case managers, this means I spend an average of at least 6 hours per month (or 1.5 hours per week) providing supervision. As the team develops, with additional case managers being recruited, the time spent providing supervision will increase.

'Figure in landscape' – the 'helicopter view'

Managers may ask, if providing supervision to case managers is a relatively time-consuming activity for Clinical Team Managers, does this arrangement help with the management of the team? My own view is that, by hearing about individual cases, the caseload management problems and other issues brought to supervision by each of the case managers in turn, the team manager is able to gain an invaluable overview of the team's caseload and the team members' attitudes, skills, strengths and weaknesses. To supervise all the case managers individually is to gain a unique collective insight into the state-of-play of the team, a perspective known in management – speak as the 'helicopter view'. Thus, the team manager gets to hear about the detail of individual cases at the same time as being able to see the 'wider area' of the team as a whole and how these 'features on the landscape' fit together. As a Clinical Team Manager, I am as concerned with the day-to-day clinical challenges the team faces, as I am with the management of that team and the development of the service. My impression is that providing individual clinical supervision to each of the case managers facilitates this process.

Staff development

The supervision process can also link into the process of staff development reviews (SDRs). Although SDRs may be seen as driven by the agenda of the employing organisation rather than by the personal and professional needs of clinicians, in practice – so long as they are conducted in a person-centred (rather than an organisation-centred) way – SDRs can be seen as a *summative* form of supervision. If according to Proctor (1987) supervision is restorative, formative and normative we might, by extension, see SDRs as a periodic *summative* time for reflection and forward-planning.

The role of group supervision

Having discussed some of the benefits of individual supervision, it is important here to highlight the important role played by *group* supervision. Part of the rationale for cultivating a 'supervision culture' in EI teams is, as has already been mentioned, to help sustain psychosocial interventions. Brennan and Gamble (2006) describe the advantages of group supervision over individual supervision when it comes to psychosocial interventions (particularly BFT). They describe a model for group supervision familiar to members of the Worcestershire EI team, (who have been trained predominantly through the Meriden West Midlands Family Interventions Programme). In this model of group supervision of family work group members take turns to share an issue and reflect on it. The facilitator is not the only one with a valid opinion any more than, in family work, any one member of the family's opinion is more valid than another's. The group supervision also allows for role play, with group members adopting the roles of family members and therapists, before returning to a group reflection on the role play.

Leff (2005) takes the view that, when it comes to supervising family work, 'several heads are better than one.' He argues that

> Supervision of family work is essential, either from an experienced therapist or from one's peer group, because the work is emotionally taxing and sometimes faces the therapists with extremely difficult problems.... The more minds that are brought to bear on a problem, the more likely it is that a creative solution will emerge. No supervisor is omniscient or infallible, and suggested interventions should be viewed as experiments that might or might not succeed.
>
> (Leff, 2005:94).

Thus, Leff makes a strong argument for group supervision of family work, with creative problem-solving in supervision mirroring the problem-solving approach families are encouraged to use in BFT. A similar argument could be made for other psychosocial interventions such as CBT, where the idea of viewing suggested interventions as 'experiments' would seem to fit well. It is with these thoughts in mind that EI team members are encouraged to attend group BFT supervision and this is also the reason we are hoping to establish group supervision of CBT in psychosis.

Evaluating supervision arrangements

Prompted by the invitation to write this chapter, I decided to attempt to survey supervision activity in the team by means of a simple survey. I designed a questionnaire which was distributed to all team members and also led a team educational session on supervision.

The educational session was attended by a cross-section of the team, including a psychiatrist, several CPNs and a psychologist. I asked the participants to feedback on what kind of supervision they currently received, how they valued it and if they had any suggestions for ways in which it could be improved. Not surprisingly, this elicited a wide range of views.

The psychologist felt she had 'an ideal set-up' in as much as her supervision was very structured, involving week-on-week clinical supervision with her psychologist colleague and 'personal and professional development supervision' from her line manager the consultant clinical psychologist. The CPNs highlighted the value of 'informal peer supervision' which occurred on an ad hoc basis as required, as well as the 'general regular supervision' with myself. The informal peer supervision was seen as a 'mutual, problem-sharing and problem-solving'. The psychiatrist felt she received supervision 'every now and then' and would have preferred 'more structured dedicated time'. For her, supervision was often 'crisis supervision or handover' and, more generally, she felt that psychiatrists tended to received 'appraisal rather than supervision'.

The group valued supervision for giving perspective to different situations, for offering alternative perspectives, reassurance, support and validation. It was seen as an opportunity to ask, 'Am I being reasonable in what I am doing?' It helped provide role clarity, to maintain professional boundaries and an opportunity to ventilate or 'off-load'. In more psychological language, it was a forum for considering 'process issues' and to be aware of when clinical issues were 'ringing personal bells'.

As for suggested improvements to existing supervision arrangements, the group suggested occasional involvement of – or partnerships with – external specialists from other 'non-psychiatric'specialities for example child development or education, as a way of promoting reflection on cases from a point of view outside of mental health. More consideration of 'early detection' as opposed to 'early intervention' was also mentioned and one CPN raised the interesting question: 'Is there anything necessarily "EI" about the way we do our supervision?' This question merits consideration later.

Following the educational session, the questionnaire (Table 30.2) was distributed to all clinical members of the team. This included an explanation that the results of the survey might be used to improve supervision for members of the team but might also, with the respondent's permission, be used as anonymised material for this chapter.

Eight questionnaires were returned (out of a possible 12). All the respondents were receiving some supervision. Two respondents were 'completely satisfied' with the supervision they were currently receiving, five were 'quite satisfied' and one was 'quite dissatisfied'.

Typical responses to what was most valued about supervision were: 'support, perspective, objectivity', 'generating some kind of way forward', 'guided reflection', 'reduces anxiety sometimes', 'encouragement to develop knowledge and skills' and 'advice and support when feeling "stuck"'. As regards suggested improvements these included: 'set an agenda before commencing session,' and 'set structured and regular time'. Several respondents suggested 'more group and peer supervision' perhaps involving 'non-psychiatric interested parties for example people involved with young adults,' but one respondent – whilst wanting to attend discipline-specific supervision – saw this, along with BFT supervision and individual clinical supervision, as 'one thing too many' and felt a need to rationalise the number of supervision sessions in any given month.

In response to the open question of 'any other comments?' respondents mentioned that 'When under pressure, supervision becomes the easy option to give up but this reduces our effectiveness', 'I think supervision is essential and needs to be seen as important in providing good, safe, clinical care', 'I find it useful to keep a record of supervision sessions' and 'difficult to identify the "EI" elements in the current supervision model'.

Implications and conclusions

By way of conclusion, I would like to return to this question: 'Is there anything necessarily "EI" about the way we do our supervision?' One answer to this is 'perhaps not'. However, if EI services are a flagship of best practice, of evidence-based, client-centred, innovative practice in a truly multi-disciplinary team approach to mental health care, then it is no surprise that a dynamic culture of supervision is present in the team (where so many mental health practitioners are still receiving little or no supervision). We should remember that supervision remains for many 'a curiosity rather than the norm' (Driscoll, 2000) and, if EI teams (with their clear focus and limited caseloads) are not 'doing supervision' then there is little chance of it becoming the norm in hard-pressed community mental health teams or inpatient units, for example.

A culture of supervision assumes that practice should be reflective and dynamic, changing in response to the varying demands of the client group, and yet careful and considered. The central role that psychosocial interventions plays in EI highlights the need for intervention-specific supervision, but individual clinical supervision is just as essential to sustain group work, family work and CBT. Practitioners will not find the time for these interventions if their caseloads and their day-to-day work with individuals is not made more manageable through individual supervision. Psychosocial interventions in EI are not be 'the icing on the cake', they are the cake. Perhaps it is the taking care of different supervisory and support needs through a rather complex web of supervision arrangements that is fairly unique to EI. That said, the suggestions about 'non-mental health' perspectives (e.g. a youth perspective or an educational perspective) need to have a greater presence in the EI culture.

Table 30.2 Educational session questionnaire

(The results from this little survey may be used to improve supervision for members of this team and, with your permission, may be used as anonymised material for a book chapter on supervision in EI. If you consent to the latter, please tick here . . .)

1. What clinical supervision do you currently receive? (Circle all that apply)

None

Individual clinical supervision

Specific supervision related to particular interventions (e.g. BFT supervision, CBT supervision, please specify)

Other (please specify)

2. What clinical supervision do you currently provide to others? (Circle all that apply)

None

Individual clinical supervision

Specific supervision related to particular interventions (e.g. BFT supervision, CBT supervision)

Other (please specify)

3. If you are receiving supervision currently, how satisfied are you with it? (Please circle one item)

Completely dissatisfied   Quite dissatisfied   Quite satisfied   Completely satisfied   Not applicable

4. If you are receiving supervision currently, what do you value most about it?
(or, if you don't currently receive supervision, what do you think you *would* value about it, were you to receive it?)

5. What changes could be made to current supervision arrangements in the EI team to improve it?

6. Any other comments?

Thank you for completing this questionnaire.

I would invite all EI teams (indeed all mental health teams) to consider the arrangements they have in place for supervision. I am not suggesting the model in place in Worcestershire's EI team is perfect. However, that all members of the team participate so actively in supervision (and are active in delivering psychosocial interventions as a core part of their work) suggests that it is highly valued. Future planning needs to be aware of the desire for "more group and peer supervision" and to balance this against the fear that any more time spent in supervision is "one thing too many." The ultimate aim must be to ensure that team members feel sufficiently supported and equipped to enjoy the challenge of providing EI to young people and their families.

Useful website addresses

http://www.meridenfamilyprogramme.com

This provides a full background to the Meriden family interventions programme referred to in this chapter. The site has been developed for use by service users, carers and family members as well as mental health staff and gives an excellent explanation of the model of family work, as well as some useful links.

http://www.infed.org

The website of 'infed' (short for 'informal education') contains some well-written and well-researched essays on supervision (and much more of interest). The website's stated aim is 'to provide a space for people to explore the theory and practice of informal education and lifelong learning. In particular, we want to encourage educators to develop ways of working and being that foster association, conversation and relationship'.

References

Brennan, G. & Gamble, C. (2006). Clinical support. In: G. Brennan & C. Gamble (eds), *Working with*

Serious Mental Illness: A Manual for Clinical Practice (2nd edition) London: Elsevier.

Butterworth, T. & Faugier, J. (1992). *Clinical Supervision and Mentorship in Nursing*. London: Chapman and Hall.

Butterworth, T., Carson, J., White, E., Jeacock, J., Clement, A. & Bishop, V. (1997). *'It Is Good to Talk': An Evaluation Study in England and Scotland*. Manchester: University of Manchester school of Nursing, Midwifery and health Visiting.

Department of Health (1993). *A Vision for the Future: Report of the Chief Nursing Officer*. London: HMSO.

Driscoll, J. (2000). Clinical supervision: a radical approach. *Mental Health Practice*, 3 (8), 8–10.

Kadushin, A. (1992). *Supervision in Social Work* (3rd edition). New York: Columbia University Press.

Kilminster, S.M. & Jolly, B.C. (2000). Effective supervision in clinical practice settings: A literature review. *Medical Education*, 34 (10), 827–840.

Leff, J. (2005). *Advanced Family Work for Schizophrenia: An Evidence-based Approach*. London: Gaskell.

Nursing and Midwifery Council (2002). *Supporting Nurses and Midwives Through Lifelong Learning*. London: NMC.

Onyett, S. (2003). *Team Working in Mental Health*. Basingstoke: Palgrave Macmillan.

Proctor, B. (1987). Supervision: A co-operative exercise in accountability. In: M. Marken, & M. Payne (eds), *Enabling and Ensuring: Supervision in practice*. Leicester: Youth Work Press.

Teasdale, K., Brocklehurst, N. & Thom, N. (2001). Clinical supervision and support for nurses: An evaluation study. *Journal of Advanced Nursing*, 33 (2), 216–224.

Chapter 31 Conclusion: Where next for early intervention

Paul French

Early intervention (EI) in psychosis has come a long way in a short time, the ideas have only been around for a couple of decades but the shift in emphasis towards this paradigm has been astounding. Only ten years ago, a search on EI in psychosis would have returned a small number of articles; today the same search will return thousands of articles on the subject. Again ten years ago in England there were only a handful of people never mind services delivering aspects of EI but over this time we have seen an explosion of services thanks to a combination of drivers. This is being replicated around the world with comprehensive EI services being established around the globe. At times the driver has been policy, at others research has driven the agenda, but perhaps the most important driver over this time has been the hearts and minds argument that late intervention cannot be right. We would not accept late intervention in any other area of health care, why should we accept it in mental health. This simple but powerful argument has been vital to help sustain the development of services. However, thanks to the expansion of evidence we can now see that not only does EI make absolute sense but there is also a substantial amount of evidence to indicate the importance of this way of working. EI has been subject to huge amounts of scrutiny perhaps more so than any other mental health service in the UK but EI has risen to this challenge. What we can see now is that EI can deliver on what should be the cornerstones of any health service in that it is able to deliver a service which (i) works, (ii) delivers an intervention that people want and, (iii) does this in a cost effective manner. Despite the investment in EI it can still save money compared to standard non-EI care (McCrone et al 2008). In fact the work of McCrone and colleagues (2008) demonstrated that it is possible to save £65 million by 2026 if EI services were available to cover 100% of the population in England. This work also hints at the potential of early detection to effect further cost savings and goes further to suggest that extending the model to Bipolar Disorder could save the NHS even more. This idea of invest to save is a contentious one and one that does not sit too easily with short-term planning cycles typical of the NHS but the economic argument presented by McCrone and colleagues (2008) must be strongly considered.

Now that EI in psychosis has established itself we need to look to the future to see where next and it would appear that one direction of travel would be moving towards providing EI not just for psychosis but extending the paradigm to encompass a range of mental health problems. It would make sense to extend this model that has been so successful to a number of mental health problems which may be just as amenable to EI strategies. For example there are emerging strategies for intervening early in disorders such as depression and borderline personality disorder. It is possible that in the next decade EI in psychosis services will be significantly different. Some of the more established EI services are moving towards the idea of a youth mental health model where EI for a range of mental health problems are provided in an integrated service for young people between the ages of 14–35. EI has focussed on this age range because it is the age group where the majority of people develop psychosis, (approximately 80% of people who develop psychosis do so within this age range) but significantly it is also the age range when lots of other mental health difficulties emerge. But it is also the place at which we currently split our services in terms of Child and Adolescent Mental Health Services (CAMHS) and Adult Mental Health Services (AMHS). There are some valid reasons for why services were originally structured in this way, however knowing what we now know it does not make sense to have such a radical split in service provision right at the point where problems begin to emerge. It would make sense that the next decade should see the evolution of services that operate within a youth model and straddle the high-risk age groups.

However, it is important that this model is not just extended; we must learn lessons from the development of EIP. The psychosis services quickly adopted new research findings and based their assessments and treatment strategies on emerging research. It is vital that we begin to research how to intervene with other mental health disorders, observing early signs and symptoms and devising reliable measures for early identification at the earliest opportunity. It is also important to remember that current EI teams have been configured to work with psychosis only populations. If teams do expand to work with other diagnostic groups then there would need to be a substantial increase in resources to manage this increase in workload. If this did not happen then it would significantly jeopardise the work that has taken place so far. It is unlikely that there would be a significant injection of funding for this type of development, instead these initiatives would need to be delivered through service restructuring. However, there are a number of existing statutory and non-statutory services who are already funded to deliver a wide range of interventions and the coordination of these groups through a youth mental health service would be an exciting prospect.

Whatever the future brings we have seen a change in service delivery for people with psychosis that has truly inspired people to believe that recovery is possible, we have entered into an era that promotes hope for people with psychosis.

References

McCrone, P., Dhanasiri, S., Patel, A., Knapp, M. & Lawton Smith, S. (2008). Paying the price: The cost of mental health care in England to 2026. Kings Fund.

Index